Environmental Economics

An Introduction   2024 Release

Barry C. Field
Department of Resource Economics
University of Massachusetts Amherst

Martha K. Field
Department of Business and Information Technology
Greenfield Community College

ENVIRONMENTAL ECONOMICS AN INTRODUCTION, 2024 RELEASE

Published by McGraw Hill LLC, 1325 Avenue of the Americas, New York, NY 10019. Copyright ©2024 by McGraw Hill LLC. All rights reserved. Printed in the United States of America. Previous editions ©2021, 2017, and 2013. No part of this publication may be reproduced or distributed in any form or by any means, or stored in a database or retrieval system, without the prior written consent of McGraw Hill LLC, including, but not limited to, in any network or other electronic storage or transmission, or broadcast for distance learning.

Some ancillaries, including electronic and print components, may not be available to customers outside the United States.

This book is printed on acid-free paper.

1 2 3 4 5 6 7 8 9 LCR 29 28 27 26 25 24

ISBN 978-1-266-54306-7 (bound edition)
MHID 1-266-54306-6 (bound edition)
ISBN 978-1-266-56200-6 (loose-leaf edition)
MHID 1-266-56200-1 (loose-leaf edition)

Associate Portfolio Manager: *Jonathan Hsu*
Marketing Manager: *Carla Villani*
Lead/Senior Content Project Manager: *Melissa Leick/Laura Payne*
Manufacturing Project Manager: *Sandy Ludovissy*
Content Licensing Specialist: *Melissa Homer*
Cover Image: *Thomas Roche/Getty Images*
Compositor: *Aptara®, Inc.*

Cover Image: *Gay Head Light, Aquinnah, Massachusetts, on the island of Martha's Vineyard, the home and ancestral land of the Wampanoag people and nation.*

All credits appearing on page or at the end of the book are considered to be an extension of the copyright page.

Library of Congress Cataloging-in-Publication Data

Names: Field, Barry C., author. | Field, Martha K., author.
Title: Environmental economics an introduction / Barry C. Field,
   Department of Resource Economics, University of Massachusetts Amherst;
   Martha K. Field, Department of Business and Information Technology,
   Greenfield Community College.
Description: 2024 Release. | New York, NY : McGraw Hill LLC, [2024] |
   Includes index.
Identifiers: LCCN 2023033633 (print) | LCCN 2023033634 (ebook) | ISBN
   9781266543067 (hardcover) | ISBN 9781266562006 (spiral bound) | ISBN
   9781266573590 (ebook) | ISBN 9781266569463 (ebook other)
Subjects: LCSH: Environmental economics. | Economic
   development–Environmental aspects.
Classification: LCC HC79.E5 F47 2024 (print) | LCC HC79.E5 (ebook) | DDC
   333.7–dc23/eng/20230720
LC record available at https://lccn.loc.gov/2023033633
LC ebook record available at https://lccn.loc.gov/2023033634

The Internet addresses listed in the text were accurate at the time of publication. The inclusion of a website does not indicate an endorsement by the authors or McGraw Hill LLC, and McGraw Hill LLC does not guarantee the accuracy of the information presented at these sites.

mheducation.com/highered

The McGraw Hill Series Economics

ESSENTIALS OF ECONOMICS

Brue, McConnell, and Flynn
Essentials of Economics
Fifth Edition

Mandel
Economics: The Basics
2024 Release

Schiller
Essentials of Economics
Twelfth Edition

PRINCIPLES OF ECONOMICS

Asarta and Butters
Principles of Economics

Colander
Economics, Microeconomics, and Macroeconomics
Twelfth Edition

Frank, Bernanke, Antonovics, and Heffetz
Principles of Economics, Principles of Microeconomics, Principles of Macroeconomics
2024 Release

Frank, Bernanke, Antonovics, and Heffetz
Streamlined Editions: Principles of Economics, Principles of Microeconomics, Principles of Macroeconomics
Fourth Edition

Karlan and Morduch
Economics, Microeconomics, and Macroeconomics
2024 Release

McConnell, Brue, and Flynn
Economics, Microeconomics, Macroeconomics
Twenty-Third Edition

McConnell, Brue, and Flynn
Brief Editions: Microeconomics and Macroeconomics
Third Edition

Samuelson and Nordhaus
Economics, Microeconomics, and Macroeconomics
Nineteenth Edition

Schiller
The Economy Today, The Micro Economy Today, and The Macro Economy Today
Seventeenth Edition

Slavin
Economics, Microeconomics, and Macroeconomics
Twelfth Edition

ECONOMICS OF SOCIAL ISSUES

Guell
Issues in Economics Today
Tenth Edition

Register and Grimes
Economics of Social Issues
Twenty-First Edition

DATA ANALYTICS FOR ECONOMICS

Prince
Predictive Analytics for Business Strategy
First Edition

BUSINESS ANALYTICS

Jaggia, Kelly, Lertwachara, and Chen
Business Analytics: Communicating with Numbers
Second Edition

Richardson and Weidenmier-Watson
Introduction to Business Analytics
First Edition

Taddy, Hendrix, and Harding
Modern Business Analytics
First Edition

MANAGERIAL ECONOMICS

Baye and Prince
Managerial Economics and Business Strategy
Tenth Edition

Brickley, Smith, and Zimmerman
Managerial Economics and Organizational Architecture
Seventh Edition

Thomas and Maurice
Managerial Economics
Fourteenth Edition

INTERMEDIATE ECONOMICS

Bernheim and Whinston
Microeconomics
Second Edition

Dornbusch, Fischer, and Startz
Macroeconomics
Thirteenth Edition

Frank
Microeconomics and Behavior
2024 Release

ADVANCED ECONOMICS

Romer
Advanced Macroeconomics
Fifth Edition

MONEY AND BANKING

Cecchetti and Schoenholtz
Money, Banking, and Financial Markets
2024 Release

URBAN ECONOMICS

O'Sullivan
Urban Economics
Ninth Edition

LABOR ECONOMICS

Borjas
Labor Economics
Ninth Edition

McConnell, Brue, and Macpherson
Contemporary Labor Economics
Twelfth Edition

PUBLIC FINANCE

Rosen and Gayer
Public Finance
Tenth Edition

ENVIRONMENTAL ECONOMICS

Field and Field
Environmental Economics An Introduction
2024 Release

INTERNATIONAL ECONOMICS

Appleyard and Field
International Economics
Ninth Edition

Pugel
International Economics
Eighteenth Edition

To Leslie, Sidney, and Tory

About the Authors

Barry C. Field is Professor Emeritus of Resource Economics at the University of Massachusetts Amherst. Previously he taught at the University of Miami and The George Washington University. He received his B.S. and M.S. degrees from Cornell University and his Ph.D. from the University of California at Berkeley.

At the University of Massachusetts he devoted many years to teaching environmental economics to students at all levels and developed an undergraduate major in environmental and resource economics.

Martha K. Field is Professor of Economics at Greenfield Community College, where she has taught environmental economics for many years. She has taught at the University of Massachusetts Amherst, Mount Holyoke College, Westfield State University, Holyoke Community College, and the Consumer Cooperative Institute at Gomel, Belarus. She received a B.S. and an M.S. from the University of Massachusetts and holds a Ph.D. from the University of Connecticut.

They reside in Leverett, Massachusetts.

Contents in Brief

SECTION ONE
Introduction 1

1   What Is Environmental Economics? 2
2   The Economy and the Environment 19

SECTION TWO
Analytical Tools 38

3   Benefits and Costs, Supply and Demand 39
4   Markets, Externalities, and Public Goods 59
5   The Economics of Environmental Quality 76

SECTION THREE
Environmental Analysis 99

6   Frameworks of Analysis 100
7   Benefit–Cost Analysis: Benefits 121
8   Benefit–Cost Analysis: Costs 141

SECTION FOUR
Environmental Policy Analysis 157

9   Criteria for Evaluating Environmental Policies 158
10   Decentralized Policies: Liability Laws, Property Rights, Voluntary Action 169
11   Command-and-Control Strategies: The Case of Standards 186
12   Incentive-Based Strategies: Environmental Charges and Subsidies 204

13   Incentive-Based Strategies: Market Trading Systems 226

SECTION FIVE
Environmental Policy in the United States 243

14   Federal Water Pollution Control Policy 244
15   Federal Air Pollution Control Policy 264
16   Federal Policy on Toxic and Hazardous Substances 284
17   State and Local Environmental Issues 307

SECTION SIX
Global Environmental Issues 323

18   Global Climate Change 324
19   International Environmental Agreements 343
20   Globalization 362
21   Economic Development and the Environment 376

APPENDIX A
Abbreviations and Acronyms Used in the Book 394

APPENDIX B
Additional Websites 399

NAME INDEX 405

SUBJECT INDEX 407

Contents

Preface xii

SECTION ONE
INTRODUCTION 1

Chapter 1
What Is Environmental Economics? 2

1-1 Economic Analysis 2
1-2 The Importance of Incentives 4
1-3 Incentives: A Household Example 5
1-4 Incentives and Climate Change 6
1-5 The Design of Environmental Policy 7
1-6 Macroeconomic Questions: Environment and Growth 9
1-7 Benefit–Cost Analysis 11
1-8 Valuing the Environment 13
1-9 Environment and Development 13
1-10 International Issues 15
1-11 Globalization and the Environment 16
1-12 Economics and Politics 17
Summary 18

Chapter 2
The Economy and the Environment 19

2-1 Natural Resource Economics 20
2-2 Environmental Economics 22
  Basic Terminology 22
2-3 The Fundamental Balance 23
2-4 The Environment as an Economic and Social Asset 26
2-5 Environmental Sustainability 28
  Green GDP and Natural Capital 29
2-6 Emissions, Ambient Quality, and Damages 30
2-7 Types of Pollutants 32
  Cumulative Versus Noncumulative Pollutants 32
  Local Versus Regional Versus Global Pollutants 33
  Point-Source Versus Nonpoint-Source Pollutants 34
  Continuous Versus Episodic Emissions 34
  Environmental Damages Not Related to Emissions 35
Summary 36
Questions for Further Discussion 36

SECTION TWO
ANALYTICAL TOOLS 38

Chapter 3
Benefits and Costs, Supply and Demand 39

3-1 Willingness to Pay 39
  Demand 41
3-2 Aggregate Demand/Willingness to Pay 43
3-3 Benefits 45
3-4 Costs 46
  Opportunity Cost 47
  Private and Social Costs 48
  Cost Curves 48
  The Shapes of Cost Curves 49
3-5 Technology 51
3-6 The Equimarginal Principle 53
3-7 Marginal Cost and Supply 54
Summary 56
Questions for Further Discussion 56

Chapter 4
Markets, Externalities, and Public Goods 59

4-1 Economic Efficiency 60
4-2 Efficiency and Equity 61

viii

4-3 Markets   62
4-4 Markets and Social Efficiency   64
4-5 External Costs   64
    Open-Access Resources   68
4-6 External Benefits   70
    Public Goods   71
Summary   73
Questions for Further Discussion   74

Chapter 5
The Economics of Environmental Quality   76

5-1 Pollution Control—A General Model   76
5-2 Pollution Damages   77
    Damage Functions   78
    Changes in Damage Functions   80
    Damages and Uncertainty   81
    Damages and Time   82
5-3 Abatement Costs   82
    Abatement Cost Functions   83
    Changes in Marginal Abatement Cost Functions   85
    Technological Change in Abatement Costs   87
    Aggregate Marginal Abatement Costs   88
5-4 The Socially Efficient Level of Emissions   89
    Changes in the Efficient Level of Emissions   92
5-5 Enforcement Costs   93
5-6 The Equimarginal Principle Applied to Emission Reductions   94
Summary   96
Questions for Further Discussion   97

SECTION THREE
ENVIRONMENTAL ANALYSIS   99

Chapter 6
Frameworks of Analysis   100

6-1 Impact Analysis   100
    Environmental Impact Analysis   100
    Economic Impact Analysis   101
    Regulatory Impact Analysis   101
6-2 Cost-Effectiveness Analysis   101
6-3 Damage Assessment   102
6-4 Benefit–Cost Analysis   104
    The Basic Framework   104
    Scope of the Program   106
    Discounting   109
    Choice of Discount Rate   110
    Discounting and Future Generations   112
    Distributional Issues   113
6-5 Risk Analysis   115
    Risk Assessment   116
    Risk Valuation   116
    Risk Management   118
Summary   118
Questions for Further Discussion   119

Chapter 7
Benefit–Cost Analysis: Benefits   121

7-1 The Damage Function: Physical Aspects   121
7-2 Measuring Damage Costs Directly   123
    Health Costs   123
    The Effects of Pollution on Production Costs   124
    Materials Damage   125
    Problems with Direct Damage Approaches   126

7-3 Willingness to Pay: Estimating Methods 127
7-4 Willingness to Pay: Revealed Preference Methods 127

The Value of Human Health as Expressed in Averting Costs 128
The Value of Human Life as Expressed in Wage Rates 128
Valuing Children's Health 130
The Value of Environmental Quality as Expressed in House Prices 131
The Value of Environmental Quality as Expressed in Travel Costs 132

7-5 Willingness to Pay: Stated Preference Methods 133

Valuing an Environmental Amenity 134
CV and Valuing Health Outcomes 135
Problems of CV Analysis 136

7-6 Problems in Benefit Estimation 137

Discounting 137
Willingness to Pay Versus Willingness to Accept 138
Nonuse Values 138

Summary 139
Questions for Further Discussion 139

Chapter 8
Benefit–Cost Analysis: Costs 141

8-1 The Cost Perspective: General Issues 141
8-2 The With/Without Principle 142
8-3 A Word on Social Costs 142
8-4 The Distribution of Costs 143
8-5 Concepts of Cost 143

Opportunity Costs 143
Environmental Costs 144
Enforcement Costs 145

8-6 Costs of Single Facilities 145
8-7 Costs of a Local Regulation 147
8-8 Costs of Regulating an Industry 148

Sources of Cost Data 149
Actual Versus Minimum Pollution-Control Costs 149
The Effect of Output Adjustments on Costs 150
Long-Run Technical Change and Pollution-Control Costs 152

8-9 Costs of National Regulation 153
8-10 Future Costs and Technological Change 155

Summary 155
Questions for Further Discussion 156

SECTION FOUR
ENVIRONMENTAL POLICY ANALYSIS 157

Chapter 9
Criteria for Evaluating Environmental Policies 158

9-1 Efficiency 158
9-2 Cost-Effectiveness 159
9-3 Equity or Fairness 160

The Idea of "Social" 161
Environmental Justice 162

9-4 Enforceability 162
9-5 Flexibility 164
9-6 Incentives for Technological Innovations 165
9-7 Materials Balance Issues 166
9-8 Moral Considerations 166
9-9 Government Failure 167

Summary 167
Questions for Further Discussion 168

Chapter 10
Decentralized Policies: Liability Laws, Property Rights, Voluntary Action 169

10-1 Liability Laws 169

The Principle 170
Common Law 171
Statutory Law 174

10-2 Property Rights 175

The Principle 175
Rules and Conditions 177

10-3 Problems with Property Rights to Internalize Externalities 177
  Transactions Costs 178
  Public Goods 178
  Absence of Markets 179
  Markets for Clean Energy 179
10-4 Voluntary Action 180
  Moral Suasion 181
  Informal Community Pressure 182
Summary 183
Questions for Further Discussion 184

Chapter 11
Command-and-Control Strategies: The Case of Standards 186

11-1 Types of Standards 187
  Ambient Standards 187
  Emission Standards 188
  Technology Standards 189
  Standards Used in Combination 191
11-2 The Economics of Standards 191
  Setting the Level of the Standard 191
  Uniformity of Standards 192
  Standards and the Equimarginal Principle 193
11-3 Standards and Incentives 196
  Political-Economic Aspects of Standards 198
11-4 The Economics of Enforcement 199
  Enforcing Emission Standards 199
  Enforcing Technology Standards 201
  The Enforcing Agency 201
Summary 202
Questions for Further Discussion 202

Chapter 12
Incentive-Based Strategies: Environmental Charges and Subsidies 204

12-1 Emission Charges or Taxes 205
  The Economics of an Emission Tax 206
  The Level of the Charge 208
  Emission Charges and Cost-Effectiveness 210
  Emission Taxes and Nonuniform Emissions 212
  Emission Charges and Uncertainty 214
  Emission Charges and Tax Revenues 215
  Emission Charges and the Incentives to Innovate 217
  Emission Charges and Enforcement Costs 218
  Other Types of Charges 219
  Carbon Taxes 219
12-2 Abatement Subsidies 220
  Deposit-Refund Systems 222
Summary 223
Questions for Further Discussion 224

Chapter 13
Incentive-Based Strategies: Market Trading Systems 226

13-1 Cap-and-Trade 227
  The Initial Rights Allocation 229
  Establishing Trading Rules 231
  Reducing the Number of Permits 231
  CAPs and Nonuniform Emissions 232
  CAPs and Enforcement 234
  CAPs and the Incentive for R&D 235
  CAPs and Uncertainty 236

13-2 Offset Trading 236
13-3 Emission Rate Trading 239
Summary 240
Questions for Further Discussion 241

SECTION FIVE
ENVIRONMENTAL POLICY IN THE UNITED STATES 243

Chapter 14
Federal Water Pollution Control Policy 244

14-1 Types of Water Pollutants 245
14-2 Federal Water Policy: A Brief History 246
14-3 Technology-Based Effluent Standards 249
   TBESs and Cost-Effectiveness 250
   TBESs and Incentives 251
   TBESs and Enforcement 252
14-4 The Municipal Wastewater Treatment Plant Subsidy Program 253
   Stormwater Runoff 255
14-5 The Safe Drinking Water Act (SDWA) 255
14-6 Accident Response: The Case of Oil Spills 257
14-7 Nonpoint-Source Water Pollution Control 258
14-8 Total Maximum Daily Load (TMDL) Program 259
   Emission Trading in Water-Pollution Control 260

Summary 262
Questions for Further Discussion 262

Chapter 15
Federal Air Pollution Control Policy 264

15-1 Federal Air Policy: A Brief History 266
15-2 National Ambient Air Quality Standards 269
15-3 Stationary-Source Control 270
   Technology-Based Effluent Standards 271
   Differentiated Control 271
   Emissions Trading in Stationary-Source Control 273
   Controlling Interstate Air Pollution 274
   Controlling Greenhouse Gas Emissions 274
15-4 Mobile-Source Air-Pollution Control 275
   New-Car Emission Standards 276
   Electric Vehicles 278
   Mobile-Source Standards and Climate Change 279
   Behavioral Economics Issues 280

Summary 282
Questions for Further Discussion 282

Chapter 16
Federal Policy on Toxic and Hazardous Substances 284

16-1 Economic Issues in Laws Governing Chemicals in Production and in Consumer Products 286
   Regulatory Criteria 287
   Differentiated Control: "Old" versus "New" 289
   Testing Chemicals and the Burden of Proof 290
   Uniform Standards 290
   Technological Change in Chemicals 291
   Globalization and Chemicals 293
   The Economics of Pest Resistance 293
16-2 Economic Issues in Federal Policy on Toxics in Water and Air Emissions 295
   Hazardous-Waste Reduction 296
16-3 The Management of Hazardous Wastes 298
16-4 Economic Issues in Handling Current Hazardous Wastes 300
   Incentive-Based Possibilities 300
   Environmental Justice 301
   Radioactive Wastes 302

16-5 Economic Issues in Handling Legacy Hazardous-Waste Sites 303
    Financing Hazardous-Waste-Site Cleanups 303
    How Clean Is Clean? 304
    Brownfields 304
    Natural Resource Damages 305
    Cleaning Up the Nuclear Buildup 305
Summary 306
Questions for Further Discussion 306

Chapter 17
State and Local Environmental Issues 307

17-1 Environmental Federalism 308
    Constitutional Issues 308
    Efficiency Issues 308
    Race to the Bottom? 310
    Policy Innovations at the State Level 310
    The States and Environmental Justice 311
17-2 The Circular Economy 311
17-3 Municipal Solid Waste 311
    Technical Options for Reducing MSW 312
    Policy Options for Reducing MSW 313
17-4 The Economics of Recycling 315
    Producer Use of Recycled Material 316
    Consumer Recycling Decisions 318
    Producer Take-Back Programs 319
17-5 Local Environmental Regulations 319
17-6 The Increasing Role of the States 320
Summary 321
Questions for Further Discussion 322

SECTION SIX
GLOBAL ENVIRONMENTAL ISSUES 323

Chapter 18
Global Climate Change 324

18-1 Global Climate Change 324
    The Physical Problem 324
    Human and Ecosystem Impacts 327
18-2 Reducing Domestic GHG Emissions 329
    Incentive-Based Approaches for Reducing GHG Emissions 330
18-3 International Agreements for Addressing Climate Change 333
    The Kyoto Protocol 333
    The Paris Agreement 334
18-4 Economics of Adaptation 336
18-5 Estimating the Social Cost of Carbon 338
18-6 Biodiversity 339
Summary 341
Questions for Further Discussion 342

Chapter 19
International Environmental Agreements 343

19-1 General Issues 344
19-2 The Economics of International Agreements 349
    Bilateral Agreements 349
    Multilateral Agreements 351
19-3 The Distribution of Costs 353
    Bargaining Issues 353
    Cost-Effectiveness in Multinational Agreements 355
19-4 A Multilateral Success Story: The Montreal Protocol 356
    The Physical Problem 356
    International Response 357
    The Economics of CFC Controls 358

Summary 360
Questions for Further Discussion 361

Chapter 20
Globalization 362

20-1 Dimensions of Globalization 362
20-2 Sorting Out Cause and Effect 363
20-3 Trade and the Environment 364
  Free Trade Versus Environmental Trade Restrictions 365
20-4 Environmental Implications of Globalization 368
20-5 Climate Change and Globalization 369
20-6 Regional Trade Agreements 371
  Environmental Trade Restrictions 371

Summary 374
Questions for Further Discussion 375

Chapter 21
Economic Development and the Environment 376

21-1 Environmental Degradation in Developing Economies 377
21-2 Economic Growth and the Environment 378
  Short-run View 378
  Sustainability 380
  Long-run Relationships 381
21-3 Environmental Policy Issues in Developing Countries 381
  Benefit–Cost Analysis 382
  Reducing Environmental Disincentives 383
  Institutional Policy: Property Rights 384
  Population Policy as Environmental Policy 386
  Policy Choice in Developing Countries 387
  The Paris Agreement and Developing Countries 389
21-4 The Role of the Developed Countries 390
  Technology Transfer 390
  Environmental Values in International Development Banks 392

Summary 392
Questions for Further Discussion 393

APPENDIX A
Abbreviations and Acronyms Used in the Book 394

APPENDIX B
Additional Websites 399

NAME INDEX 405

SUBJECT INDEX 407

Preface

This book is an introduction to environmental economics. It is about the way human decisions affect the quality of the environment, how human values and institutions shape our demands for improvement in the quality of that environment, and, most especially, about how to design effective public policies to bring about these improvements.

History is filled with bleak examples of environmental degradation, from deforestation by earlier generations to mountains of horse manure in urban areas in the days before automobiles. But today's world is different. Many people who have reached advanced levels of material well-being are questioning the value of this wealth if it comes at the cost of large-scale disruptions of the ecosystem. More fundamental, perhaps, is that with contemporary economic, demographic, and technological developments around the world, the associated environmental repercussions are much more widespread and lethal. What once were localized environmental impacts have now become widespread, even global, and may well turn out to be irreversible. Global environmental impacts from climate change are present; they are no longer future hypothetical propositions.

It is no wonder, then, that the quality of the natural environment has become a major focus of public concern. As we would expect, people have responded in many ways. Environmental interest groups and advocates have become vocal at every political level, especially in those countries with open political systems. Politicians have taken environmental issues into their agendas; some have sought to become environmental statespersons. Environmental law has burgeoned, becoming a specialty in many law schools. Thousands of environmental agencies have appeared in the public sector, from local conservation commissions to environmental agencies at the United Nations. At the scientific level, environmental problems are a focus for chemists, biologists, engineers, and many social and behavioral scientists. **Environmental economics** has become a specialty within the economics field.

Environmental economics focuses on all the different facets of the connection between environmental quality and the economic behavior of individuals and groups of people. There is the fundamental question of how the economic system shapes economic incentives in ways that lead to environmental degradation, as well as improvement. There are major problems in measuring the benefits and costs of environmental quality changes, especially intangible ones. There is a set of complicated macroeconomic questions, for example, the connection between economic growth and environmental impacts, and the feedback effects of environmental laws on growth. There are the critical issues of designing environmental policies that are both effective and equitable. Equity aspects of environmental pollution and policy especially impact people of different income levels and demographic groups.

The strength of environmental economics lies in the fact that it is analytical and deals with concepts such as efficiency, trade-offs, costs, and benefits. Many believe strongly that the times call for more direct political action, more consciousness-raising, more political-organizing, and, especially, more representation and influence of environmental interests on the political scene, essentially more action. Nobody can doubt this. Just raising the concern about environmental quality is not enough.

We live in a complicated world where human problems abound; domestically we have health care, drugs, education, violence, and other critical issues, all competing for attention and public resources. Throughout the world, vast numbers of people struggle to alter their political and economic institutions, develop their economies, and raise their material standards of living and well-being. Action to maintain or improve the quality of the natural environment has to be made within the context of these concerns.

The first edition of this book was written more than 25 years ago. Much has changed since then. Some of the environmental problems that were important then have been addressed with success, for example, the problem of acid deposition stemming from coal power-plant SO_2 emissions. And significant progress has been made during this time. Cars are much cleaner, and transition away from fossil fuel energy has begun. Many of our rivers and lakes have better water quality, and less raw sewage flows into water bodies. Emissions of ozone-depleting chemicals have been reduced substantially, and recycling is part of everyday life. These all happened through public policies of various types.

But much remains to be done. Many people are still impacted by polluted air. The quality of drinking water is a continuing problem for growing urban populations. Episodic events, like oil spills, and chemical releases happen. And we are now faced with a problem of global scale: the transformation of the global climate as a result of modern industrial energy-related emissions. The perspective of environmental economics is especially relevant.

In these settings, raising the political heat for environmental issues is necessary but not sufficient. We have to put together environmental policy initiatives that get the maximum impact for the economic and political resources spent. This is where environmental economics comes in. It is a way of examining the difficult trade-offs that all environmental issues entail. It is a valuable means of inquiring why people behave as they do toward the natural environment, and how we might restructure the current system to rectify harmful practices and inspire environmentally conscious behavior.

The subject is important enough to deserve to be widely available to the nonspecialist. This book is intended for people who have not necessarily had any economics courses, at least not yet. Economics has developed a sophisticated body of theory and applied knowledge. Courses in economics now follow a hierarchy of introductory- and intermediate-level principles that are designed to lead students along and prepare them for the more advanced applications courses. But these run the risk of closing off the subject, making it inaccessible to those who do not want to become specialists. This book was written on the assumption that it's possible to present the major principles of economics in a fairly commonsensical, although rigorous, way and then apply them to questions of environmental quality.

The basic structure and sequence of chapters in this release are unchanged from previous editions. The first section of the book is an introduction, beginning with a chapter on what environmental economics is about, followed by one on the basic relationships between the economy and the environment. The next section is devoted to studying the "tools" of analysis, the principles of demand and cost, and the elements of economic efficiency in both market and nonmarket activities. These chapters are not meant to be completely thorough treatments of these theoretical topics; however, given the objective of the book, the introductory chapters are essential. Even those who have had a course in microeconomic principles might find them valuable for purposes of review. Section 2 also contains a chapter in which these economic principles are applied to a simple model of environmental pollution control.

Section 3 is on environmental analysis. Here we look closely at some of the techniques that have been developed to answer some of the fundamental value questions that underlie environmental decision-making. We focus especially on the principles of benefit–cost analysis. After this we move to Section 4, on the principles of environmental policy design. It begins with a short chapter dealing with the criteria we might use to evaluate policies, then moves on to chapters on the main approaches to environmental quality management.

Sections 5 and 6 contain policy chapters, where we examine current developments in environmental policy with the analytical tools developed earlier. Section 5 focuses on environmental policy in the United States, covering federal policy on water, air, and toxic materials. It also contains a chapter on environmental issues at the state and local levels. Finally, the last section looks at international environmental issues: global climate change, the economics of international environmental agreements, globalization, and economic development and the environment.

The 2024 Release contains much new material, including new exhibits and updated figures and tables. It also contains new materials on:

- Forever Chemicals (PFAS) — Chapter 16
- Toxics and Drinking Water Contamination — Chapter 14
- Circular Economy — Chapters 2 and 17
- Natural Capital — Chapter 2
- Economics of Technical Change — Chapter 5
- Paris Agreement and subsequent COP meetings — Chapters 18, 19, and 21
- Environmental Justice — Chapters 9 and 16
- Economics of Subsidies & the Inflation Reduction Act — Chapter 15
- Carbon Offset Markets — Chapter 13
- Electric Vehicles and Energy Intensity — Chapter 15
- Green Technology Transfer and Developing Countries — Chapter 21

For instructors, Connect offers an Instructor's Manual available for easy download.

Supplements for the Instructor

The following ancillaries are available for quick download and convenient access via the instructor resource site available through McGraw Hill Connect. Instructor resources are password protected for security. The supplement package, which has been revised and improved, consists of the following:

Instructor's Manual: Each chapter contains objectives, main points, teaching ideas, and answers to the discussion questions.

Test Bank: Hundreds of questions test students' knowledge of key terms and concepts. All questions have been accuracy checked and are tagged with the corresponding learning objective, level of difficulty, topic, AACSB learning category, and Bloom's taxonomy for easy filtering.

Test Builder in Connect: Available within McGraw Hill Connect®, Test Builder is a cloud-based tool that enables instructors to format tests that can be printed, administered within a Learning Management System, or exported as a Word document. Test Builder offers a modern, streamlined interface for easy content configuration that matches course needs, without requiring a download.

Test Builder allows you to:
- Access all test bank content from a particular title.
- Easily pinpoint the most relevant content through robust filtering options.
- Manipulate the order of questions or scramble questions and/or answers.
- Pin questions to a specific location within a test.
- Determine your preferred treatment of algorithmic questions.
- Choose the layout and spacing.
- Add instructions and configure the default settings.

Test Builder provides a secure interface for better protection of content and allows for just-in-time updates to flow directly into assessments.

PowerPoints: The PowerPoints present a chapter-by-chapter review of the tables and figures presented in the textbook. You can print or rearrange the slides to fit the needs of your course.

Proctorio
Remote Proctoring & Browser-Locking Capabilities

Remote proctoring and browser-locking capabilities, hosted by Proctorio within Connect, provide control of the assessment environment by enabling security options and verifying the identity of the student.

Seamlessly integrated within Connect, these services allow instructors to control the assessment experience by verifying identification, restricting browser activity, and monitoring student actions.

Instant and detailed reporting gives instructors an at-a-glance view of potential academic integrity concerns, thereby avoiding personal bias and supporting evidence-based claims.

Evergreen

Content and technology are ever-changing, and it is important that you can keep your course up to date with the latest information and assessments. That's why we want to deliver the most current and relevant content for your course, hassle-free.

Environmental Economics uses an Evergreen delivery model, which means it has content, tools, and technology that are regularly updated and relevant, with updates delivered directly to your existing McGraw Hill Connect® course. Engage students and freshen up assignments with up-to-date coverage of select topics and assessments, all without having to switch editions or build a new course.

McGraw Hill Customer Care Contact Information

We understand that getting the most from new technology can be challenging. That's why our services don't stop after you purchase our products. You can reach our Product Specialists 24 hours a day to get product training online. Or you can search our knowledge bank of Frequently Asked Questions on our support website. For Customer Support, call 800-331-5094, or visit www.mheducation.com/highered/contact.html. One of our Technical Support Analysts will be able to assist you in a timely fashion.

Acknowledgments

This text is the result of teaching the subject for many years in the classroom and online, so first we want to thank all those students through the years who have listened, asked questions, and provided the feedback that shaped the book. Many people have helped review and shape previous editions of the book.

Special thanks to Jonathan Hsu, Melissa Leick, and the other folks at McGraw Hill who continue to represent the book so strongly.

Also, thanks to Dheeraj Kumar and Katy Gabel.

And finally, thanks to Tory, Sidney, and Leslie for your support, love, and insightful thoughts and comments during our dinner conversations.

Barry C. Field

Martha K. Field

A complete course platform

Connect enables you to build deeper connections with your students through cohesive digital content and tools, creating engaging learning experiences. We are committed to providing you with the right resources and tools to support all your students along their personal learning journeys.

65%
Less Time Grading

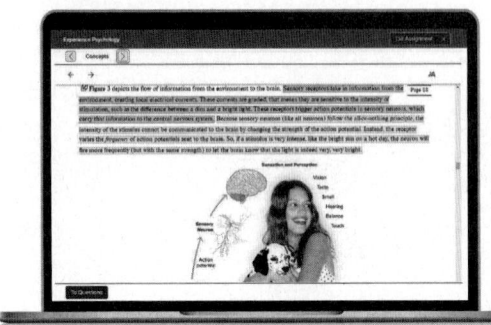

Laptop: Getty Images; Woman/dog: George Doyle/Getty Images

Every learner is unique

In Connect, instructors can assign an adaptive reading experience with SmartBook® 2.0. Rooted in advanced learning science principles, SmartBook 2.0 delivers each student a personalized experience, focusing students on their learning gaps, ensuring that the time they spend studying is time well spent.
mheducation.com/highered/connect/smartbook

Study anytime, anywhere

Encourage your students to download the free ReadAnywhere® app so they can access their online eBook, SmartBook® 2.0, or Adaptive Learning Assignments when it's convenient, even when they're offline. And since the app automatically syncs with their Connect account, all of their work is available every time they open it. Find out more at **mheducation.com/readanywhere**

"I really liked this app— it made it easy to study when you don't have your textbook in front of you."

Jordan Cunningham, a student at *Eastern Washington University*

Effective tools for efficient studying

Connect is designed to help students be more productive with simple, flexible, intuitive tools that maximize study time and meet students' individual learning needs. Get learning that works for everyone with Connect.

Education for all

McGraw Hill works directly with Accessibility Services departments and faculty to meet the learning needs of all students. Please contact your Accessibility Services Office, and ask them to email **accessibility@mheducation.com**, or visit **mheducation.com/about/accessibility** for more information.

Affordable solutions, added value

Make technology work for you with LMS integration for single sign-on access, mobile access to the digital textbook, and reports to quickly show you how each of your students is doing. And with our Inclusive Access program, you can provide all these tools at the lowest available market price to your students. Ask your McGraw Hill representative for more information.

Solutions for your challenges

A product isn't a solution. Real solutions are affordable, reliable, and come with training and ongoing support when you need it and how you want it. Visit **supportateverystep.com** for videos and resources both you and your students can use throughout the term.

Updated and relevant content

Our new Evergreen delivery model provides the most current and relevant content for your course, hassle-free. Content, tools, and technology updates are delivered directly to your existing McGraw Hill Connect® course. Engage students and freshen up assignments with up-to-date coverage of select topics and assessments, all without having to switch editions or build a new course.

Section 1
Introduction

This first section contains two introductory chapters. The first is a brief, nontechnical review of some of the main topics and ideas of environmental economics. The second contains a general discussion of the interactions that exist between the economy and the environment, and introduces some fundamental concepts and definitions that are used throughout the book.

Chapter 1
What Is Environmental Economics?

Economics is the study of how and why individuals and groups make decisions about the use and distribution of valuable human and nonhuman resources. It is not solely the study of profit-making businesses making decisions in a capitalist economy. It is much broader than this; it provides a set of analytical tools that can be used to study any situation in which the scarcity of means requires the balancing of competing objectives. It includes, for example, important questions in the behavior of nonprofit organizations, government agencies, and consumers.

Environmental economics is the application of the principles of economics to the study of how environmental resources are managed. Economics is divided into **microeconomics**, the study of the behavior of individuals and small groups, and **macroeconomics**, the study of the economic performance of economies as a whole. Environmental economics draws from both sides, although more from microeconomics than from macroeconomics. It focuses primarily on how and why people make decisions that have consequences for the natural environment. It is also concerned with how economic institutions and policies can be changed to bring these environmental impacts more into balance with human desires and the needs of the ecosystem itself.

One of our first jobs, therefore, is to become acquainted with some of the basic ideas and analytical tools of microeconomics. To do this at the very beginning, however, would risk giving the impression that the tools are more important than their uses. The tools of analysis are not interesting in themselves, but for the understanding they can give us about why the natural environment becomes degraded, what the consequences of this are, and what can be done effectively to reduce this degradation. For this reason, the first chapter is devoted to sketching out, in commonsense terms, the kinds of questions environmental economists ask and the kinds of answers they seek. After a brief discussion of some general issues, we look at a series of examples of some of the problems addressed in environmental economics.

1-1 Economic Analysis

To study economics is to study the way an economy and its institutions are set up, and how individuals and groups make decisions about transforming and managing scarce resources to increase human wealth, in its broadest sense. Environmental economics focuses on a society's natural and environmental resources, and examines the way people make decisions that lead to environmental destruction and environmental improvements.

Environmental economics is an **analytical subject.** We want not only to describe the state of the environment and changes in it, but also to understand why these conditions exist and how we might bring about improvements in environmental quality. This means we will have to introduce a specialized set of concepts and vocabulary. We will also have to use specialized means of expressing connections between important factors that are involved in the environmental quality issues we explore. To do this, economists use what are called **analytical models.** A model is a simplified representation of reality, in the sense that it isolates and focuses on the most important elements of a situation and neglects the others. The models we will use are graphical in nature, and they will be quite simple.

It is important to distinguish between:

- **positive economics**—the study of what is and
- **normative economics**—the study of what ought to be.

Positive economics seeks to understand how an economic system actually operates by looking at the way people make decisions in different types of circumstances. A study to show how the housing market reacts to changes in interest rates is an exercise in positive economics. A study to estimate how electric utilities would respond to a new tax on greenhouse gas emissions is also an example of positive economics. However, a study to determine what kind of environmental regulation we ought to adopt is a case of normative economics because it involves more than just knowing how things work; it also involves value judgments. We make use of this distinction repeatedly throughout the book.

The economic approach to environmental issues is to be contrasted with what might be called the **moral approach.** According to the latter, environmental degradation is the result of human behavior that is unethical or immoral. Thus, for example, the reason people pollute is because they lack the moral and ethical strength to refrain from the type of behavior that causes environmental degradation. If this is true, then the way to get people to stop polluting is somehow to increase the general level of environmental morality in the society. In fact, the environmental movement has led a great many people to focus on questions of environmental ethics, exploring the moral dimensions of human impacts on the natural environment. These moral questions are obviously of fundamental concern to any civilized society. Certainly one of the main reasons environmental issues have been put on the front burner of social concern is the sense of moral responsibility that has led people to take their concerns into the political arena.

But there are practical difficulties with relying on moral reawakening as the main approach to combatting pollution. People don't necessarily have readily available moral buttons to push, and environmental problems are too important to wait for a long process of moral rebuilding. Nor does a sense of moral outrage, by itself, help us make decisions about all the other social goals that also have ethical dimensions: housing, health care, education, crime, and so on. In a world of competing objectives we have to worry about very practical questions: Are we targeting the right environmental objectives, can we really enforce certain policies, are we getting the most impact for the money, and so on. But the biggest problem with basing our approach to pollution control strictly on the moral argument is the basic assumption that people pollute because they are somehow morally underdeveloped. It is not moral underdevelopment that leads to environmental destruction; rather, it is the way the economic system, within which people make decisions about how to conduct their lives, has been arranged.

We must understand, however, that incentives include more than simply the monetary aspects of a situation. Such things as time, reputation, guilt, risk and uncertainty, altruism, regret, and similar factors enter into the whole panoply of influences that shape people's decisions. In recent years, more attention has been given to these kinds of factors in explaining human actions, under the heading **behavioral economics.** Behavioral economics is an attempt to introduce psychological and perceptual factors into economic models, in order to make these models more realistic and more accurate in terms of understanding human behavior. In environmental models, for example, how people react to pollution and its alleviation will depend on how it is impacting them, and what they regard as fair in its impact on others.

1-2 The Importance of Incentives

People pollute because it is the cheapest way they have of solving a certain, very practical problem. That problem is the disposal of the waste products remaining after consumers have finished using something, or after business firms have finished producing something. People make these decisions on production, consumption, and disposal within a certain set of economic and social institutions[1]; these institutions structure the **incentives** that lead people to make decisions in one direction rather than another. What needs to be studied is how this incentive process works and, especially, how it may be restructured so that people will be led to make decisions and develop lifestyles that have more benign environmental implications.

One simplistic incentive-type statement that one often hears is that pollution is a result of the **profit motive.** According to this view, in private enterprise economies such as the Western industrialized nations, people are rewarded for maximizing profits, the difference between the value of what is produced and the value of what is used up in the production process. Furthermore, the thinking goes, the profits that entrepreneurs try to maximize are strictly monetary profits. In this headlong pursuit of monetary profits, entrepreneurs give no thought to the environmental impacts of their actions because it "does not pay." Thus, in this uncontrolled striving for monetary profits, the only way to reduce environmental pollution is to weaken the strength of the profit motive.

There is substantial truth in this proposition, but also a degree of misunderstanding. It is certainly the case that if operators of private firms make decisions without taking environmental costs into account, excess pollution will result. But this is true of anybody: private firms, individuals, and public agencies. When individuals pour paint thinner down the sink drain or buy gas-guzzling vehicles, they are making decisions without putting adequate weight on environmental consequences. The same can be said of government agencies, which have sometimes been serious polluters even though they are not profit motivated. But the most persuasive argument against the view that the search for profits is the only thing that causes pollution comes from looking at the history of Eastern Europe and the former USSR. With the collapse of these ex-Communist regimes, we became aware of the enormous environmental destruction that occurred in some of these regions—heavily polluted air and water resources in many areas, which have a major impact on human health and ecological systems. Several East Asian countries are currently experiencing the

---

1. By "institutions" we mean the fundamental set of public and private organizations, laws, and practices that a society uses to structure its economic activity. Markets are an economic institution, for example, as are corporations, a body of commercial law, public agencies, and so on.

same problem: headlong emphasis on economic development (by both public and private firms) with insufficient regard for the environmental consequences of this process. These examples show that it is not only the profit motive that can cause pollution, but any resource-using and waste-producing decisions that are made without exercising appropriate control over their environmental consequences.

In the sections and chapters that follow, we will place great stress on the importance of incentives in the functioning of an economic system. *Any* system will produce destructive environmental impacts if the incentives within the system are not structured to avoid them. We have to look more deeply into any economic system to understand how its incentive systems work and how they may be changed so that we can have a reasonably progressive economy without disastrous environmental effects.

1-3 Incentives: A Household Example

An incentive is something that attracts or repels people and leads them to modify their behavior in some way. An **economic incentive** is something in the economic world that leads people to channel their efforts at economic production and consumption in certain directions. We often think of economic incentives as consisting of payoffs in terms of material wealth; people have an incentive to behave in ways that provide them with increased wealth. But there are also nonmaterial incentives that lead people to modify their economic behavior; for example, self-esteem, the desire to preserve a beautiful visual environment, or the desire to set a good example for others.

For a simple first look at the importance of changing incentives to get improvements in environmental quality, consider the data shown in **Exhibit 1.1**. Historically, people in urban

EXHIBIT 1.1 Experience with PAYT Programs

"Pay as your throw" is a system many communities have structured to give people the incentive to reduce their waste streams and give the communities financial resources to help cover waste-management-activities. Some data put together by WasteZero[a] show how effective it has been. It covers a sample of communities in southern Maine, some with PAYT programs and some without PAYT. Some key findings are:

- For communities with PAYT programs, the average amount of trash was 356 pounds per year.
- For communities without PAYT programs, the annual trash volume per capita was 645 pounds.

- The overall recycling rate of PAYT towns was 33.1 percent. For non-PAYT communities the recycling rate averaged 20.4 percent.

These data show the effectiveness of using an incentive system to get people to increase their recycling, thereby reducing the amount of material disposed of as trash.

[a]WasteZero is an organization that partners with towns and cities to help establish effective systems for community waste management.

Source: Recycling Today, "*WasteZero releases report on impact of Pay-as-you-throw programs,*" June 8, 2018, https://www.recyclingtoday.com

areas have paid a flat annual fee to have their trash collected. The problem with this approach is that there is simply no incentive for any individual family to limit its trash production, because the family will pay the same annual trash-collection fee no matter how much, or little, it produces. This might not be a problem if there were ample landfill space and if there were no danger that the landfill would contaminate the surrounding environment, such as a nearby groundwater system. But for most communities these conditions don't hold any more, if they ever did.

Thus, many communities have introduced a system that gives people an incentive to search for ways to reduce the amount of solid waste they produce. This is done with a system of Pay-as-you-throw (PAYT) which is a charge on people for each bag of trash they put on the curb. What this does is to give families the incentive to reduce the number of bags of trash they set out. They can do this by recycling, by switching to products that have less waste, by putting food scraps in a compost pile, and so on. These have led, according to the story, to a large increase in the amount of trash recycled and a reduction in the total amount of trash. There are many other communities around the country where this system has been adopted. **Exhibit 1.1** shows how effective this system has been for a collection of towns in Maine, some of which adopted PAYT and others did not. Of course, no system is perfect. Increases in illegal dumping and difficulties with applying the plan to apartment houses are problems. Nevertheless, the new approach does illustrate in a very clear way the effects of a shift from a system where there were no incentives for people to reduce their solid waste to one where there are such incentives. The technical name for this approach is **unit pricing**.

1-4 Incentives and Climate Change

Municipal solid waste and other trash have traditionally been local problems, both because the possible environmental impacts are usually local, and because, policy-wise, local governments have had the primary responsibilities for dealing with them. Obviously, not all environmental problems are local: Traditional air pollution is usually a regional or national issue, and sometimes it is an international problem because it crosses country borders. And some environmental problems are truly global in that they have causes and impacts that involve everyone around the world, though not necessarily in equal intensity.

Of course, the global issue that is thrusting itself into the world's consciousness is the greenhouse effect, the buildup of heat-trapping gases in the earth's atmosphere that is producing long-run changes in global climate. We will have much more to say about this issue in later chapters. A major focus of environmental economists is to try to identify the most effective policy approaches to combat the emissions of substances causing the greenhouse effect, especially carbon dioxide (CO_2), but also including many other gases, such as methane (CH_4).

One way to approach this is with conventional "command-and-control" policies. This relies on laws and regulations that directly or indirectly specify pollution-control technologies or practices that polluters should use. Then standard enforcement procedures are used (inspections, monitoring, fines, etc.) to produce acceptably high degrees of compliance. Although this approach still characterizes much of the environmental policy arena, there has been a lot of attention given to incentive-based policies. There are two basic types of incentive policies: emission charges or taxes, analogous to the trash-collection fees discussed in the previous section; and market-based trading programs. We will discuss each of these at length; trading programs in **Chapter 13** and emission charges in **Chapter 12**.

Emission charges work essentially by putting a price on emissions. Many people have argued that this would be the most effective approach to getting reductions in greenhouse gas emissions. In many countries, such charges have been introduced. **Exhibit 1.2** lists some of the charges currently in effect, expressed as U.S. dollar per ton of CO_2 equivalent.

EXHIBIT 1.2 Carbon Taxes Around the World

Country/Region	U.S. $/metric ton CO_2e
Canada	43
Denmark	27
Finland	85
France	49
Iceland	34
Japan	2
Mexico	4
Norway	88
Portugal	27
Spain	17
Sweden	130
Switzerland	130
United Kingdom	24

Source: Statista, *Carbon Tax Rates Worldwide as of April 1, 2022, by Country*, 2022.

1-5 The Design of Environmental Policy

Environmental economics has a major role to play in the design of **public policies** for environmental quality improvement. There are an enormous range and variety of public programs and policies devoted to environmental matters, at all levels of government: local, state, regional, federal, and international. They vary greatly in their efficiency and effectiveness. Some have been well designed and will no doubt have beneficial impacts. Others are not well designed. Not being cost-effective, they will end up achieving much less environmental improvement than they would have if they had been designed better.

The problem of designing efficient environmental policies is often not given the emphasis it deserves. It is easy to fall into the trap of thinking that any programs or policies that flow out of the rough and tumble of the environmental political process are likely to be of some help, or that they certainly will be better than nothing. But history is full of cases where policymakers and public administrators have pursued policies that don't work; the public is frequently led to believe a policy will be effective even when any reasonable analysis could predict that it will not. All of this means that it is critically important to study how to design environmental policies that are effective and efficient.

The total social cost of environmental pollution consists of the expenditures (capital and operating) of private businesses to comply with regulations, plus the damage costs of pollution (largely health related) suffered by the exposed human population, plus the costs that the government and various public agencies incur in planning and pursuing pollution-control regulation. Although the value of the total social cost has never actually been estimated for the United States, it is clear that it is a substantial fraction of the country's GDP (which in 2022 was about $25.5 trillion). A question of great importance, however, is whether we are getting the most improvement possible in environmental quality for the money spent. Former EPA director William Reilly is quoted as saying that "at this level of expenditure, there's a very large obligation to get it right." By "getting it right," he means having programs that get the maximum improvement in environmental quality for the resources spent. Everybody has an interest in this: environmentalists, for obvious reasons; public regulators, because they are tapping a limited supply of taxpayer resources and consumer tolerance; and the regulated polluters themselves, because matters of efficiency are critical to business success.

"Getting it right" means paying attention to the factors that affect the cost-effectiveness of environmental regulations, and especially to the way they create incentives for actions taken by polluters. An important problem in environmental policy is that of **perverse incentives**—that is, incentives created by a policy that actually work against the overall objectives of that policy. Environmental policies often created perverse incentives, because environmental policymakers have too often tried to legislate results directly, rather than establish the types of regulations that harness the self-interest of polluters to move toward efficient emission reductions. **Exhibit 1.3** discusses perverse incentives in the federal program to control power plant emissions, specifically the incentive inherent in the decision to switch from old, highly polluting technology to newer, cleaner plants.

Issues related to the design of environmental policy are a major part of environmental economics. It is important to know how alternative policy approaches measure up in terms of cost-effectiveness, getting the most pollution reduction for the money spent, and, in terms of efficiency, appropriately balancing the benefits and costs of environmental improvements.

EXHIBIT 1.3 Incentive Aspects of New Source Review

The Clean Air Act, as amended, distinguishes between existing sources of air pollutants and new or modified sources. Pollution-control requirements for the latter are much more stringent than those for the former. The thinking behind this is that building pollution control into new plants is normally much less costly than retrofitting older plants. Thus, as older plants are retired in favor of new technologies, the extent of overall industry emissions would decline. But this approach actually involves incentive problems. If new or upgraded plants would be required

(Continued)

> **EXHIBIT 1.3** *(Continued)*
>
> to have expensive emission controls, the incentive would be to hold onto the old plants for as long as possible, making whatever repairs and minor changes would be required to keep them in reasonable operating shape. To counter the incentive, the EPA put into effect a procedure called New Source Review (NSR), essentially an evaluation of individual plants to make sure that any changes may have changed its classification for existing to "new," thereby requiring better pollution control. But this made the problem worse: Now plant operators had an incentive to keep operating the old plants with few or no changes, for fear of triggering an NSR if they did too much. In effect, the way the CAA was written, which seemed to foster a gradual cleaning up of the power industry as old plants were retired and newer, cleaner plants were built, actually created incentives that produced a slowing of the rate at which the industry converted to new pollution-control technologies. A straightforward way of avoiding this type of problem is to apply the same emission standards to all sources, whether new or old.
>
> **Source:** Arthur G. Fraas, John D. Graham, and Jeff Holmstead, "EPA's New Source Review Program: Time for Reform?," *Environmental Law Reporter*, 47(1), 2017, 10026–10040.

1-6 Macroeconomic Questions: Environment and Growth

The incentive issues discussed in the previous section are microeconomic problems; they deal with the behavior of individuals or small groups of consumers, polluting firms, and firms in the pollution-control industry. The macroeconomy, on the other hand, refers to the economic structure and performance of an entire country taken as a single unit. When we study topics such as changes in GDP, rates of inflation, and the unemployment rate, we are focusing on the performance of the country as a whole; that is to say, we are doing **macroeconomics**.

There are a number of important questions about the relationship between environmental issues and the behavior of the macroeconomy:

- What overall preferences do citizens have with respect to the balance between environmental protection and economic growth?
- Historically, have measures to protect the environment led to lower economic growth rates?
- How might environmental regulations be designed to minimize their impacts on growth?
- When the perspective is broadened from growth to human welfare, how do environmental protection measures stack up?

From a political standpoint, perhaps the most sensitive question is whether stricter environmental policies will tend to retard economic growth. There is little evidence that from the perspective of the total economy, environmental protection costs have been a significant economic burden. Pollution-control costs today are probably about 1 to 2 percent of GDP in the country. Costs of this magnitude are unlikely to be large enough to cause large-scale layoffs and reduced economic growth. Nevertheless, this question continues to be politically sensitive.

Environmental regulations have also been blamed for reducing employment in industries subject to the regulations. But environmental regulations also provide the incentive for growth in the envirotech industries, with the added employment this implies. **Exhibit 1.4** discusses some of these issues in the context of reducing atmospheric emissions that are causing global warming.

EXHIBIT 1.4 The Macroeconomic Cost of Reducing CO_2 Emissions: It Depends on How It's Done

Global warming is the process by which the buildup of certain gases in the earth's atmosphere increases its heat-trapping capacity sufficiently to produce an increase in mean global surface temperatures. An increase is starting to have major meteorological repercussions, with huge economic and social impacts around the world. Scientists have almost unanimously concluded that the only way of effectively forestalling global warming in the long run is to reduce the emissions of greenhouse gases, chief among which is carbon dioxide (CO_2). Emissions of CO_2 stem largely from the burning of fossil fuels, which is ubiquitous in the industrial, transportation, and domestic sectors of modern economies. But how much to try to reduce these emissions is highly controversial. Many in the environmental community believe that vigorous action is required. One of the controversial aspects of this is how much it will cost. Macroeconomic studies appear to indicate that the minimum costs of limiting U.S. carbon emissions to their 1990 level would be 1 or 2 percent of GDP. This is a relatively small number in percentage terms but a larger one in terms of dollars (1 percent of the U.S. GDP in 2022 was about $255 billion).

But this is a minimum, achievable only if greenhouse gas policies are cost-effective, and likely to be much higher if they are not. Cost-effectiveness means that the policies get the biggest "bang for the buck," in this case the biggest emission reduction for the resources spent. The fact is that the cost of reducing greenhouse gases differs a lot among industries (coal-fired power generation versus automobile manufacturing, for example) and even among firms in the same industry. For a pollution-control policy to be cost-effective, it has to take these costs differences into account. Basically, it should bring about proportionally greater emission reductions from sources with lower emission-reduction costs. How to get this result will be a major topic of this book.

Source: Jonathan M. Harris, Brian Roach, and Anne-Marie Codur, "*The Economics of Global Climate Change,*" Global Development and Environmental Institute, Tufts University, 2017.

Another macroeconomic question concerns the impacts of economic growth on environmental quality. Do higher rates of growth, that is, increases in our traditional measures such as GDP, imply greater environmental degradation, or might the opposite be true? Or, is economic growth sustainable? **Exhibit 1.5** presents a model in which pollution increases during the early stages of a country's development and then begins to diminish as countries gain adequate resources to tackle pollution problems. This happens because at low incomes, people tend to value development over environmental quality, but as they achieve greater wealth, they are willing to devote greater resources to environmental quality improvements.

EXHIBIT 1.5 Economic Growth and the Environment

One model depicting the relationship between growth and the environment is the "inverted-U" shown in the figure below. If this is in fact true (and some economists question this model), it would mean that economic growth beyond the industrial phase of development can be expected to reduce environmental pollution. We will have more to say about this phenomenon in **Chapter 21.**

1-7 Benefit–Cost Analysis

Effective decision-making requires that there be adequate information about the **consequences** of the decisions. This is as important in the **public sector,** where the issue is effective **public policy,** as it is in the **private sector,** where the main concern is with the bottom line of the profit-and-loss statement. The primary type of public-sector analysis in environmental policy questions is **benefit–cost analysis.** Policies or projects are studied in terms of the environmental benefits they would produce, and these are compared with the costs that are entailed. It was first used in this country early in the 20th century to evaluate water development projects undertaken by federal agencies. Today it is used by many government agencies to help make rational policy decisions.

Benefit-cost analysis is such an important and widely used approach that we devote several chapters to it later in the book (**Chapters 6, 7,** and **8**). In this type of analysis, as the name implies, the benefits of some proposed action are estimated and compared with the total costs that society would bear if that action were undertaken. If it is a proposal for a public park, for example, the benefits in terms of recreational experiences provided by the park are compared with the expected costs of building the park and of using the land in this way rather than in some other way. Or a proposal to build a solid-waste incinerator would compare the costs of building and operating the incinerator, including the costs of disposing of the remaining ash and the costs of possible airborne emissions, with benefits, such as reducing the use of landfills for the solid waste. **Exhibit 1.6** shows some results of a study to estimate the benefits and costs of reducing nitrogen oxide (NO_x) emissions in a group of Eastern U.S. states.

EXHIBIT 1.6 Benefits and Costs of Reducing Nitrogen Oxide (NO_x) Emissions

Nitrogen oxide (NO_x) emissions are produced from a variety of industrial and transportation sectors, as a consequence of the burning of fossil fuels. NO_x reacts with volatile organic compounds in the presence of sunlight and produces ground-level ozone, ambient concentrations of which produce a range of health damages. NO_x emissions are also precursors of particulate matter (PM), which is fine soot or dust that can be composed of a number of substances and have deleterious effects on human health. Thus, reducing NO_x emissions has been a major objective of the EPA and many state environmental agencies. To support these efforts, numerous economic studies have been done to estimate the benefits and the costs of reducing NO_x emissions. To do this, researchers examine the various types and location of sources of NO_x emissions (e.g., power plants, industrial boilers) and what it would cost these sources to reduce these emissions by a given amount. On the other side, they must estimate the effect of these reductions on ambient ozone levels, and the benefits of these reductions for people living and working in these ambient conditions.

A group of economists conducted a benefit–cost analysis of NO_x emission reductions in 19 Eastern U.S. states and regions.[1] They asked the question: What would be the benefits and costs of a 20 percent reduction in NO_x emissions from 925 large electric utility boilers in these states? To estimate the costs, they looked at the different technical options available to reduce emissions and identified the least costly alternative for meeting the emission reductions. To estimate the benefits, they used a model showing the relationship between emission reductions and changes in ambient ozone and PM, and another model to estimate the health effects of these ambient changes.

[1] Michelle S. Bergin, Jhih-Shyang Shih, Alan J. Krupnick, James W. Boylan, James G. Wilkinson, M. Talat Odman, and Armistead G. Russell, "Regional Air Quality: Local and Interstate Impacts of NO_x and SO_2 Emissions on Ozone and Fine Particulate Matter in the Eastern United States," *Environmental Science and Technology*, 41(13), 2007, 4677–4689.

(Continued)

EXHIBIT 1.6 *(Continued)*

Some of these results are as follows:

NO$_x$ reduction (tons/day)	987
Benefits ($1,000/day)	
Ozone reduction	$238
PM reduction	$1,541
Total benefits	$1,779
Costs ($1,000/day)	$914
Net benefits ($1,000/day)	$865

Note that the health benefits of PM reduction are about six times higher than those of ozone reduction. Note also that there are substantial net benefits (total benefits minus total costs). These amount to $864,000 per day, which translates into about $315 million per year. Results of benefit–cost analyses of this type can help buttress the case for tightening air-pollution-control standards under the Clean Air Act.

The benefit–cost approach implies that we need to consider both the benefits and the costs of environmental programs and policies. This often puts benefit–cost studies squarely in the middle of political controversy on many environmental issues. In the political struggles that characterize many environmental problems, groups on one side consist of people whose major concern is with the benefits, whereas groups on the other side are primarily concerned with costs. Environmental groups typically stress the benefits; business groups usually focus on the costs.

1-8 Valuing the Environment

To complete a benefit–cost analysis of an environmental program or regulation successfully, it's necessary to estimate both the benefits and the costs of the actions. One factor that complicates this type of analysis is that the benefits of environmental improvements are usually **nonmarket** in nature. If we were trying to assess the benefits to society of a program to support potato farmers, we could get a good idea of the value of potatoes by looking at how much people are willing to pay for them when they buy them at the supermarket. But suppose we have a program of air-pollution reduction that will, among other things, lower the risk that people in a certain region will have of contracting chronic bronchitis. How might we estimate the social value of this result? It cannot be done by looking directly at market behavior, as in the case of potatoes, because there is no market where people buy and sell directly the changes in health risk produced by the environmental program. Environmental economists have developed a series of **nonmarket valuation techniques** that are used to estimate these types of environmental outcomes. We will discuss some of these techniques in **Chapter 7**.

1-9 Environment and Development

Countries of the world are sometimes, perhaps misleadingly, divided into two categories: developed and developing. The latter comprises all those countries whose private and public wealth per capita are relatively low and which seek the means of developing their economies. Most developing countries have environmental issues, and many have put into place laws and regulations to deal with cases of pollution and resource degradation. Although many have embraced command-and-control policy approaches, there has also been heavy reliance on voluntary pollution-control plans.[2] The trend in the developed countries toward incentive-based (IB) programs has suggested to some that countries in the developing world also be well advised to adopt them, as their cost-effectiveness would be especially valuable in resource-scarce situations. Others have stressed that IB plans might be too complex for the special institutional characteristics of developing countries. **Exhibit 1.7** sheds some light on this question.

EXHIBIT 1.7 Incentive-Based Pollution Control in the Developing World

Incentive-based (IB) approaches to pollution control have become fairly common in the developed world, although there is still scope for their wider use. This includes emission trading in its various forms, and direct emission charges. Some people have argued that countries of the developing world would be well advised to adopt these types of programs, because they achieve, at least theoretically, cost-effective pollution control. But others have argued that the "institutional machinery" present in the developing world is often inadequate for the sophisticated monitoring and implementing that IB plans require. Weak public regulatory agencies, inadequate public laws, and substantial corruption are often the lot of developing countries, though not all of them.

In Latin America, there have been the following attempts to implement IB programs:

Chile: This was an emission trading program for air pollutants, primarily particulate matter, starting in 1993. A new public agency was created to implement the program.

Columbia: This was a plan to institute a fee for the discharge of Biochemical Oxygen Demand (BOD) and Total Suspended Solids (TSS) from a variety of point sources of these pollutants. This was begun in 1997, and included a plan for redistributing the revenues obtained from the charges.

Costa Rica: This was a program for charging a fee for the discharge of TSS and BOD. The fee was based on the concentration of these substances in the discharge stream and was meant to complement the existing program of emission standards. The program started in 2008; it also incorporated a plan for redistributing the resulting revenues.

How have these IB programs worked in these countries? The general conclusion appears to be that it is difficult to get them up and running effectively because the necessary administrative/regulatory systems are not yet in place. This means that the technical aspects of new IB programs are difficult to clarify and implement. Without effective administrative institutions, the programs are often ensnared and

(Continued)

---

2. See, for example, Allen Blackman, *Alternative Pollution Control Policies in Developing Countries*, Resources for the Future, Discussion Paper EFD DP 09-14, Washington, DC, 2009.

> **EXHIBIT 1.7** *(Continued)*
>
> hindered by political pushing and shoving among politically connected participants. What this tells us is that effective environmental policies depend on both the design of the policies and the presence of the administrative institutions that can implement them.
>
> **Source:** Marcelo Caffera, "The Use of Economic Instruments for Pollution Control in Latin America: Lessons for Future Policy Design," *Environment and Economic Development*, 16, 2010, 247–273.

1-10 International Issues

Many environmental problems are local or regional, in the sense that the causal factors and resulting damages lie within the same country. But many others are international in scope. Some are **international** simply because there is a national border between the pollution source and the resulting impacts. Airborne emissions that are carried from one country upwind to another downwind are a case in point, as is water pollution of a river that traverses several countries. There is another class of problems that are **global** in nature because they impact the global environment. One of these is the destruction of the earth's protective layer of **stratospheric ozone** by chemicals devised by humans for a number of industrial purposes. Another is the problem of **global climate change,** the possible rise in surface temperatures of the earth stemming from the accumulation of carbon dioxide in the atmosphere. The 1997 Kyoto conference featured an attempt by developed countries to agree on future cutbacks of CO_2 emissions. Cost-effective CO_2 emission reductions and the design of equitable international agreements are two topics among many on which environmental economists have worked.

The Kyoto Protocol expired in 2012, and was superceded by the Paris agreement in 2015. How this agreement to reduce emissions of greenhouse gases plays out will depend on the negotiating skills of the parties, and on the incentives that the countries have to take part in an effective agreement. What complicates this is the fact that different countries are likely to be differently affected by global warming, so they come to the bargaining table with different incentives for entering into a meaningful agreement.

To get an idea of the magnitude of this situation, **Table 1.1** shows some data for CO_2 emissions, per capita, for a small group of countries for 2016 and 2021. Note several things: A few showed increases during this period (China, Qatar); many showed modest declines. There are enormous differences among countries, for example, 30.8 tons in Qatar (2021) and 2.3 tons in Indonesia. Even among countries of the developed world there are large differences, for example, 14.9 tons in the United States and 5.2 tons in the United Kingdom. A topic of increasing interest is how differences such as this affect the willingness of countries to enter into international environmental agreements, and how the terms of these agreements might be shaped so as to motivate widespread participation. We will take up these matters in **Chapter 19.**

TABLE 1.1 CO$_2$ Emissions per Capita, Selected Countries

Country	CO$_2$ Emissions per Capita (metric tons) 2016	2021
Australia	16.0	15.1
Brazil	2.0	2.3
Canada	14.9	14.3
China	6.6	8.1
France	4.4	4.7
India	1.6	1.9
Indonesia	1.7	2.3
Mexico	3.6	3.2
Norway	6.8	7.6
Qatar	30.8	35.6
Russia	10.0	18.1
South Africa	7.4	7.3
United Kingdom	5.7	5.2
United States	15.0	14.9

Carbon dioxide emissions are those stemming from the burning of fossil fuels and the manufacture of cement.
Source: Statista, *Per Capita Carbon Dioxide Emissions Worldwide, by Country,* 2023.

1-11 Globalization and the Environment

There is another sense in which global environmental problems have recently taken on greater urgency. These are the environmental implications of globalization. **Globalization** is a term used to refer to the perceived changes that are taking place in the world economy, including the rapid growth of **trade** among nations, **privatization** of economic institutions, massive international flows of **financial capital,** and growth in the numbers and sizes of **multinational firms.** Advocates of a more integrated world economy point to its potential for stimulating economic growth and increasing wealth in the developing world. But many people also have pointed to the potential downside of globalization, one part of which may be the degradation of natural environments in developing countries.

Globalization has become a politically charged concept; it is sometimes hard to cut through the rhetoric and identify the substantive issues that are involved. One part of globalization is the substantial increase that has occurred in the volume of trade among nations. This has led to a concern about the implications of the increasing volume of trade on environmental impacts in both developed and developing countries. International trade in goods and services has been touted as an engine of growth for the countries involved. Some people take the view that the long-run environmental implications of this are positive. Many others feel that unrestricted trade will have severe environmental consequences. We will take up this topic at greater length in **Chapter 20.**

Another aspect of globalization is the growth of multinational firms and the relocation of industrial firms from developed to developing countries. Relocation is influenced by disparity in environmental regulations among countries, or even within countries, along with tax codes and infrastructure. Depending on how trade and production change geographically, emissions can be redistributed about the world and result in shifts in the burden of pollution. The fear is that some developing countries could become **pollution havens,** places to which firms move in order to have to spend less on pollution-control measures. We will look more closely at this phenomenon in **Chapter 20.**

1-12 Economics and Politics

Finally, we need to discuss briefly the question of how to achieve effective environmental policy in a highly **political policy environment.** Environmental policies not only affect the natural environment, but also affect people. This means that environmental policy decisions come out of the political process, a process where, at least in democratic systems, people and groups come together and contend for influence and control, where interests collide, coalitions shift, and biases intrude. Policies that come out of a process like this may bear little relationship to what we might think of as efficient approaches to particular environmental problems. Many people have questioned the very idea that a democratic political process could or should strive to produce policies that are efficient in some technical economic sense.

So where does that leave the environmental economist? Why spend so much time and energy on questions of efficiency and cost-effectiveness when the political process most likely is going to override these considerations and go its own way? Why worry about economic incentives and economic efficiency when "everything is political," as the saying goes? The answer is that although we know that the real world is one of compromise and power, the best way for scientists and economists to serve that process is to produce studies that are as clear and as objective as possible. It is the politician's job to compromise or seek advantage; it is the scientist's job to provide the best information he or she can. For economists, in fact, this means studies in which economic efficiency is a central role, but it means more than this. Because the policy process is one where "who gets what" is a dominant theme, environmental economics must also deal with the distribution question, on how environmental problems and policies affect different groups within society. It is also the role of scientists and economists to provide information to policymakers on alternative courses of action. Although we will focus in later chapters on what appear to be "the" most efficient policies or "the" least-cost courses of action, it has to be recognized that in the give-and-take of the political world in which policy is actually made, choosing among alternatives is always the order of the day.

But economists have no right these days to complain about their role in the environmental policy process. If anything, these are the days of the rising influence of economists. Benefit-cost procedures and results have become more widely accepted, in public policy arenas and in law courts hearing environmental cases. New pollution-control initiatives incorporating economic incentive principles are being adopted at both federal and state levels in the United States. All the more reason, then, to study and understand the basic economics of environmental analysis and policy.

Summary

The purpose of this brief chapter was to whet your appetite for the subject of environmental economics by indicating some of the main topics that the field encompasses, showing very briefly the approach that economists take in studying them. It's also to give you something to remember. When we get involved in some of the conceptual and theoretical issues that underlie the topic, it is easy to lose sight of what we are trying to accomplish. We are trying to develop these principles so that we can actually use them to address real-world problems such as those discussed in this chapter. Although the principles may appear abstract and odd at first, remember the objective: to achieve a cleaner, healthier, and more beautiful natural environment.

Chapter 2
The Economy and the Environment

The **economy** is a collection of technological, legal, and social arrangements through which individuals in society seek to increase their material and spiritual well-being. The two elementary economic functions pursued by society are **production** and **distribution.** Production refers to all those activities that determine the quantities of goods and services that are produced and the technological and managerial means by which this production is carried out. Distribution refers to the way in which goods and services are divided up, or distributed, among the individuals and groups that make up society. Distribution puts goods and services in the hands of individuals, households, and organizations; the final utilization of these goods and services is termed **consumption.**

Any economic system exists within, and is encompassed by, the natural world. Its processes and changes are of course governed by the **laws of nature.** In addition, economies make use directly of **natural assets** of all types. One role the natural world plays is that of provider of raw materials and energy inputs, without which production and consumption would be impossible. Thus, one type of impact that an economic system has on nature is by drawing upon raw materials to keep the system functioning. Production and consumption activities also produce leftover waste products, called "residuals," and sooner or later these must find their way back into the natural world. Depending on how they are handled, these residuals may lead to pollution or the degradation of the natural environment. We can illustrate these fundamental relationships with a simple schematic:

- The arrow marked (a) represents raw materials flowing into production and consumption. **Natural resource economics** is the study of this flow of nature in its role as a provider of raw materials. We must think of this broadly, as encompassing both traditional extractive uses and the services made available by natural resource preservation.
- The arrow marked (b) shows the impact of economic activity on the quality of the natural environment. **Environmental economics** focuses on the flow of materials and energy residuals back into the natural environment and the resultant impacts on the natural world.

Although pollution control is the major topic within environmental economics, it is not the only one. Human beings have an impact on the environment in many ways that are not related to pollution in the traditional sense. Habitat disruption from housing developments and scenic degradation from any number of human activities are examples of environmental impacts that are not related to the discharge of specific pollutants.

The topic of this book is environmental economics. We will study the management of waste flows and the impacts of human activity on the quality of environmental assets. But in a real sense, many of these problems originate in the earlier, raw-material phase of the nature–economy interaction. So before proceeding, we consider briefly the major dimensions of natural resource economics.

2-1 Natural Resource Economics

In modern industrial/urban societies, it is sometimes easy to overlook the fact that a large part of total economic activity still relies on the extraction and utilization of natural resources. **Natural resource economics** is the application of economic principles to the study of these activities. To get a general impression of what this discipline includes, the following is a list of its major subdivisions and examples of questions pursued in each one.[1]

Mineral economics: What is the appropriate rate at which to extract ore from a mine? How do exploration and the addition to reserves respond to mineral prices?

Forest economics: How are optimal timber harvest rates affected by forests' contribution to carbon sequestration and habitat preservation?

Marine economics: What kinds of rules need to be established for managing fisheries? How do different harvest rates affect the stocks of fish?

Land economics: How do people in the private sector (builders, home purchasers) make decisions about the use of land? How do the laws of property rights and public land-use regulations affect the way space is devoted to different uses?

Energy economics: What are the appropriate rates for extracting underground petroleum deposits? How sensitive is available energy supply to changes in energy prices?

Water economics: How do different water laws affect the way water is utilized by different people? What kinds of regulations should govern the reallocation of water from, for example, agriculture to urban users?

Agricultural economics: How do farmers make decisions about using conservation practices in cultivating their land? How do government programs affect the choices farmers make regarding what crops to produce and how to produce them?

A fundamental distinction in natural resource economics is that of **renewable** and **nonrenewable** resources:

- **Renewable resources** are living resources, such as fisheries and timber; they grow in time according to biological processes. Some nonliving resources are also renewable—the classic example being the sun's energy that reaches the earth.

---

1. Natural resource economics is the subject of a companion book written by one of the authors. See Barry C. Field, *Natural Resource Economics An Introduction*, 4th ed., Waveland Press, 2024.

- **Nonrenewable resources** are those for which there are no processes of replenishment—once used they are gone forever. Classic examples are petroleum reservoirs and non-energy mineral deposits. Certain resources, such as many groundwater aquifers, have replenishment rates that are so low that they are in effect nonrenewable.

It is easy to see that the use of nonrenewable resources is a problem with a strong intertemporal dimension; it involves trade-offs between the present and the future. If more oil is pumped out of an underground deposit this year, less will be available to extract in future years. Establishing today's correct pumping rate, therefore, requires a comparison of the value of oil now with the anticipated value of oil in the future.

But complicated intertemporal trade-offs also exist with renewable resources. What should today's codfish harvesting rate be, considering that the size of the remaining stock will affect its future growth and availability? Should this timber be cut today, or does its expected rate of growth warrant holding off harvesting until some time in the future? Biological and ecological processes create connections between the rates of resource use in the present and the quantity and quality of resources available to future generations. It is these connections that are the focus of what has come to be called **sustainability.**

A resource-use rate that is sustainable is one that can be maintained over the long run without impairing the fundamental ability of the natural resource base to support future generations. Sustainability does not mean that resources must remain untouched; rather, it means that their rates of use must be chosen so as not to jeopardize future generations. In the case of nonrenewable resources, this implies using the extracted resource in such a way that it contributes to the long-run economic and social health of the population. For renewable resources, it means establishing rates of use that are coordinated with the natural productivity rates affecting the way the resources grow and decline.

Many environmental problems also have strong intertemporal dimensions, that is, important trade-offs between today and the future. For example, many pollutants tend to accumulate in the environment rather than dissipate and disappear. Heavy metals, for example, can accumulate in water and soil. Carbon dioxide emissions over many decades have accumulated in the earth's atmosphere. What is in fact being depleted here is the earth's **assimilative capacity,** the ability of the natural system to accept certain pollutants and render them benign or inoffensive. Some of the theoretical ideas about the depletion of natural resources are also useful in understanding environmental pollution. In this sense, assimilative capacity is a natural resource akin to traditional resources such as oil deposits and forests.

A resource that resides not in any one substance but in a collection of elements is **biological diversity.** Biologists estimate that there may be as many as 10 million different species of living organisms in the world today. These represent a vast and important source of genetic information that is useful for the development of medicines, natural pesticides, resistant varieties of plants and animals, and the health of ecosystems. Human activities have substantially increased the rate of species extinctions, so habitat conservation and species preservation have become important contemporary resource problems.

One feature of the modern world is that the dividing line between natural resources and environmental resources is blurring in many cases. Many resource extraction processes, such as timber cutting and strip mining, have direct repercussions on environmental quality. In addition, there are many instances where environmental pollution or disruption has an impact on resource extraction processes. Estuarine water pollution that interferes with the replenishment of fish stocks is an example, as is air pollution that reduces agricultural yields. Furthermore, certain things, such as wildlife, may be considered both natural resources and attributes of the environment.

2-2 Environmental Economics

Basic Terminology

Throughout the book we use the following terms:

- **Ambient quality:** *Ambient* refers to the surrounding environment, so *ambient quality* refers to the quantity of pollutants in the environment, for example, the concentration of SO_2 in the air over a city or the concentration of a particular chemical in the waters of a lake.
- **Environmental quality:** A term used to refer broadly to the state of the natural environment. This includes the notion of ambient quality and such things as the visual and aesthetic quality of the environment.
- **Residuals:** Material that is left over after something has been produced. A factory, for example, takes in a variety of raw materials and converts these into some product. Materials and energy left after the product has been produced are *production residuals*. *Consumption residuals* are whatever is left after consumers have finished using the products that contained or otherwise used these materials.
- **Emissions:** The portion of production or consumption residuals that is placed in the environment, sometimes directly, sometimes after treatment.
- **Recycling:** The process of returning some or all of the production or consumption residuals to be used again in production or consumption.
- **Pollutant:** A substance, energy form, or action that, when introduced into the natural environment, results in damages from a lowering of the ambient quality level. We want to think of this as including not only the traditional things, such as oil spilled into oceans or chemicals placed in the air, but also activities, such as certain building developments, that result in "visual pollution."
- **Effluent:** Sometimes *effluent* is used to talk about water pollutants, and *emissions* to refer to air pollutants, but in this book these two words are used interchangeably.
- **Pollution:** *Pollution* is actually a tricky word to define. Some people might say that pollution results when any amount, no matter how small, of a residual has been introduced into the environment. Others hold that pollution is something that happens only when the ambient quality of the environment has been degraded enough to cause some damage.
- **Damages:** The negative impacts produced by environmental pollution on people in the form of health effects, visual degradation, and so on, and on elements of the ecosystem through disruption of ecological linkages, habitat destruction, species extinctions, and so forth.
- **Environmental medium:** Broad dimensions of the natural world that collectively constitute the environment, usually classified as land, water, and air.

- **Source:** The location at which emissions occur, such as a factory, an automobile, or a leaking landfill.

2-3 The Fundamental Balance

In this book you will find a lot of simple analytical models of situations that in reality are somewhat complex. A model is a way of trying to show the essential structure and relationships in something, without going into all of its details, much as a caricature of a person accentuates distinguishing features at the cost of all the details.

Figure 2.1 is a more complex rendering of the relationships shown at the beginning of the chapter. The elements within the circle are parts of the economic system, the whole of which is basically encapsulated within the natural environment. The economy has been divided into two broad segments, **producers** and **consumers**.

FIGURE 2.1 The Environment and the Economy

Diagram showing: Natural Environment encompassing the economy. Raw Materials (M) flow into Producers, which create Goods (G) that flow to Consumers. Producers generate Residuals (R_p), some Recycled (R_p^r) back to Producers and some Discharged (R_p^d) to the environment. Consumers generate Residuals (R_c), some Recycled (R_c^r) back to Producers and some Discharged (R_c^d) to the environment.

- The producers category includes all private firms that take inputs and convert them to outputs; it also includes units such as public agencies; nonprofit organizations; and firms producing services, such as transportation. The primary inputs from the natural environment to the producing sector are materials, in the form of fuels, nonfuel minerals, and wood; fluids (e.g., water and petroleum); and gases of various types (e.g., natural gas and oxygen). All goods and services are derived from materials with the application of energy inputs.

- The consumers category includes all of the private households to whom the vast collections of final goods and services are distributed. One could argue that consumers sometimes use inputs directly from nature, like producers; many households, for example, get their water supplies directly from groundwater aquifers rather than water distribution companies. In the interest of keeping the model simple, however, we have not drawn this type of relationship.

It needs to be kept in mind that producers and consumers actually consist of the same people in different capacities. The "us-versus-them" quality that characterizes many environmental disputes is really an internal disagreement within a single group. Society as a whole is essentially in the same position as a single household that pumps water from its own well and discharges wastes into its own septic system, which happens to be near the well.

Production and consumption create **residuals,** which is another way of saying leftovers. They include all types of material residuals that may be emitted into the air or water or disposed of on land. The list is incredibly long: sulfur dioxide, volatile organic compounds, toxic solvents, animal manure, pesticides, particulate matter of all types, waste building materials, heavy metals, and so on. Waste energy in the form of heat and noise, and radioactivity, which has characteristics of both material and energy, are also important production residuals.

Consumers are also responsible for enormous quantities of residuals, chief among which are domestic sewage, trash, and automobile emissions. All materials in consumer goods must eventually end up as leftovers, even though they may be recycled along the way. These are the source of large quantities of solid waste as well as hazardous materials such as toxic chemicals and used oil.

Let us first consider the question of production and consumption residuals from a strictly physical standpoint. **Figure 2.1** shows raw materials and energy being extracted from the natural environment (M) and residuals being discharged back into the environment.

In the early days of environmental concern, the main focus was on the end flows of discharged residuals by producers (R_p^d) and by consumers (R_c^d). By treating these residuals and otherwise changing the time and place of discharge, their impacts on humans and the environment could be substantially changed.

To consider this focus of **environmental management,** let us consider the flows of **Figure 2.1** in greater detail. From physics, the law of the conservation of matter assures us that, in the long run, these two flows must be equal. In terms of the symbols of **Figure 2.1**[2]:

$$M = R_p^d + R_c^d$$

We must say "in the long run" for several reasons. If the system is growing, it can retain some proportion of the natural inputs, which go toward increasing the size of the system through a growing population, the accumulation of capital equipment, and so on. These would be disposed of if and when the system ceases to grow. Also, recycling can delay the disposal of residuals. But recycling can never be perfect; each cycle must lose some proportion of the recycled material. Thus, the fundamental **materials/energy balance** equation

---

2. To make these direct comparisons, all flows must be expressed in terms of mass.

must hold in the long run. This shows us something very fundamental: To reduce the mass of residuals disposed of in the natural environment, it is necessary to reduce the quantity of raw materials taken into the system.[3]

To look more closely at the various options for doing this, substitute for M. According to the flow diagram,

$$R_p^d + R_c^d = M = G + R_p - R_p^r - R_c^r$$

which says that the quantity of raw materials (M) is equal to output of goods and services (G) plus production residuals (R_p), minus the amounts that are recycled from producers (R_p^r) and consumers (R_c^r). There are essentially three ways of reducing M and, therefore, residuals discharged into the natural environment.

Reduce G Assuming the other flows stay the same, we can reduce residuals discharged by reducing the quantity of goods and services produced in the economy. Some people have fastened on this as the best long-run answer to environmental degradation; reducing output, or at least stopping its rate of growth, would allow a similar change in the quantity of residuals discharged. This goal possibly could be reached with zero population growth (ZPG). A slowly growing or stationary population can make it easier to control environmental impacts, but for two reasons, it does not in any way ensure this control. First, a stationary population can grow economically, thus increasing its demand for raw materials. Increasing consumption would, in turn, raise G and, thus, M. Second, environmental impacts can be long run and cumulative, so that even ZPG can gradually degrade the environment in which it finds itself. It is certainly true, however, that population growth will often exacerbate the environmental impacts of a particular economy. In the U.S. economy, for example, although the emissions of pollutants per car have dramatically decreased over the last few decades through better emissions-control technology, the sheer growth in the number of cars on the highways has led to an increase in the total quantity of automobile emissions in many regions.

Reduce R_p Another way of reducing M, and therefore residuals discharged, is to reduce R_p. Assuming the other flows are held constant, this means essentially changing the amounts of production residuals produced for a given quantity of output produced. There are basically only two ways of doing this:

- Reduce the **residuals' intensity of production** in all sectors of the economy by inventing and adopting new production technologies and practices that leave smaller amounts of residuals per unit of output produced. For example, in later discussions of carbon dioxide (CO_2) emissions and atmospheric warming, we will see that there is much that can be done to reduce the CO_2 output per unit of output produced, especially by shifting to different fuels, and by continuing to reduce the quantities of energy required to produce a unit of final output. This approach has come to be called **pollution prevention** or **source reduction.**
- Shift the composition of final output; that is, reduce those sectors that have relatively high residuals per unit of output and expand those sectors that produce relatively few residuals per unit of output. The shift from primarily a manufacturing economy toward services is a step in this direction. This is called a **sectoral shift** because it changes the

---

3. Note that G = R_C; that is, everything that flows to the consumption sector eventually ends up as a residual from that sector.

relative shares of the different economic sectors in the aggregate economy. The rise of the so-called information sectors is another example. It is not that these new sectors produce no significant residuals; indeed, some of them may produce harsher leftovers than we have known before. The computer industry, for example, uses a variety of chemical solvents for cleaning purposes and requires energy for operations. But on the whole these sectors probably have a smaller waste-disposal problem than the traditional industries they have replaced.

Increase ($R_p^r + R_c^r$) The third possibility is to increase recycling. Instead of discharging production and consumption residuals into the environment, a portion can be recycled back into the production process. What this shows is that the central role of recycling is to replace a portion of the original flow of raw materials (M). By substituting recycled materials for raw materials, the quantity of residuals discharged can be reduced while maintaining the rate of output of goods and services (G). In modern economies, recycling offers great opportunities to reduce waste flows. But we have to remember that recycling can never be perfect, even if enormous resources were devoted to the task. Production processes usually transform the physical structure of materials inputs, making them difficult to use again. The process of energy conversion changes the chemical structure of energy materials so thoroughly that recycling is impossible. In addition, recycling processes themselves can create residuals. But materials research will continue to progress and discover new ways of recycling. For a long time, automobile tires could not be recycled because the original production process changed the physical structure of the rubber. Now with new technology, vast quantities of used tires, instead of blighting the landscape, can be incorporated into park benches, roads, and other products.

These fundamental relationships are very important. We must remember, however, that our ultimate goal is to reduce the damages caused by the discharge of production and consumption residuals. Reducing the total quantity of these residuals is one major way of doing this, and the relationships discussed indicate the basic ways this may be done. But damages can also be reduced by working directly on the stream of residuals, a fact that must be kept in mind in our later discussions.

This concept of the fundamental balance is in accord with the concept of the **circular economy.** That concept is sometimes disaggregated into "reduce, reuse, and recycle." In our terms, reduce means lowering G, reuse means lowering the leftovers of production and consumption, and recycle means increasing **R**$_p$ and **R**$_c$. As indicated, these steps are undertaken ultimately to reduce M, the flow of raw materials from nature into the economy.

2-4 The Environment as an Economic and Social Asset

One good way of thinking about the environment is as an asset that produces important services for humans and nonhuman organisms. Yet the ability of the environment to produce these services can be degraded. A way of thinking about this is in terms of a **trade-off** between conventional economic output (conventional goods and services such as cars, loaves of bread, insurance policies, etc.) and environmental quality. A trade-off of this type is depicted in **Figure 2.2.** Consider first panel (a). This shows a **production possibility curve** (PPC), which is a curve showing the different combinations of two things a society

FIGURE 2.2 Production Possibility Curves for Current and Future Generations

(a) PPC today

(b) PPC in 60 years

may produce at any time, given its resources and technological capabilities. The vertical axis has an index of the aggregate output of an economy, that is, the total market value of conventional economic goods traded in the economy in a year. The horizontal axis has an index of environmental quality, derived from data on different dimensions of the ambient environment, for example, airborne sulfur dioxide (SO_2) concentrations, urban noise levels, and water-quality data. The curved relationship shows the different combinations of these two outcomes—marketed output and environmental quality—that are available to a group of people who have a fixed endowment of resources and technology with which to work.[4]

The exact shape and location of the PPC are determined by the **technical capacities** in the economy, together with the ecological facts—meteorology, hydrology, and so on—of the natural system in which the society is situated. It says, for example, that if the current level of economic output is c_1, an increase to c_2 can be obtained only at the cost of a decrease in environmental quality from e_1 to e_2. One major objective of any society, of course, is to change the PPC so that the underlying trade-off is more favorable—in other words, so that a given economic output is consistent with higher levels of environmental quality.

Although the PPC itself is a technical constraint, where a society chooses to locate itself on its PPC is a matter of **social choice.** This depends on the values that people in that society place on conventional economic output as opposed to environmental quality. Where values come from is an open question, but it is clear that values differ from one person to another and even for the same person at different points in time. The study of the values that people place on environmental factors is a major part of environmental economics and will be discussed in more detail in **Chapters 7** and **8.**

If a society puts too much stress on increasing its measured output, it may end up at a point like (c_2, e_2) in **Figure 2.2,** panel (a), even though true social welfare may be higher at a point like (c_1, e_1).

---

4. The extremes of the PPC perhaps should be drawn with dashed lines. It's not clear what an outcome would be with "zero" environmental quality, or with "zero" economic output. Thus, these extreme points are essentially undefined, and we focus on points in the interior of the diagram.

2-5 Environmental Sustainability

We have mentioned the concept of sustainability[5] several times in this chapter. The concept is used as a criterion for evaluation actions that have environmental impacts. The idea was given its initial impetus by the influential paper put out by the World Commission on Environment and Development in 1987: *Out Common Future*. In that work it was defined as the ability to meet the needs of present generations without compromising the ability of future generations to meet their own needs. In other words, to avoid making decisions in the short run that yields negative impacts in the long run.

The distinction between the short run and the long run is fundamental in economic analysis and in environmental policy. Short-run decisions are those made on the basis of consequences that happen in the near term or of impacts as they are felt by the present generation. Long-run decisions are those in which attention is paid to consequences that occur well into the future or to future generations. There is widespread concern that many economic decisions today are not sustainable because they are being made primarily through short-run considerations, whereas environmental policy needs to be made with long-run considerations in mind. A good way of thinking about this is through the use of PPCs, introduced earlier.

Consider again **Figure 2.2**. The two panels actually show PPCs for two time periods. Panel (a) shows the trade-offs facing the current generation. Panel (b) shows the PPCs for people in, say, 60 to 80 years, the generation consisting of your great-grandchildren. According to panel (a), the present generation could choose combinations (c_1, e_1), (c_2, e_2), or any others on the curve. But the future is not independent of the choice made today. It is conceivable, for example, that degrading the environment too much today will affect future possibilities—by depleting certain important resources, by pollution that is so high it causes irreversible damage, or simply by a pollutant that is very long lived and affects future generations. In effect, this could shift the future PPC back from where it otherwise would be. This is depicted in panel (b) of the diagram. Your great-grandchildren will be confronted with a reduced set of possibilities as compared to the choices we face today. The future generation, finding itself on the inner PPC, can still have the same level of marketed output we have today (c_2), but only at a lower level of environmental quality (e_3) than we have today. Alternatively, it could enjoy the same level of environmental quality, but only with a reduced level of marketed output (c_3).

Of course, the influence of today's decisions on future production possibilities is much more complicated than this discussion might suggest. Environmental degradation affects future conditions along with technical developments and changes in human capacities. Thus, today's decisions could shift the future PPC either in or out, depending on many dynamic factors that are hard to predict. We need to be particularly alert to avoid decisions today that would have the effect of shifting the future PPC to the left. This is the essence of recent discussions about sustainability.

Sustainability means that future PPCs are not adversely affected by what is done today. It does not mean that we must maximize environmental quality today, because that implies zero output of goods and services. It means simply that environmental impacts need to be reduced enough today to avoid shifting future PPCs back in comparison to today's production possibilities.

---

5. Other types of sustainability are recognized, for example, social sustainability and economic sustainability.

Green GDP and Natural Capital

One hundred years ago, a good way to assess the status of a national economy had not yet been invented. If you wanted to know whether the economy was expanding or contracting, you had to do something like stand next to a main train line and count the number of boxcars that were passing by.

Today, we have a better way of measuring the aggregate economy of a country. It's called Gross Domestic Product (GDP), and it's a measure of the sum total of economic activity occurring in a given period of time, like a year. These days, we follow GDP numbers avidly, especially whether they are going up (economic growth) or perhaps in decline (economic recession). GDP was developed to provide this information.

In practice, GDP is an approximation because it omits activities that do not trade in markets at observed prices, such as getting paid cash to mow a neighbor's lawn or if you purchased an used item. GDP doesn't include lots of things of value, for example, the amount of work done inside the home, which doesn't get registered as a strictly economic transaction. It does include activities like health care expenditures, which depending on the ailment, may represent someone getting better (a positive) or someone becoming medically unable to work in their current job anymore (a negative). So an increasing GDP may not necessarily be a sign of improved economic or social welfare. Nevertheless, it remains a popular and valuable index of the state of an economy and whether that economy is expanding or contracting.

We know, however, that economic activity uses up things. One of those things is the stock of produced capital goods that is used in the process of production and distribution, such things as industrial machinery and buildings, and public facilities like bridges and airports. All of this infrastructure deteriorates over time, and in the course of a year, a quantity of these capital goods is used up. It is customary to subtract these out to get a measure of the net change in national output.

Also, importantly, economic activity depends on the services of nature and the environment. This entity is called **natural capital** and consists of elements of the natural world that contribute to economic output and welfare. This consists of traditional natural resources, renewable and nonrenewable. The services of clean air or water or the value of a preserved species or biodiversity preservation or the sequestration potential of a forest are not directly included in GDP. Other environmental variables that typically describe the state of the natural system, such as the presence of air or water pollutants or hazardous materials or the costs of dirty air or water, are not included in GDP as a negative value.

As yet, we do not have widely accepted, credible ways of measuring the total quantity of natural and environmental capital, and changes in it, so that we could deduct it from the standard measure of GDP to get what has been called **Green GDP**. The concept of Green GDP is based on the idea of making reasonable comprehensive adjustments to the standard GDP measure to adjust for changes in the value of the natural and environmental resources and services produced from them. Work goes on toward that end, and along the way, we will develop more accurate ways of measuring these resources, and of finding ways of valuing them so that they can be compared to the traditional valuations we use in the estimation of GDP. Both the traditional GDP measure and a Green GDP measure could enhance the tracking and the understanding of changes in aggregate social welfare and well-being.

2-6 Emissions, Ambient Quality, and Damages

Let us now focus on what happens at the end of those two discharge arrows at the right side of **Figure 2.1**. Very simply, **emissions** produce changes in ambient levels of environmental quality, which in turn cause damages to humans and nonhumans. **Figure 2.3** shows one way of sketching out this relationship. It shows *n* sources of emissions[6]; they might be private firms, government agencies, or consumers. Sources take in various inputs and use different types of technologies in production and consumption. In the process they produce residuals. How these residuals are handled then has a critical effect on subsequent stages. Some may be recovered and recycled back into production or consumption. Many can be put through treatment processes (residuals handling) that can render them more benign when emitted. Some of these processes are strictly physical (mufflers on cars and trucks, settling ponds at wastewater treatment plants, catalytic converters); others involve chemical transformations of various types (advanced treatment of domestic wastewater).

All emissions must necessarily go into one or more of the different **environmental media** (land, air, water), and there is an important relationship among them. For a given quantity of total residuals, if the amounts going into one medium are reduced, the amounts going into the others must necessarily increase. When SO_2 is removed from the stack gases of power plants, air emissions are reduced, yet the sulfur compounds have not been destroyed. Instead, we end up with a sulfurous sludge that must be disposed of some other way, perhaps by land burial. If this material is incinerated, airborne emissions result, but there will still be certain quantities of solid residuals that must be disposed of elsewhere.

In a situation involving multiple sources, emissions will often become mixed into a single flow. In the real world this mixing may be complete; for example, the effluent from two pulp mills located at the same point on a river may mix so thoroughly that a few miles downstream it is impossible to differentiate one source's effluent from the other's. When there are a million or so cars moving about an urban area, the emissions from all become uniformly mixed together. In other cases the mixing is less than complete. If one power plant is just outside the city and another is 20 miles upwind, the closer plant will normally bear a greater responsibility for deteriorating air quality in the city than the other.

This mixing of emissions is a more significant problem than might first appear. With just a single source, the line of responsibility is clear, and to get an improvement in ambient quality, we know exactly whose emissions have to be controlled. But with multiple sources, responsibilities become less clear. We may know how much we want to cut back total emissions, but the problem of distributing this total reduction among the different sources still exists. Each source then has an incentive to get the others to bear a larger share of the burden of reducing emissions. With every source thinking along the same lines, pollution-control programs face a real problem of design and enforcement.

---

6. In economic writing, the letter *n* is often used to designate an unspecified number of items, the exact value of which will vary from one situation to another.

FIGURE 2.3 Emissions, Ambient Quality, and Damages

Source: Braden, John B. and Kathleen Segerson. *Information Problems in the Design of Nonpoint Source Pollution Policy.* The Management of Nonpoint Source Pollution, Association of Environmental and Resource Economics (AERE) Workshop Papers Lexington, 1991.

Once a given quantity and quality of residuals have been introduced into a particular environmental medium, it is the physical, chemical, biological, meteorological, and so on, processes of the natural system that determine how the residuals translate into particular **ambient quality levels.** For example, wind and temperature conditions will affect whether and how residuals emitted into the air affect nearby neighborhoods, as well as people living farther downwind. In addition, because these meteorological conditions vary from day to day, the same level of emissions can produce different ambient quality levels at different times. Acid rain is produced through chemical processes acting primarily on sulfur dioxide emissions emitted far upwind; smog is also the result of complex chemical reactions involving sunlight and quantities of various pollutants. Underground hydrological processes affect the transportation of materials disposed of in landfills. And so on. Thus, to know how particular emissions will affect ambient quality levels, we must have a good understanding of the physical and chemical workings of the environment itself. This is where the natural and physical sciences come in—to study the full range of environmental phenomena, from small, localized models of groundwater flow in a particular aquifer, to complex models of large lakes and river basins, to studies of interregional wind patterns, to global climate models. The fundamental goal is to determine how particular patterns of emissions are translated into corresponding patterns of ambient quality levels.

Finally, there are damages. A given set of ambient conditions translates into particular exposure patterns for living and nonliving systems. These exposures are a function not only of the physical processes involved, and the human choices that are made about where and how to live, and of the susceptibilities of living and nonliving systems to varying environmental conditions. Last, damages are related to human values. Human beings do not have amorphous preferences over all possible outcomes of the economical/environmental interaction; they prefer some outcomes over others. A major part of environmental economics is trying to determine the relative values that people place on these different environmental outcomes, a subject to which we will turn in later chapters on benefit–cost analysis.

2-7 Types of Pollutants

Physically, the residuals identified in **Figure 2.3** consist of a vast assortment of materials and energy flowing into the three environmental media. It is helpful to distinguish among broad types of emissions according to factors that critically affect their economic characteristics.

Cumulative Versus Noncumulative Pollutants

One simple and important dimension of environmental pollutants is whether they accumulate over time or tend to dissipate soon after being emitted. The classic case of a **noncumulative pollutant** is noise; as long as the source operates, noise is emitted into the surrounding air, but as soon as the source is shut down, the noise stops. At the other end of the spectrum, there are pollutants that cumulate in the environment in nearly the same amounts as they are emitted. Radioactive waste, for example, decays over time but at such a slow rate in relation to human life spans that for all intents and purposes it will be with us permanently; it is a strictly cumulative type of pollutant. Another **cumulative pollutant** is plastics. The search for a degradable plastic has been going on for decades, but so far plastic is a substance that decays very slowly by human standards; thus, what we dispose of will be in the environment permanently. Many chemicals are cumulative pollutants; once emitted they are basically with us forever. Carbon dioxide and methane, the two main substances implicated in climate change, are cumulative over normal human life spans.

Between these two ends of the spectrum there are many types of effluent that are to some extent, but not completely, cumulative. The classic case is organic matter emitted into water bodies, for example, the wastes, treated or not, emitted from municipal waste treatment plants. Once emitted, the wastes are subject to natural chemical processes that tend to break down the organic materials into their constituent elements, thus rendering them much more benign. The water, in other words, has a natural assimilative capacity that allows it to accept organic substances and render them less harmful. As long as this assimilative capacity has not been exceeded in any particular case, the effluent source can be shut off, and in a few days, weeks, or months, the water quality will return to normal. Once emissions exceed this assimilative capacity, however, the process becomes cumulative.

Whether a pollutant is cumulative or noncumulative, the basic problem is essentially the same: trying to figure out the environmental damages and relating these back to the costs of reducing emissions. This job is much more difficult for cumulative than for noncumulative pollutants. With noncumulative emissions, ambient concentrations are strictly a function of current emissions—reducing these emissions to zero would lead to zero ambient concentrations. But with cumulative pollutants the relationship is more complex. The fact that a pollutant cumulates over time in the environment has the effect of breaking the direct connection between current emissions and current damages. This has a number of implications. For one thing it makes the science more difficult. The cause-and-effect relationships become harder to isolate when there is a lot of time intervening between them. It also may make it more difficult to get people to focus on damages from today's emissions, again because there may only be a weak connection between today's emissions and today's ambient quality levels. Furthermore, cumulative pollutants by definition lead to future damages, and human beings have shown a preference for "now" over "later" which sometimes leads to a readiness to discount future events and avoid coming to grips with them in the present.

Local Versus Regional Versus Global Pollutants

Some emissions have an impact only in restricted, localized regions, whereas others have an impact over wider regions, perhaps on the global environment. Noise pollution and the degradation of the visual environment are local in their impacts; the damages from any particular source are usually limited to relatively small groups of people in a circumscribed region. Note that this is a statement about how widespread the effects are from any particular pollution source, not about how important the overall problem is throughout a country or the world. Many pollutants, on the other hand, have widespread impacts, over a large region or perhaps over the global environment. Acid rain is a regional problem; emissions in one region of the United States (and of Europe) affect people in other parts of the country or region. The ozone-depleting effects of chlorofluorocarbon emissions from various countries work through chemical changes in the earth's stratosphere, which means that the impacts are truly global.

Other things being equal, local environmental problems ought to be easier to deal with than regional or national problems, which in turn ought to be easier to manage than global problems. If I smoke out my neighbor with my wood stove, we may be able to arrange a solution among ourselves, or we can call on local political institutions to do it. But if my behavior causes more distant pollution, solutions may be more difficult. If we are within the same political system, we can call on these institutions to arrange solutions. For a growing number of international and global environmental issues, we are far from having effective means of responding, both because the exact nature of the physical impacts is difficult to describe and because the requisite international political institutions are only beginning to appear.

Point-Source Versus Nonpoint-Source Pollutants

Pollution sources differ in terms of the ease with which actual points of discharge may be identified. The points at which sulfur dioxide emissions leave a large power plant are easy to identify; they come out the end of the smokestacks associated with each plant. Municipal waste treatment plants normally have a single outfall from which all of the wastewater is discharged. These are called **point-source pollutants.**

There are many pollutants for which there are no well-defined points of discharge. Agricultural chemicals, for example, usually run off the land in a dispersed or diffused pattern, and even though they may pollute specific streams or underground aquifers, there is no single pipe or stack from which these chemicals are emitted. This is a **nonpoint-source** type of pollutant. Urban storm water runoff is also an important nonpoint-source problem.

As one would expect, point-source pollutants are likely to be easier to come to grips with than nonpoint-source pollutants. They will probably be easier to measure and monitor and easier to study in terms of the connections between emissions and impacts. This means that it will ordinarily be easier to develop and administer control policies for point-source pollutants. As we will see, not all pollutants fit neatly into one or another of these categories.

Continuous Versus Episodic Emissions

Emissions from electric power plants or municipal waste treatment plants are more or less continuous. The plants are designed to be in operation continuously, although the operating rate may vary somewhat over the day, week, or season. Thus, the emissions from these operations are more or less continuous, and the policy problem is to manage the rate of these discharges. Immediate comparisons can be made between control programs and rates of emissions. The fact that emissions are continuous does not mean that damages are also continuous, however. Meteorological and hydrological events can turn continuous emissions into uncertain damages. But control programs are often easier to carry out when emissions are not subject to large-scale fluctuations.

Many pollutants are emitted on an episodic basis, however. Classic examples are accidental oil or chemical spills and train derailments. The policy problem here is to design and manage a system so that the probability of accidental discharges is reduced. Yet, with an episodic effluent there may be nothing to measure, at least in the short run. Even though there have been no large-scale radiation releases from U.S. nuclear power plants, for example, there is still a "pollution" problem if they are being managed in such a way as to increase the **probability** of an accidental release in the future. To measure the probabilities of episodic emissions, it is necessary to have data on actual occurrences over a long time period or to estimate them from engineering data and similar information. We then have to determine how much insurance we wish to have against these episodic events. **Exhibit 2.1** discusses the case of an episodic pollutant: pipeline spills.

EXHIBIT 2.1 Managing Episodic Sources of Pollution

Episodic, largely accidental, releases of environmental pollutants are relatively common in today's world. A source that has gained prominence in the United States is railroad tank cars. The surge in oil production has been accompanied by a large increase in petroleum shipments via long trains of tank cars. Periodic derailments have led to spills, with accompanying fires and contamination of land and water resources.

Another source of episodic spills is through pipeline breaches. The United States, like many countries, is crisscrossed with thousands of miles of underground pipelines. Breakages and spills, small and large, result from a variety of human and technical factors.

A prime element in dealing with these kinds of spills is the concept of **risk**. Risk refers to the likelihood of accidents such as these, and the benefits and costs of changing these likelihoods.

Risk can be reduced by all kinds of technical and behavioral factors: more frequent inspections, stronger pipes and tank cars, changes in operating procedures, better clean-up technology, etc.

Risky situations make it more difficult to know underlying cause and effect relationships. If we change operating procedures, how do we know that we are changing the likelihood and severity of accidents? We can try to analyze it through uncertain engineering predictions, or collect accident data over a period of time and see if probabilities have changed. Either way we are dealing with uncertainty. The other part of the equation is how people in general value reductions in risk. How much is it worth to people to reduce the chances of tank-car accidents from say one in a 100 trains, to one in 200 trains? Or to reduce pipeline leaks from one every 1,000 pipe miles to one every 1,500 pipe miles?

Environmental Damages Not Related to Emissions

So far the discussion has focused on the characteristics of different types of environmental pollutants as they relate to the discharge of residual materials or energy, but there are many important instances of deteriorating environmental quality that are not traceable to residuals discharges. The conversion of land to housing and commercial areas destroys the environmental value of that land, whether it be its ecosystem value, such as habitat or wetland, or its scenic value. Other land uses, such as logging or strip mining, or converting farmland for food crops to solar farms, can also have important impacts. In these cases, the policy problem is still to understand the incentives of people whose decisions create these impacts and to change these incentives when appropriate. Although there are no physical emissions to monitor and control, there are nevertheless outcomes that can be described, evaluated, and managed with appropriate policies.

Summary

The purpose of this chapter was to explore some basic linkages between the economy and the environment. We differentiated between the role of the natural system as a supplier of raw material inputs for the economy and as a receptor for production and consumption residuals. The first of these is normally called natural resource economics and the second environmental economics. After a very brief review of natural resource economics, we introduced the fundamental balance phenomenon, which says that in the long run all materials taken by human beings out of the natural system must eventually end up back in that system. This means that to reduce residuals flows into the environment, we must reduce materials taken from the ecosystem, and we discussed the three fundamental ways that this can be done. This led into a discussion of the inherent trade-off that exists between conventional economic goods and environmental quality and between current and future generations as regards sustainability. We also referred to the concepts of green GDP and natural capital.

We then focused more directly on the flow of residuals back into the environment, making a distinction among emissions, ambient environmental quality, and damages. The environmental damages from a given quantity of emissions can be very substantially altered by handling these emissions in different ways. Our next step was to provide a brief catalog of the different types of emissions and pollutants, as well as nonpollution types of environmental impacts such as aesthetic effects.

Questions for Further Discussion

1. Economies grow by investing in new sources of productivity, new plants and equipment, infrastructure such as roads, and so on. How does this type of investment affect the flows depicted in **Figure 2.1?**
2. What is the difference between a residual and a pollutant? Illustrate this in the context of a common airborne emission such as carbon dioxide (CO_2); with noise; with junked automobiles; with an unsightly building.
3. Why are long-lived, cumulative pollutants so much harder to manage than short-lived, noncumulative pollutants?
4. As depicted in **Figure 2.3,** most emissions from individual sources get mixed in with those of other sources, to produce the general level of ambient quality. What problems does this present in adopting emission-control policies to get a cleaner environment?
5. Consider the production and use of single-use, plastic shopping bags, and examine their flows along all parts of **Figure 2.1.** Do the same for paper shopping bags.

(Continued)

Questions for Further Discussion *(Continued)*

6. What trade-offs come into play when considering whether a country or any other political entity is spending the right amount for environmental quality improvements?
7. Suppose there is a technological change that allows firms to produce goods and services with less pollution. How would this affect the production possibilities curves of **Figure 2.2,** and where might society choose to locate itself on this curve?
8. Consider food composting. In what ways is food composting sustainable? In what ways does food composting produce residual flows? In what ways does food composting produce pollution?

Section 2
Analytical Tools

Scientific analysis consists of giving coherent explanations of relevant events and showing how other outcomes might have occurred if conditions had been different. It is to show connections among variables and to detail the ways in which they are interrelated. To do this, a science must develop a specialized vocabulary and conceptual structure with which to focus on its chosen subject matter. In this section, we cover some of the basic ideas of economics and their application to environmental problems. Those of you who have already been introduced to microeconomics can treat the next few chapters as a review. For those who are seeing this material for the first time, remember that the purpose is to develop a set of analytical tools that can be used to focus on issues of environmental quality.

Chapter 3
Benefits and Costs, Supply and Demand

This and the next chapter contain discussions of certain basic tools of **microeconomics.** The objective is to provide an understanding of fundamental concepts so that they can be used later in analyzing environmental impacts and policies. The current chapter is about benefits and costs. The juxtaposition of these two words indicates that we are going to approach things in a **trade-off,** or **balancing,** mode. Economic actions, including environmental actions, have two sides: On the one side they create value and on the other side they encounter costs. Thus, we must have basic concepts that deal with these two parts of the problem. We look first at the question of value, later at costs.

It needs to be mentioned at the very outset that microeconomic theory is **abstract.** This means that it normally proceeds with simplified models that try to capture the essence of a problem without all the details that one observes in the real world. The reason for this is that we want to reveal basic connections and relationships among the important elements of a problem, relationships that are difficult to see if we just observe the surface richness of the real world. There are dangers in this, of course; one can inadvertently overlook details that do have an important impact in reality. For example, in the past, many environmental models have been developed without considering the costs of actually enforcing environmental laws. But in the real world, **enforcement costs** are more than a detail; they can have a great impact on the outcomes of environmental regulations. Thus, we need to be careful that our abstractions truly serve to reveal basic connections and do not cover up important dimensions of problems we are trying to understand.

3-1 Willingness to Pay

The value side of the analysis is based on the fundamental notion that individuals have **preferences** for goods and services; given a choice, they can express preferences for one good over another or one bundle of goods over another bundle. How to make visible this abstract notion of preference? We need to simplify the discussion; in a modern economy there are thousands of different goods and services available, so let us focus on just one of them. We now can present the following fundamental concept: The value of this good to a person is what the person is willing and able to sacrifice for it. Sacrifice what? In a barter economy, the willingness to sacrifice for one thing would be expressed in terms of some other thing. In a market economy, it makes most sense to talk about sacrificing generalized purchasing power. Thus, the fundamental idea of value is tied to **willingness to pay;** the value of a good to somebody is what that person is *willing to pay* for it.[1] WTP is not necessarily the purchase price of a good or service.

What determines how much a person is willing to pay to obtain some good or service or some environmental asset? It's partly a question of **individual values.** Some people are willing to sacrifice a lot to visit the Grand Canyon; others are not. Some people are willing to pay a lot for a quiet living environment; others are not. Some people place a high value on trying to preserve the habitat of unique animal and plant species; others do not. It is obvious also that a person's **wealth** affects the willingness to sacrifice; the wealthier a person is, the better that person can afford to pay for various goods and services. Willingness to pay, in other words, also reflects **ability to pay.**

It is easy to misunderstand the implications of using willingness to pay as a measure of value of an outcome. It does not imply, for example, that the only thing that counts is money payments in a market. Many people speak of and genuinely feel spiritual qualities associated with nature and the natural environment. For a person holding these values, it is simply to say that they would be willing to sacrifice to attain these ends.

Let us build a graphic picture of a person's willingness to pay for pounds of organic potatoes per week. We go through the following steps:

1. Assuming someone has no organic potatoes at present, how much would they be willing to pay for one pound? Suppose the answer is $3.80.
2. Assuming someone presently possesses one pound, how much are they willing to pay for the second pound? Assume they answer $2.60.
3. Assuming someone possesses two pounds, how much would they be willing to pay for a third pound? Assume they answer $1.70.
4. How much is someone willing to pay for additional potatoes? Assume they answer $1.40 for the fourth, 90¢ for the fifth, 60¢ for the sixth, and nothing for the seventh.

These willingness-to-pay numbers are shown in **Figure 3.1.** These numbers depict a fundamental relationship of economics: the notion of diminishing willingness to pay. As the number of units consumed increases, the willingness to pay for additional units of that good normally goes down.

It is not very convenient to work with diagrams that are step-shaped as in the top of **Figure 3.1.** So we now change things a bit by assuming that people can consume fractions of items in addition to integer values. What this does is produce a smoothly shaped willingness-to-pay curve, such as the one pictured in the bottom of **Figure 3.1.** On this smooth function we have singled out one quantity for illustrative purposes. It shows that the willingness to pay for the third unit is $1.70.

---

1. It may sound as though we are limiting the analysis only to physical goods and services, but this is not true. The concept of willingness to pay is quite general, and in **Chapter 5** we will apply it to differing levels of environmental quality.

FIGURE 3.1 The Concept of Willingness to Pay

The next step is to distinguish between total and marginal willingness to pay. Suppose a person is already consuming two units of this good; according to the willingness-to-pay curve, that person would be willing to pay $1.70 for a third unit. This is the **marginal willingness to pay**—in this case, for the third unit. *Marginal* is thus a word that describes the *additional* willingness to pay of a person for one more unit. So the height of the rectangles in the top of **Figure 3.1** and the height of the curve in the bottom graph show the marginal willingness to pay for this good.

The **total willingness to pay** for a given consumption level is the total amount a person would be willing to pay to attain that consumption level rather than go without the good entirely. Suppose the person is consuming at a level of three units, their total willingness to pay for consuming this quantity is $8.10, which is the sum of the heights of the demand rectangles between the origin and the consumption level in question ($3.80 for the first plus $2.60 for the second plus $1.70 for the third). This corresponds, in the smooth version of the willingness-to-pay function, to the whole area under the willingness-to-pay curve from the origin up to the quantity in question. For three units of consumption, the total willingness to pay is equal to an amount represented by the combined areas *a* and *b*.

Demand

There is another way of looking at these marginal willingness-to-pay relationships. They are more familiarly known as **demand curves.** An individual demand curve shows the quantity of a good or service that the individual in question would demand (i.e., purchase and consume) at any particular price. For example, suppose a person whose marginal willingness-to-pay/demand curve is shown in the bottom part of **Figure 3.1** is able to purchase this item at a unit price of $1.70. The quantity they would demand at this price is three units. The reason is that this person's marginal willingness to pay for each of the first three units exceeds the purchase price. They would not push their consumption higher than this because their marginal willingness to pay for additional quantities would be less than the purchase price.

An individual's demand/marginal willingness-to-pay curve for a good or service is a way of summarizing personal consumption attitudes and capabilities for that good. Thus, we would normally expect these relationships to differ somewhat among individuals, because individual tastes and preferences vary. **Figure 3.2** displays several different demand curves. Panel (a) shows two demand curves, one steeper than the other. The steeper one shows a situation in which marginal willingness to pay drops off fairly rapidly as the quantity consumed increases; the flatter one shows marginal willingness to pay that, although lower to begin with, goes down less rapidly as quantity increases. These two demand curves could represent the case of one consumer and two different goods or services, or the case of two different consumers and the same good or service.

FIGURE 3.2 Typical Demand/Marginal Willingness-to-Pay Curves

Panel (b) of **Figure 3.2** also has two demand curves; they have the same general shape, but one is situated well to the right of the other. The demand curve above and to the right shows a good for which the marginal willingness to pay is substantially higher than it is for the same quantity of the other good. Several factors could account for the difference. They might be:

- demand curves of two different people, with different tastes and preferences;
- demand curves for the same person, the one on the right being after an income rise; or
- demand curves for the same person, before and after that person receives more information about the good (e.g., the possible presence of pesticide residues in a food item).

Note that the demand curves are in fact curvilinear, rather than straight lines. A straight-line demand relationship would imply a uniform change in the quantity demanded as its price changes. For most goods, however, this is unlikely to be true. At low prices and high rates of consumption, studies have shown that relatively small increases in price will lead to substantial reductions in quantity demanded. At high prices and low quantity demanded, however, price increases have a much smaller effect: They produce much smaller reductions in quantity demanded. This gives us a demand relationship that is convex to the origin (i.e., relatively flat at low prices and steep at higher prices). See **Example 3.1**.

EXAMPLE 3.1 The Demand for Water

Researchers have investigated the demand for water by households. Many might think that the amount of water a household uses would be related only to such things as the size of the family rather than the price of the water. This is not the case, however. In general, as the price people pay for water increases, the amount of water they use declines.

This demand is somewhat complicated. Water is used for a number of household purposes, for example, inside the house for sanitation and food preparation and outside the house for car washing, lawn sprinkling, and so forth. At higher prices, consumers will curtail unessential water uses substantially, but their water use for essential purposes will not decline as much in relative terms.

This means that the demand curve for water is shaped as in the diagram.

At low and moderate prices, increased prices will lead to a substantial drop in household water use as people cut back on unessential uses. Thus, the demand curve is relatively flat in this range. But, at higher prices where most of the water is going to essential purposes, further price increases will lead to relatively smaller drops in consumption, and hence a steeper demand curve.

Economics is sometimes misunderstood as assuming that people are driven only by thoughts of their own welfare, that they are complete egoists. Because these are individual demand curves, they do indeed summarize the attitudes of single individuals, but this does not imply that individuals make decisions with only themselves in mind. Some people may indeed act this way, but for most there are many other powerful motives that affect their demands for different goods, including altruism toward friends and relatives, feelings of civic virtue toward their communities, a sense of social responsibility toward fellow citizens, and so on. Individual tastes and preferences spring from these factors as well as from more narrow considerations of personal likes and dislikes.

3-2 Aggregate Demand/Willingness to Pay

In examining real-world issues of environmental quality and pollution-control policy, we normally focus our attention on the behavior of groups of people rather than single individuals. Our interest is in the total, or aggregate, demand/marginal willingness to pay of defined groups of people.

An **aggregate demand curve** is the summation of a number of individual demand curves.[2] What individuals are involved depends on which particular aggregation we want to look at: the demand of people living in the city of New York for Brussels sprouts; the demand of people living in New Orleans for clean water in the Mississippi River; the demand of people living in the entire country for public parks; and so on.

Figure 3.3 depicts a very simple aggregate demand curve, one in which the group consists of only three people. The aggregate demand curve is found by summing together, at each price, the quantities that are demanded by each of the three individuals, as in the following tabulation. At a price of $15, person A consumes 4 units, person B consumes 0 (the demand curve intersects the vertical axis below $15), and person C consumes 3 units; these sum to an aggregate demand of 7 units.

FIGURE 3.3 Aggregate Demand/Marginal Willingness-to-Pay Curves

	Individual Quantities Demanded			Aggregate Quantity Demanded
Price ($)	A	B	C	
8	10	6	8	24
11	6	2	5	13
15	4	0	3	7

Looked at in the other direction, we see that for a particular quantity, each consumer may have a different MWTP. When Person A is consuming 6 units, their marginal willingness to pay is $11. When Persons B and C consume, respectively, at 6 units and 8 units, they each have a marginal willingness to pay of $8, even though the quantity they each consume differs. If one more unit is made available to this aggregate, it must be distributed to Person A, Person B, or Person C, each of whom has a marginal willingness to pay of $8; thus, the aggregate marginal willingness to pay is also $8.

---

2. The term *aggregate demand* is also used in macroeconomics to refer to the total of goods and services produced in the entire economy during a given year. We are using *aggregate demand* in a more restricted sense, to refer to the combined demand of a defined group of people, sometimes, but not always, smaller than the national total.

3-3 Benefits

We now come to the idea of **benefits.** *Benefit* is one of those ordinary words to which economists have given a technical meaning. When the environment is cleaned up, people obtain benefits; when the environment is allowed to deteriorate in quality, benefits are taken away from them—they are, in fact, being damaged. We need some way of conceptualizing and measuring this notion of benefits.

The word *benefits* clearly implies being made better off. If individuals are benefited by something, their position is improved—they are better off. Conversely, if they are worse off, it must be because benefits were somehow taken away from them. How do we confer benefits on people? We do this by giving them something they value. How do we know that they value something? We know by the fact that they are willing to sacrifice, or willing to pay, for it. According to this logic, then, the benefits that people get from something are equal to the amount they are willing to pay for it. This implies that a person is willing to pay to have something reduced, like air pollution, or to have something added like enlarging a conservation area.

The logic behind this definition of *benefits* is quite strong. It means we can use ordinary demand curves to determine the benefits of making various things available to people. For example, **Figure 3.4** shows two demand curves, and on the horizontal axis two quantity levels are indicated. Suppose we wish to estimate the total benefits of increasing the availability of this item from quantity q_1 to quantity q_2. According to our previous thinking, benefits are measured by willingness to pay, and we know that total willingness to pay is measured by areas under the demand curve; in this case, the area under the demand curves between quantity q_1 and quantity q_2. So for the lower demand curve, the benefits of such an increase in availability are equal to an amount shown by area b, whereas benefits in the case of the higher demand curve are equal to the total area $a + b$.

FIGURE 3.4 Willingness to Pay and Benefits

The logic of this seems reasonable. The people with the higher demand curve must place a greater value on this item; whatever it is, they are willing to pay more for it than the people whose demand curve is the lower function. This is in agreement with common sense. The more people value something, the more they are benefited by having more of that something made available. Or, you can't damage people by taking away from them something that they don't value.

This is the fundamental logic underlying much of environmental economics. It underlies, for example, questions of measuring the damage done to people when the natural environment surrounding them is degraded. It underlies the question of evaluating the impacts of environmental programs and policies undertaken by local, state, and federal governments. This is the strength of the economic approach, the fact that it is based on a clear notion of the value that people place on different things or on different environmental attributes.

But the idea also has shortcomings. For one thing, demand and therefore benefits are often very hard to measure when it concerns environmental questions, as we will see in later chapters. For another, we have to remember that demand curves are critically affected by the ability to pay for something as well as preferences.

In **Figure 3.4,** for example, the lower demand curve could represent a group of people with lower incomes than those with the higher demand curve. The logic of the argument would lead to the conclusion that the increase in quantity of $q_2 - q_1$ would produce fewer benefits among lower-income people than among higher-income people. This may not be a very equitable conclusion, depending on the circumstances and is one underlying pillar of environmental justice. Thus, although the logic of the concept is clear, we have to be careful in using it, especially when we are dealing with groups of people with diverse income levels. The main step in doing this is to find out as clearly as possible how the various environmental policies and programs, present or proposed, affect people at different income levels.

One other possible problem exists in using conventional demand curves to measure benefits. An individual's demand for something is clearly affected by how much he or she knows about it; a person would not be willing to pay for a good if, for example, they were ignorant of its very existence. In **Figure 3.4,** the higher demand curve might be the demand for a good before it is found out that it contains a carcinogenic substance, and the lower demand curve shows demand after this fact becomes known. There is nothing especially surprising about this; people, after all, do become more knowledgeable about things over time as a matter of course.

In today's world, this could be a complication, especially with regard to the environment. We don't fully understand many of the effects of environmental degradation; furthermore, people's views about the importance of many of these effects are blown back and forth almost from day to day, by the media, by the scientific press, and so on. Care must be exercised in taking people's demand curves of the moment, influenced as they are by all kinds of real and imagined factors, as true expressions of the benefits of environmental actions.

3-4 Costs

We now switch to the other side of the picture and consider costs. Although some things in life are free—an idea, for example—it is generally true that goods and services cannot be produced out of thin air; they require the expenditure of productive resources, or inputs, in the process. The more of something that is desired, the more resources we will have to devote to its production. What is needed is a way of describing and talking about the costs of producing useful things, whether these are normal consumer goods, such as cars or hot-water bottles, or services, such as transportation or insurance, or environmental quality through the treatment of waste residuals, recycling, or land-use controls.

Imagine a simple production process. Suppose, for example, we are producing cardboard boxes. To produce boxes, many types of productive inputs are required: labor, machinery of various descriptions, energy, raw materials, waste-handling equipment, and so on. The first thing needed is a way of valuing these productive resources. If we are a private firm operating in a market economy, we would have little problem: We would value them according to what they cost to procure in the markets. Our profit-and-loss statement at the end of the year would reflect the monetary out-of-pocket costs of the inputs used in the production operation. But our concept of cost will be broader than this. From this wider perspective, the costs of these cardboard boxes are what could have been produced with these productive inputs had they not been used in box production. The name for this is *opportunity cost*.

Opportunity Cost

The **opportunity cost** of producing something consists of the maximum value of other outputs we could and would have produced had we not used the resources to produce the item in question. The word *maximum* is used for a reason. The productive inputs used to produce the cardboard boxes could have been used to produce a variety of other things, perhaps furniture, books, or pollution-control equipment. The opportunity cost of the boxes consists of the maximum value of the alternative output that could have been obtained had we used these resources differently.

Opportunity costs include out-of-pocket costs but are wider than this. Some inputs that are actually used in production may not get registered as cash costs. For example, the spouse of the cardboard box plant operator works as an unpaid assistant in the front office. This may not register as an out-of-pocket cost, but he certainly has an opportunity cost because he could have been working somewhere else if he was not working here. Even more important for our purposes, the cardboard box manufacturing process may produce waste products that are pumped into a nearby stream. Downstream these production residuals produce environmental damage, which are real opportunity costs of producing cardboard boxes, even though they do not show up as costs in the plant's profit-and-loss statement.

The opportunity cost idea is relevant in any situation in which a decision must be made about using productive resources for one purpose rather than another. For a public agency with a given budget, the opportunity costs of a particular policy are the value of alternative policies it might have pursued. For a consumer, the opportunity cost of spending time searching for a particular item is the value of the next most valuable thing to which the consumer could have devoted time.

How is opportunity cost measured? It is not very useful to measure it in terms of the number of other physical items that could have been produced. Nor is there enough information in most cases to be able to measure the value of the next best output that was forgone. In practice, therefore, opportunity costs are measured by the market value of inputs used up in production. For this to work, we have to take care that the inputs have been correctly valued. The office labor must be valued at the going rate even though it is not paid in practice. The effects on downstream water quality must be evaluated and included. Once all inputs have been accounted for, their total value may be taken as the true opportunity costs of production.

Private and Social Costs

Another important distinction is that between **private costs** and **social costs.** The private costs of an action are the costs experienced by the party making the decisions leading to that action. The social costs of an action are *all* of the costs of the action, no matter who experiences them. Social costs include private costs, but may also include much more in certain situations.

Consider the action of driving a car. The private costs of this include the fuel and lubricants, maintenance, depreciation, and even the driving time experienced by the operator of the car. The social costs include all these private costs and also the costs experienced by people other than the operator who are exposed to the congestion and air pollution resulting from use of the car. This distinction between private and social costs will be very important in later sections where we begin to analyze environmental problems with these tools.

Cost Curves

To summarize cost information, we use cost curves, which are geometric representations of the costs of producing something. And, just as in the case of willingness to pay, we differentiate between **marginal costs** and **total costs.** Consider the cost curves in **Figure 3.5.** They are meant to apply to a single producing organization, a firm, or perhaps a public agency that is producing some good or service. The graph is laid out, the same as in previous graphs, with quantity on the horizontal axis and a monetary index on the vertical axis. The quantity relates to some period of time, such as a year. The top panel shows marginal costs in terms of a step-shaped relationship. It shows that it costs $5 to produce the first unit of output. If the firm wants to increase output to two units, it must spend an added $7. The addition of a third unit would add $10 to total costs, and so on. Marginal cost is the added cost, the amount by which total costs increase, when output is increased by one unit. It is also the cost savings if production were to decrease by one unit. Thus, the reduction in output from four units to three units would reduce total costs by $15, the marginal cost of the fourth unit.

FIGURE 3.5 The Concept of Marginal Cost

It is inconvenient to work with step-shaped curves, so we make the assumption that the firm can produce intermediate quantities as well as integer values. This gives a smooth marginal cost curve, as shown in the bottom panel of **Figure 3.5.** This curve now shows the marginal cost—the added cost of one more unit of output—for any level of output. For example, at an output level of 4.5 units, marginal cost is $19.

Marginal cost curves can be used to determine **total production costs.** On the stepped marginal cost curve of **Figure 3.5,** suppose we want to know the total cost of producing five units of this item. This is equal to the cost of the first unit ($5), plus that of the second ($7), plus that of the third ($10), and so on. This total is $60; geometrically, this is equal to the total area of the rectangles above the first five units of output. Analogously, in the smoothly shaped marginal cost function in the bottom of the diagram, the total cost of producing a given quantity is the dollar amount equal to the area under the marginal cost curve between the origin and the quantity in question. The total cost of producing 4.5 units of output is thus given by the area marked *a* in the figure.

The Shapes of Cost Curves

The height and shape of the marginal cost curve for any production process will differ from one situation to another, based on several underlying factors. A key determining factor is the technology utilized in production, and we will discuss this concept later. The price of inputs is also an important factor influencing the heights of marginal cost curves. In general, if input prices increase to a firm or group of firms, their marginal cost curves will shift upward. Another important element is *time,* specifically, the amount of time that a firm has to adjust to changes in its rate of output. These factors may be better understood by looking at some actual marginal cost curves.

Figure 3.6 shows several marginal cost curves. Panel (a) shows a very typical marginal cost curve; initially it declines as output increases but then it increases as output gets larger. The initial decline comes about because of basic efficiencies achievable with larger quantities at this level. Suppose our output refers to the quantity of wastewater handled in a municipal treatment plant. At very low levels of output, the plant is not being fully utilized; thus, output increases in this range are accompanied by less-than-proportionate increases in production cost, giving marginal costs that diminish. But as output increases, the capacity of the plant is approached. Machinery must be worked longer, additional people must be hired, and so on. Thus, marginal cost begins to increase. As the capacity of the operation is neared, these problems become more acute. A point may come at which it becomes almost impossible to increase output further, which is the same as saying that the marginal costs of production at this point increase without limit. This limit is indicated by the vertical dashed line in panel (a) of **Figure 3.6.**

FIGURE 3.6 Typical Marginal Cost Curves

This marginal cost curve depicts an important generic characteristic of all marginal cost curves, namely, that although they may initially decline, they will always increase, eventually, as output becomes large enough. These increases are related to certain underlying factors, such as increased plant utilization, the need to reach farther away for raw materials, and the inevitable higher management costs that accompany larger operations. Virtually all economic studies of particular operations and industries demonstrate increasing marginal production costs, and this fact will be an important shaping element in our later discussions specifically related to environmental quality management. See **Example 3.2**.

EXAMPLE 3.2 The Marginal Costs of a Firm Producing Organic Apples

Suppose a local orchard produces organic apples, and we consider what the marginal cost curve would look like for this operation. At the very beginning of production (going from none to a small positive amount), we might expect marginal costs to be initially relatively high, because any production at all requires a certain minimum set of inputs. At slightly higher, but still low, rates of production, added output might be obtainable with relatively modest increases in cost because the existing equipment and labor force may be used more intensively and a little extra fuel and apple-picking labor may be all that would be needed. In other words, at low levels of production we might expect marginal costs of producing organic apples to be modest, or even declining. But at somewhat higher levels of output marginal costs will undoubtedly increase. Machinery must be used more intensively, resulting in added maintenance and upgrading costs. At this point we are talking about short-run marginal costs, that is, the marginal costs of increasing production with an apple orchard of given size. Clearly, when all available steps have been taken, the short-run marginal cost curve would rise rapidly, as the maximum biological capacity of the trees to produce apples is reached.

(Continued)

EXAMPLE 3.2(Continued)

But if we consider what could happen in the longer run, we would recognize that the orchard, for a cost, could be expanded by buying more land and planting more trees. Of course, additional labor inputs would be necessary. But even in the long run like this, we would expect marginal costs to be increasing. Additional land would have to be bid away from other uses, and it would probably be more difficult to coordinate and carry out decisions over an ever-increasing size of operation.

Thus, the conventional thinking among economists is that all types of production processes would display increasing marginal costs, as pictured in the accompanying diagram. How fast marginal cost rises with output would depend on the technological options available as well as the amount of time allowed for the adjustment. In later chapters, we will apply this thinking to the costs of pollution control.

Cost ($)

Organic apple production (1,000 bushels per year)

Panel (b) of **Figure 3.6** shows a marginal cost curve similar in general shape to the one in panel (a), but with less pronounced curvature. In the short run, our wastewater treatment plant had a certain capacity that was basically fixed; but in the long run, there is time to build a larger treatment plant with higher capacities. For larger outputs, the marginal costs of this larger plant will be lower than those of the smaller plant. Yet, even in these long-run situations marginal costs will eventually increase, as is depicted in panel (b). *In our subsequent discussions we will assume that we are working with long-run marginal cost curves, unless specified otherwise.*

Panel (c) of **Figure 3.6** represents a more complicated case where there is a discontinuity in the marginal cost curve. After a short downward section, the marginal costs generally trend upward, and at one point they jump upward by some amount. This might represent a "lumpy" investment in new types of technology at a certain point as output increases.

3-5 Technology

The most important factor affecting the shapes of marginal cost functions is the **technology** of the production process. By technology we mean the inherent productive capabilities of the methods and machines being employed. Any modern production requires capital goods (machinery and equipment) of various types and capacities, labor inputs, operating procedures, raw materials, and so on. The quantity of output a firm can get from a given set of inputs depends on the technical and human capabilities inherent in these inputs. The marginal cost curves pictured in **Figure 3.6** could relate to different industries because the marginal cost curves are so different. But even within the same industry, marginal cost curves can differ among firms. Some firms will be older than others; they may be working with older equipment that has different cost characteristics. Even firms of the same age may have different production techniques; past managerial decisions may have put them in different positions in terms of the marginal production costs they experience today.

This concept of technology is vitally important in environmental economics because **technological change** can provide ways to produce goods and services with fewer environmental side effects and also better ways of handling the quantities of production residuals that remain. In our simple cost model, technical advancement has the effect of shifting marginal cost curves downward. Technological progress makes it possible to produce a given increase in output at a lower marginal cost. It also reduces total production cost. Consider **Figure 3.7**. MC_1 is the firm's marginal cost curve before a technical improvement; MC_2 is the marginal cost curve after some technical improvement has been put into effect. The technical change, in other words, shifts the marginal cost curve downward. We can also determine how much total production costs are reduced as a result of the technological change. Consider output level q^*. With MC_1, the total annual cost of producing output q^* is represented by the area $a + b$, whereas after the reduction in the marginal cost curve to MC_2, the total annual cost of producing q^* is equal to area b. Thus, the reduction in total cost made possible by the technological change is equal to area a.

FIGURE 3.7 Technological Improvement

Technological change does not normally happen without effort; it normally requires research and development (R&D). R&D in environmental industries is obviously an important activity to promote, and one of the criteria we will want to use to evaluate environmental policies is whether the policies create incentives for individuals, firms, and industries to engage in vigorous R&D programs. It is vitally important, for example, that we develop new and better technologies for reducing the CO_2 content of the earth's atmosphere. The cost savings shown in **Figure 3.7** (area *a*) show part of this incentive. This is the cost savings that would result each year, and the accumulation of these annual cost savings represents the full R&D incentive.

3-6 The Equimarginal Principle

We now come to the discussion of a simple yet important economic principle, one that is used repeatedly in chapters to come. It is called the **equimarginal principle.** To understand it, take the case of a firm producing a certain product and assume that the firm's operation is divided between two different plants. For example, suppose there is a single power company that owns two different generating plants. Each plant produces the same item, so that the total output of the firm is the sum of what it produces in the two plants. Assume that the plants were built at different times and make use of different technology. The old one, Plant A in **Figure 3.8,** has older technology; it has a marginal cost curve that starts relatively low but rises steeply as production increases. The new plant, Plant B in **Figure 3.8,** uses newer technology; it has a higher marginal cost at low output levels, but marginal costs do not rise as steeply as production increases.

FIGURE 3.8 The Equimarginal Principle

Consider now a situation in which this two-plant firm wants to produce a total output of, say, 100 units. How many units should it produce in each plant in order to produce the 100 units at the *least total cost?* Would it be best to produce 50 units in each plant? This is depicted in **Figure 3.8;** at an output of 50, Plant A has a marginal cost of $12, whereas Plant B has a marginal cost of $8. Total production costs are the sum of total costs at each plant, or areas $(a + b + c) + d$. Here is the important point: The total cost of the 100 units can be lowered by reallocating production. Reduce production in Plant A by one unit and costs will fall by $12. Then increase the production in Plant B by one unit and costs there will rise by $8. Total output is still 100 units, but there has been a cost savings of $12 - $8 = $4. Thus, total cost, the sum of the costs in the two plants, has gone down.

As long as the marginal costs in the two plants differ from one another, we can continue to reallocate production—away from the high-marginal-cost plant and toward the low-marginal-cost plant—and get a reduction in total cost. In fact, the total costs of producing the 100 units in the two plants will be at a minimum only when the marginal costs of the two plants are equal, hence the "equimarginal principle." In the figure, this happens when the output in Plant A is 38 units and the output in Plant B is 62 units. Total costs in geometric terms are now $a + (d + e)$.

- The **equimarginal principle,** therefore, says the following: If you have multiple sources to produce a given product or achieve a given goal, and you want to minimize the total cost of producing a given quantity of that output, distribute production in such a way as to equalize the marginal costs between the production sources.

There is another way of saying it that may look different but actually is not: If you have a given amount of resources and you want to maximize the total amount produced, distribute total production among the sources in such a way as to equalize marginal costs. This principle will be very valuable when we take up the issue of getting maximum pollution reduction from given amounts of resources.

3-7 Marginal Cost and Supply

A critical question in the analysis of any economic system is whether private profit-seeking firms (as well as public, politically minded agencies) will produce the correct quantities of output from the standpoint of society as a whole, not only for conventional items such as cardboard boxes, but also for less conventional items such as the amounts of environmental quality. To address this question, one must understand how firms normally determine the quantities they will produce. The marginal cost of production is a key factor in determining the **supply** behavior of firms in competitive circumstances. In fact, the marginal cost curve of a firm acts essentially as a **supply curve,** showing the quantity of the good the firm would supply at different prices. Consider **Figure 3.9.** Assume that the firm with the indicated marginal cost curve is able to sell its output at a price of p^*. The firm will maximize its profits by producing that quantity of output where marginal cost is equal to p^*; that level is designated q^*. At any output level less than this, $MC < p^*$, so a firm could increase its profits by increasing output. At any output level above this, $p^* < MC$, so a firm is actually producing items for which the marginal cost is higher than price; in this case, the firm should reduce output if it wishes to maximize its profits.

FIGURE 3.9 Marginal Cost and Supply

We are often interested in the supply performance of industries composed of many firms. The aggregate supply curve of a group of firms is the sum of the individual supply curves of all the firms in the group. This is depicted in **Figure 3.10.** There are three firms, A, B, and C, with marginal cost curves as depicted in the first three panels of the figure. At a common price, say $4, Firm A supplies 10 units, Firm B supplies 8 units, and Firm C supplies 6 units. Thus, the aggregate supply at that price is 24 units, as depicted in the far right panel of **Figure 3.10.** At other possible prices, the quantities supplied by the three firms would be determined by their respective individual supply curves, and the horizontal summations of these would trace out the aggregate supply curves.

FIGURE 3.10 Derivation of Aggregate (Market) Supply from Individual Firm Supply Curves

Summary

In this chapter, we covered briefly some of the basic tools of microeconomics. Later chapters will rely heavily on these ideas, especially on the equimarginal principle and on graphs, where we will want to jump back and forth between marginal and total measures. When we begin to look at real-world problems of environmental analysis and policy design, it is easy to get pulled so far into the countless details that basic economic ideas get lost. It is the fundamental economic building blocks, such as those in this chapter, that allow us to identify the primary economic characteristics of these problems and proceed to develop solutions to them.

Questions for Further Discussion

1. Use the logic of willingness to pay to interpret the statement "I like clean air more than you do."
2. Below is the marginal willingness to pay of a consumer for fair-trade bananas. Note that the MWTP to go from 0 to 1 lb. per week is $4.00.

Consumption Level (Bananas, lbs. per week)	Marginal Willingness to Pay
0	
	$4.00
1	
	3.00
2	
	2.10
3	
	1.80
4	
	1.20
5	
	1.00
6	
	0.50
7	

   a. What is the individual's total willingness to pay to reach a consumption level of 4 lbs. of bananas?
   b. If the price of the bananas is $1.90 per lb., how many lbs. of bananas would this person consume?

(Continued)

Questions for Further Discussion *(Continued)*

3. Below are the individual quantities demanded for two consumers for lbs. of free-trade bananas.

Price	Individual Quantity Demanded Che	Zelda	Aggregate Quantity Demanded
$5.00	1	1	
$3.70	3	2	
$1.05	4.5	2.5	

a. Complete the table. At each price level, what is the aggregate quantity demanded?
b. Graph the aggregate demand curve.

4. Below are the marginal willingness-to-pay schedules for lbs. of fair-trade bananas for two individuals. Note that the MWTP for Zelda to go from eating no bananas (0 lbs.) to eating 1 lb. per week is $6.40.

Consumption Level (Bananas, lbs. per week)	Marginal WTP Che	Zelda
0	–	–
1	$5.00	$6.40
2	4.00	5.20
3	3.20	4.00
4	3.60	3.00
5	2.20	2.10
6	1.80	1.30
7	1.50	0.60
8	1.30	0.30
9	1.20	0.00

a. Construct the MWTP curves for Che and for Zelda.
b. Who would purchase fair-trade bananas if the bananas were priced at $0.25/lb.? at $6.50/lb.?
c. Would Che and/or Zelda purchase 9 lbs. of fair-trade bananas?

5. What are the advantages and disadvantages of using willingness to pay as a measure of value? What are some alternatives?

(Continued)

Questions for Further Discussion *(Continued)*

6. **Figure 3.10** illustrates the derivation of an industry supply curve under competitive conditions where each firm receives the same price for its output. What is the relationship of this procedure to the equimarginal principle discussed earlier in the chapter?
7. Consider the marginal cost curve associated with cleaning your dorm room. Label the vertical axis "time" and the horizontal axis "percent clean." What would this marginal cost curve look like?
8. Somebody invents a small machine that electrostatically is able to remove dust from rooms very quickly. What does this do to the marginal cost curve depicted in question 7?

For additional resources pertaining to the material in this chapter, see the list in **Appendix B.**

Chapter 4
Markets, Externalities, and Public Goods

This chapter has several objectives.

1. Develop the notion of **economic efficiency** as an index of examining how an economy functions and as a criterion for judging whether it is performing as well as it might.
2. Address the question of whether an unregulated **market system** can produce results that are socially efficient.

Economic efficiency is a simple idea and one that has much to recommend it as a criterion for evaluating the performance of an economic system or a part of that system, but it has to be used with care. A single firm or group of firms may be judged very efficient in their own limited way as long as they are keeping costs low and making a profit. Yet, to evaluate the *social* performance of these firms, we must use the idea of economic efficiency in a wider sense. In this case, it must include all the social values and consequences of economic decisions—in particular, environmental consequences. It is also important to discuss the relationship between **economic efficiency** and **economic equity.**

Market systems work by allowing individuals, both buyers and sellers, to seek out exchanges that are individually beneficial. People in the United States and in most of the world live in a market economy. We will see that there are a number of circumstances in which a system of private markets will not normally be able to bring about results that are efficient in this wider sense. This leads to the next chapter, where we will examine the following policy question: If the economy is not operating the way we want it to, especially in matters of environmental quality, what kind of public policy might be used to correct the situation?

Economic efficiency is a criterion that can be applied to input usage levels and to the determination of output levels. We are going to concentrate in this chapter on the second of these because ultimately we want to apply the concept to the "output" of environmental quality. There are two questions of interest: (1) What quantity ought to be produced and (2) what quantity is produced in fact? The first question deals with the notion of efficiency, the second with the way markets normally function.

4-1 Economic Efficiency

In the preceding chapter we introduced two relationships, that between the quantity of output and willingness to pay, and that between output and marginal production costs. Neither of these two relationships, by itself, can tell us what the most desirable level of output is from society's standpoint. To identify this output level, it is necessary to bring these two elements together. The central idea of **economic efficiency** is that there should be a balance between the value of what is produced and the value of what is used up to produce it. In our terminology, there should be a balance between willingness to pay and the marginal costs of production.

Efficiency is a notion that has to have a reference point. It is critical to ask: Efficient from the standpoint of whom? What is efficient for one person, in the sense of balancing costs and benefits, may not be efficient for somebody else. We want to have a concept of efficiency that is applicable to the economy as a whole. This means that when referring to marginal costs, *all* of the costs of producing the particular item in question must be included, no matter to whom they accrue. When dealing with marginal willingness to pay, we must insist that this represents accurately *all* of the value that people in the society place on the item. This does not necessarily mean that all people will place the same value on all goods; it means only that we do not leave out any missing sources of value.

How do we identify the rate of output that is socially efficient? Suppose we focus on a particular type of output; in practice it could be refrigerators, automobiles, a college education, or a certain type of pollution-control equipment. Suppose that our item is currently being produced at a particular rate, and we wish to know whether it would benefit society to have this output level increased by a small amount. To answer this requires comparing the marginal willingness to pay for that extra output with the marginal opportunity costs of the output. If the former exceeds the latter, we would presumably want the extra output to be produced; otherwise, we would not.

This can be analyzed graphically by bringing together the two relationships discussed in the last chapter. Figure 4.1 shows the aggregate marginal willingness-to-pay curve (labeled MWTP) and the aggregate marginal cost curve (MC) for the good in question. The efficient level of production for this item is the quantity identified by the intersection of the two curves, labeled q^e in the figure. At this output level, the costs of producing one more unit of this good are just exactly equal to the marginal value of it, as expressed by the marginal willingness-to-pay curve. This common value is p^e.

FIGURE 4.1 The Socially Efficient Rate of Output

The equality of the marginal willingness to pay and the marginal production cost is the test for determining if output is at the socially efficient level. There is another way of looking at this notion of efficiency. When a rate of output is at the socially efficient level, the net value, defined as **total willingness to pay** minus **total costs,** is as large as possible. In fact, we can measure this net value on the diagram. At q^e we know that the total willingness to pay is equal to an amount corresponding to the area under the marginal willingness-to-pay curve from the origin up to q^e; this area consists of the sum of the three subareas: $a + b + c$. Total cost, however, consists of the area under the marginal cost curve, or area c. Thus, the surplus is $(a + b + c) - c = a + b$, which is the triangular area enclosed by the marginal willingness-to-pay curve and the marginal cost curve. At any other quantity, the corresponding value of total willingness to pay minus total production costs will be less than this area $a + b$.

Let's be clear on what this graph is saying. We noted previously that the marginal willingness-to-pay curve is assumed to represent accurately all the benefits that people in our economy actually experience when the good becomes available. The marginal production cost curve is assumed to contain all the true opportunity costs that are required to produce this good—no hidden or overlooked costs have been left out. Thus, the quantity q^e is **efficient** because it produces a balance between the two sides—between the marginal worth of a good, as indicated by consumers' willingness to pay for it, and what it costs society to produce it, as measured by marginal costs.[1]

4-2 Efficiency and Equity

From the standpoint of society at large, production is at an efficient level when marginal benefits equal marginal production costs, that is, when net benefits are maximized, *no matter to whom those net benefits accrue.* Efficiency doesn't distinguish among people. A dollar of net benefits to one person is considered to be worth a dollar to anybody else. One hundred dollars of benefits to one person is considered to be worth the same as one dollar of benefits to each of 100 people. In the real world, an outcome that benefits very rich people at the expense of poor people would be regarded by most people as inequitable. This is simply another way of saying that an outcome that is efficient in this sense need not necessarily be equitable.

Equity is tied closely to the distribution of income and wealth in a society. If this distribution is regarded as essentially fair, then judgments about alternative output levels may justifiably be made using only the efficiency criterion. But if wealth is distributed unfairly, the efficiency criterion by itself may be too narrow. Fairness does not mean everyone holds the same level of wealth or uses identical levels of output. Having said this, however, we have to recognize that in the assessment of economic outcomes, the relative emphasis to be put on efficiency and equity is a matter of controversy. It is controversial in the political arena; it is controversial among economists themselves.

---

1. The graphs discussed in this and the preceding chapter show the production and consumption of some good or service that has positive value. In later chapters, we will adapt them to explore the production of what we might call a "bad" value, namely, environmental pollution. Then the units along the horizontal axis would be quantities of some pollutant. The marginal cost curve would show the increasing costs, or damages, to society from increasing quantities of pollutants. The demand curve, on the other hand, would show the diminishing marginal savings to polluting firms from being able to emit more pollution into the environment. We will discuss this in much greater detail in **Chapter 5.**

We will have much to say about distributional issues and equity throughout this book. **Chapter 6** contains terminology for describing the distributional impacts of environmental policies. **Chapter 9** contains a discussion of the role of economic equity as a criterion for evaluating environmental policies.

4-3 Markets

Having specified what economic efficiency means, we next ask whether a market system, a system in which the major economic decisions about how much to produce are made by the more or less unhindered interaction of buyers and sellers, gives results that are socially efficient. In other words, if we rely entirely on the market to determine how much of this item gets produced, will it settle on q^e?

Why worry about this question? Why not simply jump to the question of public policy? Doesn't this question imply that we are committed to the market system, and isn't this the system that, from an environmental point of view, has gotten us into trouble in the first place? If the market doesn't do the job, maybe we should just ignore whatever the market does and proceed through political/administrative means to bring about the desired rate of output.

The short answer to this is that, as a nation, we are in fact committed to a market-based economy. For all its faults, a market system has historically produced better environmental results overall than any other modern system. Of course, it needs to be remembered that although our system is "market based," we do not necessarily have to accept whatever results it yields. The results are acceptable only if they are reasonably efficient and equitable. We will find that in the case of environmental quality, market institutions are not likely to give us results that are socially efficient.

The slightly longer answer to the question is that the market system contains within it certain incentive structures that in many cases can be harnessed toward the objective of improved environmental quality. One of these is the cost-minimizing incentive that stems from the competitive process. Another is the incentive provided through the rewards that may be reaped through initiative in finding better, that is, less expensive, technical and organizational means of production. It will be far more effective in many cases to take advantage of these incentives than to try to do away with them. By altering them so that they take environmental values into account, the market system will yield more effective results than if we tried to jettison the whole system and adopt a different set of institutions.

A **market** is an institution in which buyers and sellers of goods and services, carry out mutually agreed-upon exchanges. When they buy or sell in a market, people naturally look for the best terms they can get. Presumably buyers would like to pay a low price, whereas sellers would prefer high prices. What brings all these conflicting objectives into balance is the adjustment of prices on the market.

Figure 4.2 shows a simple market model. Buyers' desires are represented by the **demand curve,** labeled D; it shows the quantity of the good that buyers would buy at different prices. It has the typical downward slope; the higher the price, the lower the quantity demanded, and vice versa. Underlying the demand curve are such factors as consumer tastes and preferences, the number of potential consumers in the market, and consumer income levels.

FIGURE 4.2 The Market Model

The curve labeled S is the **supply curve,** which shows the quantity of the good that suppliers would willingly make available at different prices. It is upward sloping; higher prices represent greater incentives for suppliers, and therefore larger quantities are supplied, and vice versa. The main factors affecting the height and shape of the supply curve are production costs. These, in turn, are related to the prices of inputs used in the production of this item and the level of technology inherent in the production process.

It is important to keep in mind that the demand and supply curves represent possibilities, or alternatives. During any particular time, only one quantity of a good can change hands, and sellers and buyers can be on only one point of their supply and demand curves, respectively. It is easy to see that there is only one price at which the quantity demanded by buyers is consistent with the quantity that sellers will make available. That is the price where the two curves intersect, marked p^m. Similarly, the total quantity that buyers and sellers will exchange at this price is labeled q^m.

For the market to work effectively, there must be competition among sellers and among buyers. None can be large enough that its own performance affects market prices or powerful enough that it can control how the market performs. Price must be allowed to adjust freely so that it can "discover" the quantities that bring buyers and sellers into balance. At prices higher than p^m, sellers will attempt to supply more than buyers want. In a surplus situation such as this, competition among sellers forces prices downward. If prices are temporarily lower than p^m, a shortage develops and competition among buyers will force the price to adjust upward. At the equilibrium, quantity demanded equals quantity supplied.

It is important to look at it also from the other direction. At the quantity q^m there is an equality between the marginal willingness to pay by consumers for an additional unit of the item and the marginal costs of producing the item. These are equal at the value of p^m. If price and quantity are allowed to adjust freely and competition does in fact exist, an equality will arise through the normal interaction of buyers and sellers, between the marginal valuation that consumers have for a good (their marginal willingness to pay) and the cost of making available another unit of the good (the marginal cost of production).

4-4 Markets and Social Efficiency

The next question is whether markets ordinarily produce results that are efficient from the standpoint of society. Compare **Figures 4.1** and **4.2**. They look the same, but there is actually a big difference. The first shows a socially efficient rate of output for a particular item; the second shows the rate of output and price that would prevail on a competitive market for that item. Are these two rates of output, labeled q^e and q^m, likely to be the same in the real world? The answer is yes *if*, and it is a big *if*, the market demand and supply curves, as pictured in **Figure 4.2,** are the same as the marginal cost and willingness-to-pay curves shown in **Figure 4.1**. Here is the nub of the problem: When environmental values are concerned, there are likely to be very substantial differences between market values and social values. This is called **market failure,** and it will often call for public intervention, either to override the markets directly or to rearrange things so that they will work more effectively.

In the rest of this chapter, we will discuss the performance of markets when matters of environmental quality are involved. There are two phenomena to account for, one on the supply side and the other on the demand side. Environmental effects can drive a wedge between normal market supply curves and true marginal social cost curves. On the other side of the market, environmental effects can create a difference between market demands and true social marginal willingness to pay. On the supply side the problem is *external costs*, whereas on the demand side the problem is *external benefits*.

4-5 External Costs

When entrepreneurs in a market economy make decisions about what and how much to produce, they normally take into account the price of what they will produce and the cost of items for which they will have to pay: labor, raw materials, machinery, energy, and so on. We call these the **private costs** of the firm; they are the costs that show up in the profit-and-loss statement at the end of the year. Any firm, assuming it has the objective of maximizing its profits, will try to keep its production costs as low as possible. This is a worthwhile outcome for both the firm and society because inputs always have opportunity costs; they could have been used to produce something else. Furthermore, firms will be alert to ways of reducing costs when the relative prices of inputs change. For example, we know that during the U.S. energy "crisis" of the 1970s, from 2011 to 2013 when energy inputs became much more expensive, and with the onset of the war in Ukraine, firms found ways of reducing energy inputs by using more energy-efficient machinery, changing operating procedures, and so on.

In many production operations, however, there is another type of cost that, although representing a true cost to society, does not show up in the firm's profit-and-loss statement. These are called **external costs.** They are external because, although they are real costs to some members of society, firms do not normally take them into account when they go about making their decisions about output rates. Another way of saying this is that these are costs that are external to firms but internal to society as a whole.[2] Firms do not pay for these costs.

One of the major types of external cost is the cost inflicted on people through environmental degradation. An example is the easiest way to see this. Suppose a paper mill is located somewhere on the upstream reaches of a river and that, in the course of its operation, it discharges a large amount of wastewater into the river. The wastewater is full of organic matter that arises from the process of converting wood to paper. This waste material gradually is converted to more benign materials by the natural assimilative capacity of the river water, but, before that happens, a number of people downstream are affected by the lower quality of water in the river. Perhaps the waterborne residuals reduce the number of fish in the river, affecting downstream fishers. The river may also be less attractive to look at, affecting people who would like to swim or boat on it. Worse, the river water perhaps is used downstream as a source of water for a public water supply system, and the degraded water quality means that the town has to engage in more costly treatment processes before the water can be sent through the water mains. Or, even without downstream communities, the paper mill discharge affects the downstream ecosystem. All of these downstream costs are real costs associated with producing paper, just as much as the raw materials, labor, energy, and so on, used internally by the plant. But from the mill's standpoint, these downstream costs are *external costs*. They are costs that are borne by someone other than the people who make decisions about operating the paper mill. At the end of the year, the profit-and-loss statement of the paper mill will contain no reference to these real downstream external costs.

If rates of output are to be socially efficient, decisions about resource use must take into account both types of costs: the private costs of producing paper plus whatever external costs arise from adverse environmental impacts. In terms of full social cost accounting:

Social costs = Private costs + External (environmental) costs

This is pictured in **Figure 4.3**. The top panel shows the relationship between the rate of paper production and the occurrence of these downstream external costs. It shows that the marginal external costs increase as paper production increases. The bottom panel shows several things. It shows the demand curve for paper and the marginal private costs of producing paper. The intersection of these occurs at a price of p^m and a quantity of q^m. This is the price and quantity that would arise in a competitive market where producers pay no attention to external costs. But marginal social costs are in fact higher, as shown, because they contain both the marginal private costs and the marginal external costs.[3] Thus, the full socially efficient rate of output is q^* and the associated price is p^*.

---

2. External costs are sometimes called third-party costs. The first two parties are, respectively, the producer and the consumer. So a third-party cost is one that is inflicted on people who are not directly involved in the economic transactions between buyers and sellers. It is also sometimes called a **spillover effect**.
3. Note that MEC is zero below a certain quantity. The graph is drawn under the assumption that a threshold exists: a quantity of paper production below which there are no external costs.

Compare the two rates of output and the two prices. The market output is too high compared to the socially efficient rate of output ($q^m > q^*$). In addition, the market price is too low compared to the socially efficient price ($p^m < p^*$). This is because when considering just its private costs, the firm is essentially using a productive input it is not paying for. What is this unpaid input? The unpaid input is the services of the river, which provides the firm with a cheap way to dispose of its production residuals. Although it may be cheap for the firm to do this, it may not be cheap to society; in fact, in this case we have costs being inflicted on downstream users that are being overlooked by the paper mill. So the private market system in this case produces too much paper at too low of a price compared to socially efficient results.

FIGURE 4.3 External Costs and Market Outcomes

Most of the cases of environmental destruction are related to external costs of one type or another. Many external costs stem from industrial activity. Producing electricity, especially with fossil fuels, results in downwind air pollution, and greenhouse gases, that cause a variety of health and ecosystem damages. A study found that external costs in Minnesota from power plant emissions in that state vary from $58 to $257 million per ton of emissions, depending on whether the plant is located in urban or rural areas.[4] The total dollar cost of damages from U.S. power plants was $133 billion in 2017.[5]

There are many other examples of external costs from both business and individual actions:

- Users of chemicals emit toxic fumes that affect people living in the vicinity,
- Developers build on land without taking into account the degradation of the visual environment of local inhabitants or wildlife ecosystem destruction,
- Drivers of cars and trucks, whether for businesses, organizations, or consumers, add to air pollution and traffic congestion.

---

4. Andrew L. Goodkind, and S. Polasky, *Health & Environmental Costs of Electricity Generation in Minnesota*, Report to Minnesota Center for Environmental Advocacy, 2013.
5. Stephen P. Holland, Erin T. Mansur, Nicholas Z. Muller, and Andrew J. Yates, *Decompositions and Policy Consequences of an Extraordinary Decline in Air Pollution from Electricity Generation*, NBER Working Paper 25339, Dec 2018.

Example 4.1 shows estimates of external costs in the United States from driving automobiles. Note that the largest of these cost items relates to costs of congestion and accidents. The largest conventional environmental costs are for local air pollution, which are about seven times the external costs related to global warming.

EXAMPLE 4.1 External Costs Associated with Driving Automobiles

Source of Cost	Cents/Mile[1]
Greenhouse gas emissions	1.6
Local air pollution	2.2
Congestion	1.2
Total	5.0

[1] Costs converted assuming a vehicle life of 10.6 years and mileage of 11,300 per year.

Source: Lambros K. Mitropoulos, Panos D. Prevedouros, and Pantelis Kopelias, "Total Cost of Ownership and Externalities of Conventional, Hybrid and Electric Vehicle," *Transportation Research Procedia*, 24(24), 2017, 267–274.

Most, but not all, environmental externalities are expressed through physical linkages among parties involved—that is, polluter and people damaged.

- Cases involving just two parties: one polluter and one person suffering damages. An upstream pulp mill and a downstream firm that uses the river water in its production operations provide an example.
- Cases of single polluters and multiple damaged parties, such as a power plant that emits sulfur dioxide (SO_2) affecting a group of community residents living downwind.
- Cases of multiple polluters but only one damaged party, such as the runoff from many farms that affects a local water supply system.
- Cases where both polluters and parties damaged are many in number. An example of this is urban air and noise pollution stemming from leaf blower emissions: Each user is both a producer and a recipient of the externality. The same is true of global phenomena, such as climate change.

Some externalities do not involve physical linkages. Degradation of the scenic environment through thoughtless land development is an example. In addition, some externalities involve neither physical linkages nor close proximity. People in one part of a country, for example, may feel loss when those in another region cause damage to an important environmental resource, such as a unique species of animal or plant in the Amazon rainforest.

This brings up a problem that we will state but not solve. What is the limit, if any, to be placed on external damage that people may legitimately claim? I suffer damages when someone in my vicinity plays her music too loudly, but can I legitimately claim that I suffer damages if, for example, she adopts a lifestyle with which I don't agree? If people in Boston pollute the waters of Boston Harbor, may residents in California claim that they have been damaged? If residents of New Jersey thin out the suburban deer population in order to save their flower gardens, may people in Chicago justifiably claim that they have been damaged?

The answer to these questions hinges on the notion of willingness to pay. In this approach, whether someone has or has not been affected by another action hinges on his or her willingness to pay to have that action changed. If people in New York are willing to pay to preserve clean air in Tokyo, then this is evidence that air quality in Tokyo affects the welfare of people in New York. If people in Paris are not willing to pay anything to clean up the Rhine River, we conclude that the water quality of that river has no effect on the welfare of people in Paris. The presence or absence of willingness to pay, in other words, is the economic index of whether an action may be said to affect somebody.

Open-Access Resources

One source of external costs has been widely studied by environmental economists (as well as natural resource economists):

- **open-access resource**—a resource or facility that is open to uncontrolled access by individuals who wish to use the resource.

A classic example is an ocean fishery in which anyone willing to buy a boat and take up fishing is free to do so. Other examples are a pasture that is open to anyone to graze animals, a forest where anyone may go and cut wood, or a public park open to free access.

In these situations we have, in effect, problems in property rights—their definition, distribution, and/or enforcement. If someone owns a pasture or a forest, he or she will presumably keep out encroachers, or perhaps charge them for use of the resource or otherwise control their rate of access. But when a resource or facility is open to unrestricted access, there is no way of ensuring that its rate of use is kept to the level that will maximize its overall value.[6]

To understand this, consider the following example. Suppose there are four similar firms situated on a lake. The firms use the water of the lake in producing their output and discharge emissions back into the lake. Because of the emissions, each firm must treat the water taken from the lake before it uses the water in production. The treatment costs of each firm depend on the ambient quality of the lake, which of course depends on the total emissions of the four firms. Suppose that the cost of intake water treatment is currently $40,000 per year for each firm. A new firm is contemplating starting operations on the lake. If it adds its untreated emissions to those of the current four, it will make ambient water quality worse and drive the cost of water treatment for each firm up to $60,000 per year. When the fifth firm makes its location and production decisions, it will take into account its various operating costs, which will include the $60,000 per year of water treatment costs. But the total social water-related costs of the firm's decisions are higher. There are also external costs inflicted on the other four firms, amounting to $20,000 each of added water treatment costs if the fifth firm locates on the lake. The social marginal costs of

---

6. This is what is involved in the "Tragedy of the Commons," as it was popularly termed by Garrett Hardin in "Tragedy of the Commons," *Science,* 162, 1968, 1243-1248. His example was an open-access pasture on which all farmers had the right to pasture their sheep.

water supply when the new firm locates on the lake are $140,000, consisting of $60,000 of internal costs of the new firm plus $80,000 ($20,000 × 4) of external costs inflicted on firms already on the lake. These are often called open-access externalities because they result from the fact that the firms have uncontrolled access to the lake.

We have focused on the externalities flowing from the fifth firm's decisions, but everything is symmetrical in the sense that we could say exactly the same thing about each of the other firms. Each firm will make its decisions without regard to the external costs inflicted on other firms. It is this reciprocal nature of these externalities that distinguishes them from the type we talked about before (e.g., the pulp mill upstream inflicting external costs on people downstream), but the effect is the same: externalities that lead to rates of output that are too high compared to socially efficient rates.

As another example of an open-access problem, consider a road that is open to access by anyone. A road is not a natural resource but a person-made facility. But the essence of the uncontrolled access problem is identical. It uses very simplifying assumptions in order to highlight the basic issues. There is a road connecting two cities—City A and City B. The figures in **Table 4.1** show the average travel time it takes to get from City A to City B along this road, as a function of the number of motorists using the road. Thus, for example, if there are just 10 travelers on the road, it takes 10 minutes to get from A to B (we assume a speed limit that is enforced). Likewise, when there are either 20 or 30 motorists on the road, the average travel time is still 10 minutes, but when the traffic increases to 40 travelers, the average travel time increases to 11 minutes. This is because of congestion; cars begin to get in each other's way and average speeds drop. As the number of motorists continues to increase, the congestion increases, thus driving up travel times even more.

TABLE 4.1 Travel Times Related to the Number of Cars on the Road

Number of Cars	Average Travel Time Between A and B
10	10
20	10
30	10
40	11
50	12
60	14
70	18
80	24

Now suppose you are considering using this road to go from A to B and that there are already 50 cars using it. Suppose, furthermore, that you have an alternative route that will take you 18 minutes. Assume that you know the state of the traffic and the resulting travel times. Because taking the given road will save you four minutes over the alternative, your individual decision would be to use the road. But from the standpoint of "society," in this case consisting of you plus all the other motorists on the road, this is not efficient. When you enter the highway on which there are already 50 cars, the added congestion causes an increase in average travel times of two minutes to the people already using the road. Thus, your 4-minute individual savings is offset by added travel costs of 100 minutes (50 cars times 2 minutes per car) on the part of the other motorists, meaning that if all minutes are treated as equally valuable, there is a net social loss of 96 minutes when you decide to use the road. The advent of global positioning system (GPS) units used by drivers, either in their car or on their phone, has increased the availability of traffic information. Thus, the decision process of selecting a driving route, based on congestion and travel time, has become more efficient for society.

The problem arises because there is uncontrolled access to the road, and in using it people may inflict external costs on others in the form of added congestion and higher travel times.

Other examples of the same kind of effect are:

- When a fisher enters a fishery; in catching a portion of the stock, he leaves fewer to be caught by other fishers.
- When one farmer puts animals on a common pasture, they reduce the forage available to other herds on that pasture.
- When one person cuts wood from a communal forest, she leaves fewer trees for other users and makes it more difficult for them to supply themselves with wood.

We can see that this is related to the notion of external costs. The added costs that one user of a common-property resource inflicts on other users of that resource are in fact costs that are external to that user but internal to the whole group of users. When a single individual is making a decision about whether and how much to utilize a common-property resource, she takes into account the costs and benefits that impinge directly on her. Some people might also altruistically take into account the common-property externalities they inflict on others, but most will not. The result will be, as it was with the road example, a rate of use that is higher than what is called for on grounds of social efficiency.

Thus, when external costs are present, private markets will not normally produce quantities of output that are socially efficient. This market failure may justify public policy to help move the economy toward social efficiency. This may be done sometimes by changing rules, such as property rights rules, so that the market will function efficiently. Other cases may call for more direct public intervention. We will take up these matters again in **Section 4**. We must now move to the demand side of the market and consider another important source of market failure, that of external benefits.

4-6 External Benefits

An **external benefit** is a benefit that accrues to somebody who is outside, or external to, the decision about consuming or producing the good or resource that causes the externality. When the use of an item leads to an external benefit, the market willingness to pay for that item will understate the social willingness to pay. Suppose a quieter lawn mower would provide $50 a year of extra benefits to me if I were to buy it. This is therefore the maximum that I would be willing to pay for this machine. But suppose my use of the new lawn mower would create $20 of added benefits to my neighbor because of reduced noise levels in the course of the year. These $20 of benefits to the neighbor are external benefits for me. I make my purchasing decision on the basis of benefits accruing only to me.

Thus, my marginal willingness to pay for a quieter lawn mower is $50, whereas the social marginal benefits (where "society" in this case includes just me and my neighbor) is $70 (my $50 and her $20).

As another example of an external benefit, consider a farmer whose land is on the outskirts of an urban area. The farmer cultivates the land and sells his produce to people in the city. Of course, the farmer's main concern is the income he can derive from the operation, and he makes decisions about inputs and outputs according to their effect on that income. But the land kept in agriculture produces several other benefits, including a habitat for birds and other small animals and scenic values for passers-by. These benefits, although internal from the standpoint of society, are external from the standpoint of the farmer. They don't appear anywhere in his profit-and-loss position; they are external benefits of his farming decisions. In this case, the agricultural value of the land to the farmer understates the social willingness to pay to have the land in agriculture.

Many goods do not involve external benefits. Indeed, when economists discuss the rudiments of supply and demand, the examples used are normally simple goods that do not create this complication. Farmers produce and supply so many thousand cantaloupes; individual and market demand curves for cantaloupes are easy to comprehend. If we want to know the total number of cantaloupes bought, we can simply add up the number bought by each person in the market. Each person's consumption affects no one else. In this case, the market demand curve will represent accurately the aggregate marginal willingness to pay of consumers for cantaloupes. But in cases involving external benefits, this no longer holds. We can perhaps best see this by considering a type of good that inherently involves large-scale external benefits, what economists have come to call **public goods.**

Public Goods

Consider a lighthouse. This is a service provided to mariners at sea so that they can locate themselves and avoid running aground at night. But the lighthouse has an interesting technical characteristic: If its services are made available to one mariner at sea, they immediately become available to all others in the vicinity. Once the services are made available to one person, others cannot be excluded from making use of the same services. This is the distinguishing characteristic of a **public good.** It is a good that, if made available to one person, automatically becomes available to others.

Another example of a public good is a radio signal. Once a radio station broadcasts a signal, it is available to anybody who has a receiver. Each individual can listen to the broadcast without diminishing its availability to all other people within range of the station. Note carefully that it is not the ownership of the supplying organization that makes a public good public. Lighthouses are usually publicly owned, but radio stations, at least in the United States, are typically privately owned. A public good is distinguished by the technical nature of the good, not by the type of organization making it available.

We are interested in public goods because environmental quality is essentially a public good. If the air is cleaned up for one person in an urban area, it is automatically cleaned up for everybody else in that community. The benefits, in other words, accrue to everyone in the community.

Private markets are likely to undersupply public goods, relative to efficient levels. To see why, let's look at another very simple example: a small freshwater lake, the shores of which have three occupied homes. The people living in the houses use the lake for recreational purposes, but, unfortunately, the water quality of the lake has been contaminated by an old industrial plant that has since closed. The contaminant is measured in parts per million (ppm). At present the lake contains 5 ppm of this contaminant. It is possible to clean the water by using a fairly expensive treatment process. Each of the surrounding homeowners is willing to pay a certain amount to have the water quality improved. **Table 4.2** shows these individual marginal willingnesses to pay for integer values of water quality. It also shows the aggregate marginal willingness to pay, which is the sum of the individual values.

TABLE 4.2 Individual and Aggregate Demand for Lowering Lake Pollution

Level of Contaminant (ppm)	Homeowner A	Homeowner B	Homeowner C	Aggregate MWP	Marginal Cost of Cleanup
5	–	–	–	–	–
4	110	60	30	200	50
3	85	35	20	140	65
2	70	10	15	95	95
1	55	0	10	65	150
0	45	0	5	50	240

Marginal Willingness to Pay ($ per year)

Note that the MWTP for Homeowner A to go from no clean-up at 5 ppm to 4 ppm is $110 per year, and from 4 to 3 is $85.

The table also shows the marginal cost of cleaning up the lake, again just for integer values of water quality. Note that marginal cost is increasing; as the lake becomes cleaner, the marginal cost of continued improvement increases. Marginal cost and aggregate marginal willingness to pay are equal ($95) at a water quality of 2 ppm. At higher contamination levels (higher ppm), aggregate marginal willingness to pay for a cleaner lake exceeds the marginal cost of achieving it. Hence, from the standpoint of these three homeowners together, improved water quality is desirable, but at quality levels better than 2 ppm, such as 1 or 0 ppm, total willingness to pay falls below marginal costs. Thus, 2 ppm is the socially efficient level of water quality in the lake.

Having identified the efficient level of water quality, could we rely on a competitive market system, where entrepreneurs are on the alert for new profit opportunities, to get the contaminant in the lake reduced to that level? Suppose a private firm attempts to sell its services to the three homeowners. The firm goes to person A and tries to collect an amount equal to that person's true willingness to pay. But that person will presumably realize that once the lake is cleaned up, it is cleaned up for everybody, no matter how much each homeowner actually contributed. So A may have the incentive to underpay, relative to his true willingness to pay, in the hopes that the other homeowners will contribute enough to cover the costs of the cleanup. Of course, the others may react in the same way. When a public good is involved, each person may have an incentive to **free ride** on the efforts of others. A free rider is a person who pays less for a good than their true marginal willingness to pay, that is, a person who underpays relative to the benefits they receive.

Free riding is a ubiquitous phenomenon in the world of public goods, or in fact for any good for which its consumption produces external benefits. Because of the free-riding impulse, private, profit-motivated firms will have difficulty covering their costs if they go into the business of supplying public goods.[7] Because of these reduced revenues, private firms will normally *undersupply* goods and services of this type. Environmental quality improvements are essentially public goods. Because we cannot rely on the market system to provide efficient quantities of goods of this type, we must fall back on some type of nonmarket institution involving collective action of one type or another. In the lake example, the homeowners may be able to act together privately, perhaps through a homeowners' association, to secure contributions for cleaning up the lake. Of course, the free-rider problem will still exist even for the homeowners' association, but if there are not too many of them, personal acquaintance and the operation of moral pressure may be strong enough to overcome the problem. When there are many more people involved (thousands, or perhaps millions, as there are in many large urban areas), the free-rider problem can be addressed effectively only with more direct governmental action. This opens up the huge topic of **public policy** for environmental quality, a topic we will spend much more time discussing throughout the rest of the book.

Summary

The main goal in this chapter was to discuss the operation of private markets and then apply the market model to situations in which environmental quality is an issue. Markets are places where buyers and sellers interact over the quantities and prices of particular goods or services. Buyers' desires are represented by the aggregate demand curve, which shows the quantities demanded at alternative prices. Sellers' supply capabilities are represented by supply curves, which ultimately are based on underlying production costs and show quantities that would be made available at alternative prices. The intersection of the supply and demand curves shows the unique quantity and price that can simultaneously satisfy both buyers and sellers. For many types of goods and services, market outcomes (output and price levels) may also be the outcomes that are socially efficient. Outcomes that are socially efficient are those in which the aggregate marginal willingness to pay in society is equal to the aggregate marginal social costs of production. When market results are not socially efficient, we speak of market failures.

We then discussed two main situations where market failures may result. The primary reason, on a conceptual level, is the existence of external costs and external benefits. In matters of the environment, external costs are the damages that people experience from environmental impacts that are not taken into account by the firms, public agencies, or consumers whose decisions produce them. A classic case is water pollution from an upstream pulp mill that damages people using the water downstream. Another important case is the external costs that users of an open-access resource inflict upon one another through uncontrolled use of the resource. External benefits are benefits accruing to people

---

7. This sentence emphasizes the point made earlier: It is the technical nature of the good that makes it a public or private good, not whether the organization providing it is public or private. A lighthouse (a public good) might be built and operated by a private firm; flood insurance (a private good) might be provided by a public federal agency.

other than the direct buyers or recipients of a good. The classic case of external benefits concerns what are called public goods; these are goods or services that, when they are made available to one person, automatically become available to others.

Faced with external costs and benefits, public goods, and common-property resources, markets cannot be relied upon to supply efficient levels of environmental quality. Some type of nonmarket actions by private or public groups may be called upon to rectify these situations.

Questions for Further Discussion

1. Suppose that the following discrete numbers show the integer values of MWTP and MC as depicted in **Figure 4.1**. Determine the socially efficient rate of output. Show that at any other output level, the net benefits to society will be lower than they are at the efficient level. (Remember, the marginal cost of increasing output from 4 to 5 units is $9, which is also the amount by which cost decreases in going from 5 to 4 units.)

Output	0	1	2	3	4	5	6	7	8
MWTP	$20	18	16	14	12	10	8	4	2
MC	$5	6	7	8	9	11	15	21	30

2. Following are portions of the demand curves of three individuals for the water quality in a small pond. The water quality is expressed in terms of the parts per million (ppm) of dissolved oxygen (DO). Water quality improves at higher DO levels. The demand curves show the marginal willingness to pay of each individual (A, B, C). Note that to go from 0 to 1 ppm DO, A's MWTP is $10.

   a. Complete the table. Find the aggregate willingness-to-pay curve of these three people at each DO level.

   b. If the actual marginal cost of increasing DO is $12 at all levels, what is the socially efficient level of DO in the lake, assuming these three people are the only ones involved?

   (Continued)

Questions for Further Discussion *(Continued)*

| | Marginal WTP | | | |
DO Level (ppm)	A	B	C	Aggregate WTP
0	–	–	–	–
1	$10	$10	$12	
2	6	8	10	
3	4	6	8	
4	2	4	6	
5	0	2	4	
6	0	0	2	

3. Considering the definition of public goods introduced in the chapter, is a bus a public good? Is an automatic teller machine (ATM)? Is a public park? Is a library? Discuss your reasons.

4. Consider the example of the three homeowners around the lake (the ones depicted in **Table 4.2**). Suppose the lake was cleaned up to the efficient level of 2 ppm and that the total costs of the cleanup were shared equally among the homeowners (stick to integer values here). Will all three homeowners be better off? What problems does this bring up about sharing the costs of public goods?

5. If you turn up the heating thermostat in your household, what are the private costs? What are the external costs?

For additional resources pertaining to the material in this chapter, see the list in **Appendix B.**

Chapter 5
The Economics of Environmental Quality

In the preceding chapter we concluded that the market system, left to itself, is likely to malfunction when matters of environmental pollution are involved. That is to say, it will not normally produce results that are socially efficient and equitable. This brings us to the **policy question:** If we do not like the way things are currently turning out, what steps should be undertaken to change the situation?[1]

The policy problem includes a number of closely related issues:

- Identifying the most appropriate level of environmental quality we ought to try to achieve
- Dividing the task and costs of meeting environmental quality goals
- Distributing benefits and costs across society appropriately

In this chapter we take up these issues on a conceptual basis; in subsequent chapters we will look at specific policy alternatives.

Before developing a simple policy model, we need to stress again that effective public policy depends on good information on how economic and environmental systems actually work. This might be called the scientific basis of environmental policy—that is, the study of how firms and consumers normally make decisions in the market economy, how residuals are emitted into the natural environment, and the ways in which these residuals behave in that environment to produce human and nonhuman damages. Thousands of scientists have worked and continue to work on these issues to clarify these diverse linkages. Great effort will continue to be needed to expand the scientific base on which to develop environmental policy.

5-1 Pollution Control—A General Model

Diverse types of environmental pollutants obviously call for diverse types of public policy, but in order to build up the required policy analyses, it is better to start with one very simple model that lays out the fundamentals of the policy situation. The essence of the model consists of a simple **trade-off** situation that characterizes all pollution-control activities.

---

1. This goes back to the distinction made earlier between positive and normative economics (see **Chapter 1**). Explaining why there is a certain amount of sulfur dioxide (SO_2) in the air at any particular time is a question of positive economics; deciding what best to do about it is a case of normative economics.

- On the one hand, reducing emissions reduces the damages that people suffer from environmental pollution; on the other hand, reducing emissions takes resources that could have been used in some other way.

To depict this trade-off, consider a simple situation where a firm (e.g., a pulp mill) is emitting production residuals into a river. As these residuals are carried downstream, they tend to be transformed into less damaging chemical constituents, but before that process is completed the river passes by a large metropolitan area. The people of the area use the waters of the river for various purposes, including recreation (boating, fishing) and as a source for the municipal water supply system. When the river becomes polluted with industrial waste, the people downstream are damaged by the disruption of these and other services provided by the river. One side of the trade-off, then, is the **damages** that people experience when the environment is degraded.

Upstream, the offending pulp mill could reduce the amount of effluent put in the river by treating its wastes before discharge, as well as by recycling certain materials that currently just run out of the discharge pipe. This act of reducing, or abating, some portion of its wastes will require resources of some amount, the costs of which will affect the price of the paper it produces.[2] These **abatement costs** are the other side of the basic pollution-control trade-off.

5-2 Pollution Damages

- **Damages**—all the negative impacts that users of the environment experience as a result of the degradation of that environment.

These negative impacts are of many types and, of course, will vary from one environmental asset to another. In the river pollution example, damages are to recreators, who can no longer use the river or who suffer a higher chance of picking up waterborne diseases, and to all the city dwellers who have to pay more to treat the water before they could put it into the public water mains.

Air pollution produces damage through its impacts on human health. Excess deaths from diseases such as lung cancer, chronic bronchitis, and asthma are related to elevated levels of various pollutants, such as particulate matter, asbestos fibers, and ground-level ozone emissions. Air pollution can cause damages through the degradation of materials (all of the outdoor sculpture from Renaissance Florence, Italy, has had to be put inside to protect it from air pollution) and the deterioration of the visual environment.

Besides damage to human beings, environmental destruction can have important impacts on various elements of the nonhuman ecosystem. Some of these, such as the destruction of genetic information in plant and animal species driven to extinction, will ultimately impact humans. Estimating environmental damages is one of the primary tasks facing environmental scientists and economists, and we will devote **Chapter 7** to a discussion of this problem.

---

2. The word *resources* has a double meaning in economics. On the one hand, it is a shorthand way of referring to natural resources. On the other hand, it is more generally used to refer to the inputs that are utilized to produce outputs.

Damage Functions

In general, the greater the pollution, the greater the damages it produces. To describe the relationship between pollution and damage, we will use the idea of a **damage function**. A damage function shows the relationship between the quantity of a residual and the damage that residual causes. There are two types of damage functions:

- **Emission damage functions:** These show the connection between the quantity of a residual emitted from a source or group of sources and the resulting damage.
- **Ambient damage functions:** These show the relationship between the concentration of particular pollutants in the ambient environment and the resulting damages.

Damage functions can be expressed in a variety of ways; our primary model will make use of **marginal damage functions.**

- **Marginal damage function** shows the **change** in damages stemming from a unit change in emissions or ambient concentration.

When necessary, we can also use these relationships to discuss total damages because we know that, graphically, the areas under marginal damage functions correspond to total damages.

FIGURE 5.1 Representative Marginal Damage Functions

The height and shape of a damage function depends on the pollutant and circumstances involved. Several marginal damage functions are depicted in **Figure 5.1.** The top two are marginal emission damage functions; the horizontal axes measure the quantity of an effluent emitted into the environment during some specified period of time. The exact units (pounds, tons, etc.) in any particular case depend on the specific pollutant involved. The vertical axes measure environmental damages. In physical terms, environmental damage can include many types of impacts: miles of coastline polluted, numbers of people contracting lung disease, numbers of animals wiped out, quantities of water contaminated, and so on. Every case of environmental pollution normally involves multiple types of impacts, the nature of which will depend on the pollutant involved and the time and place it is emitted. To consider these impacts comprehensively, we need to be able to aggregate them into a single dimension. For this purpose, we use a monetary scale. It is sometimes easy to express damage in monetary units, for example, the "defensive" expenditures that people make to protect themselves against pollution (e.g., heavier insulation to protect against noise or more robust railroad tank cars or home air purifiers). Usually it is very difficult, as we will see.

Panel (a) of **Figure 5.1** shows marginal damages increasing only modestly at the beginning but more rapidly as emissions get larger and larger. Work by environmental scientists and economists seems to suggest that this is a typical shape for many types of pollutants, although probably not for all of them. At low levels of emissions, marginal damages may be comparatively small; ambient concentrations are so modest that only the most sensitive people in the population are affected. But when emission levels go higher, damages mount, and at still higher levels of emissions, marginal damages become very elevated as environmental impacts become widespread and intense.

Panel (b) shows marginal emissions damage function that has the same general shape as panel (a) (i.e., it shows increasing marginal damage), but it begins much higher on the vertical axis and rises more sharply. It might represent a toxic substance that has a deadly effect even at very low levels of emission.

Panels (c) and (d) are marginal ambient damage functions. Whereas the vertical axes have a monetary index of damages, the horizontal axes have an index of ambient concentration, such as parts per million (ppm). Panel (c) shows a complicated function that increases at low concentrations, then tends to level off until much higher concentrations are reached, after which damages increase rapidly. This might apply, for example, to an air pollutant that causes marked damages among particularly sensitive members of society at relatively low concentrations, and among all people at very high concentrations, whereas in the middle ranges marginal damages do not increase rapidly. Panel (d) demonstrates an ambient marginal damage function that begins to the right of the origin and then increases linearly with ambient concentration.

Panels (a) and (d) illustrate a characteristic that is in fact quite controversial. They have:

- **Thresholds**—values of emissions or ambient concentrations below which marginal damages are zero.

Thus, the pollutant can increase to these threshold levels without causing any increase in damages. As will be seen in chapters to come, the assumed existence or nonexistence of a threshold in the damage functions for particular pollutants has had important impacts on real-world environmental control policies. There have been long, vigorous arguments about whether the damage functions of certain types of pollutants do or do not have thresholds.

Changes in Damage Functions

We need to look more deeply into the concept of the damage function because it will be used later to express and analyze a variety of different types of pollution problems and public policy approaches. Accordingly, **Figure 5.2** shows two marginal emissions damage functions.[3] It is important to remember that, like the demand and supply curves discussed earlier, these are time specific; they show the emissions and the marginal damages for a particular period of time. There are a couple of ways of thinking about this. One is to assume, for purposes of simplicity, that the graph refers to a strictly noncumulative pollutant. Thus, all damages occur in the same period as emissions. A somewhat more complicated assumption is that, for a pollutant that cumulates over time, the damage function shows the total value that people place on current and future damages. In **Chapter 6** we will discuss this concept more fully.

FIGURE 5.2 Anatomy of a Marginal Damage Function

[3]. The marginal damage function goes up to the right because the quantity on the x-axis is emissions, which start at zero and increase to the right. Reducing pollution is thus going to be a move to the left towards the origin, and the benefits this produces are shown by the reduction in marginal damages in a leftward move. In some models, however, what is indexed on the horizontal axis is *reductions* from current emission levels. Then a move to the right corresponds to a reduction in pollution, and the marginal damage function appears as a standard marginal benefit function, pictured here.

Of course either approach allows the same analysis. We chose the former (pollution upward to the right) because it means the origin corresponds to no pollution. In our models, the rising marginal damage function might suggest to you a rising marginal cost curve. In essence it is, though in this case the marginal cost refers to the marginal cost to society of increasing pollution.

Consider first just one of the marginal damage functions, the lower one labeled MD_1. In previous chapters we discussed the relationship between marginal and total quantities, for example, the relationship between marginal and total costs. We have the same relationship here. The height of the marginal damage curve shows how much total damages would change with a small change in the quantity of emissions. When the effluent level is at the point marked e_1, for example, marginal damages are $12. That is to say, if emissions were to increase by one ton from point e_1, the damages experienced by people exposed to those emissions would increase by $12. By the same token, if emissions decreased by a small amount at point e_1, total damages would be reduced by $12. Because the height of the curve, as measured on the *y*-axis, shows marginal damages, the area under the curve between the point where it is zero and some other point, such as the one labeled e_1, shows the total damages associated with that level of emissions. In the case of marginal damage function MD_1 and point e_1, total damages are equal to the monetary amount expressed by the triangular area bounded by the *x*-axis, the curve MD_1, and the effluent quantity e_1. That is area *b* in **Figure 5.2**.

What factors might account for the difference between MD_1 and MD_2 in **Figure 5.2**? Let us assume that they apply to the same pollutant. For any given level of emissions, marginal damages are higher for MD_2 than for MD_1. At emission level e_1, for example, a small increase in effluent would increase damages by $12 if the marginal damage function were MD_1, but it would increase damages by $28 if it were MD_2. Remember that any damage function shows the impacts of emitting a particular effluent in a particular time and place, so one possible explanation might be that MD_2 refers to a situation in which many people are affected by a pollutant, such as a large urban area, whereas MD_1 refers to a more sparsely populated rural area—fewer people, smaller damage. Some factors that move damage functions upward are:

a. Differences in population exposed, such as more people.
b. Different time periods, such as during the day versus after sundown.
c. Different ecosystem conditions, such as a temperature inversion that traps a pollutant over a city and produces relatively high ambient concentrations. MD_1 would be the damage function when normal wind patterns prevail so that most of an effluent is blown downwind and out of the area. Thus, the same emission levels at two different times could yield substantially different damage levels due to the workings of the natural environment.
d. New scientific estimates of increased pollution impact. Because MD_2 is above MD_1, it corresponds not only to higher marginal damages, but also to higher total damages. At emission level e_1, total damages are equal to area *b* when the damage function is MD_1, but to area $(a + b)$ when the damage function is MD_2.

Damages and Uncertainty

The damage functions just drawn give the appearance of being very clear and unambiguous. In the real world, however, they hardly ever are. Usually there is a lot of uncertainty about the connections between pollution emissions and various types of damage: health impacts on humans, ecosystem damages, and so on. When we say "uncertain," we are not implying that pollution actually causes less damage than we might have thought, but rather that the exact amount of damage caused by different levels of pollution is difficult to measure with certainty. Uncertainty in nature affects the relationship between emissions and ambient environmental conditions, and uncertainty in human reaction affects the damages that result. This is exacerbated by the fact that much of the damage can be expected to occur well off in the future, making it difficult to predict with accuracy.

Another factor of importance is the implicit assumption we are making that damage functions are **reversible.** If emissions increase, damages increase; and if emissions decrease, damages will go back to their previous level. This may fit many pollutants: more ozone, more asthma; less ozone, and cases of asthma go back down. But for many pollutants this may not be true. The buildup of global greenhouse gases could perhaps initiate global changes that are essentially irreversible. Even some local changes may be of this type; higher levels of pollution lead to ecosystem changes that take us to new situations from which there is no easy return. For example, once a groundwater aquifer is contaminated, it may never be the same again.

Environmental economists, in cooperation with environmental scientists, epidemiologists, and the like, have worked to develop means by which damage functions can be measured with greater accuracy. In the next few chapters, we will look at some of these methods. In this chapter, we will simply use the concept of the damage function to study the essential choices that face society in pollution-control decisions.

Damages and Time

Another important factor we need to recognize in the case of pollution damage functions is time. Many pollutants are persistent; once emitted they remain in the environment for many years, potentially causing damage far off into the future. For example, the emission of greenhouse gases today will contribute to a buildup in the atmosphere that will have repercussions in the future, some of which will be in the very distant future. In addition, health and ecological impacts may result from long-term exposure to pollutants, so this can create a potentially long time gap between emissions and their damages. Obviously this creates problems in estimating damage functions, i.e., being able with reasonable accuracy to predict what future damages will be from current emissions. It also brings up the problem of how we should compare future damages to current damages. We will have much more to say about this problem in the next several chapters.

Having considered the concept of damages, it is now necessary to look at the other side of the trade-off relationship. It is tempting not to do this, to conclude instead that the damage functions themselves give us all the information needed to make decisions about pollution control. One might be tempted to say, for example, that society ought to strive for emission levels around point e_2 where marginal damages are zero, or perhaps even the origin, corresponding to a point at which emissions are zero. There may be certain pollutants and situations where the efficient level of emissions is indeed zero. But to determine this we have to look at the other side of the problem: abatement costs. We consider abatement costs in the next section.

5-3 Abatement Costs

- **Abatement costs**—the costs of reducing the quantity of residuals being emitted into the environment, or of lowering ambient concentrations.

Think of the pulp mill located upstream. In its normal course of operation it produces a large quantity of organic wastes. On the assumption that it has free access to the river, the cheapest way to get rid of these wastes is simply to pump them into the river, but the firm normally has technological and managerial means to reduce these emissions. The costs of engaging in these activities are called "abatement costs" because they are the costs of abating, or reducing, the quantity of residuals put into the river.[4] By spending resources on this activity, the pulp mill can abate its emissions; in general, the greater the abatement, the greater the cost.

Abatement costs normally will differ from one source to another, depending on a variety of factors. The costs of reducing emissions of SO_2 from electric power plants obviously will be different from the costs of reducing, say, toxic fumes from chemical plants. Even for sources producing the same type of effluent, the costs of abatement are likely to be different because of differences in the technological features of the operation. One source may be relatively new, using modern production technology, whereas another may be an old one using more highly polluting technology. In the discussion that follows, keep in mind that *abatement* is used with the widest possible connotation and includes all the many ways there are of reducing emissions: changes in production technology, input switching, residuals recycling, treatment, abandonment of a site, and so forth.

Abatement Cost Functions

We represent this idea graphically using the concept of the **marginal abatement cost** function. The units on the axes are the same as with marginal damages: quantities of pollutants on the horizontal axis and monetary value on the vertical axis. Marginal emission abatement costs show the added costs of achieving a one-unit decrease in emission level, or alternatively the costs saved if emissions are increased by a unit. On the horizontal axis, marginal abatement cost curves originate at the uncontrolled emission levels, that is, emission levels prior to undertaking any abatement activities. The marginal abatement costs show the marginal costs of producing reductions in emissions. Thus, these marginal cost curves rise from right to left, depicting rising marginal costs of reducing emissions.[5] In environmental economics we usually work with emissions reductions. This means moving from an uncontrolled or elevated level of emissions to a lower one or, graphically, moving from right to left along a horizontal axes toward the origin (see **Figure 5.3**). **Figure 5.3** shows an abatement cost function for cleaning up the water of Boston Harbor.

---

4. In **Chapter 2**, this would be reducing R_p^d in **Figure 2.1**.
5. In **Chapter 3**, we showed marginal cost curves sloping upward to the right. The graph goes in the opposite direction because here we are producing *reductions* in emissions.

FIGURE 5.3 Abatement Cost Function for Cleaning up Boston Harbor

Labels on curve (from top to bottom):
- Running water; safe drinking water; secondary sewage treatment; sludge recycling
- Running water; safe drinking water; primary sewage treatment
- Running water; safe drinking water; sewage piped to harbor-no treatment
- Running water in homes; safe drinking water; no sewage pipes from homes
- No running water; no sewage pipes from homes

Y-axis: Value
X-axis: Waterborne Emissions

Figure 5.4 shows three alternative marginal abatement cost functions.

Panel (a) depicts marginal abatement costs rising very modestly as emissions are first reduced, but then rising very rapidly as emissions become relatively small.

Panel (b) shows marginal abatement costs that rise rapidly from the beginning.

Panel (c) shows a marginal abatement cost curve that has an initial declining phase, followed by increasing values; this might characterize a situation in which small reductions can be handled only by technical means that require a substantial initial investment.

FIGURE 5.4 Representative Marginal Abatement Cost Functions

Three panels (a), (b), (c), each with $ on Y-axis and Emissions on X-axis.

For somewhat larger reductions, the marginal costs actually may decline as it becomes possible to utilize these techniques more fully. Ultimately, however, marginal abatement costs increase. We have to keep in mind that in dealing with abatement costs we are dealing with a cost concept similar to that discussed in **Chapter 3.** The level of costs encountered when carrying out any particular task depends on the technology available to do the task and also on the managerial skills that are applied to the job. It is quite possible to suffer extremely high abatement costs if the wrong technology is used or if what is available is used incorrectly. In other words, the marginal abatement cost functions pictured are to be understood as the **minimum** costs of achieving reductions in emissions.

Changes in Marginal Abatement Cost Functions

To investigate more deeply the concept of marginal abatement cost, consider **Figure 5.5**, which shows two marginal abatement cost curves. For the moment we focus on the higher one, labeled MAC_2. It begins at an effluent level marked $\bar{e}$, the uncontrolled emission level. From there it slopes upward to the left. Beginning at the uncontrolled level, the first units of emission reduction can be achieved with a relatively low marginal cost. Think again of the pulp mill. This first small decrease might be obtained with the addition of a modest settling pond, but as emission levels are reduced further, the marginal cost of achieving additional reductions increases. For example, to get a 30 to 40 percent reduction, the pulp mill may have to invest in new technology that is more efficient in terms of water use. A 60 to 70 percent reduction in effluent might require substantial new treatment technology in addition to all the steps taken previously (such as screens and filters), whereas a 90 to 95 percent reduction might take very costly equipment for recycling virtually all of the production residuals produced in the plant. Thus, the larger the reduction in emissions, the greater the marginal costs of producing further reductions. This yields a marginal abatement cost function that gets steeper in slope as emissions are reduced.[6]

FIGURE 5.5 Anatomy of a Marginal Abatement Cost Curve

[6]. Remember that the quantity indexed on the horizontal axis is the quantity of emissions, starting at zero on the left. Thus, the marginal abatement costs of reducing emissions increase as you move to the left, that is, as you decrease emissions. In **Chapter 3**, we introduced marginal cost curves that had the conventional shape of increasing to the right as output increased. If we indexed the *quantity of emissions reduced* starting at zero, then the MAC curve would indeed increase to the right. We think it more intuitive, however, to have the origin correspond to zero actual emissions.

Of course, there is an upper limit on these abatement costs. The extreme option for a single plant or pollution source is to cease operations, thereby achieving a zero level of emissions. The costs of doing this depend on circumstances. If the source is just one small plant within a large industry consisting of many such plants, the costs of closing it down may not be that great. In fact, it may have very little impact on, say, the price to consumers of whatever is being produced (e.g., paper in the pulp mill), although the local impact on jobs and community welfare may be substantial. But if we are talking about the marginal abatement costs for an entire industry—electric power production in the midwestern United States, for example—the shutdown option, as a way of achieving zero emissions, would have enormous costs.

The marginal abatement cost function can express **actual** marginal costs of a source or group of sources or the **lowest possible** marginal abatement costs. Actual costs, of course, are determined by the technologies and procedures that firms have adopted in the past to reduce emissions. These could have been affected by a variety of factors, including managerial short-sightedness or public pollution-control regulations. To use the model for studying questions of social efficiency and cost-effectiveness, however, we don't want actual costs but the lowest possible abatement costs. In this case, we have to assume that sources have adopted whatever technological and managerial means are available to achieve emission reductions at the lowest possible costs. We have to assume, in other words, that sources are acting in a **cost-effective** manner.

As with any marginal graph, we can depict not only marginal but also total values. If emissions are currently at e tons per year, the value on the vertical axis shows the marginal cost of achieving one more unit of emission reduction. The area under the marginal abatement cost curve, between uncontrolled effluent at point $\bar{e}$ and any particular effluent level, is equal to the **total costs** of abating emissions to that level. For example, with the curve labeled MAC_2, the total abatement cost of achieving an emission level of e tons per year is equal to the area under the curve between e and $\bar{e}$, the area $(a + b)$; remember that we are reading the graph from right to left.

Consider now the other marginal abatement cost curve shown in **Figure 5.5,** labeled MAC_1. Its main feature is that it lies below MAC_2, meaning that it corresponds to a situation where the marginal abatement costs for any level of emissions are lower than those of MAC_2. At e tons per year of emissions, for example, the marginal costs of abating an extra ton are only c_2 in the case of MAC_1, which are substantially lower than the marginal abatement costs of MAC_2 at this point. What could account for the difference? Let us assume that we are dealing with the same pollutant in each case. One possibility is that these apply to different sources, for example, a plant that was built many years ago and another that was built more recently and uses different production technology. The newer plant lends itself to less costly emissions reduction, MAC_1.

Another possibility is that MAC_1 and MAC_2 relate to the same pollutant and the same source, but at different times. The lower one represents the situation after a new pollution-control technology has been developed, whereas the upper one applies before the change. Technological change, in other words, results in a lowering of the marginal abatement cost curve for a given pollutant. It is possible to represent graphically the annual cost that this source would save, assuming the emission rate is e before and after the change. Before the firm adopted the new technology, its total abatement cost of achieving effluent level e was equal to $(a + b)$ per year, whereas after the change, the total abatement costs are b per year. The annual cost savings from the technological change are thus a.[7]

This type of analysis will be important when we examine different types of pollution-control policies because one of the criteria we will want to use to evaluate these policies is how much cost-saving incentive they offer to firms to engage in research and development to produce new pollution-control technologies.

Technological Change in Abatement Costs

Technological change, with the shift in the marginal abatement cost function it implies, is a critical factor in the long-run effort to reduce environmental pollution. Economists have studied how technological change happens and what underlying factors encourage it. It is typically divided into three steps:

1. Research and development (R&D): Basic research that identifies potentially new procedures and techniques for reducing emissions. These may be changes in existing procedures (e.g., catalytic converters to reduce car emissions) or totally different technologies (e.g., electric vehicles).
2. Innovation: This means incorporating the results of basic research into real-world technologies that are economically feasible (e.g., new discoveries in metal behavior incorporated into battery technologies in practical ways).
3. Adoption: This means the widespread application of the technology, spreading from early adopters to entire economic sectors (e.g., the adoption among airplane manufacturers and airlines of new types of ultra-efficient engines).

Each of these functions has numerous facets, so the whole process of technological change, though very complex, is fundamental to long-run efforts to curb pollution. Some of the specific questions that need to be considered are the following:

- How to overcome the public-good aspect of information; once developed, it can be used by anybody without diminishing it in quantity.
- How to get funding. Each step takes money and resources, perhaps involving some combination of public and private sources.
- What are the risk factors that work against adopting new processes, and how can these risks be mitigated?
- What types of public procurement processes would encourage private adoption of new technologies?
- What kinds of technological lock-in result from pollution control regulations, and what are the best ways of combating this when appropriate?
- What behavioral issues may be involved with the adoption of new technologies?

The adoption of new technologies is one of the driving forces in pollution control. In terms of the concepts of this chapter, technological change impacts the costs underlying the marginal abatement cost function and therefore underlies the whole effort over time to reduce pollution.

---

7. Note that up-front capital costs are spread over the lifetime of the technology.

Aggregate Marginal Abatement Costs

The discussion of the last few pages has treated the marginal abatement cost function as something applying to a single firm, such as a single pulp mill on a river. Suppose, however, we want to talk about the marginal abatement cost of a group of firms, perhaps a group of firms in the same industry or a group of firms all located in the same region. Most environmental policies, especially at state or federal levels, are aimed at controlling emissions from groups of pollution sources, not just single polluters. Suppose, furthermore, that the individual marginal abatement cost functions differ among the various firms. To control organic pollutants in Boston Harbor or San Francisco Bay, for example, would require controlling emissions from a large variety of different sources in different industries with different production technologies, and therefore with very different individual marginal abatement cost functions. In this case, we would have to construct the overall, or aggregate, marginal abatement cost function for the collection of firms by adding together the individual marginal abatement cost curves.

Although this sounds simple, and it basically is, it nevertheless leads into one of the more important concepts underlying the design of effective environmental policy. It is critical to keep in mind the central idea of the abatement cost function. It is a function that shows the *least costly* way of achieving reductions in emissions for an individual firm if we are looking at an individual marginal abatement cost function, or for a group of polluting sources if we are considering the aggregate marginal abatement cost function.

Figure 5.6 shows, on the left, two individual marginal abatement cost functions, labeled Source A and Source B. Note that they have different shapes, although we are dealing with the same pollutant. MAC_A starts at 20 tons/week and rises rather rapidly as emissions are reduced. MAC_B also begins at the uncontrolled discharge level of 20 tons/week, but rises much less rapidly. Why the difference? Perhaps Source B is a newer plant with more flexible technological alternatives for pollution control. Or perhaps the two sources, although producing the same type of effluent, are manufacturing different consumer goods and using different production techniques. For whatever reason, they have different marginal abatement cost curves.

FIGURE 5.6 Aggregate Abatement Costs

The aggregate marginal abatement cost curve is a summation, or aggregation, of these two individual relationships. But because the individual curves are different, it makes a great deal of difference how they are added together. The problem is that when there are two (or any other number greater than one) sources with different abatement costs, the total cost will depend on how the total emissions are allocated among the different sources. The principle to follow is to add together the two individual functions in such a way as to yield the lowest possible aggregate marginal abatement costs. The way to do this is to add them horizontally. Select a particular level of marginal abatement cost—for example, the one marked w in **Figure 5.6.** This level of marginal abatement cost is associated with an emissions level of 10 tons/week from Source A and an emissions level of about 7 tons/week from Source B. On the aggregate curve, thus, a marginal abatement cost of w would be associated with an emissions level of 10 tons + 7 tons = 17 tons/week. All the other points on the aggregate marginal abatement cost curve are found the same way, by summing across horizontally on the individual marginal abatement cost curves.

In effect, what we have done here is to invoke the important **equimarginal principle,** an idea that was introduced earlier in **Chapter 4.** To get the minimum aggregate marginal abatement cost curve, the aggregate level of emissions must be distributed among the different sources in such a way that they all have the same marginal abatement costs. Start at the 10 tons/week point on the aggregate curve. Obviously, this 10-ton total could be distributed among the two sources in any number of ways: five tons from each source, or eight tons from one and two from the other, and so on. Only one allocation, however, will give the lowest aggregate marginal abatement costs; this is the allocation that leads the different sources to the point at which they have exactly the same marginal abatement costs. At the end of this chapter, we will come back to this equimarginal principle, illustrating it with a simple numerical example.

5-4 The Socially Efficient Level of Emissions

We have considered separately the marginal damage function and the marginal abatement cost function related to a particular pollutant being released at a particular place and time; it is now time to bring these two relationships together. This we do in **Figure 5.7,** which depicts a set of conventionally shaped marginal damage and marginal abatement cost curves labeled, respectively, MD and MAC. Marginal damages have a threshold at emission level $ê$, whereas the uncontrolled emission level is $é$.

- **Efficient level of emissions**—the level at which marginal damages are equal to marginal abatement costs.

FIGURE 5.7 The Efficient Level of Emissions

What is the justification for this? Note the trade-off that is inherent in the pollution phenomenon: Higher emissions expose society, or some part of it, to greater environmental damages. Lower emissions involve society in greater costs in the form of more resources devoted to abatement activities. The efficient level of emissions is thus the level at which these two types of costs exactly offset one another—that is, where **marginal abatement costs equal marginal damage costs.** This is emission level e^* in **Figure 5.7**. Marginal damages and marginal abatement costs are equal to each other and to the value w at this level of emissions.

In effect, if we are to the left of e^*, the MAC > MD and it costs society more resources than the benefits it receives in terms of reduced damages. The marginal resources could have been used to clean up other dirtier pollution problems. If we are to the right of e^*, the MAC < MD and society is getting a reduction in damages that's greater than the cost to abate, so keep reducing emissions toward e^*.

We can also look at this outcome in terms of total values because we know that the totals are the areas under the marginal curves. Thus, the triangular area marked a in **Figure 5.7** (bounded by points $\hat{e}$ and e^* and the marginal damage function) depicts the total damages existing when emissions are at level e^*, whereas the triangular area b shows the total abatement costs at this level of emissions. The sum of these two areas $(a + b)$ is a measure of the total social costs from e^* tons per year of this particular pollutant. The point e^* is the unique point at which this sum is minimized. Note that the size of area a need not equal the size of area b.

You might get the impression, on the basis of where point e^* is located on the x-axis, that this analysis has led us to the conclusion that the efficient level of emissions is always one that involves a relatively large quantity of emissions and substantial environmental damages. This is not the case. What we are developing, rather, is a conceptual way of looking at a trade-off. In the real world, every pollution problem is different. This analysis gives us a generalized way of framing the problem that obviously has to be adapted to the specifics of any particular case of environmental pollution. **Figure 5.8,** for example, depicts three different situations that might characterize particular environmental pollutants. In each case, e^* depicts the efficient level of emissions and w shows marginal damages and marginal abatement costs at that quantity of emissions.

FIGURE 5.8 Efficient Emission Levels for Different Pollutants

Panel (a) shows a pollutant for which e^* is well to the right of zero (of course, because the horizontal axis has no units, it's not clear exactly what "well to the right" actually means here). Marginal damages at this point are quite small; so are total damages and abatement costs, as shown by the small size of the triangles corresponding to these values. The reason is that this is a pollutant where both marginal abatement costs and marginal damages increase at first only very slowly.

Panel (b) shows a situation where the marginal abatement function rises moderately, then rapidly, whereas the marginal damage function rises very rapidly from the beginning. In this case, e^* is well to the right of zero, and w lies well above what it was in the first diagram (assuming the vertical axes of these diagrams all have the same scale). Note, however, that at e^* total abatement costs are substantially higher than total damages, as is indicated by the relative sizes of the triangles that measure these total values. What this emphasizes is that it is not the equality of total abatement costs and total damages that defines the efficient level of effluent, but the equality of the **marginal abatement costs** and **marginal damages.**

In panel (c) of **Figure 5.8** the efficient level of emissions is zero. There is no point of intersection of the two functions in the graph; there is no area on the graph corresponding to total damages. The only way we could conceivably get them to intersect is if we could somehow extend them to the left of the vertical axis, but this would imply that emissions could actually be negative, which is an oddity that we will avoid. What makes $e^* = 0$ is that the marginal damage function doesn't begin at zero, but rather well up on the y-axis, implying that even the first small amount of this pollutant placed in the environment causes great damage (perhaps this diagram applies to some extremely toxic material). Relative to this, the marginal costs of abatement are low, giving an efficient emission level of zero.

Changes in the Efficient Level of Emissions

The real world is a dynamic place, and this is especially true of environmental pollution control. For our purposes this implies, for example, that the level of emissions that was efficient last year, or last decade, is not necessarily the level that is efficient today or that is likely to be in the future. When any of the factors that lie behind the marginal damage and marginal abatement cost functions change, the functions themselves will shift and e^*, the efficient level of emissions, will also change.

Before taking a look at this, we need to remind ourselves of what we are doing. Remember the distinction made earlier between positive and normative economics, between the **economics of *what is*** and the **economics of *what ought to be*.** The idea of the efficient level of emissions comes firmly under normative economics, under the idea of what ought to be. We are presenting emission level e^*, the level that balances abatement costs and damage costs, as a desirable target for public policy. Do not get this confused with the actual level of emissions. If the world worked so that the actual level of emissions was always equal to, or close to, the efficient level, we presumably would have no need to worry about intervening with environmental policy of one type or another. Of course it does not, which is why we must turn to public policy.

Figure 5.9 shows several ways in which e^* might change when underlying factors change. Panel (a) shows the results of a shift upward in the marginal damage function, from MD_1 to MD_2. One of the ways this could happen is through population growth. MD_1 might apply to a municipality in 2024 and MD_2 to the same municipality in 2035 after its population has grown. More people means that a given amount of effluent will cause more damage.[8] This leads to a conclusion that is intuitively straightforward: The efficient level of emissions drops from e_1^* to e_2^*. With a higher marginal damage function, the logic of the efficiency trade-off would lead us to devote more resources to pollution control.

FIGURE 5.9 Changes in e^*, the Efficient Level of Emissions

---

[8]. This diagram could also apply, of course, to a different situation. MD_1 could be the damage function pertaining to a relatively sparsely settled rural region; MD_2 could be the marginal damage function pertaining to a more populous urban area. Everything we say about the relationship between e_1^* and e_2^* also applies to cases like this where we are comparing two different places at the same time, in addition to the previous comparison of the same place at two different times.

Panel (b) of **Figure 5.9** shows the case of a shift in the marginal abatement cost function, from MAC_1 to MAC_2. What could have caused this? The most obvious, perhaps, is a change in the technology of pollution control. As stressed earlier, abatement costs depend critically on the technology available for reducing effluent streams: treatment technology, recycling technology, alternative fuel technology, and so forth. New techniques normally arise because resources, talents, and energy have been devoted to research and development. So the shift downward in marginal abatement costs depicted in **Figure 5.9** might be the result of the development of new treatment or recycling technologies that make it less costly to reduce the effluent stream of this particular pollutant. It should not be too surprising that this leads to a reduction in the efficient level of emissions, as indicated by the change from e_1^* to e_2^*. We might note that this could lead to either an increase or a decrease in the total cost of abating emissions. Before the change, total abatement costs were an amount equal to the area $(a + b)$, that is, the area under MAC_1 between the uncontrolled level e' and the amount e_1^*. After the change, total abatement costs are equal to area $(b + c)$, and the question of whether total abatement costs at the efficient level of emissions have increased or decreased hinges on the relative sizes of the two areas a and c. This in turn depends on the shapes of the curves and the extent to which the marginal abatement cost curve has shifted; the more it has shifted, the more likely it is that the efficient level of total abatement costs after the change will exceed the costs before the change.[9]

5-5 Enforcement Costs

So far the analysis has considered only the private costs of reducing emissions, yet emission reductions do not happen unless resources are devoted to enforcement. To include all sources of cost, we need to add **enforcement costs** to the analysis. Some of these are private, such as added recordkeeping by polluters, but the bulk are public costs related to various regulatory aspects of the enforcement process.

Figure 5.10 shows a simple model of pollution control with enforcement costs added. To the normal marginal abatement cost function has been added the marginal costs of enforcement, giving a total marginal cost function labeled $MAC + E$. The vertical distance between the two marginal cost curves equals marginal enforcement costs. The assumption drawn into the graph is that marginal enforcement costs, the added costs of enforcement that it takes to get emissions reduced by a unit, increase as emissions decrease. In other words, the more polluters cut back emissions, the more costly it is to enforce further cutbacks.

---

9. These diagrams can also be used to examine some of the implications of making mistakes. For example, suppose the public control authorities think that the real marginal abatement cost was MAC_1, but, in fact, because there is a cheaper way of reducing this effluent that they do not know about, marginal abatement costs are actually MAC_2. Then we would conclude that the efficient level of effluent is e_1^*, whereas it is actually e_2^*. We might be striving toward a goal that involves excessive emissions.

FIGURE 5.10 Enforcement Costs

[Graph showing MAC, MAC+E, and MD curves with emissions on x-axis at points e_2 and e_1, and $ on y-axis]

In effect, the addition of enforcement costs moves the efficient level of emissions to the right of where it would be if they were zero. This shows the vital importance of having good enforcement technologies and policies because lower marginal enforcement costs would move MAC+E closer to MAC, decreasing the efficient emission level. In fact, **technical change in enforcement** has exactly the same effect on the efficient level of emissions as technical change in emissions abatement. We will have more to say about enforcement in later chapters, especially **Chapter 11**.

5-6 The Equimarginal Principle Applied to Emission Reductions

Before going on, we will take a very explicit look at the equimarginal principle. In the present context, the application of the equimarginal principle says the following:

> If there are **multiple sources** of a particular type of pollutant with **differing marginal abatement costs,** and if it is desired to reduce aggregate emissions at the **least possible cost** (or, alternatively, get the greatest reduction in emissions for a given cost), then emissions from the various sources must be reduced in accordance with the **equimarginal principle.**

To illustrate this, look at the numbers in **Table 5.1.** This shows explicitly the marginal abatement costs of each of two firms emitting a particular residual into the environment. If neither source makes any effort to control emissions, they will each emit 12 tons/week. If Source A reduces its emissions by 1 ton, to 11 tons/week, it will cost $1,000/week; if it reduces effluent further to 10 tons/week, its abatement costs will increase by $2,000/week, and so on. Note that the marginal abatement cost relationships of the two sources are different: that of Source B increases faster than that of Source A.

TABLE 5.1   The Equimarginal Principle

Emissions (tons/week)	12	11	10	9	8	7	6	5	4	3	2	1	0
Marginal Abatement Costs:													
Source A ($1,000/week)		0	1	2	3	4	5	6	8	10	14	24	38	70
Source B ($1,000/week)		0	2	4	6	10	14	20	25	31	38	58	94	160

Suppose that initially each plant is emitting at the uncontrolled level; total emissions would then be 24 tons/week (12 tons/week from each source). Now assume that we want to reduce overall emissions to half the present level, or a total of 12 tons/week. One way to do this would be to have **equiproportionate** cutbacks. Because we want a total reduction of 50 percent, each source is required to reduce by 50 percent. If Source A were cut 50 percent to 6 tons/week, its marginal abatement costs at this level would be $6,000/week, whereas at this level of emissions the marginal abatement costs of Source B would be $20,000/week. Total abatement costs of the 12-ton total can be found by adding up the marginal abatement costs:

Source A: $21,000 ($1,000 + $2,000 + $3,000 + $4,000 + $5,000 + $6,000)

Source B: $56,000 ($2,000 + $4,000 + $6,000 + $10,000 + $14,000 + $20,000)

Total: $77,000/week.

The overall reduction to 12 tons/week, however, can be achieved with a substantially lower total cost. We know this because the equiproportionate reduction violates the equimarginal principle; marginal abatement costs are not equalized when each source reduces its effluent to 6 tons/week. What is required is different emission rates for the two sources, where, simultaneously, they will emit together no more than 12 tons of effluent and have the same marginal abatement costs. This condition is satisfied if Source A emits 4 tons and Source B emits 8 tons. These rates add up to 12 tons total and give each source a marginal abatement cost of $10,000/week. Calculating total abatement costs at these emission levels gives:

Source A: $39,000 ($1,000 + $2,000 + $3,000 + $4,000 + $5,000 + $6,000 + $8,000 + $10,000)

Source B: $22,000 ($2,000 + $4,000 + $6,000 + $10,000)

Total: $61,000/week.

By following the equimarginal principle, the desired reduction in total emissions has been obtained, but with a savings of $16,000/week over the case of an equiproportionate reduction.

Thus, we see that an emission reduction plan that follows the equimarginal rule gives emission reduction at minimum cost. Another way of saying this is that for any particular amount of money devoted to effluent reduction, the maximum quantitative reduction in total effluent can only be obtained by following the equimarginal principle. The importance of this principle cannot be overstated.

When defining the efficient level of emissions, we were going on the assumption that we were working with the lowest possible marginal abatement cost function. The only way of achieving this is by controlling individual sources in accordance with the equimarginal rule. If we are designing public policy under the rule of equiproportionate reductions at the various sources, the marginal abatement cost function will be higher than it should be. And the extra cost spent on this pollution problem could have been spent to clean up another pollution problem. One of the results of this is that the efficient emission level will be higher than it should be, or, to say the same thing, we will seek smaller reductions in emissions than are socially efficient.

Summary

In this chapter, we have looked at a simple model of pollution control. It is based on the notion of a trade-off between environmental damages and pollution abatement costs. We introduced the notion of a **marginal damage function,** showing the marginal social damages resulting from varying levels of residual emissions or ambient pollutant levels. Then we looked at **marginal abatement cost** relationships, first for an individual pollution source and then for a group of such sources. By bringing together these two relationships, we then defined an **efficient level of emissions:** the level at which marginal damages and marginal abatement costs are equal. At this level of emissions, total social costs, the total of abatement costs and damages, are minimized.

The efficient level of emissions is subject to change as underlying factors shift. Population growth and the results of scientific studies can shift marginal damage functions; technological changes can cause marginal abatement cost functions to shift. We illustrated one case in which the efficient level of a particular pollutant is zero. Finally, we reviewed the equimarginal principle as it applies to pollution control. That principle states that when multiple sources have different marginal abatement costs, equalizing these costs will be the least-cost way of achieving a reduction in total emissions.

A word of caution is appropriate. The model presented in this chapter is very general and risks giving an overly simplistic impression of pollution problems in the real world. In fact, there are very few actual instances of environmental pollution where the marginal damage and marginal abatement functions are known with certainty. The natural world is too complex, and human and nonhuman responses are too difficult to identify with complete clarity. Furthermore, polluters come in all types and sizes and economic circumstances, and it takes enormous resources to learn even simple things about the costs of pollution abatement in concrete instances. Pollution-control technology is changing rapidly, so what is efficient today will not necessarily be so tomorrow. Nevertheless, the simple model is useful for thinking about the basic problem of pollution control, and it will be useful in our later chapters on the various approaches to environmental policy.

Questions for Further Discussion

1. Prove (graphically) that the point labeled e^* in **Figure 5.7** is indeed the point that minimizes total social costs, the sum of abatement and damage costs. (Do this by showing that at any other point, this total cost will be higher.)
2. Suppose there is a river on which are located several micro breweries, each of which discharges pollutants into the water. Suppose somebody invents a new technology for treating this waste stream that, if adopted by the breweries, could substantially diminish emissions. What are the impacts of this invention on (a) the actual level of emissions and (b) the efficient level of emissions?
3. Suppose there is a suburban community where domestic septic tanks are responsible for contaminating a local lake. What is the effect on actual and efficient levels of water quality in the lake of an increase in the number of homes in the community? Use **Figure 5.7** to show how MD and/or MAC would or would not change and the subsequent level of e^*.
4. There is one firm with two sources of emissions (a brewery with two bottling plants, for example). Each plant emits waste water, but they have different technologies for cutting back their emissions. The marginal cost of reducing quantities of waste water from the two plants are as follows:

Waste water (gallons per day)	Plant 1 Marginal cost to reduce	Plant 2 Marginal cost to reduce
100	$0	$0
90	4	2
80	6	5
70	16	9
60	20	12
50	30	14
40	44	20
30	58	30
20	72	40
10	88	55
0	105	72

Each bottling plant currently emits 100 gallons per day of waste water (a total of 200 gallons per day for the brewery). The brewery needs to reduce to a total of 100 gallons per day of waste water emitted. Use the equimarginal principle to determine the amount of waste water emitted from each plant to reach the 100-gallon total.

(Continued)

Questions for Further Discussion *(Continued)*

5. Following are the marginal abatement costs of three firms, related to the quantity of emissions. Each firm is now emitting 10 tons/week, so total emissions are 30 tons/week. Suppose we wish to reduce total emissions by 50 percent, to 15 tons per week. Compare the total costs of doing this: (*a*) with an equiproportionate decrease in emissions and (*b*) with a decrease that meets the equimarginal principle.

Emissions (tons/week)	10	9	8	7	6	5	4	3	2	1	0
Marginal Abatement Costs:											
Firm 1 ($/ton)	0	4	8	12	16	20	24	28	36	46	58
Firm 2 ($/ton)	0	1	2	4	6	8	12	20	24	28	36
Firm 3 ($/ton)	0	1	2	3	4	5	6	7	8	9	10

6. Suppose a new law is put into effect requiring oil tankers to use certain types of navigation rules in coastal waters of the United States. Suppose that the very next year there is a large tanker accident and oil spill in these waters. Does this mean that the law has had no effect?

For additional resources pertaining to the material in this chapter, see the list in **Appendix B**.

Section 3
Environmental Analysis

In the last few chapters we have used the concepts of abatement costs and damages without worrying too much about how the actual magnitudes of these concepts might be measured in particular situations. In the next three chapters this is rectified. Several types of analyses have been developed over the years to provide environmental, economic, and social valuations that can be used to inform the policy process. In the next chapter we deal with these at the framework level. From the standpoint of economics, benefit-cost analysis is the primary analytical tool, so much of the chapter will be devoted to a discussion of its major elements. Then, in the following two chapters, we look more closely at the methods available for estimating benefits and costs of environmental policy decisions.

Chapter 6
Frameworks of Analysis

Policy decisions require information, and although the availability of good information doesn't automatically mean that decisions will also be good, its *un*availability will almost always contribute to bad decisions. There are a variety of alternative frameworks for generating and presenting information useful to policymakers, calling for different skills and research procedures. We briefly review the most important of these, before focusing on benefit–cost analysis.

6-1 Impact Analysis

Impact is a very general word, meaning the effects of any actual or proposed policy. Because there are many types of effects, there are many different types of impact analyses. The basic kinds of impact analyses that affect pollution control are environmental, economic, and regulatory.

Environmental Impact Analysis

An environmental impact analysis (EIA) is essentially an identification and study of all significant environmental repercussions stemming from a course of action. For the most part, these focus on impacts that are expected to flow from a proposed decision, although retrospective EIAs are also of great value, especially when they are done to see if earlier predictions were accurate. EIAs can be carried out for any social action, public or private, industrial or domestic, local or national. They are largely the work of natural scientists, who focus on tracing out and describing the physical impacts of projects or programs, following through the complex linkages that spread these impacts through the ecosystem. They do not directly address the issue of placing social values on these impacts.

Many countries have laws requiring environmental impact studies when substantial public programs and projects are under consideration, as well as private projects in some cases. In the United States, environmental impact analyses are mandated by the **National Environmental Policy Act of 1970** (NEPA).

The resulting environmental impact statements (EISs) are primarily the work of natural scientists, yet economists have a distinct role to play. It is not only ecological linkages through which environmental impacts spread; they also spread through economic linkages. Suppose, for example, it is proposed to build a dam that will flood a certain river valley while providing a drinking water reservoir and new flat-water recreation possibilities. A substantial part of the environmental impact will stem from the inundation itself and the resulting losses in animals and plants, wild-river recreation, farmland, and so on. But much also could come from changes in patterns of behavior among people affected by the project. Recreators traveling into and out of the region could affect air pollution and traffic congestion. New housing or commercial development spurred by the recreation opportunities and sufficient water for household use could have negative environmental effects. Thus, to study the full range of environmental impacts from the dam, it is necessary to include not just the physical effects of the dam and its water impoundment, but also the ways in which people will react and adapt to this new facility.

Economic Impact Analysis

When interest centers on how some action—a new law, a new technological breakthrough, a new source of imports will affect an economic system, in whole or in terms of its various parts, we can speak of **economic impact analysis.** In most countries, especially developing ones, there is usually wide interest in the impact of environmental regulations on economic growth rates. Sometimes the focus will be on tracing out the ramifications of a public program for certain economic variables that are considered particularly important. One might be especially interested, for example, in the impact of an environmental regulation on employment, the impact of import restrictions on the rate of technological change in an industry, the effects of an environmental law on the growth of the pollution-control industry, or the response of the food industry to new packaging regulations.

Economic impact analyses can be focused at any level. Local environmental groups might be interested in the impact of a wetlands law on the rate of population growth and tax base in their community. Regional groups might be interested in the impacts of a national regulation on their particular economic circumstances. At the global level, an important question is how efforts to control carbon dioxide (CO_2) emissions might impact the relative growth rates of rich and poor countries. Whatever the level, economic impact analysis requires a basic understanding of how economies function and how their various parts fit together.

Regulatory Impact Analysis

Regulatory agencies and others are concerned with the array of possible impacts that might result from any actual or proposed regulation. **Regulatory impact analysis** (RIA) systematically and comprehensively identifies and estimates the impacts flowing from regulations. Many countries have requirements for doing these types of studies, and they differ somewhat in terms of what kinds of impacts they focus on and some of the procedures for carrying them out.[1] In the United States, RIAs essentially involve full **benefit–cost analyses** of regulatory options. We will discuss benefit–cost analysis later in this chapter.

6-2 Cost-Effectiveness Analysis

Suppose a community determined that its current water supply was contaminated with some chemical or bacteria and that it had to switch to some alternative supply. Suppose it had several possibilities: It could drill new wells into an uncontaminated aquifer, it could build a connector to the water-supply system of a neighboring town, or it could build its own surface reservoir. A drinking water crisis in Flint, Michigan, in 2014 due to lead contamination and a failure of the water system infrastructure in Jackson, Mississippi, in

---

1. Organization for Economic Cooperation and Development, "Regulatory Impact Assessment," *Government at a Glance*, Paris, 2020.

2022 are examples. A **cost-effectiveness analysis** would estimate the costs of these different alternatives with the aim of showing how they compared in terms of, say, the costs per million gallons of delivered water into the town system. Cost-effectiveness analysis, in other words, takes the objective as given, then costs out various alternative ways of attaining that objective.

Table 6.1 shows some cost-effectiveness data for reducing methane emissions in natural gas production and transmission. Methane is a potent greenhouse gas, and quantities of it escape at various points of the natural gas production and transmission cycle. Note that there is a substantial difference among the different technologies for reducing methane: The most cost-effective is only 41 cents per thousand cubic feet (Mcf) of methane reduction, while the least cost-effective is over $7.00 per Mcf.

TABLE 6.1 Cost-Effectiveness of Alternative Means of Reducing Methane Leaks in Natural Gas Operations, 2023

Technique	$Costs per Thousand Cubic Feet
Replace pump with air system	0.90
Replace pumps	4.80
Install flaring	1.90
Replace pump with electric motor	3.60
Install plunger	1.90

Source: International Energy Agency, "Strategies to Reduce Methane Emissions," *Global Methane Tracker*, 2023.

Cost-effectiveness is desirable in and of itself. Being cost-effective means getting the biggest "bang for the buck." But cost-effectiveness also underlies the idea of efficiency. For a policy to be efficient, it must at the very least be cost-effective.

6-3 Damage Assessment

Many natural resources suffer degradation due to the release of harmful materials that damage these resources. This has led to a type of study called **damage assessment**, the objective of which is to estimate the value of the damages to an injured resource so that these amounts can be recovered from those held liable by the courts. Damage assessment and the associated liability were launched in 1980 under the Comprehensive Environmental Response, Compensation and Liability Act (CERCLA or the Superfund).[2] This law allows federal, state, and local governments to act as trustees for publicly owned natural resources. The U.S. Department of Interior (DOI) was assigned the job of determining how damages are to be measured in these cases.

The conclusions of the DOI were that damages should be equal to the lesser of (1) the **lost value of the resource** or (2) the **value of restoring the resource** to its former state. Consider the following figures, which represent resource values and restoration values for several cases.

---

2. This law will be studied in more detail in **Chapter 16**.

For case A, the resource value lost from an oil or hazardous waste release is $1.2 million, but the cost of restoring the resource to its former state is only $0.6 million, so the latter is taken as the true measure of damages. In case B, the lost resource value at $1.6 million is substantially less than restoration costs of $3.8 million; therefore, the former would be used to assess damages.

	A	B
Lost resource value	$1.2 million	$1.6 million
Restoration cost	0.6 million	3.8 million

The lost economic values associated with a reduction in the quality of a natural resource can stem from many sources, for example, on-site recreation such as camping, hiking, or snow mobiling; extractive uses of natural resources, such as energy production and mining; uses of stream flows for irrigation, municipal, and industrial water supplies; and transportation services. The task of measuring these values is very similar to the steps undertaken in standard benefit–cost studies of natural and environmental resource use.

Currently, restoration costs are the preferred measure of damages. Restoration costs are defined to include restoration, rehabilitation, replacement, and/or the acquisition of equivalent resources. Some of the difficulties in estimating restoration costs are:

- The determination of what the original or baseline resource quality actually was.
- The choice among alternatives of restoring a resource in a cost-effective way.
- The determination of what is meant by a natural or environmental resource of equivalent value to a resource that was lost.

Exhibit 6.1 discusses one such case. The time frame from contamination to clean-up is often very long.

EXHIBIT 6.1   Final Restoration Plan for Maryland's 68th Street Dump Superfund Site

July 16, 2020 – The trustee agencies for the 68th Street Superfund Site released a final plan for the restoration of 109 acres of hardwood forest within the Bell Woods Environment Area in Maryland. The agreement was reached to clean up and restore natural resources injured by pollution. A $51.5 million settlement was reached in 2018. The responsible parties agreed, as part of the settlement, to implement on-site natural resource restoration, including trash reduction, invasive species control, wetlands enhancement, stream restoration, motor vehicle exclusion, and vernal pool creation. The 68th St. dump site was the site of seven former landfills that received industrial and other waste.

Source: U.S. NOAA, *Damage Assessment, Remediation and Restoration Program*, 2020.

6-4 Benefit–Cost Analysis

Benefit-cost analysis is for the public sector what a profit-and-loss analysis is for a business firm or a budget is for a household. If an automobile company was contemplating introducing a new car, it would want to get some idea of how its profitability would be affected. On the one hand, it would estimate costs of production and distribution: labor, raw materials, energy, emission-control equipment, transportation, and so forth.[3] On the other hand, it would estimate revenues through market analysis. Then it would compare expected revenues with anticipated costs. Benefit-cost analysis is an analogous exercise for programs in the public sector. This means there are two critical differences between benefit-cost analysis and the car example: It is a tool for helping to make **public decisions,** done from the standpoint of society in general rather than from that of a single profit-making firm, and it is usually done for policies and programs that have **unmarketed types of outputs,** such as improvements in environmental quality.

Benefit-cost analysis has led two intertwined lives. The first is among its practitioners: Economists inside and outside public agencies who have developed the techniques, tried to produce better data, and extended the scope of the analysis. The second is among the politicians and administrators who have set the rules and procedures governing the use of benefit-cost analysis for public decision making. In the United States, benefit-cost analysis was first used in conjunction with the United States Flood Control Act of 1936. That act specified that federal participation in projects to control flooding on major rivers of the country would be justifiable *"if the benefits to whomever they accrue are in excess of the estimated costs."* In order to determine if this criterion was satisfied for any proposed flood-control dam or large levee project, procedures had to be developed to measure these benefits and costs.

These procedures have been altered from time to time as benefit-cost analysis has evolved and matured. The status and role of benefit-cost analysis in public natural resource and environmental decision making have been the subject of continuing discussions as well as political and administrative conflicts.

Benefit-cost analysis of environmental regulations has been mandated by federal law since 1981. The requirement has been controversial. Supporters of these laws argue that such legislation is a way to ensure that costs are given appropriate weight in public regulation. Opponents say that, because many benefits are hard to measure, such requirements will make it more difficult to pursue socially beneficial public regulation.[4]

The Basic Framework

As the name implies, a benefit-cost analysis involves measuring, adding up, and comparing all of the benefits and all of the costs of a particular public project or program. There are essentially four steps in a benefit-cost analysis:

1. Specify clearly the project or program.
2. Describe quantitatively the inputs and outputs of the program.

---

3. The social external costs, such as the costs of air-pollution damage inflicted on people breathing the emissions of the new cars, would not be included.
4. For a discussion of these and other examples of the use of benefit-cost analysis in environmental policymaking, see Winston Harrington, Lisa Heinzerling, and Richard D. Morgenstern, eds., *Reforming Regulatory Impact Analysis*, Resources for the Future Press, Washington, DC, 2009.

3. Estimate the value of social costs and benefits of these inputs and outputs.
4. Compare these benefits and costs.

Each of these steps incorporates a number of component steps. In doing a benefit-cost analysis, the very first step is to decide on the **perspective** from which the study is to be done. Benefit-cost analysis is a tool of public analysis, but there are actually many publics. If we were doing a benefit-cost study for a national agency, the public typically would be all the people living in the particular country. But if we were employed by a city or regional planning agency to do a benefit-cost analysis of a local environmental program, we would undoubtedly focus on benefits and costs accruing to people living in those areas. At the other extreme, the rise of global environmental issues has forced us to undertake some benefit-cost analyses from a worldwide perspective.

Step 1 includes a **complete specification of the main elements of the project or program:** location, timing, groups involved, connections with other programs, and so on. There are two primary types of public environmental programs for which benefit-cost analyses are done:

- *Physical projects* that involve direct public production: public waste treatment plant upgrades, beach restoration projects, hazardous-waste incinerators, habitat improvement projects, seawalls, land purchases for preservation, and so on.
- *Regulatory programs* that are aimed at enforcing environmental laws and regulations: pollution-control standards, technological choices, waste-disposal practices, restrictions on land development, and so on.

Step 2 determines the full range of **consequences** that flow from it. For physical projects this amounts to specifying the inputs and outputs the project will entail. For some projects this is reasonably easy. In planning a wastewater treatment upgrade, the engineering staff will be able to provide a full physical specification of the plant, together with the inputs required to build it and keep it running. For an incinerator or combustion with energy recovery, one would need to estimate both the conventional costs of running the plant and any environmental costs stemming from whatever emissions the plant might produce.

For regulatory programs, estimating the full set of important consequences can be difficult. It involves predicting how members of the regulated community (power plants, natural gas refineries, car owners, building contractors, etc.) will respond to the new regulations in terms of altering both their behavior patterns and the technologies they might adopt for pollution-control purposes. Moreover, secondary impacts—that is, impacts in other sectors that have connections with the one being regulated—should be considered. It is in this step that we first have to recognize the importance of time. Environmentally related projects or programs do not usually last for a single year but are spread out over long periods of time. So the job of specifying consequences involves predictions of future events, often quite remote in time. This puts a premium on having a good understanding of issues such as future growth patterns, future rates of technological change, and possible changes in consumers' preferences.

Step 3 places values on the consequences—that is, to estimate benefits and costs in comparable terms. We could do this in any units we wish; typically this implies measuring benefits and costs in monetary terms. This does not mean in market-value terms because in many cases we will be dealing with effects, especially on the benefit side, that are not directly registered on markets. Nor does it imply in some fundamental manner that only monetary values count. It means that we need a single metric into which to translate all of the impacts of a project or program in order to make them comparable among themselves as well as with other types of public activities. Ultimately, certain environmental impacts of a program may be irreducible to monetary terms because we cannot find a way of measuring how much people value these impacts. In this case, it is important to supplement the monetary results of the benefit-cost analysis with estimates of these intangible impacts.

Finally, we must **compare benefits and costs.** To understand what is involved in very general terms, consider the numbers in **Exhibit 6.2.** These show the primary benefits and costs of tighter standards applied to operations of coal-fired power plants for handling the huge generation of coal-combustion residues. For the most part, these have been handled by placing the material in large impoundments (ponds for storing sludge or residue), but the failure of one of these in 2008 led to efforts to bring them under stricter regulatory control.

Benefits and costs can be compared in several ways: **Net benefits** are simply total benefits minus cost. In **Exhibit 6.2,** they are $9,520.3 million − $2,044 million = $7,476.3 million. Another criterion sometimes used is the **benefit-cost ratio,** which is the ratio of benefits to costs, or the amount of benefits produced per dollar of costs. In the example this ratio is $9,520.3 ÷ $2,044.0 = 4.6.

Scope of the Program

One important problem in benefit-cost analysis is deciding on the **scope** of the project or program. A benefit-cost analysis must be specified completely in terms of its size or scope. In reality, however, it is always possible to make a project or program larger or smaller by some amount. How can we be sure that the program we are evaluating is of the appropriate scope?

Traditionally, the scope of benefit-cost analyses has focused on the population directly affected by any environmental regulation or pollution-control program. For example, a benefit-cost analysis for a river clean-up program may be carried out by the particular state through which the river runs with benefits and costs estimated only for the residents of that state, even though some of the benefits and/or costs may accrue to residents of neighboring states. This is a limited view as externalities, both positive and negative, are being ignored in the analysis. This issue of scope is compounded when we consider the global impacts of climate change. Any benefit-cost analyses regarding control of carbon emissions or methane for example, conducted by a state or country or organization, may need to include global benefits and costs that accrue to residents throughout the world.

EXHIBIT 6.2 Benefits and Costs of New Regulations Requiring Coal-Fired Power Plants to Improve Their Handling of Coal Combustion Residues (CCR)

In response to a major industrial accident, the EPA has initiated steps to bring the control of coal combustion residues (CCR) under the regulatory structure of the Resource Conservation and Recovery Act of 1976. Its efforts included doing a series of benefit–cost studies of different technological requirements for handling this type of waste. One alternative was to require composite liners on CCR impoundments (ponds for storing sludge or residue) for all new impoundments and liners within five years for all existing impoundments. The estimated benefits and costs of this option were as follows:

	$ Millions, 2021 prices, 7% discount rate, 50-year life
Benefits:	
Value of human cancer risks avoided	51.3
Groundwater remediation costs avoided	46.6
Cleanup costs avoided	929.3
Induced future CCR beneficial use*	8,493.1
Total	9,520.3
Costs:	
Engineering controls	680.9
Ancillary regulatory requirements	148.1
Conversion to dry CCR disposal	1,215.0
Total	2,044.0
Net Benefits	7,476.3

*The assumption is that by increasing the cost of handling CCR, firms would be more creative in finding markets for CCR for beneficial use by other industries.

Source: U.S. EPA, Office of Resource Conservation and Recovery, *Regulatory Impact Analysis for EPA's Proposal RCCA Regulation of Coal Combustion Residues (CCR) Generated by the Electric Utility Industry,* 2010; updated to 2021 Bureau of Labor Statistics prices.

To explore this issue, consider **Figure 6.1.** It shows the standard emission-control model as developed in **Chapter 5,** with marginal damage (MD) and marginal abatement cost (MAC) functions. Assume that the current level of emissions is e_1; that is, emissions are essentially uncontrolled. A control program is proposed that would lower emissions to e_2. For this program, total benefits (total damages reduced) are equal to $(a + b)$, whereas total abatement costs are equal to b. Net benefits are therefore equal to area a.

FIGURE 6.1 Establishing the Size of a Public Program

For an emission-reduction program to give maximum net benefits, however, it would have to reduce emissions to e^*, the level at which MD = MAC. Here, net benefits would equal $(d + a)$.[5] The problem is that when we do a benefit-cost analysis of a specific proposal, how can we be sure that we are dealing with one such as e^* in the figure and not one such as e_2?

The general procedure here is to carry out **sensitivity analyses** on these results. This means recalculating benefits and costs for programs somewhat larger and somewhat smaller than the one shown in the example. We would analyze a program that has somewhat more restrictive emission reductions, with appropriate enforcement resources, and one that is somewhat less restrictive. If the chosen program is indeed appropriately scaled, each of the variations will produce lower net benefits.

The benefit-cost ratio is often used in public debates in describing environmental projects or programs, but the efficient program size is not the one that gives the maximum benefit-cost ratio. At emission level e^*, the benefit-cost ratio is equal to $(a + b + c + d)/(b + c)$. At emission level e_2, the benefit-cost ratio is $(a + b)/b$, which is higher than that at e^*. The benefit-cost ratio may be used to make sure that, at the very least, benefits exceed cost, but beyond this it is a misleading indicator in planning the appropriate scope of public programs.

Under some circumstances, there may be grounds for sizing programs at less than that which maximizes net benefits. Suppose there is a regional public agency in charge of enforcing air-pollution laws in two medium-sized urban areas. Suppose further that it has a fixed and predetermined budget of $1 million to spend. There are two possibilities: (1) Put it all in one enforcement program in one of the cities or (2) divide it between two programs, one in each city. Suppose the numbers are as follows:

	Costs	Benefits	Net Benefits	Benefit–Cost Ratio
One-city program	$1,000,000	$2,000,000	$1,000,000	2.0
Two-city program				
City A	500,000	1,200,000	700,000	2.4
City B	500,000	1,200,000	700,000	2.4

---

5. In Figure 6.1 net benefits are positive. Negative net benefits are possible, such as when emissions are to the left of e^*; this is a case when MAC > MD.

In this case, the agency can do better with its fixed budget by putting it into two half-sized, or equi-proportionate, programs rather than just one. In this case, the correct approach is to allocate resources so that the net benefits produced by the total budget are maximized. The equi-marginal principle could also be applied.

Discounting

We turn now to the important problem of how to compare costs and benefits that occur at very different points in time. In a pollution-control program, for example, how do we compare the high initial-year capital costs of abatement equipment with the long-run costs of maintaining it? In the global warming problem, how do we compare the very high costs today of controlling greenhouse gas emissions with the benefits that won't really start accruing for several decades? Suppose there are two programs, one with relatively high net benefits that materialize well into the future and another with smaller net benefits that occur in the near future. How do we compare these two options? The standard way to address problems such as these is through:

- **discounting**—a technique employed to add and compare costs and benefits that occur at different points in time.

Discounting has two facets: first, the mechanics of doing it; then, the reasoning behind the choice of discount rates to be used in specific cases. We take these up in turn.

A cost that will occur 10 years from now does not have the same significance as a cost that occurs today. Suppose that I have incurred a bill of $1,000 that I must pay today. To do that I must have $1,000 in the bank, or my pocket, with which to pay the obligation. Suppose, however, that I have a $1,000 bill to pay, not today, but 10 years from now. If the rate of interest I can get in a bank is 5 percent, and I expect it to stay at that level, I can deposit $613.90 in the bank today and it will compound to $1,000 in 10 years, exactly when I need it. The formula for compounding this sum is

$$\$613.90\,(1 + .05)^{10} = \$1,000$$

Now turn this around and ask: What is the **present value** (PV) to me of this $1,000 obligation 10 years from now? What would I have to put in the bank today to have exactly what I need in 10 years? This is present value and we get this by rearranging the above expression:

$$\text{Present value} = \frac{\$1,000}{(1 + .05)^{10}} = \$613.90$$

The present value is found by discounting the future cost back over the 10-year period at the interest rate, now called the discount rate, of 5 percent.[6] If it were higher—say, 8 percent—the present value would be lower—$463.20. The higher the discount rate, the lower the present value of any future dollar amount.

The same goes for a benefit. Suppose you expect someone to give you a gift of $100 at the end of six years. This would not have the same value to you today (i.e., the same present value) as $100 given to you today. If the applicable discount rate is 4 percent, the present value of that future gift would be

$$\frac{\$100}{(1 + .04)^6} = \$79.03$$

---

6. In general, the discount formula is $PV = m/(1 + r)^t$, where m is the future value, r is the discount rate, and t is the number of years involved.

Discounting is used extensively in benefit-cost analyses. Its main role is to help in aggregating a series of costs or benefits that are strung out over the life of a project or program. Consider the following illustrative numbers, showing benefits for two different programs over their short lives:

	\multicolumn{4}{c	}{Benefits ($) in Year:}	
	1	2	3	4	Total net benefits
Project A	20	20	20	20	80
Project B	50	10	10	10	80

If we simply add these benefits across the four years for each project, they have the same total: $80. But Project A has a series of equal annual benefits, whereas B has substantial benefits in the first period and lower annual benefits thereafter. To compare the total benefits of the two projects, we must calculate the **present value** of total benefits for each program. For illustrative purposes we use a discount rate of 6 percent.

$$PV_A = \$20 + \frac{\$20}{1+.06} + \frac{\$20}{(1+.06)^2} + \frac{\$20}{(1+.06)^3} = \$73.45$$

$$PV_B = \$50 + \frac{\$10}{1+.06} + \frac{\$10}{(1+.06)^2} + \frac{\$10}{(1+.06)^3} = \$76.73$$

Note first that both present values are less than the undiscounted sums of benefits. This will always be true when a portion of a program's benefits accrues in future years. Note also that the present value of benefits for B exceeds that of A, because more of B's benefits are concentrated early in the life of the program. That is to say, the time profile of B's benefits is more heavily concentrated in earlier years than the time profile of A's benefits.

Similar calculations are made for costs in order to find the present value of the stream of annual costs of a program. And the same reasoning applies: Discounting reduces the present value of a dollar of cost more the farther in the future that cost will be incurred. The present value of the stream of benefits minus the present value of costs gives the present value of net benefits. Alternatively, we could calculate for each year in the life of a project its *net benefits*, then calculate the present value of this stream of net benefits in the same way, by summing their discounted values.

Choice of Discount Rate

Because discounting is a way of aggregating a series of future net benefits into an estimate of present value, the outcome depends importantly on which particular discount rate is used. A low rate implies that a dollar in the future is very similar in value to a dollar today.[7] A high rate implies that a dollar in the near term is much more valuable than one later on. Thus,

- the higher the discount rate, the more we would be encouraged to put our resources into programs that have relatively high payoffs (i.e., high benefits and/or low costs) in the short run.
- the lower the discount rate, on the contrary, the more we would be led to select programs that have high net benefits in the more distant future.

---

7. A similar situation is how inflation decreases your real buying power in the future. With inflation, $100 today can buy you more now than $100 can buy in the future.

The choice of a discount rate has been a controversial topic through the years, and we can only summarize some of the arguments here. First, it is important to keep in mind the difference between **real** and **nominal** interest rates. Nominal rates are the rates one actually sees on the market. If you take a nominal rate and adjust it for inflation, you get a real interest rate. Suppose you deposit $100 in a bank at an interest rate of 8 percent. In 10 years your deposit would have grown to $216, but this is in nominal terms. Suppose over that 10-year period prices increase 3 percent per year on average. Then the real value of your accumulated deposit would be less; the real interest rate at which your deposit would accumulate would only be 5 percent (8 percent minus 3 percent), so in real terms your deposit would be worth only $161 after the 10 years.[8] So we have to be careful about the interest rate we use for discounting. If the cost estimates are expected real costs, that is, adjusted for expected inflation, we want to use a real interest rate for discounting purposes. If our cost estimates are nominal figures, then we use a nominal interest rate in the discounting analysis.

The discount rate reflects the way people themselves think about time. Any person normally will prefer a dollar today to a dollar in 10 years; in the language of economics, they have a positive rate of **time preference.** We see people making savings decisions by putting money in bank accounts that pay certain rates of interest. These savings account rates show what interest the banks have to offer in order to get people to forgo current consumption. We might therefore take the average bank savings account rate as reflecting the average person's rate of time preference.

The problem with this is that there are other ways of determining people's rates of time preference, and they don't necessarily give the same answer. Economists at Resources for the Future[9] completed a large survey in which they asked individuals to choose between receiving $10,000 today and larger amounts in five or ten years. The responses yielded implied rates of discount of 20 percent for a five-year time horizon and 10 percent for a 10-year horizon. These were substantially higher than bank savings rates at the time of the survey.

Another approach in thinking about the discount rate is based on the notion of the marginal productivity of investment. When investments are made in productive enterprises, people anticipate that the value of future returns will offset today's investment costs; otherwise, these investments would not be made. The thinking here is that when resources are used in the public sector for natural resource and environmental programs, they ought to yield, on average, rates of return to society equivalent to what they could have earned in the private sector. Private-sector productivity is reflected in the rates of interest banks charge their business borrowers. Thus, by this reasoning, we should use as our discount rate a rate reflecting the interest rates that private firms pay when they borrow money for investment purposes. These are typically higher than savings account interest rates.

---

8. These are slight approximations. The deposit would actually be worth $160.64, and the real rate of accumulation would be 4.89 percent.
9. Resources for the Future (RFF) is a well-known Washington organization that specializes in natural resource and environmental economics research. It publishes a quarterly newsletter discussing its work.

Discounting and Future Generations

The logic of a discount rate, even a very small one, is inexorable (see the numbers in **Exhibit 6.3**). A thousand dollars, discounted back over a century at 5 percent, has a present value of only slightly over $7.60. The present generation, considering the length of its own expected life, may not be interested in programs having very high but long-run payoffs such as this.

EXHIBIT 6.3   The Effects of Discounting

Discounting is a process that expresses the value to people today of benefits and costs that will materialize at some future time. As the time increases between today and the point where these benefits or costs actually occur, their present value diminishes. The following figure shows how much the present value of $100 of benefits, discounted at 3 percent, diminishes as the time when it will be received recedes into the future.

Similarly, for a given time period, the present value will diminish as the discount rate increases. The following figure shows how the present value of a $100 benefit, to be received 100 years from now, diminishes as the discount rate increases.

Present value of $100 to be received in the future:
- 0 years: $100.00
- 20 years: $55.37
- 40 years: $30.66
- 60 years: $16.97
- 80 years: $9.40
- 100 years: $5.20

Present value of $100 benefit received in 100 years:
- 0%: $100.00
- 1%: $36.97
- 2%: $13.80
- 3%: $5.20
- 4%: $1.98
- 5%: $0.76
- 6%: $0.29

The logic is even more compelling if we consider a future cost. One of the reasons that environmentalists have looked askance at discounting is that it can have the effect of downgrading future damages that result from today's economic activity. Suppose today's generation is considering a course of action that has certain short-run benefits of $10,000 per year for 50 years, but that, starting 50 years from now, will cost $1 million a year *forever*. This may not be too unlike the choice faced by current generations on nuclear power or on global warming. To people alive today, the present value of that perpetual stream of future cost discounted at 10 percent is only $85,000. These costs may not weigh particularly heavily on decisions made by the current generation. The present value of the benefits ($10,000 a year for 50 years at 10 percent, or $99,148) exceeds the present value of the future costs. From the standpoint of today, therefore, this might look like a good choice, despite the perpetual cost burden placed on all future generations.

But when future generations are involved, the question of what discount to use is more controversial. Most, but not all, economists and policymakers probably would agree that some positive rate of discount is appropriate. Probably most also agree that it ought to be fairly low (1 percent, 2 percent?), but beyond that there is no alternative that is widely agreed upon. This is important, especially in connection with the long-run impacts of global warming.

Distributional Issues

The relation of total benefits and total costs is a question of economic efficiency. Distribution is a matter of who gets the benefits and who pays the costs. In public-sector programs, distributional matters must be considered along with efficiency issues, which implies that benefit–cost analyses must incorporate studies of how net benefits are distributed among different groups in society.

The distribution of benefits and costs is primarily a matter of equity, or fairness. There are two main types of equity: horizontal and vertical. **Horizontal equity** is a case of treating similarly situated people the same way. An environmental program that has the same impact on an urban dweller with $20,000 of income as on a rural dweller with the same income is horizontally equitable. Consider the following numbers, which illustrate in a simple way the annual values of a particular program accruing to three different individuals who, we assume, all have the same income. Abatement costs show the costs of the program to each individual; these may be higher prices on some products, more time spent on recycling matters, higher taxes, or other factors. The reduced damages are measures of the value of the improvements in environmental quality accruing to each person.

	Person A	Person B	Person C
Reduced environmental damages ($/year)	60	80	120
Abatement costs ($/year)	40	60	80
Difference	20	20	40

Costs and reduced damages are different for individuals A and B, but the difference between them ($20/year) is the same; hence, the difference as a proportion of their income is the same. With respect to these two people, therefore, the program is horizontally equitable. It is not, however, for individual C, because this person experiences a net difference of $40/year. Because person C is assumed to have the same income as the other two people, they are clearly better off as a result of this program; horizontal equity in this case has not been achieved.

Vertical equity refers to how a policy impinges on people who are in different circumstances, in particular on people who have different income levels. Consider the numbers in **Table 6.2**. These show the impacts, expressed in monetary values, of three different environmental quality programs on three people with, respectively, a low income, a medium income, and a high income. In parentheses next to each number is shown the percentage that number is of the person's income level. For example, the "difference" row of Program 1 shows the difference between how much the person benefits from the program (in terms of reduced environmental damages impinging on them) and how much it will cost that person (in terms of the extent to which they will bear a part of the abatement costs of the program). This net difference represents 1 percent of the income of each person. This is a *proportional impact;* that is, it affects the people of each income level in the same proportion.

TABLE 6.2 Vertical Equity*

	Person A		Person B		Person C	
Income	5,000		20,000		50,000	
Program 1						
Reduced damages	150	(3.0)	300	(1.5)	600	(1.2)
Abatement costs	100	(2.0)	100	(0.5)	100	(0.2)
Difference	50	(1.0)	200	(1.0)	500	(1.0)
Program 2 (regressive)						
Reduced damages	150	(3.0)	1,400	(7.0)	5,500	(11.0)
Abatement costs	100	(2.0)	800	(4.0)	3,000	(6.0)
Difference	50	(1.0)	600	(3.0)	2,500	(5.0)
Program 3 (progressive)						
Reduced damages	700	(14.0)	2,200	(11.0)	3,000	(6.0)
Abatement costs	200	(4.0)	1,000	(5.0)	1,500	(3.0)
Difference	500	(10.0)	1,200	(6.0)	1,500	(3.0)

*Figures in this table show annual monetary values. Numbers in parentheses show the percentage of income these numbers represent.

For programs 2 and 3, the ratio, net benefit/income, varies by income. Program 3 has a *progressive* impact because net benefits represent a higher proportion of the low-income person's income (10.0) than they do of the wealthy person's income (3.0). Program 2, on the other hand, is *regressive*; it provides higher proportional net benefits to high-income people (5.0) than to low-income people (1.0). Thus, an environmental program is proportional, progressive, or regressive, according to whether the net effect of that policy has proportionally the same, greater, or less effect on low-income people as on high-income people.

Although the net effects of a program may be distributed in one way, the individual components need not be distributed in the same way. For example, although the overall effects of Program 2 are regressive, the abatement costs of that program are in fact distributed progressively (i.e., the cost burden is proportionately greater for high-income people). In this case, damage reduction is distributed so regressively that the overall program is regressive. This is the same in Program 3; although the overall program is progressive, abatement costs are distributed regressively.

These definitions of distributional impacts can be misleading. A program that is technically regressive could actually distribute the bulk of its net benefits to low-income people. Suppose a policy raised the net income of one rich person by 10 percent, but raised each of the net incomes of 1,000 low-income people by 5 percent. This policy is technically regressive, although more than likely the majority of its aggregate net benefits go to low-income people.

It is usually hard to estimate the distributional impacts of environmental programs, individually or in total. To do so requires very specific data showing impacts by income groups, race/ethnicity, or other factors. In recent years, epidemiologists have collected much better environmental and health data broken down by income, race, and other socioeconomic variables. We still lack good estimates of how program costs are distributed among these groups because these depend on complex factors related to tax collections, consumption patterns, the availability of alternatives, and so on. Despite the difficulties, however, benefit–cost analyses should try to look as closely as possible at the way in which the aggregates are distributed through the population.

Equity among populations is the focus of environmental justice. Assessing horizontal and vertical distributions can identify relative differences in net benefits and, hence, be a relative measure of environmental justice. However, the strength of any assessment is influenced by the quality of the underlying valuations of marginal damages to different population groups. Altering the many factors influencing the values (discount rate, time, benefit and cost estimates) can shift equity values and thus shift environmental justice impacts. Different political groups can use the valuation process to support or disparage a project or regulation, even though the inherent physical well-being of a person or ecosystem is not changed.

Although distributional aspects of local pollution-control programs are important to understand, issues of global equity are critical in considering such problems as climate change, and the steps that might be undertaken to combat it. Global warming affects countries in different ways. Most of the developed countries have economies that are heavily dependent on manufacturing and services, and these are not closely related to weather and climate. Things like insurance, health care, banking, and entertainment can be done most anywhere, and they can move around fairly easily. Likewise, most manufacturing is not weather dependent, although of course it is subject to short-run disruptions if it is forced to relocate. On the other hand, economies that are heavily dependent on agriculture, forestry, and fisheries are likely to be much more heavily impacted, because these activities are weather dependent. But these are the sectors that are so important in many less developed countries, which are also the countries having relatively higher numbers of people at lower levels of income and wealth. All of this means that global warming will likely continue to have a strongly regressive impact in the world, hurting poorer people much greater than it does richer ones.

6-5 Risk Analysis

The future can never be known with certainty. Uncertainty about future benefits and costs can arise from many sources. It is difficult to predict exactly the preferences of future generations, who may feel differently than we do about matters of environmental quality. The complexities of world meteorological systems make predicting future global environmental factors very uncertain. Uncertain advancements in pollution-control technologies could markedly shift future abatement costs. New chemicals, and even many that have been around for years, can have damage effects that are very uncertain.

Because of the high levels of uncertainty in environmental factors, policy analysts have sought to develop modes of analysis specifically directed at the risk factor in environmental decisions. **Risk analysis** involves essentially three actions:

- **Risk assessment:** The study of where risk comes from and how people normally respond to it.
- **Risk valuation:** The study of what values, such as willingness to pay, people place on risk reduction.
- **Risk management:** The study of how different policies affect levels of environmental risk to which people are exposed.

Risk Assessment

Suppose there is a landfill into which a hazardous chemical has been dumped for a number of years. Suppose also that the residents of a nearby community rely on a local groundwater aquifer for their water supply. Risk assessment in this case means estimating the extent of the risk that the dump site poses for the community. It consists of several steps:

1. **Exposure analysis:** Engineers, hydrologists, and others must determine the likelihood that the chemical will migrate to the aquifer, and how much the citizens of the community will be exposed to it if it does. It could be that other pathways of exposure might also have to be considered.
2. **Dose-response analysis:** Scientists must determine the relationship between exposure levels to the chemical and impacts such as incidences of cancer. Relationships like this are sought by laboratory scientists and by epidemiologists.
3. **Risk characterization:** Combining steps (1) and (2) makes it possible to estimate the specific risks faced by members of the community in terms of, for example, the number of premature deaths they could expect.

Risk Valuation

Although the work of risk assessment is the province of physical and health scientists, risk valuation falls primarily to economists. If the dump site is cleaned up, thereby leading to a reduced level of groundwater contamination and of health risk to the nearby people, how much is this actually worth to them?

When future events are probabilistic, we may be able to estimate the most likely or **expected values** of their occurrence. Consider the problem of predicting the number of excess cancer deaths caused by the hazardous waste dump site. Suppose we are told by scientists that the probabilities in any year of getting cancer deaths from this source are as shown in **Table 6.3**. These show a **probability distribution** of excess cancer deaths. For example, the probability of having no deaths is 0.80, of one death is 0.14, of two deaths is 0.05, and so on.[10] The probability of getting four or more deaths is so low that we can treat

---

10. These are illustrative numbers only.

it as zero. The expected value of cancer deaths is found by essentially taking a weighted average, where each number of deaths in the distribution is weighted by its probability of occurrence. According to this calculation, the **expected** number of deaths per year is 0.27.

TABLE 6.3 Calculating the Annual Expected Value of Cancer Deaths from Hazardous Chemicals at Landfill

Number of Deaths	Probability	Expected Value of Deaths
0	0.80	0 × 0.80 = 0.00
1	0.14	1 × 0.14 = 0.14
2	0.05	2 × 0.05 = 0.10
3	0.01	3 × 0.01 = 0.03
4	0.00	4 × 0.00 = 0.00
		Expected value: 0.27

We now can deal with the **valuation** question. Suppose it's estimated that cleaning up the hazardous waste site will lower the expected number of premature deaths from 0.27 to 0.04. How much is this worth to the people of the community? Experience has shown that the scientific results of relative risks stemming from different sources may not agree very well with how people actually feel about different types of risks. For example, people may be willing to pay substantial sums to have a chemical taken out of their water supply even though the health risk is relatively low, whereas they may not be willing to pay much for improved seat belts, which would reduce their overall risk by a great deal.

One way of looking at how people value risky situations is to look at how they react to cases that have similar expected values but quite different profiles of risk.

Consider the following numbers:

	Program A		Program B	
	Net Benefits	Probability	Net Benefits	Probability
	$500,000	0.475	$500,000	0.99
	$300,000	0.525	−$10,000,000	0.01
	Expected value: $395,000		Expected value: $395,000	

These two programs have exactly the same expected value. Suppose we have only a one-time choice between the two, which perhaps relates to the choice of the placement of a hazardous waste-storage site. With Program B, the probability is very high that the net benefits will be $500,000, but there is a small probability of a disaster in which there would be large negative net benefits. Program A has a very different profile; the net benefits are uncertain, but the outcomes are not extremely different and the probabilities are similar—it is very nearly a 50–50 proposition. If we were making decisions strictly on the basis of expected values, we would treat these projects as the same; we could flip a coin to decide which one to choose. If we did this, we would be displaying **risk-neutral** behavior—making decisions strictly on the basis of expected values. But if this is a one-shot decision, we might decide that the low probability of a large loss in the case of Program B represents a risk to which we do not wish to expose ourselves. In this case, we might be **risk averse,** preferring Program A over B.

There are many cases in environmental pollution control where risk aversion is undoubtedly the best policy. The rise of planetary-scale atmospheric change opens up the possibility of catastrophic human dislocations in the future. The potential scale of these impacts argues for a conservative, risk-averse approach to current decisions. Risk-averse decisions are also called for in the case of species extinction; a series of incremental and seemingly small decisions today may bring about a catastrophic decline in genetic resources in the future, with potentially drastic impacts on human welfare. Global issues are not the only ones for which it may be prudent to avoid low risks of outcomes that would have large negative net benefits. The contamination of an important groundwater aquifer is a possibility faced by many local communities. In addition, in any activity in which risk to human life is involved, the average person is likely to be risk averse. Thus it makes sense today to undertake costly steps in order to lower the probability of a future catastrophe.

Risk Management

Once policymakers know how people value risk and the degree of risk inherent in situations of environmental damages, they are in the position to consider policies and regulations designed to manage those risks. This may incorporate **risk-benefit analysis.**

Suppose an administrative agency, such as the Environmental Protection Agency (EPA), is considering whether a particular pesticide should be allowed on the market. It might do a study comparing the benefits farmers and consumers would gain, in the form of production cost savings, when the pesticide is used, as well as of the increased health risks to farm workers, who must handle it, and possibly to consumers if there are pesticide residues on the market crop. In essence, this is a benefit-cost analysis in which the cost side is treated more explicitly in terms of risk. Often, with policy stemming from risk analysis, we think of pesticides being banned or limited in use. However, sometimes policy can go in the other direction. In Massachusetts, as of December 2022, certain pesticides labeled for hemp are no longer prohibited for use on cannabis (marijuana) plants.

Another type of analysis is **comparative-risk analysis,** which focuses on looking at different policy options and the levels of risk they entail. For example, in the landfill example the authorities may look at the different ways of managing the landfill and water-supply system (capping the landfills, looking for an alternative water supply) in terms of the levels of risk to which each alternative exposes people in the affected communities.

Summary

In previous chapters we put the issue of environmental improvement in a trade-off type of format with willingness to pay (benefits) on one side and abatement costs on the other. In this chapter we started to focus on the problem of measuring these benefits and costs. To do this measurement, researchers have to use some underlying analytical framework to account for these benefits and costs. We considered several types of frameworks (impact analysis and cost-effectiveness analysis), then settled on the primary approach used in resource and environmental economics: benefit-cost analysis. The rest of the chapter was devoted to a discussion of the main conceptual issues involved in benefit-cost analysis. These are

- The basic analytical steps involved.
- Determining the appropriate size or scope of a project or program.
- The difference between net benefits and the benefit-cost ratio as a decision criterion.
- Discounting.
- Distributional issues and Environmental Justice.
- Risk analysis.

Having discussed the basic structure of benefit-cost analysis, we turn in the next two chapters to a discussion of the problems of actually measuring the benefits and costs of specific environmental programs.

Questions for Further Discussion

1. Air-pollution-control authorities in southern California proposed to control mobile-source emissions by requiring that 100% of all new cars sold in the region be electric by 2035. Contrast the different perspectives that would be involved in analyzing this proposal with (*a*) economic impact analysis, (*b*) cost-effectiveness analysis, and (*c*) benefit-cost analysis.

2. Suppose we are comparing two ways of increasing nonfossil fuel energy production: expanding solar arrays (short run) or developing off-shore wind power (longer run). How would changes in the discount rate be likely to affect the comparison among these two options?

3. Following are some illustrative numbers for benefits and costs arising from a program to restrict emissions of a pollutant. Current emissions are 10 tons per month. Identify the emission level at which net benefits would be maximized. Show that this is not the same as the emission level that gives the highest benefit-cost ratio. Explain the discrepancy.

Emissions (tons/month)	10	9	8	7	6	5	4	3	2	1	0
Benefits ($ mil)	0	4	8	18	32	44	54	62	68	72	74
Costs ($ mil)	0	2	4	6	9	14	21	36	48	64	86

4. Suppose the costs of an environmental pollution-control program are expected to be equal to $80 per year, and that benefits will be $50 per year for 50 years, then $150 per year thereafter. At a discount rate of 4 percent, what are the net benefits of this program? What would the net benefits be at a discount rate of 2 percent? Comment on the difference.

(Continued)

Questions for Further Discussion *(Continued)*

5. When setting public policy on environmental risks, should we base it on the levels of risk to which people think they are exposed or on the risk levels as scientists have determined them to be in fact?

For additional resources pertaining to the material in this chapter, see the list in **Appendix B.**

Chapter 7
Benefit–Cost Analysis: Benefits

Remembering the provisos about the distribution of income and the availability of information, we already have made the connection between benefits and willingness to pay. The benefits of something are equal to what people are willing to pay for it. The question is: How is willingness to pay to be estimated in specific cases? For goods and services sold on markets it may be relatively easy to estimate willingness to pay. To estimate people's willingness to pay for potatoes, for example, we can observe them buying potatoes—so many potatoes at certain prices—and develop a good idea of the value people place on this item. This will not work, however, when valuing changes in environmental quality. There are no markets where people buy and sell units of environmental quality directly. Instead, we have to fall back on indirect means. As one environmental economist put it: "Benefit estimation often involves a kind of detective work for piecing together the clues about the values individuals place on [environmental services] as they respond to other economic signals."[1]

The measurement of benefits is an activity pursued on many levels. For an analyst working in an environmental agency, it can turn into a plug-in-the-numbers exercise. So many acres of clam bed destroyed (information provided by a marine biologist) times the going price of clams (provided by a quick trip to the local fish market) equals damages of water pollution in the "X" estuary. At the other extreme, for an environmental economist whose interest is in extending the technique, it can be an excursion into sophisticated means of squeezing subtle information from new sets of data. Our path in this chapter lies between these extremes. We review the main techniques environmental economists have developed to measure the benefits of improvements in environmental quality. The objective is to understand the economic logic behind these techniques, without getting bogged down in the theoretical and statistical details.

7-1 The Damage Function: Physical Aspects

When environmental degradation occurs, it produces damages; the emissions control model of **Chapter 5** is based in part on the relationship between emissions and marginal damages. Thus, the **benefits** of environmental quality improvements stem from the reduced damages. To measure an emissions damage function, it's necessary to go through the following steps:

1. Measure **emissions.**
2. Determine the resulting levels of ambient quality through the use of **diffusion models.**
3. Estimate the resulting **human exposure** that these ambient levels would produce.
4. Estimate the **physical impacts** of these exposure levels.

---

1. A. Myrick Freeman III, "Benefits of Pollution Control," in U.S. Environmental Protection Agency, *Critical Review of Estimating Benefits of Air and Water Pollution Control*, Washington, DC, EPA 600/ 5-78-014, 1978, 11–16.

5. Determine the **values** associated with these physical impacts.

The primary work of environmental economists is in step 5, and we will devote most of the chapter to this activity. Let us begin, however, with some brief comments on human exposure and health.

Some of the most important damages caused by environmental pollution are those related to human health. Air pollution, especially, leads to increases in mortality and morbidity[2] among people exposed to it, certainly in the episodic releases of toxic pollutants, but also from long-run exposure to such pollutants as sulfur dioxide (SO_2) and particulate matter (PM). Diseases such as bronchitis, emphysema, lung cancer, and asthma are thought to be traceable in part to polluted air. Water pollution also produces health damages, primarily through contaminated drinking water supplies. So the measurement of the human health damages of environmental pollution is a critical task for environmental economists.

Many factors affect human health—lifestyles, diet, genetic factors, age, and so on—besides ambient pollution levels. To separate the effects of pollution, one has to account for all the other factors or else run the risk of attributing effects to pollution that are actually caused by something else (e.g., smoking). This calls for large amounts of accurate data on health factors, as well as the numerous suspected causal factors. The major work here is that of **epidemiologists,** who derive statistical results from large data sets to measure relationships between ambient pollution exposure and adverse health effects. One of the first such studies of air pollution and human health in the United States was done by Lave and Seskin in the 1970s.[3] The data were for 1969 and refer to published information on standard metropolitan statistical areas (SMSAs). They concluded that a 1 percent reduction in air pollution produces a 0.12 percent reduction in death rates. In the last few decades, literally thousands of additional studies have been done to investigate the linkage between pollution and human health, in terms of both premature mortality and morbidity. A study sponsored by the California Air Resources Board (CARB) showed clear relationships in children between exposure to air pollutants and reduced lung function.[4] A study by Ritz and colleagues showed a relationship between birth defects and the exposure of pregnant women to air pollutants.[5] Zhang and colleagues studied national data and showed a pronounced relationship between levels of ozone and PM and adverse health outcomes.[6] During the worldwide COVID-19 pandemic, the many people in lock down caused global activity to drop drastically. Air pollution dramatically lessened with an associated decrease in the very short term of damages; air became cleaner to breathe and vistas expanded for people to see.

The next step, where environmental economics comes into play in a major way, is to value these outcomes so that the information can be used in classic benefit–cost type studies.

---

2. Morbidity refers to the incidence of ill health and can be expressed in many ways, for example, days missed from work, days spent in the hospital, and the duration of particular symptoms.
3. Lester B. Lave and Eugene P. Seskin, *Air Pollution and Human Health*, Johns Hopkins Press, Baltimore, MD, 1977.
4. California Air Resources Board, *The Children's Health Study*, CARB, Sacramento, 2015.
5. Beate Ritz et al., "Ambient Air Pollution and Risk of Birth Defects in Southern California," *American Journal of Epidemiology*, 155(1), 2002, 17–25.
6. Y. Zhang et al., "Long-term Trends in the Ambient PM2.5 and O_3 Related Mortality Burdens in the United States Under Emission Reductions From 1990 to 2010," *Atmospheric Chemistry and Physics*, 18, 2018, 15003–15016.

7-2 Measuring Damage Costs Directly

There are a number of situations where it would appear possible to measure directly the monetary costs of health and other types of outcomes.

Health Costs

The greatest concern about diminished air and water quality is the impacts these have on human health. One approach to assessing damages in this case is to estimate the increased medical and other costs associated with particular pollution-related illnesses. This is called the **cost of illness** (COI) approach. For example, **Table 7.1** shows data from a study of this type on asthma, which is believed to be related to air pollution. The estimates are divided into direct and indirect costs. Direct costs are the costs of medical visits to hospitals or doctors' offices, together with the costs of medications used to fight asthma. Indirect costs are related to the opportunity costs of lost work time for people who become ill, lost school days, and lost economic productivity of people who die prematurely from asthma.

With the COI perspective, the benefits of pollution control are the reduced health-related costs they produce. This could be regarded as a minimum, or lower-bound, assessment of these benefits, because the improved health also produces a better quality of life for those who are impacted. Many researchers in the health area have sought to create health indices that capture the improvements in physical health parameters that less environmental pollution would produce. This involves assigning numeric values to various health states, both mortality and morbidity, to develop aggregate measures of health outcomes. These indices are sometimes "monetized" to develop estimates of values of health outcomes that can be compared with the monetary costs of pollution control. They do not rely, however, on the basic concept of willingness to sacrifice as a measure of value. We will take this up later in this chapter.

TABLE 7.1 Estimated Cost of Asthma in the United States

	Annual Per Person 2015 Dollars
Prescriptions	1,830
Office visits	640
Hospitalization	529
Outpatient care	176
Emergency room	105
Total	3,280
	Aggregate Costs (2008–2013) $ Billion
Lost school days	3.0
Mortality	29.0
Medical costs	50.3
Total	82.3

Source: Tursynbek Nurmagambetov, Robin Kuwahara, and Paul Garbe, "The Economic Burden of Asthma in the United States 2008–2013," *Annals of the American Thoracic Society,* 2018.

The Effects of Pollution on Production Costs

- Air pollution can reduce yields of exposed crops; it can also reduce the growth rates of commercially valuable timber.
- Water pollution can adversely affect firms and municipalities that use the water for production purposes or for domestic use. Diminished water quality can also have a negative impact on commercial fishing industries.
- Soil contamination can have serious impacts on agricultural production.
- Workplace pollution can reduce the effectiveness of workers and often can increase the rate at which machinery and buildings deteriorate.

In these cases, the effects of pollution are felt on the production of goods and services. The damage caused by the pollution comes about because it interferes in some way with these production processes, in effect making it more costly to produce these outputs than it would be in a less polluted world.

How we actually measure production-related benefits of reducing pollution depends on circumstances. Suppose we are looking at a small group of agricultural producers living in a certain region who will be affected by reduced airborne emissions coming from an upwind factory. Pollutants from the factory have depressed yields, so reducing emissions will cause yields to increase. The crop being produced is sold in a national market, and its price will be unaffected by the output changes in this one region. This situation is depicted in **Figure 7.1**. In this diagram, S_1 is the supply curve for this group of farms before the improved air quality; S_2 is the supply curve after the improvement. The price of the output is p_1. Before the change, these farmers produce at an output level of q_1, whereas after the improvement, their output increases to q_2.

One way of approximating the benefits of this environmental improvement is to measure the value of increased output produced by this group of farms. This is the increased output, $q_2 - q_1$, multiplied by the price of the crop. This gives an estimate corresponding to the area $(d + e)$ in **Figure 7.1**.

FIGURE 7.1 Benefits from Reduced Production Costs

Numerous studies have been done along these lines.[7] Murphy et al.[8] studied the effects on agriculture of eliminating ozone precursor emissions from motor vehicles in the United States. They estimated that the benefits to the agricultural sector of this change would amount to between $3.5 and $6.1 billion annually. Lobell et al. followed with a 2018–2020 study and identified that a 25% reduction in nitrous oxides (NO_x) increased crop yields in China by 25%, 10% in Western Europe, and 8% in South America.[9] Another example of this approach is in estimating the benefits of forestalling climate change (at least in part) by estimating the reduction in lost future output that current reductions in greenhouse gases will produce.

The problem with taking just the value of the increased output is that production costs may also have changed. When air pollution diminishes, farmers actually may increase their use of certain inputs and farm this land more intensively. How do we account for this possibility? In **Figure 7.1** we can analyze the full change by using the net incomes of the farmers (total value of output minus total production costs).

The situation before the change:

$$\text{Total value of output: } a + b + c$$
$$\text{Total costs: } b + c$$
$$\text{Net income: } a$$

The situation after the change:

$$\text{Total value of output: } a + b + c + d + e$$
$$\text{Total costs: } c + e$$
$$\text{Net income: } a + b + d$$

Thus, the improvement in net incomes is $(a + b + d) - a$, or an amount equal to area $b + d$ in **Figure 7.1**.

How we measure this amount depends on how much information we are able to get. If we have studied these farms and know their supply curves before and after the change, we can measure the increased net income directly. If the supply curves are not known, we might look at the increased values of agricultural land in the area. In many cases, added net incomes of this type will get capitalized into land values, and we can use the **increased land values** to estimate the benefits of the environmental improvements.

Materials Damage

Air pollutants cause damage to exposed surfaces, metal surfaces of machinery, stone surfaces of buildings and statuary, and painted surfaces of all types of items. The most heavily implicated pollutants are the sulfur compounds, particulate matter, oxidants, and nitrogen

---

7. These are reviewed in Gardner M. Brown Jr. and Mark L. Plummer, "Market Measures of User Benefits," in *Acid Deposition: State of Science and Technology*, Report 27, Methods for Valuing Acidic Deposition and Air Pollution Effects, National Acid Precipitation Assessment Program, Washington, DC, U.S. Superintendent of Documents, 1990, 27–73.
8. James Murphy, Mark Delucchi, Donald McCubbin, and H. J. Kim, *The Cost of Crop Damage Caused by Ozone Air Pollution from Motor Vehicles*, Institute of Transportation Studies, Paper UCD-ITS-REP-99-03, April 1, 1999, **http://repositories.cdlib.org/itsdavis/UCD-ITS-REP-99-03**.
9. David Lobell et al., "Globally Ubiquitous Negative Effects of Nitrogen Dioxides on Crop Growth," *Science Advances*, 8(22), June 2022.

oxides. For the most part, the damage is from increased deterioration that must be offset by increased maintenance and earlier replacement. In the case of outdoor sculpture, the damage is to the aesthetic qualities of the objects.

In this case, the dose-response relationship shows the extent of deterioration associated with exposure to varying amounts of air pollutants. The basic physical relationships may be investigated in the laboratory, but in application to any particular area, one must have data on the various amounts of exposed materials that actually exist in the study region. Then it is possible to estimate the total amount of materials deterioration that would occur in an average year of exposure to the air of the region with its "normal" loading of various pollutants. One must then put a value on this deterioration. Taking a strict damage-function approach, we could estimate the increased cost of maintenance (labor, paint, etc.) made necessary by this deterioration, but this would be an underestimate of the true damages from a willingness-to-pay (WTP) perspective. Part of the damages would be aesthetic—the reduced visual values of less-sightly buildings and painted surfaces. We might arrive at these values through contingent valuation methods, discussed later. In addition, the maintenance cost approach would not be complete if pollution causes builders to switch to other materials to reduce damages.

Problems with Direct Damage Approaches

The basic problem with direct damage estimates is that they are almost always seriously incomplete. Consider the case of measuring health damages by lost productivity and medical expenditures. We note, first, that these tend to be market measures. They measure the value of marketed goods and services a person might, on average, produce. So the many nonmarket contributions people make, both inside and outside the home, sometimes don't get counted. This method would also assign a zero value to a person unable to work due to disabilities or to a retiree. There are also numerous monetary, as well as psychic, benefits received by others—friends and relatives, for example—that the productivity measure does not account for. Nor does it account for the pain and suffering of illness. Similar conclusions may be drawn about using medical expenditures to estimate damages from reduced environmental quality. Suppose we estimate the damages to you of getting a head cold. We come up with an estimate of $1.87, the cost of the aspirin you consume to reduce the discomfort. This probably would be a serious understatement of the true damages of the cold. If you were asked how much you would be willing to pay to avoid the cold, the answer is likely to be substantially more than the cost of the aspirin. This is perhaps an unfair example because major medical expenditures for a person suffering from air pollution-induced lung cancer are much more significant than a bottle of aspirin. But the principle is valid.

Another problem with attempts to measure damage functions directly is that people and markets normally will change and adjust to environmental pollution, and a full accounting of the damages of pollution must take these adjustments into account. Farmers raising crops affected by pollution may shift to other crops, while the prices of the damaged crops may change, affecting consumers. People often will change their behavior when faced with polluted air or water, engaging in what is called **averting behavior,** or making major changes in lifestyle, such as substituting bottled water for tap water. These effects are difficult to measure when using a direct approach to damage measurement. For this reason, we must turn back to our fundamental concept for determining value: willingness to pay.

7-3 Willingness to Pay: Estimating Methods

There are essentially three ways of trying to find out how much people are willing to pay for improvements in environmental quality. We can illustrate them by considering a case of noise pollution. One feature of the modern world is high-speed roadways (expressways, freeways, and turnpikes), and a major characteristic of these roads is that the traffic on them creates noise. Thus, the people who live nearby suffer damages from this traffic noise. Suppose our job is to estimate the willingness to pay of people living near expressways to reduce traffic noise. How might we do this?

1. The homeowners themselves may have made expenditures to reduce the noise levels inside their homes. For example, they may have installed additional insulation in the walls of their homes or put double-thick glass in the windows. When people make expenditures such as these, they reveal something about their willingness to pay for a quieter environment. In general, then, if we can find cases where market goods are purchased in order to affect a consumer's exposure to the ambient environment, we may be able to analyze these purchases for what they say about the value people place on changes in that ambient environment. The technical term for this is the study of **averting costs.**

2. The noise in the vicinity of the road may have affected the prices that nearby residents may have paid for their houses. If two houses have exactly the same characteristics in all respects except the level of exterior noise, we would expect the one in the noisier environment to be less valuable to prospective buyers than the one in the quieter environment. If the housing market is competitive, the price of the noisier house would be lower than the price of the other one. Thus, by looking at the difference in house prices, we can estimate the value people place on reduced noise pollution. In general, therefore, any time the price of some good or service varies in accordance with its environmental characteristics, we may be able to analyze these **price variations** to determine people's willingness to pay for these characteristics.

3. The third way is deceptively simple. It is to conduct a survey among homeowners and ask them how much they would be willing to pay for reductions in noise levels around and inside their homes. This direct-survey approach has received a lot of attention from environmental economists primarily because of its flexibility. The primary method in this survey-type approach is called **contingent valuation.** Virtually any feature of the natural environment that can be described accurately to people can be studied by this method.

The first two of these methods involve the study of individuals' choices so as to uncover the implied values that have led them to make these decisions. For this reason they are often called **revealed preference** methods, as individuals are essentially revealing their underlying values. The third method involves asking people directly what their willingnesses to pay are, and are therefore called **stated preference** approaches.

7-4 Willingness to Pay: Revealed Preference Methods

The thought behind these indirect approaches is that when people make market choices among certain items that have different characteristics related to the environment, they reveal the value they place on these environmental factors.

Using willingness to pay to measure health benefits has the virtue of being consistent with other types of economic-demand studies, and it recognizes that even with something as important as health care, it is people's evaluations of its worth that should count. But the concept must be used with care. In any real-world situation, willingness to pay implies ability to pay; one cannot express a willingness to pay for something if one lacks the necessary income or wealth. So we must be sensitive to the income levels of people whose demand we are trying to measure. If the analysis includes a substantial number of people with low incomes, the measured willingness to pay may be lower than what might be justified. We may not want to lower the estimated health benefits of an environmental program simply because the target population has lower-than-average incomes.

Another feature about health care as a normal economic good is that people may be willing to pay for the health of others. I do not care if my daughter eats meat; her own willingness to pay is a good expression of her demand for meat. I do care about her health, however, and, to her own willingness to pay for good health, I would be willing to add a substantial sum of my own. Thus, strictly individualistic measures of willingness to pay for health improvements may underestimate the true benefits of programs that increase health.

The Value of Human Health as Expressed in Averting Costs

Air and water pollution can produce a variety of adverse health conditions, ranging from slight chest discomfort or headaches all the way to acute episodes requiring hospital care. People often make expenditures to try to avoid, or avert, these conditions, and these averting costs are an expression of their willingness to pay to avoid them. A number of studies have been done in which these averting expenditures have been analyzed for what they tell about willingness to pay.[10] One early study was done of a sample of people in the Los Angeles area in 1986 and looked at expenditures they made to avoid a variety of respiratory symptoms. Expenditures included such things as cooking with electricity rather than gas, operating a home air conditioner, and driving an air-conditioned car. Their estimates of the willingness to pay to avoid various respiratory symptoms ranged from $0.97 for shortness of breath to $23.87 for chest tightness.

One place where averting-cost analysis has been done is to value water quality, because of the usually ready availability of alternatives to water of dubious quality, such as water filtration devices and bottled water. Water hardness, taste, and color are subject to averting costs when people hold well-formed perceptions of quality.[11] At the other extreme, averting behavior has been studied to deduce the value of a statistical life (VSL).[12]

The Value of Human Life as Expressed in Wage Rates

Diminished air quality and contaminated water can lead to deteriorated health and death. How are these impacts to be valued? It is tempting to say that "human life is beyond measure," but that is not the way people behave in the real world. We can see by casual observation that individuals do not, in fact, behave as if prolonged life, or the warding

---

10. These are reviewed in Maureen L. Cropper and A. Myrick Freeman III, "Environmental Health Effects," in John B. Braden and Charles D. Kolstad, eds., *Measuring the Demand for Environmental Quality*, North-Holland, Amsterdam, 1991, 200-202.
11. Bruno Lanz and Allen Provins, "Using Averting Expenditures to Estimate the Demand for Public Goods: Combining Objective and Perceived Quality," *Resource and Energy Economics* 47, 2017, 20-35.
12. Glenn C. Blomquist, "Self Protection and Averting Behavior, Values of Statistical Lives, and Benefit Cost Analysis of Environmental Policy," *Review of Economics of the Household*, 2(1), 2004, 89-110.

off of disease, is in some sense an ultimate end to which all their resources must be devoted. We see people engaging in risky activity, in some sense trading off risk for the benefits received. Almost everybody drives a car, some people smoke, some rock climb, many strive to get tans, and so on. We also see people allocating portions of their income to reducing risk: buying locks, installing smoke alarms, staying away from dark places at night, applying sunscreen. In addition, we observe people making differential judgments of their own worth: Parents with children buying more life insurance than single people, and so on. All of this suggests that people treat the risk of death in a reasonably rational manner, and that we could use willingness to pay as a way of evaluating the benefits of reducing the risk of death or illness.

But we must be clear on exactly what is involved. There is a joke about the stingy millionaire, walking down a street, who gets held up. The robber points a gun at her and says, "Your money or your life," and the victim replies: "Ah, let me think about that." Estimating the WTP value of a human life does not involve this kind of situation. People are not asked for their willingness to pay to save their own lives. Under some circumstances a person presumably will be willing to give everything he or she owns, but these are not the kinds of situations people normally face. When I express a willingness to pay for reducing air pollution, the relevant concept is the **value of a statistical life** (VSL), not the life of some particular individual. Another term for this concept is **value of reduced mortality risk.**[13] This does not imply that people are assumed to care only about the average, or random, person and not about specific people. People obviously feel closer to their relatives, friends, and neighbors than to strangers. What is involved is the value people place on rearranging the living conditions of a large group of people by, for example, reducing their exposure to environmental pollutants in order to lower the probability that some **randomly determined individual** from the group will suffer illness or premature death. Suppose, for example, that the average person in a group of 100,000 people would be willing to pay $20 to lower the probability of a random death among members of that group from 7 in 100,000 to 6 in 100,000. Then the total willingness to pay is $20 (100,000) = $2,000,000, which is the VSL based on willingness to pay.

The most fully developed revealed preference approach to measuring the willingness to pay for reducing risk to life is through **industrial wage rate studies.** Suppose there are two jobs similar in all respects except that in one, because of the type of machinery used, the risk of death is somewhat higher than in the other. Suppose that initially the wage rates in the two industries were the same. In this case, it would obviously be preferable to work in the safer industry—same wage, lower risk. Workers would then seek to move from the dangerous industry to the safer industry. This would tend to drive down the wage in the safer industry and increase the wage in the other, as firms sought to keep workers from leaving that industry. Thus, a wage differential would evolve between the two industries; the amount of that differential would show how workers valued the differences between them in terms of risk of death. The wage differential, in other words, represents an implicit valuation of a statistical life.

---

13. For a work discussing VSL in depth, see W. Kip Viscusi, *Pricing Lives Guideposts for a Safer Society,* Princeton University Press, 2018.

A similar relationship of wage rate to pollution level would evolve if the pollution varied by city or job location rather than by industry. Assuming other factors are equal, jobs in cleaner cities would have lower wage rates than in more polluted cities. By analyzing wage differences such as this, we can get a measure of the benefits people would get from reducing pollution-related premature deaths.

Table 7.2 summarizes some results of wage-rate studies aimed at estimating the VSL in the United States. Note that the estimates range from $1.5 million to over $10 million. What accounts for these differences? Different data and statistical techniques probably account for most of them. These studies are difficult because there are many other factors that have to be taken into account and because it is hard to get exactly the right data. For example, most worker accident and wage data apply to industry groupings, and within these groups there may be substantial variation among individual firms, not only because of technological differences among them, but also because some firms may have done a lot more than others to make the workplace safer. It is also the case that wage-rate studies such as these are predicated on the reasonably efficient working of the labor market, and this may not be the case in some industries. Union agreements, collusion among firm managers, and lack of information can upset the competitive wage-making process in some industries. These problems do not mean that these studies are not useful, only that we have not yet reached a point where they are giving us a consistent story.

TABLE 7.2 Implied Value of a Statistical Life as Estimated in Labor Market Studies

A Statistical Study	Estimated Value of Statistical Life ($ million)
Moore and Viscusi (1990)	20.8
Kniesner et al. (2012)	4.0–10.0
Leigh (1995)	8.1–16.8
Viscusi and Addy	6.8–9.5
Rose (2014)	3.2
Lott and Manning (2000)	12.4
Banzhaf (2022)	2.4–14.0

Sources: J. P. Leigh, "Compensating Wages, Value of a Statistical Life, and Inter-Industry Differentials," *Journal of Environmental Economics and Management,* 1995; J. R. Lott and R. L. Manning, "Have Changing Liability Rules Compensated Workers Twice for Occupational Hazards? Earnings Premiums and Cancer Risks," *Journal of Legal Studies,* 2000; M. J. Moore and W. Kip Viscusi, "Models for Estimating Discount Rates for Long-Term Health Risks Using Labor Market Data," *Journal of Risk and Uncertainty,* 1990; J. Rose, "Official Estimates for the Value of Statistical Life for Road Accidents in Selected Countries," *Transport Economics,* 2014; T. J. Kniesner, W. Kip Viscusi, C. Wook, and J. P. Ziliak, "The Value of a Statistical Life, Evidence from Panel Data," *Review of Economics and Statistics,* 2012; H. Spencer Banzhaf, *The Value of Statistical Life: A Meta-Analysis of Meta-Analyses,* Cambridge University Press, 2022.

Valuing Children's Health

Most WTP studies in the health area are focused on the valuations of adults. But a large percentage of the people impacted by environmental pollution are children, and it is not clear that the WTP estimates of adults are applicable also to children. Children may be more heavily impacted than adults by given concentrations of pollutants in the air and water. And children themselves are in no position to offer WTP information on their health. Thus, what we need are WTP estimates of adults for reducing health risks to children, and these may be quite different than their WTP to reduce health risks to themselves. For example, Hammitt and Haninger found that people valued the child VSL higher ($12.4 million) than the adult VSL ($7.5 million).[14] But Adamowicz et al. found that parents are willing to pay, on the margin, equal amounts to reduce environmental risks to themselves and to their children.[15]

The Value of Environmental Quality as Expressed in House Prices

The wage-rate studies we just looked at estimate the willingness to pay to be exposed to a lower risk of death, which is a specific consequence of being exposed to lower levels of environmental pollution. But there are wider benefits to a cleaner environment than simply health benefits. A more inclusive approach is to examine people's willingness to pay to live in a less polluted environment. This would include the health effects and other dimensions such as aesthetic impacts.

Suppose you had two houses that were exactly the same in terms of all of their physical characteristics—number of rooms, floor area, age, and so on—as well as in locational factors—distance to neighbors, distance to shopping, schools, and so forth. Assume, however, that one house is located in an area of substantial air pollution, whereas the other is located in an area with relatively clean air. We would expect the market prices of these two houses to differ because of the air quality difference. This conclusion generalizes to a large housing market involving many properties. The surrounding air quality is essentially a feature of the location of a house so, as houses are bought and sold in the house market, these air quality differences would tend to get "capitalized" into the market prices of the houses. Of course, homes differ in many respects, not just in terms of air quality. So it is necessary to collect large amounts of data on many properties and then use statistical techniques to identify the role played by air pollution, as well as other factors.[16]

Assuming we had collected enough data and conducted the appropriate statistical analyses, we might end up with a relationship such as that shown in **Figure 7.2**. This shows that as the particulate content of the surrounding air increases, house prices decrease, everything else held equal. Information of this type can then be used to estimate homeowners' marginal willingness to pay (benefits) for small decreases in particulate exposure.

The same kind of approach might be used with some cases of water pollution. In **Chapter 4,** we used lake pollution to introduce the concept of a public good. Suppose a lake is surrounded by a number of residences. The market price of these homes will be affected by many things: their age, size, condition, and so on. They will also be affected by the water quality of the lake. If this water quality degrades over time, we would expect the market values of the surrounding properties to go down. The deteriorating water quality means that homeowners will obtain less utility from living in that vicinity, other things remaining equal,

---

14. J. K. Hammitt and K. Haninger, "Valuing Fatal Risks to Children and Adults: Effects of Disease, Latency and Risk Aversion," *American Journal of Agricultural Economic*, 89(5), 2007, 1170–1175.
15. W. Adamowicz et al., "Household Decision Making and Valuation of Environmental Health Risks to Parents and Their Children," *Journal of the Association of Environmental and Resource Economics*, 1(4), 2014, 481–519.
16. The technical name for this type of approach is "hedonic" analysis. When the price of something is related to the many characteristics it possesses, we can study patterns of price differences to deduce the value people place on one of those characteristics.

and this will get capitalized into the values of the houses. One approach to measuring the benefits of cleaning up the lake is to estimate the overall increase in property values among the homes in the vicinity of the lake. We have to remember, however, that this is likely to be only a partial estimate of total benefits. If nonresidents have access to the lake or park, they would also be gaining benefits, but these would not show up in property value changes. Property value changes to measure benefits from pollution reduction can also be used in other situations, for example, in valuing the damage from noise around airports and major highways and in measuring the benefits flowing from urban parks.

FIGURE 7.2 Relationship of Ambient PM Concentration and House Prices

House price studies can also be used to value the impact of flood risks, a growing concern of homeowners who may be affected by rising coastal sea levels, especially with increased hurricane risk.[17] However, many variables affect pricing in real estate markets, such as mortgage rates; also, the influence of the supply and demand for housing stock varies along the coastline.[18]

The Value of Environmental Quality as Expressed in Travel Costs

One of the first approaches that environmental economists ever used to estimate the demand for environmental amenities is a method that takes travel costs as a proxy for price. Although we don't observe people buying units of environmental quality directly, we do observe them traveling to enjoy, for example, recreational experiences in national and state parks, swimming and fishing experiences in lakes and streams, and so on. Travel is costly; it takes time as well as out-of-pocket travel expenses. By treating these travel costs as a price that people must pay to experience the environmental amenity, we can estimate, under some circumstances, a demand function for those amenities.

---

17. A. A. Aliya et al., "Impact of Flooding on Residential Property Values: A Review and Analysis of Previous Studies," *Proceedings of the Academic Conference of Nightingale Publications & Research International on Sustainable Development*, 2(2), 2016.
18. D.C. Rodziewicz et al., "Housing market impairment from future sea-level rise inundation," *Environment Systems and Decisions*, 42, 2022, 637–656.

By getting travel cost data for a large number of people, we can build up estimates of the aggregate willingness to pay for particular environmental amenities. Of course, information must be obtained on more than just their travel costs. Families will differ in terms of many factors, not just in terms of their travel costs to this park. They will have different income levels, they will differ in terms of the presence of alternative parks and other recreational experiences available to them, etc. So surveys have to collect large amounts of data on many visitors to be able to statistically sort out all these various influences on park visitation rates.

This approach may be used to estimate the benefits of improving the quality of the environment at the visitation site, for example, by improving the water quality at a recreation lake so that fishing is better. To do this we must collect information not only on the travel costs of recreators to a single recreation site but also on the travel costs to many different sites with differing natural characteristics. Then we can parse out the effects on visitation of various qualitative aspects of different sites. From this we can then determine their willingness to pay for improvements in these qualitative changes.

7-5 Willingness to Pay: Stated Preference Methods

We now come to what might seem as a more direct way of assessing willingness to pay. This is a **stated preference** approach, because it involves asking people directly to indicate their willingness to pay for some environmental feature, or some outcome that is closely connected to the state of the environment.

The best known stated preference method is a technique called **contingent valuation** (CV). In this method, individuals are asked to make WTP responses when placed in contingent situations. If we were interested in measuring people's willingness to pay for something like potatoes, we could station ourselves at stores and see them choosing in real situations. But when there are no real markets for something, such as an environmental quality characteristic, we can only ask them to tell us how they would choose *if* they were faced with a market for these characteristics.

Contingent valuation methods have been utilized in two different types of situations: (1) to estimate valuations for specific features of the environment, for example, the value of view-related amenities, the recreational quality of beaches, preservation of wildlife species, congestion in wilderness areas, hunting and fishing experiences, preservation of wild rivers, and others[19]; and (2) to estimate the valuations people place on outcomes that are related to environmental quality. A major justification for more stringent environmental regulations has always been the improvements in human health that these would produce. What is important here are the valuations that people place on such things as reduced risk of premature mortality, decreased risk of chronic lung disease, decreased risk of asthma, and so on.

---

19. For the classic discussions of CV analysis, see Robert Cameron Mitchell and Richard T. Carson, *Using Surveys to Value Public Goods: The Contingent Valuation Method*, Resources for the Future, Washington, DC, 1989; and Ronald G. Cummings, David S. Brookshire, and William D. Schulze, *Valuing Environmental Goods: An Assessment of the Contingent Valuation Method*, Rowland and Allanheld Publishers, Totowa, NJ, 1986. Also, see Patricia A. Champ, Kevin J. Boyle, and Thomas C. Brown, *A Primer on Nonmarket Evaluation*, Amsterdam, Springer Science and Business Media, 2017.

The basic steps in a CV analysis are the following:

1. Identification and description of the environmental quality characteristic or health outcome to be evaluated
2. Identification of respondents to be approached, including sampling procedures used to select respondents
3. Design and application of a survey questionnaire, interview, or focus group
4. Analysis of results and aggregation of individual responses to estimate values for the group affected by the environmental change

The nature of CV analysis can best be understood by looking more closely at the questionnaire design phase.

Valuing an Environmental Amenity

In this case, the questionnaire is designed to elicit from respondents their willingness to pay for some feature of the environment. The questionnaire would normally have three components:

1. A clear statement of exactly what the environmental feature or amenity is that people are being asked to evaluate
2. A set of questions that will describe the respondent in economically relevant ways, such as income, residential location, age, and use of related goods
3. A question, or set of questions, designed to elicit WTP responses from the respondent

The central purpose of the questionnaire is to elicit from respondents their estimate of what the environmental feature is worth to them. In economic terms, this means getting them to reveal the maximum amount they would be willing to pay rather than go without the amenity in question.

Numerous techniques have been used to get this response:

- **No prompting** – The most obvious is to ask people outright to provide the number with no prompting or probing on the part of the interviewer.
- **Bidding techniques**
    - **Low bid** – The interviewer starts with a bid at a low level and progressively increases the value until the user indicates that the limit has been reached.
    - **High bid** – Alternatively, the interviewer could start with a high figure and lower it to find where the respondent's threshold value is located.
- **Range** – Another method is to give the respondents a selection of a range of values and then ask the respondents to check off their maximum willingness to pay.

One great advantage of contingent valuation is that it is flexible and applicable to a wide range of environmental amenities, not just those that can somehow be measured in conjunction with some marketable good. Virtually anything that can be made comprehensible to respondents can be studied with this technique. Also, CV methods have been combined with averting cost estimates which were discussed earlier in this chapter.[20]

---

20. Jennifer Orgill-Meyer et al., "Comparing Contingent Valuation and Averting Expenditure Estimates of the Costs of Irregular Water Supply," *Ecological Economics*, 146, 2018, 250–264.

- CV was first used in 1963 by Bob Davis to estimate the benefits of outdoor recreation opportunities in the Maine backwoods. He found that the modal willingness to pay per family for the use of a wilderness recreation area was between $1.00 and $2.00 per day.[21]
- Loomis and colleagues found that the average respondent in their CV survey would be willing to pay $21 per month for improved water quality in the Platte River.[22]
- Banzhaf and colleagues found that residents in the Adirondack region of New York would be willing to pay between $48 and $107 for ecological improvements in air and water that might flow from currently proposed environmental regulations.[23]
- Holmes et al., using a CV approach, found that riparian landowners along the Little Tennessee River would be willing to pay $89.50 per foot along the river for restoration activities.[24]
- Qiao et al., found education, income, and environmental knowledge to have a positive effect on WTP for rubber plantation ecological restoration in China through the use of CV, while age had a negative effect on WTP.[25]
- Czajkowski et al., used CV methods to study people's attitudes to recycling.[26]

CV and Valuing Health Outcomes

Contingent valuation studies have been done to value these health impacts, or their avoidance, in terms of willingness to pay. The studies have been of two general types: those estimating respondents' willingness to pay to avoid premature mortality, and those estimating willingness to pay to achieve certain reductions in morbidity. The latter can be further subdivided into studies of chronic diseases, such as bronchitis and asthma, and temporary but acute health conditions.

In the mortality studies the outcomes have been expressed probabilistically, that is, the willingness to pay for a reduction of a certain amount in the probability of premature death. Kochi et al. reviewed 45 CV studies aimed at estimating the value of a statistical life (VSL) showing that the average estimate was $3.5 million.[27] Studies of chronic illnesses have also usually been aimed at probabilistic measures, for example, willingness to pay to

---

21. Robert K. Davis, "The Value of Big Game Hunting in a Private Forest," in *Transactions of the Twenty-ninth North American Wildlife Conference*, Wildlife Management Institute, Washington, DC, 1964.
22. John Loomis, Paula Kent, Liz Strange, Kurt Fausch, and Alan Covich, "Measuring the Total Economic Value of Restoring Ecosystem Services in an Impaired River Basin: Results from a Contingent Value Survey," *Ecological Economics*, 33(1), 2000, 103–117.
23. H. Spencer Banzhaf, Dallas Burtraw, David Evans, and Alan J. Krupnick, *Valuation of Natural Resource Improvements in the Adirondacks*, paper presented at National Center for Environmental Economics, Environmental Protection Agency workshop, 2004.
24. Thomas P. Holmes, John C. Bergstrom, Eric Huszar, Susan B. Kask, and Fritz Orr III, "Contingent Valuation, Net Marginal Benefits, and the Scale of Riparian Ecosystem Restoration," *Ecological Economics*, 49(1), 2004, 19–30.
25. Dan Qiao, "Chasing the Unbiased Willingness to Pay: Using an Integrated Contingent Valuation Survey in Estimating the Non Market Value of Rubber Plantation Ecological Restoration Programs in China," *Frontiers in Ecology and Evolution*, Nov 2022.
26. Mikolaj Czajkowski, Nancy Hanley, and Karina Nyborg, "Social Norms, Morals and Self-interest as Determinants of Pro-environment Behaviours: The Case of Household Recycling," *Environment and Resource Economics*, 66(4), April 2017, 647–670.
27. Kochi et al., "An Empirical Bayes Approach to Combining and Comparing Estimates of the Value of a Statistical Life for Environmental Policy Analysis," *Environmental and Resource Economics*, 34, 2006, 385–406.

lower the probability of having chronic bronchitis. Acute health conditions have usually been valued as though they were certain to be avoided, for example, willingness to pay to avoid a common cold, or a visit to the emergency room of a hospital.

Table 7.3 shows some results on health-related benefits produced by a plan proposed by the Environmental Protection Agency to reduce the interstate flow of air pollution from power plants. These estimates are primarily based on WTP studies of health outcomes. Note that the greatest source of health-related benefits is the reduction in premature deaths from air pollution. A study of European Union countries found that measures of increased air pollution ($PM_{2.5}$) in some regions correlated with increased worker absenteeism and reduced labor productivity resulting in explaining 90% of a drop in GDP with the agricultural and construction sectors being the most affected.[28]

TABLE 7.3 Benefits and Costs of a Proposal for Controlling Power Plant Emissions in Order to Reduce Interstate Air Pollution

Benefits	Millions (2007 U.S. dollars)
Premature mortality	$270,000
Chronic bronchitis	$4,200
Nonfatal heart attacks	$1,700
Hospital admissions	$130
Other health	$50
Recreational visibility	$4,100
Other nonhealth	$1,500
Total	*$281,680*
Costs	$810

Sources: U.S. EPA, Office of Air and Radiation, *Regulatory Impact Analysis for the Federal Implementation Plan to Reduce Interstate Transport of Fine Particulate Matter and Ozone in 27 States*. Correction of SIP Approvals for 22 States, 2011.

Problems of CV Analysis

The most problematic aspect of contingent valuation is its hypothetical character. When people buy potatoes, to go back to our example, they have to "put their money where their mouth is," as the saying goes. It is a real situation, and if the wrong choices are made, people suffer real consequences. In a CV questionnaire, however, the same real-world implications are not present. People face a hypothetical situation to which they may give hypothetical responses not governed by the discipline of a real marketplace. In thinking about this, two types of questions come up: First, will people know enough about their real preferences to be able to give valid responses, and, second, even if they know their preferences, will they have incentives to misrepresent them to the investigator?

Everyone develops experience buying some things, but not others, on the market. In 17th-century New England, people were used to buying and selling pews in the church. In some countries, official papers from public officials require standard monetary bribes.

---

28. Antoine Dechezleprêtre et al., "The Economic Cost of Air Pollution: Evidence from Europe, Organization for Economic Co-operation and Development," *Economics Department Working Papers No. 1584,* August 2020.

In contemporary society there are going prices for cantaloupes and insulin for diabetes. When people face market prices for a good or service over a period of time, they have time to learn about their values, adjust their purchases, and settle on a willingness to pay that accurately represents their preferences. But when asked to place a monetary value on something that does not normally carry a price, it may be much more difficult to state one's true willingness to pay. What would you be willing to pay for 10 more beautiful sunsets per year? People also develop ideas over time about the appropriate extent of the market in allocating certain goods and services; when asked to put a value on something that is currently beyond the market, their answers may reflect not just the value of a particular item, but something about what kind of an economic system they want to live in, which is a much broader question.

The other question is whether respondents could normally be expected to have incentives to misstate their true willingness to pay. Environmental quality characteristics are public goods, as we saw in **Chapter 4.** People can be expected to understate their preferences for these kinds of goods when they expect that their answers will be used to establish payment schedules for the goods. Yet, in CV studies, there is no threat that responses could be used, for example, to set taxes to pay for the item being evaluated. So, perhaps, this source of bias is unlikely. The opposite bias may be more likely. People may be led to give an inflated estimate of their willingness to pay hoping, perhaps, that others will do the same thing, realizing that their share of the cost of making the item available will, in any case, be very small.

There have been hundreds of contingent valuation studies carried out to estimate people's willingness to pay for environmental quality. Despite the difficulties, CV analysis offers flexibility and a chance of estimating values that no other technique can match.

7-6 Problems in Benefit Estimation

Many problems remain in estimating the benefits of improved environmental quality. Good data are always hard to come by. Better techniques are always useful to separate out the effects of other factors and isolate the true environmental impacts. More thought has to be given to the conceptual problems that remain. We will indicate very briefly some of the latter.

Discounting

One of the most important is the matter of **discounting.** Should we discount future benefits, as we talked about in **Chapter 6,** and, if so, what discount rate is appropriate? When we discount the future value of something, we reduce its present value, and the longer in the future these benefits will be realized, the lower their present value. So discounting tends to decrease the relative value of programs that produce benefits far in the future and increase those that produce benefits in the next few years. This might make sense with certain types of benefits. People today presumably would put more value on reducing environmentally related premature deaths next year than they would on premature deaths 50 years from now. But there are some significant environmental issues, such as climate change, where substantial impacts are expected to occur in the future, and in this case discounting tends to reduce substantially the importance of programs addressing this problem.

There is no easy answer to this problem. We cannot simply reject discounting altogether; even future generations would be unlikely to agree with that if they could make their wishes known. In ordinary affairs, however, the present generation is undoubtedly too oriented to the short run; too much reliance is placed on recent history and not enough on future possibilities. For society as a whole, a longer-run perspective is appropriate. Perhaps the best approach is to combine discounting with sustainability. Discounting is appropriate as long as it does not lead to a reduction in the long-run environmental capital of the society.

Willingness to Pay Versus Willingness to Accept

An alternative way of approaching the problem of valuing environmental improvements is to ask people how much they would be **willing to accept** to give up some environmental amenity. To value better air quality, we could ask either how much people would be willing to pay for a small improvement or how much they would have to receive to compensate them for a small reduction in air quality. Suppose public authorities are contemplating locating a hazardous waste incinerator in a particular community. As a measure of the damages suffered by the community, we could take the amount of money required for community members willingly to accept the incinerator (rather than, in other words, the amount they would be willing to pay to keep it out).

Clearly, willingness to accept is not constrained by one's income, as is willingness to pay. So it may be no surprise that when people are asked willingness-to-accept questions, their answers are usually higher than their WTP responses for the same item. To some extent it may depend on what they are asked. For a small change, we would expect the two measures to be close. Suppose what is involved is a single cantaloupe. If I am willing to pay $4.49 for one more cantaloupe, that is also probably close to what it would take to compensate for my loss of a single cantaloupe, but for large changes (what are called nonmarginal changes) this may not be the case. If we are talking, for example, of large changes in air pollution in my neighborhood that will substantially change my welfare, the two measures may be quite different.

Economists have taken several approaches to resolving this problem. One is to look closely at the questionnaire and the way questions are asked of respondents. Experience has shown that responses will differ according to how questions are phrased; therefore, one possibility is that the differences between willingness to pay and willingness to accept are traceable primarily to the way questions are being framed. The other approach is to replace the standard economic principles, which imply that there should be no difference between these two measures, with new concepts that can explain the difference.

Nonuse Values

When people buy potatoes, we assume that they do so because they expect to eat them; the value of potatoes to people lies in their *use* value. This reasoning also extends to environmental assets, but in this case there may be more. When people voluntarily donate money for the preservation of unique environmental assets that they may never even see, except perhaps in photographs, such as polar bears in the Arctic, something other than use value must be involved.

People's willingness to pay for these environmental characteristics must also involve certain **nonuse values:**

- **Option value** – Although someone may not currently be in a position to experience directly a particular environmental asset, they often want to preserve the option to do so in the future. Option value is the amount a person would be willing to pay to preserve the option of being able to experience a particular environmental amenity in the future.
- **Existence value** – People may even be willing to pay to preserve something they, in all likelihood, will never see–Amazon wildlife, for example. In this case, what is involved is existence value, a willingness to pay simply to help preserve the existence of some environmental amenity.
- **Bequest value** – Altruistic values may be focused to some extent on future generations, preserving resources so future generations can experience them.
- **Stewardship value** – This value is not related necessarily to the human use of the environment but rather to maintaining the health of the environment for the continued use of all living organisms.

One of the reasons contingent valuation studies have become more common is that questions can be phrased so as to get at these nonuse values.

Summary

Benefit measurement is a major focus of study within environmental economics. Various techniques are used to uncover values that previously were hidden from view. From legislatures and courts, a brisk demand exists for benefits information on which to base laws and legal settlements. Public environmental agencies have devoted considerable time and effort to generating benefits estimates in order to justify their policy rulings. After reviewing briefly what we mean by *benefits*, we discussed some of the main techniques environmental economists use to measure these benefits. Health impacts, previously assessed by direct damage estimation, utilize WTP procedures, especially wage-rate studies showing how people value risks to health. We also covered house-price studies, production cost studies, and travel cost studies. Finally, we reviewed the technique of contingent valuation. This technique allows benefits to be measured over a much wider range of environmental phenomena than other techniques permit. Discounting and issues related to current versus future generations are important considerations. CV techniques allow analysts to explore some of the less tangible, but no less real, sources of environmental benefits, such as option value, existence value, and stewardship value.

Questions for Further Discussion

1. Suppose you were hired by the homeowners located around a lake to determine the benefits of improving the water quality in the lake. How might you go about doing it?

(Continued)

Questions for Further Discussion *(Continued)*

2. A region is proposing an expansive project to install adaptation technology to control anticipated future sea water rise to protect an urban area along the seacoast. Compare and contrast how individuals living in the urban area would evaluate the benefits versus how individuals living in the hilly, rural area to the north would evaluate the benefits. How would each set the discount rate to fit their view?

3. Suppose you want to determine the aggregate willingness to pay among students at your school for increasing the number of electric vehicle charging stations at the school. How might you do this?

4. What is the usual meaning that economists give to the expression "the value of a human life"? What are the different ways of estimating this value?

5. Design some contingent valuation-type questions for evaluating the value to people of improving the air quality in the Grand Canyon. Identify non-use values that may influence respondents.

6. Survey 10 other students, asking them how much they would be willing to pay for one visit to their favorite beach. What qualifying questions did your respondents ask you before they could assign a dollar value? What are some factors influencing people's willingness-to-pay value?

For additional resources pertaining to the material in this chapter, see the list in **Appendix B.**

Chapter 8
Benefit–Cost Analysis: Costs

In this chapter we look at the cost side of benefit-cost analysis. The importance of accurate cost measurement has often been underestimated. The results of a benefit–cost analysis can be affected as easily by overestimating costs as by underestimating benefits. In developing countries, where people place a high priority on economic growth, it is critically important to know how environmental programs will affect that growth rate and how costs are distributed among different social groups. In industrialized countries, opposition to environmental policies frequently centers on their estimated costs, which means that those doing benefit-cost analyses of these programs are well advised to get the cost estimates right. In this chapter we will first take up some general considerations about costs, then look at some specific issues and examples of cost estimation.

8-1 The Cost Perspective: General Issues

Cost analysis can be done on many levels. At its simplest, it focuses on the costs to a single community or firm of an environmental regulation or of a single environmental project, such as a wastewater treatment plant, incinerator, or beach restoration project. The reason for calling these the simplest is that they usually proceed by costing out a definite engineering specification that has clear boundaries and for which the "rest of the world" can rightly assume to be constant.

At the next level we have costs to an industry, or perhaps to a region, of meeting environmental regulations or of adopting certain technologies. Here it is no longer possible to rely on simple engineering assumptions; we must do things such as predict with reasonable accuracy how groups of polluting firms will respond to changes in laws on emissions or how they will respond to changes in recycling regulations. Problems will arise because not all firms will be alike—some small, some large, some old, some new, and so on—and each of them will usually have multiple possibilities for reacting to regulations.

At a still higher level, our concern may be with the costs to an entire economy of achieving stated environmental goals. Estimating costs at the national level calls for an entirely different approach. Here everything is connected to everything else; when pollution-control regulations are imposed, adjustments will reverberate throughout the economy. Tracing them out requires macroeconomic data and usually fairly sophisticated aggregate models. After taking a look at several general issues in cost estimation, we will deal with the subject at these different levels.

8-2 The With/Without Principle

There is an important principle that has to be kept in mind in this work. In doing a benefit–cost analysis of how firms will respond to new laws, we want to use the **with/without** principle and not the **before/after** principle. We want to estimate the differences in costs that polluters would have with the new law, *compared to what their costs would have been in the absence of the law.* This is not the same as the difference between their new costs and what their costs used to be before the law.

- Before/after are two different periods of time, while with/without are different conditions in the same time period.

Consider the following illustrative numbers that apply to a manufacturing firm for which a pollution-control regulation has been proposed:

Estimated production costs:

Before the regulation:	$100
In the future without the regulation:	$120
In the future with the regulation:	$150

It would be a mistake to conclude that the added costs of the pollution-control regulation will be $50 (future costs with the regulation minus costs before the law). This is an application of the before/after principle and does not accurately reflect the true costs of the law. This is so because in the absence of any new law, production costs are expected to increase (e.g., because of increased fuel costs unrelated to environmental regulations). Thus, the true cost of the regulation is found by applying the with/without principle. Here, these costs are $30 (costs in the future with the regulation minus future costs without the regulation). Of course this makes the whole job of cost estimation harder because what we want to know is not the historical costs of a firm or an industry but what its future costs would be if it were to continue operating without the new environmental laws.

The with/without scenario calls for **baseline analysis,** the estimation of what future cost levels could be expected to be in the absence of the regulation. What makes baseline analysis so difficult is that future technical change (better procedures, better equipment, etc.) will lower costs, and it is normally very hard to predict with accuracy how fast this technical change will take place.

8-3 A Word on Social Costs

In **Chapter 3** we made a distinction between private and social costs. Social costs are all the costs stemming from an action, and are equal to private costs plus external costs. When a power plant produces electricity and air pollution, taking steps to reduce air pollution involves both a reduction in social costs, here the damages from air pollution, and increased production costs as a result of adopting and operating pollution-control technology. In effect, power production without pollution-control requirements amounts to a public subsidy to power producers. Adopting pollution-control policy is a gain in social welfare.

There are many other examples of public subsidies leading to distorted output levels, which could be ameliorated by appropriate public policies.

Consider, for example, **coastal zone flood insurance** in the United States. Commercial insurance for property constructed in the coastal zone would normally have such high premiums, because of the expected losses from floods, that few coastal homeowners could afford it. The U.S. government, and sometimes state governments, will often subsidize coastal zone insurance so that people building in these areas can get insurance at substantially less than commercial rates. The effects of this have been to reduce the private monetary costs of building and maintaining houses in the coastal zone; thus, substantial development has occurred there, with attendant environmental impacts. A reduction in these public subsidies to coastal homeowners not only would work to reduce these environmental impacts but also would lead to an increase in national income. Of course, coastal homeowners would suffer losses.

There are many other examples such as this. **Agricultural subsidies** in many developed countries have provided the incentive to develop intensive, chemical-based production methods, which have resulted both in increased agricultural output and in the nonpoint-source water and air pollution to which these methods lead. Reducing these agricultural subsidies would increase national income and reduce the environmental impacts, though of course some farmers would be worse off.

8-4 The Distribution of Costs

The overall social costs of environmental regulations are important in assessing their cost-effectiveness. Beyond this, however, a major factor behind many policy controversies is how these total costs are **distributed** among different groups in society. Environmental regulations initially may lead to increased production costs in the industry to which the regulation applies, as firms undertake the pollution-control steps required by the regulations. But changes will not be confined to this one industry. As firms alter production technology, input mixes, and other aspects of their operations, their **prices** are likely to change, for both outputs and inputs. So some, or perhaps all, of the consequences of the regulation will be shifted to consumers and input-supplying firms. Employees of the regulated firms will be impacted when production rates increase or decrease in the affected industries. Very often there will be important regional differences in these impacts because industries are more concentrated in certain regions than in others. It is important, then, to be concerned not only with total costs, but also with how these costs are distributed.

8-5 Concepts of Cost

Opportunity Costs

In economics the most fundamental concept of costs is **opportunity costs.** The opportunity cost of using resources[1] in a certain way is the highest value these resources would have produced had they not been used in the manner under consideration. If resources are used to produce cars, they can't be used to produce something else. If resources are used

---

1. Remember that *resources* is a word that can have two meanings: It can be a short way of saying *natural resources* or a general reference analogous to the word *inputs*. Here we are using it in the second sense.

to enforce air-pollution regulations, they can't be used to implement land-use regulations. It is the forgone values of these alternative uses that constitute the opportunity costs of pursuing a particular course of action.

Costs are incurred by all types of firms, industries, agencies, and other groups. From the perspective of a private firm, the opportunity cost of producing a good or service is what it could have produced if it had chosen a different output. We must differentiate **private costs** from **social opportunity costs.** The latter represent the costs to society of using resources in a particular way, meaning all costs, no matter to whom they accrue. We discussed in **Chapter 4** how social costs include private costs and **external costs,** in the form of pollution damage costs incurred by third parties, whenever they exist.

Sometimes items that a private group might consider a cost (e.g., a tax) are not a cost from the standpoint of society. Sometimes items that particular decision makers do not consider as costs really do have social costs. Suppose a community is contemplating building a bicycle path to relieve congestion and air pollution downtown. Its primary concern is what the town will have to pay to build the path. Suppose it will take $1 million to build it, but 50 percent of this will come from the state or federal government. From the town's perspective, the cost of the bike path will be a half million dollars, but from the standpoint of society the full opportunity costs of the path are $1 million.

When most people think of cost they usually think of money expenditure. Often the monetary cost of something is a good measure of its opportunity costs, but frequently it is not. Suppose the bike path is going to be put on an old railroad right-of-way that has absolutely no alternative use, and suppose the town must pay the railroad $100,000 for this right-of-way. This money is definitely an expenditure the town must make, but it is not truly a part of the opportunity costs of building the path because there is no other use for the old right-of-way.

We must also distinguish between opportunity costs and **transfer payments.** The latter are monetary amounts that flow from one person or group to another without affecting actual resource commitments or true opportunity costs. In **Chapter 12** we discuss pollution taxes (sometimes call "charges"). This is where polluters are charged for whatever quantities of emissions they produce. In evaluating the social costs of this type of program, we would include any real costs that polluters incur to reduce their emissions. But the monetary charges they pay to the administering government agency are actually transfer payments going from one group (the polluting firms) to another (the beneficiaries of the tax payments).

Environmental Costs

It may seem paradoxical to think that environmental protection-control programs might have environmental costs, but this is in fact the case. Most specific emissions-reduction programs are media based; that is, they are aimed at reducing emissions into one particular environmental medium such as air or water or land. So when emissions into one medium are reduced, they may increase emissions into another. Reducing untreated domestic waste outflow into rivers or coastal oceans leaves quantities of solid waste that must then be disposed of, perhaps through land spreading or incineration or private homeowner septic systems. Reducing airborne sulfur dioxide (SO_2) emissions from power plants by stack-gas scrubbing also leaves a highly concentrated sludge that must be disposed of in some way. Incinerating domestic solid waste creates airborne emissions.

Media switches are not the only source of environmental impacts stemming from environmental improvement programs. There can be direct effects, for example, sediment runoff from construction sites for new treatment plants or sewer lines. There can also be unforeseen impacts when firms or consumers adjust to new programs. Gasoline producers eliminated lead in their product, but because consumers still insisted on high-powered performance they added other compounds, which ended up having environmental impacts in their own right. The adoption of electric vehicles (EVs) will reduce CO_2 emissions yet will increase demand for mining rare earth minerals. With the beginning of community programs to charge consumers for solid waste disposal, some have been faced with substantial increases in "midnight dumping," that is, illegal dumping along the sides of roads or in remote areas.

Some of the potential environmental impacts from these public projects or programs can be **mitigated;** that is, steps can be taken to reduce or avoid them. More enforcement resources can help control illegal dumping, extra steps can be taken to reduce construction-site impacts, special techniques may be available to reduce incinerator residuals, and so on. These mitigation costs must be included as part of the total costs of any project or program. Beyond this, any remaining environmental costs must be set against the overall reduction in environmental damages to which the program is primarily aimed.

Enforcement Costs

Environmental regulations are not self-enforcing. Resources must be devoted to monitoring the behavior of firms, agencies, and individuals subject to the regulations and to sanctioning violators. Public environmental facilities, such as wastewater treatment plants and incinerators, must be monitored to be sure they are being operated correctly.

Many environmental laws are enforced by agencies whose enforcement budgets are not strictly tailored to the enforcement responsibilities they are given. Thus, budgets can be stable, or even declining, at the same time that new environmental laws are passed. Enforcing the new laws may require shifting agency resources away from the enforcement of other laws. In this case the opportunity costs of new enforcement must include the lower levels of compliance in areas that now are subject to less enforcement.

8-6 Costs of Single Facilities

Perhaps the easiest type of cost analysis to visualize is that for a single, engineered project. There are many types of environmental quality programs that involve publicly supported construction of physical facilities (although the analysis would be the same whatever the ownership), such as public wastewater treatment plants, of which hundreds of millions of dollars' worth have been upgraded over the last few decades. Other examples include flood control projects, solid-waste handling facilities, combustion with energy recovery systems, beach-restoration projects, public parks, wildlife refuges, and so on.

Facility-type projects such as these are individualized and substantially unique, although of course they have similar objectives and use technology that is similar to that used for many other projects. To estimate their costs, primary reliance is placed on engineering and technical specifications, developed largely through experience with similar types of facilities. The data of **Table 8.1** show costs for a representative 200 megawatt land-based wind turbine power plant. These are based on survey and engineering data obtained by the National Renewable Energy Laboratory, a unit within the U.S. Department of Energy. Naturally these types of costs will vary depending on the location and topography of the plant site, as well as other factors. The rated capacity of the plant would be 200 megawatts, but how much power it actually produces during a year would of course depend on wind velocity and duration.

TABLE 8.1   Typical Costs of a 105-Turbine, 200 Megawatt Wind Energy Plant

	Total ($1,000)	Annual ($1,000)
Capital Costs		
Site preparation	10,500	
Turbines	238,000	
Assembly	21,000	
Electrical infrastructure	31,000	
Finance	10,500	
Contingency	21,000	
Other	18,000	
Decommissioning	(not estimated)	
Total	350,000	28,000*
Annual Costs		
Operations		2,800
Maintenance		5,600
Land lease		1,600
Total		10,000
Environmental Costs	(not estimated)	
Capital costs per installed kw $1,750		

*Based on an interest rate of 5 percent and a life of 20 years.

Source: C. Mone, A. Smith, B. Maples, and M. Hand, *Cost of Wind Energy Review*, National Renewable Energy Laboratory, Technical Report NREL/TP-5000-63267, 2015.

The table shows capital costs, the up-front costs of procuring and installing the turbines, along with the costs of connecting them to the grid. These are shown in total, and in annualized form. The latter are the capital costs allocated to one year's operation and depend on assumptions about the discount rate and years of life. The annual operation and maintenance costs are also shown.

In **Table 8.1**, estimated environmental costs have not been included. Costs of this type that have been identified in other studies include:

- Costs of wildlife disruption, especially birds
- Noise pollution
- Degradation of scenic values

These costs will clearly vary greatly from one site to another, and will be difficult to measure with convincing accuracy, especially as they are not directly observable in market transactions. We will discuss possible estimation methods in the next chapter.

With the exception of unmitigated environmental costs, these cost items are all expenditure figures, and only close inspection can tell if they represent true social opportunity costs. Suppose, for example, that in the construction phase numerous local unemployed people are hired. Although the construction costs include their wages, their opportunity costs would be zero because society had to give up nothing when they went to work on the plant. It might be that the land on which the plant is to be placed is town land that is to be donated. In this case, there will be no specific cost entry for land, but there will be an opportunity cost related to the value the land could have had in its next best use, such as a location for a fire station. Suppose that the construction firm is able to get subsidized loans from local banks (i.e., borrow money at lower-than-market rates). Then the true opportunity costs of construction will be higher than the monetary costs indicated. This also goes for any operating costs that could potentially qualify for renewable energy subsidies. There are no specific rules for making these adjustments; only a knowledge of the specific situations can reveal when it is important enough to make them and where sufficient data are available to do the job.

8-7 Costs of a Local Regulation

Environmental regulations are frequently enacted at the local level and have an impact on local people and firms. In fact, in the political economy of pollution control, it is often the fear of these local impacts that deters communities from enacting the regulations. Fears of lost payrolls and the secondary losses to other firms from shrinking local markets loom large at the local level; from a national perspective the opportunity costs are less severe.

Suppose in a particular small town there is a large apple orchard that provides substantial local employment. Suppose further that presently the orchard managers use relatively large applications of chemicals to control apple pests and diseases, and that the chemical runoff from this activity threatens local water supplies. Assume the community enacts an ordinance requiring the orchard to practice **integrated pest management** (IPM), a lower level of chemical use coupled with other means to compensate for this reduction. Assume further, for purposes of illustration, that the IPM practices increase the costs of raising apples in this orchard.[2] What are the social costs of this regulation?

If the orchard raises and sells the same number of apples it previously did, the true social opportunity costs of the regulation are the increased production costs. If local consumers are willing to pay somewhat higher prices for locally grown apples, some of this cost gets passed on to these consumers. Suppose, however, that competitive conditions make it impossible for the orchard to sell its apples for any higher price than pertained before. In this case, the higher production costs must be reflected in lower incomes of the apple orchard owners themselves, or perhaps of the orchard workers, if they will accept lower wages.

---

2. In fact, various authorities and scientific studies suggest that some IPM practices can actually lower costs relative to chemical-intensive growing techniques.

Suppose the orchard was just breaking even before the local IPM ordinance, and that the statute leads to such cost increases that production is substantially curtailed; in fact, assume for purposes of argument that the orchard goes out of business. Clearly there will be local costs: lost payrolls of orchard workers, lost income to the local orchard owners, lost income to local merchants because their markets shrink. But these lost incomes are not likely to be social opportunity costs in their entirety, unless the workers become permanently unemployed. Assuming other employment is available and they transfer to other job opportunities, their new incomes will offset, at least partly, the lost incomes they were earning previously. There may be certain valid opportunity costs in the form of adjustment costs, as workers and owners have to move to new places of employment.

What about the value of the apples no longer produced in this orchard? If we assume that there are many other orchards in neighboring towns and other regions to take up the slack with essentially no cost increases, then this lost production is offset by others, consumer prices are stable, and the social opportunity costs of this marginal rearrangement of apple production are basically nil. However, without other operating orchards nearby, consumers, too, will suffer an opportunity cost.

To summarize, when we are dealing with a single local ordinance affecting one firm and the economy is at or near full employment, ensuing resource adjustments ensure that social opportunity costs are small, limited to the costs of actually carrying out the adjustments. From the standpoint of the affected community, of course, costs will seem high, because of lost local incomes brought about by the increased apple production costs.

8-8 Costs of Regulating an Industry

These conclusions do not follow when we impose an environmental regulation on an entire industry. Higher production costs for the industry are true social opportunity costs because they require added resources that could have been used elsewhere. But in dealing with whole industries, we cannot make the assumption, as we did with the one apple orchard, that its production could easily be picked up by the others.

Consider first the standard approach to estimating increased industry production costs, which is to measure the **added expenditures** that an industry would have to make to come into compliance with an environmental regulation. Cost estimation in this case requires the analyst to predict how polluters will respond to environmental regulations and then to estimate the costs of this response. If the regulation is very specific, requiring, for example, that manufacturing firms install a certain piece of pollution-control equipment or that farmers adopt certain cultivation practices to avoid soil runoff, the cost estimation may be fairly straightforward. But if the regulation leaves the polluters considerable latitude in making their response, it may be hard to predict exactly what they will do, and therefore what their costs will be.

Suppose, for example, several dairy farms are required to reduce their manure emissions by some percentage, and that we (a public agency) wish to estimate the impact of this on the production costs of the firms in the industry. In effect, we want to estimate the aggregate marginal abatement cost function for this group of firms. To do this with reasonable accuracy requires enough knowledge about the dairy business to be able to predict how the firms will respond, what treatment techniques they will use, how they might change their internal production processes, and so on. Or suppose we wanted to estimate the costs among electro-plating firms of a ban on a certain type of solvent. In this case, the analyst would want to identify the alternatives that plant operators had available to replace this chemical, what impacts this would have on productivity, how much additional labor and other inputs they would use, and so on.

Sources of Cost Data

Where does one get the cost data necessary to construct these representative firms? Many of the basic data are generated through **cost surveys** of existing firms. In effect, questionnaires are sent to these firms asking them to supply information on number of employees, processes used, costs of energy and materials, and so on. With a sufficiently detailed questionnaire and a reasonably high response rate by firms, researchers hope to get a good idea of basic cost conditions in the industry and how they might be affected by environmental regulations.

One problem with cost surveys is that they are usually better at getting information on past cost data than on future costs under new regulations. Firms can probably report past cost data with more reliability than they can estimate future costs of meeting environmental constraints. Historical data may not be a good guide to the future, especially because environmental regulations almost by definition confront firms with novel situations. In these cases, it is common to supplement survey data with technical engineering data that can be better adapted to costing out the new techniques and procedures that firms may adopt.

The "representative firm" approach, although dictated by the large number of firms in an industry, has its own problems, especially when those firms are substantially heterogeneous among themselves. In following this procedure, for example, the EPA runs into the problem of whether costs of the real plants in the industry, each of which is to some degree unique, can be accurately represented by a composite cost estimate. In this case *accurately* means close enough that individual firms will not be inclined to take the agency to court on grounds that their own unique cost situations are misrepresented by the figures for the "representative" firm. Many court battles have been fought over this issue.

Because the regulated firms themselves are the source of much cost data used to develop the regulations, there is clearly a question of whether these firms will supply accurate data. By overstating the costs of reaching certain reductions in emissions, firms may hope to convince agencies to promulgate weaker regulations than they would if the agencies had an accurate idea of costs.

It is a very common sight in public hearings on establishing emission-control regulations to see firms making vigorous claims that the regulations will be unduly costly for them to meet. There is evidence that many of these claims have been exaggerated in the past. This issue will come up numerous times when we examine the incentives surrounding different types of environmental policies. In effect, regulated firms have private information about their costs that regulating agencies often don't have.

Actual Versus Minimum Pollution-Control Costs

There is an important question of whether costs are the *least* costs necessary to achieve an emission reduction sought in the law. This is an important point because, as we saw in **Chapter 5,** the efficient level of emissions or ambient quality is defined by the trade-off of emission abatement costs and environmental damages. If abatement costs used to define the efficient level are higher than they need to be, the point so defined will be only a **pseudo-efficient** outcome.

When there is a single facility involved, we must rely on engineering judgment to ensure that the technical proposal represents the least costly way of achieving the objectives. When what is involved is an entire industry, both technical and economic factors come into play. As discussed earlier, in order for the overall costs of a given emission reduction to be achieved at minimum cost, the equimarginal principle has to be fulfilled.

Frequently, environmental regulations work against this by dictating that different sources adopt essentially the same levels of emission reductions or install the same general types of pollution-control technology. Although simple, usually this may lead to inefficiencies for each firm within an industry and higher aggregate costs for the entire industry. As will be seen in later chapters, many environmental laws are based on administratively specified operating decisions that firms are required to make. These decisions may not lead, or allow, firms to achieve emission abatement at least cost.

There is no easy way out of this dilemma. If one is called on to do a benefit–cost analysis of a particular environmental regulation, one presumably is committed to evaluating the regulation as given. In cases such as this it would no doubt be good policy for the analyst to point out that there are less costly ways of achieving the benefits.

The Effect of Output Adjustments on Costs

The increase in abatement expenditures may not be an accurate measure of opportunity costs when an entire industry is involved. This is because **market adjustments** are likely to alter the role and performance of the industry in the wider economy. For example, when the costs of a competitive industry increase, the price of its output increases, normally causing a reduction in quantity demanded. This is pictured in **Figure 8.1,** which shows supply and demand curves for two industries. For convenience, the supply curves have been drawn horizontally, representing marginal production costs that do not vary with output. Consider first panel (a). The initial supply function is C_1, so the initial quantity produced is q_1. The pollution-control law causes production costs to rise, represented by a shift upward in supply from curve C_1 to C_2. Suppose we calculate the increased cost of producing the initial rate of output. This would be an amount equal to the area $(a + b + c)$. In panel (b) the comparable cost is $(d + e + f)$. This approach to measuring costs, however, will overstate the true cost increase because when costs and prices go up, quantity demanded and output will decline.

How much output declines is a matter of the steepness of the demand curve or the sensitivity of consumers to the change in price from p_1 to p_2. In panel (a), output declines only from q_1 to q_2, but in panel (b), with the flatter demand curve, output will decline from r_1 to r_2, a much larger amount. The correct measure of the cost to society is $(a + b)$ in panel (a) and $(d + e)$ in panel (b). Note that the original approach to cost estimation, calculating the increased cost of current output, is a much better approximation to the true burden on society in panel (a) than in panel (b). This is because the output adjustment is much larger in the latter. The lesson here is that if increased expenditures are to be taken as true opportunity costs, they must be calculated taking into account price and output adjustments that occur in the industries affected by the environmental regulations.

FIGURE 8.1 Output Adjustments in Industries Subject to Pollution-Control Regulations

Figure 8.1 can also illustrate something about the distribution of pollution-control costs. Firms in the affected industries bear these costs in the beginning, but the final burden depends on how the cost increase is passed forward to consumers or backward to workers and stockholders. Note that in both panels (a) and (b), the market prices of the goods increased by the amount of the cost increase, but the quantity response is quite different. In panel (a) consumers continue buying close to what they did before; little adjustment is called for in terms of output shrinkage in the industry. Thus, workers and shareholders in this industry will be little affected, in relative terms. In panel (b) the same price increase leads to a large drop in output. Consumers have good substitutes to which they can switch when the price of this output goes up; in effect, they can escape from the full burden of the price increase. However, the industry-level adjustment is large. Resources, particularly workers, will have to flow out of the regulated industry and try to find employment elsewhere. If they can, the costs may be only temporary adjustment costs; if not, the costs will be much longer run.

Long-Run Technical Change and Pollution-Control Costs

In the short run, firms must make whatever adjustments they can within the constraints of available technology and operating procedures. In the long run, however, costs can change because these technologies and procedures can be altered. Scientific and engineering research and development (R&D) yield new and better (less costly) ways of controlling emissions. Some are straightforward, such as a new way of handling and treating residuals; some are more profound, such as a change in the basic technology of production so that fewer residuals are produced in the first place. When firms are subject to emission reduction requirements, they have an incentive to engage in R&D to find better emissions abatement technology. There is some evidence that in reality this may draw resources away from output-increasing R&D efforts, thereby affecting the firm's ability to reduce costs in the long run. There is also evidence that environmental regulations have led to unanticipated, marketable products or processes stemming from their research. After investing in pollution-control R&D, some firms have reduced their long-run production costs. In cases such as this, the short-run cost increases arising from pollution-control regulations are not accurate estimates of the long-run opportunity costs of these regulations.

Critical to the success of any effort to innovate in pollution-control technology is the economic health of the **envirotech industry.** This is the industry consisting of firms producing goods and services that are used by other firms to reduce their emissions and environmental impacts, such as firms that make catalytic converters or landfill linings or solar panels. It also contains firms that engage in environmental cleanup, such as the cleanup of past hazardous-waste dump sites or asbestos removal. A healthy envirotech industry is one that produces a brisk supply of new pollution-control technology and practices. The growth of this industry will influence how fast marginal abatement costs come down in the future (see **Exhibit 8.1**).

EXHIBIT 8.1 The Environmental Industry

The U.S. environmental industry in 2017 had total revenues of over $388 billion. More than half of the industry actually comprises services, whereas the rest are technology and equipment based. Employment has grown. The early growth of the industry was based on cleaning up the sins of the past, or controlling emissions from outdated facilities. Growth in the future will depend more on developments in pollution prevention, renewable energy, and climate change adaptation.

(Continued)

EXHIBIT 8.1 *(Continued)*

Environmental Industry—Revenues and Employment, by Industry Segment: 2017

[59.0 represents $59,000,000,000. Covers approximately 59,000 private and public companies engaged in environmental activities.]

Industry Segment	Revenue (Billion $) 2017
Industry total	388.0
Analytical services[1]	1.9
Wastewater treatment works[2]	55.9
Solid-waste management[3]	57.9
Hazardous-waste management[4]	10.8
Remediation/industrial services	14.2
Consulting and engineering	28.9
Water equipment and chemicals	30.5
Instrument manufacturing	6.3
Air-pollution control equipment[5]	16.0
Waste-management equipment[6]	12.2
Process and prevention technology	2.1
Water utilities[7]	54.6
Resource recovery[8]	29.1

[1] Covers environmental laboratory testing and services.

[2] Mostly revenues collected by municipal entities.

[3] Covers such activities as collection, transportation, transfer stations, disposal, landfill ownership, and management for solid waste.

[4] Transportation and disposal of hazardous, medical, and nuclear waste.

[5] Includes stationary and mobile sources.

[6] Includes vehicles, containers, liners, processing, and remediation equipment.

[7] Revenues generated from the sale of water.

[8] Revenues generated from the sale of recovered metals, paper, plastic, and so on.

Source: Department of Commerce, International Trade Administration, 2017, www.trade.gov/topmarkets/pdf/Environmental_Technologies_Executive_Summary.pdf.

8-9 Costs of National Regulation

We finally come to the most aggregate level for which cost studies are normally pursued, the level of the **national economy**. The usual question is what is the macroeconomic cost burden of the environmental regulations a country imposes, or might be planning to impose, in a given period of time. Sometimes interest centers on the totality of the regulations put in place. Sometimes the focus is on specific regulations that will nevertheless have a broad impact on a national economy, such as a program of carbon emissions reduction.

There are basically two ways of approaching this question:

- **bottom up**–looks at expenditures made throughout the economy by individual firms for pollution-control purposes, or
- **top down**–looks at whether, and how much, pollution-control programs may change national economic performance.

Firms in the economy are subject to a number of pollution-control regulations. In response, they install and operate a wide variety of technological means to reduce emissions. These expenditures detract from other outputs (assuming full employment) because of the input diversion.

It is sometimes asserted that environmental regulations affect smaller firms disproportionately more than large firms. Some research suggests this is not the case, but rather that large firms spend more on pollution control than do small firms.[3] In addition, expenditures for plant, equipment, labor, and other inputs for reducing emissions can affect other economic sectors not directly covered by environmental regulations, and macroeconomic interactions of this type need to be accounted for to get the complete picture. An industry subject to environmental controls, and trying to lower its emissions, puts increasing demand on the pollution-control industry, which expands output and puts increasing demands on other sectors, for example, the construction sector, which respond by increasing output.

The long-run economic change–growth or decline–is a matter of the accumulation of capital: human capital and inanimate capital. It also depends on technical change, getting larger amounts of output from a given quantity of inputs. So an important question is how environmental laws will affect the accumulation of capital and the rate of technical innovation. Diverting inputs from conventional sectors to pollution-control activities may lower the rate of capital accumulation in those conventional sectors. This may be expected to reduce the rate of growth of productivity (output per unit of input) in the production of conventional output and thus slow overall growth rates. The impacts on the rate of technical innovation in the economy are perhaps more ambiguous, as mentioned previously. If attempts to innovate in pollution control reduce the efforts to do so in other sectors, the impact on future growth could be negative; however, efforts to reduce emissions might have a positive impact on the overall rate of technical innovation, which would have a positive impact. More research is needed on this question. This trade-off reflects the production possibilities frontiers discussed in **Chapter 2**.

A top-down analysis uses **macroeconomic modeling.** The basic question is whether, and how much, pollution-control expenditures result in a lowering of national economic performance; or, as the case regarding global warming, result in a future generational increase in national welfare. To explore this, mathematical models are constructed using the various macroeconomic variables of interest, such as total output, perhaps broken down into

---

3. Randy Becker, Carl Pasurka Jr., and Ronald J. Shadbegian, *Do Environmental Regulations Disproportionately Affect Small Businesses? Evidence form the Pollution Abatement Costs and Expenditure Survey*, Center for Economic Studies, U.S. Census Bureau, CES12-25R, 2013.

several economic subsectors: employment, capital investment, prices, pollution-control costs, and so on. The models are first run using historical data, which show how various underlying factors have contributed to the overall rate of growth in an economy. Then they are rerun under the assumption that the pollution-control expenditures were in fact not made. This generates new results in terms of aggregate output growth, employment, and so on, which can be compared with the first run including pollution control. The differences are attributed to the pollution-control expenditures.

8-10 Future Costs and Technological Change

Many of the big controversies in environmental policy involve differences of opinion about what future pollution-control costs are likely to be, especially the future cost consequences of today's decisions. A good example of this is the cost of CO_2 emission reduction to reduce the effects of global warming. In the United States, much of the stated opposition to undertaking vigorous reductions in CO_2 stems from a concern that the future costs of doing so will be too high. Others say that the costs need not be high if the most effective policy approaches are used.

If the time horizon is short, future costs will depend on the adoption by polluters of currently available technologies. These technologies may be reasonably well known (e.g., heat pumps for cooling and heating homes), in which case it will not be too hard to estimate what these new pollution-control costs will be. Much of the earlier discussion in this chapter is based on this perspective.

But when the relevant time horizon is longer, say 10 or 20 years or more (as with climate change), it is no longer easy to know what technological changes will occur, when they will be available for widespread adoption, and what impact they will have on pollution-control costs. Much discussion and research have been directed at the large-scale changeover to an electric fuel system in cars and trucks, for example. But it is not easy to see the rate at which that might arrive and what its impacts may be, like battery development and deployment. In the long run, in other words, estimating future costs is likely to be very difficult.

One of the important aspects of this is how research, development, and adoption of new pollution-control technologies respond to environmental policies and regulations.

Summary

In this chapter we reviewed some of the ways that costs are estimated in benefit–cost studies. We began with a discussion of the fundamental concept of opportunity costs, differentiating this from the notion of cost as expenditure. We then looked at cost estimation as it applies to different levels of economic activity. The first was a cost analysis of a single facility, as represented by the estimated costs of a wind turbine facility. We then considered the costs of an environmental regulation undertaken by a single community, distinguishing between costs to the community and opportunity costs to the whole society.

We then shifted focus to cost estimation for an entire industry, giving special attention to the difference between short-run and long-run costs and the problem of achieving minimum costs. We finally expanded our perspective to the national economy as a whole, where cost means the loss in value of marketed output resulting from environmental regulations. All of these long-run aspects are affected by technological change.

Questions for Further Discussion

1. Over the last two years, emission abatement costs in industry X have been about $1 million per year. A new regulation will lead to abatement costs of $1.8 million per year. Does this mean that the regulation will cause increased abatement costs of $800,000 per year? Explain.

2. In order to protect the quality of its nearby water resources, a community places a restriction on any housing development closer than 100 feet to a wetland. How might you estimate the social costs of this regulation?

3. Consider a small home project or a simple activity to help the climate that you, and maybe some friends, could do. Itemize and estimate the costs, including opportunity costs, of the project or activity if done by one person. Adjust your estimates if it expands to 10 people doing the activity or project. Then adjust your estimates if the activity or project expands for 5 years into the future. Discuss.

4. A tax on gasoline is proposed in order to raise money for the pollution-control activities of several public agencies. The tax will be 10¢ per gallon, and last year 10.3 million gallons of gasoline were used by motorists (this is strictly an illustrative number). Does this mean that we can anticipate $1,030,000 in revenues from this tax? Explain and use a graph to answer this question.

5. Most industries are composed of firms that, though perhaps producing roughly the same thing, are very different; some are large and some small; some are profitable and others not; some are located in one part of the country and some in others; some perhaps have undertaken a certain amount of voluntary emissions reductions and some have not. How does this complicate the job of estimating the total social costs of pollution-control regulations?

For additional resources pertaining to the material in this chapter, see the list in **Appendix B**.

Section 4
Environmental Policy Analysis

The public policy problem arises when there is a discrepancy between the actual level of environmental quality and the preferred level. How can this state of affairs be changed? Something has to be done to change the way people behave on both the production and consumption sides of the system. The available public policy approaches for doing this are as follows:

Decentralized policies

    Liability laws

    Property rights

    Voluntary action

Centralized policies

    Command-and-control

    Standards

Market-based policies

    Taxes and subsidies

    Transferable discharge permits (Cap-and-trade)

    Offset trading

In the chapters of this section we discuss each of these policy approaches, but before that we must address briefly a prior question: What criteria are appropriate to evaluate alternative policies and identify the one best suited to any particular environmental problem? We consider a number of these criteria in the next chapter, then analyze in depth the specific policy approaches just listed.

Chapter 9
Criteria for Evaluating Environmental Policies

There are many different types of environmental policies. Each type anticipates that administrators and polluters will respond in particular ways. Each type has specific characteristics that make it more likely to succeed in some circumstances and not in others. When we evaluate the effectiveness and appropriateness of a policy for addressing a given problem in environmental pollution control, it is important to have clearly in mind a set of **policy evaluation criteria**.[1] The criteria to be used in later chapters to discuss specific environmental policies are the following:

- Efficiency
- Cost-effectiveness
- Equity (Fairness)
- Enforceability
- Flexibility
- Incentives for technological innovations
- Moral considerations

9-1 Efficiency

A state of affairs is efficient if it is one that produces for society a maximum of net benefits. Note that we have said "society." Efficiency is sometimes misconstrued to mean the maximum of somebody's net income. Although efficiency does not rule that out, it involves substantially more than this; it involves the maximum of net benefits, considering everybody in the society.

Efficiency in the case of pollution control implies a balance between abatement costs and damages. An efficient policy is one that moves us to, or near, the point (either of emissions or of ambient quality) where marginal abatement costs and marginal damages are equal.

One way of thinking about environmental policies is along a continuum from **centralized** to **decentralized**. A centralized policy requires that some controlling administrative agency be responsible for determining what is to be done. To achieve efficiency in a centralized policy, the regulatory agency in charge must have knowledge of the relevant marginal abatement cost and marginal damage functions, then take steps to move the situation to the point where they are equal.

---

1. Another way of describing the content of this chapter is as a discussion of "instrument choices." "Instrument" is a term often used to describe a specific type of action plan in an environmental law or regulation. We will use "instrument" as synonymous with "policy."

A decentralized policy gets results from the interaction of many individual decision makers, each of whom is essentially making his or her own assessment of the situation. In a decentralized approach, the interactions of the individuals involved serve to reveal the relevant information about marginal abatement costs and marginal damages and to adjust the situation toward the point where they are equal.

9-2 Cost-Effectiveness

It is often the case that environmental damages cannot be measured accurately. This sometimes makes it useful to employ **cost-effectiveness** as a primary policy criterion. A policy is effective if:

- it produces the maximum environmental improvement possible for the resources being expended or, equivalently,
- it achieves a given amount of environmental improvement at the least possible cost.

For a policy to be efficient it must be cost-effective, but not necessarily vice versa. A policy might be cost-effective even if it were aimed at the wrong target. Suppose the objective is to clean up New York harbor, regardless of what the benefits are. We would still be interested in finding policies that did the job cost-effectively; however, for a policy to be socially efficient, it must be cost-effective and balance costs with benefits. To be efficient, the harbor-cleaning project must balance marginal benefits with marginal cleanup costs.

The capability of a policy to achieve cost-effective emission reductions (i.e., yield the maximum improvement for the resources spent) is also important for another reason. If programs are not cost-effective, the policymakers and administrators will be making decisions using an aggregate abatement cost function that is higher than it needs to be, leading them to set less restrictive targets in terms of desired amounts of emission reductions. This is shown in **Figure 9.1,** for a case of sulfur dioxide (SO_2) emissions. With a *cost-ineffective* policy, the perceived marginal abatement cost is the higher one, labeled MAC_1; whereas with a cost-effective approach, marginal abatement costs would be MAC_2. Thus, with the MD function as shown, the emissions level a_1 appears to be the efficient level of pollution, whereas with a cost-effective program, the efficient level would be a_2. The real problem with having costs higher than they need to be is that society will be inclined to set its objectives too low in terms of the amount of emission reduction sought.

Efficiency and cost-effectiveness are important because, although preserving environmental resources is critically important, it is only one of the many desirable things that people seek. Advocates are usually convinced that their objectives are automatically worth the cost, but success depends on persuading large numbers of other people that environmental policies are efficiently designed. Thus, the resources devoted to environmental quality improvement ought to be spent in ways that will have the greatest impact. This is especially important in less developed economies, where people have fewer resources to put in environmental programs and can ill-afford policies that are not cost-effective and efficient. Cost-effectiveness may become an important issue in industrialized countries during times of recession or economic stagnation, or when deciding between a program for pollution control or food security, for example.

FIGURE 9.1 Mistaking the Efficient Emissions Level When Abatement Technologies Are Not Cost-Effective

Cost-effectiveness (and efficiency, as cost-effectiveness is part of efficiency) clearly involves pollution-control costs in a major way. But accurate information about pollution-control costs is for the most part **private information** in a market system. Public policymakers typically do not have totally accurate information about the pollution-control costs that firms and industries face in the real world. What we have here is what economists call **asymmetric information;** polluters have better information about the costs of different pollution-control technologies than do public policymakers. As we shall see, different types of pollution-control policies create different levels of incentives for polluters to achieve cost-effective pollution control by making full use of their own private information regarding the costs of alternative pollution-control technologies.

9-3 Equity or Fairness

Fairness, or **equity,** is another important criterion for evaluating environmental policy (or any policy, for that matter). Equity is, first and foremost, a matter of morality and the concerns about how the benefits and costs of environmental improvements ought to be distributed among members of society. Fairness does not necessarily mean equal. Fairness is important from the standpoint of policy effectiveness, because policies may not be supported as enthusiastically in the political arena if they are thought to be inequitable. Having said this, however, it has to be recognized that there is no agreement on how much weight should be put on the two objectives: efficiency and distribution. Consider the following hypothetical example which might relate to the costs and benefits of several alternative approaches to controlling air pollution in a given region.

The first three columns show total costs, total benefits, and net benefits for each program. Suppose Groups X and Y refer to a low-income group and a high-income group, respectively. Programs A and B have the same net benefits, but these are distributed more progressively in B than in A, i.e., Group X (low-income) receives more of the net benefits in Program B than Group Y. We might agree that B is preferable to A because it has the same net benefits and "better" distributional effects.

Program	Total Costs	Total Benefits	Net Benefits	Distribution of Net Benefits Group X	Group Y
A	50	100	50	25	25
B	50	100	50	30	20
C	50	140	90	20	70
D	50	140	90	40	50

Compare Programs B and C. The net benefits of Program C are much higher than in B. Unfortunately, they are not distributed as progressively as those of B; in fact, they are distributed more toward high-income people (70 vs. 20). How should we choose between B and C? Some might argue that B is best, for equity reasons; others might argue for C on overall efficiency grounds.

Now compare Programs B and D. In this case, D has the advantage in overall efficiency (net benefits are 90), although, as in the case of C, more of the net benefits go to high-income people (50 vs. 40). Here we also see that low-income people would be better off in absolute terms, although not relatively, with D than with B. On these grounds, D might be preferred.

Suppose, on the other hand, that Groups X and Y refer to people in two different regions of the country rather than to income. Now we see that there is an issue of **interregional equity.** If we knew, for example, that the Group Y region was where the problem originated that is being addressed by these possible programs, C and D might definitely be regarded as inequitable, because most of the net benefits go to Group Y, the region that caused the problem. For example, an upstream-industrial manufacturing city versus a downstream-coastal community.

Equity considerations also loom large in the making of international environmental policy. As we will discuss later in chapters on global and international environmental problems, countries at different stages of development have different views on how the burdens of international pollution-control programs should be distributed. These views are driven by considerations of what seems fair in the light of the wide economic disparities around the globe.

The Idea of "Social"

We have talked about efficiency, equity, and other criteria somewhat in the abstract. It has to be kept in mind that when we talk about such concepts in "social efficiency," we must have some particular "society" in mind. If we are discussing global issues, the reference is presumably to the entire global society. But most environmental policy discussions and controversies take place at a lower level, especially national units or, increasingly, sub-national regions. In the United States, the individual states are playing a growing role in environmental policy, as major federal initiatives slowed. What is socially efficient from the perspective of a single state may not be from a national viewpoint because a state may not take account of externalities running to other states. When evaluating different environmental regulations and programs, one has to keep in mind the perspective from which this evaluation is done.

Environmental Justice

Equity considerations are prominent in the movement for **environmental justice.** The concern is that racial and ethnic minorities and low-income people are disproportionately exposed to environmental contaminants, both those outside the home such as air and water pollution and those within the home and workplace such as lead and drinking water. In some cases, exposure to low environmental quality correlates with socioeconomic conditions. Another consideration for environmental justice is the involvement of potentially impacted people in the development and implementation of environmental policy in a meaningful political manner, essentially giving people voice in the policy process.

One concern has been largely about exposure to the pollutants coming from hazardous-waste sites. The question is whether hazardous-waste sites are disproportionately located in areas where there are relatively large populations of low-income people and people of color and, if that is so, what to do about it from a policy perspective. For example, ending strip mining of coal in Black Mesa, Arizona, simultaneously stops environmental destruction and eliminates jobs and a tax base for the local Hopi and Navajo Nations. Replacing with living-wage, green industry jobs and income security are part of the overlap of environmental and social justice.[2] We will take up these matters at greater length in **Chapter 16.**

Another concern is the multitudes in poverty living along low-lying seacoasts. With climate change these regions are increasingly susceptible to storm-water pollution along with floods and rising water levels.

9-4 Enforceability

There perhaps is a natural tendency among people to think that enacting a law automatically leads to the rectification of the problem to which it is addressed. Among some in the environmental community, this tendency is depressingly strong. But anybody with even a cursory understanding of public policy knows this is not true. Regulations have to be **enforced.** Enforcement takes time and resources, just like any other activity, and because public budgets are always limited, the requirements of enforcement have to be balanced with those of other public functions.[3] The importance of the issues can be appreciated by looking at reports of Environmental Protection Agency (EPA) enforcement. An example of public transparency concerns about enforcement is shown in **Exhibit 9.1.** Since 2000, EPA personnel has dropped by about 20%, equivalent to approximately 2,500 full-time equivalents; this naturally decreases enforcement even though rules for enforcement remain intact. All of this means that policy enforceability is an important criterion for judging particular policies.

---

2. See Tory Field and Beverly Bell, *Harvesting Justice*, Otherworlds, 2013.
3. It is also clear that enforcement is a political football. Public officials can increase or decrease enforcement activity to match their positions on how stringent environmental regulations ought to be.

EXHIBIT 9.1 The Importance of Enforcement

Public transparency of reported emissions and the enforcement of regulations have increased with the use of electronic records and the expansion of internet access. Private firms and public agencies often report their actions on various websites. This action lends itself to monitoring, for example:

- are records uploaded in a timely manner?
- are records validated?
- are records searchable?

- are remote monitoring sensors working properly and physically checked in the field?

The Pipeline and Hazardous Materials Safety Administration, for example, inspects interstate natural gas and hazardous liquid pipelines, investigates accidents, and enforces laws and regulations. Information about its enforcement activities is posted on its public Enforcement Transparency website. The website, in turn, is monitored for confirming the following specific requirements:

Website Criteria	2022 Findings	Recommendations
• Engage with users	Met	None
• Fully describe the data	Met	None
• Provide free and unrestricted data	Partially met	Provide data that is downloadable
• Provide data in useful formats	Partially met	Update data to be interoperable with other data sets
• Facilitate data discovery for users	Partially met	Enable searching by regulation violated

Source: U.S. Government Accountability Office. *Pipeline Safety: Fully Implementing Key Practices Could Help Improve Transparency of Enforcement Website.* Washington, D.C. 2022. Report GAO-23-105537.

There are two main steps in enforcement:

- **monitoring** refers to measuring the performance of polluters in comparison to whatever requirements are set out in the relevant law.
- **sanctioning** refers to the task of bringing to justice those whom monitoring has shown to be in violation of the law.

The objective of enforcement is to get people to comply with an applicable law. Thus, some amount of monitoring is normally essential. Monitoring polluting behavior is far more complicated than, say, keeping track of the temperature. Nature doesn't really care, and so it won't willfully try to outwit and confound the monitoring process. Polluters, however, can often find ways of frustrating the monitoring process. The more sophisticated and complicated that process, the easier it may be for polluters to find ways of evading it. Great strides have been made in developing monitoring technology, particularly for large sources of airborne and waterborne pollutants.

Sanctioning refers to the task of bringing to justice those whom monitoring has shown to be in violation of the law. This may sound like a simple step; if violators are found, we simply take them to court and levy the penalties specified in the relevant law, but things are much more complicated than this. Court cases take time and energy and resources. With many laws and many more violators, the burden on the legal system of trying to bring all violators to justice may be overwhelming. The data underlying the sanctions can be imperfect, leading to challenges and costly conflicts. To create a demonstration effect it may be desirable for authorities to sanction only a few of the most egregious violations, but this opens up the problem of trying to determine just which violators to single out. Very often authorities try to achieve voluntary compliance and encourage violators to remedy the situation without penalty.

There is a paradox built into the sanctioning process. One might think that the greater the potential sanctions—higher fines, long jail terms for violators, and so on—the more the law would deter violators. But the other side of the coin is that the higher the penalties, the more reluctant courts may be to apply them. The threat to close down violators, or even to levy stiff financial penalties, can in turn threaten the economic livelihoods of large numbers of people. Courts are usually reluctant to throw a large number of people out of work, and so may opt for less drastic penalties than allowed by the law. The sanctioning process can become much more complicated than the simple model implies.

9-5 Flexibility

A valuable characteristic of any policy or instrument is that it be sufficiently flexible to be adapted to changing circumstances. Most environmental regulations are put in place in accordance with what is known about the situation to which they are applied, for example, the known or estimated benefits and costs of the case. When these change, such as new estimates of benefits and/or costs become available, the policies ought to be altered. Flexible policies would allow for technological changes and implementation of research and development (R&D). In the real world of policy institutions and political strength, policies that meet stringent efficiency criteria may be less effective in the long run than policies that may be less efficient but easier to adapt to new circumstances.

It has been argued, for example, that the command-and-control provisions of the Clean Air Act, though somewhat inefficient if looked at in the short run, have been substantially more efficient in the long run.[4] This is because it contains an array of provisions that permit its frequent adjustment and adaptation to new circumstances. A cap-and-trade plan, for example, may be efficient at first, but not over time if the overall cap cannot be readily adjusted as underlying conditions change.

---

4. Dallas Burtraw, *The Institutional Blind Spot in Environmental Economics,* Resources for the Future, Discussion paper 12-41, 2012.

9-6 Incentives for Technological Innovations

In our studies of environmental policy, much of the focus normally gets put on the performance of public officials because they appear to be the source of that policy. What needs to be kept clearly in mind, however, is that it is private parties, firms, and consumers whose decisions actually determine the range and extent of environmental impacts,[5] and the incentives facing these private parties determine how and where these impacts will be reduced. Thus, a critically important criterion that must be used to evaluate any environmental policy is whether that policy provides a strong **incentive** for individuals and groups to find **new, innovative ways of reducing their impacts** on the ambient environment. Does the policy place all the initiative and burden on public agencies, or does it provide incentives for private parties to devote their energies and creativities to finding new ways of reducing environmental impacts?

It is easy to miss the importance of this by concentrating on particular abatement cost and damage functions in the standard analysis. These show the efficient level of emissions with current technology, but over the longer run it is important that we try to shift the functions with new technology. It is especially important to try to shift downward the marginal abatement cost function, to lower the social cost of reductions in emissions, because this will justify higher levels of environmental quality.

Technological change, flowing from programs of R&D, shifts the marginal abatement cost function downward. So do education and training, which allow people to work and solve problems more efficiently. Ultimately we want to know whether, and how much, a particular environmental policy contains incentives for polluters to seek better ways of reducing pollution. The greater these incentives, the better the policy, at least by this one criterion. As we shall see, a major criticism of much of historic environmental policy has been that it does not create strong incentives of this type to find improved solutions.

The development and widespread adoption of new pollution-control technology is a complex socioeconomic process. It involves resources being devoted to invention and development, patent and copyright laws, decisions about adoption by existing and new sources, as well as by firms that supply portions of necessary infrastructure for the new technologies. Inventions, and the ideas giving rise to them, are in the nature of public goods, and we saw earlier that private markets will normally undersupply public goods—which means that the rate of technological change in pollution control may be too slow in the absence of the public policy to promote it.

A major factor here is the incentive effect produced by stringent pollution-control regulations. It is hard to suppose, for example, that society will get enough effort devoted to technical change to reduce the cost of carbon dioxide (CO_2) emission reductions if there is essentially no public policy requiring that these emissions be reduced. In some cases policymakers may utilize **technology-forcing** regulations—that is, regulations that will require polluters to find innovative technology in order to meet pollution-control targets with reasonable cost.

---

5. However, many serious cases of environmental destruction have been caused by public agencies.

A major factor in technological innovation is the status of the **envirotech industry.** As shown in the last chapter,[6] this industry consists of a wide variety of firms that produce new technology and operating procedures for use by polluting firms to help reduce their emissions more cost-effectively. The health and vigor of the envirotech industry, therefore, is of paramount importance for long-run improvements in technology. The economic health of this industry is directly related to the nature and stringency of environmental regulations.

9-7 Materials Balance Issues

Remembering back to **Chapter 2,** we need to remind ourselves of the **materials-balance** aspects of pollution control. Given a certain quantity of residuals, if the flow going into one environmental medium (e.g., the water) is reduced, the flow going into the others (air and/or land) must increase. Thus, one important dimension of a pollution-control policy is how well it addresses these potential **cross-media transfer** problems. The first thing is to be able to recognize cases where important problems of this nature might be encountered. The next thing is to shape the policies so as to reduce their potential impact. This might be done by simply proscribing certain actions or, if enough information is available, by specifying acceptable trade-offs across technologies and environmental media—that is, by allowing only transfers that substantially reduce total damages from a given quantity of residuals. For example, an electric vehicle (EV) has zero tailpipe emissions, but when coal is used to generate the power for the EV, positive net benefits are significantly reduced.

9-8 Moral Considerations

We earlier discussed questions of income distribution and the impacts of different environmental policies on people with different levels of wealth. These are ethical issues on which different people will have varied opinions, but they are important to discuss when deciding on alternative public policies. But moral considerations extend beyond these distributional questions. The innate feelings that people have about what is right and wrong undoubtedly affect the way they look at different environmental policies. These have to be weighed in the balance along with the more technical criteria discussed previously.

Take, for example, the question of choosing between effluent taxes and effluent subsidies. Both are economic-incentive policies, and both might have roughly the same effect in given cases of pollution control. From the standpoint of effectiveness, one might argue that subsidies would be better. Polluters might very well respond quicker and with greater willingness to a subsidy program than to one that is likely to cost them a lot of money. Strictly from the standpoint of getting the environment cleaned up as soon as possible, subsidies might be the most effective; however, this may run counter to the ethical notion that people who are causing a problem ought not to be "rewarded" for stopping, which is how subsidies are sometimes viewed.

Some people would take this idea further, arguing that because we should regard polluting behavior as essentially immoral to begin with, we should adopt policies that tend to recognize it as such. By this criterion, policies that declare outright that certain types of polluting behavior are illegal are to be preferred to policies that do not. Another idea grounded in

---

6. See Exhibit 8.1.

morality is that those who cause a problem ought to bear the major burden of alleviating it. We see this, for example, in discussions of global environmental issues. The industrial nations, especially the most economically developed among them, are largely responsible for the atmospheric buildup of CO_2 and climate change. Many people take the view that these countries ought to bear the major burden in rectifying the situation.

9-9 Government Failure

In **Chapter 4,** we discussed the idea of market failure, a situation where, because of externalities of one type or another, unregulated markets may not yield efficient and equitable results. This is especially true in the case of pollution because of the public-good nature of environmental quality. This leads, in turn, to the conclusion that public policy is called for to rectify the situation.

It is important to recognize another type of failure, however, that makes the outcome of public policy somewhat problematic. This is called **government failure,** which refers to systematic tendencies and incentives within legislatures and regulating agencies that work against the attainment of efficient and equitable public policy.

If public action were always undertaken by reasonable people seeking rationally to advance the public interest, we could perhaps be confident that these public policies were consistently making the pollution problem better. But this unfortunately doesn't fit reality. The policy process is a political phenomenon as well as a problem-solving one. As such, policy outcomes are also affected by the vagaries of the political struggle, by the change of elected officials with time-prescribed elections, by the continuous attempts to accumulate and wield influence, and by simple grandstanding and political theatrics. What comes out of this process may not resemble anything like informed, rational public policy that advances the welfare of society. This is not a justification for doing nothing; rather, it is a reason for making sure that environmental policies and regulations have clearly stated objectives, well-designed means, and transparent ways of assessing results.

Summary

The purpose of this chapter is to review a number of criteria that may be useful in evaluating environmental policies in different circumstances. These criteria are

- Efficiency
- Cost-effectiveness
- Equity (Fairness)
- Enforceability
- Flexibility
- Incentives for technological innovations
- Moral considerations
- Government failure

With these criteria at hand, it is now time to launch into discussions of the various types of environmental policies. We will begin with several traditional decentralized approaches, following this with a look at the use of standards, a centralized approach that has been the most frequently used historically. Finally, we will look at incentive-based policies.

Questions for Further Discussion

1. "Efficiency implies cost-effectiveness, but cost-effectiveness does not imply efficiency." Explain this statement.
2. Investigate the recycling policy in the city where you live. How might you interpret the policy using the concepts or policy criteria presented in this chapter?
3. Do you think that the impacts of the program to control automobile pollution are progressively or regressively distributed by income levels? How about the program to ensure the quality of public water supply systems?
4. Is there ever a justification for adopting an environmental regulation that cannot be, or will not be, enforced?
5. Catalytic converters are required on all new cars to reduce tailpipe emissions. Explain how this technology could have a beneficial impact in the short run but a less beneficial impact in the long run.
6. "The costs of achieving emission reductions in the future will depend greatly on the types of policies used to reduce emissions today." Explain.
7. Identify a specific pollution problem and the specific environmental media (see **Figure 2.3** for a review) it affects. Create a possible policy to reduce that pollution, and explain how your policy would affect cross-media transfer into another environmental media.
8. Explain how market failure differs from government failure. Give an example of each.

For additional resources pertaining to the material in this chapter, see the list in **Appendix B.**

Chapter 10
Decentralized Policies: Liability Laws, Property Rights, Voluntary Action

By **"decentralized"** policies we mean policies that essentially allow the individuals involved in a case of environmental pollution to work it out themselves. Think back to the previous example of water quality in a lake. Suppose there are several industrial plants around the lake. One is a brewery, and the water of the lake is an important input in its operation. The other is a food processing plant that uses the lake for waste disposal. How is it possible to balance the pollution damage suffered by the first firm with the abatement costs of the second? A decentralized approach to finding the efficient level of ambient water quality in the lake is simply to let the two plants seek solutions between themselves. They might do this either through informal negotiations or through more formal interaction in a local court of law. Decentralized approaches can have several real advantages over other types of public policy:

- Because the parties involved are the ones producing and suffering the environmental externalities, they have strong incentives to seek solutions to the environmental problems.
- The people involved may be the ones with the best knowledge of damages and abatement costs; therefore, they may be best able to find the right balance among them, that is, to find efficient solutions.

10-1 Liability Laws

Almost everybody has an intuitive notion of **liability** and **compensation.** To be liable for some behavior is to be held responsible for whatever untoward consequences result from that behavior. Compensation requires that those causing the damage compensate those damaged in amounts appropriate to the extent of the injury.

One approach to environmental issues, therefore, is to rely on liability laws. This would work simply by making polluters liable for the damages they cause. The purpose of this is not simply to compensate people after they have been injured, although that is important. The real purpose is to get would-be polluters to make careful decisions. Knowing that they will be held liable for environmental damages in effect **internalizes** what would otherwise be ignored **external effects.**

The Principle

Consider **Figure 10.1**. It's the familiar model of environmental pollution showing marginal abatement costs and marginal damages, both related to the rate at which some production residual is emitted.[1] Suppose that the actual emission rate is initially at e_1, substantially above the efficient rate e^*. Suppose also that there is a new law requiring polluters to compensate those damaged in an amount equal to the damages caused. The effect of the law is to internalize the environmental damages that were external before the law. The damages now become costs that polluters will have to pay and therefore will want to take into account when deciding on their emission rate. At e_1, the total damages, which equal the amount of the compensation payment, would be a monetary amount equal to the area $(b + c + d)$.

FIGURE 10.1 Policy Options: Liability and Property Rights Approaches

This polluter could reduce its compensation payments by reducing emissions. As it does that, of course, its marginal abatement costs increase. But as long as the marginal abatement costs are less than marginal damages, it would have an incentive to move to the left—that is, to reduce its rate of emissions. In theory, then, a liability system could automatically lead this polluter to emission level e^*. We say "automatically" because it would not require any centralized control authorities to intervene and mandate emission reductions. It requires, rather, a system of liability laws that would permit those damaged by pollution to be compensated for damages suffered.

Theoretically, this approach appears to address the incentive question—getting people to take into account the environmental damages they may cause—as well as the question of compensating those who are damaged. It may appear to solve the problem of determining just where e^* is along the emission axis. But whether this is actually true or not depends on the legal process through which the amount of liability and compensation is established. In the United States and other countries with similar legal traditions, this might be established through common law processes. Alternatively, it might be the result of statutory enactments by legislators.

---

1. Liability laws are often used in the case of short-run environmental damage caused by accidents; in this case the horizontal axis would index the amount of pollutant released as the result of an accident. These laws cover cases where there is the threat of damage.

Common Law

Common law systems rely on court proceedings in which plaintiffs and defendants meet to make claims and counterclaims, and in which juries are often called on to decide questions of fact and amounts of compensation. Judgments normally are based on precedent established from similar cases in the past. Common law cases usually involve actions of one private party, the polluter, that damage another private party. They may also involve cases, under the **public trust doctrine** of public or private actions, that damage **publicly held resources** (e.g., a fresh- or saltwater fishery in public waters).

Doctrines of liability have developed through the evolution of court decisions. The law now recognizes:

- **strict liability,** which holds polluters responsible for damages regardless of circumstances. A firm handling hazardous materials might be held strictly liable for damages done by these wastes. Thus, any damages that resulted, regardless of how careful the firm had been in handling the waste, would require compensation; and
- **negligence,** which holds polluters responsible only if they do not take appropriate steps to avoid the damage. Negligence would hold it responsible only if it failed to take appropriate steps to ensure that the materials did not escape into the surrounding environment.

As an example, after years of litigation, British Petroleum (BP) was found negligent in the 2010 Deep Water Horizon oil rig explosion in the Gulf of Mexico because BP did not replace a malfunctioning valve identified during a safety inspection.

Another distinction is between **joint and several** and **nonjoint** liability. In the former, one party can be held liable for all of the damages stemming from a collective act of pollution, for example, one party may have to come up with the entire cleanup costs of a site to which it and many others polluted. In nonjoint liability, a party will be held liable only for its portion of the total.

The critical factors in a liability system are where the burden of proof lies and what standards have to be met in order to establish that proof. In the United States, those who believe they may have been injured by pollution must file an action within a specified time period, typically two or three years, and then in court must establish a direct causal link between the pollution and the damage. This involves two major steps:

1. Showing that the polluting material at issue was in fact the cause of the damage, and
2. Showing that the polluting material did in fact come from the specific defendant who appears in court.

Both steps are difficult because the standards of proof required by the courts may be more than current science can supply. Most chemicals, for example, are implicated in increased disease only on a **probabilistic basis;** that is, exposure to the substance involves an increased probability of disease, not certainty. Even though we know that smoking causes lung cancer, for example, this causal link remains probabilistic; an increased number of people will get lung cancer if they smoke, but we can't tell exactly which ones. In Woburn, Massachusetts, contamination of well water was estimated by some epidemiologists to have probably caused 6 of the 12 excess cases of leukemia in the town. But under traditional standards of proof, a plaintiff could not conclusively prove that a *specific* cancer was caused by the water contamination. In other words, without being able to show explicitly how the polluting material operated in a particular body to produce cancer, the plaintiff cannot meet the standard of proof historically required in U.S. courts.[2]

The other link in the causal chain is to show that the material to which one was exposed came from a particular source. This won't be difficult in some cases; the oil on the Louisiana shoreline definitely came from the Deepwater Horizon oil rig explosion, the hazy atmosphere over the Grand Canyon definitely comes from the power plant, and so on. But in many cases this direct linkage is unknown. For an urban dweller in New York or Los Angeles, which specific industrial plant produced the sulfur dioxide (SO_2) molecules that a particular person may have breathed? For the people living in towns of the Connecticut Valley, which specific tobacco farms were responsible for the chemicals that showed up in their water supply? Without being able to trace a polluting substance to specific defendants, those who have been damaged by it may be unable to obtain compensation.

An important problem with using common law to address environmental damage is that economics and the law may use different criteria for identifying who is damaged from pollution. Under standard principles of economics, a person is "damaged" if he or she would be willing to pay to have the pollution reduced. On these grounds, for example, a person in New York could claim to be damaged by the Exxon BP Deep Water Horizon oil spill even though he or she was never on the U.S. Gulf coast. But legal doctrine requires that people have legal **standing** to proceed with a lawsuit. This requires normally that they show a close nexus between the degraded environment and their physical health and welfare. Thus, a person in New York may genuinely be worse off because of the Gulf oil spill, in the economic sense, but lack legal standing to proceed with a case in court.

Another major point about liability systems relates to the concept of **transactions costs.** In general terms, transactions costs are the costs of reaching and enforcing agreements. The concept was first introduced in economics to apply to the costs that buyers and sellers encounter in making a successful transaction: costs of searching out information, costs of bargaining over terms, and costs of making sure an agreement is actually carried out. The transactions costs also apply to liability systems in a court of law to determine the question of liability and the appropriate amounts of compensation. In this case, transactions costs are all the legal costs associated with gathering evidence, presenting a case, challenging opponents, awarding and collecting damages, and so on.

If the case is relatively simple, with one party on each side and a reasonably clear case of damage, the liability system may function, with a minimum of transactions costs, to give something approaching the efficient level of emissions. In the case of the two small factories on a small lake, the two can go to court and argue about the economic values to each of them of using the lake for their purposes. Because these values are comparable, it presumably would not be too difficult for a judge to determine the extent of the damages that the one firm is inflicting on the other. But transactions costs in many cases are likely to be very high. Complicated scientific questions often are involved, and judges and juries may find it virtually impossible to sort them out clearly (see **Exhibit 10.1**). And there may be many, many more than two parties involved, making it very difficult to agree on comprehensive solutions. In the

---

2. In some cases the law recognizes the special characteristics of pollution-caused damage. For example, statutes of limitation are being changed to count from the time the disease first becomes apparent, in recognition of the fact that many pollution-caused diseases may not show up for many years after exposure. Some courts are allowing statistical cause-and-effect linkages.

case of the Deep Water Horizon oil rig explosion, for example, about a half million people filed damage claims, hundreds of lawyers represented all the different sides, and numerous environmental groups, government organizations, and business groups were involved.

EXHIBIT 10.1 Common Law Courts and Questions of Science

The citizens of Woburn, Massachusetts, thought they had found the cause of the excess cases of childhood leukemia in the town: the industrial chemicals that had contaminated their water groundwater supplies. Furthermore, they believed they had found the culprit, or at least two of them: manufacturing companies that had been in operation near the town and had engaged in questionable, probably illegal, disposal methods for their used chemicals.

So they sued in state court, alleging that the companies had improperly dumped their chemicals, that these chemicals had then migrated to the town's water supply, and that the contaminated water led to the deaths of the children. The case proceeded to a jury trial, and this is where things became complicated.

For a plaintiff to win a common law case, it's necessary to show clearly who committed the action and how this action affected the people claiming damage. The folks of Woburn thought the connection was clear, and wanted the jury simply to find for the plaintiff or the defendant.

But the judge thought that the case, as it proceeded, would require much more data: who dumped what, when, and how; definitive information on when the material reached the town wells; and what damage it might have caused. Epidemiologists could provide probabilistic answers to the last question, though this was subject to challenge by the companies. But the process by which the water might have gotten contaminated was much more complicated. The plaintiffs tried to keep it simple; the defendants sought to open up new possibilities and uncertainties. Eventually, it came down to a series of very complex technical questions on which the jury was asked to render judgment. At one point the judge said: "My God, to ask them a question like that: You're talking to plain folks, you know. You've got to cast these in some form of language that is not hedged around with reservations and clauses and subclauses and commas and all that."[1]

In fact, these questions were basically unanswerable by juries composed of ordinary people. "Science could not determine the moment when these chemicals had arrived at the wells with the sort of precision Judge Skinner was demanding of the jurors. The judge was, in effect, asking the jurors to create a fiction that would in the end stand for truth. Or, if they found themselves unable to do that, to end the case by saying they couldn't answer the questions based on the evidence. If these questions really were necessary to a just resolution of the case, then perhaps the case was one that the judicial system was not equipped to handle."

[1]**Source of quotes:** Jonathan Harr, *A Civil Action*, New York, Random House Vintage, 1996, 368–369.

To summarize: Liability laws and the incentive they create can help generate efficient pollution levels when

- Relatively few people are involved,
- Causal linkages are clear, and
- Damages are easy to measure.

Statutory Law

Another way to institute a system of liability for pollution is to include the appropriate provisions within statutory pollution-control laws. Numerous countries, individually and in international agreements, have sought to use this means to address the problem of maritime oil spills. One particularity of oil tanker spills is that it is very difficult to monitor the behavior of the polluters. It is an episodic emission, so there is no continuous flow to measure, and spill probabilities depend on many practices (navigation, tanker maintenance, etc.) that are difficult for public authorities to monitor continuously. When polluter behavior is difficult to monitor, liability provisions may give the polluters an incentive to undertake the appropriate steps to reduce the probability of accidents. The U.S. Oil Pollution Act of 1990 details the acts for which compensation is required and how the amounts will be determined. The law requires companies, prior to operations, to provide financial assurances showing that they will be able to meet payments if conditions require. In 2010 the non-profit Marine Well Containment Company was established and funded by 10 petroleum-related companies. Its purpose is to provide capping equipment for use in the Gulf of Mexico in case of accidental deep-sea blowouts, in order to limit damage, and thus liability compensation. In addition to national laws, several international agreements have been directed at specifying the liability requirements of companies whose tankers release, accidentally or not, large quantities of oil into the ocean.

Worker's compensation laws normally allow compensation for damages to individuals from workplace exposure to pollutants, such as toxic chemicals and excessive noise. The Radiation Exposure Compensation Act of 1990 provides for compensation to individuals damaged by radiation from nuclear weapons testing or working in uranium mines.

Another major law that incorporates liability provisions is the **Comprehensive Environmental Response, Compensation, and Liability Act** of 1980 (CERCLA). In effect, it holds polluters liable for two types of costs:

- **clean-up costs** at certain legacy dump sites in which companies may have disposed of toxic materials in the past. The amount of compensation is related to the costs of cleanup, which may not be associated very closely with the amounts of damages actually caused, and
- **compensation** for damages to public resources stemming from intentional or accidental releases of hazardous materials into the environment. Compensation is more closely connected to damages, and major controversy surrounds how to measure these damages in particular cases.

We will study CERCLA in greater detail in **Chapter 16.**

How well these types of statutory liability laws work in providing the correct incentive for polluters depends heavily on the formulas specified for determining the exact amount of the liability. The laws can provide the correct incentives only if the compensatory payments required from each polluter approach the actual amounts of damage they cause.

10-2 Property Rights

In the previous section we discussed the case of a small lake that one firm used for waste disposal and another for a water supply. On deeper thought, we are led to a more fundamental question: Which one of the firms is really causing damage and which firm is the one suffering damages? This may sound counter-intuitive because you might naturally think that the waste-disposing firm is of course the one causing the damage. But we might argue just as well that the presence of the brewery inflicts damages on the waste-disposing firm because its presence makes it necessary for the latter to take special efforts to control its emissions. (Assume for purposes of argument that there are no other people, such as homeowners or recreators, using the lake.) The problem may come about simply because it is not clear who has the initial right to use the services of the lake—that is, who effectively owns the **property rights** to the lake. When a resource has no owner, nobody has a very strong incentive to see to it that it is not overly exploited or degraded in quality.

Private property rights are, of course, the dominant institutional arrangement in most developed economies. Many other countries are moving in that direction. So we are familiar with the operation of that institutional system when it comes to person-made assets such as machines, buildings, and consumer goods. Private property in land is also a familiar arrangement. If somebody owns a piece of land, he or she has an incentive to see to it that the land is managed in ways that maximize its value. If somebody comes along and threatens to dump something onto the land, the owner may call upon the law to prevent it if he or she wants to. By this diagnosis, the problem of the misuse of many environmental assets comes about because of ambiguously specified property rights in those assets.

The Principle

Consider again the case of the lake and the two firms. Apparently, there are two choices for vesting ownership of the lake. It could be owned either by the polluting firm or by the firm using it for a water supply. How does this choice affect the level of pollution in the lake? Would it not lead to zero emissions if owned by one firm and uncontrolled emissions if owned by the other? Not necessarily, if owners and nonowners are allowed to negotiate. Of course, this is the very essence of a property rights system. The owner decides how the asset is to be used and may stop any unauthorized use, but also may negotiate with anybody else who wants access to that asset.

Look again at **Figure 10.1.** Suppose the marginal damage function refers to all the damages suffered by the brewery—call this Firm A. Assume the marginal abatement cost curve applies to the firm emitting effluent into the lake—call this one Firm B. We have to make some assumption about who owns the lake, Firm A or Firm B. We will see that, *theoretically,* the same quantity of emissions will result in either case, provided that the two firms can come together and reach an agreement about how the lake is to be used.

In the first case, suppose that Firm B owns the lake. For the moment we need not worry about how this came about, only that this is the way it is. Firm B may use the lake any way it wishes. Suppose that emissions initially are at e_1. Firm B is initially devoting no resources at all to emissions abatement. But is this where matters will remain? At this point marginal damages are $r, whereas marginal abatement costs are nil. The straightforward thing for Firm A to do is to offer Firm B some amount of money to reduce its effluent stream; for the first ton any amount agreed on between 0 and $r would make both parties better off. In fact, they could continue to bargain over the marginal unit as long as marginal damages exceeded marginal abatement costs. Firm B would be better off by reducing its emissions for any payment in excess of its marginal abatement costs, whereas any payment less than the marginal damages would make Firm A better off. In this way, bargaining between the owners of the lake (here Firm B) and the people who are damaged by pollution would result in a reduction in effluent to e^*, the point at which marginal abatement costs and marginal damages are equal.

Suppose, on the other hand, that ownership of the lake is vested in Firm A, the firm that is damaged by pollution. In this case we might assume that the owners would allow no infringement of their property, that is, the emission level would be zero or close to it. Is this where it would remain? Not if, again, owners and others may negotiate. In this second case, Firm B would have to buy permission from Firm A to place its wastes in the lake. Any price for this lower-than-marginal abatement costs but higher-than-marginal damages would make both parties better off. And so, by a similar process of bargaining with payments now going in the opposite direction, the emissions level into the lake would be adjusted from the low level where it started toward the efficient level e^*. At this point any further adjustment would stop because marginal abatement costs, the maximum the polluters would pay for the right to emit one more ton of effluent, are equal to marginal damages, the minimum Firm A would take in order to allow Firm B to emit this added ton.

So, as we have seen in this little example, if property rights over the environmental asset are clearly defined, and bargaining among owners and prospective users is allowed, the efficient level of effluent will result irrespective of who was initially given the property right. In fact, this is a famous theorem, called the Coase theorem, after the economist who developed it.[3]

The wider implication is that by defining private property rights (not necessarily individual property rights because private *groups* of people could have these rights), we can establish the conditions under which decentralized bargaining can produce efficient levels of environmental quality. This has some appeal. The good part of it is that the people doing the bargaining may know more about the relative values involved—abatement costs and damages—than anybody else, so there is some hope that the true efficiency point will be attained. Also, because it would be a decentralized system, we would not need to have some central bureaucratic organization making decisions that are based mostly on political considerations instead of the true economic values involved. Ideas like this have led some people to recommend widespread conversion of natural and environmental resources to private ownership as a means of achieving their efficient use.

---

3. Ronald H. Coase, "The Problem of Social Cost," *Journal of Law and Economics,* 3, 1960, 1–44.

Rules and Conditions

How well is this property rights approach likely to work in practice? In order for a property rights approach to work well—that is, to give us something approaching the efficient level of environmental pollution—essentially three main conditions have to be met:

1. Property rights must be well defined, enforceable, and transferable.
2. There must be a reasonably efficient and competitive system that allows interested parties to come together and negotiate about how these environmental property rights will be used.
3. There must be a complete set of markets so that private owners may capture all social values associated with the use of an environmental asset.

If Firm A cannot keep Firm B from doing whatever the latter wishes, of course, a property rights approach will not work. In other words, owners must be physically and legally able to stop others from encroaching on their property. To be transferable, owners must be able to sell their property to any would-be buyer. If owners cannot sell the property, this will weaken their incentives to preserve its long-run productivity. This is because any use that does draw down its long-run environmental productivity cannot be punished through the reduced market value of the asset. This is a particularly strong problem in countries where ownership rights are incomplete (i.e., they do not have all the required conditions specified earlier), people do not have strong incentives to see that long-run productivity is maintained.

10-3 Problems with Property Rights to Internalize Externalities

In some cases property rights might be used creatively to advance the preservation of natural and environmental resources. **Exhibit 10.2** discusses one of these: the protection of forests in places where their destruction is a major threat. But in modern cases of environmental pollution control, there are real problems in using property rights to internalize externalities.

EXHIBIT 10.2 Payments for Environment Services (PES)

A farmer owns a tract of land that developers would like to buy and convert into a large commercial development. A forest owner could gain by selling the timber from his land and converting it to agricultural fields. In each case the land currently has ecological value because it provides services such as habitat for diversity, flood control, and carbon sequestration. Markets for environmental services have increased and owners are able to realize their value and have an incentive to preserve them. Key types are carbon sequestration, biodiversity or watershed protection, and landscape protection.

(Continued)

> **EXHIBIT 10.2** *(Continued)*
>
> One role for public authorities in this situation might be to enhance the demand side for such a market. This could be done by offering to pay the landowners an amount equal to the wider ecological value of the land, provided these ecological values were not impaired by the landholders' use of the land.
>
> Around the world this type of program has come to be called **payment for environmental services.** Governments or other organizations identify critical ecosystem assets and pay landowners amounts large enough to ensure their preservation. Of course there are lots of problems that have to be solved for this type of property rights approach to work effectively:
>
> - How ecological services are to be measured accurately
> - How to make sure that ecological services are actually preserved
> - How to ensure that political considerations don't enter the decisions to preserve ecosystem values.

Transactions Costs

We saw previously that the efficient use of the lake depended on negotiations and agreement between the two interested firms. Negotiating costs, together with the costs of policing the agreement, could be expected to be fairly modest. What we are referring to here is **transactions costs,** the idea that we introduced in the preceding section. In the simple lake case, transactions costs would probably be low enough that the firms would be able to negotiate on the efficient level of emissions. But suppose Firm A, the firm using the lake as a water supply source, is replaced with a community of 50,000 people who use it not only for a water supply, but also for recreational purposes. Now the negotiations must take place between a single polluting firm on one side and 50,000 people, or their representatives, on the other side. For each of these individuals the value of improved water quality is small relative to the value to the firm of polluting the lake. Moreover, the level of water quality in the lake is a public good for these individuals. This seriously increases the transactions costs of negotiating an agreement among different users.

To make matters worse, suppose that instead of one polluting firm there are 1,000 polluting firms, together with a few thousand homeowners who are not yet hooked into the public sewer system and so are using septic tanks on the shores of the lake. Here the possibilities of vesting the ownership of the lake in one person, and expecting negotiations between that person and prospective users to find the efficient levels of use, essentially vanish.

Public Goods

A factor that exacerbates transactions cost problems is that environmental quality improvements are **public goods.** So we could expect **free riding,** especially when the number of affected individuals is large. In negotiating with polluters over the ambient quality levels to be achieved, some, perhaps many, potential beneficiaries could be expected to keep their true preference hidden in order to escape their fair share of the cost of pollution control. When public goods are involved, decentralized approaches such as property rights systems will not bring about efficient outcomes.

Absence of Markets

For private property institutions to ensure that an environmental asset is put to its best use, the process must work in such a way that the owner is able to capture the full social value of the resource in that use. Suppose you own a small island in the Florida Keys. There are two possible uses: develop a resort hotel or devote it to a wildlife refuge. If you build the hotel, you get a direct flow of monetary wealth because the tourism market is well developed in that part of the world and you can expect customers to find your hotel and pay the going rate for your services. But there is no comparable "market" for wildlife refuge services. The value of the island as a refuge may well be much higher than its value as a resort, in terms of the actual aggregate willingness to pay of all the people in the country and the world. But there is no good way for them to express that value; there is no ready market such as the one in the tourism market where they in effect can bid against the tourists who would visit the island. You might think that a **nature conservancy** could buy up the island if its value as refuge really is higher than its value as hotel. But nature conservancies run on the basis of voluntary contributions, and islands and other lands are in effect public goods.[4] We saw earlier that when public goods are involved, voluntary contributions to make something available are likely to be a lot less than its true value because of **free-riding behavior.** The upshot is that, while you as an owner could certainly expect to reap the full monetary value of the island as a resort, you would not be able to realize its full social value if you held it as a preserve.

Or consider again the case with the lake on which are located the food-processing company and the brewery. Suppose there was a unique fish species in the lake that was of no value to either company but of high value to society at large. In this case assigning exclusive property rights to either of the companies would not be an effective way of protecting the fish.

In recent years, policymakers, especially those in developing countries, have sought to develop an innovative property rights plan to preserve important ecosystem resources. It's called **payment for environmental services** and is discussed in **Exhibit 10.2.**

Markets for Clean Energy

Once property rights are established, might new private markets be formed that could move the economy toward improved environmental quality? Among the citizenry at large, there is steadily growing concern about the impacts of environmental pollution. This represents an opportunity for private entrepreneurs to make available goods and services that are produced in more environmentally benign ways. Consider **Figure 10.2 (a),** for example. It shows a demand function by consumers for clean energy (sometimes referred to as green power), that is, electricity generated in a way that produces less air pollutants than standard fossil-based technologies. This function is labeled D_1 in the figure. If the

---

4. The Nature Conservancy is an international group that seeks to protect sensitive resources from damage by buying them outright. Founded in 1951, they have helped to protect more than 125 million acres of ecologically sensitive land around the world; some has been transferred to other public and private conservation groups; the rest still belongs to the Nature Conservancy. Many individual states within the United States also have conservancy groups.

technological options available to produce green power (solar, wind, etc.) give a supply function of S_1, we could expect private markets to come into being and produce about q_1 units of green power, at a price of p_1. If better technology is made available, the clean energy supply function might shift to S_2, increasing the amount of green power sold on the market to q_2 and lowering its price to p_2.[5]

The significance for this can be seen in **Figure 10.2 (b)**, which shows the demand for fossil-based, or conventional, power. The lowering price in the clean energy market serves to shift back the demand curve for fossil power, because these two goods are substitutes for one another. In other words, the growth in a voluntary green power sector would lead to a shift back in the demand for dirty power.

How much might we expect private markets of this type to come into being and lead to reduced pollution? Clearly some will develop, because we can actually see growing markets in renewable energy, organic food, recycled paper, and so on. Will they be able to provide the socially efficient amount of pollution reduction? Not likely. When I buy clean power, I am conferring benefits not only on myself, but also on others whose air is made cleaner as a result and contributing to a reduction in global warming. My purchase, in other words, produces a public good, and we have seen that private markets, left to themselves, will undersupply public goods. So although this means can move us part of the way toward efficient pollution reduction, it most assuredly cannot do the whole job.

FIGURE 10.2 Private Markets for Clean Energy

10-4 Voluntary Action

By **voluntary action** we mean cases where individuals (including individual firms) engage in pollution-control behavior in the absence of any formal, legal obligation to do so. One might think that in this market-driven, competitive world, voluntary pollution control would be quite scarce, but this may not be true. There are many who feel that programs based on voluntary restraint can be used quite effectively. **Table 10.1** is a partial list of voluntary programs that have been used in the United States. There are various social forces that presumably must be in operation for these programs to be effective. One of these is **moral suasion;** another is **informal community pressure.**

---

5. The economic parameter of prime importance here is the *price elasticity of demand*, defined as the percentage change in quantity demanded of something produced by a 1 percent change in its price. The bigger this elasticity (in a negative sense, as p and q are moving in opposite directions), the bigger the quantity increase that would result from a price drop such as that from p_1 to p_2 in the diagram.

TABLE 10.1 Examples of Voluntary Pollution Reduction Programs (VPRPs) in the United States

Program Type	Examples
Public programs aimed at individuals and based mostly on moral suasion	"Give a hoot, don't pollute"; "Pitch-in"; community recycling programs
Environmental Protection Agency (EPA) programs that encourage, but do not require, environmentally friendly process changes	**Green Lights**—encourage firms to adopt energy-efficient lighting technologies to reduce electricity consumption **Design for the Environment (DfE)**—encourage firms to meet "DfE" green labeling standards
Statutory or voluntary programs that provide information about the environmental performance of polluters	**Toxic Release Inventory**—make available toxic release data for public to use in programs of **informal pressure** or to design regulations
Voluntary programs of information release	**Energy Star Program**—publicize names of firms that adopt energy efficiency plans **Drift Reduction Technology (DRT)**—gives 1 to 4 stars for labeling for safer pesticide spray products that reduce pesticide drift
Programs undertaken unilaterally by polluters without the participation of public agencies	**Responsible Care**—program of the American Chemical Association to foster safe development and handling of chemicals **ISO14001**—voluntary international standards for environmental management systems **LEED certification**—certification from the Leadership in Energy and Environmental Design for buildings with green design and operation practices
Industry-specific programs	**Voluntary Program (airlines)**—reduces pollution associated with using Aircraft Deicing Fluid **Green Clean Project (laundry and drycleaners)**—reduces use of toxic chemicals

Moral Suasion

A classic case of moral suasion is the Smokey Bear and Woodsy Owl effort of the National Forest Service, a publicity campaign aimed at getting people to be more sensitive about littering in the woods and about avoiding actions that would raise the risk of forest fires. Although there are fines and penalties for doing these things, the campaign was not based on threats of penalties as much as it was on appealing to people's sense of civic morality. "Reduce, Reuse, Recycle" campaigns are essentially the same type of approach.

In the early days of recycling, communities often mounted voluntary efforts, where appeals were made on the basis of civic virtue. In some cases these efforts were successful; in others they fell flat. Today there are many mandatory recycling programs, although it is true that they still must rely heavily on moral suasion to get high rates of compliance. Other situations clearly exist where appeals to civic morality may be effective public policy. This is especially the case with emissions such as litter, where violators are normally scattered throughout a population in a way that makes it impractical to monitor them and detect violations as they occur.

High-profile individuals can emphasize the moral aspects of environmental causes. Pope Francis penned *Laudato Si'*, the encyclical for climate prayer and action, while Greta Thunberg spurred the youth movement "Fridays for Future" by chastising governments for not taking action on global warming.

The good thing about moral suasion is that it may have widespread spillover effects. Whereas an effluent tax on a single type of effluent will have no impact on emissions of other types of waste products, appeals to civic virtue for one problem may produce side effects on other situations.

Of course, not all people are equally responsible from an ethical standpoint. Some people will respond to moral arguments; others will not. The burden of this policy will fall, therefore, on the part of the population that is morally more sensitive; those who respond less to moral arguments will be free riding on the others, enjoying the benefits of others' moral restraint but escaping their rightful share of the burden. Some electric companies issue neighborhood use reports which compare electricity consumption by one household to electricity use by neighbors within a geographic area.

It is easy to be cynical about moral suasion as a tool for environmental improvement. With increasing internet access and social media use, tough-minded policymakers may be naturally drawn toward environmental policies that have more teeth in them. This would probably be a mistake. It perhaps is true that we cannot rely very heavily on moral suasion to produce, for example, a significant reduction in air pollution in the Los Angeles basin or substantial drops in farm use of groundwater-contaminating chemicals. But in our search for new, effective public policy devices to address specific pollution or global warming problems, we perhaps underestimate the contribution of the overall climate of public morality and civic virtue. A strong culture in this sense makes it possible to institute new policies and makes it easier to administer and enforce them. We can also deduce the importance of politicians and policymakers speaking for and doing things that replenish this moral climate rather than erode it.

Informal Community Pressure

Another means through which some voluntary programs work is through **informal pressure** on polluters to reduce their emissions. It is informal because it is not exercised through statutory or legal means, and it is pressure because it attempts to inflict costs on those who are responsible for excessive pollution. The costs are in terms of such things as loss of reputation, the loss of local markets (perhaps going so far as to involve boycotts), or a loss of public reputation leading to declines in the stock values of firms that are publicly owned. The pressure is exercised through activities of local citizens groups, grass roots campaigns, social media posts, demonstrations, discussions with polluters, and so on. See **Exhibit 10.3**.

EXHIBIT 10.3 A Case of Informal Economic Pressure

Antipollution groups have long sought means of inflicting economic pressure on polluters. Attempts to boycott the products of polluting firms have been minimally successful. Disinvestment in the stock of polluting firms has been encouraged, also with modest success. Another tack that has been tried recently is to convince banks to reduce the credit they normally make available to polluting firms. Mountain-top coal mining in some eastern states has left a trail of denuded landscape and polluted water courses in many areas. Firms engaged in the practice often use short-term loans to finance these operations. Environmental groups have convinced some of the lending banks to cut back on these loans, thereby increasing the costs, and reducing the profitability of mountain-top mining. However, the withholding of credit by banks was short lived. When coal mining firms came out of bankruptcy, some banks resumed and increased lending to the industry. As of 2022, $1.5 trillion has been channeled from banks to coal.

Sources: For more information, see Andrew Ross Sorkin, "A New Tack in the War on Mining Mountains," *New York Times*, 10, 2015, B1; Emily Flitter, "Think Big Banks have Abandoned Coal? Think Again," *New York Times*, 2018, B1; and Sam Meredith, "Banks haven't Quit Coal...," *Sustainable Future CNBC*, Feb. 15, 2022.

A major factor in voluntary actions of this type is the information that is available about polluters' emissions. If good data are lacking on the quantity and quality of emissions from particular sources, it will be difficult to mobilize public concern and focus it on the responsible parties. This is one of the motivations behind the U.S. Toxic Release Inventory, a program established under the **Emergency Planning and Community Right to Know Act** (1986) and the **Pollution Prevention Act** (1990), whereby polluters are required to report their toxic emissions, which are then published in such a way that communities can identify emissions that directly affect them. The 2014 federal hydrological fracturing rules established Frac Focus, an industry listing of chemicals and liquids used for fracking. Sometimes called "sunshine laws" because they shed light on and disclose information available to the public, this public disclosure approach is also being pursued in other countries.

Summary

In this chapter we began the exploration of different types of public policies that might be used to combat environmental pollution. The chapter discussed two main decentralized types of approaches to environmental quality improvement. The first was to rely on liability rules, which require polluters to compensate those they have damaged. In theory, the threat of liability can lead potential polluters to internalize what would ordinarily be external costs. By weighing relative compensation and abatement costs, polluters would be brought to efficient emission levels. Although liability doctrines may work well in simple cases of pollution where few people are involved and cause-and-effect linkages are clear, they are unlikely to work reliably in the large-scale, technically complicated environmental problems of contemporary societies.

The second major approach we discussed was reliance on the institution of private property rights. Looked at from this perspective, environmental externalities are problems only because ownership of environmental assets is often not clearly defined. By establishing clear property rights, owners and others who would like to use environmental assets for various purposes can negotiate agreements that balance the relative costs of different alternatives. Thus, negotiations among parties theoretically could bring about efficient emission rates. But problems of transactions costs, especially related to the public goods aspects of environmental quality, and lack of markets for environmental services, work against relying primarily on traditional property rights institutions in environmental quality issues. We will see in a subsequent chapter, however, that some new types of property rights approaches may hold greater promise.

Finally, we mentioned the idea of moral suasion, which may be useful when it is impossible to measure the emissions stemming from particular sources. The problem of moral free riding was discussed. Increased transparency through public disclosure is another means of encouraging ethical behavior in environmental matters.

Questions for Further Discussion

1. It would seem that neighbors could easily negotiate among themselves to settle problems of local externalities such as noise and unsightly land uses. Yet most communities control these problems with local laws and regulations. Why?
2. Suppose courts changed rules regarding burden of proof, requiring polluters to show that their emissions are harmless, rather than pollutees to show that they have been harmed. What impact might this have?
3. Suppose a community weighed each resident's solid-waste disposal when it was picked up and published the individual totals each year in the local newspaper. Do you think this would lead to a reduction in the total quantity of solid waste disposed of in the community? If they were published monthly? Explain your reasoning.
4. For what types of pollution problems is voluntary action likely to be the most effective policy approach?

(Continued)

Questions for Further Discussion *(Continued)*

5. Accidents with trucks carrying hazardous wastes are fairly common. Suppose regulators enact a rule requiring that the perpetrators of such an accident be liable for a sum equal to the average damages of all such accidents in the industry. Would this lead trucking companies to take the socially efficient amount of precaution against such accidents?

6. Identify a case of moral suasion in the city or neighborhood or campus where you live, that influences people's behavior toward a particular action.

For additional resources pertaining to the material in this chapter, see the list in **Appendix B.**

Chapter 11

Command-and-Control Strategies: The Case of Standards

A **command-and-control (CAC)** approach to public policy is one where, in order to bring about behavior thought to be socially desirable, political authorities simply mandate the behavior in law, then use whatever enforcement machinery—courts, police, fines, and so on—that is necessary to get people to obey the law. In the case of environmental policy, the command-and-control approach consists of relying on **standards** of various types to bring about improvements in environmental quality. In general, a standard is simply a mandated level of performance that is enforced in law. For example, a maximum level of a toxic, such as ppm (parts per million) of arsenic in drinking water. A speed limit is a classic type of standard; it sets maximum rates that drivers may legally travel. An emission standard is a maximum rate of emissions that is legally allowed. The spirit of a standard is, if you want people not to do something, simply pass a law that makes it illegal, then send out the authorities to enforce the law.

Figure 11.1 is our familiar graph showing marginal abatement costs and marginal damages related to the rate at which some production residual is emitted into the environment. Suppose that initially the actual level of effluent is at e_1, a rate substantially above the efficient rate of e^*. To achieve e^* the authorities set an emission standard at that level; e^* becomes a mandated upper limit for the emissions of this firm. The standard is then enforced by sending out whatever enforcement authorities are necessary to measure and detect any possible violations. If infractions are found, the source is fined or subject to some other penalty. If the firm reduces emissions in accordance with the standard, it will be incurring an amount equivalent to area a per year in total abatement costs. These total abatement costs are the **compliance costs** of meeting the standard.

Standards are popular for a number of reasons. They appear to be simple and direct. They apparently set clearly specified targets. They appeal, therefore, to the sense that everybody has of wanting to come directly to grips with environmental pollution and get it reduced. Standards also appear to be congenial to our ethical sense that pollution is bad and ought to be declared illegal. The legal system is geared to operate by defining and stopping illegal behavior, and the standards approach conforms to this mind-set.

We will see, however, that the standards approach is a lot more complex than might first appear. Standards appear to offer a method to take away the freedom of sources to pollute, replacing it with mandated changes in behavior. In fact, a very practical reason for the popularity of standards is that they may permit far more flexibility in enforcement than might be apparent. What appears to be the directness and unambiguousness of standards becomes a lot more problematic when we look below the surface.

FIGURE 11.1 Emission Standards

[Figure 11.1: A graph with Emissions (tons/year) on the x-axis and $ on the y-axis. A downward-sloping "Marginal abatement costs" curve and an upward-sloping "Marginal damages" curve intersect at e^*. Points labeled on x-axis from left to right: e_t, e_o, e^*, e_1. A shaded region labeled a appears between e^* and e_1 under the marginal damages curve.]

11-1 Types of Standards

There are three main types of environmental standards:

- **Ambient**—Ambient environmental quality refers to the qualitative dimensions for the surrounding environment. For example, in August 2022, two beaches on Bde Maka Ska and one beach on Lake Hiawatha in Minneapolis were closed because the level of E. coli bacteria measured above 1,260 organisms per 100 milliliters (mL) of water.
- **Emissions**—Emission standards are never-exceed levels applied directly to the quantities of emissions coming from pollution sources. For example, beginning August 2023, the Ultra Low Emission Zone (ULEZ) expands to all London boroughs; it requires petrol cars to meet tighter exhaust emissions standards such as 0.025 g/km for particulate matter (PM) or face a daily charge.
- **Technology**—Technology standards are the technologies, techniques, or practices that potential polluters must adopt. For example, all food service establishments in California are required to install, operate, and maintain an approved type and adequately sized grease interceptor.

Ambient Standards

An **ambient standard** is a never-exceed level for some pollutant in the ambient environment. It could be the ambient quality of the air over a particular city or the ambient quality of the water in a particular river. For example, an ambient standard for dissolved oxygen in a particular river may be set at 3 parts per million (ppm), meaning that this is the lowest level of dissolved oxygen that is to be allowed in the river. Ambient standards cannot be enforced directly. Enforcing various emissions can lead to ambient quality levels. To ensure that dissolved oxygen never falls below 3 ppm in the river, we must know how the emissions of the various sources on the river contribute to changes in this measure, then introduce some means of controlling these sources.

Ambient standards are normally expressed in terms of average concentration levels over some period of time. For example, the current U.S. national primary ambient air quality standard for carbon monoxide (CO) is 9 ppm based on an 8-hour averaging time and 35 ppm based on a 1-hour averaging time. Neither can be exceeded more than once per year. The reason for taking averages is to recognize that there are seasonal and daily variations in meteorological conditions, as well as in the emissions that produce variations in ambient quality. Averaging means that short-term ambient quality levels may be worse than the standard, so long as this does not persist for too long and it is balanced by periods when the air quality is better than the standard.

Emission Standards

Emission (or effluent) standards are normally expressed in terms of quantity of material per some unit of time, for example, grams per minute or tons per week. Continuous emissions streams may be subject to standards on "instantaneous" rates of flow, for example, upper limits on the quantity of residuals flow per minute or on the average residuals flow over some time period.

Setting emission standards at a certain level does not necessarily entail meeting a set of ambient standards. Between emissions and ambient quality stands nature, in particular the meteorological and hydrological phenomena that link the two.

Research to study the linkage between emission levels and ambient quality levels is an important part of environmental science. The environment usually transports the emissions from point of discharge to other locations, often diluting and dispersing them along the way. Chemical processes occur in all environmental media that often change the physical character of the pollutant. In some cases this may render the emitted substance more benign. Organic wastes put in rivers and streams will normally be subject to natural degradation processes, which will break them down into constituent elements. Thus, the ambient quality of the water at various points downstream depends on the quantity of emissions as well as the hydrology of the river: its rate of flow, temperature, natural reaeration conditions, and so on.

The link between emissions and ambient quality can also be vitally affected by human decisions. A classic case is automobiles. As part of the mobile-source air pollution program, emission standards have been set for new cars in terms of emissions per mile of operation. Although these standards were designed and adopted for internal combustion engine (ICE) vehicles, the emissions standards apply to electric vehicles (EVs) and any other new car. But because there is no effective way of controlling either the number of cars on the roads or the total number of miles each is driven, the aggregate quantity of pollutants in the air, and thus, ambient air quality, is not directly controlled.

Emission standards can be set on a wide variety of different bases. For example:

1. Emission rate (e.g., pounds per hour).
2. Emission concentration (e.g., parts per million of biochemical oxygen demand, or BOD, in wastewater).
3. Total quantity of residuals (rate of discharge times concentration times duration).
4. Residuals produced per unit of output (e.g., SO_2 emissions per kilowatt-hour of electricity produced).
5. Residuals content per unit of input (e.g., SO_2 emissions per ton of coal burned in power generation).
6. Percentage removal of pollutant (e.g., 60 percent removal of waste material before discharge).

In the language of regulation, emission standards are a type of **performance standard** because they refer to end results that are meant to be achieved by the polluters that are regulated. There are many other types of performance standards, for example, workplace standards set in terms of maximum numbers of accidents or levels of risk to which workers are exposed. A requirement that farmers reduce their use of a particular pesticide below some level is also a performance standard, as is a highway speed limit.

Technology Standards

Technology standards don't actually specify an end result. The requirement that ICE cars be equipped with catalytic converters or seat belts is a technology standard. When electric utilities were required to install stack-gas scrubbers to reduce SO_2 emissions,[1] these would be, in effect, technology standards because a particular type of technology is being specified by central authorities. This type of standard includes what are often called design standards or engineering standards.

There are also a variety of product standards specifying characteristics that goods must have and input standards that require potential polluters to use inputs meeting specific conditions. Organizations may face a mandatory specification for using a product, such as Massachusetts requiring all state offices to purchase copy paper having at least 30 percent post-consumer recycled content.

At the edges, the difference between a performance standard and a technology standard may become blurred. The basic point of differentiation is that an emission standard sets a constraint on some performance criterion and then allows people to choose the best means of achieving it. A technology standard dictates certain techniques to be used, such as particular equipment or operating practices to be used by polluters.

For illustrative purposes, **Exhibit 11.1** shows some typical standards, applicable in this case to snowmobiles. The carbon monoxide, hydrocarbon, and noise limits are emission standards; the limit on snowmobiles entering Yellowstone National Park can be thought of as a technology standard, as it restricts the use of certain machines in this setting.

---

1. A scrubber is a device that treats the exhaust gas stream so as to remove a substantial proportion of the target substance from that stream. The recovered material then must be disposed of elsewhere.

EXHIBIT 11.1 Standards Applicable to Snowmobiles[1]

Snowmobiling is a major wintertime activity in the United States. Historically, snowmobiles were built with two-stroke engines, the same kind of engine that has been used to power lawn mowers and outboard motors. In a two-stroke engine, fuel enters the combustion chamber at the same time that exhaust gases are expelled from it. As a result, as much as one-third of the fuel passes through the engine without being combusted. This causes poor fuel economy and high levels of emissions. While many snowmobile models emit the maximum limit for carbon monoxide, the same models emit half the maximum limit for hydrocarbons. They are also very noisy. Historically, there has been a political struggle over emission standards applicable to snowmobiles. Another aspect of the fight has been over efforts to control the entrance of snowmobiles into national parks, especially Yellowstone National Park. The tabulation shows standards adopted by the EPA after extensive review, mediation, and court battles, as the snowmobile industry regards them as too restrictive, and environmental groups regard them as not restrictive enough.

Emission Standards Applicable to New Snowmobiles (2-stroke engines are not allowed)	Carbon Monoxide g/kw-hr	Hydrocarbons g/kw-hr
Before 2006	397	150
2006/2007	275	100
2010	275	75
2012	200	75
Yellowstone 2003	120	15
Yellowstone 2015–2023	90	15

Yellowstone Entry Standards	Number of Snowmobiles Allowed (vehicles/day)
2003	0
2007	950
2011–2012 season	318
2015–2016 season	480[2]
2018–2019 season	510[3]
2021–2023 season	480[4]

Noise Standards for Yellowstone	Decibels
Yellowstone 2015–2023 season	67 dBA

[1] Snowcoaches, another type of oversnow vehicle (OSV), have another set of specific emissions and noise standards.

[2] Limited to 48 transportation events with up to 10 snowmobiles per event.

(Continued)

EXHIBIT 11.1 *(Continued)*

[3] Limited to 51 guided groups of up to 10 snowmobiles each per day, plus 4 unguided groups of 5 snowmobiles each per day.

[4] Limited to 460 commercially guided snowmobiles per day (46 events with 10 snowmobiles per event), plus 20 non-commercially guided snowmobiles per day (1 group with up to 5 snowmobiles permitted to enter through each of the four park entrances).

Sources: Department of the Interior, National Park Service, *Special Regulations; Area of the National Park System; Yellowstone National Park; Winter Use,* Final Rule Federal Register 78(205), 23, 2013, 63069–63093; National Park Service Yellowstone, *Oversnow Vehicle (OSV) Noise Emissions Testing,* 2015–2016 update; Yellowstone Center for Resources. *Winter Use Monitoring: Summary of Findings 2014–2020,* October 2021.

Standards Used in Combination

In most actual pollution-control programs, different types of standards are used in combination. National air pollution-control policy contains all three, as we will see in **Chapter 15**. In the Total Maximum Daily Load program for water pollution control, authorities establish ambient standards for water quality, emission standards to reduce incoming pollution loads, and technology standards in the form of **best management practices**. We will encounter this program in **Chapter 14**.

11-2 The Economics of Standards

It would seem to be a simple and straightforward thing to achieve better environmental quality by applying standards of various types. Standards appear to give regulators a degree of positive control to get pollution reduced, but standards turn out to be more complicated than they first appear. The discussion in the rest of this chapter will focus on the efficiency and cost-effectiveness of standards, as well as the problem of enforcement.

Setting the Level of the Standard

Perhaps the first perplexing problem is where to set the standard. We saw in the case of the decentralized approaches to pollution control—liability laws and property rights regimes—that there was, at least, the theoretical possibility that the interactions of people involved would lead to efficient outcomes. But with standards we can't presume this; standards are established through some sort of authoritative political/administrative process that may be affected by all kinds of considerations.

The most fundamental question in setting standards, is whether authorities should take into account only damages, or both damages and abatement costs. Look again at **Figure 11.1**, particularly at the marginal damage function. One approach in standard setting has been to try to set ambient or emission standards by reference only to the damage function.

A principle used in some environmental laws has been to set the standard at a "zero-risk" level: that is, at the level that would protect everyone, no matter how sensitive, from damage. This would imply setting emission standards at the **threshold** level, labeled e_t in **Figure 11.1**. This concept is fine as long as there is a threshold. In some cases, toxicologists and other scientists indicate that there may be no threshold for many environmental pollutants, that in fact marginal damage functions are positive right from the origin. If we followed a zero-risk approach, we would have to set all standards at zero. This may be appropriate for some substances, certain highly toxic chemicals, but it would be essentially impossible to achieve for all pollutants.

The standard might instead be set at a level that accepts a "reasonably small" amount of damages, for example, e_0, the point where the marginal damage function begins to increase very rapidly. Here again, however, we would be setting the standard without regard to abatement costs. A different logic might suggest that in setting the standard, damages ought to be balanced with abatement costs. This would put us squarely within the logic used in discussing the notion of economic efficiency and, in this way, lead us to set the standard at e^*, the efficient emission level.

Note that there is, in effect, a certain amount of "balancing" going on when standards are set on the basis of an average over some time period. Short-run periods, when ambient quality is relatively low, are considered acceptable as long as they do not last too long. A judgment is being made, in effect, that it is not necessary to install enough abatement technology to hold ambient quality within the standard under all conceivable natural conditions. In other words, an implicit trade-off is being made between the damages that will result from the temporary deterioration of ambient quality below the standard and the high costs that would be necessary to keep ambient quality within the standard under all conditions.

Uniformity of Standards

A very practical problem in standard setting is whether it should be applied uniformly to all situations or varied according to circumstances. This can be illustrated by using the problem of the spatial uniformity of standards. The ambient air quality standards in the United States, for example, are essentially national. The problem with this is that regions may differ greatly in terms of the factors affecting damage and abatement cost relationships, so that one set of standards, uniformly applied across these local variations, may have serious efficiency implications.

Consider **Figure 11.2.** It shows two marginal damage functions, one (labeled MD_u) is assumed to characterize an urban area, whereas the other (labeled MD_r) applies to a rural area. MD_u lies above MD_r because there are many more people living in the urban area, so the same quantity of emissions will affect the health of more people there than in the rural region. Assume that marginal abatement costs (labeled MAC) are the same in the two regions. Because the marginal damages are much higher in the urban than in the rural area, the efficient ambient level of benzene is much lower in the urban e_u than in the rural region e_r. Thus, a single, uniform standard cannot be efficient simultaneously in the two regions. If it is set at e_u, it will be overly stringent for the rural area, and if it is set at e_r, it will not be tight enough for the urban region. The only way to avoid this would be to set different standards in the two areas. This confronts us with one of the great policy trade-offs:

- the more a policy is tailored so that it applies to different and heterogeneous situations, the more efficient it will be in terms of its impacts, but the more costly it will be in terms of getting the information needed to set the diverse standards and enforcing them once they have been established.

FIGURE 11.2 Regional Variation in Efficiency Levels

[Figure: Graph showing MAC curve decreasing and two marginal damage curves MD_u (steeper) and MD_r (flatter) increasing; intersections at e_u and e_r on the horizontal axis labeled "Ambient levels of benzene"; vertical axis in $.]

The curves in **Figure 11.2** could be used to represent other heterogeneous situations as well as differences in geographical regions. For example, MD_u might represent marginal damages in a particular region under some meteorological conditions such as high humidity, or in one season of the year, whereas MD_r could represent the marginal damage function for the same area but under different meteorological conditions, like windy conditions, or at a different time of year. Now a single standard, enforced throughout the year, cannot be efficient at all points in time; if it is efficient at one time, it will not be at the other.[2]

Standards and the Equimarginal Principle

Having discussed the issue of setting the standard at the efficient level of emissions, we need to remember that the efficient level itself is defined by the minimum marginal abatement cost function. This means that where there are multiple emissions sources producing the same effluent,[3] the **equimarginal principle** must hold. The principle states that in order to get the greatest reductions in total emissions for a given total abatement cost, the different sources of emissions must be controlled in such a way that they have the same marginal abatement costs. This means that different sources of a pollutant would normally be controlled to different degrees, depending on the shape of the marginal abatement cost curve at each source. A major problem with standards is that there is almost always an overwhelming tendency for authorities to apply the same standards to all sources. It makes regulation much simpler, and it gives the impression of being fair to everyone because all are apparently being treated alike. But identical standards will be cost-effective only in the unlikely event that all polluters have the same marginal abatement costs.

Consider **Figure 11.3,** showing the marginal abatement cost relationships for two different sources, each emitting the same waste material. For Firm A, the marginal abatement cost function increases much less rapidly as emissions are reduced than they do for Firm B.

---

2. Uniformity is an issue in other environmental cases, for example, California setting water-use restrictions at 25% for all except agriculture.
3. That is, in cases of "uniformly mixed" emissions.

Why the difference? They may be producing different outputs with different technologies. One firm might be older (MAC_B) than the other, and older technology may be less flexible, making it more costly to reduce emissions than at the plant with the newer equipment. One plant may be designed to use a different type of raw material input than the other. This, in fact, mirrors the situation in the real world. Normally one can expect considerable heterogeneity in abatement costs among groups of firms even though they are emitting the same type of residual. Recall from policy criteria that equity or fairness does not necessarily mean equal.

FIGURE 11.3 Marginal Abatement Costs for Two Sources

Emission Level (tons/month)	Marginal Abatement Costs ($) A	B
20	0.00	0.00
19	1.00	2.10
18	2.10	4.60
17	3.30	9.40
16	4.60	19.30
15	6.00	32.50
14	7.60	54.90
13	9.40	82.90
12	11.50	116.90
11	13.90	156.90
10	16.50	204.90
9	19.30	264.90
8	22.30	332.90
7	25.50	406.90
6	28.90	487.00
5	32.50	577.00
4	36.30	677.20
3	40.50	787.20
2	44.90	907.20
1	49.70	1,037.20
0	54.90	1,187.20

The essential numbers from **Figure 11.3** are summarized in **Table 11.1.** Uncontrolled emissions are 20 for each firm, and control costs, marginal and total, are zero.

TABLE 11.1 Illustrative Values for Polluters Shown in Figure 11.3

	Firm A	Firm B	Total
Beginning Solution			
Emissions (tons)	20	20	40
Marginal abatement costs	$0	$0	$0
Total abatement costs	$0	$0	$0
Equiproportionate Reduction			
Emissions (tons)	10	10	20
Marginal abatement costs	$16.50	$204.90	
Total abatement costs	$75.90	$684.40	$760.30
Equimarginal Reduction			
Emissions (tons)	5	15	30
Marginal abatement costs	$32.50	$32.50	
Total abatement costs	$204.40	$67.90	$272.30

Under an equiproportionate rule,[4] each firm would cut back by 50 percent, to 10 tons each. Marginal control costs are then unequal, $16.50 for A and $204.90 for B. Total pollution control costs are $75.90 for A and $684.40 for B, for a total of $760.30.[5]

With equimarginal cutbacks, A goes to 5 tons and B to 15 tons. Pollution control costs total $272.30 for this situation. Compliance costs for a cutback that satisfies the equimarginal criterion are only about 36 percent of compliance costs in an equiproportionate reduction.

To summarize: Standards are usually designed to be applied uniformly across emission sources. This practice is almost inherent in the basic philosophy of the standards approach, and to many people this strikes them as an equitable way to proceed. But if marginal abatement costs in the real world vary across sources, as they usually do, the equal-standards approach will produce less reduction in total emissions for the total compliance costs of the program than would be achieved with an approach that satisfied the equimarginal principle. The greater the differences in marginal abatement costs among sources, the worse will be the performance of the equal-standards approach. We will see in the chapters ahead that this difference can be very large indeed.

Could command-and-control standards be set in accordance with the equimarginal principle? Unless the applicable law required some sort of **equiproportional cutback,** there may be nothing to stop the authorities from setting different standards for the individual sources. To get an overall reduction to 20 tons/month in the previous example, they could

---

4. An equiproportionate cutback is one that reduces each source by the same percentage of its original emissions. In the example, the 10-ton cutback for each source is equal in absolute terms and is equiproportionate (50%), as each source is assumed to be initially at an emission level of 20 tons per month.
5. Note total abatement costs in Table 11.1 are the sum of MAC from Figure 11.3.
   Firm A: $1.00 + 2.10 + 3.30 + 4.60 + 6 + 7.60 + 9.40 + 11.50 + 13.90 + 16.50 = \$75.90$
   Firm B: $2.10 + 4.60 + 9.40 + 19.30 + 32.50 + 54.90 + 82.90 + 116.90 + 156.90 + 204.90 = \$684.40$

require Source A to reduce to 5 tons/month and Source B to cut back to 15 tons/month. The difficult part is that to accomplish this, the authorities must know what the marginal abatement costs are for the different sources. This point needs to be stressed:

- for almost any real-world pollution problem, there will normally be multiple sources. For a public agency to set individual standards in accordance with the equimarginal principle, it would have to know the marginal abatement cost relationship for each of these sources.

We talked in **Chapter 9** about the problem of asymmetric information. Polluters normally have a substantial amount of **private information** about pollution-control costs. These costs will usually vary among sources, so for the regulators to establish cost-effective pollution-control regulations, they will have to find some way to obtain this information. The primary source of data would have to be the polluters themselves, and there is no reason to believe they would willingly share this information. In fact, if they realize, as they certainly would, that the information would be used to establish individual source standards, they would have every incentive to provide the administering agency with data showing that their marginal abatement costs rise very steeply with emission reductions. Thus, there are real problems with authorities attempting to establish source-specific emission standards. Nevertheless, a considerable amount of this is done informally, through the interactions of local pollution-control authorities, charged with enforcing common standards, and local sources, each of which is in somewhat different circumstances. We will come back to this later when we discuss issues of enforcement.

11-3 Standards and Incentives

An important issue for any policy is whether it creates incentives for sources to reduce emissions to efficient levels and in cost-effective ways. The command-and-control approach based on standards is seriously deficient in this regard. A basic problem is that standards are all or nothing; either they are being met or they are not. If they are being met, there is no incentive to do better than the standard, even though the costs of further emission reductions may be quite modest. By the same token, the incentives are to meet the standards, even though the last few units of emission reduction may be much more costly than the damages reduced.

It is easy to deal with the case of technology standards. Here, the incentives to find cheaper ways (considering all costs) of reducing emissions are effectively zero. If control authorities dictate in detail the specific technology and practices that polluters may legally use to reduce emissions, there are no rewards to finding better approaches. A polluter using a better but different technology than in the regulation could be fined. Technology standards are stultifying on these grounds because they substantially drain the incentives for entrepreneurs in the pollution-control industry to develop new ideas.

Now consider emission standards. **Figure 11.4** shows marginal abatement costs of a firm in two situations: MAC_1 refers to such costs before a given technological improvement; MAC_2 is the marginal abatement cost curve the firm could expect to have after investing resources in a research and development (R&D) effort to develop better treatment or recycling technology. Without any pollution-control program at all, there is absolutely no incentive to spend the money on the R&D. But suppose the firm is now faced with having to meet emission standards of e_2 tons/year. With the original marginal abatement costs the total annual cost of compliance for this firm is $(a + b)$ per year. If the R&D program is successful and MAC_1 reduces to MAC_2, compliance costs would be only b/year. The difference, a/year, is the amount by which compliance costs would be reduced and represents, in fact, the incentive for engaging in the R&D effort. This is more than we could say for technology standards, in which case the firm is stuck with MAC_1.

FIGURE 11.4 Cost Savings from Technological Change: The Case of Standards

To understand fully the incentive effects of standards, one has to look closely at the details. **Figure 11.4** depicts a standard applied to total emissions. Historically, most standards have been applied to emissions **per unit of input or output** of industrial firms. For electric utilities, an emission standard per unit of fuel burned is a standard per unit of input. There are important incentive implications of setting standards this way.

Consider the following expression, showing how total emissions from an industrial operation are related to underlying performance factors:

$$\text{Total emissions} = \text{Total output} \times \text{Inputs used per unit of output} \times \text{Emissions per unit of input}$$

Suppose authorities apply an input standard to, for example, coal-burning power plants. The standard could be expressed in terms of maximum amounts of SO_2 emissions allowed per ton of coal burned. This is a standard applied to the last term of the equation, and so the power plant will presumably reduce its emissions per unit of input to the level of the standard. There are two other ways of reducing total emissions, as depicted in the first two terms to the right of the equals sign. One is to reduce total output through, for example, encouraging consumers to conserve electricity. The other is to reduce the amount of coal needed per unit of electricity generated, in other words, for the plant(s) to increase **fuel efficiency.** But the plants will have no incentive to reduce emissions in these last two ways because the standard has been written in terms only of the last factor in the expression.

With **output-based standards,** standards are expressed in terms of allowable emissions per unit of output.[6] If you multiply together the last two terms of the expression, you get **emissions per unit of output.** If you place a standard on this factor, polluters can reduce emissions in two ways: by reducing inputs per unit of output and by reducing emissions per unit of input. The incentives of the polluters have been broadened. In the case of a power plant, an output-based standard would involve both incentives: to reduce emissions per unit of coal burned (perhaps by switching to low-sulfur coal) and to become more fuel efficient (perhaps by upgrading the boilers of the plant). With this approach a producer can decide the most efficient and best method for the firm to meet the output-based standard.

Political-Economic Aspects of Standards

The theory of standards is that they are established by regulatory authorities, then responded to by polluters. In fact, this process can lead to patterns of political give-and-take between the parties that will substantially affect the outcome and create:

- **perverse incentives**—an incentive that actually works against the objectives of the regulation.

Suppose that the authorities are making every effort to set the standard at something approaching the efficient level of emissions. In **Figure 11.4,** e_2 is their view of the efficient level before the technical change. A new technology lowers the marginal abatement cost curve, and this will reduce the efficient level of emissions. Suppose the authorities estimate that, given their view of marginal damages, the new technology shifts the efficient emission level to e_3 in **Figure 11.4,** and that they now change the standard to reflect this. Before the new technology and e_3, compliance costs were $(a + b)$. Now the firm's compliance cost will be $(b + c)$ per year. The difference is now $(a - c)$. If $(b + c) > (a + b)$, the firm would be worse off with the new technology than with the old methods. Setting standards in this case has undermined the incentive to produce new pollution-control technology. In this case, standard setting can work against long-run improvements in pollution-control technology.[7]

If emission standards create incentives for technological change, is it not desirable to establish very stringent standards so as to increase that incentive? This is another place where political considerations come into play. If, in **Figure 11.4,** the standard is set at e_3 right at the beginning, this would mean cost savings of $(a + d + e)$ with the new technology (MAC_1) rather than just a as it would be with the standard set at e_2. The principle is:

- **technology forcing**—setting standards that are unrealistic with today's technology in the hope that it will motivate the pollution-control industry to invent ways of meeting the standard at reasonable cost.

But stricter standards also create another incentive: the incentive for polluters to seek relief from public authorities by delaying the date when they become applicable. In an open political system, firms may take some of the resources that might have gone for pollution-control R&D and devote them instead to influencing political authorities to delay the

---

6. Automobile emission standards have always been in terms of output, for example, grams of pollutant per mile driven. We will talk about this in Chapter 15.
7. There is another perverse incentive lurking in equiproportionate reductions. If polluters realize that they will be subject to an equiproportionate cutback in the future, it is better for them to increase their base now by increasing their emissions. When the cutback is imposed, they will be able to emit higher amounts than they would have had they not inflated their base.

onset of strict standards. The stricter and more near-term the standards, the more of this activity there is likely to be. Thus, technology forcing is another one of those strategies where the effectiveness of moderate amounts does not imply that more will be even more effective. Emissions standards are better in this respect, as we have seen.

11-4 The Economics of Enforcement

All pollution-control programs (perhaps with the exception of voluntary programs, mentioned in the last chapter) require enforcement. Much of the ongoing political conflict over environmental regulations involves questions of enforcement, with one side often saying that it is too harsh, the other side maintaining that it isn't harsh enough. In this section we deal briefly with some economic issues related to enforcement, discussing these particularly in their relation to enforcing standards. In later chapters we will discuss enforcement issues related to other types of policy instruments.

Enforcing Emission Standards

Let's consider the two primary dimensions of enforcement: monitoring and sanctioning. **Figure 11.5** shows a marginal abatement cost function representing as usual the marginal costs to the firm of reducing emissions. But on the other side, instead of a marginal damage function as in the standard model, there is a **marginal penalty function.** The line marked MPC represents the expected penalties that firms can be expected to face for violating an emission standard. Penalties arise when firms are detected to be exceeding their emission standard and fines or other penalties are levied as a result. Suppose a standard is set at e^*. What is relevant here is the way firms will actually be motivated to reduce their emissions.[8] MPC is zero below e^*; the firm is only penalized for emissions in excess of the standard, and the shape of the MPC curve shows how penalties would increase as the size of the violation increases.

FIGURE 11.5 The Economics of Enforcement

---

[8]. In chapter 10 we discussed liability rules as a way of controlling emissions. In penalty function terms, liability rules turn the marginal damage function into an MPC curve, because they would make firms responsible for paying for the damages their emissions produce.

If current emissions are at e_0, the firm will clearly reduce them because marginal abatement costs at this point are well below the marginal penalty costs currently in effect (MPC). But it will stop reducing emissions at e_1, because to go lower than this would require higher abatement costs than it would save in terms of reduced penalties. Unless something changes, therefore, the firm's emissions will end up at e_1, and the amount of noncompliance will be $e^* - e_1$.

The only way to reduce noncompliance is to raise the penalty function. Basically, there are two ways of doing this: raise monitoring activities so as to be better able to detect noncompliance, or raise fines for those who have been detected as noncompliant. If the authorities do both, the penalty function could be raised to something like the dotted line labeled MPC', which would then ensure a noncompliance rate of zero. Emissions would be reduced to e^*.

This analysis shows several things:

- there is a trade-off in enforcement; to get higher levels of compliance, authorities will normally have to devote more resources to enforcement.
- there is also a trade-off between monitoring and fines. The MPC curve of **Figure 11.5** can be raised or lowered by changes in either one of these enforcement elements.

We should also note that monitoring in this case requires measuring, or estimating, the quantities of emissions, because the MPC function is essentially expressed in terms of deviations of actual emissions from the emission levels set in the standard. This deviation could apply to hourly, daily, or annual quantities. Over the years, there have been major advances in monitoring technology. In the early days of rigorous pollution control, much of the enforcement effort depended on **self-monitoring,** where sources themselves kept the books on emissions flows over time. This permitted the agencies to visit firms periodically to audit the records at each source. Agencies could also make random checks to measure emissions. The rate of auditing and random visits could be varied according to agency budgets. More recently, technologies have been developed for undertaking **continuous measurement** with electronic reporting of emissions and **remote monitoring technology.**

The other main factor behind the MPC function of **Figure 11.5** is the size of the fines or other sanctions (e.g., jail terms). Most pollution-control statutes contain provisions on the size of the fine or jail term that may be levied against violators if and when they are caught and found guilty. In many cases, fines have been set too low, lower than the abatement costs required to meet the standards. In these situations firms can actually save money by dragging their feet on compliance. With low sanctions like this, enforcement is therefore likely to be much more difficult and costly than if sanctions are higher. Sources faced with the possibility of having to pay substantially higher fines would presumably have a stronger incentive to come into compliance.

It needs to be kept in mind that sanctioning ordinarily involves using the court system to pursue legal action, and this may put some limits on what enforcing agencies may do. For example, if monetary fines or other penalties expressed in the law are very high, courts may be reluctant to hold sources in rigorous noncompliance because of the economic dislocation this may produce.

Enforcing Technology Standards

Technology standards require that sources adopt and operate approved technical means of pollution control. In this case an important distinction is between:

- **initial compliance**—where a polluter charged with meeting a particular technology standard installs the appropriate equipment, and
- **continued compliance**—where a polluter verifies that the adopted technology is functioning as prescribed and is routinely used or operating.

To monitor initial compliance it is necessary to have inspectors visit the site, check to see that the equipment is installed, and make sure it will operate in accordance with the conditions of the standard. Having ascertained this, the administering agency can then give the firm the necessary operating permit, but this does not ensure that the equipment will continue to be operated in the future in accordance with the terms of the permit. It may deteriorate through normal use, it may not be maintained properly, future operating personnel may not be properly trained, and so on. Without some amount of monitoring, therefore, there is no assurance that the source will continue to be in compliance. But here, again, the administering agency has great flexibility in setting up a monitoring program. It can vary from very infrequent visits to randomly selected sites all the way up to permanent observers stationed at each source, like resident inspectors in the nuclear power industry.

The Enforcing Agency

When enforcement costs are included in the analysis, the question arises of whether standards should be set, at least in part, with enforcement costs in mind. Stricter standards may involve larger enforcement costs because they require larger operating changes on the part of sources. Less strict standards may be achievable with fewer enforcement resources for the opposite reason. Public environmental agencies are usually faced with budget stringencies. In some cases, greater overall reductions in emissions may be obtained by using less strict standards that can be easily enforced than by stricter standards involving higher enforcement costs.

One very common feature of environmental standards is that they are usually set and enforced by different groups of people. Standards often are set by national authorities; enforcement is usually done by local authorities. For example, the air quality standards established under the Clean Air Act are set at the federal level, yet enforcement is mostly carried out by state agencies. This has a number of important implications. One is that standards are often set without much thought to costs of enforcement; it is more or less assumed that local authorities will find the necessary enforcement resources. Of course, this is not the case in practice. With limited enforcement budgets and/or with cuts in the number of people employed in enforcement of standards, local authorities may react to new programs by reducing resources devoted to other programs.

Another implication is that, in practice, environmental policies incorporating standards end up having a lot more flexibility than might at first appear. Laws written at national levels are specific and apparently applicable everywhere. But at the local level, "where the rubber meets the road," as they say, it's a matter of local pollution-control authorities applying the law to local sources, and in this process there can be a great deal of informal give-and-take between the authorities and local plant managers, with participation by local environmental groups as well. Some people might favor standards because of the very fact that in the real world of tight public agency budgets, they permit partial or incomplete compliance due to weak enforcement. Policies using standards permit flexibility in enforcement which some see as an advantage and others as a disadvantage.

Summary

The most popular approach to environmental pollution control historically has been the setting of standards. This has been called the command-and-control approach because it consists of public authorities announcing certain limits on polluters, then enforcing these limits with appropriate enforcement institutions. We specified three primary types of standards: ambient, emission, and technology. Initial discussion centered on the level at which standards should be set and the regional uniformity of standards.

A leading problem with standard setting is the question of cost-effectiveness and the equimarginal principle. In most standards programs, the administrative bias is to apply the same standards to all sources of a particular pollutant. But pollution control can be cost-effective only when marginal abatement costs are equalized across sources. When marginal abatement costs differ among sources, as they almost always do, uniform standards cannot be cost-effective. In practice, differences among sources in their marginal abatement costs often are recognized informally by local administrators in applying a uniform national standard.

We also dealt at length with the question of the long-run impact of standards through their effects on the incentives to look for better ways of reducing emissions. Technology standards completely undermine these incentives. Emission standards do create positive incentives for R&D in pollution control, although we will see that these are weaker than those of economic-incentive types of pollution-control policies, the subject of the next two chapters. Finally, we discussed the all-important question of enforcement.

Questions for Further Discussion

1. Environmental protection programs are frequently designed to require all polluters to cut back emissions by a certain percentage. What are some perverse incentives built into this type of program?
2. If emission standards are ruled out because of, for example, the impossibility of measuring emissions (as in nonpoint-source emissions), what alternative types of standards might be used instead? Discuss how they would work.
3. In **Figure 11.2,** show the social cost of setting a uniform national standard, applicable to both rural and urban areas (to do this, you can assume that the national standard is set at either e_u or e_r).

(Continued)

Questions for Further Discussion *(Continued)*

4. Consider the example of **Figure 11.3.** Suppose we define as *fair* a cutback in which the two sources have the same total costs. Would an equiproportionate reduction be fair in this sense? A reduction meeting the equimarginal principle? Is this a reasonable definition of *fair*?

5. It is sometimes suggested that the most equitable way to resolve issues in international trade agreements would be for all countries to adopt the same emission standards. What are the pros and cons of this from an economic standpoint?

6. Suppose you want to reduce the level of trash disposed by your household. Develop an emission standard, a technology standard, and an ambient standard that would accomplish the reduction. Develop a plan to monitor and enforce your standard.

For additional resources pertaining to the material in this chapter, see the list in **Appendix B.**

Chapter 12
Incentive-Based Strategies: Environmental Charges and Subsidies

In the last chapter we discussed some of the advantages and disadvantages of using a standards approach to pollution control. Although standards seemingly offer direct control of polluting activities, in many applications they have serious drawbacks by virtue of their tendency to treat all sources alike even though they may be very different, and to lock in certain technologies. A major problem is that they typically are unable to take advantage of the private information that polluters have about means and procedures they could use to reduce pollution. **Incentive-based** (IB) environmental policies are designed to rectify these drawbacks. IB plans work by having public authorities first set overall objectives and rules, and then leaving firms enough latitude that their normal commercial incentives will lead to the adoption of cost-effective pollution-control procedures and technologies.

There are basically two types of incentive policies:

1. **Charges (taxes) and subsidies,** and
2. **Market-based systems.**

Both require centralized policy initiative to get started and then rely on flexible firm responses to attain efficient pollution control. In the first, firms are given latitude to respond however they wish to what is essentially a new price for using the services of the environment. The second is designed to work more or less automatically through the interactions among polluters themselves or between polluters and other interested parties. Many countries have relied upon environmental charges to motivate emission reductions, as well as raise public revenues. **Exhibit 12.1** notes some of the plans adopted in Europe. In this chapter we examine the economics of environmental charges and subsidies. In **Chapter 13** we will consider market-based systems.

Environmental economists have long favored the idea of incorporating IB approaches more thoroughly into environmental policies. These can serve to put more teeth into environmental policies and substantially improve the cost-effectiveness of these policies. They are especially important to consider for the difficult task of reducing emissions of greenhouse gases (GHGs).

Keep in mind something said before: No single type of policy is likely to be the best in all circumstances. IB policies are no exception. They have strengths and they have weaknesses. The strengths are sufficiently strong to encourage greater reliance on them in many circumstances. But there are many types of environmental problems where they may not be as useful as other approaches.

EXHIBIT 12.1 Environmental Taxes in Europe

Charge or Tax	Description
France	Aircraft noise charges, based on maximum take-off weight, certified noise performance, and time of day
Hungary	Emissions charges on SO_2, NO_x, and nontoxic dust
Norway	User charges on wastewater treatment, based on costs of treatment facilities
Sweden	Taxes on nitrogen-oxide emissions and CO_2 emissions
United Kingdom	Climate charge levy, varying charges on carbon content of different fuels—a carbon tax
Ireland	Landfill tax charged per ton of waste delivered to an approved disposal side
Denmark	Pesticide taxes, levied on wholesale prices of pesticides
Netherlands	Energy tax, on energy products used for heating and electricity production
Latvia	Taxes on estimates of airborne emissions of a variety of pollutants

Source: OECD, Database on Policy Instruments for the Environment, 2017.

12-1 Emission Charges or Taxes[1]

Firms pollute because they do not take into account the social damage their actions cause. Essentially the price for the use of some parts of the environment is zero. Although many consumers and producers accept paying a price for disposing of trash, that concept has not been widely adopted yet for greenhouse gases, for example. Thus, the most straightforward approach to controlling emissions is for authorities to charge a price for these emissions. This can be done in two ways:

- By charging for each unit of emissions, or
- By giving a subsidy for each unit of emissions that the source cuts back.

We deal first with **emission charges,** also called **emission taxes.** In a charge system polluters are told: "You may discharge any amount of residuals you wish, but your emissions will be measured and you will be required to pay a certain charge for every unit (e.g., ton) of effluent you discharge."[2] For example, one of the first emission charges proposed in the United States was in 1970, when President Nixon recommended a tax of 15 cents per pound on sulfur emissions from large power plants. It was never adopted by Congress.

---

1. Terminology varies in this subject. Some people prefer to talk of emission **charges,** others prefer emissions **taxes.** For our purposes, charges and taxes are synonymous and are used interchangeably.
2. The idea of taxing "bads" was first put forth by A.C. Pigou in his *Economic of Welfare,* London, Macmillan, 1920. Thus, Pigouvian taxes are taxes meant to achieve changes in the behavior of, in this case, polluters, in contrast to standard taxes, whose purpose is primarily to raise public revenues.

When an emission charge is put into effect, firms responsible for emissions must essentially pay for the services of the environment—transportation, dilution, chemical decomposition, and so on—just as they must pay for all other inputs used in their operations. And just as they have always had an incentive to conserve on scarce labor and other conventional production inputs, they will now have an incentive to conserve on their use of environmental services. How do they do this? Any way they wish (within reason). This may sound flippant but in fact it represents the main advantage of this technique. By leaving polluters free to determine how best to reduce emissions, this type of policy attempts to harness their own energy and creativity and their desire to minimize costs, to find the least-cost way of reducing emissions. It could be any combination of treatment, internal process changes, changes in inputs, recycling, shifts to less polluting outputs, and so on. The essence of the charge approach is to provide an incentive for the polluters themselves to find the best way to reduce emissions, rather than having a central authority determine how it should be done. And in so doing, they will have a strong incentive to use the private information they have about the pollution-control costs of alternative technologies.

The Economics of an Emission Tax

The essential mechanics of an emission tax are depicted in **Figure 12.1.** The numbers refer to a single source of a particular pollutant. The top panel shows the analysis numerically, while the bottom shows essentially the same information graphically. The tax has been set at $120/ton/month. The second column in the top panel shows the firm's marginal abatement costs and the third column shows total abatement costs. The last two columns show the total monthly tax bill the firm would pay at different emission levels, and the total cost, consisting of the sum of abatement costs and the tax bill. We see that the minimum total cost of $855 occurs at an emission rate of 4 tons/month. Let's pursue the logic of this by considering marginal abatement costs.

Suppose the firm is initially emitting 10 tons/month. If it does not reduce emissions, the firm's tax, or payment for using the environment, is $1,200. The firm has an incentive to reduce emissions. If it were to cut emissions to 9 tons, it would cost $15 in abatement costs, but it would save $120 in total tax bill, clearly a good move because total costs drop to $1,095. Following this logic, it could improve its bottom line by continuing to reduce emissions as long as the tax rate is above marginal abatement costs. The rule for the firm to follow is thus:

- Reduce emissions until marginal abatement costs are equal to the charge on emissions.

This is shown diagrammatically in the bottom part of **Figure 12.1.** With a continuous marginal abatement cost function, it's possible to talk about fractions of tons of emissions, something we could not do in the upper panel. So the graph is drawn to agree with the integer values above; that is, the charge of $120 leads the firm to reduce emissions to exactly 4 tons/month.

FIGURE 12.1 An Emissions Charge

Emissions (tons/month)	Marginal Abatement Cost	Total Abatement Cost	Total Tax Bill at $120/Ton	Total Costs
10	0	0	1,200	1,200
9	15	15	1,080	1,095
8	30	45	960	1,005
7	50	95	840	935
6	70	165	720	885
5	95	260	600	860
4	120	375	480	855
3	150	525	360	885
2	185	710	240	950
1	230	940	120	1,060
0	290	1,230	0	1,230

After the firm has reduced its emissions to 4 tons/month, its total (monthly) tax bill will be $480. Its monthly abatement costs will be $375. Graphically, total abatement costs correspond to the area under the marginal abatement cost function, labeled *b* in the figure. The total tax bill is equal to emissions times the tax rate, or the rectangle labeled *a*. Under a charge system of this type, a firm's total cost equals its abatement costs plus the tax payments to the taxing authority.

Why wouldn't the firm simply disregard the charge, continue to pollute as it has been doing, and just pass the charge on to consumers in the form of higher prices? If the firm stayed at 10 tons of emissions, its total outlay would be $1,200/month, consisting entirely of tax payment. This is much higher than the $855 it can achieve by cutting back to 4 tons/month. The assumption in an emissions charge program is that **competitive pressures** will lead firms to do whatever they can to minimize their costs. Thus, when there is competition in the industry subject to the emission tax, it will lead firms to reduce emissions in response to the tax. By the same token, however, we must recognize that if competition is weak, firms may not respond in this way. Electric power plants, for example, are usually operated by regulated monopolies subject to oversight by public utility commissions. They may not respond to charges on sulfur dioxide (SO_2) emissions in the same way as firms that operate in more competitive economic climates.

For competitive firms, the amount of the response will depend on several factors. The higher the charge, the greater the reduction, and vice versa. In the example of **Figure 12.1**, a tax of $50/ton/month would have led the source to reduce emissions only to 7 tons/month, whereas one of $180 would have produced a cutback to 2 tons/month; that is, the firm would select an emissions quantity closest to where MAC equals the charge. Also, the steeper the marginal abatement cost function, the less emissions will be reduced in response to a tax. We will come back to this later.

Compare the charge approach with an emission standard. With the tax the firm's total outlay is $855. Suppose that, instead, the authorities had relied on an emission standard set to 4 tons/month. In that case, the firm's total outlay would be only the $375 of abatement costs. Thus, the charge system ends up costing the firm more than the standards approach. With a standard, the firm has the same total abatement costs as in the charge system, but it is still essentially getting the services of the environment free, whereas with a charge system it has to pay for those services. Although in most circumstances, polluting firms would thus prefer standards to emission charges, there are good reasons why society would often prefer taxes over standards.

The Level of the Charge

In competitive situations, higher charges will bring about greater reductions in emissions, but just how high should the charge be set? If we know the marginal damage function, the answer presumably would be to set the charge so as to produce the efficient level of emissions, as in **Figure 12.2**. At a tax rate of t^*, emissions are e^*, and marginal damages equal marginal abatement costs. The firm's total costs of emission control are divided into two types: total abatement costs (compliance costs) of e and total tax payments of $(a + b + c + d)$. The former are the costs of whatever techniques the firm has chosen to reduce emissions from e_0 to e^*, whereas the latter are tax payments to the control agency covering the charge on the remaining emissions. From the standpoint of the firm, of course, these are both real costs that will have to be covered out of revenues. From the standpoint of *society,* however, the tax payments are different from the abatement costs. Whereas the abatement costs involve real resources and therefore real social costs, the emission taxes are actually **transfer payments,** payments made by the firms (ultimately by people who buy the firms' output) to the public sector and eventually to those in society who are benefited by the resulting public expenditures. When a firm considers its costs, it will include both abatement costs and tax payments.

FIGURE 12.2 An Efficient Emission Charge

[Figure 12.2: Graph showing marginal abatement costs (downward sloping curve) and marginal damage (upward sloping curve) intersecting at emission level e^* and tax rate t^*. The horizontal axis shows Emissions (tons/year) with points e_1, e^*, and e_0. Areas labeled a, b, c, d, e, and f are shown between the curves.]

The reduction of emissions from e_0 to e^* has eliminated damages of $(e + f)$. Remaining damages are $(b + d)$, an amount less than the firm pays in taxes. This underscores the idea that the emission charge is based on the right to use environmental resources, not on the notion of compensation and not on the notion of punishment. But a "flat tax" like this (one tax rate for all emissions) has been criticized because it would often lead to situations where the total tax payments of firms would substantially exceed remaining damages. A way around this is to institute a **two-part emission charge.** We allow some initial quantity of emission to go untaxed, applying the charge only to emissions in excess of this threshold. For example, in **Figure 12.2** we might allow the firm e_1 units of emissions free of tax and apply the tax rate of t^* to anything over this. In this way the firm would still have the incentive to reduce emissions to e^*, but its total tax payments would be only $(c + d)$. Total abatement costs, and total damages caused by the e^* units of emissions, would still be the same.

How might the charge be set if regulators do not know the marginal damage function? Emissions are connected to ambient quality; the lower the emissions, the lower the ambient concentration of the pollutant, in general. However, tracking the subsequent charge in ambient quality could take a long time. In responding to a charge, polluters would invest in a variety of pollution-control devices and practices, many of which would have relatively high up-front costs. This investment process could be substantially upset if, shortly after setting one tax rate, the authorities shift to a new tax rate. Any agency trying to use this method to find the efficient charge rate would undoubtedly find itself embroiled in a brisk political battle. Rather than planning to make successive adjustments in the tax rate, there would be a strong incentive for policymakers to determine the correct rate at the beginning. This would put a premium on prior study to get some idea of the shapes of the aggregate abatement and damage cost curves.

Emission Charges and Cost-Effectiveness

Perhaps the strongest case for a policy of effluent charges is to be made on grounds of their effects in controlling multiple sources of emissions in a way that satisfies the **equimarginal principle**. If the same tax rate is applied to different sources with different marginal abatement cost functions, and each source reduces its emissions until its marginal abatement costs equal the tax, then marginal abatement costs will automatically be equalized across all the sources.

This is depicted in **Figure 12.3**. We assume here that there are two sources of a particular type of emission, labeled Sources A and B. Also assume that these emissions, after they leave the respective sources, are uniformly mixed together, so that the emissions of the two plants are equally damaging in the downstream, or downwind, impact area. The marginal abatement costs for the two sources are shown in graphical form at the bottom of **Figure 12.3**. The marginal abatement costs of Source A increase much less rapidly with reductions in emissions than do those of Source B. In the real world, differences like this are normally related to the fact that the firms are using different production technologies. They may be producing different outputs (e.g., a pulp mill and a food-canning firm), or they may be plants in the same industry but using different production techniques (e.g., coal-fired and natural gas-fired electric power plants). According to the graphs, the production technology used by Source B makes emission reduction more costly than it is at Source A. If we impose an effluent charge of $33/ton on each source, the operators of Source A will reduce their emissions to 5 tons/month; those at Source B will cut back to 15 tons/month (dealing only with integer values). After these reductions, the two sources will have the same marginal abatement costs. The total reduction has been 20 tons per month, which the effluent charge has automatically distributed between the two firms in accordance with the equimarginal principle.

Note very carefully that the emission tax has led Source A to reduce its emissions by 75 percent, whereas Source B has reduced its emissions by only 25 percent. The emissions tax leads to larger proportionate emission reductions from firms with lower marginal abatement costs. Conversely, firms having steeper marginal abatement costs will reduce emissions less, in proportionate terms.

Suppose that instead of the charge the authorities had instituted a **proportionate** cutback on the grounds that "everybody should be treated alike"; therefore, they require each source to reduce emissions by 50 percent. Our two sources in **Figure 12.3** both reduce emissions to 10 tons/month. At this point their marginal abatement costs would be different. Furthermore, we can calculate total abatement costs by remembering that total cost is the sum of marginal costs. Thus, for example, for Source A the total costs of 10 tons of emissions would be $(1.0 + 2.1 + \cdots + 16.5) = \$75.90$.

CHAPTER 12 Incentive-Based Strategies: Environmental Charges and Subsidies 211

FIGURE 12.3 Emission Charges and the Equimarginal Rule

Emission Level (tons/month)	Marginal Abatement Costs ($) Source A	Marginal Abatement Costs ($) Source B
20	0.0	0.0
19	1.0	2.1
18	2.1	4.6
17	3.3	9.4
16	4.6	19.3
15	6.0	32.5
14	7.6	54.9
13	9.4	82.9
12	11.5	116.9
11	13.9	156.9
10	16.5	204.9
9	19.3	264.9
8	22.3	332.9
7	25.5	406.9
6	28.9	487.0
5	32.5	577.0
4	36.3	677.2
3	40.5	787.2
2	44.9	907.2
1	49.7	1,037.2
0	54.9	1,187.2

The following tabulation compares the compliance costs of the equiproportionate reduction and the effluent charge with equimarginal rules.

	Total Compliance Costs ($/month)	
	Equiproportionate Reduction	**Effluent Charge with Equimarginal Rules**
Source A	75.90	204.40
Source B	684.40	67.90
Total	760.30	272.30

Note how much the totals differ. The total compliance cost of an equiproportionate cutback is about 2.8 times the total cost of an emission tax. The simple reason is that the equiproportionate cutback violates the equimarginal principle; it requires the same proportionate cutback regardless of the height and shape of a firm's marginal abatement costs. The difference in total costs between these two approaches is quite large with these illustrative numbers. The extra money spent by firms with the equiproportionate percentage could have been used to further reduce pollution.

The higher the tax rate, the more emissions will be reduced. In fact, if the tax rate were increased to something over $55/ton, Firm A would stop emitting this residual entirely. The marginal abatement cost function for Firm B increases so rapidly, however, that an extremely high charge (more than $1,187/ton) would be required to get this source to reduce emissions to zero. A single effluent charge, when applied to several firms, will induce a greater reduction by firms whose marginal abatement costs increase less rapidly than from firms whose marginal abatement costs increase more rapidly. Because the firms are paying the same tax rate, they will have different total abatement costs and different tax bills. In **Figure 12.3,** the total abatement costs are equal to area *b* for Source A and area *d* for Source B. On the other hand, the monthly tax bill sent to Source A would be only *a,* compared to a bill of *c* sent to Source B. Thus, the less steeply the marginal abatement cost of a firm increases, the larger that firm's emission reduction will be and the smaller its tax bill.

It needs to be emphasized that the efficiency results of the emission charge approach (i.e., that it satisfies the equimarginal principle) are achievable *even though the administering agency knows nothing about the marginal abatement costs of any of the sources.* This is in clear contrast with the standards approach, where the public agency has to know exactly what these marginal abatement costs are for each firm in order to have a fully efficient program. In a charge approach, the only requirement is that firms pay the same tax rate and that they are cost minimizers. After each one has adjusted its emissions in accordance with its marginal abatement costs (which we can expect them to know themselves), they will all be emitting at the appropriate rates to satisfy the equimarginal principle.

Emission Taxes and Nonuniform Emissions

So far the discussion has proceeded under the assumption that the emissions of all sources are uniformly mixed together; that is, the emissions from one source have the same marginal impact on ambient quality levels as those from other sources. In the real world this is usually not the case. Very often the situation is something like, although of course more complicated than, that depicted in **Figure 12.4**. Here there are two sources. Source A is about twice as far away from the center of population as Source B. This means that emissions from Source A do not produce as much damage in the urban area as emissions from Source B. If the two sources are emitting some material into a river that flows toward the city, the emissions of Source A have a longer time in the water to be broken down and rendered less harmful than do the emissions from Source B. Or if it is a problem of air pollution, Source A is much farther upwind than Source B, so there is more time for its emissions to be spread out and diluted than there is for the emissions from Source B. There could be other reasons than location differences for the different impacts; for example, they may emit residuals at different times of the year when wind patterns are different. Studying the location problem allows us to examine the general problem of nonuniform emissions.

FIGURE 12.4 Nonuniform Emissions

In this case a single emission charge applied to both sources would not be fully efficient. A single charge addresses only the problem of differences in marginal abatement costs, not differences in damages caused by the emissions from different sources. In **Figure 12.4**, a one-unit reduction in emissions from Plant B would improve environmental quality (reduce damages) in the urban area more than a one-unit reduction in emissions from Plant A. This fact must be taken into account in setting emission charge rates. Suppose emission reductions at Source B are twice as effective at reducing damages as reductions in emissions at Source A. This means, in effect, that the effluent tax paid by Source B must be twice as high as the effluent charge paid by Source A.[3] Thus, after adjustment to these tax levels the marginal abatement cost of Source B would be twice the marginal abatement cost of Source A. But the damage reduction *per dollar spent in reducing emissions* would be equalized across the two sources.

The logic of the preceding discussion implies that in these cases we would have to charge different emission charges to each source. Another response here might be to institute what is called a **zoned emission charge**. Here the administering agency would divide a

---

3. The technical concept here is called a "transfer coefficient." A transfer coefficient is a number that tells how the emissions from any particular source affect ambient quality at some other point. In the previous example, suppose 1 thousand cubit feet (Mcf) of methane (CH_4) emitted by B would increase CH_4 concentration over the urban area by 0.1 ppb. Then a ton emitted from Source A would increase the ambient concentration by 0.05 (assuming an effect that is strictly proportional to distance). If the transfer coefficient for Source B is 1, that for Source A is 0.5, so the tax at A has to be half the tax at B. More generally, if the transfer coefficient at A is t_1, and that of B is t_2, then the tax at A should be t_1/t_2 times the tax at B.

territory into separate zones; the actual number of zones would depend on the circumstances of the case. Within each zone the agency would charge the same emission charge to all sources, whereas it would charge different charges in different zones.

Naturally, the zones would be identified by grouping together sources whose emissions have similar effects on ambient quality levels. **Figure 12.5,** for example, shows the schematic of a river with a dozen different sources of emissions and one urban area where water quality is measured and water quality targets are established. The 10 upstream sources are strung along the river at increasing distances from the urban area. Thus, each has a different impact on measured water quality at the monitoring station, and a fully cost-effective program of emissions reductions would have to account for this fact *in addition to* their different marginal abatement costs. But it would be administratively very costly to apply a different emissions charge to each source. We might, in this case, fall back on a zoned emission charge.

FIGURE 12.5 Zoned Emissions Charge

Key: ■ Emission sources
⊗ Water-quality monitoring station

We first define different zones along the river, then apply the same tax to all sources within the same zone, and different taxes to sources in different zones. Each zone would contain sources whose emissions have roughly the same impact on measured water quality. In **Figure 12.5,** for example, four upstream zones along the river are sketched out. The three sources in Zone 1 would pay the same charge, as would the four sources in Zone 2, and so on. Sources 11 and 12 are downstream from the urban area and may not get taxed at all. Of course, this is a simplified diagram to show the basic idea; in the real world, there would also very likely be downstream damages. By using a zone system, we can achieve a certain amount of administrative simplification while recognizing differences in the locations of different groups of sources.

Emission Charges and Uncertainty

When administrators set taxes at certain levels, they face **uncertainty** about how much emission reduction will ensue, for that depends on how sources respond to the tax. This is one of the drawbacks of emission charges. It may be difficult to predict accurately how much total emissions will decrease because exact knowledge of marginal abatement costs is often lacking. Observe **Figure 12.6.** It shows two different marginal abatement cost functions, a steep one (MAC_1) and one that is much less steep (MAC_2).

FIGURE 12.6 Emission Charges, Uncertainty, and Tax Revenues

Consider MAC_1. If the tax were set at the relatively high rate of t_h, this source would reduce emissions to e_1, whereas if it were set at the low rate of t_l, it would adjust emissions to e_2. These two emission rates are relatively close together. In other words, whether the tax is high or low, the emissions rate of this source would not vary much; we could count on having an emissions rate of something in the vicinity of e_1 and e_2.

But for the firm with the less steep marginal abatement costs (MAC_2), things are much more unstable. If the tax were set low, it would change emissions to e_4, whereas with a high tax emissions would go all the way down to e_3. In other words, for given changes in the tax rate, this firm would respond with much larger changes in emission rates than would the source with the steeper MAC curve.

The upshot of this discussion is that if most firms in a particular pollution problem have relatively flat MAC functions, regulators may have trouble finding the charge rate that will give us just the amount of reduction in total emissions we want. Because they don't know exactly where the MAC functions really are, they don't know exactly how high to set the tax. If they set it a little high or a little low, these firms will respond with large changes in their emissions. This is one of the main reasons administrators opt for standards: They seem to offer a definite control on quantities of emissions produced. In the next chapter, we will discuss an incentive approach that addresses this problem.

Emission Charges and Tax Revenues

Another important aspect of emission charges is that they lead to **tax revenues** accruing to the government. Carrying this line of thought further has suggested to many people that society could benefit by replacing certain existing taxes with emission taxes. Many countries tax employment, for example. When firms hire workers, they must pay employment taxes to cover such things as the public costs of unemployment insurance and social security payments. But employment taxes lead to reduced levels of employment because, in effect, they make hiring workers more expensive. A government, therefore, might reduce its employment taxes and increase emission taxes in such a way as to keep its total tax revenue the same. In this case, society would gain both from the emissions taxes (through reduced emission damage) and from reduced employment tax (through increased employment).

But predicting the revenue impacts of emission taxes may be difficult. Suppose, in **Figure 12.6,** an emission tax was increased from t_l to t_h. If the aggregate marginal abatement cost of the affected firm is MAC_1, total tax revenue will increase from $(b + c)$ to $(a + b)$. But if the marginal abatement cost is actually MAC_2, raising the emission tax will cause tax revenues to decrease from $(e + f)$ to $(d + e)$. This is because in the case of MAC_2 the tax increase leads to a large decrease in emissions, while in the case of MAC_1 it does not. Thus, if the tax authorities don't know much about the shape and location of the relevant marginal abatement, they may be in for some major surprises in terms of changes in tax revenues.[4]

There are two primary impacts of emission charges on the distribution of income and wealth:

1. Effects from the expenditure of tax funds generated by the charges, and
2. Impacts on prices and output of goods and services affected by the charges.

Effluent charges can involve substantial sums going from consumers of the goods produced by the taxed industry to the beneficiaries, whomever they may be, of the funds collected by the taxing authorities. These funds could be used for any number of purposes; how they are used would determine their impacts:

- They might be distributed to lower-income people to offset the effects of price increases.
- They might help finance the purchase of pollution-control technology.
- They might be used to pay for other environmental initiatives in places where direct public action is called for.
- They even might be used to reduce overall budget deficits, with benefits flowing to general taxpayers.

Also, businesses subject to a charge will experience an increase in costs because of both the abatement costs and the tax payments, which the firm will presumably pass on to consumers just as with any cost of production. Whether and how much the firm can do this depends on competitive conditions and the conditions of demand. If the charge is applied to a single firm or small group of firms within a competitive industry, it will not be able to push its price above the market price, and so will have to absorb the cost increase. In this case the impacts will be felt entirely by owners of the firm and the people who work there. Many firms fear, or pretend to fear, being in precisely this situation and base their public objections to taxes on this outcome. If the charge is applied to an entire industry, prices will go up and consumers will bear part of the burden. How much prices go up depends on demand conditions.[5] For taxes applied directly to consumer goods, such as gasoline or heating oil, market prices would respond according to the supply and demand characteristics of the markets.

Price increases often are thought of as regressive because, for any given item, an increase in its price would affect poor people proportionately more than higher-income people. For something that both poor and well-off people consume, such as electricity, this conclusion is straightforward. For price increases on goods consumed disproportionately by higher-income people (e.g., airline travel), the burden would be mostly on them.

---

4. See Don Fullerton and Gilbert E. Metcalf, "Environmental Taxes and the Double-Dividend Hypothesis: Did You Really Expect Something for Nothing?," *Chicago-Kent Law Review,* 73(1), 1998, 221–256.
5. This was discussed in greater detail in Chapter 8.

The burden on workers is tied closely to what happens to the rate of output of the affected firms. Here again, the extent of the output effect depends on competitive conditions and the nature of the demand for the good. If the emission tax program is applied to a single firm in a competitive industry or if the demand for the output of an industry is very responsive to price, output adjustments will be relatively large and workers could be displaced. The long-run burden is then a matter of whether good alternative sources of employment are available.

We have to remember that the charge program is creating substantial benefits in the form of reduced environmental and health damages. To know how a program affects any particular group, we would also have to account for how these benefits of reduced damages are distributed.

Emission Charges and the Incentives to Innovate

In a dynamic world, it is critical that environmental policies encourage technological change in pollution control. One of the main advantages of emission charges is that they provide strong incentives for this. This is shown in **Figure 12.7,** which shows two marginal abatement cost curves for a single firm. MAC_1 represents the current condition. It shows the costs the firm would experience in cutting back its emissions with the particular technology it currently uses. MAC_2, on the other hand, refers to abatement costs that the firm would experience after engaging in a relatively expensive research and development (R&D) program to develop a new method of reducing emissions. Assume the firm has a reasonably good idea of what the results of the R&D will be, although of course nothing is ever a sure thing. We can use it to measure the strength of the incentives for this firm to put money into the R&D program.

FIGURE 12.7 Emission Charges and the Incentive for R&D

Suppose the firm is subject to an effluent tax of t/ton of emissions. Initially it will reduce emissions to e_1; at this point its total pollution-related costs will consist of $(d + e)$ worth of abatement costs and a tax bill of $(a + b + c)$. If it can lower its marginal abatement cost curve to MAC_2 through the R&D activities, it would then reduce its emissions to e_2. At this point it would pay $(b + e)$ in abatement costs and a in taxes. The reduction in total costs has been $(c + d)$. If the firm had instead been faced with an emissions standard of e_1, its cost savings with the new technology would have been only d, as we saw in the last chapter. Also, as we saw in the last chapter, if public authorities shift the standard to e_2 when the new technology becomes available (giving the same emissions reduction as the tax would have), the firm could actually experience an *increase* in costs because of its R&D efforts.

Thus, under a policy of emission charges:

- A firm's R&D efforts will lead to a bigger reduction in its pollution-control costs (abatement costs plus tax payments) than under a standards approach.
- A firm would automatically reduce its emissions as it found ways to shift its marginal abatement cost function downward, whereas under the standard no such automatic process would result.
- Polluters must pay for emissions as well as for abatement costs, whereas with standards they only need to pay abatement costs.
- Potential cost savings from new pollution-control techniques are much larger under the charge program.

Emission Charges and Enforcement Costs

Charges pose a different type of **enforcement** problem than standards. Any charge system requires accurate information on the item to be taxed. If emissions are to be taxed, they must be measurable at reasonable cost. This means that residuals flowing from a source must be identifiable so that monitoring is possible. This rules out most nonpoint-source emissions because they are spread thinly over a wide area in a way that makes them impossible to measure. It would normally be impossible to tax the pollutants in city street runoff because the diffuse nature of the "emissions" makes them impossible to measure. This may also rule out certain toxic chemical emissions, which, in addition to being nonpoint source, often involve such small quantities that their flow rates are difficult to measure.

With emission charges the taxing authorities would be sending a tax bill to the polluting firms at the end of each month or year, based on their total quantity of emissions during that period. So the agency would require information on cumulative emissions from each source. This is more involved than just information on rate of discharge because cumulative discharge is rate times duration. There are several ways of getting this information:

- Ideal would be to have permanent monitoring equipment that measure emissions continuously over the time period in question, or
- Lacking such technology, have periodic checking of the rate of emissions, with an estimate of the duration based on normal business considerations or self-reporting by firms, or
- Engineering studies might be carried out to determine prospective emission quantities under specific conditions of operation, inputs used, and so on.

It is probably fair to say that the **monitoring requirements** of an emissions charge policy are more stringent than those for the typical standards program. Polluters, of course, have incentives to find ways, legal and otherwise, to get their tax bills reduced. One way to do this is to influence the monitoring process enough so that reported emissions are smaller. Once they do get their tax bills, recipients will have every incentive to contest them if they appear to be based on uncertain data or have other technical weaknesses. The lack of high-quality monitoring and reporting procedures has undoubtedly contributed to the unpopularity of effluent charge policies for environmental quality control.

Other Types of Charges

So far we have discussed only one type of charge, an effluent or emissions tax. Because it is the emission of residuals that leads directly to environmental pollution, charges on emissions presumably have the greatest leverage in terms of altering the incentives of polluters. When it is impossible or impractical to levy charges directly on emissions, an **upstream** tax may be more practical. A good case of this is the problem of water pollution from fertilizer runoff in agriculture. It is impossible to tax the pounds of nitrogen in the runoff because it is a nonpoint-source pollutant and thus not directly measurable. The same problem applies to agricultural pesticides. What may be feasible instead is to put charges on these materials as they are bought by farmers—that is, say, a charge per ton of fertilizer or per 100 pounds of pesticide purchased. The charge is to reflect the fact that a certain proportion of these materials ends up in nearby streams and lakes. Because they are paying higher prices for these items, farmers would have the incentive to use them in smaller quantities. Higher prices also create an incentive to use the fertilizer in ways that involve less wastage, for example, by reducing the amounts that run off.

Placing a charge on something other than emissions is usually a "second-best" course of action made necessary because direct emissions can't be closely monitored. In cases such as this we have to watch out for distortions that can come about as people respond to the charge, distortions that can substantially alleviate the effects of the tax or can sometimes make related problems worse. We mentioned in **Chapter 1** the move by many U.S. communities to tax household trash. One technique is to sell stickers to the residents and require that each bag of trash has a sticker on it. The rate of tax is determined by the price of the stickers, and it is relatively easy to monitor and enforce the system through the curbside pickup operations. But the per-bag tax will produce an incentive to pack more into each bag, so the reduction in total quantity of trash may be less than the reduction in the number of bags collected.

Carbon Taxes

A major challenge of contemporary environmental management is dealing with global climate change. It is imperative to reduce emissions of the substances that are behind the global greenhouse effect. The chief greenhouse gas (GHG) is carbon dioxide, and the primary source of this is the burning of fossil fuels. The logic of emission taxes would be to put a charge on the emissions of CO_2 coming from fossil fuel use. The practicality of this, however, is questionable, given the need to monitor and measure emissions for a large number of diverse point and nonpoint sources. What we would like is for the prices of goods and services to be adjusted to take into account their carbon footprints.

- The **carbon footprint** of an item (a physical good, or a service) is the total emissions of GHGs occurring in the production and consumption of the item, usually expressed in equivalent tons of CO_2 (1 ton of CO_2 is equivalent to 0.27 tons of carbon).

A way of accomplishing this is to levy a tax on fossil fuels at the source, that is "upstream" where they are first extracted or imported. The tax would then filter through the system, affecting more heavily the prices of those goods and services that have large carbon footprints and less heavily on prices of those with low or negligible footprints. This process is depicted schematically in **Figure 12.8.**

FIGURE 12.8 A Tax on Carbon

An "upstream" tax on the carbon content of:

Coal   Natural gas   Petroleum

↓ ↓ ↙

Input markets

↓

Output markets

↙ ↓ ↘

Large Carbon footprint (e.g., cars, fossil fuels, snowmobiles)	Intermediate Carbon footprint (e.g., furniture, clothing, local food)	Small Carbon footprint (e.g., insurance, hiking, wind energy)
Large price increase	Moderate price increase	Low, or no, price increase

As with other pollution, without a charge for emitting carbon into the atmosphere, the air as a resource for carbon disposal is used for free. Society experiences a negative externality. The goal of any carbon tax is to provide an incentive to reduce carbon emissions. Like other taxes, the money collected becomes revenue to the public authority, most likely a state, regional, or national government. That revenue could be used in an unlimited variety of ways: subsidizing the purchase of e-bikes, decreasing income taxes, expanding a food security program, funding battery recycling, etc. There need not be a direct link between carbon tax revenue and government spending or outlays.

12-2 Abatement Subsidies

An emission charge works by placing a price on the environmental asset into which emissions are occurring. Essentially, the same incentive effects would result if, instead of a charge, we instituted a **subsidy** on emission reductions. Here a public authority would pay a polluter a certain amount per ton of emissions for every ton it reduced, starting from some benchmark level. The subsidy acts as a reward for reducing emissions. More formally, it acts as an **opportunity cost;** when a polluter chooses to emit a unit of effluent, it is in effect forgoing the subsidy payment it could have had if it had chosen to withhold that unit of effluent instead. **Table 12.1,** using the same numbers as in the preceding discussion on emission charges, shows how this works in principle. The firm's base level is set at its current emissions rate: 10 tons/month. It receives $120 per ton for every ton it cuts back from this base. The fourth column shows its total subsidy revenues, and the last column shows total subsidies minus total abatement costs. This net revenue peaks at 4 tons/month, the same emissions level the firm would choose with the $120 tax. In other words, the incentive for the firm is the same as for the tax.

TABLE 12.1 An Abatement Subsidy

Emissions (tons/month)	Marginal Abatement Cost	Total Abatement Cost	Total Subsidy at $120/Ton	Total Subsidy Minus Total Abatement Costs
10	0	0	0	0
9	15	15	120	105
8	30	45	240	195
7	50	95	360	265
6	70	165	480	315
5	95	260	600	340
4	120	375	720	345
3	150	525	840	315
2	185	710	960	250
1	230	940	1,080	140
0	290	1,230	1,200	−30

Although an abatement subsidy like this would have the same incentive for each individual source, total emissions may actually increase. To understand why, note the difference in the financial position of this firm when it emits 4 tons of pollutant under the two programs: With the tax it has total costs of $855 (see **Figure 12.1**), whereas with the subsidy it has a total *revenue* of $345. Thus, the financial position of the firm is much different. In effect, it will be earning higher profits after the imposition of the subsidy, and this can have the effect of making this industry more attractive for potential new firms. There is the possibility of having the emissions per firm go down while the number of firms in the industry increases, and therefore total emissions increase. This feature is a major drawback of simple subsidies like this.

Exhibit 12.2 lists a variety of subsidy programs that are meant to further the goals of pollution reduction. Some subsidy programs target the adoption of specific pollution-control or climate-change technologies. These can come in the form of tax credits for firms that develop or produce the technology and for firms that adopt it. Some subsidy programs give consumers money to purchase climate-change technology. Depending on competitive conditions, the consumer subsidy money may end up being transferred to sellers of the technology as sellers charge higher prices due to the subsidy.

EXHIBIT 12.2 Types of Environmentally Related Subsidies

Subsidies in the Form of	Example(s)
Tax benefits	Tax exemptions for pollution-control equipment or recycling equipment
	Exemptions of ethanol-blended gas from federal taxes
Reduced environmental fines	Reduction in normal fines if firms undertake extensive pollution-control plans
Public grants to encourage environmental programs	EPA grants to communities to fund "brownfields" programs[1]
	Grants to farmers to adopt conservation practices
	Grants to businesses or communities to establish recycling programs
Development rights purchase programs	Public purchases of agricultural development rights to maintain land in agriculture or open space
Public support of environmental market development	Public rules of procurement of products made from recycled materials
	Cash payments for people who turn in old, high-emitting automobiles
	Cash payments for purchase of electric vehicles (EVs)
Cost-sharing grants	Grants made to localities to cover a portion of the cost of upgrading wastewater treatment facilities
Accelerated depreciation	Decrease in time over which costs can be deducted on environmental investments and environmentally favorable products like EVs
Renewable energy subsidies	Tax credits for renewable energy investments like solar panel installations on homes (Inflation Reduction Act of 2022)

[1]Brownfields are contaminated industrial sites that pose relatively low risks, but may be avoided by private developers because of potential liability problems.

Deposit-Refund Systems

One place where subsidies may be more practical is in deposit-refund systems. A deposit-refund system is essentially the combination of a tax and a subsidy. For example, a subsidy (the refund) is paid to consumers when they return an item to a designated collection point. The purpose of the subsidy is to provide the incentive for people to refrain from disposing of these items in environmentally damaging ways. The funds for paying the subsidy are raised by levying taxes (the deposit) on these items when they are purchased. In this case, the purpose of the tax is not necessarily so much to get people to reduce the consumption of the item, but to raise money to pay the subsidy. The tax is called a deposit and the subsidy a refund.

Deposit-refund systems are particularly well suited to situations where a product is widely dispersed when purchased and used, and where disposal is difficult or impossible for authorities to monitor. In the United States, a number of individual states[6] have enacted deposit-refund systems for beverage containers, both to reduce litter and to encourage recycling. This approach has also been widely used in Europe. With inflation, the real value of any deposit-refund (e.g., 5¢ per bottle) will fall, thus reducing the incentive.

Germany instituted a deposit-refund on waste lubricating oil. Each year very large quantities of waste oil are disposed of improperly, putting many air, water, and land resources under threat. In the German system, new lubricating oil is subject to a tax (a deposit), the proceeds of which go into a special fund. This fund is then used to subsidize (the refund side) a waste oil recovery and reprocessing system. The terms of the subsidy are set so as to encourage competition in the recovery/reprocessing system and to provide an incentive for users to reduce the extent to which oil is contaminated during use.

In Sweden and Norway, deposit-refund systems have been instituted for cars. New-car buyers pay a deposit at the time of purchase, which will be refunded when and if the car is turned over to an authorized junk dealer. Experience with these systems shows that success depends on more than just the size of the deposit-refund. For example, it is essential that the collection system be designed to be reasonably convenient for consumers.

Other items for which deposit-refund systems have been instituted are consumer products containing hazardous substances, such as batteries containing lithium, and car batteries.[7] Automobile tires might also be handled this way. The deposit-refund system might also be adaptable to conventional industrial pollutants. For example, users of fossil fuels might pay deposits on the quantities of sulfur contained in the fuels they purchase; they would then get refunds on the sulfur recovered from the exhaust gas. Thus, they would lose their deposit only on the sulfur that went up the stacks.

Summary

Emission charges attack the pollution problem at its source, by putting a price on something that has been free and, therefore, overused. The main advantage of emission charges is their efficiency aspects: If all sources are subject to the same charge, they will adjust their emission rates so that the equimarginal rule is satisfied. Administrators do not have to know the individual source marginal abatement cost functions for this to happen;

---

6. As of 2023 these were California, Connecticut, Hawaii, Iowa, Maine, Massachusetts, Michigan, New York, Oregon, and Vermont, plus Guam.
7. As of 2023, 30 U.S. states had deposit-refund systems for lead-acid car batteries. For lithium-ion batteries, the EPA Office of Resource Conservation and Recovery has been focusing on disposal and recycling only since 2023.

it is enough that firms are faced with the charge and then left free to make their own adjustments. A second major advantage of emission charges is that they produce a strong incentive to innovate, to discover cheaper ways of reducing emissions.

The apparent indirect character of emission charges may tend to work against their acceptance by policymakers. Standards have the appearance of placing direct control on the thing that is at issue, namely, emissions. Emission charges, on the other hand, place no direct restrictions on emissions but rely on the self-interested behavior of firms to adjust their own emission rates in response to the tax. This may make some policymakers uneasy because firms apparently are still allowed to control their own emission rates. It may seem paradoxical that this "indirect" character of effluent taxes can sometimes provide a stronger inducement to emission reductions than seemingly more direct approaches.

Emission charges require effective monitoring. They cannot be enforced simply by checking to see if sources have installed certain types of pollution-control equipment. If emission charges are to have the appropriate incentive effects, they must be based closely on *cumulative emissions*.

An advantage of emission charges is that they provide a source of revenue for public authorities. Many have recommended that tax systems be changed to rely less on taxes that have distorting economic effects and more on emissions charges. Efforts to combat global climate change have led many to recommend carbon taxes; these have become quite popular in Europe.

Emissions subsidies would have the same incentive effect on individual polluters, but they could lead to increases in total emission levels. One place where subsidies have been used effectively is in deposit-refund systems, which are essentially tax and subsidy systems in combination.

Questions for Further Discussion

1. How might an emission charge program based on odometer readings be designed to reduce automobile emissions?
2. Explain how the same dollar emission charge satisfies the equimarginal principle while the same percent emissions reduction (equiproportional) results in higher societal costs.
3. Opponents of emission tax policies sometimes assert that they are simply a way of letting firms buy the right to pollute. Is this a reasonable criticism?
4. When emission charges are put into effect, who ultimately ends up paying for them? Is this fair?
5. Emission charges are sometimes seen as creating a "double burden": Firms must pay the costs of reducing emissions and also pay the government for polluting discharges. How might a charge system be designed to reduce this double burden?

(Continued)

Questions for Further Discussion *(Continued)*

6. Refer to **Figure 12.1.** Suppose the emissions tax is $95/ton/month. Find the efficient level of emissions for the firm. Explain why the firm would not reduce its emissions to 1 ton/month.
7. How does the slope of a MAC curve affect the total taxes paid for an emissions charge?
8. Refer to **Exhibit 12.1.** Visit the OECD (**www.oecd.org**) and select a country. Investigate an environmental tax or charge implemented in that country. Explain how firms or individuals may change their behavior due to the tax.

For additional resources pertaining to the material in this chapter, see the list in **Appendix B.**

Chapter 13
Incentive-Based Strategies: Market Trading Systems

An effluent charge (emissions tax) requires that some central public authority establish a charge rate, monitor the performance of each polluter, and then collect the tax bills. It is essentially an interaction between polluters and public authorities in which we might expect the same type of adversarial relationship we get in any tax system. In this chapter we take a look at some policy approaches that, while incorporating economic incentives, are designed to work in a more decentralized fashion. Rather than leaving everything to a centralized public agency, they work through market interactions.

- Polluters buy and sell emission permits, and emissions are controlled by linking them with the number of permits held (Cap-and-trade or CAP).
- Firms, or individuals, cover their emissions by buying offsets, which are linked to the reduction of emissions by others at some other location (offset trading).

Cap-and-trade programs have proliferated. One of the earliest in the United States was the sulfur dioxide (SO_2) trading scheme introduced as part of the Clean Air Act of 1990. A nitrous oxide (NO_x) trading plan was used by a group of eastern states from 1999 to 2009. California has several programs within its own borders. The European Union (EU) has inaugurated a multicountry trading plan to reduce carbon dioxide (CO_2) emissions. It may at first seem odd that cap-and-trade allows polluters to purchase emission permits. But permits must normally be bought from other polluters. The price at which they transact becomes the price of the emissions, analogous to an emission charge as we discussed in **Chapter 12**.

The perspective of offset markets is to view the world as a global, interconnected ecosystem with pollution anywhere creating negative externalities globally. This fits well for carbon emissions because greenhouse gases (GHGs) emitted anywhere impact the world level of global warming. The Paris Agreement includes the Clean Development Mechanism (CDM), which was adopted under the Kyoto Protocol and initiated carbon offset markets internationally.

We can distinguish three types of trading systems for achieving more efficient pollution control:

- Cap-and-trade (CAP)
- Offset trading
- Emission rate trading

13-1 Cap-and-Trade

The first step in a CAP program is to make a centralized decision (by a regulatory agency or some other collective entity) on the aggregate quantity of emissions to be allowed. Permits are then written in accordance with this quantity. These permits are then distributed among the sources responsible for the emissions. Some formula must be used to determine how many permits each source will receive. Assuming that the total number of permits is fewer than current total emissions, some or all emitters will receive fewer permits than their current emissions.

Suppose, for example, that a CAP program has been instituted to reduce the amount of sulfur dioxide emitted by a group of power plants. Current total emissions are, say, 150,000 tons of sulfur per year, and policymakers have decided that this must be reduced to 100,000 tons per year. Let's focus on the situation of one of the power plants, which is depicted in **Figure 13.1**. We suppose it is emitting 5,000 tons of sulfur currently. Under the program, the plant is initially given 2,500 discharge permits. The plant manager now has three choices:

1. Reduce the emissions to the level covered by the number of permits the plant was initially awarded.
2. Buy additional permits and emit at levels higher than the original award level (e.g., buy 1,000 permits to add to its 2,500 initial distribution, so its emissions would now be 3,500 tons/year).
3. Reduce emissions below the level of the original award, then sell the permits it doesn't need (e.g., reduce emissions to 1,800 tons/year and sell 700 permits).

FIGURE 13.1 Individual Firm Choices Under a Cap-and-Trade Program

Note that whether the firm is a buyer or seller of permits depends on the relationship of the price of permits and their marginal abatement costs at the emission level corresponding to their initial permit holding.

1. If the original award is 1,800 permits, the firm's marginal abatement costs would be $60/ton; with a permit price of $40, it can improve its situation by buying 700 permits and increasing its emissions to 2,500 tons.
2. If its original allocation is 3,500 permits, its marginal abatement costs would be lower than the permit price; it can improve its situation by selling 1,000 permits and reducing its emission to 2,500 tons.

Think of a situation involving an industry where there are a large number of firms and each one is emitting a pollutant we wish to control with a cap-and-trade program. An overall level of aggregate emissions is set by the authorities, and transferable permits are allocated to each firm according to some formula. Marginal abatement costs can be expected to differ among firms, based on different production and pollution-control technologies available to each. Some sources will be potential buyers of permits (MAC > permit price), and some firms will be potential sellers (MAC < permit price). There are **gains from trade** to be had by the sources, by buying and selling permits, in effect rearranging the total number of permits (which has been fixed by the authorities) among the plants.

Now each firm will be in a situation analogous to the one depicted in **Figure 13.1**. By buying or selling permits, they move to a situation where marginal abatement costs are equal to the price of permits. Assuming there is a single overall market for permits, and therefore a single market price for them, this means that the trading of permits among the firms will result in a cost-effective reduction in total emission, because each firm will end up equating its marginal abatement costs to the single permit price.

Cost-effectiveness in cap-and-trade programs requires that there be a single market for permits, where suppliers and demanders may interact openly and where knowledge of transactions prices is publicly available to all participants. The normal forces of competition would then bring about a single price for permits. The permits would in general flow from sources with relatively low marginal abatement costs to those with high marginal abatement costs.

A permit market is depicted in **Figure 13.2**. The demand for permits is simply the aggregate marginal abatement cost functions of all the firms participating in the market. The supply of permits is the quantity in the cap as initially established by public authorities; the supply curve is vertical at that quantity.

As in any competitive market, the price of permits is determined by the interaction of supply and demand. If the cap is set at q_1 in **Figure 13.2,** the price of permits will settle at p_1. A more restrictive cap, such as q_2, would give a higher permit price, the case at p_2.

It's important to understand that the permit price in a CAP program is what provides the incentive for emission reductions by participating firms. In this sense it is analogous to the emission tax as discussed in **Chapter 12.** But note that the two approaches proceed differently:

- With a cap-and-trade program, a quantity restriction (the cap) is set, and a permit price results as firms adjust their emission levels.

- With an emission charge program, the tax level is set by authorities, and a change in the quantity of aggregate emission results as firms adjust their emission levels.

FIGURE 13.2 The Market for Discharge Permits

Table 13.1 lists some CAP programs in effect. Some of the largest programs have to do with air pollution. On the water pollution-control side there has been a proliferation of programs for particular water bodies. Also, some address greenhouse gases.

Unlike effluent charge approaches, which basically make people pay for something they were once getting for free, CAP programs begin by creating and distributing a new type of right. These rights will have a market value as long as the total number of permits created is limited. From a political standpoint, it is perhaps easier for people to agree on a pollution-control policy that begins by distributing valuable new rights than by notifying people they will be subject to a new tax. Of course, like any pollution-control policy, CAP programs have their own set of problems that must be overcome if they are to work effectively. What looks in theory like a neat way of using market forces to achieve efficient pollution reduction must be adapted to the complexities of the real world.

The Initial Rights Allocation

The success of the CAP approach in controlling pollution depends critically on limiting the number of rights in circulation; this is the "cap." Because individual polluters will no doubt want as many as they can get in the first distribution, the very first step of the program is one of potentially great controversy: what formula to use to make the original distribution of emission rights. Almost any rule will appear to have some inequities. For example, they might be distributed equally among all existing sources of a particular effluent. But this would encounter the problem that firms vary a lot in size. Some pulp mills are larger than others, for example, and the average size of pulp mills, in terms of value of output, may be different from the average size of, say, soda bottling plants. So giving each polluter the same number of permits may not be fair.

TABLE 13.1 Selected Trading Programs

Program	Item Traded
1990 Clean Air Act	Tons of SO_2 emissions from power plants
Southern California Reclaim	Tons of SO_2 and NO_x from large industrial sources
California Trading Program	Tons of greenhouse gases
New Zealand Trading Program	Tons of greenhouse gases
Kyoto Protocol Clean Development Mechanism	Tons of greenhouse gases from projects in developing countries
European Trading Scheme	Tons of greenhouse gases from large power, industrial, and cement plants
Regional Greenhouse Gas Initiative	Tons of greenhouse gases from large plants in Northeastern and mid-Atlantic United States
Renewable Energy Certificates (in states where renewable energy portfolio standards exist)	Certificates for each 1,000 kWh of renewable energy produced
China Trading Program	Tons of CO_2 emissions
Long Island Sound Nitrogen Trading Program	Pounds of waterborne nitrogen emissions from wastewater treatment plants
Chesapeake Bay Agreement	Pounds of waterborne nutrients (nitrogen and phosphorus)
Minnesota Water Quality Trading	Pounds of phosphorus emissions
Ohio Wetlands Mitigation Program	Acres of restored, enhanced, or preserved wetlands

Permits might be allocated in accordance with the existing emissions of a source. For example, each source might get permits amounting to 50 percent of its current emissions. This may sound equitable, but, in fact, it may have built-in incentive difficulties. A rule like this does not recognize the fact that some firms already may have worked hard to reduce their emissions. One could easily argue that those firms that have already invested in emission reduction should not now be penalized by receiving emission permits in proportion to these lower emission levels. It would seem to reward firms that have dragged their feet in the past.[1] If polluters believe that permits will soon be allocated in this way, they may have the incentive to *increase* today's emission rate because this would give them a larger base for the initial allocation of permits. Each allocation formula has its problems, and those setting the cap must find some workable compromise.

Closely related to this issue is the question of whether the rights should be given away or perhaps sold or auctioned. In principle it doesn't matter as long as the permits get distributed fairly widely. Subsequent market transactions will redistribute them in accordance with the relative marginal abatement costs of polluters, whatever the original distribution may have been. But free distribution of permits will confer windfall gains on the recipients,

---

1. This is another example of the perverse incentives built into any program that asks everybody to cut their consumption by x percent from their current rate. It favors those who have consumed at high rates in the past and hurts those who have tried hard to live frugally.

the amount of which would depend on the market price of the permits. What a sale or auction would do is transfer some of the original value of the rights into the hands of the auctioning agency. This might be a good way for public agencies to raise funds for worthy projects, but it has to be recognized that a plan like this would create political objections. A hybrid system would be to distribute a certain number of permits free and then auction some number of additional permits.

Establishing Trading Rules

For any market to work effectively, clear rules must exist governing who may trade and the trading procedures that must be followed. Furthermore, the rules should not be so burdensome that they make it impossible for market participants to gauge accurately the implications of buying or selling at specific prices. This implies a hands-off stance by public agencies after the initial distribution of the rights. The general rule for the public agency should be to set simple and clear rules and then allow trading to proceed.

One basic rule that would have to be established is who may participate in the market. Is this to be limited to polluters, or may anyone trade? For example, may environmental advocacy groups or individuals buy permits and retire them as a way of reducing total emissions? The EPA's Acid Rain Program allows any for-profit firm or non-profit organization or individual to purchase an SO_2 permit. The effect of a non-polluter purchasing a permit is to retire the permit which reduces the number of outstanding permits thus lowering emissions.

Reducing the Number of Permits

Controlling the total number of permits (the CAP) is usually handled by a public agency such as the Environmental Protection Agency (EPA) in the U.S. or by the European Commission for the European Union Emissions Trading System (EU-ETS). One question that presents itself is, how does the total number of permits get reduced over time? If the efficient level of emissions is going down because of technological change, how do authorities reduce the overall number of permits in circulation?

The most direct way is that in the initial distribution each permit is dated according to the year in which it may be used. Then each participating emitter would be issued a declining series of dated permits. In this way, the annual total permit holdings would decline according to the formula adopted in the overall program. **Exhibit 13.1** depicts this for the California CAP for reducing greenhouse gas emissions.

Another way the total cap may be reduced over time is for organizations, or individuals, to enter the market, buy allowances, and retire them. The Adirondack Council, a private conservation group in New York, purchased CO_2 emission permits in the Regional Greenhouse Gas Initiative of the Northeastern and Middle Atlantic States (REGGI). The EU Emissions Trading Scheme (EU ETS) realigned and decreased the CAP to match the 2030 EU goals of the Paris Climate Change Agreement. In the past, students at various colleges, such as the Bates College Environmental Economics class, purchased SO_2 permits.

EXHIBIT 13.1 The Carbon Market of California

In the absence of action on the federal level to combat climate change, some states have taken the initiative. One of these is the carbon cap-and-trade program initiated in 2012 in California. It applied to power plants and large industrial plants; as of 2015 it was extended to suppliers of fuel, such as gasoline, natural gas, diesel, and propane. Covered emissions included CO_2, plus other greenhouse gases such as methane, NOx, and hydrofluorocarbons, recorded in terms of their CO_2 equivalent values. The goal is to cut greenhouse gases by 85 percent below 1990 levels to reach carbon neutrality by 2045. Emission allowances were distributed free to initial participants; additional allowances were auctioned by the managing agency, the California Air Resources Board. Fuel suppliers added to the program in 2015 were required to purchase allowances covering the greenhouse gas content of the fuels they delivered. In early 2014, this allowance market was linked to a similar cap-and-trade market in Quebec, Canada. The emission allowances of the California program can be exchanged one for one with allowances in the Quebec program. Prices of allowances fluctuated greatly during the first year of the program, and then settled down to around $13 to $14 per ton of CO_2 equivalent in 2013. Since 2020, they have fluctuated around $25 to $30 per ton.

For added information, see
www.carboncredtis.com/carbon-prices-today/

CAPs and Nonuniform Emissions

Suppose we are trying to design a CAP program to control total airborne SO_2 emissions in a region where there are numerous different sources—power plants, industrial plants, and so on—scattered rather widely around a region. A schematic of this situation is depicted in **Figure 13.3**. All of the emission points are not equally situated relative to the prevailing wind or to the area of highest population density. Some sources are upwind, others are downwind, of the populated area. We assume they are not all equal in terms of marginal abatement costs, but neither are they equal in terms of the impact of their emissions on ambient SO_2 levels over the populated area. Even with a larger geographic region which includes multiple cities, impacts will vary. In technical terms, they have different **transfer coefficients** linking their own emissions with damages in the urban area.

Having distributed discharge permits, we now allow them to be traded. As long as the number of permits in circulation is held constant, we have effectively controlled total SO_2 emissions. If we allow straight trading, unit for unit, of permits among all sources, the damage caused by that total could change. If a downwind firm sold permits to an upwind firm, the total number of permits would remain the same but there would now be more emissions upwind of the population, and therefore more damage. This is called the "hotspot" problem.

FIGURE 13.3 Nonuniform Emissions and CAP Programs

Key: ☒ Locations of each emission point
☐ Highest population density
--- Zones for permit trading

One way to get around this might be to adjust the trading rules to take into account the impacts of individual sources. Suppose the emissions from Source A were twice as damaging as the emissions of Source B simply because of the location of the two sources. Then the administrators of the program might set a rule that if Source A is buying permits from Source B, it must buy two permits to get one. If this principle is extended to a situation with many sources, things can quickly get very complicated. Authorities would have to determine, for each source, how many permits would have to be purchased from each other source in order for the purchasing source to be credited with one new permit. If there were five sources, the agency would have to figure out only 10 such trading ratios, but if there were 20 different sources, it would have to estimate 190 of these ratios.[2]

A zoned system could address this problem; it is analogous to a zoned effluent charge we talked about earlier. Authorities would designate a series of zones, each of which would contain sources that were relatively similar in terms of their location and the impact of their emissions on ambient quality. Four such zones are shown in **Figure 13.3**. Authorities then could do one of two things:

1. allow trading by firms only with other firms in the same zone, or
2. make adjustments for all trades across zone boundaries.

For example, if sources in Zone A were judged to have transfer coefficients twice the size, on average, as sources in Zone B, any trade between sources in these two zones would be adjusted by that same factor of two: Any firm in Zone A buying permits from any firm in Zone B would have to buy two permits in order to get credit for one new one; any source in Zone B would have to buy only half a permit from a firm in Zone A to get credit for one new permit.

---

2. In general, if there were n sources, there would have to be $[n(n-1)]/2$ trading ratios established.

As with the location of toxic or hazardous-waste sites, environmental justice issues can arise with zones for the heavier polluters. Those production facilities needing higher number of permits due to higher levels of emissions may be disproportionately located in poorer neighborhoods.[3]

Markets work best when there is substantial **competition** among buyers and among sellers; they work significantly less well if there are so few buyers or sellers that competitive pressures are weak or absent. In cases where there are few traders, one of them, or perhaps a small group, may be able to exercise control over the market, colluding on prices, perhaps charging different prices to different people, using the control of discharge permits to gain economic control in its industry, and so on. From the standpoint of fostering competition, we would like to set our trading zones as widely as possible, to include large numbers of potential buyers and sellers.

However, this may work against the ecological facts. In many cases there may be meteorological or hydrological reasons for limiting the trading area to a relatively narrow geographical area. If the objective was to control airborne emissions affecting a particular city, we would probably not want to allow firms located there to trade permits with firms in another city. Or if our concern is controlling emissions into a particular lake or river, we could not allow sources located there to trade permits with sources located on some entirely different body of water. For local environmental reasons, it may well be desirable to have trading areas restricted, whereas for economic reasons we would want to have trading areas defined broadly. There is no magic rule to tell exactly how these two factors should be balanced in all cases. Authorities can only look at specific cases as they arise and weigh the particularities of the environmental features with the subtleties of the competitive conditions in the industries where trading will occur.

CAPs and Enforcement

The directly controlling aspect of a CAP program is that sources are constrained to keep their emissions at a level no greater than the total number of discharge permits in their possession. Thus, an administering agency must essentially keep track of two things:

1. the number of permits in the possession of each source and
2. the quantity of emissions from each source.

The agency must have some way of keeping track of permit transactions among market participants.

Also, polluters must be monitored to see whether emissions at each source exceed the number of permits held. If permits are expressed in terms of total emissions over some period of time, a means has to be available to measure cumulative emissions at each source. This is the same requirement as with an effluent charge. If there were reasonable certainty that emissions were fairly even throughout the year, authorities could get a check on cumulative emissions by making spot checks of instantaneous rates. For most industrial sources of pollution, however, there are considerable daily, weekly, or seasonal variations in emissions; therefore, more sophisticated monitoring would be required.

---

3. Lara Cushing et al. Carbon Trading, Co-Pollutants, and Environmental Equity: Evidence from California's Cap and Trade Program (2011–2015), *PLoS Medicine*, 15(7), 2018, e1002604.

CAPs and the Incentive for R&D

One of our main criteria for judging an environmental policy is whether or not it creates strong incentives for firms to seek better ways of reducing emissions. Emission standards are weak in this regard, whereas emission charges are much stronger. CAP programs in this respect are identical to emissions charges, at least in theory. Consider the firm in **Figure 13.4**. Suppose that at present the firm's marginal abatement cost function is MAC_1. Emission permits sell for p each, and let us assume that this price is not expected to change. The firm has adjusted its holdings so that it currently owns e_1 permits.[4] Its emissions are therefore e_1 and its total abatement costs are $(a + b)$. The incentive to do research and development (R&D) is to find a less costly way of controlling emissions, so the firm can cut emissions and sell the surplus permits. How much would it be worth to get marginal abatement costs shifted to MAC_2? With MAC_2, the firm would shift to an emissions level of e_2. Its total abatement costs here would be $(b + d)$, but it would be able to sell $(e_1 - e_2)$ permits for a revenue of $p(e_1 - e_2) = (c + d)$. The change in its position would thus be:

$$\begin{array}{c}\text{Total abatement costs}\\ \text{with } MAC_1\end{array} - \begin{array}{c}\text{Total abatement costs}\\ \text{with } MAC_2\end{array} + \begin{array}{c}\text{Receipts from}\\ \text{CAP sale}\end{array}$$

or $(a + b) - (d + b) + (c + d)$, which equals $(a + c)$. Check this with the savings under an effluent charge (see **Chapter 12**). It is exactly the same. The market price of the permit has the same incentive as a pollution charge; by not reducing their emissions, firms are forgoing the increased revenues they could have obtained by selling some of their permits.

FIGURE 13.4 Transferable Emission Permits and Technological Change

---

4. These marginal abatement cost functions apply to a year; that is, they are the costs per year of changing emissions. The price p is therefore a one-year purchase (or sale) price–what it would cost to buy or sell a permit for just one year.

CAPs and Uncertainty

- A policy of emission charges to reduce pollution is a *price-based* system, because it starts with an emission charge, which leads to a reduction in the quantity of emissions. When marginal abatement costs are uncertain, we cannot be sure about how much of a reduction of emissions we would get from a given emission charge.
- A CAP program is a *quantity-based* system, because it starts with the setting of a quantitative limit on total emissions, which then produces a certain price for emission permits. If emission control costs are uncertain, we cannot be certain what price permits will trade for when the quantity of the cap is set at some particular level. If the cap is set too high, permit prices will be too low, weakening their incentive effect. If the cap is set too low, permit prices could be very high, leading to economic disruption and volatile permit markets.

This has led recently to the idea of a *safety valve* in CAP programs. This is an upper limit price that, if it is reached, would trigger an increase in the supply of permits. If permit prices reach this limit, firms would be able to buy additional permits from the governmental authorities operating the program. This effectively puts an upper limit on permit prices during periods when demand exceeds available supply in the permit market.

13-2 Offset Trading

Emissions trading also includes offset trading. An offset is a real, or promised, emission reduction by one entity that can be sold to another entity that seeks to get credit for reducing emissions. Purchasers of offsets are entities who wish to compensate for their increase in emissions; sellers of offsets are entities who will reduce emissions in a quantity sufficient to compensate for the emissions of the buyers.

Any activity that reduces emissions could be designated as an offset and offered for sale at a value or price agreeable to a buyer, thus creating a market for that offset. Offsets focused on addressing climate change, mostly target forest and wetland restoration or conservation, renewable energy production, and transportation. Examples of offsets are:

- an acre or hectare of forest that would be planted or not harvested
- a quantity of EVs manufactured
- an installation of solar panels on a roof or construction of a large solar array

Buyers of offsets fall into a couple of categories:

- Compliance offsets—firms or organizations or countries facing emission reduction requirements
- Voluntary offsets—firms or organizations or individuals desiring to compensate their actions as a polluter by investing in a non-polluting activity elsewhere

Compliance demand may result from firms subject to legal limits on their activities. Many states have statutory requirements that power companies generate some portion of their output from renewable sources, such as wind, solar, and geothermal. It is acceptable, in most cases, that they are allowed to meet this requirement in part by buying renewable power offsets, usually from firms that build and operate new plants that use renewable energy.

A substantial international market has developed in strictly voluntary offset trading. Voluntary offsets are those sold to entities that wish to compensate for their emissions but are not strictly required to do so. The market for voluntary carbon credits is likely to be worth upwards of $50 billion by 2030.[5] In these markets, emitters looking to purchase offsets seek to find suppliers of offsets who are willing to sell. Many of these offsets address climate change and hence are called carbon offsets. An individual can compensate for their personal carbon footprint in this manner. For example:

- Purchasing an airline offset to compensate for the carbon emitted on a flight.
- Purchasing Ben and Jerry's brand of ice cream helps to capture manure solids and reduce methane emissions via the Green Dream Methane Reduction Project.
- Purchasing an Ecotourist pass to offset driving an ICE vehicle 3000 miles across the United States.

Greenhouse gas (GHG) offset markets began at the international level with the adoption of the Clean Development Mechanism (CDM) in the Kyoto Protocol and were later included in the Paris Agreement. The CDM allowed developed countries that could not meet carbon emission reduction goals domestically to reach their emission reduction goals by purchasing offset credits from developing countries. The major carbon offset supplying countries include Peru, Brazil, Kenya, Zimbabwe, Bolivia, Indonesia, and Cambodia with most of the activities being reforestation or land-use activities such as the creation of timber plantations.

Greenhouse gas emissions, regardless of where the emissions originate, eventually impact the overall increase in warming globally. The earth and its atmosphere disperse the warming temperatures according to the physical characteristics of the earth and the climate change impact is not traceable to the original location of the emissions. Hence, a reduction in GHG emissions from any location can offset an increase in GHG emissions from another location. A key assumption of the international carbon offset market is that an activity to reduce GHG emissions in one area of the world can physically impact a negative externality from emissions in another part of the world. This assumption differs from more localized emissions, such as water-borne emissions, in which pollution upstream impacts ambient water quality downstream.

Transactions in offsets are somewhat different from transactions in physical goods. Offsets require emission reductions or altered technology by offset suppliers. This creates the problem of validating that the changes have actually been made to supply the offset, that is, that a supplier has actually reduced their emissions. In response to this, the specialty has developed with third-party consultants specializing in authenticating legitimate offsets.

For an activity to produce a legitimate offset, it must be:

- Verifiable—the activity actually occurring and can be confirmed by a third party,
- Unique—the activity can be counted once and not sold to multiple buyers, i.e., no double counting, and
- Additional—the activity must add to overall emissions reduction; the activity cannot be such that it would have happened anyway.

---

5. Christopher Blaufelder, Cindy Levy, Peter Mannion, and Dickon Pinner. *A Blueprint for Scaling Voluntary Carbon Markets to Meet the Climate Challenge*. McKinsey Sustainability, January 2021.

Equity and environmental justice questions arise with offsets. The argument can be made that only people with enough income are able to purchase and thus offset their behavior rather than taking steps to reduce their personal carbon footprint. Given the list of predominantly developing or poorer nations supplying offsets, people in richer more developed nations are able to use the resources of those countries to support a lifestyle that has already created extensive global warming. The term "climate colonialism" has been associated with these carbon offsets because the buyers who are mostly located in developed countries could exert pressure and influence on developing countries, although the activities being influenced are under the umbrella of sustainability.[6]

These points raise the notion of "greenwashing." Many companies and organizations offer their customers the opportunity to purchase an offset to go with their service or product. **Exhibit 13.2** discusses this situation.

EXHIBIT 13.2 Carbon Offset Markets: Real or Greenwashing?

The market for carbon offsets has been growing rapidly. Spending on global voluntary carbon offsets grew from $54 million in 2007 to $341 million in 2021, and the trend continues. Supposedly, the money went to tree planting, solar energy, wind farms, and other means of reducing carbon dioxide emissions. This money was spent by people and corporations wanting to offset the increase in atmospheric carbon dioxide produced by their products or activities: buying and using a computer, taking a trip on an airplane, driving a new car, and so on.

Many carbon credit providers are in business and claim to promote sustainability. They vary in terms of their focus, price, and location. Some examples are: Sustainable Travel International (travel), Nature Energy (wind, solar, hydro energy), and ClearSky Climate Solutions (forests). Firms, and some nonprofits, such as Terra Pass and Carbon-fund, are intermediaries between those who are supposedly producing carbon reductions, through either reducing emissions or increasing carbon sequestration, and corporations and individuals wanting to buy these reductions to offset their own emissions.

But the question is, how are buyers of offsets to know whether the producers of offsets are actually reducing atmospheric carbon as part of the deal? Or, in the case of Terra Pass, are investments in cleaner or renewable energy projects being made? Is there any way of making sure that, at the end of the line, somebody is reducing carbon as a result of your buying some offsets?

The Federal Trade Commission (FTC), charged with consumer protection, has initiated steps to look into advertising claims made by suppliers of carbon offsets. It comes under the heading of green marketing, and is aimed at making sure that suppliers of carbon offsets can substantiate their claims that carbon is actually reduced after people buy offsets.

(Continued)

---

6. Jess Wang, *Carbon Offsets, a New Form of Neocolonialism News from Climate and Society*. Columbia University, May 2021.

EXHIBIT 13.2 *(Continued)*

Also, it serves to protect honest businesses from questionable competitors. The FTC issues *Guides for the Use of Environmental Marketing Claims* ("Green Guides").

The FTC's objective is to make sure that people are not engaged in *greenwashing*, that is, selling carbon offsets without being able to substantiate that the offsets have led to real carbon reductions, which could be intentional, or simply mistaken because of lack of information.

The Dutch National Advertising Code Commission (ACC) filed litigation against KLM airlines for exaggerating their "CO$_2$ZERO" campaign with reforestation projects in Panama. Similar litigation is pending in France and Denmark.*

The FTC recognizes that it is a market that depends on accurate information flowing through the long line between producers and consumers. If I buy a car and it doesn't work right, I can take it back. But if I buy some carbon offsets, it's almost impossible to know if carbon has actually been reduced somewhere. This function is now being served by third-party consultants who claim to physically check carbon offset projects.

*Marlies Hesselman, "A New Frontier in (Dutch) Climate Litigation: Greenwashing Advertisements on CO$_2$ Compensation." *Climate Law* (blog). *Columbia Law School*. July 12, 2022.

13-3 Emission Rate Trading

Emission rate trading was used to phase out of leaded gasoline in the United States. In the 1950s, the practice of adding lead to fuel to augment its performance became common among gasoline refiners. As leaded gas became popular, the lead content of urban air began to show an alarming increase, and concern mounted over the resulting health effects. In addition, lead in gasoline interfered with catalytic converters, the technology of choice for reducing other emissions. The federal response was to establish a timetable for the elimination of lead in gasoline. The program included a **trading system** to help reduce the overall cost of a transition to lead-free gasoline. To decrease the lead content of gas but maintain normal octane ratings, refineries had to install new equipment and institute new operating procedures. But conversion costs differed among refineries, especially between large and small operations. Some could switch to lead-free gas quickly and at reasonably low cost, whereas for others conversion would take longer and be more costly. A lead trading program was introduced to allow more flexibility and lower costs in the conversion process.

Refineries were given (by the EPA) annual base rates for the amount of lead in the gas they produced. The rate declined over time, so all production of leaded gas was ended by 1988. Suppose, for example, the base rate for a given year was 1 g/gallon. If a refinery reduced its rate to, say, 0.5 g/gal for that year, and produced 100,000 gallons of gas in that year, it would have 100,000 × 0.5 = 50,000 of allowances (sometimes called lead credits) to sell to refineries which produced that year at a lead rate over the base level.

The lead market, which was national in scope, was widely used in the transition to low-lead gas. The EPA estimates that it probably saved several hundreds of millions of dollars in total transition costs. Its success has been chalked up to two main points:

- initial widespread agreement on the overall goal of phasing out leaded gas and
- the ease of monitoring the amount of lead in gas.

Although the lead trading program was a success in easing the lead "phase-down," getting lead out of gas was not achieved without compensating environmental costs. People wanted less lead, but they also still wanted high engine performance. Thus, the octane ratings of gasoline were to some extent maintained by substituting other compounds for lead.

A potential exists for implementing a policy like the one for lead-free gasoline to GHG reduction by point-source emissions. Such a system may provide an incentive to move from internal combustion engines to hybrids to electric vehicles at a faster pace.

Summary

Programs of transferable discharge permits have become popular. One of the first such programs was the SO_2 control CAP in the 1990 Clean Air Act Amendments. CAP programs for the control of greenhouse gas emissions have been initiated in Europe and in California. The spirit behind this approach, the transfer of emission rights from sources with low control costs to those with high costs, is also behind developments in the control of nonpoint-source waterborne emissions; we will discuss these in the chapter on water pollution (see **Chapter 14**). The cap-and-trade approach gives us pollution control at a substantially lower cost than the system of technology-based effluent standards, and a sense that, politically, these programs are more acceptable than emission charges.

But CAP programs come with their own set of problems. Most especially, CAP programs take some of the burden of pollution control out of the hands of engineers and place it under the operation of a market. There are a host of important factors: Who gets the permits at the beginning, the strength of their incentives to minimize costs, the degree of competition in the market, the transaction rules set by the administering public agency, the ability to monitor and enforce compliance, and so on.

Besides CAP programs, several other trading systems are common. Offset markets, both voluntary and regulatory, are widespread, particularly in efforts to reduce global greenhouse gas emissions. Carbon offsets allow any entity engaging in an activity that reduces carbon to compensate or sell the value of that reduction to another entity that desires to compensate for its carbon emissions. The most frequent activities are reforestation, renewable energy projects, and transportation. Emission rate trading systems have also been used, for example, in phasing out leaded gasoline.

Both transferable discharge systems and emission charge systems seek to take the burden and responsibility of making technical pollution-control decisions out of the hands of central administrators and put them into the hands of polluters themselves. They are not, we should stress, aimed at putting pollution-control *objectives* themselves into the hands of the polluters. It is not the market that is going to determine the most efficient level of pollution control for society. Rather, these systems are the means of enlisting the incentives of the polluters themselves in finding more effective ways of meeting the overall objective of reducing emissions.

Questions for Further Discussion

1. How might you design a transferable discharge permit system for solid waste? For phasing out of use a certain type of plastic? For phasing in a program for using recycled newsprint in newspapers?
2. Explain how a program of transferable discharge permits works to satisfy the equimarginal principle.
3. Following are the marginal abatement costs of two sources. They currently emit 10 tons each.

    a. What would the total abatement costs be for a cutback to a total of 10 tons by closing Source B? by closing Source A?
    b. What would the total abatement costs be for an equiproportional cutback to a total of 10 tons?
    c. Suppose we print up 10 transferable discharge permits, each of which entitles the holder to 1 ton of emissions. We distribute them equally to the two sources. What will the final emissions be for each of the two sources, and the total abatement costs after all adjustments have been made?
    d. Show that if the permits are originally distributed in a different way (say all to one source and none to the other), the final results will be the same in terms of total and individual emissions, but the distribution of the gains from trade will be different between the two sources.

	Marginal Abatement Costs	
Emissions (tons)	Source A	Source B
10	0	0
9	2	4
8	4	8
7	6	14
6	8	20
5	10	30
4	12	42
3	14	56
2	18	76
1	28	100
0	48	180

(Continued)

Questions for Further Discussion *(Continued)*

4. What are the pros and cons of letting *anybody* (banks, private citizens, environmental groups, government agencies, etc.) buy and sell transferable discharge permits, in addition to emission sources themselves?

5. Most of the carbon offsets traded globally are being bought by corporations, many of which are not currently subject to emission restrictions. Why do you think this is the case?

For additional resources pertaining to the material in this chapter, see the list in **Appendix B.**

Section 5
Environmental Policy in the United States

Having looked at the principles of designing effective environmental policy, we now turn to an examination of actual policies. Most of the remainder of the book consists of chapters about public policies that have been put in place to deal with environmental problems of various types. This section contains four chapters on U.S. environmental policies. There are three chapters on federal policy on problems of water, air, and hazardous materials. Then there is a chapter on environmental policies of the states, including recycling. Each of these policy areas is extremely complex, with its own history, character, and vocabulary. The chapters aim to summarize the main elements of each policy area, utilizing the ideas discussed in the preceding chapters. Pollution-control policy is rife with acronyms. **Appendix A** contains a list of acronyms used in the book.

Chapter 14
Federal Water Pollution Control Policy

Water is biologically necessary for life, but, beyond this, water resources play a vital and pervasive role in the health and welfare of a modern economy. Water for direct human consumption is a small but critical part of the domestic system, which also includes water used in food preparation, cleaning, and sewage disposal. Water is an essential element in many industrial and commercial production processes, again both as an input and as a medium of waste disposal. Large amounts of water are used by farmers for irrigation, especially in the western United States. Also, water-based sports and recreation, both freshwater and saltwater, have become very popular.

The water resource system itself consists of a vast array of interconnected components, from the grandiose to the tiny. The surface-water system includes the huge main-stem rivers and Great Lakes, as well as the thousands of small neighborhood streams and ponds. Add to these the innumerable person-made components, from the mill ponds of the first industrial era to the vast reservoirs and canals of today. Swamps and wetlands abound, ranging from small local bogs to the huge Everglades in southern Florida. And then there is the vast, but unseen, system of groundwater aquifers, exceeding surface waters in terms of sheer quantity of water. Saltwater resources are also of vital importance. Marshes and coastal lowlands are critical for fish and wildlife resources; beaches and scenic coasts are important recreational resources; coastal waters provide transportation and pleasure boating services; and saltwater fisheries are a major source of food.

The nation's water system is important in two respects: its water supply characteristics or quantity, and its water quality aspects. Water supply issues from surface and underground sources vary in degree from eastern regions with relative water abundance to western regions where water is scarce and often a source of contention and conflict. Quantitative aspects of water are studied in resource economics. In this chapter, we focus on water quality.

Efforts to protect the quality of water resources have gone on for a long time. In this chapter we look at federal water pollution–control policy. Our objective is to review the main elements of that policy with the economic concepts developed in preceding chapters. We also look at policies that seek to make use of economic incentives to achieve improvements in water quality. Most states and localities have active water pollution–control efforts, some of which are tied into the federal programs; we will consider some of these in a later chapter.

14-1 Types of Water Pollutants

There are many different types of waterborne pollutants. Within the policy arena it is common to differentiate the following categories:

Conventional pollutants: These represent some of the first water pollutants that were subject to control. They include biochemical oxygen-demanding (BOD) wastes, total suspended solids (TSS), bacteria, fecal coliform (FC), oil, grease, and pH.

Nonconventional pollutants: These include chemical oxygen demand (COD), total organic carbon (TOC), nitrogen, and phosphorous. Fertilizers, sewage, manure, and detergents are sources of these substances.

Toxic pollutants: These include 65 named (in the Clean Water Act) chemicals, consisting of natural and synthetic organic chemicals as well as metals discharged from industrial sources. From this list of chemicals, a list of "priority pollutants" is derived, for which testing and control programs are created.

Waterborne emissions include all the different types of discharges discussed in **Chapter 2**. **Point sources** include outfalls from industry and domestic wastewater treatment plants. **Nonpoint sources** include agricultural runoff of pesticides and fertilizers and the chemicals and oils that are flushed off urban streets by periodic rains. Many sources, especially point sources, have **continuous** emissions related to the rate of operation of the industrial plant or the domestic sewer system. There are also many **episodic emissions,** such as accidental releases of toxic materials, oil-tanker accidents, or occasional planned releases of industrial pollutants.

In **Chapter 2** we also spoke of cumulative and noncumulative pollutants. In water-pollution control, it is more common to speak of **persistent** and **degradable** pollutants. Degradable waterborne pollutants undergo a variety of biological, chemical, and physical processes that change their characteristics after emission. Especially important are the oxygen-using chemical processes that rely on the oxygen contained in receiving waters to degrade the wastes.[1] The reason for focusing on oxygen requirements is that oxygen plays a critical role in water quality. High levels of dissolved oxygen (DO) are usually associated with high-quality water, water that will support high-quality animal and plant life, recreational uses, and domestic water-supply systems.

Because DO is used up in the degradation process, one way of measuring the quantity of waste emitted is through **biochemical oxygen demand,** or BOD, the amount of oxygen required to decompose the organic material under specified conditions of temperature and time.[2] A substantial proportion of the BOD load introduced into the water resources of the country comes from municipal waste-treatment plants. Much of this consists of wastewater from treated domestic waste, which contains a variety of degradable organic compounds. Industrial sources also contribute large amounts of BOD wastes, some stemming from the sanitary facilities within the plants, and more importantly from the great variety of water-using steps in the production processes, such as cleaning, product formation, waste removal, and product transport.

---

1. Degradable wastes include a variety of infectious bacterial agents that can cause such diseases as typhoid, cholera, and dysentery. Waste heat is also a degradable pollutant; it comes mostly from large-scale industrial processes that use water for cooling purposes.
2. For example, BOD10 is a quantity of material requiring 10 pounds of oxygen in order to be completely converted to its constituent elements during a period of 10 days and at a temperature of 20°C.

When a BOD load is put into a river or body of water, it produces a temporary reduction in the DO level of that water as the oxygen is used to degrade the waste. Over time, through natural aeration processes, the DO content of the water will normally recover. The **DO profile** would thus look like **Figure 14.1** (where the discharge point is marked x). This can be thought of as the average DO level at various distances downstream from the point at which a BOD load is introduced, or the DO level at various times after a BOD load has been introduced into a lake. This is called a DO "sag," and it illustrates the degradation process by which the water body is assimilating the BOD load. The important thing to see is that the DO reduction is reversible. It is also noncumulative—if the BOD source were stopped, the DO sag would shortly disappear.

FIGURE 14.1 Dissolved Oxygen Profile in Water After a BOD Load Has Been Introduced

Early water pollution–control efforts were centered on conventional pollutants such as BOD wastes, suspended solids, and so on, for which there are common water quality measures such as DO, turbidity, acidity, and coliform count. More recent programs also focus on **toxic pollutants.** Toxicity is often a matter of concentration; substances that are toxic at high concentrations may not be at low concentrations. This implies that the diluting ability of water is a valuable quality in addition to its capacity to transform degradable substances.

Persistent water pollutants are those that remain for a long period of time, either because they are nondegradable or because the rate of degradation is very slow. This category includes thousands of inorganic and organic chemicals. Industrial wastes contain many such persistent pollutants. Wastes from mining operations can contain various metals as well as acid-mine drainage.

Agriculture is the source of pesticides, fertilizers, and soil runoff. The concept of "persistent" does not mean permanent in a technical sense; many chemicals, oils, and solvents break down but over a long period of time. In the process they pose a persistent threat. Radioactive waste is physically degradable over very long periods, but measured in terms of a human scale it is essentially a persistent pollutant. Viruses are also in this category.

14-2 Federal Water Policy: A Brief History

In the "sanitary awakening" of the mid-19th century, the public began to appreciate the importance of water quality for human health. Many states instituted public boards of health in response.[3] The first federal law of any note covering water-pollution control was the

---

3. The first such agency was in Massachusetts in 1869.

1899 Refuse Act empowering the U.S. Army Corps of Engineers to grant permits to anyone desiring to put refuse of any kind into any navigable waterway (see **Table 14.1**). The primary objective of this act was to ensure navigation, not to control water pollution per se.

TABLE 14.1 Major Federal Legislation on Water Pollution Control

1899 Refuse Act
Required permit from the U.S. Army Corps of Engineers before refuse of any kind could be put into a navigable water. Primary purpose was to ensure navigability.
1948 Water Pollution Control Act (WPCA)
Federal government was authorized to conduct investigations, research, and surveys; however, no federal authority was established to enforce laws, set standards, or limit discharges. Authorized federal government to make loans to municipalities to construct sewage treatment facilities.
1956 WPCA Amendments
Authorized the states to establish criteria for determining desirable levels of water quality; introduced the idea of an "enforcement conference," sponsored by federal agencies to bring together state and local interests to develop enforcement plans. Authorized federal government to make grants for municipal waste-treatment facilities, with federal share up to 55 percent of construction costs.
1965 Water Quality Act
Required the states to develop *ambient quality* standards for interstate water bodies and implementation plans calling for effluent reductions from specific sources. State actions required federal approval, with a strengthened "enforcement conference" procedure.
1972 WPCA Amendments
Provided for a federally mandated system of *technology-based effluent standards*, with federal enforcement through the granting of discharge permits. Phase I (starting in 1977) permits were based on "Best Practicable Technology" (BPT); Phase II (starting in 1983) permits were based on "best available technology" (BAT); states could ultimately take over the permitting process. Declared a goal of zero discharge to be attained by 1985. Made a large increase in the municipal treatment plant grant program, with federal share increased to 75 percent of construction costs. Mandated secondary treatment in municipal treatment plants. Changed the definition of "federal waters" from one based on navigability to simply "the waters of the United States."
1974 Safe Drinking Water Act (SDWA)
Requires the EPA to set maximum contaminant levels for drinking water; requires public authorities to protect, monitor, and test water supplies. Amended in 1986 and 1996.
1977 Clean Water Act (CWA)
Established procedures for control of toxic effluent in addition to the conventional effluent on which previous acts had focused; sources were required to meet "best conventional technology" (BCT) for conventional pollutants and BAT for toxics, starting in 1984; increased authorization for treatment plant subsidies.

(Continued)

TABLE 14.1 (Continued)

1981 Municipal Wastewater Treatment Construction Grant Amendments
Reduced federal share to 55 percent and substantially decreased total funding.
1987 Water Quality Act (WQA)
Postponed some of the deadlines for adopting *technology-based effluent standards*; changed the waste-treatment subsidy program from federal grants to federal contributions to state revolving funds; requires states to develop and implement programs to control nonpoint sources of pollution, particularly with best-management practices (BMP).
2014 Water Infrastructure Finance and Innovation Act (WIFIA)
Established a federal loan program for clean water, drinking water, along with wastewater infrastructure projects. The act expanded grantees to include private ventures or joint ventures of private corporations with government or tribal entities.

The 1948 act authorized a program that over the years would become a major element of the federal effort: subsidies to municipalities to construct waste-treatment facilities. That act also developed new enforcement institutions, so-called enforcement conferences, where federal, state, and local administrative authorities would come together and hammer out water pollution-control policies. In 1965 came the Water Quality Act, which, besides extending many provisions of past laws and refunding the municipal waste-treatment subsidy program, sought to encourage the states to develop **ambient standards** for water quality.

The early 1970s saw a rapid growth in the environmental movement and in environmental advocacy. The Environmental Protection Agency (EPA) formed in 1970 and this gave environmental issues more visibility and greater political representation. The primary approach was an ambient-based one. States were supposed to establish ambient water quality standards, then translate these into specific emission reductions by the many firms and treatment plants contributing to the problem. The 1972 Water Pollution Control Act Amendments established a powerful, direct federal role in controlling water pollution.

Federal authorities set specific effluent standards for individual point sources of water pollutants. These were enforced with federally issued **discharge permits.** Each source of waterborne emissions required a permit specifying the time, place, and maximum quantity of emissions. To provide the basis for these permits, the EPA would promulgate **technology-based effluent standards** (TBESs) for all sources discharging wastes into the nation's waters. These are essentially emission standards that are tied to particular types of pollution-control technology. Thus, the primary approach to water-pollution control was changed from an ambient-based to a technology-based system for point sources.

The Water Quality Act of 1987 directed attention to **nonpoint sources** and used a technology-based approach to pollution control. A substantial focus of the program has been to encourage operators (especially farmers, whose operations account for a large part of nonpoint-source emissions) to adopt **best-management practices** (BMPs). A BMP is a federally approved (and often subsidized) procedure or technique whose adoption will reduce the runoff of NPS water pollutants. Agricultural BMPs might include, for example, changes in certain cultivation practices, construction of dikes or barriers, or planting of buffer zones around fields.

14-3 Technology-Based Effluent Standards

The Clean Water Act (CWA) charges the EPA with establishing effluent standards for industrial facilities and publicly-owned treatment works (POTWs). Technology-based effluent limitation guidelines identify the alternative pollution-control technologies available to firms in each industry. These guidelines form the basis for identifying the appropriate emission standard.

A TBES, therefore, is an effluent standard set at the level of emissions that a source would produce if it were employing a particular type of abatement technology. Firms emitting waste materials or energy usually face a choice among different technologies and methods for reducing emissions. Different packages of technologies and operating procedures lead to different costs as well as a different level of emissions.

It would require enormous effort to establish effluent standards for each and every individual source. Thus, the EPA sets standards for categories of polluting sources. For example, consider sugar-beet processing plants.[4] This is a process that uses a large amount of water for cleaning purposes; thus, the wastewater may contain large amounts of suspended solids and BOD wastes. **Table 14.2** shows hypothetical costs and emissions performance of five different technology options for plants in this industry. Each technological option refers to a particular collection of treatment equipment, operating procedures, fuels, and so on, that the plants might adopt.

TABLE 14.2 Estimated Total Costs and Emissions from Sugar-Beet Plants Using Alternative Emission Abatement Technology

	No Control	A	B	C	D	E
Emissions (kg/kkg of raw product processed)						
BOD*	5.8	3.6	2.2	1.05	0.23	0.0
TSS†	10.2	5.7	2.5	1.02	0.30	0.0
Total costs ($ mil/year)	0.0	8.0	14.4	23.40	36.50	78.8

*Biochemical oxygen demand.
†Total suspended solids.

Lower levels of emissions can be obtained with greater costs; emissions into water bodies could be reduced to zero at a very high cost. To pick one set of emission levels for the standard requires that the EPA use some sort of criterion. The WPCA of 1972 states that the EPA should initially set emission standards on the basis of the **best practicable technology** (BPT) currently available to the firms. This was Phase I, to be achieved by 1977. Then, starting in 1983, firms would be subject to Phase II effluent standards, based on **best available technology** (BAT).

---

4. Sugar-beet processing uses substantial quantities of water. Some is used simply to move the product around the plant, whereas some is used in actual processing. Hydrated lime is used as a purifying agent, which leaves a large amount of "lime mud" to dispose of. Emission control can be done with a variety of water recycling and recirculation processes, screening, settling, stabilization ponds, and land disposal.

In Phase I suppose the EPA decides that technology C, with an estimated cost of $23.4 million per year, represents the BPT for this type of processing industry. Then it would set emission standards at 1.05 kg/kkg for BOD waste and 1.02 kg/kkg for TSSs. All sugar-beet processing plants would then be subject to this emission standard.

In Phase II EPA would be called on to select the BAT for this type of industry. BAT would appear to be a more stringent standard than BPT because it includes all technologies that are available, whether or not they are practicable. But the rules also specify that BAT has to be "economically achievable." On this basis, technology E in **Table 14.2** might be regarded as the BAT for sugar-beet processing plants. On the other hand, some (especially those in the industry) might argue that such technology doesn't realistically exist, that it is too costly to be considered "available" in any economic sense, in which case the EPA might select D as the BAT.

Setting TBESs for an industry is obviously a time-consuming business. It requires large amounts of economic analysis and hinges on an agency judgment about what *available* and *practicable* mean when applied to pollution-control technology. It is also politically controversial, with industries ready to challenge in court when they feel the standards are too constraining.

The CWA changed and after 1984 sources were to meet standards based on **best conventional technology** (BCT), which allows more weight to be put on the costs of installing and operating the technology. The notion of conventional technology is different, and weaker, than the idea of available technology; it presumably allows more weight to be put on the costs of installing and operating the technology. The EPA also sets TBESs, called pretreatment standards, for firms discharging wastes into public sewer systems. Their role is to reduce the burden on public wastewater treatment plants.

TBESs and Cost-Effectiveness

For a policy to be efficient, it must balance damages and control costs. The TBESs are designed, however, to be applied on a national basis. The same standards for, say, leather processing plants will be applied to all leather plants in the country, whether they are located on a river just upstream from a large urban area or on a river in some remote part of the country. Strict efficiency would call for different levels of pollution control for sources in different circumstances as regards the water resource on which they are located.

Cost-effectiveness questions whether the policy is designed so that when sources on a given water resource are in compliance they will have the same marginal abatement costs. There is nothing in the logic of the TBES process that moves polluters in the direction of meeting the equimarginal condition. The procedure leads instead to the application of the same standards to all firms within each subcategory. For example, all sugar-beet processing plants in the country are subject to the same effluent standards. These will be cost-effective only if all individual plants in each category and on the same water resource have exactly the same marginal abatement costs.

The EPA has designated around 600 subcategories of water-polluting industries, for each of which TBESs have been promulgated. Studies of cost-effectiveness show generally that costs of the actual CWA standards have been substantially more costly, often by a factor of two, than least cost systems. But we must bring other criteria into play. The analytical administrative and political costs of applying different standards to all sources in different locations would undoubtedly be very high. On these grounds, a reasonable second best may have been to apply similar standards across all firms in each industry.

In assessing the actual experience with TBESs, an obvious question is, how much has the nation's water quality been improved as a result of the system? This question is extremely complicated. The country's waters are very diverse, consisting of many different streams, rivers, lakes, estuaries, and aquifers, all variously situated with respect to both natural and human factors. It's reasonably easy to draw conclusions of a single, small water body, but very hard to do it for the entire system. EPA studies show that the CWA, which has been primarily aimed at point sources, has moved us much closer to zero-discharge levels for point sources. This is a significant accomplishment. However, it is also apparent that there are limits to the extent to which all watercourses could be restored to swimmable category solely through point-source control. The results do not touch on water pollution in other parts of the water system, namely, ponds, lakes, coastal areas, estuaries, and underground aquifers must be addressed.

TBESs and Incentives

The discussion in **Chapter 12** showed that emission standards lead to weaker incentives to innovate in pollution control than economic-incentive types of policies. In the case of TBESs, incentives are made even weaker by linking the emission standards to particular control technologies. When polluters are faced with this type of technology-linked standard, compliance tends to become a matter of adopting the technology the authorities have used to set the standard. Because permanent emissions monitoring is quite costly, administering authorities can check compliance by making periodic inspections to ascertain whether sources are using approved emissions-control technology. To minimize the risk of being penalized for noncompliance, polluters have the incentive to adopt the particular technology that EPA used to establish the standard. The result is that although the TBESs are nominally just emission standards, they end up tending to dictate the particular effluent-control technologies chosen by firms. This substantially undermines the incentives to search for other, cheaper ways to meet the standards.

Figure 14.2 shows an abbreviated sketch of a typical residuals and emissions loop. The primary focus of the program of TBESs has been on technology in box (2), that is, on getting point sources to adopt new technological means of handling and testing residuals. This is known as an **end-of-the-pipe** program orientation, because it focuses only on the last step in the residuals/emissions process. There is another important dimension of these incentive effects. Emissions can be reduced at other points along the production process through **pollution prevention** to reduce the residual stream by[5]:

- developing better recycling technology.
- introducing changes in the production process itself that lower the quantity of residuals produced.
- using fewer inputs in the production process.
- reducing the rate of output itself (e.g., efforts to get consumers to conserve energy).

5. Refer to Figure 2.1.

FIGURE 14.2 End-of-the-Pipe Pollution Control Versus Pollution Prevention

```
                           Recycling
          ┌──────────────────┬──────────────────┐
          ↓                  │                  ↓
Raw materials  ┌──────────┐ Residuals ┌──────────┐ Emissions
─────────────→ │Production│──────────→│ Residuals│─────────→
               └──────────┘           │ Handling │
                                      └──────────┘
                   (1)                    (2)
```

By encouraging firms to concentrate on changing end-of-the-pipe technology, the regulatory program has weakened the incentives to take vigorous steps in the direction of pollution prevention.

TBESs and Enforcement

Effluent standards are enforced through a system of **discharge permits.** To discharge wastes into a river or body of water, a firm must have a permit issued through the relevant EPA-backed state permitting program. The permit specifies the allowable emissions the source may make and is subject to enforcement by state authorities. Given the enormous number of discharge points and the difficulties of monitoring emissions, enforcement becomes a critical program element. One response has been to distinguish between major and minor emitters, using criteria such as quantity, toxicity, conventional pollution load, and impact of emissions. In this way more enforcement resources can be devoted to the major sources, which account for the largest proportion of total emissions.

When emission standards are tied to certain technologies, enforcing authorities can try to confirm compliance by checking to see if firms have put in place the criterion technology. The problem here is that there is a difference between **initial compliance** and **continued compliance.** The fact that a firm has installed certain pollution-control equipment does not necessarily mean that this equipment will be operated efficiently in the years to come. If operating costs are substantial and if nobody is effectively monitoring emissions, the incentive will be to save on operating costs by not operating the pollution-control equipment and let emissions increase.

The TBES engineering-based approach may be far less effective than it appears. From an economic standpoint, it is likely to be seriously cost ineffective; for the money that is being devoted to pollution control under this system, substantially greater improvements in water quality could be achieved with other policy approaches. The apparent technological definiteness of the approach (BPT, BAT, BMP, etc.) is less effective in practice. The EPA is required to make countless engineering decisions in order to develop these standards. Not only is this very difficult for an administrating agency, but each of these decisions is a place where political interests can focus influence. The apparent concreteness of TBESs is also substantially undermined by the monitoring and enforcement problem. What looks like a straightforward technological fix becomes, in reality, a policy with a great deal of hidden flexibility.

14-4 The Municipal Wastewater Treatment Plant Subsidy Program

A large proportion of waterborne emissions into the nation's waterways comes not from private industries but from people themselves, especially from the public sewer systems of urbanized areas. Water sanitation is a particular hallmark of U.S. water policy. Compared to the mid-1800s, with outhouses, open septic, and street-side drainage, wastewater treatment and sanitation has been financially well supported at the federal level. This has led to decreased water contamination from disease and human waste, thus improving human health.

Whereas in the case of industrial pollution, federal authorities adopted a policy of having polluters themselves pay for reducing emissions, the response toward public-sector pollution has been different. Here the major approach has been **federal subsidies** to construct treatment plants. The inspiration for this type of approach probably comes from two sources: the normal public works mentality of the Congress and the fact that it is better politics to "get tough" on industrial polluters than on cities, towns, and voters.

Treatment of domestic wastes uses both physical and biological processes and is fairly standardized. The different degrees of treatment are designated *primary, secondary,* and *tertiary,* according to the process used and the extent of treatment given to the wastes:

- Primary treatment is essentially a set of physical steps built around a basic sedimentation process; it can remove about 35 to 40 percent of the primary BOD waste in the original waste stream.
- Secondary treatment uses biological means (e.g., "activated sludge") to further treat the waste.

Primary and secondary processes together can reduce BOD waste by between 85 and 90 percent. These processes, although quite effective in removing BOD load, are less so in handling plant nutrients such as nitrogen and phosphorus.

- Tertiary treatment makes use of a variety of chemical processes and can reduce waste loads even more.

The sequence of primary, secondary, and tertiary processes is subject to increasing marginal abatement costs; the greater the reduction one wants in BOD waste or other pollutants in the waste stream, the higher the marginal cost of getting it.

The 1972 WPCA Amendments mandated that all municipal sewer systems have at least secondary treatment within 11 years. Congress authorized a program of federal subsidies to local municipalities to cover 75 percent of the costs of designing and constructing public wastewater treatment plants. Large sums were appropriated for the program. The figures in **Table 14.3** seem to show the impact of the program. From 1960 to 1988, the percentage of public sewer systems discharging untreated waste declined from 63 percent to less than 1 percent, whereas the percentage having at least secondary treatment increased substantially.

TABLE 14.3 Progress in Public Wastewater Treatment Facilities

	1960	1980	1996	2000	2008	2012	2019
Total U.S. population (millions)	180	224	264	270	284	314	328
Percentage served by waste-treatment systems	61	71	72	77	79	76	84
Percentage of served population with:							
No treatment	61	1	<1	0	0	0	0
Primary treatment only	33	31	9	<1	<1	0	0
At least secondary	4	68	91	97	97	99	100
Advanced	N/A	N/A	23	40	45	60	N/A

Sources: Environmental Protection Agency, *2012 Clean Water Needs Survey, Report to Congress*, U.S. EPA, Office of Wastewater Management, 2016; Environmental Protection Agency, *Clean Watersheds Needs Survey 2012, Report to Congress Summary*, U.S. EPA, Office of Wastewater Management, 2012; Center for Sustainable Systems, *U.S. Wastewater Treatment Factsheet*, University of Michigan, Pub. No. CSS04-14, 2022.

From these numbers it is clear that great strides have been made in community wastewater treatment. The federal program added large sums to the construction of publicly owned treatment works (POTWs) or wastewater treatment plants (WWTPs). It was originally feared that federal money would simply displace funding by states and communities, but this does not appear to have happened.[6]

Federal subsidies for WWTPs covered capital construction costs, but not operating costs. Thus, there was a built-in incentive to build plants with excess treatment capacity. A community that expects to pay only 5 or 25 cents on the dollar may have less incentive to control construction costs than if they had to pay for the entire project. Excess capacity could accommodate future population growth and may attract new industrial growth. A program of emission standards called **pretreatment standards** was developed. These are standards applied to wastewater streams entering public sewer systems from private business sources. The objective is to get industrial polluters to undertake some treatment themselves before they put their wastes into the public sewer system.

Industrial pollution and the POTW program have become more closely interrelated. At the present time most industrial polluters are **indirect dischargers;** their emissions are sent to a WWTP for treatment and are subject to the requirements of the pretreatment program. These are somewhat akin to emission charges, and may be having the predicted effect—that is, providing an incentive for industrial polluters to search for ways of reducing their waterborne emissions.

States continue to receive federal grants, but states now must provide matching funds equal to 20 percent of the federal funds. The combined funds are used to establish **state revolving funds** (SRFs), which are used to make loans to communities to build wastewater treatment plants. The loans made from the funds are largely paid back (this is why they are called "revolving funds"). This reshaped local incentives because local groups are responsible for covering the actual costs of constructing their treatment plants.

---

6. See: David A. Keiser and Joseph S. Shapiro, "Consequences of the Clean Water Act and the Demand for Water Quality," *The Quarterly Journal of Economics*, 134(1), 2019, 348-396.

Stormwater Runoff

Stormwater runoff refers to runoff that flows across streets, parking lots, and other paved areas into storm drains and then into the environment. Often, stormwater bypasses wastewater treatment facilities and flows directly into waterways. Many municipalities use the SRF to finance WWTP upgrades. These are particularly necessary to reach a tertiary treatment level and to increase capacity for handling larger volumes of stormwater runoff. When stormwater runoff becomes too great for a WWTP to handle, particularly during large storms, the WWTP cannot treat waste coming into the system, and untreated or raw waste and sewage move directly into rivers.

This issue has become critical in some municipalities where quantities exceed permit levels. Stormwater trading is an alternative compliance approach used by jurisdictions subject to Municipal Separate Storm Sewer System permits. A stormwater crediting program may be established to provide compliance flexibility for development sites subject to post-construction regulations, or to achieve regional water quality objectives cost-effectively. Credits might be generated through the installation of urban green infrastructure or through agricultural conservation practices. Stormwater credit buyers include municipal governments, real estate developers, and departments of transportation.[7]

14-5 The Safe Drinking Water Act (SDWA)

Aging infrastructure and drinking water contaminants such as lead, and algae blooms from nutrient pollution, all contribute to drinking water deterioration. These issues are addressed by the Clean Water Act and the Safe Drinking Water Act of the biennial National Water Program. A similar SRF program to wastewater treatment has been established to help communities build drinking water treatment facilities. Approximately 95 percent of the population of the United States obtains its drinking water from public water supply systems. Although these are exclusively local and community organizations, public and private, the SDWA of 1974 requires the federal government to regulate these local systems and to ensure the facilities meet national primary drinking water standards.

The SDWA requires the EPA to set maximum contaminant levels (MCLs) for each recognized contaminant; currently about 100 contaminants have been identified. MCLs are, in effect, never-exceed levels, and determining where they should be is not easy. For each substance the EPA must set a maximum contaminant level goal (MCLG), "at a level at which no known anticipated adverse health effects occur and that allows for an adequate margin of safety."[8] For carcinogens and microbes the MCLGs must be set at zero. To establish an enforceable MCL, the EPA is permitted to take into account the feasibility of achieving lower contaminant levels, considering the technologies available to do so and the costs involved. Also, there are numerous unregulated contaminants that are monitored for future regulation. See **Exhibit 14.1**. The Lead and Copper Rule (LCR) particularly addresses water contamination at schools and childcare centers. A similar focus on lead in paint occurs in the housing market. Both strive to achieve a lead-free goal.

---

7. National Network on Water Quality Trading, *Breaking Down Barriers: Priority Actions for Advancing Water Quality Trading*, 2018.
8. Mary Tiemann, *Safe Drinking Water Act: Implementation and Issues*, Congressional Research Service, Report IB10118, 2003.

> ### EXHIBIT 14.1 Potential Water Contamination
>
> In an effort to save city taxes and spending, the drinking water source for Flint, Michigan was shifted in 2014 from Lake Huron to the Flint River. Unfortunately, old pipes, leaching, and insufficient water treatment resulted in drinking water contamination and crisis.
>
> The risks of contaminated drinking water are high on the list of concerns among people on public water supply systems. The EPA has the mission of advising local water-supply systems about substances that could contaminate water-supply systems. It is a challenge to stay ahead of the situations and substances that appear in the modern economy. Here are some examples:
>
> - Hydrologic fracturing is a technique that extracts natural gas from deep underground shale formations. There have been reports in parts of the country of contamination of groundwater and related surface water with the chemical additives used by operators in the high-pressure water stream, as well as by the methane that is released as a result of the drilling.
> - Producers of skin products began adding tiny plastic microbeads to their products, which on rinsing would end up in wastewater and the water bodies into which the wastewater was returned.
> - Increased use of fluoridated dental products and the consumption of food made with fluoridated water have led the EPA to establish a minimum contaminant level for fluoride in drinking water.
> - Regulations have been developed governing underground injection wells, looking to the day when there may be large quantities of carbon dioxide that are destined for long-term storage possibly near underground aquifers.
> - Widespread appearance of PFAS-type chemicals in drinking water, in 2023, led the EPA to propose the National Primary Drinking Water Regulation (NPDWR) and to limit the maximum contaminant level (MCL) to 4.0 nanograms per liter (4.0 parts per trillion) for PFOA and PFOS.

In the 1996 amendments to the SDWA, some concern was expressed that feasible MCLs for large, better-financed systems might not be feasible for small communities where costs might loom larger and potential benefits smaller. Thus, language was put in the law allowing the EPA to establish standards based on a comparison of both the benefits and the costs of the standard.

Thus, in setting standards under the SDWA, the EPA can identify goals based solely on health impacts, but set enforceable standards at a less stringent level that is based on an analysis of both the benefits and costs of achieving them. This is a case of making trade-offs in pollution control. The approach also goes under the name *balancing* and is controversial in its application to environmental regulations. Environmental groups, in particular, are likely to look askance at balancing because they think it may give undue prominence to the costs of achieving pollution reduction. Others look on balancing as an essential part of achieving greater efficiency and cost-effectiveness in pollution-control programs.

Economic changes, especially new technologies, have always presented society with new problems in controlling environmental pollution. This is certain to continue in the future. The technology associated with fracking for extracting deep underground natural gas, raises concern for groundwater contamination. See **Exhibit 14.1**.

14-6 Accident Response: The Case of Oil Spills

The United States has historically been a net importer of crude oil. But with the rise of fracking, it has become an exporter. This means much larger quantities of oil being shipped within the country and in its coastal waters. And this has meant the increasing incidence of oil spills. Offshore spills are often revealed in dramatic ways by accidental releases from tankers and barges that are transporting oil in coastal waters. Ship and barge transportation in these waters has historically been regulated with a complex mix of state, federal, and international laws. Over the last 30 years, the number of significant spills and the quantity of oil released from these spills have dropped substantially, as **Figure 14.3** shows.

FIGURE 14.3 Volume and Number of Oil Spills for Incidents in Navigable U.S. Waters, 1985–2021

Source: Bureau of Transportation Statistics. Petroleum Oil Spills Impacting Navigable U.S. Waters, 2022.

Note: In 2010, the Deepwater Horizon oil spill reached 207 million gallons.

The 1989 major oil spill in U.S. waters of the Exxon *Valdez* in Alaska led directly to the federal Oil Pollution Act of 1990. This law made comprehensive changes in the law through two means: expanding federal response authority and increasing spill liability. It also incorporated specific technology standards, such as requiring double-hulled tankers and a variety of performance requirements for operators. Another oil-spill problem is water contamination stemming from accidents on off-shore oil drilling platforms.

Onshore, major quantities of oil are being transported by rail and pipeline. Spills have become common, and arguments rage about which transport mode is less risky. Both modes involve risk, and policy issues abound as regards the management of these risks. There are two main dimensions of this, reducing the incidence of spills, and ameliorating the damage when spills occur.

To reduce the number of spills, companies must have strong incentives to deploy strong accident reduction technology. This can be done by:

1. having an effective regulatory system in place, for example, requiring blowout protectors, double-hulled vessels, and effective braking systems for rail cars.
2. giving firms incentives to act, for example, having liability arrangements whereby oil companies will be held liable for any damages caused by spills.

To reduce the damage once a spill has occurred, adequate spill response procedures have to be in place. The EPA and numerous other federal and state agencies have accident response programs that involve reporting functions as well as clean-up technology and labor mobilization procedures that are meant to be readily available.

14-7 Nonpoint-Source Water Pollution Control

The EPA estimates that nonpoint-source (NPS) emissions are responsible for more than 50 percent of water quality standards violations at the beginning of the 21st century. Major NPSs are agricultural runoff, urban street runoff, and activities related to land clearance and building construction. The fact that NPS emissions are diffuse and not concentrated into specific outfalls has made them very difficult to control. NPS pollutants are also normally weather related, which makes the runoff patterns more difficult to monitor.

Difficulties of control explain why NPS pollution has not been addressed as vigorously as point-source emissions, despite its importance. Early federal water quality laws directed state agencies to consider NPS pollution in their water quality programs, but did not require that specific steps be taken. The 1987 law gives it somewhat more prominence and authorizes federal money to subsidize local efforts to control NPS pollution. In fact, there is a major contrast between the national, uniform policy that has been followed to control point-source emissions and the policy for NPS pollution. In the latter case federal authorities have essentially thrown the problem into the hands of the states. Their reasoning is that "the application of uniform technological controls . . . is not appropriate for the management of NPSs. Site-specific decisions must consider the nature of the watershed, the nature of the water body, . . . and the range of management practices available to control NPS pollution."[9]

Passing the major initiative to the states has led to a great variety of programs for NPS pollution control.[10] Traditional approaches such as emission standards are not common, because of the difficulties of measuring emissions with accuracy. This has pushed back the locus of control onto regulating activities and technologies that typically lead to NPS emissions. These are mostly what we have called **design standards.** These are standards that require certain techniques or practices to be used by sources whose activities lead

---

9. U.S. Environmental Protection Agency, *Report to Congress: Nonpoint Source Pollution in the U.S.*, 1984.
10. US EPA, State and Tribal Nonpoint Source Management Programs, **https://www.epa.gov/nps/nonpoint-source-news-notes**.

to NPS emissions. Standards that rule out agricultural cultivation on steep, easily eroded land; standards specifying the design of urban storm sewers; and standards requiring homebuilders to take certain steps to control construction site runoff are types of design standards. The 1987 Water Quality Act, for example, establishes a program of federal subsidies for farmers to adopt **best-management practices** to control agricultural pollution. Although design standards may be necessary in the case of NPS emissions, we should keep in mind the difficulties inherent in their use. They require administrative determination of what particular technologies and techniques will be allowed in different circumstances. These involve substantial amounts of pushing and shoving among regulators and polluters, and probably the weakening of individual incentives to find new and better ways of reducing emissions.

Another method of controlling NPS emissions is to put a charge on those activities or materials that lead to the emissions, rather than the emissions themselves. Charges might be put on fertilizer used by farmers, for example, or on lawn chemicals used by suburban dwellers. The objective in this case is to induce a reduction in the use of materials that may ultimately end up in rivers, lakes, or groundwater aquifers.

In ocean and lake coastal regions, a major non-point source of water pollutants is septic tanks, both domestic and industrial. One important source of algae blooms along coasts is nitrogen runoff or seepage from the septic systems of oceanfront properties. Nitrogen is a natural effluent in home wastewater and sewage. The prime pollutant here is nitrates, which can leak from tanks and spread over a wide area. This has led many states, the major players in this form of pollution control, to enact new technical specifications for these installations. In some coastal states, such as Rhode Island and Massachusetts, septic systems within designated ocean impact regions must be built or retrofitted with nitrogen-reducing technology so less nitrogen enters leach fields and nearby water bodies.

14-8 Total Maximum Daily Load (TMDL) Program

The national system of TBESs has been criticized from its beginnings, especially by economists, for its relative inflexibility and cost ineffectiveness. A nationally mandated program based on the premise that all sources should be subject to the same standards is bound to make water quality improvements much more costly than they have to be. Furthermore, there has been a disconnect between the permit program and ambient water quality improvement goals. It is quite conceivable, for example, that all of the sources on a particular body of water, such as an estuary, could have adopted the legally mandated emission-control technologies, but for the water quality in the estuary to be substantially diminished. One way this could happen is through a growth in the number of pollutant sources as the economy expands; total emissions would increase, even though each individual source had adopted the BCT. Therefore, federal water quality regulators have sought to reestablish an **ambient-based** orientation in water-pollution control.

Although the 1972 Clean Water Act gave federal water-pollution control a technology orientation, it also contained a section that in effect requires an ambient approach. In cases where the quality of water bodies is impaired, even after technology-based controls, states are required to develop **total maximum daily loads** (TMDLs) for these waters. The purpose of a TMDL is to restore an impaired water body to water quality conditions under which applicable water quality standards can once again be attained. TMDLs incorporate the following steps:

1. Identification of water resources that have impaired quality.
2. For individual bodies of water, the determination of the TMDL of individual pollutants that the water body can receive without violating ambient water quality standards set for that water body.
3. The identification of all the sources, both point source and nonpoint source, that contribute to the degraded water quality.
4. An allocation of the total daily load, that is, a daily effluent limit, among the relevant sources located on the water body.

According to the law, the states are supposed to take the lead in establishing TMDLs, with backing from the EPA.[11] Establishing a TMDL for a waterbody may be the least controversial aspect of the program. To do this requires drawing a connection between total pollutant loadings and resulting water quality. In some cases this connection may be reasonably simple, whereas in others it is complex. One issue is when there is accumulated pollution in a water body; setting the TMDL must allow for this.

No doubt the much harder job politically is allocating the total loading among the various pollution sources. There is the standard public goods problem here, as each source has the incentive to shift as much of the total control cost as possible onto other sources. In many cases NPS emissions, particularly those from agriculture, are the major contributing factor in water quality degradation. It has been much more difficult to develop effective regulatory programs for NPSs than it has for point sources, and this problem intensified with the TMDL program.

Despite these difficulties the states made substantial progress in drawing up TMDLs until 2008. Since then, because of budget cuts and a notable shift toward more difficult TMDLs, progress has been erratic. In 2013, the EPA updated the long-term vision and goals for protection, restoration, and assessment under the CWA. This effort facilitated the listing of more TMDLs for impaired waterbodies.

Emission Trading in Water-Pollution Control

If total pollutant loads have been established for a body of water, and those loads have been allocated among the sources of emissions, it is only natural to think about **emission trading**. As we saw in **Chapter 13,** trading can often (but not always) offer substantial improvements over traditional approaches in terms of cost-effectiveness, leading to much greater pollution reduction per dollar of cost.

Water quality trading and offset programs are operating throughout the United States; some were established in the 1990s and continue today. The EPA has encouraged states, interstate agencies, and tribes to devise trading plans for polluted water bodies in their jurisdictions, and has published guides to help in designing them.[12]

---

11. The EPA maintains information on all aspects of the TMDL program. See **https://www.epa.gov/tmdl/overview-total-maximum-daily-loads-tmdls.**
12. U.S. Environmental Protection Agency, *Water Quality Trading,* **https://www.epa.gov/npdes/water-quality-trading.**

The National Network on Water Quality Trading started in 2013 to help guide implementation of most emerging trading programs in the country. Efficient water quality trading programs are limited to sources discharging into particular water bodies, as the water quality issues of these individual bodies are hydrologically distinct from one another. In the nutrient trading plan for the Chesapeake Bay, for example, trading is limited to within the sources of each of the major tributaries of the Bay. See **Exhibit 14.2.** Limitations of this type may lead to problems if the number of sources is small, because markets tend to work better when there are many potential participants.

EXHIBIT 14.2 Nutrient Pollution Trading

The Chesapeake Bay is a large, complex body of water, with many significant tributaries, and the recipient of huge volumes of water pollution from industrial, municipal, and agricultural operations. A major feature of pollution control on the Bay is a nutrient trading system, established in 2005. The program initially featured trading among point sources, under an overall cap established in reference to the TMDL applied for portions of the Bay.

The trading system was subsequently expanded to include nonpoint sources, particularly urban storm water and agricultural runoff. It allows offset trading, whereby sources may reduce their emissions to create offsets, which may then be traded. In this type of system regulators have to put in place very specific and practical requirements for creating offsets. Some of these are:

- Establishment of a baseline, an emission level that must be attained before further reductions would qualify as offsets.

- Additionality: No tradable credit may be generated for practices already in place, or reductions that would have occurred anyway without the trading program.

- Steps taken to create offsets must conform to "best management practices," as approved by the Chesapeake Bay Program.

- Any pollution reduction resulting from funding under a different program (e.g., support for agriculture) may not be used to create offsets.

- Absence of "leakages." Leakage is when reduction in emissions in one location create the conditions for increased emissions at another location.

For further information, see Virginia Cooperative Extension. *Virginia Citizens Guide to Environmental Trading Programs: An Overview.* ANR-173P, 2022.

There is also the problem of potential hotspots. Many water bodies (such as the Chesapeake just mentioned) have subsections that have somewhat distinct hydrologic systems. If sources in these types of areas are able to purchase additional emission permits from elsewhere, local water quality may be reduced even though overall water quality is not. Under the law, trading cannot lead to any localized diminishment in water quality.

Trading among individual sources implies that individual emissions can be monitored and measured. Nonpoint emissions are extremely difficult to measure with accuracy, so suitability of trading is questionable. Thus, the stress is on using technological approaches such as voluntary or required adoption of BMPs. However, there are exceptions; in the Central Valley of California, selenium discharges from agriculture have caused great damage to wildlife resources in the region. In this case circumstances are such that total and individual selenium runoff can be monitored, making it possible to implement an effective trading program for reducing this material.[13]

Summary

The initial federal effort to control U.S. water pollution was focused on the promulgation and enforcement of technology-based effluent standards (TBESs). These are emission standards stemming from the EPA's findings as to the "best available technology" or "best practicable technology" for specific industries. These technology-based standards, with enforcement by the individual states, had a number of drawbacks, in terms of cost effectiveness and incentives for technological change. Despite this, great progress has been made in cleaning up the water resources of the country. More recently, federal water-pollution policy has shifted toward an ambient-based approach, through the total maximum daily load (TMDL) system.

We also discussed the federal program of subsidies for municipal waste-treatment facilities. Over the last several decades the proportion of the U.S. population being served by advanced (secondary or tertiary) treatment facilities has been substantially increased. To address stormwater runoff and nitrogen effluent, coastal regions are requiring financing for advanced technological solutions.

One objective of a major revision of federal water pollution–control policy will be to try to find greater opportunities for using incentive-based strategies to combat water pollution. Most problems about water pollution are local or regional, implying that the permit markets in water-pollution control will have to operate with relatively small numbers of traders.

Questions for Further Discussion

1. Distinguish between a "technology-based" water pollution–control program and an "ambient-based" program.
2. In order to meet TMDL limits in a cost-effective manner, what is the appropriate role of the equimarginal principle? What about the economic efficiency principle?

(Continued)

---

13. World Resources Institute, *Nutrient Trading by Municipal Stormwater Programs in Maryland and Virginia: Three Case Studies*, WRI 2017.

Questions for Further Discussion (Continued)

3. Controlling the residuals from the production of bleached paper towels is about five times costlier than controlling the residuals from unbleached paper towels. Analyze this difference with our standard pollution-control model. What does it suggest in terms of public policy toward water pollution control?

4. What are likely to be the main problems in establishing cap-and-trade programs for water pollution control?

5. Refer to **Figure 14.3.** Select a year when the gallons of oil spilled were over 7 million. Research the spill(s) for that year. Was the amount due to one oil spill or multiple oil spills? Investigate the cause of the accident(s) and propose how incentives could have been adjusted to prevent the spill.

6. Consider the behavioral effects and incentives where a coastal town proposes to prohibit people from eating foods that contribute to a relatively high level of nitrogen in their toilet wastewater. Suggest a policy that could be proposed to reduce the density of nitrogen in household wastewater. Discuss how people may try to circumvent your policy.

For additional resources pertaining to the material in this chapter, see the list in **Appendix B.**

Chapter 15
Federal Air Pollution Control Policy

As it travels through space, planet earth takes along with itself an enveloping, but relatively thin, layer of gases, without which it would be a cinder. That layer of atmospheric gases provides two critical services: direct life support for living organisms on the earth's surface and control over the radiation exchange between earth and space. Both of these services can be upset by human activity.

For human beings and other living organisms, the air is what water is for fish. Unless you wear a gas mask, there is no escaping what the air has to offer. The surface air (the troposphere) normally contains about 78 percent nitrogen, 21 percent oxygen, small amounts of other gases, and varying amounts of water vapor. It may also have many, many other things put there through special acts of nature and the activities of human beings. The upper layers of the earth's atmosphere (collectively called the stratosphere) contain only about 5 percent of the planet's air, but they have a critical role to play in making it habitable. Trace gases in the stratosphere, particularly ozone, filter out about 99 percent of incoming ultraviolet radiation, acting like a giant sun block, without which we would be exposed to damaging levels of radiation. Other trace gases in the stratosphere provide greenhouse services; they trap some of the infrared radiation that is reflected back from the earth's surface, warming it and making it more hospitable to living organisms. Both of these vital phenomena can be disrupted by human activity.

Human disruptions of the atmosphere are not new; instances of local smoke pollution have occurred for centuries. With the post-industrial age, the potential severity of air-pollution problems has grown more acute, owing to the sheer scale of airborne residuals released and the exotic nature of some of the emitted substances. There are thousands of potential air pollutants: for example, oxides of carbon, nitrogen, and sulfur; volatile organic compounds (VOCs); suspended particulate matter; photochemical oxidants; radioactivity; heat; and noise. These pollutants cause a diverse set of damages, including human health impacts. Prolonged exposure to airborne substances can lead to lung cancer, bronchitis, emphysema, and asthma; accidental releases can have acute impacts. Air pollution also causes damage to plants, as in, for example, the destruction of forests and reduced crop yields stemming from acid deposition. Air pollution can lead to severe damage of exposed materials, such as the surface erosion and discoloration of stone and concrete work and the corrosion of metals. Stratospheric ozone depletion and enhanced global warming have significant implications for humans and the earth's ecosystem. Not all air pollution is outdoors; in fact, indoor air pollution is a critical problem in many homes, factories, mines, and farms.

In this chapter we discuss issues concerning the control of conventional air pollutants. The problem of global climate change stemming from emissions of CO_2, methane, and other heat trapping chemicals will be addressed in **Chapter 16**.

Many airborne pollutants are emitted on a continuous basis. The sulfur dioxide (SO_2) emissions from power plants, for example, are continuously produced as long as the plants are in operation. For individual motor vehicles with internal combustion engines (ICE), emissions start and stop with their operation, although for an entire urban area, auto and truck emissions vary continuously throughout the days and seasons according to the rhythms of economic activity. Episodic emissions have been the cause of severe air-pollution incidents, such as large-scale releases from accidents at chemical plants. The links between emissions and ambient air quality levels can be complicated because of the complexities of meteorological phenomena, such as winds, storms, and air temperature inversions, when local weather conditions trap air pollutants sometimes for extended periods of time.

Annual expenditures in the United States for air-pollution control have increased substantially since the early 1970s. Has this had an impact? **Table 15.1** shows aggregate U.S. emissions for major air pollutants for several years between 1980 and 2021. All of these have declined over this time period. Sulfur dioxide emissions are largely from stationary sources, and these have decreased substantially over this time period. Nitrogen oxides (NO_x), on the other hand, are largely from mobile sources; there have been sharp decreases in these emissions in the more recent years. The biggest success story has been with lead emissions; these have decreased dramatically from both mobile and stationary sources.

TABLE 15.1 National Emissions Estimates for Common Pollutants and their Precursors

	\multicolumn{7}{c}{Millions of Tons per Year}
	1980	1990	2000	2005	2013	2017	2021
Carbon monoxide (CO)	178	144	102	81	59	47	43.7
Lead	0.074	0.005	0.002	0.001	0.001	0.001	NA
Nitrogen Oxides (NO_x)	27	25	22	20	13	11	7.6
Volatile Organic Compounds (VOC)	30	23	17	16	14	14	11.8
Particulate Matter (PM)							
PM_{10}	6	3	3	4	3	2	2
$PM_{2.5}$	NA	2	3	3	2	1.4	1.4
Sulfur Dioxide (SO_2)	26	23	16	14	5	3	1.8

Notes: For CO, NO_x, SO_2, and VOC emissions, fires are excluded because they are highly variable; for direct PM emissions, both fires and dust are excluded.
Source: U.S. Environmental Protection Agency, *Air Quality Trends*, 2017; Statista, *U.S. Air Pollutant Emissions by Type 1970–2021*, 2023.

Emission data like these do not tell us directly whether pollution-control policies have been effective. To know this, one needs a with/without analysis: what emissions were compared to what they would have been if the policies had not been pursued.

15-1 Federal Air Policy: A Brief History

The major federal air-pollution statutes since the 1960s are summarized in **Table 15.2.** There was little federal concern or statutory activity in air-pollution matters prior to the late 1960s; in this respect, it was similar to water pollution. Air pollution was regarded as primarily a local concern, to be dealt with under **local nuisance laws.** Federal activity was regarded as best directed at helping the states deal with growing air quality problems. In the 1967 Air Quality Act, the Department of Health, Education, and Welfare was charged with establishing criteria through which ambient air quality standards could be set for six common air pollutants: SO_2, NO_x, ozone, particulate matter, CO, and lead. These became known as the **criteria pollutants,** and ambient standards for these six were to be set by the states. The CAA Amendments of 1970 represented an aggressive assertion of federal power into air-pollution matters. It established the basic contours of air-pollution policy that persist to the present: national ambient air quality standards (NAAQSs), a variety of technology-based emission standards (TBESs) for stationary sources, and stricter emission standards for automobiles.

TABLE 15.2 Major Federal Air-Pollution Laws

Air Pollution Control Act (APCA) of 1955
Authorized the Secretary of Health, Education, and Welfare (HEW) to spend up to $5 million a year to do research and to help the states in training and technical assistance on matters of air pollution. Extended in 1959 and 1962.
Motor Vehicle Exhaust Study Act of 1960
Directed the Secretary of HEW to do a study on "Motor Vehicles, Air Pollution and Health" within two years.
Clean Air Act (CAA) of 1963
Authorized federal grants to states to develop state and local air pollution–control programs; established a conference system to deal with problems of interstate air pollution; extended authorization for federal research on air pollution.
Motor Vehicle Air Pollution Control Act of 1965
Authorized the Secretary of HEW to set *emission standards* for new cars (but no deadline was established); dealt with international air pollution and called for more research.
CAA Extension of 1966
Extended the CAA of 1963 and added authority to make grants to states to support air pollution–control programs.

(Continued)

TABLE 15.1 *(Continued)*

Air Quality Act (AQA) of 1967

Provided for additional grants to states to plan air pollution–control programs; provided for interstate air pollution–control agencies, expanded research on fuels and vehicles; required HEW to establish air quality regions of the country and publish air quality criteria and control technology reports for the common pollutants; required states to establish ambient air quality standards for the "criteria" pollutants and develop attainment programs; authorized HEW to give financial assistance to states to establish motor-vehicle inspection programs.

CAA Amendments of 1970

Established national ambient air quality standards (NAAQSs) for criteria pollutants; required the establishment of new-car emission standards along with certification programs; EPA was to establish emission standards for major toxic or hazardous pollutants; EPA to establish technology-based emission standards for all *new sources* (NSPS) of the common air pollutants; required state implementation plans (SIPs) to control existing stationary sources of air pollutants.

CAA Amendments of 1977

Established the goal of "prevention of serious deterioration" (PSD) in areas already cleaner than the national standards; established three classes of already clean areas:

Class I areas: no additional air quality deterioration permitted (includes national parks, etc.).
Class II areas: some air quality deterioration to be permitted (includes most PSD regions).
Class III areas: air quality to be allowed to deteriorate to level of NAAQSs.

Established a technology standard "lowest achievable emission rate" (LAER) for new sources in nonattainment areas and "best available control technologies" (BACT) for new sources in PSD regions.

CAA Amendments of 1990

Established tougher tailpipe standards for new cars, with longer warranty period; mandated pilot program of "clean" cars in some cities, reformulated fuels in some cities, Phase II pumps at gas stations, and onboard fume canisters on cars; streamlined stationary-source permitting procedures; provided for reduction of 189 toxic airborne emissions; provided for stricter local plans to reduce ozone, carbon monoxide, and particulates in the worst cities; outlined further rules for phasing out of CFCs (chlorofluorocarbons); provided for a system of transferable discharge permits among power plants to reduce sulfur dioxide emissions.

Inflation Reduction Act (IRA) of 2022

Includes provision for inflation reduction, health care, and environmental provisions, particularly for the transition to electric vehicles (including cars, bikes, buses, and government and military fleets) and renewable energy sources. Provides subsidies through tax reductions for shifting to non-fossil fuel technology. EV and renewable energy adoption can lower greenhouse gas emissions and other toxic vehicle emissions, thereby improving ambient air quality.

There was widespread concern after the 1970 law that cities in areas with air quality already better than the national ambient standard could compete unfairly for new industrial development. The 1977 CAA amendments differentiated **PSD areas** (PSD stands for "prevention of significant deterioration") and **nonattainment areas.** Different TBESs would apply to PSD regions than to nonattainment regions.[1]

There were some significant policy innovations that occurred during this time. One was the EPA's decision to allow emission trading among sources; to accommodate economic growth and efficient pollution control, emission reduction credits could be traded between firms as well as intra-firm.

The CAA Amendments of 1990 contain five main sections dealing with:

- motor vehicles and fuels
- acid rain
- air toxics
- urban air quality, and
- stratospheric ozone problems

The continued problem of motor-vehicle pollution was addressed by a further tightening of new-car emission standards and expansion of state **inspection and maintenance** (I&M) programs. In addition, the law mandated many new technologies, such as reformulated fuel, fume-catching nozzles at gas stations, and the development of a generation of clean cars.

To combat the ecological effects of SO_2 emissions from power plants, the 1990 CAA introduced an innovative plan for a transferable discharge permit program. The law also attempted to deal more directly with **toxic air pollutants.** The 1990 act specifically lists 189 toxic materials that are to be controlled and requires that the EPA establish effluent standards incorporating maximum achievable control technology (MACT), defined as technology based on the "best control technologies that have already been demonstrated" in the designated industrial categories.

The 1990 Act sought to recognize degrees of nonattainment in different metropolitan areas. The law specified increasingly stringent control techniques for cities according to the degree of nonattainment achieved.

Efforts to protect the earth's stratospheric ozone layer are a response to scientific results showing that this layer was being degraded by the release of certain chemicals in industrial and domestic use. The 1990 program was put in place to implement the country's responsibilities as part of the Montreal Protocol to phase out the use of ozone-depleting chemicals.

Current federal air-pollution policies are long and complex, but they can be boiled down to the following:

- NAAQS for criteria pollutants, with pollution-control programs of varying stringency based on the severity of the air pollution in different regions.
- Command-and-control type emissions standards for stationary sources of criteria pollutants and hazardous pollutants, with differential stringency depending on age and location of source.

---

1. The PSD regions were differentiated into three classes; see the detail in Table 15.2.

- State Implementation Plans (SIPs): plans developed by the individual states and approved by the EPA, showing how they will meet the ambient standard.
- Emission standards for new cars, with I&M programs in some states.
- A variety of new technology specifications for automobile pollution (clean cars and widespread adoption of the California timeline, reformulated fuel, and on-board vapor-catching devices).
- Increased efforts to utilize market trading mechanisms to reduce airborne emissions.

The EPA was tasked with evaluating the national benefits and costs of the 1990 Clean Air Act. They looked at the criteria for pollutants (those shown in **Table 15-1**) and concluded that the benefits of the law had exceed the costs by a substantial margin.[2] We can conclude that the policies have led to substantial emission reductions, and therefore to improved air quality. What also should be asked is whether the sums of money that the nation has put into pollution control have achieved as much improvement as possible. For this, we need to look more closely at the policies themselves.

15-2 National Ambient Air Quality Standards

The 1970 CAA specifies a system of **national ambient air quality standards** (NAAQS) for criteria pollutants, to be applied uniformly across the country. In **Chapter 11** we discussed the question of uniformity in standards. Unless marginal damage and marginal abatement costs happen to be the same in all regions, uniform national standards will not be efficient. They will be overly stringent where marginal damages are relatively low and/or marginal abatement costs relatively high, or not stringent enough where marginal damages are relatively high and/or marginal abatement costs relatively low. But the political spirit of the times was that everybody was entitled to the same level of air quality. Furthermore, it would be costly for each state to set and enforce its own standards. This made national ambient standards the preferred approach.

The current standards for criteria pollutants are shown in **Table 15.3**. There are two levels of standards established in the CAA: primary and secondary. The legal criteria to be used by the EPA in establishing these are as follows:

- **Primary standards:** To be set at whatever level is required to protect the **public health,** with an "adequate margin of safety." The latter clause has been interpreted to require that the standards be set to protect the health of the more sensitive members of the population, such as children, people with asthma, and the elderly.
- **Secondary standards:** To be set at the level necessary to protect the **public welfare.** This has been interpreted to include such things as protection from decreased visibility and damage to crops, animals, vegetation, and buildings.

2. Congressional Research Service. *Cost and Benefit Consideration in Clean Air Act Regulation.* CRS Report R44840, May 5, 2017.

TABLE 15.3 National Primary and Secondary Ambient Air Quality Standards as of 2023

Pollutant	Primary/Secondary	Averaging Time	Level
Carbon monoxide	Primary	8 hours	9 ppm
		1 hour	35 ppm
Lead	Primary and secondary	Rolling 3-month average	0.15 $\mu g/m^3$
Nitrogen dioxide	Primary	1 hour	100 ppb
	Primary and secondary	Annual	0.053 μ/m^3
Ozone	Primary and secondary	8 hours	0.070 ppm
Particle pollution, PM$_{2.5}$	Primary	Annual	12 μ/m^3
	Secondary	Annual	15 μ/m^3
	Primary and secondary	24 hours	150 μ/m^3
Particle pollution, PM$_{10}$	Primary and secondary	24 hours	35 $\mu g/m^3$
Sulfur dioxide	Primary	1 hour	75 ppb
	Secondary	3 hours	0.5 ppm

Major battles have been waged over these standards. Some argue that the standards should be set without reference to the cost of meeting them. Others take the position that trade-offs are inevitable, so costs should be part of the decisions. Of the 67 sections of the Clean Air Act that authorize health-related standards, 34 of them specifically mention costs as being a factor that can be brought into the consideration. Over the years, the EPA has developed legally defensible procedures for establishing these standards.

The standards as set imply that the damage functions associated with these criteria pollutants have **thresholds,** below which damages are minimal or nonexistent. When the standards were set, relatively little was known about the damage functions. Even today we are unsure if these thresholds exist. Recent results suggest that they may not, that in fact damages may occur even at very low levels of these pollutants. But the costs of achieving zero levels of these pollutants would be enormous.

15-3 Stationary-Source Control

A strictly ambient-based approach to air-pollution control would take the ambient standards as given, and then determine the specific steps needed to attain them. The 1972 CAA involved a change to a technology-based system. It gave the EPA the authority and responsibility to establish emission standards that would, in effect, specify the technologies that polluters would have to install and operate to reduce emissions. A stationary source emits pollution from a fixed location, such as a smoke stack at a power plant or a chimney on a house. The law specified that the EPA uses a system of technology-based effluent standards (TBES) to combat emissions from stationary sources.

Technology-Based Effluent Standards

Emissions standards are never-exceed levels for the emissions of various pollutants coming from industrial sources. In theory, an emission level could be established while leaving the polluter free to figure out the best way (presumably the cheapest way) to achieve the standard. But that is not the way the 1970 CAA was written. The relevant language in the act is the following:

> The term "standard of performance" means a standard for emissions of air pollution which reflects the degree of emission limitation achievable through the application of the best system of emission reduction which (taking into account the cost of achieving such reduction and any nonair quality health and environmental impact and energy requirements) the Administrator determines has been adequately demonstrated.

This is an emission standard that is tied to technology. In other words, the standard has to "reflect" the control achievable through a system that is in some sense the "best" one available. In this case the criterion seems to be technology that has been "adequately demonstrated." In other cases the EPA was instructed to set emission standards based on other criteria, as we will discuss below.

What initially might have sounded like a straightforward emissions standard (lower your emissions to the standard level using whatever means you want) in practice turned into a technology standard; the EPA identified acceptable technologies and provided incentives for firms to adopt these particular technologies. Firms treated these EPA-designated technologies as technology standards primarily because of monitoring difficulties and the need to assume compliance.

Differentiated Control

The standards differ between existing and new sources and between nonattainment and PSD regions as shown in **Table 15.4**. Distinctions between existing and new sources are a prominent feature in environmental control programs. New sources means pollution from newly constructed stationary sources, or existing sources that are modified in some major way; they are usually held to stricter standards than existing, established sources, which are much older. In the air quality program, new sources in nonattainment areas are subject to a LAER (lowest achievable emission rate) standard,[3] which is meant to be more restrictive than the RACT (reasonably available control technology) standard applied to existing sources in those areas. In PSD regions, new sources are held to standards based on BACT (best available control technology), whereas existing sources are, in effect, not subject to any standard.

The 1970 CAA incorporated this tradition by specifying **new source performance standards (NSPS)** for new and modified stationary sources, while leaving much of the regulation of existing sources to the discretion of states. In the 1977 amendments a new wrinkle was added: **new source review (NSR)**. NSR required new or modified sources to get a permit before building or changing, with the permit to be given only if the sources adopted the approved technology. The case for holding new sources to stricter standards (**new-source bias**) than those applied to existing sources is usually made on the basis of

---

3. LAER is defined as the lowest achievable emission rate specified in any state implementation plan, whether or not any source is currently achieving that rate.

cost; it normally costs more to retrofit existing plants with pollution-control equipment than to incorporate the equipment into new plants when they are being built. In effect, the argument is that the marginal abatement costs of existing plants are normally higher than those of new plants, so cost-effectiveness justifies more restrictive emission standards for the former than for the latter. To a large extent, this is probably an economic argument being used to justify a course of action that is politically expedient. It is easier to put stricter limits on new sources than on existing ones because, by definition, the former will have less political clout than the latter. And existing firms may not be so opposed to applying stricter controls that make it relatively costly for new competitors to get into business. From an administrative standpoint, a new-source bias is also easy to understand. In any given year, there are many times more existing sources than there are new or modified sources. A focus on new sources also implies a gradualist approach because it means that stricter standards will gradually spread through the various industries as old capital is replaced with new.

TABLE 15.4 Technology-Based Effluent Standards (TBESs) for Control of Large Stationary Sources of Air Pollutants

Nonattainment Regions	
Existing sources:	RACT: reasonably available control technology
New sources:	LAER: lowest achievable emission rate
Prevention of Significant Deterioration (PSD) Regions	
Existing sources:	None
New sources:	BACT: best available control technology

But the price paid for holding new sources to stricter standards may be high. The problem is that a new-source bias creates incentives to hold on to existing or older plants because they will be subject to less strict environmental standards than new or modernized plants. So in trying to ease the transition to lower pollution levels through a new-source bias, the regulations may inadvertently slow up the rate of adoption of pollution-abatement technology. A fierce battle has gone on through the years over how regulators define a "new" versus an "existing" plant.

Virtually all of the observations we made about TBESs in water-pollution control are also applicable to air pollution–control policy:

- They encourage uniform compliance among sources. When marginal abatement costs differ across sources, this cannot be cost-effective. In some cases, reliance on uniform TBESs is substantially more costly than if more cost-effective regulation were pursued.
- The initiative and responsibility for pollution control tends to be in the hands of administrative agencies rather than the polluters themselves.
- Much of the energy and creativity of polluting firms is devoted to finding ways of avoiding compliance rather than devising better means of controlling emissions.
- The incentives for research and development (R&D) to develop new techniques of pollution control or to reach back into the production process to reduce residuals in the first place are weakened.

We need to be mindful, however, of the idea that efficiency and cost-effectiveness are not the only criteria on which pollution-control policies should be evaluated. Another is flexibility, or adaptability, and on this criterion, technology-based effluent standards may be more effective. Since they depend on substantial regulator discretion, adjustments can sometimes be made in concepts, definitions, monitoring, enforcement, and other dimensions to adapt to new circumstances without triggering acrimonious political battles.

We also need to remember the emission data shown at the beginning of this chapter. Under the regime of TBES employed under the CAA, there have been substantial reductions in the major air pollutants since the act has been in force. Research has shown that it is the CAA that is responsible for the reductions.[4]

Emissions Trading in Stationary-Source Control

While the central regulatory mechanism of the CAA continues to be command-and-control standards, a number of emission trading plans have been implemented. In **Chapter 13** we referred to the emission reduction credit trading that was initiated under the CAA so that economic growth could be accommodated in nonattainment areas.

A number of complete **cap-and-trade (CAP)** programs have been put in place to address some of the nation's most significant air-pollution problems:

- The national SO_2 emission trading program addressed the acid rain problem, due mainly to SO_2 emissions from coal-fired power plants. The first phase included 263 of the most polluting plants, while the second phase included almost all of the coal-fired plants in the U.S. Ambient sulfate concentrations decreased by about 75 percent in the Eastern United States between 1986 and 2016. For particulate matter ($PM_{2.5}$), all plants in New England are now compliant. The intensity of acid rain throughout the northeast substantially improved, along with a reduction in its effects. Acid rain, a common problem of the late 20th century, is no longer a major environmental concern because of policy success.

- Pollution-control authorities in Southern California began the Regional Clean Air Incentive Market (RECLAIM) in 1993. It applies to emissions of nitrogen oxides (NO_x) and sulfur oxides (SO_x). Initially about 350 firms participate in the NO_x market and 40 in the SO_x market. NO_x emissions have declined by about 80 percent, and SO_x emissions by a comparable percentage.[5]

- From 2003 to 2008, 13 northeastern U.S. states/regions began a CAP program to control emissions of NO_x. By interstate agreement, the total NO_x emissions for the group are allocated among the states, then each state allocates its total emissions as tradable permits among sources in the state. Trading among sources, which are mostly electric utilities and large industrial boilers, may be both intra- and interstate. This program was later expanded to include 10 midwestern states and led to a dramatic reduction in NO_x emissions, especially in the summer months. This plan was effectively replaced by federal policy on interstate pollution.

---

4. Joseph S. Shapiro and Reed Walker, "Why is Pollution from U.S. Manufacturing Declining? The Roles of Environmental Regulation, Productivity, and Trade," *American Economic Review,* 108(12), 2018, 3814-3854.
5. For more information, consult **http://www.aqmd.gov.**

- Harris County in Texas established a CAP program to reduce highly reactive volatile organic compounds (VOCs). The objective is to satisfy the NAAQS for ozone in that county. Other states have introduced similar programs.
- Many states have initiated CAP programs to control greenhouse gases. We deal with these in **Chapter 18.**

Controlling Interstate Air Pollution

The original Clean Air Act focused on intrastate air pollution: any state in which the ambient standards were violated was tasked with finding ways to reduce emissions from sources in that state. It is widely recognized that ambient conditions in many states, especially those "downwind" (mostly eastern states) are strongly affected by emissions from sources in other states. Addressing this issue has been very difficult because it involves interstate politics, and interstate pollution control plans put forward by the EPA have been routinely set aside by the courts. One plan, called the "Cross-State Air Pollution Rule," would require upwind states to join an ozone emission trading plan in order to reduce downwind state ozone levels. This problem will no doubt continue to be controversial.

Controlling Greenhouse Gas Emissions

The need to control GHG emissions to ameliorate global climate change has become a matter of urgency in the United States and around the world. The first major attempt to do this in the United States was a proposal for a national CAP program for carbon emissions. The U.S. Congress was unable to come to agreement on its design and push it to enactment. Subsequently, the Supreme Court ruled that new legislation was not in fact necessary, and that the EPA had the power under the CAA, to regulate GHG emissions, even though they were not explicitly mentioned in that law.

This put the initiative back in the White House, which in 2014 proposed a new plan for control of GHGs from power plants. The essence of the program, called the Clean Power Plan (CPP), is to set specific state-level targets for power plant emissions, then essentially leave it up to the states, alone or in combination, to achieve the targets. The plan was not adopted.

The plan that was adopted was the "Inflation Reduction Act of 2022," which, despite its title, contains important provisions for curbing greenhouse gases: consumer subsidies for purchasing electric cars and producer subsidies for producing electricity with renewable forms of fuel.

Consumer Subsidies

The Inflation Reduction Act has many features, one of which is subsidies for consumers to lower the cost to them of buying an electric vehicle. The social objective is to get the private automobile fleet to turn over more rapidly into one that contains more electric cars and therefore burns less fossil fuel. The situation is depicted in **Figure 15.1**. The subsidy works to lower the supply price of electric cars, effectively shifting the supply curve facing consumers from S_1 to S_2 by the amount of the subsidy. The new equilibrium quantity of electric cars bought goes from Q_1 to Q_2. How much this quantity increases depends on the amount of the shift in supply, and also the elasticity (related to the slope) of the demand function. The greater the slope (i.e., the higher the price elasticity of demand), the larger the overall effect. It is vital to remember, however, that this depends on there being stiff competition among alternative suppliers of the item. If there are only a few suppliers, it may be possible for one or all of them to increase the price of their product, thereby appropriating the value of the subsidy. Consumers would still believe that they were getting a subsidy, but in effect it would be flowing into the bank account of the supplier.

FIGURE 15.1 Consumer Subsidies

Producer Technology Subsidies

These subsidies are based on the idea that the transition costs for power companies to shift to renewable forms of energy are too high and uncertain and therefore need to be reduced through public subsidies. The operational means of doing this are through producer tax rebates for investing in renewable power and for producing electricity with renewable sources. In effect, this means subsidies to firms for shifting to a production means that have substantially lower marginal abatement costs.

15-4 Mobile-Source Air-Pollution Control

The other major part of the federal air quality program is control of mobile-source emissions. Although there are thousands of stationary sources of air pollution, there are many millions of mobile sources. They are most often associated with transportation vehicles, such as cars, trucks, planes, railroads, and ships. Furthermore, the political fundamentals of mobile-source control are totally different from those of stationary-source emissions. It is often good politics to be seen chastising the polluting behavior of the businesses, especially corporations, responsible for stationary sources. It is quite different to take an aggressive stance against the millions of people whose cars cause the pollution but who also vote. So the spirit of the mobile-source program has been to reduce emissions, but in a way that avoids placing an obvious burden on individual drivers.

The total quantity of mobile-source emissions in a given period can be expressed in the following way:

Equation 15.1

$$\text{Total quantity of emissions} = \text{Number of vehicles} \times \text{Average miles traveled} \times \text{Emissions per mile}$$

If we were devising a cost-effective way of reducing the total quantity of emissions, we would want to balance the three factors on the right side of this equation according to the **equimarginal principle.** In fact, the federal mobile-source pollution-control program has focused almost completely on the last of these variables, emissions per mile. Clearly, the most important factor in the split between fossil-fueled vehicles with internal combustion engines (ICEs) and electric vehicles (EVs) is with this variable. Although car makers have been quite successful in producing ICE cars with ever-lower emissions per mile and reaching the CAFE standards, EVs have zero emissions per mile when driven. However, the other two factors in **Equation 15.1** are also critical.

Economic and demographic growth has added to the number of vehicles on the road. Such an increase in the first variable in **Equation 15.1** would thereby increase the total quantity of emissions. Countries with a lower number of ICEs per 1,000 people tend to have lower aggregate CO_2 emissions from mobile sources. There are many governmental programs that partially subsidize the purchase of EVs to give incentives for drivers to buy zero-emission vehicles rather than ICE vehicles. However, increasing the number of EVs sold may or may not impact total emissions if ICE vehicle driving does not change. There is no necessary one-to-one relationship between buying an EV and no longer driving an ICE. This highlights the second factor in **Equation 15.1,** average miles traveled.

The total mileage driven continues to increase, with the exception of the COVID-19 pandemic affected years (2020–2021), as the following tabulation shows:

Year	Total Miles Driven (billions)
1970	1,120
1980	1,520
1990	3,147
2000	2,747
2010	2,967
2014	3,038
2019	3,250
2020	3,238
2021	2,886

Source: U.S. Department of Transportation Federal Highway Administration, "Moving 12-Month Total on All US Highways, 2022.

New-Car Emission Standards

The main emissions from mobile sources are hydrocarbons (sometimes called volatile organic compounds or VOCs), NO_x, CO, and particulate matter. Lead used to be a major mobile-source pollutant but, since the advent of lead-free gas, this is no longer the case.[6]

---

6. Historically, the transition to lead-free gas was a federal policy to eliminate the use of lead in gasoline to reduce the level of lead in the air we breathe. The EPA policy was adopted, implemented, and completed successfully from 1970 to 1995. Conceptually, the policy was a technology standard with the maximum allowable lead in gasoline used in automobiles set to zero and included trading.

The first two of these (VOCs and NO$_x$) are smog precursors; that is, after they are emitted, they react with sunlight and among themselves to form the smog and elevated ozone levels that characterize so many urban areas.

The primary federal approach to controlling mobile-source emissions was set in the 1970 CAA. It consists of a **new-car certification program**—essentially a program of mandated emission standards on new cars. Manufacturers are required to certify that the emissions of new cars do not violate the legally mandated standards. Violations may lead to a variety of penalties, up to and including shutting down the assembly lines that produce the offending vehicles. **Table 15.5** shows the emission standards established in federal laws. The first row shows emissions for a typical car of around 1970, based on average performance and gas mileage data. Subsequent rows show more recent standards. The last row shows standards as they are expected to come into effect in future model years.

TABLE 15.5 Automobile and Light Trucks Emission Standards, Past and Future

	VOCs	CO	NO$_x$	PM	HCHO
	Grams per Mile					
Uncontrolled emissions	8.7	87.0	3.5		
1974	3.0	28.0	3.1	n/a	n/a
1990	0.41	3.4	1.0	n/a	n/a
2009	0.09	4.2	0.07	0.01	0.18
2017†	NMOG* 0.086	2.1		0.003	0.004
2022†	NMOG* 0.056			0.003	
2025†	NMOG* 0.03				

VOCs: volatile organic compounds, now called nonmethane organic gas; CO: carbon monoxide; NO$_x$: nitrogen oxides;
PM: particulate matter; HCHO: formaldehyde.
† Standards as they would apply beginning with these model years.
*As of 2002 VOCs (volatile organic compounds) and NO$_x$ (nitrogen oxides) have been combined into a single form: NMOG (nonmethane organic gas).

It is clear that current and prospective future emissions are very small relative to earlier years. It must be remembered that these apply to new vehicles (cars and light trucks), so that how widespread and how soon they become in actuality depends on how fast the vehicle fleet is replaced as people trade in old cars and replace them with new ones. The fleet turnover ratio (new car sales in a year divided by total cars registered) is affected by many factors, most notably by the state of the economy. In the 2008–09 recession, for example, it fell to very low levels then recovered.

These reductions in tailpipe standards have been controversial. Critics, especially automobile companies, maintained that they were unrealistic when they were enacted. But advocates held that unrealistic standards were useful because they provided the incentive for car companies to search for new control technologies. This approach goes under the name of **technology forcing.** Technology forcing is one of those things, of which there are many others, that are good in moderation but perhaps counterproductive if used in excess. The very stringent emission standards written into the 1970 clean-air legislation were in fact not met; rather, they were postponed and not finally achieved until the early 1980s. We do not know whether more realistically timed emission standards might have led the automobile companies to spend more money on research and less on political efforts to get the standards postponed.

Although the emission standards have been progressively lowered through time, this trend actually overstates the reduction in emissions performance by cars in actual operation. The problem is that emissions performance of cars progressively deteriorates as the cars age and accumulate mileage. The federal program attempts to attack this problem in two ways. First it required pollution-control equipment on automobiles to be long-lived enough to ensure that emissions standards will continue to be met for a given number of miles (the "warranty" program). It is set at 140,000 miles. In addition, it mandated that states with severe air-pollution problems initiate inspection and maintenance (I&M) programs, whereby individual cars can be checked for emissions. Owners whose cars exceed emission standards can then be held liable for repairs to bring them into compliance. However, in some states, when cars reach an age of 20 years, emissions standards no longer are enforced. The irony here is that old cars tend to be heavier polluters than newer vehicles.

Besides tightening emission standards, the CAA also incorporated many federally mandated technology standards that are supposed to allow nonattainment areas to move toward attainment even without any direct controls on the overall number of cars. These standards include:

- "Reformulated" fuels, the use of oxygenated fuels at certain times of the year. At the federal level this requirement ended in 2007, but it remains in certain areas, such as California.
- Renewable fuels, in particular a requirement that ethanol be added to gasoline produced in the United States to reduce fuel imports.
- A requirement that the sulfur content of fuel be reduced, since lower sulfur content makes it easier to achieve reduced pollutant emissions.

The mobile-source parts of the law are a veritable jungle of technological specifications and requirements. It carries on the historic command-and-control tradition of pollution-control policy. Also, it is an ongoing arena of great conflicts over detailed technical specifications and regulations in which economic and political incentives are thoroughly intertwined and opaque to the outsider.

Electric Vehicles

Research, development, and innovation have proceeded rapidly for ICE alternatives. For the most part, this has focused on electric vehicles, those that operate on electricity from stored on-board batteries. Most car and truck manufacturers are offering EVs on the market. California has mandated (2023) that by 2035, all new vehicles sold in the state must be EVs. Although many states have adopted California's low-emission vehicle (LEV) and zero-emission vehicle (ZEV) standards, five have set restrictions on selling new, non-EVs cars by 2035. Several European countries have moved toward this adoption as well. Questions remain about states having the appropriate infrastructure, in particular having a sufficient number of charging stations to support the growth in these numbers. One issue is the rural versus urban divide as regards charging station access. Other questions have come up regarding the sufficiency of the electric transmission infrastructure and the availability of a larger base of renewable power generation facilities.

To lower total emissions via EVs, the proportion of miles driven by EVs, **EV intensity,** must increase. Suppose TM is the total miles driven in a period of time; ICEM is the miles driven by ICE vehicles; and EVM is the miles driven by EVs.

$$TM = ICEM + EVM$$

Rearranging the above expression gives:

$$ICEM = TM - EVM \quad \text{or} \quad = TM(1 - m)$$

where m is the EV intensity, or EVM/TM. There are essentially two ways to reduce ICEM:

1. Reduce the overall miles driven and/or
2. Increase the EV intensity by increasing the miles driven by EVs by a greater proportion than the increase in TM.

Total miles can be reduced by more people "working from home" more often, thus reducing commuting miles, increasing use of public transportation, walking, biking, etc. EVs are often second cars and tend to be used for short trips around town or commuting to work. One current constraint is access to and availability of charging stations. Larger ICE vehicles pose less risk for running out of fuel on longer, higher-mileage trips. Rural areas with fewer charging stations and longer distances between destinations can inhibit EV adoption.

While EV transition programs and the installation of charging stations become more numerous, federal mobile-source pollution-control programs that apply to ICE vehicles remain in force and operative. They consist of the following elements:

- At the manufacturing level, a "new-car certification" program that essentially sets emission standards on new cars, together with a warranty program that is meant to ensure the continued emissions performance of automobiles after they have left the plant.
- In some states, I&M programs aimed at ensuring that the emissions performance of automobiles does not deteriorate as they are used.
- In nonattainment areas, a variety of technological specifications dealing with vehicles, fuels, and other components of the transportation system.

Mobile-Source Standards and Climate Change

When national mobile-source emission control was first adopted, the focus was NO_x and hydrocarbon vehicle emissions. Now global climate change has become a major issue, and policy questions abound in trying to do something about it. Many countries around the world have imposed GHG restrictions on vehicles, sometimes directly, usually through fuel economy measures.

Table 15.6 shows U.S. mpg standards for selected years, 1978–2026, and shows GHG standards in term of grams of CO_2e per mile. CAFE (corporate average fuel economy) standards, set in the 1970s, is a fuel-efficiency level set for the average of all vehicles produced by a manufacturer. It is not the minimum fuel efficiency for every vehicle. If, in a particular year, a manufacturer produces an EV or an LEV, it can produce other vehicles with mpg below CAFE standards as long as the average stays above the standard. CAFE only addresses tailpipe emissions when driving and does not apply to the emissions or environmental impacts of manufacturing vehicles.

TABLE 15.6 U.S. CAFE and GHG Standards for Automobiles, Selected Years, 1978–2026

Year	Mileage Standard (mpg)	GHG Standard (g CO_2e/m)
1978	18.0	None
1985	27.5	None
1990	27.5	None
2010	27.5	None
2012	33.2	261
2013	34.4	253
2016	38.2	225
2019	37.0	222
2022	43.0	190
2025	56.2	163
2026	49.0	NA

Source: National Highway Traffic Safety Administration, *Summary of Fuel Economy Performance,* 2011; U.S. Environmental Protection Agency, *EPA and NHTSA Set Standards to Reduce Greenhouse Gases and Improve Fuel Economy for Model Years 2017–2025 Cars and Light Trucks,* Office of Transportation and Air Quality, EPA-420-F-12-051, 2012; EPA. "MYs 2021–2026 CAFE Proposal - by the Numbers Fact Sheet," EPA-420-F-18-90, 2018; National Highway Traffic Safety Administration, *CAFE standards MYs 2024–2026,* 2022.

CAFE standards are set by the National Highway Traffic Safety Administration in the Department of Transportation, while GHG standards are set by the EPA. They are not the same because there are some ways of reducing vehicle GHG emissions in addition to increasing fuel economy, for example, improving vehicle air conditioning systems.

Behavioral Economics Issues

The CAFE and mobile GHG programs are essentially a continuation of the focus on technology-based solutions to mobile-source emissions, in which improvements are sought through a series of technological fixes.

In addition, little attention has been directed at behavioral factors associated with the fully mobile lifestyle, such as multiple-car families, dispersed living patterns, and long-distance voyaging. The basic fact is that mobile-source emissions are linked not only to the technical characteristics of cars and fuel systems, but also to the millions of decisions that individuals make about where, when, and how to travel.

A car that has better mileage means that the cost per mile of overcoming distance has gone down. One expects this to lead to the average consumer driving longer distances, thus exacerbating the total miles driven phenomenon. Or, with better mileage, people drive at higher speeds which requires more fuel.

Other things equal, buying cars with better mileage will cost more than a car with lower mileage. The purchase involves an investment, in the sense that there is usually an upfront cost that is recovered over a period of years through reduced energy consumption. Studies have shown that there is often a general hesitancy on the part of consumers to make these investments, even though engineering-type studies show that substantial savings in energy costs would result. This is sometimes called the **energy-efficiency gap.**

What is it about consumer behavior that leads to this phenomenon? Why aren't consumers willing to buy more fuel-efficient vehicles when it appears that in the long run, and not too long at that, they would save more money than they cost? Some possible answers to the conundrum are the following[7]:

1. Consumers may use higher discount rates than we believe they do for the future savings in energy costs.
2. Although technical data seem to show potential for future cost savings, consumers may be responding to the uncertainty inherent in making any decision about the future; they may hold back until these uncertainties are resolved.
3. Consumers may lack convenient access to credit (liquidity) required for up front purchases of energy-efficient goods, including fuel-efficient cars.
4. New work in psychology and economics, called **behavioral economics,** has documented many cases where consumers do not necessarily behave as fully informed, rational, decision makers. Rather, consumers may be normally subject to biased beliefs, inattention, and self-control issues that lead them to make decisions that appear to be suboptimal in the classic sense.

Some of these factors imply a need for incentive-based policies that impact people's decisions about automobile use. One approach that has been suggested is to levy a significantly higher tax on gasoline. With gasoline more expensive, motorists would have the incentive to think more about their driving habits, organize their driving more coherently, reduce total miles traveled, shift to more fuel-efficient vehicles, use mass transit to a greater extent, and so on. The effects of the higher fuel price would filter throughout the transportation system and lead people to shift their behavior in places where the marginal costs of doing so are lowest, much as they do when gasoline prices spike. Gasoline or carbon taxes might also help reduce traffic congestion in some cases. Taxes on gas have historically been levied at the state level. This might make it possible to adapt the tax to the level of air pollution in the region, but it also complicates the policy from a political point of view.

Another suggestion is to place a charge directly on vehicle emissions. As part of the state I&M programs, inspectors could record each year the total mileage that a vehicle had been driven. This total mileage could be multiplied by the emissions per mile, also measured at the time of inspection, to yield an estimate of total emissions in the preceding year. A charge could then be levied on these emissions. Unlike a fuel tax, which would have no direct incentive for drivers to worry about emissions, a charge on emissions would create an incentive to look at all the ways of lowering them, including reducing total miles driven, driving low-polluting vehicles, and so on. One attractive aspect of this approach is that the

---

7. For further discussion, see Kenneth Gillingham and Karen Palmer, *Bridging the Energy Efficiency Gap, Policy Insights from Economic Theory and Empirical Evidence*, Resources for the Future, Discussion Paper DP13-02-REV, 2013; Virginia McConnell, *The New CAFE Standards: Are They Enough on Their Own*, Resources for the Future, Discussion Paper 13-14, 2013.

charge could be varied among regions to match the severity of regional air quality problems. Frequency of paying such an emission tax would need examination so that people's change in driving behavior could be closely reinforced by a change in the emissions tax.

Summary

The federal effort to control airborne emissions has had several main elements. National ambient air quality standards have been established "to protect the public health," with an "adequate margin of safety," irrespective of the costs and irrespective of efficiency considerations as we have discussed them. In fact, the essential trade-offs between costs and benefits were left for administrators to work out behind the scenes. A distinction is made between nonattainment areas, where ambient standards are not met, and PSD regions, where they are. To meet the ambient standards in the case of stationary sources, primary reliance is placed on technology-based emission standards. These TBESs are based on a number of different concepts, such as lowest achievable emission rate (LAER) for new sources in nonattainment areas and maximum achievable control technology (MACT) for hazardous emissions. Most economic studies of these TBESs in air-pollution control show that for the total amount of money spent on pollution control, they achieve only a fraction of the emission reduction that a fully cost-effective program would attain.

The 1990 Clean Air Act contained an innovative national program of transferable emission permits, in this case applied to SO_2 emissions from large power plants. Emission permits were allocated to existing power plants; these permits could then be traded. The market in SO_2 permits has been heavily impacted by programs to combat interstate pollution. Other trading programs are being developed to achieve efficient reductions in GHG emissions. Mobile-source emission reductions have been sought almost entirely through establishing emission standards for new cars, and then trying to ensure that emissions do not increase as the cars are being used. Technological changes have been mandated such as low-polluting vehicles and EVs. Less attention has been given to the important behavioral factors and other incentives to reduce total vehicle miles. Recently subsidies for purchasing EVs have been adopted.

Questions for Further Discussion

1. Discuss the importance of the question of whether air-pollution damage functions have thresholds for establishing ambient air quality standards.
2. Suppose that engineers invented an accurate and reliable means of monitoring and measuring the emissions from individual automobiles throughout the year. What possibilities would this open up for new types of mobile-source emission control programs?
3. The federal mobile-source air-pollution program means that new cars sold in rural regions meet the same emissions standards as cars sold in urban areas. Because there are fewer cars in rural areas, this means that air quality will be a lot better there than in the cities. Is this efficient? Is it equitable?

(Continued)

Questions for Further Discussion *(Continued)*

4. What are the advantages and disadvantages of a "new-source" bias in stationary-source air-pollution control? Consider especially its impacts on the incentives of the operators of existing sources.
5. If people ordinarily will invest in items that save money in the long run, why is the CAFE program necessary at all?
6. Discuss current and potential environmental justice issues regarding society's transition from ICE vehicles to EVs.
7. Select a 48-hour period and drive slightly below the speed limit whenever you drive during that time. Keep a journal about your behavior, experience, and feelings. How did this affect your time allocation for travel? How did passengers in your vehicle respond? Try to keep track of your gas or fuel consumption. For highway driving, repeat this activity by driving 5 mph below the speed limit.

For additional resources pertaining to the material in this chapter, see the list in **Appendix B**.

Chapter 16
Federal Policy on Toxic and Hazardous Substances

Within the general domain of environmental analysis and policy there is a class of pollutants that have come to be called "toxic" substances and "hazardous" materials. Although all pollutants are damaging to some extent, these have been singled out for their special short- or long-run potency. Most are chemicals, the person-made organic and inorganic compounds that are now ubiquitous throughout all industrialized economies, and even widespread in developing countries. From virtually nothing in 1950, the field has grown in exponential fashion, and today chemicals and chemical products have permeated into every corner of the world economy. In product improvements, new materials, food safety, health innovations, and many other dimensions, chemicals have enriched the lives of almost everyone. There is, however, a downside. A large number of these substances may cause human and ecosystem damages, certainly from exposure to concentrated doses, but also from long-run exposure to the trace amounts that show up virtually everywhere in workplaces, consumer products, and the environment.

The call to arms on chemicals in the environment was made by Rachel Carson in her book *Silent Spring* published in 1962. She documented the ecosystem damage caused by the popular pesticide DDT, which was subsequently banned in the United States in 1972 and in Europe in 1986. Other events have multiplied concern. Health damages to workers exposed to chemicals in the workplace, such as vinyl chloride and certain potent agricultural chemicals, have occurred with disconcerting frequency. In 1978, in the infamous case of Love Canal, people found chemicals oozing into their houses built on top of an abandoned hazardous-waste disposal site. Accidental releases of chemicals have become a growing problem, from the legendary spills like that in Bhopal, India (1984), to the Husky Energy Refinery explosion in Wisconsin (2018), the Westlake Corporation chemical tank explosion (2022), and to innumerable smaller airborne and waterborne accidents.[1] There is rising concern about the damages from long-term exposure to chemical residues in food, clothing, and other consumer products, such as endocrine disruptors in plastics. Some toxics are referred to as **forever chemicals** because they are highly persistent, in that they do not break down chemically, and do not occur naturally in the environment.

A primary concern is the impact of chemicals on human health. Health damages from accidental releases and workplace exposure are relatively easy to identify. Those from long-run exposure to trace amounts of chemicals in water, air, and soil are much harder to measure. Ecosystem damages are also important. Accidental waterborne chemical releases

---

1. An appreciation for the ongoing seriousness of this problem can be gained by looking at the website of the National Response Center, **http://www.nrc.uscg.mil.**

have wreaked havoc among fish and other organisms in enclosed bodies of water. Agricultural and industrial runoff has substantially damaged many rivers and estuaries around the world.

Hazardous and toxic materials have characteristics that present unique problems for monitoring and control.

1. They are **ubiquitous** in the modern economy; each year sees the development of new chemicals. This makes it difficult even knowing what substances are being used and in what quantities. It accounts for the fact that much public policy has been directed at simply getting better information about quantities of hazardous and toxic materials at various places in the system.
2. With the thousands of substances in use, each with different chemical and physical properties, it is extremely difficult to be fully informed about the **levels of danger** that each one poses to humans and other parts of the ecosystem.
3. In many cases, the quantities used are **relatively small,** as are the quantities that end up as effluent. This substantially increases monitoring problems. It also makes it easier for users to carry out surreptitious disposal. It is easy to see the plume of smoke coming out of the stack of an industrial plant; it is harder to track the much smaller quantities of chemicals used in production.
4. The damages caused by exposure to hazardous materials often can take many years, even decades, to show up. And whenever there is a **long time gap** between cause and effect, there is a tendency to downgrade the overall seriousness of the problem.

The policy world governing these materials is a jungle. There are numerous major and minor laws at the federal level. Many federal agencies are involved, with territories staked out and objectives pursued in ways that are often inconsistent. Then there are public agencies at state and local levels that are actively pursuing efforts to come to grips with these types of pollutants. And all of this is within a setting where thousands of different substances are in use, hundreds more are introduced each year, massive uncertainties exist about the human and nonhuman effects of most of them, and public concerns flare up and die down in unpredictable ways.

The laws on toxic and hazardous substances essentially create a strong regulatory structure to be pursued by federal agencies. The regulations can be tightened by one administration (e.g., that of President Obama) and loosened by others (e.g., President Trump). Thus the impact and achievements of regulations can change a lot over time.

To help sort out these complexities we have organized the following discussion under three groupings:

1. laws governing chemical use in industrial and agricultural production processes and in consumer goods;
2. laws governing airborne and waterborne emissions of toxic materials; and
3. laws governing hazardous waste handling, treatment, and disposal.

We will deal in each section with some of the important economic issues these laws, and their implementation, present.

16-1 Economic Issues in Laws Governing Chemicals in Production and in Consumer Products

The objective of the management of chemicals in consumer products and in the workplace is to ensure that these products and workplaces are reasonably safe. Household and work environments are not, properly speaking, parts of the natural environment and, in these cases, the relations of consumers to producers, and of workers to firm owners, are played out directly through markets. Nevertheless, environmental concerns have to some extent reached out to subsume certain elements of the private environment as well as the world of nature properly speaking, so we follow that lead here. Homeowners exposed to flame retardants in carpet padding or maintenance workers exposed to fumes from cleaners are subject to the same kinds of actual and potential damages as are individuals exposed to toxic emissions coming from a neighborhood factory.

Issues of workplace safety and consumer product safety have been around for a long time. During the Industrial Revolution, the rush to produce often led to unsafe working conditions and led to inadvertent, and sometimes intentional, product adulteration. The rise of the chemical economy in the later 20th century has substantially complicated these relationships and has led to a number of federal laws, the most important of which are indicated in **Table 16.1**.

TABLE 16.1 Federal Laws Dealing with Chemicals in Production and Consumer Products

Statute	Responsible Agency	Coverage
Federal Insecticide, Fungicide, and Rodenticide Act (1974)	EPA	Requires that all pesticides be registered with the EPA
Pesticide Registration Improvement Act (2003)	EPA	Created a system for pesticide registration and set maximum residue levels for food and feed
Food, Drug, and Cosmetic Act (1938) and amendments	FDA	Basic coverage of food and color additives, drugs, animal feed, medical devices, and cosmetics
Section 346(a) of the Food, Drug, and Cosmetic Act (1954)	FDA	Establishes tolerances for pesticide residues in human food and animal feeds
Federal Hazardous Substances Act (1960)	CPSC	Toxic household and consumer products
Consumer Product Safety Act (1972)	CPSC	Dangerous consumer products
Poison Prevention Packaging Act (1970)	CPSC	Packaging of dangerous children's products
Lead-Based Paint Poison Prevention Act (1991)	CPSC	Use of lead paint in federally assisted housing

(Continued)

TABLE 16.1 (Continued)

Statute	Responsible Agency	Coverage
Reduction of Lead in Drinking Water Act (2011)	EPA	Lowers maximum lead content of wetted surfaces of plumbing products
Federal Meat Inspection Act (1907)	USDA	Food, feed, and color additives and pesticide residues in meat and poultry products
Poultry Products Inspection Act (1957)	USDA	Poultry products
Egg Products Inspection Act (1970)	USDA	Egg products
Federal Mine Safety and Health Act (1977)	MSHA	Coal mines or other mines
Toxic Substances Control Act (1976)	EPA	Requires premanufacture evaluation of all new chemicals (other than food, food additives, drugs, pesticides, alcohol, tobacco); allows the EPA to regulate existing chemical hazards
Frank Lautenberg Chemical Safety for the 21st Century Act (2016)	EPA	Tightens TSCA; requires risk analysis, mandates testing of existing chemicals, provides funding source for EPA
Occupational Safety and Health Act (1970)	OSHA	Establishes permissible exposure levels to chemicals in the workplace
Food Quality Protection Act of 1996	EPA	Sets maximum levels of pesticides in food

Note: EPA = Environmental Protection Agency; FDA = Food and Drug Administration; OSHA = Occupational Safety and Health Administration; CPSC = Consumer Product Safety Commission; USDA = United States Department of Agriculture; MSHA = Mine Safety and Health Administration.

Regulatory Criteria

Perhaps the most important question in the use of chemicals is the criterion for determining acceptable levels of exposure or protection. What principle should regulating agencies follow in setting exposure standards, for example, in setting the benzene or cotton dust standards in workplaces or the formaldehyde regulations for building materials, or the acceptable application levels of a weed killer? In discussing our general model of environmental pollution control in **Chapter 5,** we developed the idea of the efficient level of environmental pollution as being a trade-off between control costs and damages. Applying the same logic to the case of chemicals means that in setting chemical exposure levels, society would try to determine the point where the benefits of reducing health or other risks are just balanced by the costs of decreasing the production and use of the chemical. This trade-off is pictured in **Figure 16.1.**

FIGURE 16.1 Cost–Benefit Balancing in Regulating Exposure to a Chemical

The curvature of the marginal control costs and marginal damages curves will vary depending on the toxicity level. Also, underestimating or overestimating marginal damages would shift the marginal damages curve lower or higher. Banning a chemical would shift marginal control costs, as replacements are found. These would all affect the optimal level of chemical exposure (e^* on previous graphs).

The original Toxic Substances Control Act (TSCA) mandates the regulation of chemicals that pose an "unreasonable risk of injury to human health or the environment." In addition, in setting regulations the Environmental Protection Agency (EPA) is required to take into account "...the reasonably ascertainable economic consequences of the rule, after considering the effect on the national economy, small business, technological innovation, and public health."

The provision, which is similar to those in the Federal Insecticide, Fungicide, and Rodenticide Act (FIFRA) and the Food, Drug, and Cosmetic Act (FDCA), though not in OHSA,[2] mandated a balancing, or benefit–cost, approach to decisions about the use of chemicals.

The 2016 amendments to TSCA sought to change the criterion for regulation, from a balancing criterion to a strictly risk-based criterion. Chemicals are now evaluated to determine whether they pose an unreasonable risk to exposed populations, especially to those

---

2. The standard under FIFRA is "unreasonable risk to human health," and under FDCA is "reasonable certainty of no harm."

who might be especially susceptible, such as children. However, the law also says that the EPA, in issuing regulations, must take into account the economic costs of regulation "to the extent practicable." This will have the effect of introducing a type of balancing into the chemical regulation process.

There is no question that the data and analytical requirements of chemical regulation are high. It requires good dose-response information, exposure data, and estimates of the benefits of reducing risks to workers and consumers. In the nature of the case, chemical damages, especially those associated with health impacts, are likely to be much more difficult to estimate than are the costs of reducing the chemical's use. Under the circumstances, the concern is that costs may be accorded greater weight in decisions, essentially biasing outcomes away from decisions to regulate. An illustration is the conflict over the impact of pesticides on honeybees as discussed in **Exhibit 16.1**.

EXHIBIT 16.1 Honeybees and Neonicotinoids

Honeybees are a critical element in the production of many agricultural crops for the pollination services they provide and the honey they produce. In the last decade, however, honeybee numbers have been in decline. One causal factor for this is thought to be the use of pesticides on agricultural and horticultural crops. One major point of debate is whether a widely used class of insecticides called neonicotinoids (neonics for short) damages honeybees as they go about their work. These chemicals were introduced in the 1990s and gained wide acceptance because they are less toxic to mammals and incorporate a new seed-based treatment. Producers of neonics have claimed that damages to honeybees are minimal, particularly when best practices are followed for pesticide application and for monitoring seed coatings, compared to the benefit that would be lost if they were banned. But evidence of damages from a 2012 risk assessment by the European Food Safety Authority (EFSA) led the European Union in 2013 to ban these chemicals on a number of agricultural crops and seeds, with use only allowed for enclosed greenhouses. Several U.S. manufacturers produce neonics under the United Nations Code of Conduct on Pesticide Management. Control of toxics by one country can impact other nations when the regulations are expanded to international trade. As of 2022, the EU lowered the residue level of neonics permitted on imported foods and animal feed. As of 2026, all imports must have a zero residue level for neonics; thus effectively banning neonic use for any country that exports to the EU. In the U.S., neonic use restrictions are set by each individual state.

Differentiated Control: "Old" versus "New"

The discussion of water- and air-pollution policy, especially the latter, showed that the major laws have differentiated between "old" sources and "new" sources, regulating the latter more stringently than the former. We also discussed some of the problems this leads to. In toxics control the same thing exists, especially under TSCA. This act differentiates between existing chemicals and new chemicals and, in effect, sets more stringent testing requirements for the latter. The same is true of FIFRA. This may provide an incentive for chemical producers and users to hold on to older, more toxic chemicals, rather than develop replacements that are less toxic but that would have to go through more rigorous testing.

The EPA has been slow in evaluating the risks of chemicals already in use when TSCA was first enacted. The 2016 Lautenberg Act requires that the agency identifies high priority chemicals currently in use and sets a time table for testing these.

Testing Chemicals and the Burden of Proof

For the thousands of chemicals that existed at the time TSCA was enacted, testing has been contentious and slow. This is because of the issues related to the **burden of proof**.

Burden of proof refers to the question of which party has the responsibility of providing information sufficient to decide the issue of a chemical's safety. In the decision of whether or not to regulate a chemical, the burden could be on the EPA, to show it is dangerous; or on the chemical company, to show that it is not dangerous. Since testing is expensive, the placement of the burden of proof is not an insignificant issue.

TSCA permits the EPA to require information from producers about the safety of particular chemicals. But for this request to be legal according to the wording of the original law, the EPA had to find that the chemical in question may present an unreasonable risk to human health or the environment. This put the EPA in a "catch 22" dilemma: To obtain safety data from the companies it had the burden of proof to show that the chemical may be dangerous. This procedure for finding that an existing chemical must be tested has been a substantial administrative hurdle for the EPA, with the result that progress in testing existing chemicals (i.e., chemicals already in use when TSCA was enacted) has been slow. The procedure was changed in 2016. The new law allows the EPA to require testing when it finds that the chemical presents an unreasonable risk to human health.

Chemical testing procedures have improved over the last several decades. The search is one for cheap, effective ways of testing a chemical for toxicity to humans. In the meantime, it has to be recognized that there is still a lot of uncertainty surrounding the average estimate of risk arising from using a particular chemical, and this has to be taken into account in making balancing decisions about its use. A special issue is the shape of dose–response curves, and whether the large numbers of chemicals that are present in food are truly nontoxic at very low levels, as is maintained by many of the producers of these substances.

Uniform Standards

The problem of toxic materials in the workplace and in consumer products has been addressed largely by establishing standards of various types. This brings up several important issues. One is the issue of whether the standards should be **uniform.** Another is the issue of how **markets** ordinarily function to take account of risks present in workplaces and consumer products.

In other words, the normal working of the labor market may function in such a way as to produce higher wages in riskier situations. An example is higher wages for hazardous-materials removal jobs. Workers contemplating employment would face an array of wages and risks, and each could choose the combination that most closely matched his or her own preferences. Moreover, this would also produce an incentive for firms to find ways of reducing risks in the workplace because they would gain through the savings in wages this would produce.

If the labor market worked smoothly like this, there would perhaps be no need for public efforts to set standards. For the labor market to work smoothly, it must be reasonably **competitive** and, to be competitive, people on both sides of the market must have reasonably good alternatives. Often they do not. More important, competitive labor markets require that all participants know the risks involved in different job situations. This knowledge is often lacking. Very often workers are not fully aware of the chemical risks to which they are exposed, either because they do not know what chemicals are in the workplace, or more likely because they lack knowledge of the effects, especially long-run effects, of these substances. This suggests a strong role for public action to see to it that workers are more fully informed about workplace risks.

Technological Change in Chemicals

The problem of chemical regulation is compounded by the fact that to regulate one substance, we need more than just information on the risks and benefits of that one material. If a chemical is banned, either altogether or in particular uses, the full impact depends on what other substance might be used as a **replacement.** Thus, to assess a particular substance we have to know not only its own characteristics, but also what products would replace it, and what the full characteristics of these substitutes are. The possibility exists that a substitute chemical could have a greater negative impact than the one being considered for prohibition.

Testing will continue to be impacted by rapid change in chemical substances. **Nanotechnology** has led to new materials and the prospects of many more. These are substances composed of extremely small particles that may have unknown, and perhaps negative, impacts on humans and nonhuman organisms. The existing laws applying to chemicals may be ill-equipped to deal with new materials such as these, because they do not put a high enough burden of proof on their originators that they are reasonably safe. The continued development of new technology and materials will ensure that these issues and problems will continue to be with us.

The incentive for replacing chemicals that serve a social benefit can yield a cycle of development, followed by retraction, followed by more development. (See **Exhibit 16.2.**) Having flexible policies can address this cyclicality problem by ensuring that new chemicals face established rules. Policy construction is a fluid process needing continual adjustments to change.

EXHIBIT 16.2 Fire Retardants and the Replacement Cycle

The development of fire retardants and firefighting materials illustrates the cyclicality of toxics replacement: a cycle of use, health issues identified, production bans, phase-out, new toxics developed, and repeat.

(Continued)

EXHIBIT 16.2 *(Continued)*

The EPA first defined asbestos as a toxic in 1971. Phase out began in 1975, and in 1995, the EPA issued a final rule banning most asbestos-containing products. Removal of asbestos-contaminated building materials is addressed under CERCLA (Comprehensive Environmental Response, Compensation, and Liability Act), and those places are considered Superfund sites. A couple of decades later, PFOS or PFOA (per- and polyfluoroalkyl substances) appeared as part of a group of fluorine-containing chemicals and were used as protective, non-stick coatings. They were used extensively as fire retardants, much in the same way that asbestos was used as a fire retardant before it. PFOS and PFOA were first identified as toxic in the 1970s when they were used on military bases; these chemicals persist in the environment without degradation. The EPA published health advisories in 2009, followed in 2016 with lifetime health advisories and a phase-out by manufacturers completed in 2022. Most manufacturers of non-stick cookware stopped using it by 2013. (Non-stick cookware made prior to 2014 may be toxic and should be replaced in the home and disposed of properly, which means do not pass along to others for reuse.) Imports into the United States of raw chrysotile asbestos and AFFF (Aqueous Film Forming Foam) are not banned, nor are products that contain PFAS.

Firefighting foam and non-stick coatings yield positive benefits to society. Post-2013, another substitute steps in – GenX. GenX is a hexafluoropropylene oxide with similar performance properties as the PFAS chemicals it replaces. Aqueous Film Forming Foam (AFFF) is part of the GenX chemical group. However again, the EPA in June 2022 released a report stating that, although GenX was intended to be less environmentally persistent than PFOA, it persists in water supplies.

As of January 2022, AFFF is prohibited from discharge and use in the United States. It is no longer produced in the United States. However, imports into the United States of raw chrysotile asbestos, PFAS products, and AFFF are not banned.

For cleanup and mitigation of PFOS at military sites, procedures set forth by CERCLA are followed. As with asbestos, the cycle of clean-up is repeated.

What are the next replacements? The strong incentive for firefighting foam continues with fluorine-free foams (3F foam) or Green FFFs developed and promoted as environmentally friendly alternatives. The same applies to green non-stick cookware. Tests using new generation foams are undergoing. All these products are currently commercially available.

Because none of these chemicals are directly ingestible by humans or used as additives in food, testing prior to the approval of production and use is not mandated under the burden of proof in TSCA (Toxic Substances Control Act). A long time gap from exposure to health effects characterized these toxics, as it does for many hazardous materials.

Will the cycle repeat? Addressing replacement cyclicality is a difficult aspect of policy design.

Source: Environmental Protection Agency. "Fact Sheet: Human Health Toxicity Assessment for GenX." 822-F-21-006. October 2021.

Environmental Protection Agency. "Human Health Toxicity Assessments for GenX Chemicals." January 13, 2022. https://www.epa.gov/chemical-research/human-health-toxicity-assessments-genx-chemicals.

Globalization and Chemicals

The chemicals industry has developed, as most industries have, under the influence of the forces of globalization. The huge chemical industries in Europe and the United States, and the growing industry in China, have been accompanied by ever increasing quantities of chemicals entering international trade. The way chemicals are managed in one country, especially as regards testing and safety issues, will be substantially impacted by developments of chemicals policy elsewhere.

The use of some of the most hazardous chemicals is restricted on an international basis under the Stockholm Convention on Persistent Organic Pollutants (POPs), which was adopted in 2001 by the United Nations Environment Program (UNEP), has been ratified by 186 parties (185 countries plus the EU). The conditions of the agreement are that each nation will prohibit and/or take legal and administrative action necessary to eliminate high-risk POPs and devise a plan for their disposal, while also reducing or minimizing the impact of all future chemicals that could be used in the same capacity. The idea is to minimize the impact on the environment and health risks. Of the top 12 most toxic pesticides or chemicals, called the "dirty dozen," that had been listed when the convention was formed, ten have been eliminated while the remaining two are restricted in use. In 2009, another nine chemicals were added to the convention.

The European Union (EU) adopted an aggressive registration system (similar to FIFRA in the United States) which involves, among other things, more rigorous protocols for determining chemical safety. REACH (Registration, Evaluation, Authorisation and Restriction of Chemicals) allows the administering agency to designate "substances of high concern" and requires producers to carry out risk studies. In effect it puts the burden of proof on chemical producers and importers, rather than on the regulating agencies.[3]

Another decision concept widely used in Europe, which impacts the way benefits and costs are evaluated, is the **precautionary principle.** It is intended to introduce greater caution into public decisions in cases where there could be substantial future costs (damages) that are currently unknown. It stems from well-known cases of many countries where the introduction of a product or material that had substantial up-front benefits turned out in the end to have some very high costs that were not foreseen. Asbestos is an example, as are chlorofluorocarbons (CFCs). The precautionary principle essentially states that if there is a perceptible threat of serious and/or irreversible damage in undertaking some action, these future costs should not be overlooked or discounted simply because they are scientifically uncertain. In a sense, the principle emphasizes the burden-of-proof issue in environmental decision-making: Should the burden of demonstrating that a new product or practice is safe be put on those who introduce it, or on those who might question its safety?

The Economics of Pest Resistance

When a pesticide is used repeatedly, the organisms toward which it is directed are subject to selection pressure, such that they will tend to evolve resistance toward the pesticide. Genes that would confer resistance to a pesticide normally occur at very low frequencies among members of that species, because they are not important to its survival. Once a pesticide is applied, however, individuals possessing the resistance gene will survive, while

---

3. For added information, see European Commission at **https://ec.europa.eu/environment/chemicals/reach/reach_en.htm** and the European Chemical Agency (ECHA) at **https://echa.europa.eu/regulations/reach/understanding-reach.**

those not possessing that gene will be killed off. Thus, the gene conferring resistance will increase in frequency among individuals in the population. Eventually, if pesticide use is kept up, the resistance gene may become so common that it seriously reduces the overall effectiveness of the pesticide.

We have here a public goods type of problem. Were any pesticide user to reduce its application, a benefit, in terms of extending the effectiveness of the pesticide, is conferred not only on that one operator, but also on everyone else who is using that material. Under normal market conditions, we saw that public goods will be underprovided. The implication here is that pesticide users, each making their own individual decisions, will overuse the pesticide and contribute to the target pest becoming resistant.[4]

As **Exhibit 16.3** discusses, effective policy requires joint action on the part of pesticide users, in this case joint action among them to keep the gene conferring resistance from becoming dominant in the target pest population.

EXHIBIT 16.3 Pesticides and the Evolution of Resistant Bugs

Insect pests account for hundreds of millions of dollars of losses each year in agricultural crops. Pesticides can help to reduce these losses. But high levels of pesticide use, besides causing damage of the traditional sort, can lead to pest resistance, thereby increasing losses and producing incentives for even higher pesticide applications.

Pests evolve resistance because in any insect population the susceptibility to a particular pesticide will vary among individual bugs. The pesticide tends to kill off the highly susceptible ones and leave those that are less susceptible. Over time the latter grow in proportion until a whole pest population can become essentially resistant.

This goes for pesticides applied in the traditional way as well as for newer types. Some species of corn, cotton, soybeans, and other crops have been engineered to express a protein of *Bacillus thuringiensis* (Bt), a soil microbe that can kill caterpillars and some other insect pests. But the concern is that Bt-resistant insects will evolve just as they have with traditional chemicals (the first instances of pesticide resistance were noted almost a century ago in 1914).

In recent years weed control in agriculture has encountered the same problem: Weeds have started to show resistance to the very popular herbicide called "Roundup." What to do about this problem? It's important to understand that this is a resource conservation problem, the "resource" here being the susceptibility of a pest to the pesticide. Steps taken to conserve this resource are actually supplying a public good, and therefore will be "undersupplied" if it's left up to individual farmers with standard commercial incentives. Round-up can now be purchased in a less concentrated formula by consumers for home gardens; this increases the potential for future resistance to grow.

(Continued)

---

4. Exactly the same phenomenon occurs in the overprescription of antibiotics to treat human illnesses.

EXHIBIT 16.3 *(Continued)*

Possible public policy steps include:

1. Standard integrated pest management practices: reduced spraying, cultural practices, crop rotation, and so on.
2. Alternate different insecticide classes so insects will be less likely to gain resistance to a single pesticide that is used repeatedly.
3. In the case of Bt crops, get farmers to plant a certain proportion of their fields with non-Bt crops. In the United States, the EPA has required seed companies to ensure that farmers do this; similar regulations have been imposed in Canada. The objective here is to allow for interbreeding between pests that may have developed resistance to Bt and pests that remain susceptible to Bt but feed on the non-Bt crop. Crop "refuges" of this type can be required by law, or can be encouraged through a variety of incentive-type programs.

16-2 Economic Issues in Federal Policy on Toxics in Water and Air Emissions

Toxic emissions come in a great variety of forms, from small airborne releases of cleaning fluid from dry cleaning establishments to large-scale releases of toxics from substantial industrial plants. Also included are the concentrated accidental releases that have spurred public concern about toxics in the environment. Not all toxics are chemicals; some, like heavy metals (mercury, cadmium, etc.), are by-products of various industrial and mining operations, and some toxics are natural, like arsenic in soil which has impacted rice farming.

When emissions-control policies at the national level were first being hammered out, the main focus was on the management of conventional airborne and waterborne pollutants. For air this meant the criteria pollutants—sulfur dioxide (SO_2), carbon monoxide (CO), ozone (O_3), nitrous oxide (NO_x), total suspended particulates, and lead—and for water it meant biochemically oxygen-demanding (BOD) waste, suspended solids, coliform count, and so on. Even in these early days, however, it was known that there was a potentially serious class of toxic emissions stemming from industrial production operations, as well as from household sources. The main laws governing toxic emissions are part of the primary pollution control statues and their amendments, namely the Clean Air Act, the Clean Water Act, the Safe Drinking Water Act, and the toxic release inventory. The CAA sets industry-specific rules for hazardous air pollutants (HAPs) standards, which control the maximum emissions levels of each toxic. The CWA focuses on ambient quality levels of watersheds, and the SDWA sets rules for maximum contaminant levels (MCLs) of specific toxics that could be in drinking water and the pipes through which drinking water flows.

The primary approach to regulating toxic emissions has been the use of technology-based effluent standards (TBES). For example, with mercury:

- Under the CAA, mercury and air toxic standards (MATS) set TBES for mercury emitted by coal and oil power plants at an MCL of 2 parts per billion (ppb). For mercury ore processing plants and mercury cell chlor-alkali plants, the rule prohibits mercury emissions as of 2022, with a 3-year compliance period.
- Under the SDWA, point-source mercury discharge rules fall under the National Pollutant Discharge Elimination System (NPDES) and are set at an MCL of 0.002 mg/L or 2 ppb.
- Under the Emergency Planning and Community Right-to-Know Act (EPCRA), any mercury or mercury compounds emitted by any industrial or federal facility must be reported in the toxic release inventory.
- The Food and Drug Administration (FDA) and the Occupational Safety and Health Administration (OSHA) also administer rules regulating mercury.

Hazardous-Waste Reduction

The early laws on hazardous waste were aimed at managing the flow of hazardous emissions coming from firms in order to reduce potential impacts, especially on human health. In this respect the method mirrored the approach taken with conventional pollutants. But toxic emissions are more difficult to manage. Smaller quantities make them much more difficult to monitor, even though in many cases, small quantities can be quite damaging. This has led policymakers to attack the toxics problems by "moving back up the line," that is, by trying to reduce the amounts of material that are in need of disposal. **Waste reduction** can be done in two ways:

1. by recycling residuals back into the production process and
2. by shifting technologies and operations so that the amount of residuals actually generated by firms is reduced.

By changing production processes and adopting new technologies and operating procedures, firms can substantially reduce the quantities of hazardous waste they produce per unit of final product. For example:

- A firm might find a new way to operate a material cleaning process to get the same effect but with less cleaning solvent, or
- a firm might shift from using a process requiring a toxic material to one involving a nontoxic substance, or
- an end product might be redesigned in a way that permits its fabrication using smaller quantities of hazardous materials.

Waste reduction is complicated and firm-specific. Different processes lend themselves to different waste reduction procedures, and the costs of achieving significant waste reduction in one situation will be very different from the costs of other cases. This is a setting where it is essentially impossible to achieve efficient controls by having a regulatory agency dictate particular technology choices for firms using toxic substances. The technical aspects of production processes and the situation of each firm are too heterogeneous for this approach.

Can **liability and compensation laws** give firms the appropriate incentives for waste reduction? We discussed the issue of liability conceptually in **Chapter 10**. By requiring polluters to compensate those whom they have damaged, these costs can become internalized, which would lead firms to take them into account in making their decisions. This could also operate through an insurance market if premiums for hazardous-waste damage policies could be set so as to reflect accurately the risks of damage associated with a firm's hazardous-waste actions. The real problem is whether enough is known about risks to be able to rely on an efficient insurance market and compensation system. Although there are thousands of chemicals in use, we have very little hard information on exactly how much damage they may cause to humans; most of the dose–response information we have comes from studies on animals, especially mice. Under the circumstances, there is not enough information about risks and damages to be able to establish consistent compensation awards or insurance premium rates that reflect true risks.

Several possibilities exist for using incentive mechanisms to control toxic or hazardous substances:

- Apply **emission charges** to toxics: Because of the relatively small volumes involved, taxing emissions would provide a strong incentive for firms to dispose of toxics illegally. The widespread **dispersion** of these materials throughout the economic sector, together with the fact that many are emitted in nonpoint modes, makes widespread monitoring very difficult. Taxes on waste disposal, however, may be somewhat more feasible.

- Levy a **tax on the feedstocks**: Apply a tax on the inputs used to manufacture chemicals, as these would be fewer in number and easier to measure than the chemicals themselves once they have moved into production channels.

- Institute **deposit–refund systems** for chemicals: Firms would pay a deposit along with the purchase price when the chemicals were bought. They could recover that deposit, or a portion of it, by documenting a reduction of emissions, that is, the recovery of the chemical from the normal waste stream.

- Increase transparency about release of toxic materials: Incentives for waste reduction have been created by making **information** more widely available through the public Toxic Release Inventory (TRI).

The Emergency Planning and Community Right-to-Know Act of 1986 requires facilities with 10 or more employees that manufacture, process, or use chemicals in quantities above some threshold level to report their chemical emissions to the EPA and state authorities. These are compiled and published periodically in the EPA's TRI.[5] Communities can then find out what hazardous materials are being used and discharged in their areas. The negative publicity of this revelation has motivated many firms to seek ways of reducing their use of hazardous materials. The law is a fairly blunt tool, however; it provides no guidance on what actual damages may be coming from the hazardous-materials releases and, in some cases, real damages and public concern may not be closely connected.

---

5. The EPA makes TRI available at **https://www.epa.gov/toxics-release-inventory-tri-program,** where visitors can easily access TRI data for their local areas. The webpage has data on criteria air pollutants, ambient concentrations of some hazardous chemicals, and hazardous-waste sites, organized so that users can see the data for their local regions.

16-3 The Management of Hazardous Wastes

The control of airborne and waterborne toxic residuals does not address the major issue of the large quantities of hazardous materials that are left over after production (and recycling) is completed, and which must then be disposed. This is the problem of **hazardous wastes**. Hazardous waste consists of a diverse set of materials. In liquid form there are waste oils, solvents, and liquids containing metals, acids, PCBs, and so on. There are hazardous wastes in solid form, such as metals dust, polyvinyls, and polyethylene materials. There are many materials between liquid and solid, called sludges, such as sulfur sludge; heavy metal, solvent, and cyanide sludges; and dye and paint sludges. Then there are a variety of mixed substances such as pesticides, explosives, lab wastes, and the like. In legal terms, the EPA and various state environmental agencies have power to define what is considered a hazardous waste; in past years, the definitional net they have thrown over the full physical list of substances has left out some significant materials (e.g., waste oil).

Table 16.2 shows the results of an EPA survey to find out how hazardous wastes were being disposed of in 2019. The greatest proportion was disposed of in injection wells, that is, deep wells driven into underground geologic formations (salt caverns and aquifers). From an industry standpoint, this method is relatively cheap and flexible. About 6 percent of hazardous waste generated is subject to some type of recovery (recycling) operation, and about 7 percent is burned, roughly half of which is done to produce useful heat. Although these numbers do not show it directly, about 80 percent of all hazardous waste generated in the United States is disposed of on-site, that is, at the site of the industrial plant where it was manufactured and/or used. Only 20 percent was transported to off-site disposal facilities.

TABLE 16.2 Hazardous-Waste Quantities Managed in 2019, by Management Methods

Management Method	Percent of total tons managed
Thermal treatment	~3%
Land disposal	~78%
Recovery operations	~6%
Other	~8%

Source: U.S. Environmental Protection Agency. "RCRA Biennial Report Summary." Management Methods, Washington, DC, 2019.

The two major pathways leading to damage are through accidental releases and releases stemming from improper handling, either at the site of use or at waste-disposal facilities. Accidents have led to severe and obvious damages, to humans and to other parts of the ecosystem. It has been less easy to document the damages coming from long-run exposure to small amounts of hazardous wastes. Ecosystems in the vicinity of industrial waste dumps are sometimes visibly affected. Human health effects have been harder to show, particularly when what is at issue is long-run exposure to small quantities of hazardous materials. Much more epidemiological and laboratory work remains to be done.

Federal policy has been directed at two types of problems:

- developing a system to manage the storage, transportation, and disposal of current hazardous wastes, and
- cleaning up land disposal sites where large quantities of hazardous wastes were dumped in years past.

The major laws addressing these problems are shown in **Table 16.3**.

TABLE 16.3 Basic Laws Dealing with Handling, Storage, Treatment, and Disposal of Hazardous Wastes

Statute	Responsible Agency	Coverage
Resource Conservation and Recovery Act (1976) and Amendments	EPA	Defines hazardous wastes and sets standards for landfills; establishes a manifest system
Maritime Protection, Research, and Sanctuaries Act (1972)	EPA	Ocean dumping
Comprehensive Environmental Response, Compensation, and Liability Act (1980)	EPA	"Superfund"; sets procedures for cleaning up hazardous-waste sites, and establishes a liability program for damages to natural resources
Hazardous Materials Transportation Act (1975)	DOT	Transportation of toxic substances generally
Federal Railroad Safety Act (1970)	DOT	Railroad safety
Ports and Waterways Safety Act (1972)	DOT	Shipment of toxic materials by water
Dangerous Cargo Act (1871)	DOT	Shipment of toxic materials by water
Nuclear Waste Policy Act of 1982 (amended 1987)	DOE	Requires DOE to find and develop a repository for high-level nuclear waste
Low-Level Radioactive Waste Policy Act of 1980 (amended 1985)	States	Encourages states to enter into compacts to establish landfill sites for low-level radioactive waste
National Defense Authorization Acts	DOD DOE	Allocate funds to DOD for cleaning up military bases, and to DOE for cleaning up nuclear weapons sites

Note: EPA = Environmental Protection Agency; DOT = Department of Transportation; DOE = Department of Energy; DOD = Department of Defense.

16-4 Economic Issues in Handling Current Hazardous Wastes

The primary policy here is the Resource Conservation and Recovery Act (RCRA) of 1976.

Hazardous and Solid Waste Amendments of 1984 ▸ Federal Facilities Compliance Act of 1992 ▸ Land Disposal Program Flexibility Act of 1996

RCRA does essentially four things:

1. Defines **hazardous waste.**
2. Creates a **manifest system,** essentially a document trail, so that material can be tracked through the system from production to disposal.
3. Requires a set of **standards** for treatment, storage, and disposal facilities.
4. Establishes a **permit system** for approval of RCRA landfills and incinerators.

RCRA is largely a command-and-control system, requiring the EPA to set technical and managerial requirements for handling hazardous waste.[6]

Incentive-Based Possibilities

There may be useful programs that could be installed to reshape the incentives relating to using and disposing of hazardous materials. Taxes on hazardous wastes, levied at the place where they are generated or where they are disposed of, are a feasible way of providing the incentive for reducing the quantities produced, as well as directing the flow of wastes toward various channels. These have come to be called **waste-end taxes.** The monitoring problem is much less a factor than with toxic emissions because wastes are often in bulk form that lends itself to quantitative measurement. Many states and local transfer stations have established waste-end charges for sites within their jurisdictions. Charges of this type would stimulate industry efforts at waste reduction. They would also lead to increases in the prices of products that produce substantial quantities of waste in their manufacture.

Any kind of tax placed on hazardous material creates an incentive for disposers to conceal material discharged, perhaps by disposing of it on-site, into a public sewer system, or in some unapproved landfill. Also, many hazardous wastes are in small quantities that are difficult to monitor. One way of turning these incentives around is to offer a subsidy for hazardous materials disposed of in approved ways. This, of course, would require a source of funds. A possibility would be to institute **deposit–refund** systems for hazardous materials. Firms would pay a deposit per unit of hazardous chemical at the time of purchase from a chemical supplier. They would then be paid a refund on materials when they were properly disposed.[7]

One area in which RCRA incorporates some incentive-based provisions is in making hazardous-waste handlers and operators liable for certain costs associated with their operations. Thus, operators of hazardous-waste landfills are liable for closure, cleanup,

---

6. RCRA also contains requirements for nonhazardous-waste landfills, particularly those handling municipal solid waste (MSW), essentially trash from households and public agencies. This material can contain significant amounts of hazardous waste, for example, used electronic devices.
7. For more on this idea, see Margaret A. Walls, *Deposit–Refund Systems in Theory and Practice*, Resources for the Future, RFF DP 11-47, 2011.

and restoration costs associated with the sites. RCRA also holds owners and operators of underground storage tanks responsible for cleanup costs in the event that they leak, which many do.

As we discussed in **Chapter 10,** liability requirements are, at least in principle, effective ways of getting polluters to take potential environmental costs into account in their decision-making. If they know they will be held liable for certain environmental costs, they will balance this prospect with their costs of taking actions to reduce the risk, thus arriving at an "efficient" outcome. The actual outcome may be somewhat different, however. Liability provisions in these laws set up a complex game between regulators and private firms that are motivated to find ways of reducing their exposure to the provisions. One aspect of this is that firms can shield themselves from liability by going out of business or declaring bankruptcy. For small firms (e.g., an operator of a gas station) faced with large liability costs, this may be an attractive alternative. To counter this, many environmental statutes combine liability provisions with **financial assurance rules.** These are requirements that owners and operators demonstrate financial resources sufficient to cover their potential environmental liabilities. The full impact of these rules is unclear. In some cases (e.g., leaking underground storage tanks), states have set up financial funds to help operators and owners meet these obligations, thus potentially weakening some of their impacts on incentives.

Environmental Justice

All environmental issues involve **distributional** questions, having to do with which particular individuals or groups from among the whole population bear the costs and experience the benefits of environmental programs. **Environmental justice** is the term used to describe the search for programs that are equitable to the less advantaged members of society. Much of the environmental justice focus has been on the location of hazardous-waste sites in relation to communities in which there are relatively large numbers of low-income residents and people of color. This issue gained prominence in the early 1980s, largely as the result of efforts to site a large hazardous-waste dump in Warren County, South Carolina, a county with a predominantly African–American population. In 1983, the U.S. General Accounting Office concluded in a study of eight southeastern states that a positive correlation exists between siting and majority Black and low-income communities. A 2002 study found that in non-U.S. OECD countries, a correlation with low-income communities exists.

The preponderance of evidence to date indicates that RCRA sites tend to be located in areas where there are relatively large numbers of low-income and minority populations. Having established this pattern, the next question is, why has it occurred? There are essentially two ways this could have occurred:

1. The siting process itself has worked against people of color and poor people. This could be either because of rank discrimination, in which undesirable activities are foisted onto certain people, or because in the political process surrounding these siting decisions, certain people lack the political influence necessary to ward off these facilities. Legislative redistricting may add to this problem.
2. The dynamics of the land and housing market may lead to this type of pattern, even though the original siting decisions were not discriminatory. If these hazardous waste facilities make local neighborhoods less desirable, higher-income people may be motivated to move out. Furthermore, if the facility works so as to depress land prices,

it could make housing there more attractive to low-income families. This could also happen if income discrimination in general relegates certain people to less desirable neighborhoods.

All of these factors are at work, though at specific sites one factor may be substantially more important than the other.[8] It is clear that policymakers need to look carefully at the siting decision process to make it more democratic and remove its discriminatory features. It's also clear that economists need to learn much more about how the land and property markets function so that we can identify situations where certain people will end up being unfairly exposed to environmental risks.

For steps toward addressing future hazardous waste locations, the permitting process could include benefit–cost analysis, risk assessment, and socio-economic impacts on the potentially affected communities.

Radioactive Wastes

Radioactive wastes are governed by a separate set of statutes. There are two types of radioactive wastes:

- **high-level wastes** (HLWs) are made up primarily of spent fuel from nuclear power plants and wastes from government nuclear processing facilities, and
- **low-level wastes** (LLWs) come from a variety of industrial and medical processes that utilize small amounts of radioactive material and include the material itself together with all manner of items that have become contaminated in normal production operations.

The primary problem in HLW is to find a secure, *permanent* storage site, because the rate of radioactive decay is so slow that these wastes will be lethal essentially forever by human standards. The Nuclear Waste Policy Act of 1982 requires the Department of Energy (DOE) to find and develop a permanent underground depository for nuclear HLW. This has proved to be an immensely complicated task and one full of political conflict. The effort is funded by a tax of one-tenth of a cent per kilowatt-hour of electricity generated at all nuclear power plants. The standards for storage have been set by the EPA, in terms of the maximum allowable rate of release of radionuclides from the repository for the next 10,000 years! It is difficult, if not essentially impossible, to identify underground geological formations that are sure to be secure for the next 10,000 years. It is even more difficult to convince people living near candidate sites that no damage will come their way and that this is the best use of a portion of their landscape. Thus, the projected year of opening for the depository has been continuously set back, and appears to be off in the indefinite future.

Low-level radioactive wastes are disposed of for the most part in approved landfills. Prior to 1980, there were three landfill sites in the United States accepting low-level radioactive waste. The Low-Level Radioactive Waste Policy Act of 1985 encouraged states to enter into interstate compacts to open sites that would accept all the waste from states in each

---

8. See, for example, David Schlosberg, "Defining Environmental Justice: Theories, Movements, and Nature," *Ethics in International Affairs,* 22(3), 2008, 335–338; H. Spencer Banzhaf, *The Political Economy of Environmental Justice,* Stanford University Press, Redwood City, CA, 2012.

compact. Although ten interstate compacts, involving 42 states, have formed, there are only four active LLW disposal sites in the United States: Washington, Utah, Texas, and South Carolina.

16-5 Economic Issues in Handling Legacy Hazardous-Waste Sites

The main law governing legacy hazardous-waste sites is the Comprehensive Environmental Response, Compensation, and Liability Act (CERCLA) of 1980. The law has come to be called Superfund, perhaps in reference to the massive sums of money involved. CERCLA was enacted in response to heightened public fears about the health impacts of past, and often forgotten, hazardous-waste disposal sites. In some cases, as in the notorious Love Canal incident, people were exposed directly to hazardous materials that migrated through the soil; in other cases, the fear was, and is, of groundwater contamination from these old dump sites.

The law established:

1. A **financial fund** derived from taxes on petroleum and chemical feedstocks, a corporate environmental tax, and payments made by those responsible for past dumping. The fund is used to carry out site investigations and cleanup actions. The legal authority for the taxes expired in 1995. Since then it has been financed from general tax revenues, and from firms whose waste created the problem sites, as discussed below.
2. The **National Contingency Plan** (NCP) that specifies procedures for identifying and investigating sites, determining cleanup plans, and deciding on who will pay for it. Part of the procedure involves a state–federal effort to create the list of sites that are in greatest need of action; this is called the **National Priorities List** (NPL), and it involves a hazard-ranking system taking into account the types and quantities of hazardous materials at the site and the possibility of human exposure.
3. Authority for the EPA to clean up sites itself or to identify responsible private parties to clean up the sites.
4. A **liability provision** for natural resources damage. Besides cleanup liability, CERCLA has a provision for holding responsible parties liable for damages to natural resources stemming from spilled or released toxic materials. Thus, if a chemical is accidentally released into a river, the people causing the spill can be held liable for the damages this causes; or if an old landfill leaks toxic compounds, responsible parties may be held liable not only for cleaning up the site but also for damages to surrounding groundwater resources.

Financing Hazardous-Waste-Site Cleanups

Progress under Superfund has entailed a continuing battle between the EPA and the private firms that are responsible for the sites.

- **Potentially responsible parties** (PRPs) are firms or organizations that were involved with hazardous-waste contamination of land or a site at any time in the past.

The courts have ruled that PRPs may be held to a standard of strict, joint, and several liability in Superfund cleanups. Strict liability means that they are liable even though their actions were at the time legal. Joint and several means that when more than one firm has dumped hazardous wastes into the site, the EPA may nevertheless sue and recover total cleanup costs from just one of the responsible parties. So, for example, a company that has dumped only a small portion of the wastes into a site can nevertheless be held responsible for the total cleanup costs at the site. The effect of this is to provide an incentive for this one firm to identify and recover costs from other parties that were responsible for dumping at the site. But there are disadvantages as well. Firms may be reluctant to come forward voluntarily to enter cleanup agreements if they feel they could get stuck with a substantial amount of the total costs of the cleanup. Firms will also be very reluctant to acquire land that may be contaminated if they think this will expose them to liability. These and other problems have made the law highly contentious and litigious, with firms spending enormous amounts of money suing one another, the EPA, municipalities, states, insurance companies, and so on.

How Clean Is Clean?

Superfund activity has produced a continuing debate over how thorough the cleanup should be at any particular site. Should all sites be restored to pristine condition? Should cleanup actions be undertaken in the light of how the site is likely to be used in the future? Criteria as to how to clean up sites have largely been established with the objective of making each site totally risk free under the worst possible future development scenario. Thus, at many sites very costly cleanup techniques have been used in cases where the risk of damage to humans is relatively low. An economic analysis of 150 randomly selected Superfund sites concludes that the expected number of cancer cases averted at each cleanup site is less than 0.1 and that the cost per cancer case averted was on average greater than $100 million.[9] What this indicates is that perhaps a more explicit benefit-cost approach might be able to adapt cleanup techniques at each site more closely to the benefits to be expected in terms of human exposures. This would allow more sites to be cleaned up with a consequent increase in overall human protection, given the total amount of money that is spent on the program.

Brownfields

As of the 2022, there were 1,329 Superfund sites listed on the NPL. Since 1982, 25 percent of sites have completed cleanups and been removed from the NPL list. One can argue, therefore, that despite its inefficiencies, the Superfund program has made a real dent in the number of sites needing attention. The EPA has also identified over 10,000 other sites where light to moderate contamination is suspected or has been confirmed. Superfund, as it was originally developed, does not address these many sites that are contaminated to a lesser degree. Substantial portions of these additional sites are within urban and suburban areas and have potential for industrial or commercial redevelopment.

There may be important incentive problems associated with these sites. Developers may avoid them in favor of sites in pristine environments in order to avoid the possibility of being made legally responsible for cleaning them up. This possibility has led the EPA, and many of the states, to develop special programs dealing with these types of sites, which

---

9. Keely Maxwell et al., *How Clean Is Clean: A Review of the Social Science of Environmental Cleanups*, Environmental Research Letters, 1–16, August 2018.

are called **brownfields**. The programs consist of efforts to relax potential liability problems at the sites, and funding assistance to assess and ameliorate contamination problems at the sites. Some brownfields have turned into economic development projects as they have been remediated and cleaned up to allow for non-hazardous waste-producing manufacturers or retailers.

Natural Resource Damages

Besides providing a program for cleaning up legacy hazardous-waste sites, CERCLA also contains a provision making polluters **liable for damages to public resources** stemming from their activities. This has been used primarily against those responsible for accidental releases of oil and toxic chemicals. The Oil Pollution Act, approved after the Exxon *Valdez* accident in Alaska, also has provisions for assessing natural damages and identifying reasonable parties. These provisions were applied to the Deepwater Horizon oil rig explosion in the Gulf of Mexico in 2010. An early study of 46 cases listed the following:

- Sites where industrial activities are accompanied by releases of a variety of hazardous substances into rivers, harbors, marshlands, and other wetlands, as well as disposal to the ocean.
- Sites where mines and associated waste piles contaminate surface waters and groundwater with acid drainage and leachate containing heavy metals.
- Cases where vessels run aground; cargo oil spills, the ships' own fuel spills, and ships run onto coral reefs causing damage to the reef.
- Oil pipeline ruptures.
- Cases where retaining walls rupture, allowing gypsum slurry releases in to rivers.
- Train derailments result in spills of diesel fuel and chemicals.
- Oil well accidents that release oil and other liquids into bayous.
- Cases where containers of a toxic chemical are lost overboard in rough seas.

The biggest issue in NRD cases is how to measure the damages. Part of these damages consists of the costs of restoring the resource to its original condition. The other, and probably harder, part is to estimate the actual damages that the release inflicted on people, either in the vicinity or elsewhere. Environmental economics has provided a tool, **contingent valuation** (CV), for doing this.[10] Controversies over the techniques used in CV analysis, and the answers it has given in particular cases, have continued.

Cleaning Up the Nuclear Buildup

During the height of the **cold war (1970s and 80s),** the development and production of nuclear weapons took place at a large number of sites around the United States. The stress at that time was on military needs, not potential environmental damage. There are more than 100 sites across the country where massively contaminated soil, water, structures, and equipment pose serious health threats to nearby people and ecosystems. Many ex-military bases have contamination, including waste oil and waste ordinances from ex-bombing practice sites. Some islands used for this purpose, such as Nomans Land Island off of Cape Cod, Massachusetts, are now designated a National Wildlife Refuge (NWR). The Northwestern Hawaiian Island Chain, along with Midway Atoll and Kure Atoll, are also designated as NWRs.

10. See Chapter 7.

Summary

The coming of the chemical society has led to new sources of environmental damage and opened up new requirements for managing toxic and hazardous materials. The policy world governing these materials is a jungle. At the federal level, numerous major laws deal with toxic and hazardous substances, and numerous federal agencies are responsible for their administration. For the most part the laws incorporate a variety of command-and-control measures to identify and monitor the use of toxic materials in workplaces and consumer products, to control toxic emissions from production, and to manage the complex process of disposing of hazardous materials. The most important laws are TSCA, FIFRA, FDCA, and OSHA.

Important points exist where the management of toxics could be substantially improved. One of these is to improve the procedures for "balancing" the costs and benefits of using chemicals in particular products and processes. We also discussed the new emphasis on waste reduction, that is, changes in production systems that lead to lower quantities of hazardous waste requiring disposal. Finally, we discussed the federal laws governing the handling and disposal of hazardous waste, the cleaning up of past dump sites (CERCLA), and radioactive waste.

Questions for Further Discussion

1. Handlers of hazardous wastes, that is, firms that accept hazardous materials and transport them for disposal, sometimes dispose of the materials illegally or in unapproved landfills. How might a deposit-refund system be designed to provide incentives to dispose of hazardous materials in approved ways?
2. Discuss the connection between a brownfield located in a municipality and the economic development for that municipality. Are brownfields located where you live? Investigate.
3. What are the advantages and disadvantages of using the doctrine of strict, joint, and several liability for Superfund sites?
4. What are the two primary explanations for the demographic patterns found in the vicinity of many hazardous-waste dump sites?
5. In conducting a balancing analysis for a particular chemical or pesticide, what role is played by people's attitudes toward risk?
6. In what way does TSCA put the burden of proof for a chemical's safety on the EPA?
7. When considering banning a toxic chemical, why should replacement substances or processes be part of the decision?

For additional resources pertaining to the material in this chapter, see the list in **Appendix B**.

Chapter 17
State and Local Environmental Issues

Environmental policy is undertaken at many levels: from small neighborhood or community groups, to towns and cities, to states, to regional groupings, to the federal level, to the international level. Policies usually are more successful when they are a blend along this continuum. In the 1950s and 1960s there was no strong federal presence in U.S. environmental policy; what initiative there was lay mostly at the state level. In the 1970s this changed dramatically, as strong federal laws were written that essentially shifted the policy center of gravity toward Washington. The U.S. Environmental Protection Agency (EPA) was founded in 1970. Since that time, many of the states have become much more active in pollution control activities.

States and communities play three primary roles:

1. Contributing to federal laws; most federal policies permit, require, or encourage some type of contributing state action, especially in enforcement. About three quarters of the environmental enforcement actions undertaken in the United States are carried out by the states. States generate more than 90 percent of the data that feed federal environmental databases.
2. Adopting companion policies that express the particular environmental values, goals, or circumstances of individual states; these have often been a source of innovative policy ideas.
3. Dealing with certain major issues that have been left for the most part to the states.

There is substantial diversity among the states in terms of their environmental problems and policy responses:

- Air pollution is much more severe in some states than others; New Jersey compared to Wyoming, for example.
- Hazardous-waste releases, although occurring in every state, are nevertheless concentrated in certain ones, particularly Texas and Louisiana.
- Water quality problems are widespread and are pronouced in Florida because of the Everglades and its reliance on groundwater.
- Coastal states have special problems in managing their coastal resources.
- Mining regulation is a particular problem for some states, as is agricultural runoff in others.

Given these great variations, equal state expenditures on environmental programs do not necessarily imply equal concern about environmental quality or equal achievements in pollution control.

17-1 Environmental Federalism

Environmental federalism refers to the question of whether, and to what extent, environmental regulations ought to be established at the national or federal level, or decentralized for independent actions of the individual states. There are several dimensions to this question.

Constitutional Issues

The U.S. Constitution governs the division of powers between the federal government and the states. In cases where valid (i.e., constitutional) environmental laws have been enacted at the federal level, these normally **preempt** state action. Thus, for example, federal laws to control coastal tanker traffic so as to reduce the threat of oil spills will usually preempt any state actions aimed at the same result. In cases where the federal government has not acted, states may do so provided they do not exceed constitutional limits. The most important of these is that states may not pass laws that discriminate against interstate commerce. In environmental matters, this has been held to bar states from passing laws restricting the importation of solid waste from other states. But virtually all state environmental actions will have some impact on interstate commerce, so the federal courts have become the arena for ongoing controversy about the legitimacy of state environmental actions.

One ongoing controversy is that between California and the federal authorities over setting automobile mileage standards. California has historical rights, via the Clean Air Act, to set automobile emission standards for cars sold in that state. The only practicable way of doing this at the present time is to require that cars get substantially better mileage, as CO_2 emissions per mile are directly related to fuel use per mile. But Congress has preempted the setting of automobile mileage standards, in the CAFE program enacted in 1975. This program was discussed in **Chapter 15**.

Efficiency Issues

Economic efficiency in environmental regulation is, as we have discussed many times, a matter of finding the appropriate balance between environmental damages and abatement costs. Will this balance be realizable more closely with a national system of pollution control, or a decentralized one? Consider a simple case, one in which the emissions from sources in each state produce damages only within that state. This is an extreme assumption; it means that no individual in any other state will be affected in any way by the level of emissions in any one state. This would appear to call for a completely decentralized determination of environmental regulations; each state would set its own standards and enjoy its own level of environmental quality.

Now consider a different case at the other end of the spectrum. Suppose the emissions from each state are uniformly mixed with those of all others in such a way that the emissions from any state affect everybody, in state and out of state, to the same extent as emissions from any other state. In this case we would have an efficiency argument for a purely centralized regulatory regime. No state has control over its own environmental quality. All emissions spill over and affect all other states. A centrally determined emission standard applicable to all states would presumably be efficient.

There are some pollutants that meet these two cases: perhaps municipal solid waste (MSW) for the first one and CO_2 emissions for the second. But many pollutants fall along the continuum between these cases: interstate air pollution, for example. In this case the appropriate degree of decentralization is somewhere between none and complete. In the United States, for example, it might call for environmental regulations to be established at the regional level. In fact, the mixed case has been addressed largely by states taking active roles in coordinating and managing federally initiated programs.

Water Pollution Control

Virtually all federal programs have provisions for substantial state and local participation. Federal water-pollution law (incorporating technology-based effluent standards) works through a **permitting system;** sources must obtain permits for waterborne emissions and are supposed to operate in accordance with the terms specified in the permits. For the most part, it is the states that actually operate the permit system, though there are a few (e.g., New Mexico, New Hampshire, and Massachusetts) where federal authorities are still responsible. Federal water law also requires the states to establish ambient water quality standards in the various bodies of water within their boundaries. Traditionally these standards have been expressed in terms of the functions that particular water quality levels would allow, for example, standards for fishable/swimmable water and standards for drinkable water. In recent laws, states have also been given the responsibility of setting ambient standards for waterborne toxics.

Air Pollution Control

States have many responsibilities in controlling air pollution. A major activity is the design and operation of State Implementation Plans (SIPs). These are plans of action through which national ambient air quality standards are to be reached in current nonattainment regions. The states have permitting authority to achieve these SIPs. The 1990 Clean Air Act Amendments allows them to operate fee systems for these permits, similar to the water program. Permit fees can be charged and these can be based on emission levels, but fees are only supposed to be high enough to cover the costs of running the permit program. They may not be used, in other words, as full incentive-changing emission charges such as those we discussed in previous chapters. This type of "dedicated funding" system is being increasingly relied upon by states to fund their environmental programs. Rather than fund these efforts from general state revenues, they are turning to using sources in particular programs—permit fees, fines, trust funds, and so on—to get the money to run these programs. Examples include dedicating the money collected through wastewater discharge fees to other types of water-pollution control projects. In times of economic hardship, these dedicated funds sometimes are raided to cover budget shortfalls.

Hazardous Waste

States may also regulate hazardous wastes, but, according to the Resource Conservation and Recovery Act (RCRA), the state regulations must be at least as strict as applicable federal regulations. Many states have done this in various areas: definition of hazardous wastes, standards for incinerators, requirements for the manifest system, location requirements for hazardous-waste disposal sites, insurance requirements for hazardous-waste facility operators, and so on. State hazardous-waste regulations are almost exclusively performance and technology standards:

- Some states have enacted their own Superfund laws to supplement the federal law. These are designed in the image of the Comprehensive Environmental Response, Compensation, and Liability Act (CERCLA), with a response fund, a site priority list, and various action criteria.
- States have also taken varying degrees of responsibility for actions at some of the National Priorities List (NPL) sites.

Race to the Bottom?

States compete among themselves to attract business and investment so as to provide employment and economic growth for growing populations. This leads to a concern that they might use weak environmental regulations to attract investment. The concern is that this could lead to a competitive weakening of state environmental laws in what is known as a "race to the bottom." Although it is possible theoretically to explain the conditions that would lead to such a race, most empirical evidence to date suggests that such a race has not happened. In fact, if anything, there has been a race to the top, fueled perhaps by the concerns of states for having quality living conditions to attract economic activity.[1]

Policy Innovations at the State Level

States have been a source of some innovative environmental policy initiatives. This is especially true of California, which has been the source of several policy initiatives that have later spread to other states and the federal level. Chief among these has been mobile-source pollution control. The Los Angeles area was the first in the nation to experience smog, and the California response in the early 1960s was to require technological improvements in cars to reduce emissions. Since that time, vehicles sold in California have had to meet more stringent state emission standards. The standards have not been legally preempted by federal emission limits, and in recent years some other states have adopted the California standards as a way of dealing with increasingly severe urban air pollution. The new federal standards for some pollutants, discussed in **Chapter 15**, will bring federal and California standards in harmony.

California has been a pioneer in air pollution control, especially the use of tradable emission permits to control airborne emissions. The South Coast Air Quality Management District, a regional organization whose objective is to manage air-pollution reductions in the Los Angeles basin, developed a cap-and-trade program covering greenhouse gas emissions in that region. California is now leading the switch to electric vehicles.

Many other environmental programs that have become law at the federal level were initially developed by one or more of the states. The pesticide DDT was first banned by Wisconsin; this later became a national effort. The Federal Strip Mining Control and Reclamation Act of 1977 was substantially modeled after the Pennsylvania strip mining reclamation law. The federal Toxics Release Inventory (TRI) program is an idea that originated with programs in New Jersey and Maryland.

---

1. Eric Sjöberg, "An Empirical Study of U.S. Environmental Federalism: RCRA Enforcement from 1998 to 2011," *Ecological Economics*, 147, 2018, 253–263.

The States and Environmental Justice

Environmental policy and political concerns at the state level are bound to be heavily involved with the fine-grained application of federal programs to the specific circumstances of local groups. So it is with the issue of environmental justice. At the national level, it exists largely at the hortatory level; at the local level, it involves real people with a degree of political access and with specific values and needs. In theory, environmental justice refers to the idea that the cost of pollution control should not be disproportionately borne by low-income families or people of color; and that the benefits of pollution control should not be systematically biased toward well-off individuals and families. Many states have developed very specific environmental justice programs:

- Michigan requires that a portion of the revenue from environmental fines be directed to disadvantaged communities.
- New Jersey identifies overburdened communities and sets new requirements for locating new facilities such as incinerators and sewage treatment plants in these communities.
- Massachusetts requires special environmental reports for new projects located within five miles of any environmental justice community.
- California requires that disadvantaged communities receive financial benefits from that state's cap and trade programs.
- Colorado requires that a special environmental task force identify specific communities that are disproportionately affected by state environmental regulations.

17-2 The Circular Economy

The concept of the **circular economy** has become popular among students of environmental pollution control. It refers to a system in which materials extracted from nature are taken by a return flow back for use, essentially recycled back into the economy. Materials follow a closed loop, or circle, from extraction to processing, to consumer or producer use, to reprocessing if necessary, and then back to reuse. The goal of a circular economy is to have a sustainable, waste-free economy with as much use of renewable resources as possible. Another way of thinking about it is as a system of complete recycling, with recycled materials going back through regenerative technology to render it into a form that is competitive with raw materials. The dominant paradigm of the circular economy is "reduce, reuse, recycle." We turn next to an important element in this paradigm, namely, municipal solid waste.

17-3 Municipal Solid Waste

In the rest of this chapter we deal in some detail with several important environmental problems that traditionally have been left to states and localities. The first of these is **solid waste,** the disposal of which has emerged as a leading problem in many cities and towns across the country. Landfilling, for a long time the preferred disposal method for urban solid waste, has come up hard against rising land shortages in many places, leading some localities to ship their solid wastes long distances for disposal. In addition, rising fears of groundwater contamination from landfills and of air pollutants from incineration have turned what once was a disposal activity to which nobody gave a second thought into a prime environmental concern.

The **municipal solid waste (MSW)** stream is actually a trickle at the end of a long and very large flow of materials used in any economy. The Environmental Protection Agency (EPA) estimates that the total quantity of materials of all types generated per person per day is almost 300 pounds. Most of this is industrial waste. Municipal solid waste consists of trash or garbage from homes, businesses, and institutions. In 2018 there were an estimated about 5 pounds per person per day of MSW generated in the country. This was up from 2.7 pounds in 1960 (see **Table 17.1**). Half of this MSW was disposed of in landfills in 2018, down from about 80 percent in 1980. Over the last 60 years, the amount of MSW that is recycled and composted has increased, from 6.3 percent in 1960 to 32 percent in 2018 with a doubling since 1990. A food management pathway was added by the EPA for monitoring in 2020 and pertains to wasted food generation and how it is directed through donation, land application, animal feed, biochemical processing, etc.

These are aggregate numbers, which hide substantial variation among states and communities in the country. The MSW problem is not equally acute everywhere. In localities with large populations and/or constrained landfill space, the problem is one of immediate concern; in areas with the opposite characteristics, it is much less so.

TABLE 17.1 Municipal Solid Waste, Selected Data

	1960	1970	1980	1990	2000	2010	2015	2018
Total quantity generated (mil. tons)	88.1	121.0	151.6	196.9	238.3	249.9	262.4	292.4
Quantity generated per capita (lbs./person/day)	2.7	3.3	3.7	4.3	4.6	4.4	4.5	4.9
Disposal, percent of total:								
Landfill	63.0	72.6	81.4	66.7	54.7	54.2	52.5	50.0
Combustion with energy recovery	30.6	20.7	9.0	16.2	16.2	11.7	12.8	11.8
Recycled and composted	6.3	6.6	9.6	17.2	29.1	34.1	34.7	32.1
Food waste management pathway	NA	NA	NA	NA	NA	NA	NA	6.1

Source: U.S. Environmental Protection Agency, *Advancing Sustainable Materials Management: 2018 Fact Sheet*, December 2020.

Technical Options for Reducing MSW

We define the following terms: TM is total materials used, by a firm or industry or economy, in a period of time; VM is virgin materials used, sometimes called raw materials; and RM is recycled materials used. Then it must be true that for any time period:

$$TM = VM + RM.$$

Materials-balance considerations, as discussed in **Chapter 2**, tell us that all materials inputs taken into an economic system must eventually end up back in the environment in some fashion. The form may change, as when solid materials are burned to yield energy and waste products. The time span can differ; some materials do not lend themselves to reuse and so are discarded almost immediately, whereas others can be recycled, perhaps many times. But recycling can never be perfect because of conversion losses, waste in consumption, and so on. This means we should focus on the quantity of virgin materials used. Rearranging the above expression gives:

$$VM = TM - RM, \quad \text{or} \quad = TM(1 - r)$$

where r is the **rate of reuse**, or RM/TM. There are essentially two ways to reduce the use of virgin materials: (1) reduce the overall quantity of materials (TM) and/or (2) increase the reuse rate, r, that is, increase waste reduction and recycling.

Total materials use can be reduced in two ways: by reducing the rate of economic activity or by reducing the **materials intensity** of that activity. By "materials intensity" we mean the quantity of materials used per unit of production or consumption. This is the "reduce" part of the reduce-reuse-recycle paradigm. And this in turn can be done in two ways:

1. by rearranging the composition of output and consumption away from products that use relatively large amounts of materials and toward those that use less (e.g., a shift away from tangible goods toward services) and
2. by decreasing the materials intensity of particular products (e.g., reducing the amount of packaging material in consumer electronics or food products, or increase in online payments).

Also, there must be awareness of substitution behavior that can shift discharge from one environmental medium to another. For example, although online shopping decreases individual vehicle trips and the associated tailpipe emissions, there is a correlated increase in packaging and delivery truck miles.

The other alternative is **reuse**. This means reaching into the waste stream to extract materials that may be reused. Some may be reused directly, as when consumers reuse clothing. Consignment shops are healthy businesses in many communities; some used cloth can be redirected to building insulation.

Lastly is **recycling**. The separation, transportation, and reprocessing technologies that are available critically affect the costs of recycled materials, and thus their ability to displace raw materials. Some communities in the Netherlands practice a circular economy with a goal of VM equal to zero.

Policy Options for Reducing MSW

The present policy picture is very complicated, as you would expect from the nature of the physical problem, the large number of materials involved, and the thousands of municipalities, small and large, searching for solutions. **Table 17.2** lists some of the various measures that are, or have been, pursued in various states. For the most part these focus on some facet of recycling. When MSW first became an issue, it was regarded primarily as a disposal issue—people were taking to the landfill materials and products that could be recycled. Thus, the initial response of most communities was to think about materials recovery and recycling. Voluntary recycling programs began in the 1970s (the first was in Oregon). In some communities recycling has become mandatory for items that are recyclable. Data show that about 24 percent of MSW is currently recycled. As **Table 17.3** shows, the recycling rate for different materials varies from a high of 68 percent for paper to a low of 4 percent for food wastes. About 12 percent is combusted with energy recovery.

TABLE 17.2 MSW Reduction and Recycling Actions Undertaken in States and Communities

Product bans: plastic nondegradable plastic bags, plastic-coated paper, polystyrene containers, disposable diapers, plastic six-pack rings, cans containing both plastic and metal, plastic bag purchases by state or local agencies.

Returnable disposal fees: fee on newsprint that is returned for recycling, returnable deposits on tires and car batteries.

Taxes on virgin materials content.

Consumer fees on MSW: fees per bag or bin of unsorted MSW.

Prohibitions on landfilling certain products, such as yard clippings, metal, and tires.

Bottle deposits.

Mandatory recycled content of purchased material by public agencies.

Voluntary or mandatory material separation and curbside recycling.

Recycled or recyclable labels on products.

Technical assistance for recycling programs.

Grants and loans to municipalities for recycling programs.

Public construction of waste separation and reprocessing plants.

Public construction of waste-to-energy plants: combustion with energy recovery.

Tax credits and exemptions for recycling equipment and other investments by private businesses.

Food waste composting requirements for large restaurants, schools, grocery stores, etc.

TABLE 17.3 Municipal Solid Waste Generated and Recovered in the United States, 2018

	Waste Generated (million tons)	Materials Recovered (percent of generation)
Paper	67.4	68
Yard waste	35.4	63
Plastics	35.7	9
Metals	25.6	34
Wood	18.1	7
Food waste	68.1	4
Glass	12.3	25
Textiles	17.3	15
Total	292.4	24

Source: U.S. Environmental Protection Agency, *Advancing Sustainable Materials Management: 2018 Fact Sheet*, December 2020.

17-4 The Economics of Recycling

The complete materials recycling loop is actually a complex process involving a number of stages and interconnections. A schematic outline of this loop is depicted in **Figure 17.1**. It shows the primary actors at each stage and how the flow of materials goes from one stage to the next. At each stage there is also some material disposal, depicted by the dashed arrows. The connections among actors at each stage are worked out through markets; these markets are depicted by small supply/demand figures between each stage of the recycling loop.

FIGURE 17.1 Recycling Consists of a Number of Markets Linking Generators and Users

The size and composition of the material flows are determined by the many decisions made by the demanders and suppliers in these markets. Producers and packagers design products and the materials used for them; they make decisions on the total quantities of materials used and the amounts of virgin and recycled feedstocks they will use. Consumers choose products that contain different types and amounts of material; they also decide how to dispose of the various materials after the products have been consumed. There is a stage consisting of collectors: firms that collect, transport, and sort material and make it available to materials reprocessors. The latter, in turn, convert the various materials of the solid-waste stream into materials that may be reused by producers/packagers, thus closing the loop.

Solid waste is a problem because of pricing difficulties in the various markets around the loop. For example,

- The harvesting of raw materials leads to a variety of economic costs. In most cases these costs are external to the harvesting firms, making the prices of raw materials too low from the standpoint of social efficiency.

- Because of low prices for raw materials, it is difficult for entrepreneurs to be competitive in supplying materials pulled from the waste stream and reprocessed into reusable forms. This is sometimes called **regeneration**.

- Discarded solid waste involves environmental costs that ought to be reflected in prices paid by consumers facing different disposal options. Pay-as-you-throw (PAYT) systems are common and give incentives for recycling as a waste-disposal method for households. By increasing recycling the household has less trash and incurs less PAYT fees. Some communities even penalize households that include recyclable materials in their trash, even though the household can pay-to-throw. When solid waste-disposal services are paid through flat fees levied to cover the cost of collection and disposal, there is no incentive, other than moral obligation, for consumers to be concerned about the amounts of solid waste they discard. Also, there is no incentive to reduce the excess packaging materials that accompany their purchases; for example, electing to use cloth, reusable shopping bags rather than one-use plastic shopping bags.
- Originally the approach to recycling placed the responsibility of sorting of recyclable materials on the consumer. A system called **single-stream recycling** shifts this responsibility and thus the cost from the consumer to the waste-management facility. Single Stream Recycling is a system whereby a variety of recyclable items can be collected together in a single container, hauled off site, and later sorted at the sorting facility. Such a system increases convenience at the point of recycling, and thereby the incentive to recycle, because consumers don't have to decide among mixed paper (newspapers, copy paper, junk mail, etc.) or containers (bottles, cans, certain types of plastics, etc.) or trash, the decision rule is simplified to trash or recycle.

However, because the mix of recyclables is so varied and can include more types of materials (all kinds of paper tossed in with all kinds of plastic) distinguishing trash is more difficult for the consumer with single stream. This has led to more loads of recycled materials contaminated with trash, thus making the recyclable materials unusable and many loads intended for recycling to end up in landfills. With the adoption of mandatory recycling policies expanding in many countries, an international market has developed in recycled materials. The United States recycles about 66 million tons of material each year, and about one-third of this is exported. Tighter requirements on the level of contaminant material in a load have put a huge burden on the sorting that single stream collection requires. Some communities have tried to shift some of the sorting burden back to the consumer at town transfer stations or with curbside pick-up, but the effect of this has been modest.

Producer Use of Recycled Material

Let us take a closer look at the top-most market in **Figure 17.1**, the market in which producers of goods and services use various amounts and types of material. This market is modeled in **Figure 17.2**. The demand curve applies to a firm or industry; it shows the quantity demanded of a particular type of material in a given period, such as a year. There are two sources of this material: virgin and recycled. We assume that this firm or industry is small relative to the total use of this material; thus, it can obtain virgin material in whatever quantity it wishes at a constant price. This price is marked p_v and is shown as a horizontal line intersecting the demand curve at a quantity level q_0. But this material may also be obtained from recycled sources. Here, however, the procurement cost picture is more complicated. Reaching into the waste stream for recycled materials involves a number of special costs—of collection, separation, transportation, reprocessing, and so on. We assume that these costs increase with the amount of recycled material used. The supply curve of recycled material to this firm or industry is therefore an increasing function such as S_1 or S_2. These two supply curves refer to situations with different recycling technology. For S_1, costs go up relatively rapidly; S_2 increases much less rapidly. Consider for the moment the recycled material supply curve labeled S_1. If this is the one faced by this firm or industry, it will end up using q_1 of recycled materials. In other words, the producer will use recycled materials up to the point where its cost is equal to the price of virgin materials. Because the total materials use is q_0, the difference $(q_0 - q_1)$ consists of virgin materials.

FIGURE 17.2 Use of Recycled Materials in Production

The reuse ratio, the proportion of total materials coming from recycled feedstock, is q_1/q_0. This ratio can be increased in three ways: increase q_1 while holding q_0 constant, decrease q_0 while holding q_1 constant, or both. Most community efforts at recycling are aimed at the first of these. For example, public curbside sorting and collection programs are ultimately aimed at making the supply of recycled material more abundant and, hence, less costly to producers. In terms of the model of **Figure 17.2**, these programs have aimed at shifting the recycled supply curve downward, say, from S_1 to S_2. If this is done, recycled materials use increases to q_2, the recycling rate increases to q_2/q_0, and use of virgin materials drops to $(q_0 - q_2)$.

Another way of increasing the recycling ratio is to reduce the demand for materials in general while holding constant the use of recycled materials. Diagrammatically this means shifting the whole materials demand curve back. This might be done, for example, by finding ways of producing output using fewer materials. It might also simply happen as consumers shift away from materials-intensive products, such as consumers purchasing in bulk rather than individual packages. Finally, there is one way of simultaneously reducing total materials used and increasing recycled materials: Increase the price of virgin materials. If, in **Figure 17.2**, we lift the virgin materials price to, say, p_2 through a tax, this will lead to a move both up the recycling supply curve and up the materials demand curve.

This means an increase in the quantity of recycled materials and a decrease in the quantity demanded of materials in total. Raising the price on raw materials with a tax thus has a double effect on the reuse ratio, because it works at both ends of the problem.

We can use this simple model to examine proposals for **recycled-content standards** in materials-using industries. Early enthusiasm for community recycling efforts led to situations in which the amounts of collected material outstripped technical ability to turn it into useful raw material, and in the absence of demand, large quantities of sorted and collected material actually ended up in landfills. Thus, policy efforts have turned toward trying to increase the strength of demand for the recycled material. Numerous states have thought to try this by introducing minimum-content standards for materials-using production processes. Minimum-content standards require that all materials-using products manufactured or sold within a given state contain some specified percentage of recycled material.

We have talked many times of the cost-ineffectiveness of uniform standards in the face of heterogeneous emissions withholding costs. In the case of uniform content standards for materials, the same principle applies, but here the important factor is heterogeneity across materials-using firms in terms of the costs of obtaining and using recycled materials. For a truly cost-effective approach to the problem, we would want to achieve equality across industries and materials in terms of **marginal recycling costs.** What this implies is having higher rates of recycled materials use by industries whose recycling costs are relatively low and lower rates for industries with relatively high recycling costs. One way to achieve this is to apply a tax on raw materials. As mentioned previously, a tax of, say, $p_2 - p_v$ per unit of raw materials, charged to all firms, would lead each to increase its recycling ratio in a way that satisfied the equimarginal principle. A transferable permit system in the recycling market is a possibility but not yet one that has been adopted.

In the real world, of course, things are a lot more complicated than they appear in this simple model. For example, one underlying assumption built into **Figure 17.2** is that recycled material and virgin material are physically interchangeable. This is hardly ever true in practice. Although newspaper can be produced largely from recycled newspaper, some virgin newsprint is usually necessary to achieve minimum quality levels. The same is true of many recycled metals. It is also true that the recycling market, like any economic market, is very dynamic, whereas the model displayed in **Figure 17.2** is essentially static; that is, it is limited to events happening in a single time period.

Consumer Recycling Decisions

Let us now take a look at the second and third markets depicted in **Figure 17.1**, where consumers purchase goods and services and make decisions about solid-waste disposal. Consumers can be expected to purchase products based on their private net benefits: benefits minus purchase price minus disposal costs. Historically most private disposal costs have been small, so getting rid of containers, packaging, and so forth has not been a big issue for consumers. But with landfills filling up, and environmental contamination looming as a problem in many places, there is an added social cost of disposal. In effect, the full social costs of disposal are now the private costs just mentioned, plus the environmental damage costs that may be caused by the disposal of products. These damage costs are external costs, a concept that we have discussed at length in this book.

With trash, one way to reduce these environmental damages is for consumers to extract certain items from their waste stream and make them available for recycling. If recycling is voluntary, the incentive for this comes either from public exhortation or from the "warm glow" effect. Substantially greater recycling effort can normally be induced by putting a charge, per bag or per can, on material that is thrown away rather than recycled. This charge is an example of an emissions tax, where "emissions" in this case refer to material discarded rather than recycled. See the discussion of unit pricing in **Chapter 1**. These may be accompanied by regulations that prohibit certain items from going to landfills that may risk substantial damage to the environment, for example, florescent light bulbs and oil-based paints.

To avoid consumer disposal of certain recyclable items, a number of states have instituted deposit–refund programs. Charging a deposit on these items provides funds that can be used to offer refunds for their return to designated locations. If the deposit refund is high enough, including the ease of accessing the refund, it provides the incentive for the consumer to keep these items, or at least a substantial proportion of them, out of the waste stream.

Producer Take-Back Programs

Take-back programs create a greater direct incentive for front-end improvements in product design as compared to situations where the consumer assumes total responsibility for recycling. Incentives enhance the recyclability of materials in end-of-life electronics and reuse. Take-back programs are useful by-products of selling in reusable packaging; those containing energy value after their useful life, such as power tools and batteries; those containing useful components, such as printer cartridges and computers; and those becoming obsolete quickly, such as electronics and appliances. A variety of companies have voluntary take-back programs. Ford Motor Company's Core Recovery Program seeks to refurbish or recycle fuel injectors, wiper motors, headlights, underbody shields, battery trays, and carpets, for example. Plastic car bumpers are melted and reformed into plastic taillight housings and new bumpers. Take-back programs tend to be concentrated in the technology sector. A number of communities and states have started mandatory take-back programs, for such items as car batteries and paint. Attempts to start mandatory U.S. federal programs have not been successful.

The European Commission adopted a mandatory directive on Waste from Electrical and Electronic Equipment (WEEE) that delegates the responsibility to the producer to manage the electronic product throughout its product life cycle. The producer is required to assume the physical and financial responsibility, including the cost of the disposal of e-waste, with consumers being able to return their equipment free of charge.

17-5 Local Environmental Regulations

In this chapter we have focused on local programs for the management of household solid waste. Many communities have also enacted regulations dealing with other environmental issues, for example:

- Protection of wetlands (no building in or near wetlands)
- Protection of scenic values and views (no building on ridge lines)

- Water quality (no road salt near streams or ponds)
- Noise pollution (no loud parties on weekends)

These regulations (often called ordinances) come under the exercise of the police power, which confers on communities the constitutional right to enact environmental (and other) regulations, provided they are reasonable, clearly related to public welfare, and are not arbitrary, or discriminatory. In effect, we have, at the community level, the same regulatory problem that is posed by our standard economic model of pollution control: how to balance the benefits of public regulation with their costs.

From the standpoint of public health, there may be little difficulty barring development in sensitive wetlands, on the grounds that these are linked into the hydrological systems on which many people depend for water supply. But when public health is not so directly involved, things can be much less clear. Suppose there is a particular farm in a community and that over time the people of the community have come to value the scenic qualities of that land. Clearly the land has environmental (scenic) value, but may the town pass a regulation saying that it may not be developed because of the scenic value? In doing this, the town is essentially putting on the farm the entire burden of providing these scenic values.

In issues of this type, much of the outcome depends on the impacts of environmental regulations on land values. One of the most contested issues in using local land-use controls for environmental protection purposes is the **takings** problem. The Fifth Amendment to the U.S. Constitution contains the following language: "No person shall be . . . deprived of life, liberty, or property, without due process of law; nor shall private property be taken for a public use, without just compensation." This authorizes the government to "take" private property, but only if it is for a public purpose and only if the owners receive just compensation. Land may be taken physically (e.g., for a sidewalk, public park, or highway) under **eminent domain,** and the main question will revolve around how much the compensation should be.

When a community passes land-use regulations—for example, to protect water quality or scenic views—the issue is not a physical taking, but whether the regulations substantially reduce the value of the affected property, constituting what is known as a **regulatory taking.** If it does, then compensation is due to the affected landowners. The regulatory takings issue hangs over the community exercise of the police power for environmental purposes. If affected individuals must be compensated for regulations, it makes these regulations, in effect, more costly for the community.

17-6 The Increasing Role of the States

At the beginning of the 21st century, continued political divisiveness and stasis at the federal level has worked against new national pollution-control statutes. One result of this is to shift more initiatives to the states, many of which have developed notable analytical and administrative competencies in environmental matters. Although California has long been in the forefront of this effort, other states' actions are now more widespread. They grapple with problems that are unique to particular states (such as coastal pollution in Rhode Island), and to address issues of national significance on which the U.S. Congress is unable to act.

State-level programs are paramount for controlling nonpoint source water pollution, now considered the largest remaining source of water quality impairments.

Regulations to control mercury emissions, especially from power plants, have been in contention for well over a decade at the federal level. So a number of states have sought to enact mercury regulations on their own initiative.[2]

In the absence of federal action to upgrade national procedures for approving chemicals, some states have tried to install their own programs for testing and approving chemicals. The 2016 update of TSCA contains stronger provisions for federal preemption of toxics testing.

Steps to control e-waste have been undertaken by numerous states.[3] As of 2023, there has been essentially no U.S. federal action to confront the growing problem of electronic waste. Contrastingly, the European Union has had an e-waste directive since 2003 with amendments in 2014.

Even new initiatives at the federal level are recognizing the greater capabilities of the states. Recent efforts to shape a national program on greenhouse gas control have leaned heavily on the ability of individual states to design cost-effective pollution-control programs for sources within their boundaries.

Summary

State and local efforts have become more important in environmental policy matters. As greater attention shifts to problems of enforcing environmental policies and regulations, state-level efforts in this respect have become more critical. States have also served as the source of innovation in many areas of environmental policies, spurring federal efforts and trying out new ideas in the control of emissions. The leading role of California in fostering more aggressive air-pollution control is especially notable.

States and localities have had the primary responsibility for solid-waste management, land-use controls, and the protection of groundwater resources. Community efforts at recycling are a major part of the effort to address solid-waste issues. We saw how recycling decisions depend on complex incentive situations facing consumers in their buying and disposal decisions, and producers whose demands for recycled materials may lead them to reach into the solid-waste stream for sources of raw materials. Producer take-back programs push responsibility for reducing MSW up the supply chain. Communities are also active in enacting environmental regulations, which have to be shaped in accordance with constitutional limits on the police power.

---

2. Howard A. Learner, "Restraining Federal Preemption when there is an 'Emerging Consensus' of State Environmental Laws and Policies," *Northwestern University Law Review*, 102(2), 2008, 649–663.
3. For a list of state initiatives see: Recycle Nation, "Each States Rules on Electronic Recycling," 2021, **https://recyclenation.com/**.

Questions for Further Discussion

1. What are the implications for cost-effective recycling programs of regulations that establish the same recycling ratios for all sectors of the economy?
2. How might a system of transferable permits be designed to achieve an aggregate recycling target cost-effectively?
3. Another way of increasing the use of recycled material by industry is to subsidize its purchase of materials taken from the waste stream. How would you analyze this in terms of **Figure 17.2**?
4. What are the factors, both economic and environmental, that make a problem more properly a local issue rather than a state issue?
5. Investigate the rules for recycling and solid-waste disposal for a local community with which you are familiar. What are the incentives that increase the rate of reuse (r)?
6. Refer to **Figure 17.2**. Assume the price of virgin materials is p_2. Identify the level of total materials on the graph, the level of recyclable materials and virgin materials used via curve S_1. Repeat for curve S_2.

For additional resources pertaining to the material in this chapter, see the list in **Appendix B**.

Section 6
Global Environmental Issues

In the last four chapters we have dealt with economic issues of domestic U.S. pollution control. It is now time to turn to international issues. The prospects for the 21st century are for nations to become increasingly interconnected. These interactions will grow in environmental matters. Regional and global problems will demand greater levels of cooperation and more effective international institutions.

We turn first, in **Chapter 18,** to environmental issues that are global in scale. Of course the most critical of these is global climate change. Coming to grips with climate change is going to require effective international agreements, so this is the subject of **Chapter 19.** Next we turn to the phenomenon called globalization, environmental issues arising from the growing interdependence among economies of the world. Finally, the last chapter discusses some economic aspects of environmental issues facing countries of the world that are putting a strong emphasis on economic development.

Chapter 18
Global Climate Change

People all around the world are struggling to come to grips with local environmental problems and improve their immediate surroundings. But over the last few decades, people have also had to broaden their outlooks to recognize that there is a **global environment** that is critical to human welfare. Moreover, the scale of human activities has become so widespread and intense that it has begun to have an impact on our global environment in significant ways.

For all of history, one of the ways humans have reacted to local environmental destruction is migration. But at the planetary level this option is not available. There is no escape if we inadvertently make our planet less habitable.

Complementing the daunting physical facts are the sobering political/economic facts that have made it very difficult for the world's nations to act collectively. There is a race on between the accumulating scientific data that scientists are straining to interpret and the growing efforts to develop international institutions and perspectives that will make concerted action possible.

18-1 Global Climate Change

The Physical Problem

Clearly the most important global problem facing us today is the possibility that, because of our current behavior, we are rendering the planet substantially less habitable, for humans as well as other members of the biosphere. This sometimes goes under the name of "climate change," or the global "greenhouse" effect. The principle of a greenhouse is that the enclosing glass or plastic allows the passage of incoming sunlight, but traps a portion of the reflected infrared radiation, which warms the interior of the greenhouse above the outside temperature. Greenhouse gases (GHGs) in the earth's atmosphere play a similar role; they serve to raise the temperature of the earth's surface and make it habitable. With no GHGs at all, the surface of the earth would be about 30°C cooler than it is today, making human life impossible.

Under preindustrial conditions, trace amounts of GHGs were in global balance. They were given off by decaying plant and animal materials and absorbed by forests and oceans. Into this rough balance came human beings and one of their greatest cultural and economic developments: the Industrial Revolution. That event was basically a revolution in energy use, involving a vast increase in the extraction of energy from fossil fuels—first coal and later petroleum and natural gas. Combustion of fossil fuels, together with deforestation and high-density animal agriculture, has led to vast increases in emissions (see **Exhibit 18.1**) and to an increase in the carbon dioxide (CO_2) content of the atmosphere by about 45 percent from the beginning of the Industrial Revolution. In 1986, CO_2 reached 350 ppm and may reach 550 around 2050. Although CO_2 is an important **greenhouse gas,** it is not the only one. Another is methane, which is in fact 25 times more potent as a GHG than CO_2. Analysis of ice cores shows that over the last 800,000 years atmospheric concentrations of methane have never exceeded 750 parts per billion. Today it is about 1,900 parts per billion. The main GHGs, their approximate proportionate contribution to global warming, and their major sources are shown in **Table 18.1**.

EXHIBIT 18.1 The Quick Story

The data below show very quickly the nature of the problem in global climate change. They show emissions of CO_2, the main GHG, for a few selected countries and for the global total, at points over the last 30 years. Key observations are:

- For the total, a modest increase in the last decade of the 20th century, then a 45 percent jump over the next 19 years.
- Some evidence that emission increases have been contained in the United States and Europe (though the Great Recession of 2008–09 was probably responsible for a substantial part of this).
- Almost a tripling in China in the last 19 years.
- Emissions in India have more than doubled over the last 19 years, though from a low base.
- A lower level occurred in early 2020s mostly due to the COVID-19 pandemic and lock down, with a subsequent rise post-Covid.

Emissions of CO_2 (billion tons)

	1990	2000	2010	2019
United States	5.07	5.92	5.57	5.11
European Union (15 countries)	4.41	4.12	3.92	3.30
China	2.44	3.72	9.20	11.60
India	0.60	0.99	1.76	2.60
Global Total	22.70	25.70	34.00	38.00
% increase between time periods		13%	32%	12%

Source: J. G. J. Olivier, K. M. Schure, and J. A. H. W. Peters, "Trends in Global CO_2 and Total Greenhouse Gas Emissions: 2020 Report," PBL Netherlands Environmental Assessment Agency, Table A.1.

TABLE 18.1 Major Greenhouse Gases

	Global Warming Potential (GWP)	Emissions 2020 Metric ton of Carbon Dioxide equivalent (MMT CO₂e)
Carbon dioxide (CO₂)	1.0	4,715.7
Methane (CH₄)	25	650.4
Nitrogen oxide (NOₓ)	298	426.2
Hydrofluorocarbons (HFCs)	124–14,800	178.8
Sulfur hexafluoride (SF₆)	22,800	5.4
Perfluorocarbons (PECs)	7,390–9,300	4.4
Nitrogen trifluoride (NF₃)	17,200	0.6
Total Emissions		5,981.0

Source: U.S. Environmental Protection Agency, *Inventory of U.S. Greenhouse Gas Emissions and Sinks: 2020*, EPA 430-f-22-001, April 2022.

Climate change is a long-term phenomenon that is characterized by changing atmospheric and ocean current patterns throughout the globe. These macro patterns affect weather, which, contrastingly, is highly variable in the short term compared to climate change. One cause of climate change is global warming. When economic activity slowed drastically, for example, during the great recession of 2008-09 and during the global lockdown of the COVID-19 pandemic in 2020-21, increases in global accumulation of GHGs decreased significantly. Air pollution subsided and ambient air quality improved for a brief time. However, climate change did not abate and when economic activity came back online and surged following these slowdowns, GHGs climbed again.

Accompanying this buildup of GHGs has been a rise in mean surface temperatures around the globe. Study of temperature records, the composition of long-lived glaciers, and other sources shows that the earth has warmed about 1.0°C (1.8°F) since 1900. Some scientific models predict that by the year 2100, temperatures could rise 2°C to 4°C. The rate of heating is put at about 0.32°C per decade. This may not sound like a very rapid change, but historical studies have shown that in past episodes of warming and cooling, during which agricultural societies of the time suffered major dislocations, climate change occurred at a rate of only about 0.05°C per decade. Today's rate of change, in other words, is expected to be very much faster than those faced by humans in the past.

Global warming is bringing about a general rise in sea level because of the expansion of sea water, the melting of glaciers, and the breaking up of polar ice sheets. It will have different local impacts on tidal and current patterns. Changes in meteorological patterns will also vary widely among regions. In the northern hemisphere, Arctic polar regions are warming faster than equatorial zones; on the continental landmasses, the centers will become drier than the peripheries, and so on. There is also, very importantly, an increased risk of a rapid and catastrophic change in the global climate, brought about by positive and negative feedback loops in the earth's geophysical processes. Our ability to predict these changes will improve as the global climate models of atmospheric scientists are better developed.

Human and Ecosystem Impacts

Although this is a problem of the global environment, its impacts on humans and the ecosystem will vary greatly from one country and region to another. Sea-level rise (SLR) is having devastating impacts in certain societies, such as those of the Pacific islands or those concentrated in low river deltas. Impacts will be relatively less in countries where development may be redirected toward interior regions. The drowning of coastal wetlands throughout the world could have impacts on fisheries, and thus on societies that rely heavily on marine resources. Another potential impact of great importance is the increased acidification of the oceans caused by higher levels of atmospheric CO_2, which reacts with water to create carbonic acid. There will be very substantial impacts on ecosystems and individual species of plants and animals, not just because of the amount of change but also because the rate of change will be fast by evolutionary standards. In ice ages of the past, weather changes have happened slowly enough to allow species of plants and animals to migrate and survive. The rapid pace of change expected in the greenhouse phenomenon may be too quick for many organisms to adjust to changing habitats. This will put a severe strain on species that occupy narrow ecological niches because relatively small changes in weather patterns can destroy the habitats on which they depend. For example, along the eastern Atlantic seaboard, there is a migration of lobsters north as ocean temperatures have slightly increased.

Some of the biggest impacts on humans will be through the effects of changed climate patterns on **agriculture and forestry.** Here the story gets very complicated because weather patterns will be differently affected throughout the world, and because crops, and the systems of cultivation adopted by farmers, vary a lot in terms of their ability to withstand changes in temperature and water availability. The agricultural impacts of atmospheric warming hit developing nations harder than developed countries. It is expected that African nations will bear the greatest impact particularly due to extended droughts over larger geographical areas. Some studies conclude that agriculture can be adapted to future climate changes through crop development and technical changes. But others cast some doubt on the ability of many developing countries to do this because many of their crops are already closer to the limits of tolerance for warmer temperatures.

All respectable scientific judgment is that human produced global climate change is occurring, and will get worse, if nothing is done about it. Exactly how much worse? That is the unknown. In **Chapter 6** we introduced a few concepts to help in analyzing situations involving risk, in particular, the concept of risk aversion in cases involving small probabilities of very large losses. There is uncertainty about the extent of global warming in the future, but the potential negative consequences are so great that it behooves us to be risk averse. In plain terms: better to be safe than sorry. All of this suggest strongly that significant steps need to be undertaken today to reduce the level of serious global warming in the future.

To get an overall view of the current world production rate of CO_2 and how it may be altered, consider the following equation (GDP is a gross domestic product):

Total CO_2 Emissions (mil tons CO_2)	=	Population (millions)	×	GDP/Person (1,000)	×	Energy/GDP (tons oil equiv.)	×	CO_2/Energy (tons CO_2)

The quantity of CO_2 emissions depends on the interaction of four factors:

- The first is **population.** Other things remaining equal, larger populations will use more energy and therefore emit larger amounts of CO_2.
- The second term is **GDP per capita,** a measure of the domestic output of goods and services per person. We normally associate increases in this factor with economic growth.

Neither population nor per capita GDP can be considered likely candidates for reducing CO_2 emissions in the short run. Deliberate population control measures are unlikely to be effective, and no country is likely to be willing to reduce its rate of economic development. In the long run, however, the interaction of these two factors will be important, as history seems to show that lower population growth rates can be achieved by substantial improvements in economic welfare.

Significant near-term CO_2 reductions will have to come from the last two terms in the expression:

- The third factor, **energy per GDP,** is what we mean by **energy intensity.** This is the amount of energy used per dollar (or per euro or rupee or cedi) of output. The key here is to move toward technologies of production, distribution, and consumption that require relatively smaller quantities of energy.
- The last term is **CO_2 produced per unit of energy used.** Because different energy forms have markedly different CO_2 outputs per unit, reductions in CO_2 can be achieved by switching to less CO_2-intensive fuels. The move toward renewable energy comes into play here, as does the switch from coal to natural gas.

What has happened to this equation over time? World population has increased in conjunction with population increases in almost every country. For the countries or regions of the world that contribute the most to GHG (United States, European Union, China, and India), there has been a substantial drop in CO_2 emissions per unit of energy consumed (the last term in the equation); this is called **decarbonization.** This is mostly due to a worldwide shift away from coal and toward oil, natural gas, and non-fossil power sources. In 2022, the U.S. use of renewable energy sources surpassed the use of coal for the first time. While the U.S. and the EU are using less energy per dollar of GDP, China and India are using more energy per dollar of GDP. Although shifts around the world are reducing the CO_2 intensity of fuel use, growth in population, and especially rapid GDP growth in some countries, such as China and India, is leading to the continued global increase in CO_2 emissions.

Although the equation points to addressing any of the terms as a way to reduce total CO_2 emission, in a sense there are three fundamental social choices for this problem:[1]

- **mitigation**—refers to taking steps today to reduce GHG emissions so as to delay or reduce global temperature increases, and/or
- **adaptation**—refers to the efforts of future generations to adjust in ways that will substantially reduce the negative impacts of these temperature increases, and/or

---

1. The policy issues surrounding the climate-change phenomenon have been, and are being, much researched and discussed and written about. A good place to explore them is the Energy and Climate program of Resources for the Future (http://www.rff.org) and the Intergovernmental Panel on Climate Change (https://www.ipcc.ch).

- **migration**—refers to the movement of people away from living in areas with a high probability of becoming unlivable due to climate changes, such as sea-level rise or fires. However, the movement does not necessarily lower carbon emissions on a global scale; it only shifts them to a different geographic area.

It needs to be recognized, however, that there are many things that could be done to mitigate CO_2 emissions, and that these come at different costs and trade-offs. It is very important, therefore, to keep the concept of **cost-effectiveness** clearly in mind when developing contemporary mitigation steps. The primary means of reducing the warming lies in reducing the output of GHG and/or augmenting the GHG-absorbing capacity of the natural world. Because CO_2 is the main GHG, we focus on the issue of reducing global CO_2 emissions.

18-2 Reducing Domestic GHG Emissions

Effective global action to combat global warming will require individual countries to undertake steps to reduce their GHG emissions. The question is: How should this be undertaken? In the short run, say over the next 20 years or so, the emphasis will be on getting increases in fuel conservation and efficiency, switching to low-carbon fuels, and reducing the use and emissions of chemicals with high greenhouse impacts. From a policy perspective, perhaps the first thing to note is that there is no single source we could call on to get drastic reductions in GHG production. Instead, changes need to be made across the spectrum of stationary- and mobile-source emissions, from households, industries, transportation, and agriculture. These needed changes are both technological—for example, a switch to more energy-efficient equipment, low carbon fuels, and zero emissions vehicles—and behavioral—for example, a change in driving habits and the adoption of less energy-intensive lifestyles.

The big question is, how much is it going to cost to reduce GHG emissions significantly? And the answer to this is: It depends on how it is done. Given the long histories of command-and-control policies in the United States and other countries, many are likely to be attracted to technology or emission standards. This has been the tradition in the United States (as well as most other countries), so first efforts here have been directed at subsidizing, or requiring, technology options. This includes, for example, biofuel and renewable energy mandates, and performance requirements for vehicles in the Corporate Average Fuel Economy (CAFE) program. As we have discussed many times in this book, mandated technology and performance standards are highly unlikely to be cost-effective, meaning that going this route to combat global warming will be much more costly to society than the alternatives.

This is because there are really substantial differences among technical options in terms of GHG control costs. **Table 18.2** shows some cost-effectiveness comparisons. Some of the technologies are estimated to have a negative cost; these are approaches that would pay for themselves without even considering GHG removal, primarily through savings in energy costs. Those with positive costs are in the range of $12 to $131 per ton. Considering that the total quantity of global GHG emissions is about 58 gigatons of CO_2e today with it possibly reaching 62 $GtCO_2e$ by 2030, one can get a rough idea of the costs of decreasing these emissions by a substantial fraction. These are also marginal costs; that is, the costs of reducing GHG emissions starting with where we are today. If we ever succeed in moving to a much more energy-efficient economy, the costs of making further reductions in GHG emissions will no doubt increase, probably a lot.

TABLE 18.2 Cost-Effectiveness of Alternative Means of Reducing GHG, 2022

Means	Costs per ton of carbon dioxide equivalent ($ CO_2e)
Coal-fired power plants; carbon capture, utilization, and storage (CCUS)	131
Biofuels	47
Nuclear power	17
EV buses	12
Hybrid cars	−41
Commercial building efficiency	−40
Wind power	27
Solar power	33

Source: International Energy Agency, *GHG Abatement Costs for Selected Measures of the Sustainable Recovery Plan*, Paris, Licence: CC BY 4.0, 2023.

Some cost figures that stand out are the low estimates for afforestation, as essentially an add-on to the current conservation reserve program, and the high costs of GHG removal through CO_2 capture and storage. Afforestation is not an emission reduction method, but an attempt to augment the CO_2-absorbing capacity of the earth's ecosystem. Afforestation looks like a good buy for CO_2 removal, but the other side of the coin is that because of the relatively small numbers of acres involved, the total amount of CO_2 that could be removed through this means in the United States is relatively modest. Note also the low (in fact negative) costs of achieving greater fuel efficiency and emissions reduction for cars and trucks. The potential for cost-effective GHG reduction through these means is tremendous, as is demonstrated by the rapid rise of EVs.

These technical options are diverse and subject to change, and new ones will undoubtedly be found and developed. What is vitally important is that we have strong incentives permeating through the economy to bring about these changes. And this implies that the best policies to combating the greenhouse effect are ones that create strong incentives for reducing GHG emissions.

Incentive-Based Approaches for Reducing GHG Emissions

When there are substantial differences among sources and technologies in terms of the costs of reducing GHG emissions, the use of incentive-based policies can get a substantially bigger economic impact than traditional command-and-control policies. In the United States, and many other countries, therefore, analysts and policymakers are emphasizing the several major types of incentive-based approaches: cap-and-trade plans, emission taxes or charges, and subsidies.

Efforts in the United States to implement CAP programs for GHG have been frustrated at the national level. However a number of states have taken the lead. The best known is the Regional Greenhouse Gas Initiative (RGGI), a program among nine northeastern states to reduce emissions of GHG. A declining total emission cap has been allocated among the states, and among power plants in each state. Sources may trade allowances, among other sources in the same state, or with sources in another RGGI state. So far over the life time of the program, total emissions of greenhouse gases have been reduced by more than 50 percent.

Countries of the EU instituted a large, intercountry cap-and-trade (CAP) program targeting CO_2 emissions; this is described in **Exhibit 18.2**. In that agreement, the EU collectively agreed to reduce its CO_2 emissions to a level 7 percent below its 1990 emissions. Under the European Green Deal, setting forth that the EU reach climate neutrality by 2050, the EU ETS sets another goal of reducing emissions by 43 percent below 2005 levels. Individual country goals vary around this, depending on their own circumstances. In their national plans, each country is to allocate a portion of its total cutback requirement to the firms of four sectors: energy, iron and steel, minerals (cement, glass), and pulp and paper. These firms may then trade emission allowances among themselves and with sources in other EU countries.

The specifics of setting goals for reducing emissions can be identified in a couple of ways. One is that the percentage of reduction to be attained can be altered and amended. A second is that the baseline year from which to measure the reduction can be altered. For the EU ETS, the baseline year changed from 1990 to 2005, while the percentage reduction goal changed from 7 percent to 43 percent.

EXHIBIT 18.2 Details of the European Trading Scheme

The European Union Emissions Trading Scheme (EU ETS) began in 2005. The aggregate European-wide cap consisted of a collection of national caps, as specified by the individual countries themselves in their national allocation plans. They applied only to CO_2. The total number of allowances originally distributed exceeded actual emissions in the six industrial sectors included (electricity and heat production, oil refineries, coke ovens, metal ore and steel operations, cement kilns, glass and ceramic producers, and pulp and paper mills). Over the next few years allowance prices dropped from a peak of 30€ per ton to almost zero.

The second phase of the program ran from 2008 to 2012. While initial allowance allocations were given away free, a small quantity were now auctioned. Allowance prices at first recovered, but then collapsed again under the influence of the worldwide recession of those years. Controversy arose over extending the system to other sectors, especially airlines. Fines for noncompliance were increased, from 40€ per ton in the first phase, to 100€ per ton in the second phase. Limited amounts of allowance banking were allowed.

(Continued)

EXHIBIT 18.2 *(Continued)*

Phase III runs from 2013 to 2020. The concern that free allowance allocation was leading to windfall profits led to an increased reliance on allowance auctions; in electricity production it is anticipated that 100 percent of the allowances will be auctioned. Phase III will also involve a shift away from individual country caps, to an overall European cap set by the European Union. Continued weakness in allowance prices has led authorities to back load the allowance allocation procedure, meaning to push back the allocation of 900 million allowances until 2019–2020. Authorities also established a market stability reserve essentially a central bank for allowances, to reduce the over allocation problem.

Source: Sidney M. Field, *Carbon-Trading in the Air: Why Europe Should Clamp Down on International Aviation Emissions*, unpublished paper, 2015. See also: European Commission, *European Trading Scheme (EU ETS)*, https://ec.europa.eu/clima/policies/ets_en.

As discussed in **Chapter 13,** cap-and-trade is a quantity-based plan, in which a quantitative limit is placed on emissions and prices are established on emission permit markets. Another option is a carbon tax, or a tax on CO_2 emissions. The use of emission taxes, **Chapter 12,** is a price-based policy, where a monetary fee on emissions is set and the quantity of emissions is adjusted as polluters react to that fee.

There are also advocates of an international program of carbon taxes. Levied upstream, at points of fuel production, these taxes would filter through economies and shift prices of goods and services according to their contribution to global warming. Many individual countries, especially those of Europe, have instituted carbon taxes.

In the United States, carbon taxes have been politically rejected, primarily because of the possible political ramifications of having price increases, even when the carbon tax is linked to an income tax rebate.[2] A national cap and trade program has also been rejected. Instead, political authorities have resorted (in the Inflation Reduction Act of 2022) to subsidies, for both producers and consumers. Companies, including fossil fuel companies, are being offered additional subsidies to produce electricity with renewable power. A disadvantage of subsidies is that any beneficial or promising technology R&D not supported by a subsidy program may not advance. The law offers tax credits for investing in and adopting technologies, such as solar and wind energy and carbon capture and storage.

The opposite of reducing GHG emissions is capturing and sequestering carbon either before it is emitted into the atmosphere or post-emission. Reforestation and land-use conservation is one method of carbon capture that is tied closely to carbon credits (see **Chapter 13**). Waste to energy (WtE) combustion transfers the energy from trash incineration into heat and steam energy is another technological advance. These adaptation strategies augment mitigation of GHGs.

---

2. See, for example, Gilbert E. Metcalf, *Paying for Pollution: Why a Carbon Tax Is Good for America,* Oxford University Press, 2019.

18-3 International Agreements for Addressing Climate Change

Climate change is a global problem, requiring concerted and coordinated action by the countries of the world. Joint action by groups of countries is not easy to get in this time of strong nationalistic attitudes. Any plan for global action will impact countries differently and will imply different criteria for distributing the responsibility among them. The UN Framework Convention on Climate Change (UNFCCC) has recognized "common but differentiated responsibilities and respective capabilities in light of different national circumstances." What formula might be followed in assigning individual responsibilities? Consider the following possibilities:

- Equiproportionate reduction in emissions.
- Ability to pay: base emission reductions and transfer payments on current income levels.
- Polluter pays principle: base emission reductions on current or past contributions to the problem.
- Equal per capita emissions: base emission reductions on the principle that everyone is entitled to the same level of use of the global environment.

The Kyoto Protocol

The original attempt to get international reductions in GHG emissions was the **Kyoto Protocol,** an agreement negotiated under the auspices of the United Nations in 1997.[3] It covered six GHGs and established emission reduction targets that countries were obligated to reach by the years 2008 to 2012. The targets were in terms of aggregate anthropogenic CO_2e emissions, expressed as a percentage of 1990 emissions in the various countries. The agreement contained commitments from 39 countries and the European Union. These were primarily European countries and the former Communist countries of Eastern Europe, together with the United States, Canada, Russia, and Japan.

The Kyoto Protocol came into force on February 16, 2005, after being ratified by the requisite number of countries. The agreement set specific goals for participating countries, in terms of greenhouse gas emissions. It required relatively large cutbacks of GHGs by countries of the developed world, but none by developing countries, such as India and China. Overall emissions in 2009 were below the Kyoto targets, but there is a question as to how much of this was attributable to the protocol. Large reductions occurred in Russia and Eastern Europe, mainly because of the general economic contractions in these countries. Many of the other countries experienced economic recessions in the 2000s and 2010s, contributing to the decline. But some efforts, especially in Europe, had an impact, and in general we may conclude that the protocol has helped to keep the issue on the front burner of policy battles around the world.

---

3. The Kyoto Protocol is a furtherance of the United Nations Framework Convention on Climate Change, which was completed in 1992.

The agreement included **flexibility mechanisms** that would presumably help countries meet their cutback targets with a lower overall cost. Flexibility focuses attention on the goal of reducing GHGs for the earth as a whole regardless of where the GHGs originate. Flexibility approaches include the following:

- International emission trading: Some countries could alter their GHG cutback responsibilities by buying or selling emission quantities among themselves. Thus, one country could cut emissions by more than that is required, and sell the excess to another country, which may then cut back by a smaller amount.
- Joint implementation: Countries could undertake joint projects (e.g., a reforestation project in the United States partly funded by another country) and transfer emission allowances on the basis of the projects.
- Clean development mechanism: Some countries could finance emission reductions in other countries and gain credits toward their GHG cutback responsibilities.

The Kyoto Protocol was the first effort internationally to address GHG control, and few expected it to make much of a dent in the overall global problem. Its deficiencies have been widely discussed:

- It set quantitative limits on GHG emissions without regard to any specific objective in terms of atmospheric carbon content or future increase in global temperatures.
- It did not involve in any significant way for participation of the countries of the developing world, several of which are becoming major GHG emitters.
- It paid insufficient attention to implementation and enforcement.
- It focused entirely on short-term goals without sufficient consideration of the long-term needs of the global atmosphere and its management.

The Paris Agreement

Although the Kyoto Protocol lapsed, the UNFCCC continued holding periodic meetings called the Conference of Parties (COP). At the 21st meeting (COP21) in 2015, the Paris Agreement on climate change was discussed and concluded by 196 countries. It contains the following principles:

- The aggregate **quantitative targets** of GHG reductions that should be aimed for, in the short and long runs. **Countries individually commit** to their own quantitative targets.
- The **benefits and costs** of achieving these targets, with particular emphasis on having policies and procedures that are cost-effective.
- **Equity** concerns on burden sharing: how the burden of emission reductions should be distributed among rich and poor countries.
- **Flexibility** concerns in terms of the ability to shift plans in the face of new scientific information and R&D, and to change the terms of participation by countries within and outside the agreement.

In accordance with these principles, the major provisions of the Paris Agreement are:

1. Intended Nationally Determined Contributions (INDC)—Each participant country is to put forth specific steps it will take to contribute to the reduction of global climate change. The steps may differ from one country to another. They may include:

    a. Specific limits on national GHG emissions.
    b. Commitments to decarbonization, for example, reduction in CO_2 per unit of energy consumed.
    c. Commitments to reach peak GHG emissions as of a certain year.
    d. Commitments to have a certain amount of renewable energy as of a certain year.
    e. Specific goals for energy efficiency or afforestation.

2. Commitment by all countries to offer INDCs, not just developed countries.
3. Transparency—commitment by all countries to monitor, report, and verify progress with respect to their INDCs.
4. Agreement to rule out any attempt by any country to seek damage payments from any other country that is a party to the agreement, as relates to climate change.
5. Provisions for encouraging and facilitating policy linkages among signatory countries, for example, emission trading among countries.

In the U.S. the Obama administration (2009-2017) enthusiastically embraced the Paris Accord. The EPA at the time introduced a plan for reducing GHG emissions from power plants. This plan was abandoned by the Trump administration, which also pulled the country out of the Paris Agreement. Many U.S. states, cities, businesses, organizations, and individuals continued to pursue goals expressed in that agreement and people attended COP meetings as unofficial observers. In 2021, the United States re-signed the Paris Agreement. Some of these efforts were discussed earlier in this chapter and in **Chapter 15**. Efforts encourage new technologies, such as solar and wind power, next generation heating and cooling, electric vehicles, and advanced batteries.

Some COP meetings since the Paris Agreement have assessed risk, articulated action steps and timing, and addressed social justice issues. Other post-Paris COP meetings advanced GHG mitigation and INDCs. The Green Climate Fund under the Paris Agreement conceptually transfers financial assistance from those countries with more resources to those with less financial resources to address climate change, or to enable technology transfer to these developing countries. No money has been put into the Green Climate Fund as of yet. The monetary struggle and environmental justice issues between countries with significantly larger, poorer populations and richer, more developed countries continue.

The Global Methane Pledge (GMP) was adopted during COP26 (year 2021) to reduce methane by 30 percent from 2020 levels by 2030. The GMP has the same features as other mitigation policies:

- A percentage reduction
- A base year from which the reduction is measured
- A goal year for accomplishing the reduction

Methane tends to be more point-source based than non-point-source pollution in that methane sources can be identified more readily than ubiquitous CO_2 sources. Plugging methane leaks is a readily implemented technology, unlike the continuing development of EVs.

In international agreements, real questions come up about monitoring and enforcement. Self-monitoring by the individual countries is likely to be the only practical solution to this issue because it is unlikely that countries would willingly permit international monitoring efforts. The United Nations lacks executive power to enforce international environmental agreements. The International Court of Justice (ICJ) acts chiefly as a place for discussing disputes and lacks mechanisms to enforce rulings. This leaves enforcement up to a combination of moral pressure and whatever unilateral actions states might take, such as trade sanctions.

Until COP20 in 2014 mitigation was the primary, and in some conventions only, policy approach discussed; adaptation rose to prominence with COP21's Paris Agreement. Effective collective action on mitigation may not be forthcoming, in which case countries will be forced into adaptation. In addition, the perceived costs of adaptation are likely to place limits on the extent to which any particular country will readily accept CO_2 emission reduction requirements, as no country is likely to want to spend more in control costs than the cost of adapting to the change. Because of the effect of global warming on SLR, adaptation has focused on reducing flooding in low-lying coastal areas. For cooler countries in higher latitudes, with relatively little critical shoreline, adaptation costs may be fairly modest. Countries in the opposite situation will have very high costs of adapting to higher temperatures and rising sea levels.

Countries differ also in terms of agricultural adaptability, the ability to shift crops, crop varieties, cultivation methods, and so on, to maintain production in the face of climate changes. So countries are likely to have very different perceptions about how they will be affected by global warming. The obstacles to an effective international agreement on GHG reduction are many, and the need for creative treaty diplomacy is great.

18-4 Economics of Adaptation

Enormous efforts are now being directed at mitigation or at slowing the rate of global climate changes. It seems clear, however, that these efforts are unlikely to be soon enough or strong enough, to ward off substantial changes in the global climate. This means there will have to be major efforts devoted to adaptation. Adaptation means doing what we can to protect human welfare and ecosystems in a world with vastly different, and threatening, climate characteristics. Some examples of adaptation are flood control investments, building structures that are less vulnerable to wind and water events, raising road and other transportation networks above flood levels, hardening power and communication networks, developing food crops that will be productive in much warmer temperatures, and providing for emergency facilities for displaced people.

Adaptation will not be a once-and-for-all activity. Modest steps in adaptation are happening now. As climate changes progress, adaptation will also have to progress. How fast depends on their cost, and on how people evaluate and react to the rising risks of climate-induced changes.

Adaptation will consist of some combination of **individual and collective** action, especially governmental action. Individuals will be taking actions on the basis of their understandings of the risks that are involved and how those risks are borne by themselves and others. How fast this takes place depends on how people evaluate and react to the rising risks of climate transformation. It also depends on the costs of taking action and of inaction. In this, humans have not become known for acting with a long vision. Rather, the tendency has been to **discount** the future heavily. Behavioral economists have made it clear that people often react irrationally to risky situations. A part of effective adaptation, therefore, will be determining and making intelligible the **degree of risk** facing people in their particular circumstances, for example, the risks of coastal flooding, or the risks of more severe storms.

We have talked in this book about the importance of incentives, the configuration of personal benefits and costs that lead people toward, or away from, sound decisions. In a similar way, incentives can move people toward or away from sound adaptation decisions. Individual decisions about living in fire-prone areas, or in areas where very high temperatures are expected, or much more severe storms are predicted, need to be made in light of the best available risk estimates and straightforward arrangements for individuals to bear that risk. By straightforward arrangements we mean the extent to which individuals themselves bear these risks, or whether all or a part of them are shifted to society in general. For example, climate change is widely expected to raise ocean levels and produce more coastal flooding. Decisions about living and building in coastal flood plains have historically been distorted by the availability of publicly provided, below-cost flood insurance. Adaptation would decrease availability of coastal flood insurance and possibly rewrite zoning rules to limit rebuilding on beach-front properties following coastal storms.

One role of public agencies will be to provide good risk estimates. Another will come through the demand for **infrastructure** that will function in a world of more severe weather. These presumably will run the gamut, from modest changes in existing systems (a protective sea wall, elevated roadway) to vast new projects (new power grids, new planned communities, new water and sewer systems). A concept we have stressed throughout this book is cost-effectiveness; achieving the greatest value for money spent. With the enormous costs that infrastructure changes will require, long-run planning is the only way of ensuring that cost-effectiveness is given sufficient weight in decision-making. Many of these infrastructure decisions are likely to be made in an atmosphere of emergency response, and amid much political pulling and shoving.

Among some communities, there is a growing emphasis on **resilience** planning. Resilience is the ability of communities to implement preparatory and recovery steps in response to disasters due to climate change and to reduce the time for a community to re-establish normality. A huge issue in this is who will bear the large costs of infrastructure changes. The scarcity of local capital, both private and public, will tend to shift these actions to higher levels of government.

Another important element in adaptation is the regulatory environment, consisting of the public agencies and their regulatory output at local, state, and federal levels. Public agencies can act to hinder change, or can facilitate the kinds of transformation that adaptation requires. For example, land use regulations that shape the way communities grow and expand can have a major effect on communities' vulnerability to climate-related incidents. Regulations are also necessary to make sure people have the best available risk estimates associated with climate events, and that infrastructure improvements are equitably distributed.

18-5 Estimating the Social Cost of Carbon

In **Chapter 6** we discussed briefly the concept of **regulatory impact analysis.** This kind of analysis is required when federal agencies introduce new regulations, or change existing ones. Essentially the requirement is to estimate the benefits and costs of the regulations, with the presumption that any proposed regulation would not go forward unless **net benefits** were positive. Among the regulations that the contemporary EPA is required to promulgate are those having the objective of reducing future GHGs. Thus it must have some notion of what it is worth to reduce future GHGs by any given amount. The term for this is the **social cost of carbon** (SCC). SCC is the estimated future damages of carbon emitted today. It is a marginal value: a monetary estimate of the global external costs of one CO_2-equivalent ton of GHGs.

It's obvious that estimating the value is fraught with difficulties. It requires estimating the long-run future costs of all the impacts expected to occur: more frequent and intense storms, sea-level rise, higher production costs, human health effects, ecosystem devastation, and so on. It also requires estimates of future demographic and economic growth. These impacts must be expressed in a common metric; usually this is in dollars of reduced future GDP. So estimating the SCC involves dealing with all the uncertainties of climate change, both the uncertainties of scientists who are trying to understand the physical effects and natural and social scientists trying to predict impacts on humans and other elements of the biosphere.

In 2010 a federal working group brought together the results from a large number of climate/economy simulation models used to predict future impacts. Their estimate of the social cost of carbon, using a discount rate of 3 percent, was $39 (in 2011 dollars).[4] Another thorough study was done by economists in 2020. It concluded that the social cost of carbon, discounted at 3 percent, was $61, and discounted at 2 percent was $168.[5]

We have mentioned that the estimates may be useful in guiding regulatory decisions by the EPA. Another is a guide to setting carbon taxes. Recall that a carbon tax of, for example, $46 per ton would provide emitters of CO_2 (and CO_2 equivalent) an incentive to abate emissions up to the point where marginal abatement costs are equal to the tax ($46 per ton). Since $46 is the SCC, emissions at that point would be at the socially efficient level.

There is at least one dimension of this result that is problematic. Estimates of the SCC are usually global. National policies of carbon taxes, if they are to be politically acceptable, may have to be based on estimates of nation-specific damages.

---

4. Environmental Protection Agency, *EPA Fact Sheet Social Costs of Carbon,* November 2013.
5. Kevin Rennert et al. *The Social Cost of Carbon,* Brookings Paper on Economic Activity, 2021.

18-6 Biodiversity

Another problem that has been prominently recognized is the worldwide reduction in diversity among the elements of the biological system. This can be discussed at a couple of levels:

- diversity in the stock of genetic material, species diversity, or
- diversity among ecosystems.

The long-run health of the global ecosystem requires that there be diversity among its parts. Biological uniformity produces inflexibility and a weakened ability to respond to new circumstances; diversity gives a system the means to adapt to change. Climate change adds pressure to biodiversity preservation.

The human population cannot maintain itself without cultivating certain species of animals and plants. But the continued vigor of this relationship actually depends also on the stock of wild species. This dependence can manifest itself in a variety of ways. About 25 to 50 percent of the **prescription drugs** in the developed societies are derived from plants. Diseases are not static; they evolve in response to efforts made to eradicate them. Thus, wild species of plants constitute a vital source of raw material needed for future medicines. Wild species are also critical for **agriculture.** Through traditional plant and animal breeding, and even more through modern methods of **biotechnology,** genetic material and the qualities they entail may be transferred from wild species into cultivated ones. For example, a species of wild maize resistant to an important crop virus was discovered in a remote corner of Mexico. When transferred to species of domestic corn, this characteristic substantially enhanced the agricultural value of that crop.

The stock of species at any particular time is a result of two processes: the random mutations that create new species of organisms and the forces that determine rates of extinction among existing species. Scientists currently are uncertain about the number of extant species on earth. Approximately 1.5 million have been described. When a species goes extinct, we lose forever whatever valuable qualities that organism may have had. The long-run rate of species extinction has been estimated at about one extinction per million species per year. Thus, this is a rate at which the genetic information contained in the species stock vanishes. At several times in the geological past, the rate of extinctions has been very much higher. One of these times was the period, millions of years ago, during which the dinosaurs died off. Another is today. But while the earlier period was the result of natural causes, today's rapid destruction of the stock of species is due primarily to the actions of human being.[6]

Some species go extinct because they are **overexploited.** However, the vast majority is under pressure because of **habitat destruction.** This comes primarily from commercial pressures to exploit other features of the land: logging off the trees for timber or wood, converting the land to agricultural uses, clearing the land for urban expansion, and so on. This has been a particular problem in many developing countries, which contain a disproportionately large share of the world's wild species, but which are also under great pressure to pursue modern economic development.

---

6. For more discussion see: *The Sixth Extinction* by Elizabeth Kolbert.

The information contained in the global stock of genetic capital has consistently been undervalued. This is partly because we do not know what is there or what portions of it may turn out to be important in the future. It is also because, almost by definition, it is impossible to know the value of the genes in a species that has gone extinct; we cannot miss something we never realized we had. But primarily the undervaluation of the stock of wild germ plasm is a function of the **institutions** governing the management of wild species. Whereas the market values of conventional products ensure that their production will be pursued with vigor, there are normally no comparable market values for the information contained in the wild gene pool.

In the United States, the Endangered Species Act (ESA) of 1973 was enacted to help preserve individual species. When a species is listed as either "endangered" or "threatened," steps may be undertaken toward its preservation. This includes prohibitions on the "taking" (killing or wounding) of any individual of that species, and a requirement that actions authorized or funded by any federal agency not put in jeopardy the continued existence of the species. This ESA type of approach is pursued in a number of other federal animal protection statutes (e.g., the Bald Eagle Protection Act of 1940, the Marine Mammal Protection Act of 1972, and the Salmon and Steelhead Conservation and Enhancement Act of 1980). Each state also has its own endangered species laws. Although these laws have had some success in preserving individual species, they are relatively ineffective at preserving diversity, which is not a matter of a single species but of a relationship among a large number of species.

The effective maintenance of biodiversity depends on the **maintenance of habitats** or ecosystems in amounts big enough that species may preserve themselves in complex biological equilibria. This involves first identifying valuable habitats and then protecting them from development pressures that are incompatible with preserving the resident species. In the United States, a large network of reserved lands has been preserved in the public domain, national parks, wilderness areas, wildlife refuges, and the like. The fact of the matter is, however, that the world's primary areas of genetic and species abundance and diversity are in developing countries in Central and South America, Africa, and Southeast Asia.[7]

Efforts have been made in some of these countries, sometimes vigorously and sometimes not, to protect areas of high biological value by putting them into some sort of **protected status**—sanctuaries, reserves, parks, and so on. But here the situation is usually much more complicated by high-population pressures. People who are struggling to get enough resources to achieve some degree of economic security and well-being may not view biological diversity as a valuable trade-off. Land reservation for species preservation is essentially a zoning approach, and it suffers the same fundamental flaw of that policy: It does not reshape the underlying incentives that are leading to population pressure on the habitats.

At the recent (2023) international conference on biodiversity preservation, primary attention was directed at setting goals for preserving habitat. A target was set for establishing some degree of protection over at least 30 percent of the earth's land surface by 2030. "Some degree of protection" means any one of the many ways that land use and land conversion can be restricted so as to maintain its value as habitat for biodiversity resources.

---

7. The countries especially recognized for biological diversity are Mexico, Colombia, Brazil, Madagascar, South Africa, Ecuador, Venezuela, and Indonesia.

One suggestion for change is to create a more complete **system of property rights** over genetic resources. At the present time, property rights are recognized for special breeder stock, genetically modified organisms, and newly developed medicines. This provides a strong incentive for research on new drugs and the development of improved crops. But this incentive does not extend backward to the protection of wild gene plasm, especially in developing countries. Thus, the suggestion is to clarify property rights in wild species and let countries themselves exercise these property rights in world markets for genetic information. By allowing them to sell the rights to parts of the genetic stock, countries would have a way of realizing the values inherent in these stocks and would therefore be motivated to devote more effort and resources to their protection.

In some places of the world, a market has developed for the services of endangered species in the form of **ecotourism.** Conservation by landowners and others creates value in the sense that people are willing to pay the landowner for opportunities to observe or photograph species in their preserved natural habitat. Ecuador manages the Galapagos Islands for this benefit.

Especially important is how this type of approach would filter down to affect individuals who are actually using the land. It is highly doubtful if substantial amounts of land could be put off limits to any type of development if **population pressure** continues high. So attention needs to be directed also at developing modes of commercial agriculture that are compatible with genetic and species preservation. Production based on retaining natural habitat requires two things: that cultivators have secure property rights and that there be strong markets for the types of crops produced in this kind of system.

Summary

In recent years we have seen the rise of truly global environmental problems, especially those dealing with the disruption of the global atmosphere. In these cases it is as if all the nations of the world were homeowners living around a small lake, each one dependent on the lake for water supply, but each one also using the lake for waste disposal.

The greatest problem facing the global community is climate change, stemming from atmospheric buildup of CO_2, methane, and other greenhouse gases that are affecting the earth's radiation balance and leading to an increase in mean global temperatures. Substantial impacts are expected on weather patterns around the globe. These are expected to disrupt agricultural operations in significant ways. A rise in the sea level will have profound impacts on coastal communities. A substantial attack on the phenomenon will require cutting back on the use of fossil fuels and emissions of GHGs. Virtually all countries are dependent to a greater or lesser extent on fossil fuels to power their economies. Thus, we must emphasize cost-effective policies to improve energy efficiency and to switch to fuels that emit less GHG. As part of this effort, much attention has been given to estimating the social cost of carbon. The Kyoto Protocol was the first major international effort to reduce GHGs. This has been superseded by the Paris Agreement on climate change, characterized by countries setting their own goals for mitigation of GHGs and adaptation to climate change.

The destruction of biological diversity is a subtler global problem, but it may be just as costly in the long run. Dealing with this problem will require greater efforts to preserve habitat and develop agriculture that is compatible with species preservation. Effective action will mean doing something about the incentives that currently lead to species destruction.

Questions for Further Discussion

1. The condition of the global climate, in terms of its CO_2 content, is a public good. How does that affect the global effort to reduce CO_2?
2. In the absence of a worldwide agreement to reduce CO_2 through a carbon tax, how effective might it be if just one country, or a small number of countries, instituted a tax unilaterally?
3. Rather than placing a tax on fuels or the carbon content of fuels, taxes might be put on fuel-using items, such as gas-guzzling cars, large, flat-screen TVs, or houses with poor insulation. Which type of tax would be more efficient? Which type of tax would have greater equity? Discuss.
4. Suppose every country in the world is asked to reduce their CO_2 emissions by the same proportion. What are the equity and efficiency implications of this?
5. What is the effect of varying the discount rate on estimates of the social cost of carbon?
6. Select one industry in one country and investigate the GHG emissions for that industry. Discuss policies related to incentives in that industry as they affect GHG emissions, and trade-offs the industry faces.

For additional resources pertaining to the material in this chapter, see the list in **Appendix B.**

Chapter 19
International Environmental Agreements

In the last chapter we discussed several global environmental issues. As countries grow, more and more environmental problems will spill beyond national borders. There are an increasing number of environmental externalities inflicted by people in one country on those of another. So while environmental policies continue to evolve within individual countries, **multicountry** approaches to environmental problems are growing.[1] In this chapter we take a look at some of the economic issues involved in the creation of **international environmental agreements**.

International environmental policy has a distinctly different character from national policies. The most salient difference is that on the international level the available enforcement mechanisms are much weaker than at the national level. Within any country, authoritative regulatory authorities can be called upon to enforce whatever laws are passed, although this does not imply by any means that all environmental laws will be adequately enforced. But on the international level enforcement authorities do not exist. Thus, environmental policy at this level consists essentially of international agreements among sovereign states, where each country pledges to follow certain specified courses of action regarding emissions reductions or other steps for environmental protection. Enforcement then has to be carried out either through voluntary means such as moral suasion, or else through retaliation by whatever pressure a country or group of countries may be able to exert on recalcitrant countries. Sometimes environmental agreements are incorporated into international trade agreements, so that relaxation of restrictions on the trade of goods and services becomes linked to environmental regulations. For example, regulations pertaining to emissions of vehicles that are used for transport across the Mexican, United States and Canadian borders are part of the United States–Mexico–Canada Agreement (USMCA). Trade restrictions are also part of the Montreal Protocol for reducing ozone-depleting substances.

In this chapter we review some of the main features of international environmental agreements, focusing especially on the incentive situations facing countries that are considering an agreement. The discussion begins with a brief descriptive section that shows the great variety of international environmental agreements that have been concluded to date. It then moves to cases that involve just two countries, **bilateral,** followed by the

---

1. The international scope of many environmental problems was first highlighted by the 1972 United Nations Conference on the Human Environment (the Stockholm Conference or the first earth summit), which led to the United Nations Environment Program (UNEP) and the earth summits of Rio de Janeiro in 1992, Johannesburg in 2002, Rio+20 in 2012 in Canada, and the Paris conference on climate change (COP21) in 2015. Details of the Paris Agreements are presented in Chapter 18.

case of multiple-country agreements, **multilateral**. The chapter ends with a discussion of a successful international environmental agreement, the Montreal Protocol on Substances that Deplete the Ozone Layer.

19-1 General Issues

The history of international agreements on natural resource matters goes back many centuries, to the time when countries sought to agree on navigation rules to cover ocean passages. In the 20th century, international treaties proliferated as a result of the rapidly expanding list of environmental problems involving multiple countries. Now in the 21st century, climate change dominates treaty negotiations. **Table 19.1** shows a partial list of **current multilateral agreements** pertaining to natural and environmental resources. The number of countries, or signatories, involved varies from 3 to 194.

TABLE 19.1 Selected International Environmental Agreements

Name of Agreement	Date of Adoption	Date of Entry into Force	Number of Signatories
Marine Pollution			
International Convention for the Prevention of Pollution of the Sea by Oil (as amended 11/4/62 and 10/21/69)	1954	1958	69
Agreement for Cooperation in Dealing with Pollution of the North Sea by Oil	1969	1969	8
International Convention on Civil Liability for Oil Pollution Damage (as amended)	1969	1975	64
International Convention Relating to Intervention on the High Seas in Cases of Oil Pollution Casualties	1969	1975	75
Convention on the Prevention of Marine Pollution by Dumping of Wastes and Other Matter ("London Dumping")	1972	1975	82
International Convention for the Prevention of Pollution from Ships, 1973	1973	1983	113
Convention on the Prevention of Marine Pollution from Land-Based Sources	1974	1978	13
Convention for the Protection of the Mediterranean Sea Against Pollution	1976	1978	21
International Rivers			
Protocol Concerning the Constitution of an International Commission for the Protection of the Mosel Against Pollution	1961	1962	3

(Continued)

TABLE 19.1 (Continued)

Name of Agreement	Date of Adoption	Date of Entry into Force	Number of Signatories
Agreement Concerning the International Commission for the Protection of the Rhine Against Pollution	1963	1965	6
Convention on the Protection of the Rhine Against Chemical Pollution	1976	1979	6
Convention Creating the Niger Basin Authority and Protocol Relating to the Development Fund of the Niger Basin	1980	1982	9
Flora and Fauna			
European Treaty on the Conservation of Birds Useful to Agriculture	1902	1905	10
Convention Relative to the Preservation of Fauna and Flora in Their Natural State	1933	1936	10
Convention of Nature Protection and Wildlife Preservation in the Western Hemisphere	1940	1942	22
International Convention for the Regulation of Whaling (as amended)	1946	1948	40
International Convention for the Protection of Birds	1950	1963	15
International Plant Protection Convention	1951	1952	111
International Convention for the High Seas Fisheries of the North Pacific Ocean (as amended)	1952	1953	3
Convention on Fishing and Conservation of the Living Resources of the High Seas	1958	1966	57
International Convention for the Protection of New Varieties of Plants (as amended)	1961	1968	46
Convention on the African Migratory Locust	1962	1963	16
African Convention on the Conservation of Nature and Natural Resources	1968	1969	43
European Convention for the Protection of Animals During International Transport	1968	1971	20
Benelux Convention on the Hunting and Protection of Birds (as amended)	1970	1972	3
Convention on Wetlands of International Importance Especially as Waterfowl Habitat	1971	1975	124
Convention for Conservation of Antarctic Seals	1972	1978	12

(Continued)

TABLE 19.1 (Continued)

Name of Agreement	Date of Adoption	Date of Entry into Force	Number of Signatories
Convention on International Trade in Endangered Species of Wild Fauna and Flora	1973	1975	182
Agreement on Conservation of Polar Bears	1973	1976	5
Convention on Conservation of Nature in the South Pacific	1976	1990	6
Convention on Migratory Species	1979	1983	75
Convention on Biological Diversity	1992	1993	178
Nuclear			
Convention on Third Party Liability in the Field of Nuclear Energy (as amended)	1960	1968	16
Vienna Convention on Civil Liability for Nuclear Damage	1963	1977	35
Treaty Banning Nuclear Weapon Tests in the Atmosphere, in Outer Space and Under Water	1963	1963	117
Treaty on the Prohibition of the Emplacement of Nuclear Weapons and Other Weapons of Mass Destruction on the Sea-Bed and the Ocean Floor and in the Subsoil Thereof	1971	1972	79
Convention on Early Notification of a Nuclear Accident	1986	1986	97
Air Pollution			
Convention on Long-Range Transboundary Air Pollution	1979	1983	49
Protocol to the 1979 Convention on Long-Range Transboundary Air Pollution on Long-Term Financing of the Cooperative Programme for Monitoring and Evaluation of the Long-Range Transmission of Air Pollutants in Europe	1984	1988	38
Protocol to the 1979 Convention on Long-Range Transboundary Air Pollution on the Reduction of Sulphur Emissions or Their Transboundary Fluxes by at Least 30 Percent	1985	1987	22
Protocol to the 1979 Convention on Long-Range Transboundary Air Pollution Concerning the Control of Emissions of Nitrogen Oxides or Their Transboundary Fluxes	1988	1991	29

(Continued)

TABLE 19.1   (Continued)

Name of Agreement	Date of Adoption	Date of Entry into Force	Number of Signatories
Vienna Convention for the Protection of the Ozone Layer	1985	1988	176
Montreal Protocol on Substances that Deplete the Ozone Layer	1987	1989	197
Kyoto Protocol to the United Nations Framework Convention on Climate Change	1999	2005	140
ASEAN Agreement on Transboundary Haze Pollution	2002	2003	8
Paris Agreement on Climate Change	2015	2016	194
Miscellaneous			
The Antarctic Treaty	1959	1961	44
European Convention on the Protection of the Archaeological Heritage	1969	1970	25
Ramsar Convention on Wetlands	1971	1975	124
Convention on the Prohibition of the Development, Production and Stockpiling or Bacteriological (Biological) and Toxin Weapons, and on Their Destruction	1972	1975	145
Convention Concerning the Protection of the World Cultural and Natural Heritage	1972	1975	98
Treaty for Amazonian Cooperation	1978	1980	8
Convention on the Conservation of Antarctic Marine Living Resources	1980	1982	21
Convention Concerning Occupational Safety and Health and the Working Environment	1981	1983	34
United Nations Convention on the Law of the Sea	1982	—	161
Convention on the Regulation of Antarctic Mineral Resource Activities	1988	—	17
Basel Convention on the Control of the Transboundary Movements of Hazardous Wastes and Their Disposal	1989	1992	188
Stockholm Convention on Persistent Organic Pollutants	2001	2004	176

Source: *Register of International Treaties and Other Agreements in the Field of the Environment*, United Nations Environment Programme, December 2005; United Nations Treaty Collection, 2023.

Numerous treaties have been concluded on marine pollution, beginning with oil-pollution agreements and later extending to more general pollution-control measures. Although much attention has been given recently to the issue of protecting the resources of biological diversity, the first international treaties on flora and fauna were actually made decades ago. Now there are many such treaties, including the important 1973 Convention on International Trade in Endangered Species (CITES). There has been a gradual shift away from species-specific agreements toward agreements focusing on ecosystems. This is a general acknowledgement of the scientific interconnectedness of flora and fauna and the environment.

International agreements come in several forms:

- A **convention** is an agreement in which countries define a problem and jointly commit to addressing it, but without specifying exactly the concrete steps that will be undertaken to meet its objectives.
- A **protocol** is an agreement that attempts to fill in some of the details of a convention: what specific actions signatories will undertake, what institutions will be established to implement the agreement, and so on.
- A **treaty** is a fully developed agreement specifying problems, actions to be undertaken by signatories, steps to be taken under implementation and enforcement.

A **bilateral agreement** is one entered into by two countries to manage a particular resource. For example, the China–Australia Migratory Bird Agreement and the Columbia River Treaty between the United States and Canada.

Multilateral agreements, as the name implies, are agreements among groups of countries with the objective of managing an important resource. This includes **regional agreements,** which are groups of propinquitous countries whose concerns focus on a resource of local interest.

A standard international agreement will contain provisions specifying the actions to be undertaken by each signatory country, as well as numerous institutional and logistical matters, such as what kind of governing agency is to be established, how its work is to be funded, what information is to be shared, and so on.

Many of the multilateral treaties are actually regional in scope. This includes, for example, the treaties concerning water-and air-pollution control among the countries of Europe. The United Nations has sponsored a number of regional agreements involving countries bordering particular seas (Mediterranean Sea, Red Sea, Southeastern Pacific Ocean, Western African coastal waters, Caribbean Sea, etc.). Besides the multilateral treaties there are hundreds of bilateral treaties, addressing the environmental problems of just two countries. The United States and Canada have concluded a number of bilateral agreements, including agreements dealing with acid rain and with the management of the Great Lakes. The United States and Mexico have also worked out several environmental agreements dealing with hazardous waste shipments, the use of the Colorado and Rio Grande rivers, and other matters. The European Commission on Environment oversees agreements among the member countries of the EU.

19-2 The Economics of International Agreements

When international agreements are being negotiated, the focus is usually on political issues. This is natural, as what is going on are complex negotiations among sovereign states. But underlying the political interactions—national sovereignty, political assertiveness, creative diplomacy, and so on—lie many bedrock economic factors that affect the **perceived benefits and costs** accruing to the different participants and the incentives they have for entering into environmental agreements. In the next few sections we discuss some of these issues.

Bilateral Agreements

Consider the case of just two countries—call them Country A and Country B. B is downwind from A, so sulfur dioxide (SO_2) emissions from A contribute to acid rain both at home and in B. In B, SO_2 emissions contribute to acid rain only in that country; because of prevailing wind patterns, there is no reciprocal acid rain externality inflicted by B upon A.[2] This situation is pictured in **Figure 19.1**. It shows the marginal abatement costs in A (MAC_A) and the marginal damage functions associated with the emissions of that country. Marginal damages arising in A itself are shown as MD_A, whereas MD_T are aggregate marginal damages for both A and B. The marginal damages in B from A's emissions, in other words, are ($MD_T - MD_A$). If A were managing its emissions without regard to the externalities produced in B, it would regard point e_1 as the efficient level of emissions.

FIGURE 19.1 Bilateral Transboundary Pollution and the Economics of Reaching an Agreement

Emissions of country A

---

2. This situation is characteristic of prevailing wind patterns that sweep across North America, and Europe, from west to east.

But for emissions in A to be internationally efficient, it is necessary to take into account the effects on B. The **globally efficient** level of emissions is e_2. The added abatement cost in A to achieve this further reduction in emissions is an amount equal to the area $(d + f)$. But this is more than offset by a reduction in damages totaling $(c + d + f)$, of which f represents damage reduction in A, whereas $(d + c)$ is damage reduction in B.

We saw in **Chapter 10** that negotiations between polluters and those damaged can result in efficient emission levels, given that property rights are clearly defined and that transactions costs are minimal. On the international level, direct negotiations between private parties involved are essentially ruled out, because under international law private citizens of one country do not have the right to sue private citizens in another country. Instead, negotiations must be carried out among political authorities of the two countries. This is where diplomacy comes in because, in the example, the reduction in A's emissions from e_1 to e_2 involves negative net benefits *in that country*—added costs of $(d + f)$ and reduced damages of only f. So, in effect, authorities would be asking people in Country A to make a sacrifice to benefit people in another country. This kind of thing happens all the time within individual countries. But across countries the institutions of policy are weaker, depending essentially on diplomatic skills and whatever international sanctioning can be carried out through moral, economic, or political means.

According to the precedents in international law, cases like this are supposed to be covered by a **polluter pays principle** (PPP). The *Trail Smelter* case of 1935 is an important source of that precedent. Trail Smelter was a metal refinery in British Columbia whose SO_2 discharges damaged farm crops across the border in the United States. The tribunal finding in favor of the farmers stated that under the principles of international law, "no State has the right to use or permit the use of its territory in such a manner as to cause injury by fumes in or to the territory of another."[3] This declaration was embodied in the Declaration of the 1972 United Nations Conference on the Human Environment (the first earth summit), which covered all types of transboundary pollution. Most international agreements seek to incorporate the PPP.

Because international agreements are voluntary, it may be supposed that individual countries will never sign any agreement that makes them worse off. In other words, all prospective signatories must regard the agreement as leaving them at least as well off as they would be without it. In our example, this means that the two countries may have to shift partially to a **victim pays principle** (VPP). The net loss to A in going from e_1 to e_2 would have to be compensated by Country B. Country A has added abatement costs of $(d + f)$ in going from e_1 to e_2, but it also experiences added benefits (reduced damages) of f, so its extra costs are equal to d. Because B's damage reduction totals $(c + d)$, it could compensate A for these costs and still be ahead by an amount equal to c.

It is not straightforward politically for countries to make payments of this sort (sometimes called **side payments**) as part of an environmental agreement. They sometimes do occur, however. For example, the convention on controlling chlorine pollution in the Rhine River involved payments from downstream countries to sources in upstream countries. Numerous treaties for allocating water rights have involved direct payments. Sidebar agreements that address environmental issues are not necessarily monetary payments. They have been attached to basic trade agreements, such as the United States–Mexico–Canada Agreement (USMCA) or the European Union-Vietnam Free Trade Agreement (EVFTA).

---

3. Quoted in William A. Nitze, "Acid-Rain: A United States Perspective," in Daniel Barstow Magraw (ed.), *International Law and Pollution*, University of Pennsylvania Press, Philadelphia, 1991, 346.

Rather than direct payments, countries may be able to arrange side payments by shaping their normal trade agreements. Countries that are trying to reach environmental agreements will usually be involved in commercial interactions of exports and imports. Side payments can thus be arranged by altering some of these trade interactions. Hilary Sigman has shown that the greater the interaction among countries in terms of trade, the lower the pollution levels in shared rivers.[4] This presumably happens because countries that have a lot of mutual trade have more leverage over one another to conclude formal or informal environmental agreements.[5]

Multilateral Agreements

Consider now a situation where a number of countries contribute to an environmental problem that affects all of them. Examples are acid rain pollution stemming from SO_2 emissions, pollution of a regional sea by riparian countries, stratospheric ozone depletion through emissions of chlorofluorocarbons (CFCs), and the greenhouse effect stemming from CO_2 emissions. In these cases the damages suffered by each country are related to the level of total emissions, present and probably past, of all the countries. From an economic standpoint there are both **efficiency** and **equity** issues in these types of international agreements. There is the basic efficiency question of balancing overall benefits and costs. For most international agreements, especially the truly global ones, there are enormous difficulties in estimating total global benefits with any accuracy. The impacts are too massive, and there are extraordinarily difficult problems of trying to compare benefits across countries that are in very different economic circumstances. So on the benefit side we usually settle for an enumeration of the physical impacts of various environmental changes and some idea of how these impacts might be distributed among countries. This means that most of the emphasis is likely to be placed on abatement costs and their distribution.

There are two major issues related to cost:

1. what methods to adopt in various countries to meet the performance required by the agreements and
2. how to share the overall costs among the participating countries.

Of course, the questions are related because cost-effective measures undertaken by signatory countries can substantially reduce the costs of the overall program that must be shared. The importance of cost distribution arises because these global emission control agreements supply **global public goods.** The benefits accruing to any particular country from, say, a 20 percent cut in CO_2 will be the same no matter where, and by whom, the CO_2 is reduced.[6] Thus, each country has some incentive to get other countries to bear as much of the total global abatement costs as they can. The incentive difficulties are very similar to those we discussed when introducing the concept of **public goods** in **Chapter 4.** They can be illustrated with a simple numerical example.

---

4. Hilary Sigman, "Does Trade Promote Environmental Coordination? Pollution in International Rivers," *Contributions in Economic Analysis and Policy*, 3(2), Article 2, 2004.
5. In addition, John Krutilla's early study of the Columbia River Treaty between the United States and Canada shows that the distribution of costs in the treaty was primarily related to the desire of the United States to stimulate economic development in Canada. See John V. Krutilla, *The Columbia River Treaty: A Study of the Economics of International River Basin Development*, Johns Hopkins Press, Baltimore, MD, 1968.
6. This does not mean that the benefits will be the same for all countries—we know this is not true because of the way the global meteorological system works—only that the effects on any particular country are invariant to the source of the reduction.

Suppose a country (call it Country A) is trying to decide whether to invest $10 billion in reducing CO_2 emissions. These emissions contribute to a global problem of temperature increases. Suppose that the proposed action is part of a multilateral effort by countries all around the world to reduce global emissions by getting each country to reduce its emissions. There are three situations that might occur. The following tabulation shows the benefits and costs to Country A in each of these cases:

Situation	Costs	Benefits	Net Benefits
1. All countries agree to reduce emissions.	10	20	10
2. No agreement is reached.	0	−5	−5
3. All other countries agree to reduce emissions, but Country A does not.	0	19	19

If all countries follow the agreement, Country A devotes $10 billion to control costs and then experiences, for example, $20 billion in benefits. The net benefits to Country A in this case are $10 billion.

If there is no agreement, however, Country A has no control costs. But it now experiences negative benefits, in the form of environmental costs, of $5 billion. Its net benefits in this case are therefore negative $5 billion. It would seem rational for Country A to be part of the global agreement.

In the third possible situation, Country A may try to take advantage of an agreement entered into by all the other countries. It could do so by staying out of the agreement and experiencing zero control costs. Its benefits would then appear to be $19 billion (a billion less than if it were to join the agreement because it won't be cutting back its own emissions), so its net benefit would be $19 billion. It can gain with an agreement, but it could gain even more by staying out of the agreement put together by the other countries. In this case Country A is **free riding** on the control efforts of the others.

The problem is, if one country perceives that it could better its circumstances by trying to free ride, other countries can have the same perception. In that case there would be no agreement. Situation 3 can arise when a country joins an agreement at an international level, and domestic regulations or legislation prevent the private firms in that country from adopting and implementing the treaty's protocols.

In some cases, private firms can adopt a treaty's protocols, even if the country's government does not endorse or ratify the treaty. This would change the net benefits in Situation 3. An example would be when, in 2018, the United States withdrew itself as a signatory of the Paris Agreement on climate change. At the time, private firms and some states in the U.S. still adopted practices that reduce GHGs, which are part of the agreement's protocols. Some U.S. states adopted carbon emission reduction goals as well.

19-3 The Distribution of Costs

The control costs that a country experiences can be affected in three ways:

1. In the choices it makes about reducing its own emissions, for example, through strict command-and-control measures or through greater reliance on incentive-based policies. This factor is important whether or not a country is part of a large multilateral agreement.
2. Through the choice of the rules chosen in an international agreement as to how overall emission reductions will be distributed among countries.
3. Through side payments made by some countries to others as part of an international agreement to help offset costs in the recipient countries.

Side payments can take many forms. In the Montreal Protocol dealing with global CFC reductions, discussed later in this chapter, the advanced economies agreed to help the developing countries through **technology transfer,** a process whereby the recipient countries are aided financially and technically to adapt and adopt technologies produced in the developed countries for reducing CFC use.

Bargaining Issues

Numerical examples such as those used in the last section are useful to depict the incentives facing individual countries that might be considering signing on to an international environmental agreement. It's impossible to use them to predict the results of such agreements because international negotiations on environmental treaties are only one dimension of the full set of international interactions among countries. How an individual country behaves in bargaining over, for example, a treaty reducing CO_2 emissions depends not only on the merits of that particular problem but also on the whole gamut of international relationships in which it is involved. If it is involved simultaneously in negotiations on other matters, it may be more concerned with the total outcome and be willing to compromise in some areas in return for concessions in others. In addition, when countries are involved in many negotiations, they may be concerned particularly with shoring up their reputations as hard bargainers, which may lead them to behave in certain cases in ways that look to be inconsistent with their self-interest. The outcomes of treaty negotiations depend on context and the strategic possibilities that the times have made available, which is another reason we use the simple examples of the previous section for depicting the underlying economic logic of international agreements and not for actually predicting events.

The Paris Agreement on climate change was adopted in Paris on December 12, 2015. The agreement was part of the Conference of the Parties' 21st meeting (COP21) of the United Nations Framework Convention on Climate Change (UNFCCC). The COP first met in Berlin, Germany, in 1995. There have been various milestone protocols agreed upon by this multilateral group. Among these are the Montreal Protocol in 1987 (see below) with the Kigali amendment (COP27) and the Kyoto Protocol (COP3) in 1997 (see **Chapter 18**).

COP meetings are organized and managed around the concept of consensus. Consensus means that 100 percent of attendees support, in some form, the resolutions proposed by the group. A country could enter a supporting vote, yet mean that they:

- agree fully with the resolution,
- agree with reservations, or
- agree not to vote against the resolution.

All three options yield a supporting vote, and, hence, 100 percent consensus. Consensus often involves much negotiation and discussion prior to a vote so that all parties are in support to some degree with a resolution. Of course, a consensus in which many participants agree fully is stronger than when many participants agree with some reservations.

The time, effort, and funding associated with negotiations can be considered transactions costs to achieving an agreement. Because consensus requires 100 percent support, transactions costs can be high prior to a vote, as details and concerns about a resolution are negotiated. However, with more participants in agreement at the front-end, implementation of a resolution post vote can proceed readily. One key negotiation piece of COP21 was the incorporation of subsidies to developing and newly industrialized countries for technology transfer, for example, solar and wind power technology to India.

Contrary to consensus, majority rule may apply as a form of organization for voting on a resolution or agreement. Many countries use majority rule internally. Majority rule means that greater than 50 percent of voting participants support a resolution. Transactions costs for negotiation and discussion under majority rule can be much less than with consensus rule because half the number needs to agree to support. Although majority rule enables faster adoption, implementation post vote can be more problematic than with consensus because more reservations need to be resolved after a vote. Transactions costs in this case migrate to the implementation stage.

Some governing bodies use super majority rule, which means that 67 percent, or two-thirds, of a body must vote to support a resolution. This increases transactions costs on the front-end and conceptually increases implementation readiness post vote or after adoption of a resolution.

A key feature of the Paris Agreement resulting from negotiations is the incorporation of goals being set by each country or signatory rather than goals being set by the overarching governing UNFCCC. This is a change from Kyoto which established overarching goals from the UNFCCC to the individual countries. In essence, instead of top-down protocol, we have bottom-up protocol in the Paris Agreement. This should enable a more efficient trade-off of marginal damages and marginal abatement costs within each country. It is important to recognize that the nonuniformity of goal setting does increase transactions costs on a global scale because each country must set, monitor, and report their progress.

Following the COP21 consensus vote, the Paris Agreement needed ratification by at least 55 countries and covering at least 55 percent of global carbon emissions for entry into force to occur. Ratification was achieved on November 4, 2016.[7]

---

7. See Chapter 18 for more discussion of the Paris Agreement.

Cost-Effectiveness in Multinational Agreements

The previous discussion was couched in terms of an international agreement to secure certain emission reductions from each of the participating countries. This is the way most international agreements are shaped; there is a strong bias toward treating each country in the same way by applying the same reduction goals to each.

We have discussed the efficiency aspects of this approach many times. The main problem is that it does not take advantage of differences in marginal abatement costs among sources, meaning countries in this case. To accomplish this would require larger cutbacks from nations with relatively low marginal abatement costs and less reduction from those with higher costs. But these nonuniform reductions appear to run counter to the principle of treating everybody alike.

Suppose each of two countries would benefit the same amount from cutbacks in emissions, but have different marginal abatement cost functions. These are pictured in **Figure 19.2.** The marginal abatement costs of Country A rise much more steeply than those of Country B. Current emissions are 100 from Country A and 80 from Country B. An agreement requiring a uniform 50 percent reduction would put A at 40 and B at 50. But the costs of achieving this would be much higher for A $(a + b + c)$ than for B $(d + e)$. Country A might very well fail to agree with uniform reductions when there would be such a large discrepancy in total abatement costs. If it were desired nonetheless to specify a treaty in terms of specific cutbacks from each, they could perhaps be set so that the total abatement costs of each country were the same (assuming each country had reliable information about the other country's abatement costs). In **Figure 19.2**, that would be along the level of the tax with a reduction to 60 for Country A and to 30 for Country B. But this would violate the uniform emission reduction principle, and it would not be cost-effective.

FIGURE 19.2 Cost-Effectiveness in International Agreements

When abatement costs differ among countries, in other words, it will be difficult to achieve cost-effectiveness if there is strong allegiance to the same type of equiproportionate rule.

So, although incorporating country differences in abatement abilities increases the economic efficiency of a treaty, negotiating those differences takes more time and, thus, increases the costs of the negotiation process. Shifting the focus to prioritizing total reduction for the aggregate of both countries, and applying the polluter pays principle with the victim pays principle, can enhance the cost-effectiveness of emissions reductions.

19-4 A Multilateral Success Story: The Montreal Protocol

One outstanding success in achieving a meaningful multilateral agreement is the 1987 Montreal Protocol on Substances that Deplete the Ozone Layer.

The key features of the protocol yielded a model for future international environmental agreements:

- Recognition of country differences in development: The ability to come to an agreement between developed and developing countries that acknowledged their different growth rates. Developing countries could have a different time frame for implementation than developed countries.
- Private firm participation: Buy-in from private firms that could readily adapt to substitutes and actually gain a competitive advantage by implementing the Montreal Protocol.
- Flexibility to adapt: Possible to revisit protocol steps with an organizational or implementation structure that could apply to new chemicals coming under the same agreement.

This flexibility came to fruition in 2016, when the Kigali amendment to the Montreal Protocol was adopted (currently there are 197 signatories). The Kigali amendment addressed climate change and added hydrofluorocarbons (HFCs) to the treaty; HFCs have high global warming potential values. HFC production and consumption would be phased out by 80 percent by 2033. Like the original Montreal Protocol, there is broad participation and separate phase down scheduled for developed countries (beginning reductions in 2019) and developing countries (beginning in 2024, with some in 2029).

The Physical Problem

At sea level, ozone is a pollutant produced when emissions of hydrocarbons and nitrogen oxides interact in the presence of sunlight. Various health problems and agricultural crop damages have been traced to elevated levels of surface ozone. But most of the ozone in the earth's atmosphere is located in the stratosphere, a zone extending from about 10 km to about 50 km in altitude. This stratospheric ozone is critical in maintaining the earth's radiation balance. The atmosphere surrounding the earth essentially acts as a filter for incoming electromagnetic radiation. The atmospheric gas responsible for this is ozone, which blocks a large percentage of incoming low-wavelength, or ultraviolet, radiation.

Significant atmospheric ozone reduction has been linked to a variety of manufactured chemicals, which, released at ground level, slowly migrated to higher altitudes. The culprits (ozone-depleting substances or ODSs) are substances called **halocarbons,** and the primary halocarbons are called **chlorofluorocarbons,** which have molecules consisting of combinations of carbon, fluorine, and chlorine atoms.

CFCs were developed in the 1930s as a replacement for the refrigerants in use at the time. Their use spread quickly as refrigerants and also as propellants for aerosols (hair sprays, deodorants, insecticides), industrial agents for making polyurethane and polystyrene foams, and industrial cleaning agents and solvents. Halons are widely used as fire suppressors. When these substances were introduced, attention was exclusively focused on their benefits; there was no evidence that they could have long-run impacts on the atmosphere. After surface release, they drift up through the troposphere into the stratosphere, where they begin a long process of ozone destruction.

There are two main sources of damage to humans: **health impacts** and **agricultural crop losses**. Health damages are related to the increased incidence of skin cancers and eye disease. Increased UV_B radiation can also be expected to increase food production costs because of the physical damages it produces in growing plants.

International Response

Under the auspices of the United Nations, 24 nations signed in 1987 the *Montreal Protocol on Substances That Deplete the Ozone Layer*. The agreement committed these nations to phase out the production and consumption of ozone-depleting substances. In subsequent amendments countries agreed to phase out the production of CFCs completely by the year 2000, to add carbon tetrachloride and methyl chloroform to the list, and to introduce a longer-run schedule for phasing out hydrochlorofluorocarbons (HCFCs). By 2012 the agreement had been ratified by 197 countries, including India and China.

Table 19.2 shows the consumption freeze and phaseout schedules for the main ozone-depleting substances covered in the agreement. Note the several decade phaseout period: from 1995 to 2040.

One of its important features is that it treats developed and developing countries differently: The latter have delayed phaseout schedules relative to the former, in deference to their needs to foster economic growth. Monitoring is a key part to meeting the phaseout schedule.

The Montreal Protocol has been a success in many ways:

- It has found wide agreement among nations of the world.
- It very effectively focused attention on the burgeoning body of scientific evidence of ozone depletion, using it to motivate political agreement.
- It created conditions where both developed and developing countries could find agreement.

TABLE 19.2 Phaseout Schedules Contained in the Montreal Protocol and Subsequent Amendments

	Developed Countries		Developing Countries	
Substance	Consumption Freeze	Phaseout	Consumption Freeze	Phaseout
Chlorofluorocarbons (CFCs)	1 July 1989	1 January 1996	1 July 1999	1 January 2010
Halons	—	1 January 1994	1 January 2002	1 January 2010
Other fully halogenated CFCs	—	1 January 1996	—	1 January 2010
Carbon tetrachloride	—	1 January 1996	—	1 January 2010
Methyl chloroform	1 January 1993	1 January 1996	1 January 2003	1 January 2015
Hydrochlorofluorocarbons (HCFCs)	1 January 1996	1 January 2030	1 January 2016	1 January 2040
Methyl bromide	1 January 1995	1 January 2005	1 January 2002	1 January 2015

Source: *Montreal Protocol*, United Nations Development Program.

The protocol deals essentially with a restricted set of substances. In all producing countries, the CFC-producing industry is composed of a few large chemical companies. So international policy has been driven not only by scientific results, but also by international competition in this industry.

As of the 35th anniversary (2022), the Montreal Protocol appears to have been very successful. The overall abundance of ozone-depleting substances continues to decline.[8] Scientists are predicting that the ozone hole will be substantially diminished by 2070. Note the very long time lag between policy steps and rectification of the problem. Total column ozone is expected to recover in the Antarctic by 2066, the Arctic by 2045, and globally on average by 2040.

The Economics of CFC Controls

In economic terms, the problem here was similar to the phasing out of leaded gasoline. The objective was reasonably clear and widely shared; the basic problem was how to bring it about in different countries. In advanced economies, the main focus has been put on technological change by developing **substitute chemicals** that will perform the same tasks as CFCs—as refrigerants, cleaning agents, and so on—but have little or no ozone-depleting impact.

The main provisions of the Montreal Protocol are the following:

- Requirements for individual countries to **phase out** the production and consumption of designated substances.
- A **multilateral fund** into which industrialized countries could contribute funds that would be used to help developing countries achieve the control measures specified in the agreement.

---

8. WMO (World Meteorological Organization), *Scientific Assessment of Ozone Depletion: 2022 - Executive Summary*, GAW Report 278, 56, Geneva, Switzerland, 2022.

- A provision for **trade restrictions,** banning trade between signatories and nonsignatories in designated ozone-depleting chemicals. It also bans trade in products containing these substances, such as refrigerators and air conditioners.

To meet the conditions of the protocol, all CFC-producing countries had to phase out their production levels. The policy enacted in the United States was to create declining production quotas for each of the firms producing CFCs, quotas that would eventually reach zero. To reap the benefits of the differential costs of reducing CFC output, these production quotas were made transferable, similar to the transferable quota program that was used in the phasing out of leaded gasoline.

A major problem with setting production ceilings in this way was that it could lead to unwarranted increases in profits for current manufacturers of CFCs. In effect it gave firms in the industry, which may have been operating as rivals, a way of acting like monopolists. **Figure 19.3** illustrates this with a simple market model. It shows a typical downward-sloping demand curve for CFCs, together with a flat marginal cost curve. Left to itself, competitive forces would lead to a production level of q_1 and a price that equals marginal production costs. But if public authorities limit production to q_2, the price will increase to p_2, which is substantially above production costs. Thus, an amount equal to area a becomes potential **excess profits** earned in the industry because of the output restrictions.

FIGURE 19.3 Government-Imposed Production Limitations Lead to Monopoly Profits

To tighten CFC controls and phase out CFCs faster, the United States adopted a tax on the production of CFCs. In theory, a tax equal to $(p_2 - p_1)$ would transfer all of the excess profits to the public. The funds then could be used for any number of purposes, perhaps put into general revenues or used specifically to help the CFC conversion process.

The system that was adopted established a base tax rate, then set different taxes on the various ozone-depleting chemicals according to the formula:

Tax rate = Base rate × Ozone-depleting potential[9]

The base rate was originally set at $1.37 per pound but has since been increased. The rate in 2019 was $16.15 per pound.

The 1990 Clean Air Act Amendments contained a number of other parts on ozone depletion. They established a phaseout program for HCFCs, with production to be eliminated by 2030. They established a national recycling program for CFCs used in refrigerators and air conditioners, and they introduced prohibitions on the venting of CFCs from equipment currently containing these substances.

The Montreal Protocol contains a provision for trading. This is the trading of **emission reduction credits** among countries. Thus, if a country failed to meet its required production cutback because of the needs of "industrial rationalization," it was supposed to offset the excess emissions by getting comparable reductions in other countries. Some of the organizational structure of the Montreal Protocol can be found in the Paris Agreement, although the difference between the developed and developing countries is more substantial in the Paris Agreement.

Summary

With environmental issues becoming more international in scope and significance, there are more international agreements. International agreements are much more problematic than domestic policies because enforcement is much weaker on the international level. International externalities are essentially of two types. In the first, one country's pollution causes damage in another country. Here the problem of who pays (polluter or victim) when agreements are negotiated is of primary relevance. In the second, each country's emissions affect all countries, including the home country itself. Here the basic problem is how to get individual countries to forgo attempts to free ride on the control efforts of others. The strength of the incentive to free ride depends on a country's perceived benefits and costs of an international agreement, together with whatever side payments, money subsidies, technology transfers, and so on, are part of the agreement.

One successful multilateral agreement has been the Montreal Protocol. Depletion of the earth's protective ozone layer has been a result of the widespread use of ozone depleting substances (ODSs), such as chlorofluorocarbons (CFCs) for refrigerants, solvents, and other uses. Chemical companies have had success in developing substitutes for ODSs. This greatly facilitated the signing of the Montreal Protocol, an international agreement among most of the nations of the world that is leading to a phaseout of the production and consumption of ODSs over the next few decades. One of the factors contributing to the success of the Montreal Protocol is that developing countries have been given more time for the phaseout than developed countries. Some of the organizational and implantation structure of the Montreal Protocol has been applied in the Paris Agreement.

---

9. The ozone-depleting potential (ODP) of a substance is a number showing its relative ability to destroy atmospheric ozone. CFC-11 has an ODP of 1.0, and other substances range upward and downward from this.

Questions for Further Discussion

1. Following are illustrative numbers indicating benefits and costs to Country A of taking specific actions on an international treaty to reduce CO_2 emissions. The choice for Country A is either to adhere to the CO_2 emissions cutbacks called for by the treaty or to disregard the treaty.

	Costs	Benefits	Net Benefits
All countries adhere to treaty	15	30	15
No countries adhere to treaty	0	−10	−10
Other countries adhere to treaty, Country A does not	0	25	25

   What is the incentive for Country A to free ride on the abatement efforts of other countries? If all countries become free riders, what is the result?
2. We talked about side payments given to countries to lower the costs to them of joining international environmental agreements. What types of side payments might be effective?
3. What is free-riding in the context of international agreements and what might be some ways of overcoming it?
4. "International environmental agreements are very much shaped by the fact that enforcement on the international level is difficult, if not impossible." Discuss.
5. When CFCs were first introduced, their benefits were obvious, and nobody appreciated the long-run impacts they might have. How do we guard ourselves against unforeseen long-run effects such as this?
6. Select an agreement from **Table 19.1** and investigate the details.

For additional resources pertaining to the material in this chapter, see the list in **Appendix B.**

Chapter 20
Globalization

Few economic stories have caught the public attention and imagination more in recent years than the phenomenon called **globalization**. Globalization appears to involve inexorable, worldwide forces that are producing fundamental changes in the way people live. Proponents point out the advantages of globalization and the positive impacts it can have on the welfare of people in diverse circumstances around the world. Critics stress the economic and social threats to which many people will be exposed as globalization rolls onward in apparently ever strengthening waves.

Our subject in this chapter will be the environmental implications of globalization. We will first look at the kinds of changes that globalization entails, then discuss a number of ways in which globalization and environmental issues appear to be closely interwoven.

20-1 Dimensions of Globalization

First let us be clear about what globalization actually is. Globalization has a number of dimensions:

- Increasing trade among nations: Over the last 60 years, the pre-COVID-19 pandemic annual growth rate of total economic activity in the world has been about 3.5 percent; the annual growth rate in total global exports has been about 6.2 percent. In other words, international trade has grown about twice as fast as overall economic growth. Economies are becoming increasingly interconnected through trade.
- Interconnectedness of financial markets: money and other financial assets can be, and are, moved about the world very rapidly. The flows are large, and they can be volatile, moving into and out of a country so fast that they can destabilize economies, especially those that are relatively small by international standards.
- Globalization also involves movements of people: Every year millions of people in the world move from one country to another (and there is even more moving around within countries). The movement is response to many things, but a primary factor is economic migration, where people move from one country to another in search of better economic prospects. Demographic factors (e.g., differentiated fertility rates) are also important here.

The world COVID-19 pandemic during 2019-2020 affected all of these dimensions: global disease transmission despite lockdowns, supply-chain shortages, and a sudden global recession with exceptionally high unemployment. In addition to these very direct and obvious impacts of globalization, there are others that perhaps are less obvious:

- Changes in economic institutions: Globalization is often thought to involve a general predisposition for shifting economic activity toward private sector and market-oriented institutions. This has been stressed especially in the developing world, where substantial fractions of the economies have been run by state-owned and/or operated firms. On the other hand, a huge impetus to global trade has been the ascendency of China, which has encouraged the growth of **managed trade,** using large public, or combination of public/private, enterprises. The Nairobi Expressway, built by the China Road and Bridge Corporation in Nairobi, Kenya, is an example of an infrastructure project that supports trade.
- Significant realignments in political power: Many observers feel that globalization will have important local political impacts, especially shifting political power away from national governments and toward international bodies. Two types of institutions are singled out: multinational companies and international policy bodies. By opening up their economies to the full forces of international commerce, nations may give large international companies (the multinationals) greater power over domestic economic policy, at the expense of local authorities. This would not necessarily be bad if these multinational companies had the interest of the local citizenry at heart, but they often do not. Globalization may also shift political power toward large international agencies such as the World Bank, the International Monetary Fund (IMF), and the World Trade Organization (WTO).
- Greater inequalities in income and wealth: A major point of contention on globalization is whether it is leading to greater levels of **economic inequality** among and within countries. Critics say it does; others say it doesn't. In fact, the distribution of income and wealth and its connection with trade and economic development have been much studied. While there have been small changes in the worldwide distribution of wealth over the last 50 years, these are nowhere near the extreme changes that took place in the first half of the 19th century, when some countries were embracing the industrial revolution aggressively.
- Cultural and economic homogenization: The term cultural homogenization is sometimes taken to imply an increased attachment to the "cultural products" of the developed world, especially American products. Likewise, economic homogenization usually refers to a situation in which people strive to achieve a material standard of living characteristic of the developed world as opposed to the local, subsistence-based economies of much of the developing world. However, awareness of cultures from developing countries has spread to people living in industrialized nations.

20-2 Sorting Out Cause and Effect

While globalization is obviously a major force in the world, the extent and direction of its impacts are matters of great controversy. In sorting out the causes and effects of these impacts, it is important to guard against several modes of thought. One is to attribute everything that happens to globalization. The problem with this is that there are many other profound changes taking place around the world: political, social, religious, and so on. These developments are important drivers of world events in their own right. For example, we have seen a profound demographic revolution in the last 50 years; for every world citizen at the beginning of this time there are now 2.1 people. Much of the turmoil and conflict around the world can be attributed to this population explosion. Some have argued that integration of world economies may have had the effect of actually ameliorating the impacts of this phenomenon.

In analyzing the impacts of globalization, we must also guard against drawing general conclusions based on anecdotal evidence. It is abundantly clear that globalization does not benefit everyone. But looking at the circumstances of individual components may not be a reliable way to draw conclusions about overall trends. For example, reading a story about a highly polluting company relocating to a developing country doesn't necessarily mean that low-income countries are becoming havens for polluting firms headquartered elsewhere. To find out whether this incident is part of a larger trend we have to look at all the data in a comprehensive way.

Additionally, it is important to keep in mind the opposite tendency: looking only at averages without breaking these down to examine subgroups of populations. The movement of averages (e.g., rising average income levels) can sometimes mask the fact that important subgroups of a population are moving in the opposite direction. A drop in the average levels of urban air pollution, for example, doesn't necessarily mean that air pollution in each and every urban area has been reduced.

20-3 Trade and the Environment

What are the interactions, or connections, between trade and the environment? The most direct question that could be asked is: does trade, in and of itself, involve higher environmental costs?

As we have discussed throughout the book, environmental damages in production and consumption are the result of externalities and public goods. If, in a producing country, the production of a tradable good is also producing environmental damage of one type or another, increased export demand will clearly result in increased environmental damage.

History, and experience, is replete with instances in which added production for export has added to the burden of environmental damage. China's export-driven growth can be taken as a macro example of this. But micro cases are also common, as **Exhibit 20.1** illustrates.

One could argue effectively that in cases like this it is not the trade that leads to environmental costs, but the lack of effective pollution-control technology and institutions by the trading countries. If there is sufficient control over detrimental externalities in the affected countries, added trade will not produce excessive environmental costs. This essentially means that it is a question of the political economy of the environmental policy within exporting countries.

EXHIBIT 20.1 The Plundering of Nauru

Nauru is a tiny (8-square mile) speck of an island in the Western Pacific, home to about 12,000 people. In the early 1900s, a valuable deposit of phosphate was discovered on the island. One might think that this would have been a great boon to the people of Nauru, whose livelihoods had been sorely constrained by the natural limits of the island. The extraction and export of phosphate should have been a source of rising incomes and improved welfare. It was not, however.

For many years extraction and export were controlled by colonial powers, chiefly, Australia. Net incomes (revenues minus costs) were chiefly to these powers, not to the local people. Most importantly, scant attention was given to the consequences of the extraction operation.

The people of Nauru achieved independence in 1968, by which time two-thirds of the phosphate was gone. Phosphate continued to be extracted and exported, now under local control, and several funds were set up to rehabilitate the land and provide for social services. Phosphate resources were exhausted in 2006 and left 80 percent of Nauru's land uninhabitable. With the income from the resource extraction exhausted, Nauru is dependent on aid from the United Nations. Sea level rise due to climate change is also affecting fisheries and coral reefs.

Nauru is clearly a case where an open economy and world trade led to environmental degradation and not to sustainability.

For more information, see *Paradise Well and Truly Lost, Economist,* December 22, 2001; Naazneen H. Barma, K. Kaiser, T. Minh, and L. Viñuela, *Rents to Riches? The Political Economy of Natural Resource-Led Development,* Washington, DC, The World Bank, 2012.

Free Trade Versus Environmental Trade Restrictions

Over the last four decades or so, the countries of the world have made special efforts to foster free and unhindered trade. This has been done in the name of improved economic welfare. **Free trade** allows countries to prosper by giving them expanded markets for things on which they have a comparative advantage in production and gives them greater opportunities to procure goods for which they have a comparative disadvantage. The prosperity of many countries, both developed and developing, depends critically on international trade. The problem is whether the emphasis on moving toward free trade may make it more difficult for countries to protect the environmental resources that they value.

The main international institution governing trade is the World Trade Organization.[1] Its purpose is to set out a list of rules and procedures to be followed by nations in their international trade relationships. It is especially aimed at reducing the barriers to trade, to get nations to refrain from putting tariffs and quotas on imports or subsidies on exports, and in general to move toward conditions of free trade among the world's nations, almost all of which are members of the WTO. One section of the WTO agreement also outlaws what

---

1. WTO is the successor to the General Agreement on Tariffs and Trade (GATT), which came into being in the 1940s as an international effort to foster an increase in world trade.

are called nontariff barriers such as excessive inspection requirements, excessive product specifications, and the like. But there is a very broad list of conditions that are exceptions to WTO rules; one is that governments are allowed to set restrictions in order to achieve the "protection of human, animal or plant life or health," and the "conserving of natural resources."

Consider the analysis of **Figure 20.1.** It shows the behavior of producers and consumers of a product in a particular country that also relies upon imports for a large part of its supply. The demand curve (D) is domestic demand for the product, whereas S is the domestic supply curve, that is, the supply curve of domestic producers. Without imports, price and quantity would settle at the intersection of these two curves. But let us introduce an import supply curve, labeled I. This supply curve is actually horizontal because we assume that a relatively large amount of this item is produced in the world, so this importing country could import larger or smaller quantities without affecting the world price. With the addition of imports, this country now ends up with a total consumption at q_0. Domestic production, meanwhile, is q_1. The difference, $(q_0 - q_1)$, is imported. With imports, the domestic price is also equal to the world price.

FIGURE 20.1 Effects of Environmental Regulations on Domestic Production and Imports

WTO rules allow governments to set import restrictions on products that have direct health implications, as long as it is done in a nondiscriminatory way. Suppose the good in question is automobiles, the use of which causes air pollution. Setting tight emission standards increases the production costs for automobiles and therefore their prices. The importing country may require imported cars to meet strict emission standards, which would have the effect of lifting the import supply curve to I'. This is nondiscriminatory as long as domestic producers are held to the same standards, in effect shifting the domestic supply curve to S'. The result of this is first to lower the total quantity of cars purchased by people in this country, from q_0 to q_2. Second, assuming that the emission standards increase the costs of domestic supply as much as they do imports, the pollution control applied to both domestically produced cars and imports will leave domestic production unchanged but reduce imports, from $(q_0 - q_1)$ to $(q_2 - q_1)$.

In this case the purpose of the strict emission standards was to protect human health. When it is not a matter of human health but, say, one of environmental aesthetics or sustainability, the case may be less clear and far more protracted over time. In 1981, Denmark placed a ban on the use of nonrefillable drink containers. Then in 1998, the European Commission stated the ban was non-compliant and could not be enforced. Since 2002, the ban was replaced by a deposit fee structure. Recycling facilities and options are widespread; the current recycling rate is 93 percent.

Things become decidedly less clear when it is not the consumption of a good that causes pollution but its production. Suppose that a production process causes a certain amount of air pollution. Suppose further that it adopts an air-pollution program to curb emissions from this industry. Suppose even further that the item is produced in other countries and imported, and that the countries from which it is imported do not undertake any type of pollution-control efforts. The producers of the importing country are now at somewhat of a cost disadvantage because they have to operate under environmental constraints and their competitors don't. Can this country legally (i.e., within the WTO rules) put a tariff on the importation of this item to equalize the cost burden? One might argue that this would tend to protect people in other producing countries who are exposed to air pollution from the firms making this item; however, WTO rules presumably allow countries to take action only to protect their own citizens, not those in other countries. And a tariff against the good may have no impact on lessening air pollution in other countries; the only way that could be done would be through explicit pollution-control programs in those countries, and there is certainly no way for the first country to enforce such programs.

The interrelationship of environmental issues and trade problems raises the possibility that environmental standards will be co-opted by those whose interest is primarily to protect themselves against international competition. Representatives of some industry that feel threatened by producers in other countries appeal to political authorities for a tariff or some other barrier against imports and use environmental factors to support their view. If they can plausibly argue that the foreign competitors are causing damage to environmental resources, they may be better able to justify the trade barrier. The key is whether the environmental impacts of foreign producers are legitimately a concern of the importing country.

In one case, the United States barred imports of tuna from Mexico that had been caught using methods that cause excessive mortality among dolphins and sea turtles. The question that needs to be sorted out is whether consumers really do have a substantial willingness to pay for protecting dolphins or sea turtles, wherever they may be, or whether this was just being used as an excuse by U.S. tuna companies to shield themselves from foreign competition. Labeling products such as "dolphin safe" or "pole and line caught" can appeal to consumers and enable sellers to expand demand and raise the price due to the environmental attributes of the product.

20-4 Environmental Implications of Globalization

Opponents of globalization sometimes paint a bleak picture about the impact it might have on environmental regulations throughout the world. The supposed scenario goes something like this: Trade and finance liberalization increases international commerce and the flow of investment among countries. More people around the world, in both developed and developing countries, become dependent on international markets for their livelihoods and prosperity. In an increasingly competitive world economy, countries and regions look for ways of boosting the competitiveness of their local businesses. This means trying to find ways of lowering the costs of production and distribution. Governments are pressured to relax environmental regulations so that firms can avoid costly pollution-control measures. Countries that have had higher environmental standards have to lower them to keep their businesses from fleeing to countries with the lower standards. Pollution levels surge as countries engage in competitive lowering of their environmental standards in order to give their own firms an advantage in international markets.

The phrase sometimes used to describe this phenomenon is **race to the bottom,** a progressive weakening of environmental standards brought on by the desire to be competitive in an increasingly integrated world economy.

Closely allied to the race-to-the-bottom idea is the pollution-haven hypothesis. A major part of globalization is the international fluidity of capital. Financial capital can flow easily and rapidly among most countries, often with destabilizing effects. Investment capital is also globally mobile, as firms in one country can invest in new or existing firms in others. Thus, many have expressed fears that heavily polluting firms in countries of the developed world, rather than undertaking the costs of lowering their emissions, would relocate to countries where effective environmental standards are less restrictive. Countries with lower standards would thus tend to attract firms with relative large emissions; they would become, in other words, **pollution havens.**

Are these concerns well founded? Are we actually seeing a general race to the bottom in environmental regulations as a result of globalization? There has been a lot of close analysis of this question in the last decade or so, and the clear answer is: no. Around the world we see general improvements in environmental quality and increasingly stringent environmental regulations. There has been many an anecdote that globalization critics can point to in apparent support of their argument. An example is the ship-breaking industry. Every year hundreds of very large, old, oceangoing tankers and freighters are dismantled; the separated parts and materials are then recycled. This activity is currently concentrated in coastal enclaves located in several developing countries, India, Bangladesh, and Pakistan. One of the attractions of these locations is that there are no effective environmental regulations governing the activity; to this extent it is a pollution-haven story. Beyond this, however, it is largely a story of low labor costs; the work is extremely labor intensive and supplies of low-wage labor are abundant in these locations.

But anecdotes do not make trends, and the trends are clearly in the other direction. Most integrated economies grow faster, and the higher incomes and wealth this produces lead societies to pursue more stringent standards, not weaker ones.

Many studies have been done to determine whether the race-to-the-bottom effect exists, and if it does, how strongly. There appears to be evidence for a weak effect but not one that is very strong.[2] Thus the race-to-the-bottom hypothesis, as a generalized phenomenon, is false. If the diagnosis is wrong, so is the implied prescription: that countries should either restrict trade, or all agree to adopt the same set of environmental standards governing their industries.

But let us not be overly glib about this relationship. Environmental pollution from industrial firms is an externality, an impact that takes place away from perpetrators, downstream or downwind. Getting polluters to do something about these effects doesn't just happen automatically as a country's economy grows. It requires the development of legal structures and the growth of politically active groups who will raise the necessary questions and work for their resolution. These laws and groups are more likely to materialize in situations where the economic welfare of people is improving.

The behavior of multinational firms in developing countries is also an issue. Suppose a large manufacturing firm in a developed country is moving to a developing country. Suppose further that environmental standards in the two countries differ. They are quite strict in the firm's home country and much less so in the adopted country, either because the standards themselves are weaker or because they are badly enforced or both. Which standards should the firm follow in its new home? There are two extreme points of view on this. One is that the company should seek to adopt the local practices with respect to acceptable emission controls and emissions. This means recognition of local laws, as well as "normal" behavior vis-à-vis the local authorities who enforce these laws. The other is that the firm should continue to follow the stricter pollution-control practices of its original country, with the same technology and practices that would have governed its operations had it not moved. But there is also an intermediate ground. A company may, for example, move toward local standards, but operate with progressive attitude; that is, it could obey local rules even though they may not be energetically enforced or showcase new pollution-control methods that local firms might be persuaded to adopt.

20-5 Climate Change and Globalization

Climate change advances the forces of globalization. The effects of climate change are not going to be uniform around the world. Some countries, and regions, can expect to be impacted much more than others. Food production is becoming much more difficult in some places, and perhaps enhanced in others. Trade patterns are shifting to balance regional supplies and demand of food. Overlaid on this is the massive urbanization that is happening—the growth of mega cities around world. Living conditions in some regions, particularly with sea level rise, will be substantially diminished. Although climate change is not intentionally distributed by class, it's clear that people with fewer resources will be disproportionately affected. These changes will produce powerful incentives for people to migrate.

---

2. Ian Sheldon, "Trade and Environmental Policy: A Race to the Bottom?" *Journal of Agricultural Economics,* Wiley Online Library, 2006; Jeffrey A. Frankel and Andrew K. Rose, "Is Trade Good or Bad for the Environment? Sorting Out the Causality," *Review of Economics and Statistics,* 87(1), 2005, 85-91; Katharina Holzinger and Thomas Sommerer, "'Race to the Bottom' or 'Race to Brussels'? Environmental Competition in Europe", *Journal of Common Market Studies,* Wiley, 49(2), 2011, 315-339.

Also, globalization implies increased trade, which involves large quantities of goods and services entering international transport. Transport requires the expenditure of fossil fuels. From which it may be concluded that more trade will increase the **carbon footprint** of global output. This conclusion depends, however, on the carbon intensities of production in the countries involved in trade.

- **Carbon intensity** is defined as the output of greenhouse gases per dollar of GDP.

If producing firms in two countries involved in trade have the same carbon intensity then trade between them will not affect total carbon emissions. But if a country with a relatively low carbon intensity imports from a country with a higher carbon intensity, trade will affect global carbon emissions. For example, the average carbon intensity of the United States in 2019 was 0.2 kilograms CO_2 per dollar of GDP. The average carbon intensity of firms in China is 0.5. Thus, if trade displaces production from the United States to China, it will result in (on average) higher global carbon emissions. With Zambia at 0.1, exporting a good from Zambia to China may well offset the carbon intensity of the product being produced and consumed locally in China. Differences in average carbon intensities for an entire country do not necessarily hold for the carbon intensities of individual products, as shown in **Exhibit 20.2**.

EXHIBIT 20.2 Carbon Footprints

The complexity of measuring embodied carbon is illustrated in Blanke's (2006) life-cycle analysis of apples, which compares the primary energy consumed for both imported and home-grown apples in the Rhein-Ruhr area in Germany in the month of April. The primary energy to produce home-grown apples included energy for five months of cold storage, compared to the energy requirements of transporting apples from New Zealand (28 days transport) or South Africa (14 days transport).

The increased energy required to import fresh fruit from overseas was partially offset by the energy needed for cold storage of domestic apples. But in order to *fully* offset the differences in embodied carbon for fruit imports from South Africa or New Zealand, home-grown apples had to be stored locally for nine or 18 months, respectively, that is, in the latter case beyond the next harvest. As such, in this case, the embodied carbon differential between local and imported goods changed with the month of the year and the age of the local produce.

The type of fuel used for each production step in this example affects the carbon footprint. As renewable energy sources increase, the carbon footprint of storage and transport will change along with the carbon differential between local and imported apples.

Source: Jiang Kejun, Aaron Cosbey, and Deborah Murphy, "*Embodied Carbon in Traded Goods,*" International Institute for Sustainable Development, June 2008.

20-6 Regional Trade Agreements

The WTO agreement is worldwide in scope, meant to address trade-related issues among all the countries of the world. There have also been many bilateral or regional trade agreements among smaller groups of countries, and these have had, and will continue to have, important environmental implications. Examples include: United States–Mexico–Canada Agreement (USMCA, formerly the North American Free Trade Agreement or NAFTA); Asia-Pacific Trade Agreement (APTA); the African Continental Free Trade Agreement (AfCFTA); and economic cooperation unions, such as the European Union (EU). Agreements of this type are controversial, because the general desire for increased trade opportunities sometimes conflicts with other goals. Environmental factors play an important role. Most countries have public regulations to protect the environment, though not all are vigorously enforced. It is important that the enthusiasm for more trade opportunities not be used to weaken current environmental regulations or the need to tighten these regulations as conditions change.

From the standpoint of the United States and its neighbors, an important trade agreement has been NAFTA (1994) that was renegotiated in 2018 and adopted as the United States–Mexico–Canada Agreement (USMCA). This is an agreement negotiated among the United States, Canada, and Mexico primarily to reduce tariffs and other barriers to trade among the three countries by expanding markets for the goods and services they produce or might produce in the future. A separate side agreement was reached on the environment. There were, and still are, substantial differences of opinion about how NAFTA/USMCA has impacted environmental quality in the participating countries. The specific concerns have been:

- Increased pollution in the countries, especially Mexico, because of increased economic activity accompanied by pollution-control regulations that are too lax, or are not sufficiently enforced.
- Increased cross-border pollution as a result of the economic stimulus USMCA gives to the Manufacturing and Export Services Industry (IMMEX) Maquiladora program. This Maquiladora program allows firms in Mexico to import production supplies and equipment duty free if the resulting output is exported. Although there are few limits on where these firms may locate in Mexico, in practice they have concentrated near the Mexico/U.S. border.
- Pressure for reduced environmental standards, particularly in the United States and Canada, so firms in those countries can better compete in a liberalized trade environment. This is the familiar race-to-the-bottom argument.

One chapter of USMCA is the Environmental Cooperation Agreement. Its principle aims are to reduce pollution, enhance environmental governance, and implement natural resource sustainability. Because one of the stated objectives is to seek ways to strengthen environmental cooperation, the organizational structure of the USMCA can address climate change, although that term does not appear in the agreement.

Environmental Trade Restrictions

In some cases international environmental agreements involve trade agreements.[3]

---

3. See Chapter 19, International Environmental Agreements.

Montreal Protocol

As part of the international effort to reduce ozone-depleting chemicals, the Montreal Protocol prohibits exports of controlled substances (basically CFCs) from any signatory nation to any state not a party to the protocol. Furthermore, signatory countries may not import any controlled substance from any nonsignatory state. The purpose of these trade regulations is to ensure that production of CFCs and other ozone-depleting chemicals does not simply migrate to nonsigning countries.

London Guidelines on Chemicals

As we have discussed many times throughout this book, one major obstacle to controlling environmental pollutants is lack of information—information on pollutant emissions, damages, control costs, and so on. On the international level the problem is even more severe than it is domestically because of the different ways countries have approached pollution-control problems and the vastly different information requirements and availabilities among them. The London Guidelines for the Exchange of Information on Chemicals in International Trade, under the auspices of the United Nations Environment Program (UNEP), require that any country banning or severely restricting a particular chemical notify all other countries of its actions, so that the latter can assess the risks and take whatever action they deem appropriate. The guidelines also encourage "technology transfer," stating that states with more advanced chemical testing and management technology should share their experience with countries in need of approved systems.

Basel Convention on Transboundary Movements of Hazardous Wastes

This agreement, enforced in 1992, is aimed at the issue of international trade in hazardous wastes. It does not prohibit this trade but does put requirements on it, especially information requirements. It puts an obligation on countries to prohibit any export of hazardous wastes unless appropriate authorities in the receiving country have consented in writing to the import and unless it has assurances that the waste will be properly disposed. It also has provisions on notification, cooperation on liability matters, transmission of essential information, and so on. Basel expanded in 2019 to include all hazardous and non-hazardous plastics, including plastics being transported for recycling and all international trade in plastic scrap. As of 2023, the Basel Convention has been signed, but not ratified, by the United States.

Convention on International Trade in Endangered Species of Wild Fauna and Flora

Roughly 35,000 species of animals and plants, whether they are traded as live specimens, leather accessories or herbs, are protected under the Convention on International Trade in Endangered Species of Wild Fauna and Flora (CITES). CITES came into force in 1975; 182 countries are parties to CITES. Each country establishes its own permit system to control the movement of wildlife exports and imports, and must designate a management body to handle the permit system and a scientific body to determine whether trade is likely to be detrimental to the survival of the species. Species are separated into three classes:

Class I.   Species threatened with extinction, in which commercial trade is banned and noncommercial trade regulated;
Class II. Species that may become threatened if trade is not held to levels consistent with biological processes, for which commercial trade is allowed with conditions; and

Class III. Species that are protected in at least one country and international cooperation is appropriate, for which trade requires permits.

Efforts to control endangered species trade is considered by many to be a qualified success, although much more remains to be done, especially in improving national permit processes. There are some simple lessons to be derived from considering this type of trade restriction, which we will pursue by looking at an international supply-and-demand model of an endangered species. The same conclusions can apply to other cases, such as export restrictions on logs to protect rain forests.

Consider the market model of **Figure 20.2**. This shows the world, or aggregate, supply and export demand conditions for a species of wildlife. The supply function is based on the costs of hunting, transporting, processing, recordkeeping, and so on, necessary to bring the wildlife to the point of export. It is an aggregate supply function made up of the supply function of the various countries in which that species lives. The demand function shows the quantities that the export market will take at alternative prices. The intersection of the two functions shows the market price and quantity of this type of wildlife that will be traded in a year's time.

FIGURE 20.2 Effects of Trade Policy on the International Market in an Endangered Species

Quantity of trade in an endangered species

Two types of trade constraints could be used to reduce the quantity of this species moving in international trade:

- export controls and
- import controls

Each will reduce the quantity traded, but they will have very different impacts on price.

Export controls work by essentially making exporting more costly, which has the effect in **Figure 20.2** of shifting the supply function leftward from supply curve S_0 to supply curve S_1. The result of this is a reduction in quantity traded, in this case to q_1. The amount that quantity falls depends on the extent to which the supply curve shifts and also on the slope of the demand function; the steeper this slope, the less quantity will contract. This approach to trade reduction leads to an increase in price, from the original price p_0 to p_1. This price increase could have several impacts, depending essentially on property rights.

Imagine a case where the endangered species is subject to private ownership, either by individuals or by small, well-defined groups. Perhaps the habitat of the species is under private ownership, for example. The higher price for the species now becomes a signal for its owners to be more concerned about its safety and welfare because, in this circumstance, efforts at conservation will have a direct market payoff.

However, when property rights in the endangered species are ill-defined or completely absent, which is the usual case, the added price will have the opposite effect. Most of the habitats for the world's endangered species are common property, in the sense that either everybody has the right to enter and harvest the animal or plant, or that, as in public parks, authorities are unable to keep people from taking the species illegally, i.e., poaching. We saw, in **Chapter 4,** the problem to which common-property resources are prone: Because other users cannot be kept out, nobody has an incentive to conserve the resource. It's either use it or lose it to some other harvester. The increased price for the endangered species in this case will work against conservation. It will encourage higher rates of extraction or timber cutting, higher rates of poaching on common-property habitats, and thus higher pressure on the endangered species.

Import controls, however, drive the price downward. Import controls have the effect of reducing the demand for the imported species. In **Figure 20.2** this leads to a backward shift in demand, from D_0 to D_1. This has been drawn so as to give the same quantity reduction as before. But in this case the price drops to p_2. The effect of this price decrease is to decrease the incentives discussed in the previous paragraphs. In particular, where endangered species are subject to common-property exploitation, the lower price would lead to reduced pressure to harvest and less rapid population decline. Something of this sort has happened recently as a result of an international ban on ivory imports. The ban led to a substantial drop in the world price of ivory, which has reduced the pressure of poachers on the elephant in many parts of Africa. However, cultural factors and changing consumer preferences can cause demand to increase and negate the effects of an import ban.

Summary

Globalization is the increased integration of national economies around the world, involving greater international flows of goods and services, financial assets, and people. It may also lead to significant institutional change and altered power relations. There are important questions about the interaction of trade and the natural environment. If national environmental regulations are unchanged, increased trade will lead to greater environmental damages. This has led in many cases to calls for trade restrictions to protect environmental values. Trade also opens up the opportunities for strategic behavior among countries, such as the potential "race-to-the-bottom" and the "pollution-haven" phenomena. With climate change, increased trade may increase the carbon footprint of the global economy. The contemporary efforts to foster regional trade agreements have led to conflicts over their possible environmental impacts, and some established environmental agreements incorporate trade limits. Yet, with more regional economic cooperation, synergy of environmental regulations among countries has improved.

Questions for Further Discussion

1. Suppose Country A imports a product from Country B, and that Country B lacks environmental laws governing the production of the item. Under what conditions might Country A be justified in putting a tariff on the imported item?
2. If all countries adopted the same emission standards in similar industries, would this tend to equalize production costs and put each country on the same footing with respect to environmental matters? Explain.
3. Which of the dimensions of globalization do you think will have the greatest long-run impact on environmental quality around the world? Explain.
4. How might globalization and the growth of multinational corporations in the envirotech industry be a positive force for environmental protection in the countries of the world?
5. Why has trade policy been effective in protecting some endangered species and not others?
6. What do we mean by "race to the bottom" in environmental regulation? As countries discuss climate change mitigation options, how does race-to-the-bottom relate to establishing GHG reductions among countries?
7. Select a species covered by CITES. Investigate the trade regulations for that species, identify the countries of concern for export and import, and how the regulations are impacting the longevity of the species.

For additional resources pertaining to the material in this chapter, see the list in **Appendix B.**

Chapter 21
Economic Development and the Environment

There was a time when problems of environmental quality were widely regarded as being unique to developed, industrial economies. Industrial development was associated with air and water pollution, overreliance on chemicals, visual blight, and so on. Developing countries, however, were thought to have fewer environmental problems because their preindustrial technology was more environmentally benign, and because they had not yet committed themselves to a materialistic style of life, with the negative trade-offs many believe that this implies.

It has become clear, however, that massive environmental degradation has occurred in the developing world. Rural areas have seen large-scale soil erosion and water quality deterioration, deforestation, and declining soil productivity. Urban areas have experienced seriously diminished air and water quality. Furthermore, this environmental deterioration in developing countries is not just a matter of aesthetics or quality of life, but rather a more serious issue involving the diminishment of economic productivity and the acceleration of social dislocation. In addition, developing countries obviously wish to put a strong priority on **economic growth,** as a way to improve well-being and to lift people out of poverty. The interaction between this growth and the quality of the environment is of paramount importance.

In this chapter we explore the interrelationship of economic development and the environment among the nonindustrialized countries of the world. In keeping with the distinction made in **Chapter 2**, we approach it on two levels: the positive and the normative. From the positive standpoint, the problem is to understand how development and environmental degradation are reciprocally related and what factors account for this interrelationship. From a normative standpoint, the problem is to deal with questions about the types of public policies that may be the most appropriate for countries of the developing world.

It is common to distinguish between **economic growth** and **economic development.** There is a simple, as well as a more complicated, way of distinguishing between these concepts. In simple terms, growth refers to increases in the **aggregate level of output,** whereas development means increases in **per capita output.** Thus, a country could grow, but not develop, if its population growth exceeded its rate of economic growth. The more complicated way is to say that economic growth refers to increases in economic activity without any underlying change in the fundamental economic structure and institutions of a country, whereas development also includes a wider set of technological, institutional, and social transformations. Changes in such things as education, health, population, transportation infrastructure, and legal institutions are all part of the development process. The overall well-being of a population and its national welfare are part of development. This should alert us to the fact that when talking about environmental issues in developing countries, we will usually be talking about situations where the social and technological milieu can be very different from that in industrialized countries. At the same time it implies that in environmental policy matters, a wider set of choices may be available because of the institutional transformations taking place in many developing countries. Furthermore, policy instruments deemed best for the developed world may not be for developing countries because of differences between them in political, economic, and cultural factors.

In speaking of these issues, we tend to divide the world into just two parts: developed and developing.[1] Of course, any brief classification such as this is an enormous oversimplification of the real world. At the very least we should think not of a simple categorization such as this but of a continuum, running from the poorest to the richest, or along any other dimension of interest. The countries of the world are spread along that continuum, although not necessarily evenly. It's also true that **national aggregates** can tend to obscure some important development problems within particular countries. Many countries that look reasonably good on the basis of national macrodata have pockets of poverty and underdevelopment that would be sufficient to put these regions in the less-developed ranks if national political boundaries were drawn differently.

21-1 Environmental Degradation in Developing Economies

Many people in the developed world have been brought to a realization of the existence of environmental problems in the developing world through recent global concerns, such as climate change and the rapid pace of species extinction.

A disproportionately high number of the world's endangered species are residents of developing countries, so efforts to preserve the habitats of these species have brought people to focus on the development–environment linkages in nonindustrialized countries. Similarly, the developed world's concern about global warming has heightened concern about deforestation because forests act to absorb atmospheric carbon dioxide (CO_2). In many developing countries the harvesting of fuel wood and timber and the conversion of forested lands to agricultural uses have led to high rates of deforestation. Thus, large-scale deforestation has the potential to worsen the global greenhouse effect.

From the standpoint of the developing countries themselves, their worst environmental problems are probably the water and air pollution they suffer, especially in their expanding urban areas. In the developed world, the chemical treatment of water supplies, together with the treatment of wastewater, has largely neutralized the water system as a source of widespread human disease; continued water-pollution control is justified on recreational and aesthetic grounds. This is not the case in many developing countries, where water pollution is still responsible for vast amounts of disease and death. Lack of treatment facilities leads to widespread exposure to disease-bearing human wastes. In places where there has been an expansion of industry, mining, and the use of agricultural chemicals, rivers have become contaminated with toxic chemicals and with heavy metals. Seepage of

---

1. Other terms sometimes used are industrial, newly-industrialized countries, less-developed countries, and low-income countries.

hazardous materials from industrial sites and waste dumps is increasingly threatening the groundwater resources toward which many countries are turning as surface waters become more heavily contaminated.

The World Bank made the following assessments:

- One of the top causes of death in 2019 in low-income countries is diarrhoeal diseases which are usually associated with poor water quality.
- Economic costs of environmental degradation have been estimated at 4 to 8 percent of gross domestic product (GDP) per year in many developing countries.
- Climate change threatens to further undermine long-term development and the ability of many poor people to escape poverty, especially in low-lying coastal regions susceptible to sea level rise.

In many countries auto and truck emissions lead to serious damages from airborne pollution. Indoor air pollution is also a more serious problem than in developed countries, owing to the continued heavy reliance on biomass fuels for cooking and heating with poor ventilation.

Another important phenomenon is **urbanization.** In the United States about 86 percent of the population lives in urban and suburban areas. In Asia this percentage is about 50, while Africa's is 43 percent and has been increasing rapidly and is expected to continue in the future. The United Nations expects 68 percent of world population to live in cities by 2050, with Africa at 56 percent and Asia at 64 percent. It is also true that no country has ever achieved substantial economic growth without large-scale urbanization; in most countries rapid industrialization has been accompanied by huge environmental problems. Understanding the incentives behind these population increases in urban areas is key to achieving future sustainability.

21-2 Economic Growth and the Environment

Issues related to economic growth in the less-developed countries have been uppermost for many years and have pre-dated global concern for environmental problems. This emphasis on economic development will continue as countries strive to close the economic gap with the developed economies. What needs to be examined, therefore, is the relationship between economic development and environmental quality.

Short-Run View

Probably the most frequently mentioned viewpoint on these matters is that developing countries simply cannot afford high levels of environmental quality. According to this view, the situation of these countries, in comparison to developed economies, can be pictured by the production possibilities curves (PPCs) of **Figure 21.1.** The PPC chart shows a trade-off between environment quality on one axis and marketed goods on the other axis.

Marketed output refers to the conventional types of goods and services produced and distributed through economic markets. The PPC labeled A is for a typical developed country, while B refers to a developing nation. Because of past resource exploitation, or population pressures, or less sophisticated technology, B lies entirely within A. Thus, to achieve higher levels of marketed income, which it must if it is to develop, it must be willing to put up

FIGURE 21.1 Production Possibilities Curves of Developed and Developing Countries

```
Marketed
output
         A
            A: Developed country
            B: Less-developed country
         B
    c₁ ┆---------------┆
       ┆               ┆
       ┆               ┆
       ┆               ┆
       e₂              e₁
         Environmental quality
```

with lower levels of environmental quality. For example, for the developing country to reach a level of marketed output of c_1, it must trade off environmental quality back to the level e_2. The developed country, because of the factors mentioned previously, can have c_1 of marketed output with a much higher level of environmental quality—e_1 instead of only e_2. As one economist put it:

> The poorer countries of the world confront tragic choices. They cannot afford drinking water standards as high as those the industrial countries are accustomed to. They cannot afford to close their pristine areas to polluting industries that would introduce technical know how and productive capital and that would earn urgently needed foreign exchange. They cannot afford to bar mining companies from their unexploited regions. Nor can they afford to impose antipollution requirements on these companies that are as strict and expensive as those in richer industrial countries. They should always realize that environmental protection measures are financed out of the stomachs of their own people; the multinationals cannot be made to pay for them.[2]

Developing countries, according to this view, cannot afford the high levels of environmental quality sought in the developed world because this would mean lower monetary incomes and a lessened capacity to support their populations.

There is another side to this argument, however. The PPC approach sees marketed output and environmental quality as **substitutes,** with more effort devoted to reducing environmental impacts leading to lower monetary incomes. But in the developing world there are clear cases where environmental quality and measured GDP are **complementary.** Most developing countries depend proportionately more on primary industries than do developed ones. For example, they usually have a greater proportion of their population involved in agriculture. Thus, degradation of environmental resources has the potential for

---

2. Robert Dorfman, "An Economist's View of Natural Resources and Environmental Problems," in Robert Repetto (ed.), *The Global Possible,* Yale University Press, New Haven, CT, 1985, 67–76.

being more highly destructive of productive assets in developing countries. In industrial countries, environmental quality issues hinge primarily on matters of human health and the aesthetic quality of the environment.

Furthermore, technological developments have decoupled, to a considerable extent, the resource-using sector from the rest of the economy. In developing countries, however, environmental issues are related to human health and productivity and also to the degradation of the future productivity of the natural resource base on which many people are directly dependent. Conversely, improvement in environmental quality, particularly land, can yield greater agricultural productivity. According to this argument, the environment and the economy are not so much substitutes as they are complements. A healthier environment can encourage healthier economic development.

Sustainability

The above are essentially short-run arguments, and the essence of economic development is long-run change. So the relevant question is: How is long-run economic development likely to affect environmental quality? The normal expectation is that development would shift the production possibility curve of **Figure 21.1** outward. More marketed goods and a higher level of environmental quality level could be attained by pushing PPC for B toward PPC for A. As economies change, becoming less tied to natural resources, and as less-polluting technologies are adopted, this outward shift would improve the potential trade-offs between marketed output and environmental quality. Developing countries could then devote more resources to improving environmental quality.

Sometimes the opposite has happened, however; the short-run effort to increase or maintain marketed incomes, in effect, tended to shift the PPC curve to the left and worsen the available choices. This has occurred when the search for short-run economic growth has led to **irreversible** reductions in the productivity of some part of a country's environmental assets. Here we are defining **environmental assets** very broadly, to include such things as soil fertility and forestry resources along with clean urban air and water. The concept that has become widely used to talk of this phenomenon is **sustainability.** A practice is sustainable if it does not reduce the long-run productivity of the natural resource assets on which a country's income and development depend.[3]

Sustainability is fundamentally a matter of **renewable** resources. When **nonrenewable** resources are used, they automatically become unavailable to future generations. The rule to follow here is to use them at the correct rate—neither too fast nor too slow—and to see to it that the natural wealth that they represent is converted into long-lived human-made wealth as they are used. Thus, for example, the mineral resources of many developing countries must be converted to long-term productive capital, both private and public, if they are to contribute to the long-run economic development of the extracting country. By productive capital we mean physical capital (roads, factories, etc.), human capital (education, skills), and what we might call institutional capital (an efficient legal system, effective public agencies, etc.).

---

3. The concept of "sustainability" received its major impetus in the influential report put out by the World Commission on Environment and Development, *Our Common Future,* Oxford University Press, Oxford, England, 1987. This report is popularly called "The Brundtland Report" because the Commission, created by the United Nations in 1983, was headed by Prime Minister Gro Harlem Brundtland of Norway.

Long-Run Relationships

World economic cycles of recessions and expansions affect developing and developed countries; growth rates of 3 to 6 percent a year are often considered healthy targets by economists. What impacts can be expected on environmental quality in these countries? If all technological factors were to stay the same over this period, environmental impacts and damages would increase along with this economic growth. But these factors are unlikely to remain constant. Economic development brings with it many changes. The most obvious is an increase in per capita incomes. As people's economic welfare improves, so does their ability to afford greater levels of pollution control. Developing economies usually also experience a variety of structural changes, often in the direction of replacing relatively high-polluting industries with those that pollute less.

There are essentially three types of relationships we see between environmental quality and income:

1. Environmental quality declines as incomes increase: This applies to access to safe water and sanitation facilities, which countries can presumably more easily afford as incomes rise, but which also are normal goods in the sense that as incomes increase people are willing to pay larger amounts for them.
2. Environmental quality first increases but then decreases with income: This tends to apply to ambient conditions, such as amounts of particulates and sulfur dioxide (SO_2). This pattern is probably due to the fact that in its early stages industrial development leads to greater air pollution, whereas with continued development there is a shift in industry type toward cleaner industries, as well as a rising public demand in more well-to-do countries for pollution control.
3. Those showing a steady increase with income gains: This applies to municipal solid wastes and CO_2 emissions per capita. The first is a reflection of the growth in material standards of living as incomes increase, whereas the second results from the increasing demand for energy, particularly fossil-based, that normally accompanies development.

These relationships can be taken as general tendencies, which may be different in particular countries, depending on technology choices adopted as well as the preferences of their citizens. It points out that for many environmental problems, the situation is likely to get better as development occurs; indeed, economic development may be seen as a way of combating these problems, which is why continued efforts need to be directed at encouraging equitable growth and open political processes in the developing world.

21-3 Environmental Policy Issues in Developing Countries

Although it may be true that development can help to alleviate some environmental problems, there is nothing automatic about this; appropriate public policies are necessary. This is especially true for those factors, such as CO_2 emissions and solid waste, that get worse with development. Most discussions of the strengths and weaknesses of alternative policies have been directed toward developed countries. There is an important question about how much the lessons learned in this context also apply to developing countries.

Although the environmental problems are in principle the same, involving externalities, common-property resources, public goods, and so on, the political and economic situations are markedly different from those in most developed countries.

Benefit–Cost Analysis

The basis of effective policy is in the analysis of the benefits and costs of different courses of action. Much more than in developed countries, damages in developing countries affect economic productivity through impacts on human health, soil fertility, resource depletion, and the like. In addition, with relatively low incomes and high importance given to matters of economic development, it is important to understand, and place in priority, the various steps that might be taken to achieve environmental improvement. Thus, there is a critical need to be able to assess the benefits and costs of alternative environmental policies and regulations in countries of the developing world.

There are several important issues regarding the use of standard techniques of **benefit–cost analysis** in developing countries.

- **Willingness to pay** does not equate to **ability to pay.**

One is the emphasis on willingness to pay (WTP) as a measure of the benefits of pollution reduction. Willingness to pay reflects not only tastes and preferences, but also ability to pay. In many developing economies, poverty is widespread, so a standard WTP approach to valuing environmental damages may yield only modest estimates of these damages. In the face of extensive poverty, WTP estimates may be quite small despite what look to be high rates of environmental degradation. Thus, if WTP approaches are used, they must be used with frank recognition that the distribution of income is heavily skewed, and value judgments are called for making decisions on environmental quality programs. This also argues for putting more emphasis on lost productivity, particularly in the long run, in assessing the damages of environmental degradation.

- **Discounting** – immediate versus longer-term pay-offs

Another special difficulty in applying benefit–cost analysis of environmental programs to developing countries is discounting. In developed economies, discounting is a relatively benign procedure that helps make choices among programs with different time profiles of benefits and costs. But in developing countries the focus is more on long-run development, and here the role of discounting is less clear. It's often asserted that people in developing countries, especially those with lower incomes, discount the future very highly, preferring to emphasize actions that will pay off in the short run because of their immediate need for family income to supply enough food, clothing, and shelter.[4] Thus, environmental improvement programs, if they deliver the bulk of their benefits only in the long run, may take lower priority than economic development projects that pay off more quickly.

- **Intergenerational equity** – how today's decisions impact future generations

High rates of discount can lead people to overlook negative environmental impacts that occur far off in the future; this is a matter of fairness between generations. The present value of even severe long-run environmental damage can be quite low when it is evaluated

---

4. Recall that lower discount rates put greater weight on long-run future costs and benefits, while higher discounts rates put greater weight on near-term costs and benefits.

with a positive discount rate.[5] For some people these arguments imply using a very low, perhaps even zero, discount rate in evaluating environmental and developmental projects in developing countries. But this would make it impossible to coordinate public policies and development projects with decisions being made in the private sector and would treat a dollar of net benefits 10 years from now as equivalent to a dollar of net benefits today. It is perhaps better to utilize a standard discount rate in evaluating programs, and augment the typical benefit–cost study in developing countries with an analysis of the impacts of the program on long-run **sustainability** and intergenerational equity.

Valuation Issues

Valuation, as we discussed in **Chapter 7**, refers to analyses that attempt to measure the relative worth of environmental improvements of various kinds. Indirect studies utilize secondary data (house prices, travel distances, wage rates, etc.), whereas direct studies, such as contingent valuation, use survey data generated specifically for the analyses.

Some studies which apply valuation techniques to the developing world include:

- Estimating the value of willingness to pay for improved water sanitation in low-income Kenyan cities.[6]
- Valuation of forest ecosystem benefits in Nepal.[7]
- Valuing the proximity of urban amenities such as clean water and open space in India.[8]
- Estimating industrial and service value added for renewable energy consumption in low-income countries.[9]
- Estimating the benefits of maintaining beachfront quality in Thailand.[10]

Reducing Environmental Disincentives

Environmental policy is usually regarded as requiring activist intervention to remedy the problems of uncontrolled externalities, the undersupply of public environmental goods, and so on. But many times environmental improvements can be had by altering current policies that have negative environmental impacts. In many cases these policies have

---

5. We are not talking here about unpredictable consequences; rather, those that are predictable but far into the future. When chlorofluorocarbons (CFCs) were introduced as refrigerants in the early 20th century, nobody predicted the impacts they would have on the global atmosphere. Likewise, nobody foresaw the negative effects of the pesticide DDT. At the time these substances were introduced, science was not well enough advanced to have predicted these outcomes. There is a difference, however, between consequences that are not predictable and those that are predictable but far enough in the future to be neglected in today's decision-making.
6. Charisma Acey et al., "Cross-Subsidies for Improved Sanitation in Low Income Settlements: Assessing the Willingness to Pay of Water Utility Customers in Kenyan Cities," *World Development,* 115, 2019, 160–177.
7. Rajesh K. Rai, and Helen Scarborough, "Nonmarket Valuation in Developing Countries: Incorporating Labour Contributions in Environmental Benefits Estimates," *The Australian Journal of Agricultural and Resource Economics,* August 28, 2014, online version.
8. Pradeep Chaudhry, M.P. Sharma, G. Singh, and Arun Bansal, "Valuation of Urban Environmental Amenities in Developing Countries: A Case Study from Chandigarh, India," *Global Journal of Science Frontier Research,* 13(2), September 2013.
9. Mehdi Ben Jebli, Sahbi Farhani, and Khaled Guesmi, "Renewable Energy, CO_2 Emissions and Value Added: Empirical Evidence from Countries with Different Income Levels," *Structural Change and Economic Dynamics,* 53, 2020, 402–410.
10. Colin Cushman, Barry C. Field, Tom Stevens, and Dan Lass, "External Costs from Increased Island Visitation: Results from the Southern Thai Islands," *Tourism Economics,* 10, 2004, 220–240.

been put in place in the belief that they will spur economic growth. However, their impact creates distortions in local economies that lead both to lower growth rates and to environmental degradation.

A good example of this is the practice many governments have of subsidizing pesticide or fertilizer use by farmers. In many cases these subsidies were undertaken in the belief that they would spur farmers to adopt new crop varieties and intensive methods of cultivation. But the subsidies often continue well after their usefulness in this regard has ceased. The result of these subsidies is predictable: the overuse of agricultural chemicals and the damages that result. These include heavy pesticide exposure of farm workers, contamination of nearby surface- and groundwater resources with excess nitrogen, and the rapid development of immunity by target pests. Numerous developing countries have sought to reduce their pesticide and chemical fertilizer subsidies in the light of the impacts they have had.

Other agricultural subsidies, for example, on irrigation water and fertilizer, have similar effects. Much attention has also focused on overly rapid rates of deforestation in developing countries. In many cases this happens because of government policies. Policies that underprice the value of timber concessions offered to logging companies increase the incentive to harvest timber at a high rate. Uncontrolled private access to communal forest resources reduces the incentive to conserve timber stocks. Timber harvesting may be a one-time activity to convert land for cattle grazing, or soybean or avocado production, or other non-forestry purpose. Misguided public road building can open up large areas to timber harvesting.

In some cases land grants to individuals cannot become permanent unless and until the land is cleared and put into agricultural production, which obviously creates the incentive to get rid of the trees as soon as possible. The result of these policies is timber harvest that is higher than it should be, and pursued in places it should not be, with the resulting impacts in soil loss, polluted water, reduction in the global carbon sink, and so on.

We should not think, however, that distorting public policies with negative environmental impacts are features solely of the developing world. In fact, the developed world also has many such policies. In the United States, agricultural price supports coupled with land-use restrictions have led to excessive rates of pesticide or chemical fertilizer use in certain crops. Publicly subsidized flood insurance has led people to develop shoreline property, or to rebuild after storms, that might best be left undisturbed.

Institutional Policy: Property Rights

Economic development usually implies wide-ranging economic and political transformations. An important part of this is developing modern economic institutions that can provide the appropriate incentive structures to shape the decisions that will lead toward development. Inappropriate property rights institutions often have been singled out for having environmentally destructive consequences. Thus, one major avenue for policy to protect environmental resources is to alter property rights institutions.

In a classic study of resource depletion in Ethiopia, the author lists a series of stages through which a portion of the rural economy had evolved.[11]

---

11. Kenneth J. Newcombe, "An Economic Justification for Rural Afforestation: The Case of Ethiopia," in Gunter Schramm and Jeremy J. Warford (eds.), *Environmental Management and Economic Development,* Johns Hopkins Press for the World Bank, Baltimore, MD, 1989, 117–138.

Stage 1: Because of population pressure, the average harvest of fuel wood begins to exceed the average rate of wood production.

Stage 2: Farmers begin to use straw and dung for fuel; thus, less of these are available for maintaining soil fertility.

Stage 3: Almost all tree cover is removed, all dung is sold for cash, and wheat yields begin a serious decline.

Stage 4: Soil erosion becomes dramatic because of reduced tree cover and declining fertility.

Stage 5: There is a total collapse of fertility; farmers abandon their land, swelling urban populations.

The basic question is: Why did this sequence of stages take place? It might be more instructive to ask this the opposite way: Why didn't something like the following scenario happen?

Stage 1: Fuel wood harvest increases because of increasing demand, and this increases the price of fuel wood because of increased scarcity.

Stage 2: Farmers see the increasing incomes to be made by growing and selling fuel wood, so they devote portions of their land to growing fuel wood.

Stage 3: Farmers act to conserve the remaining supplies in the face of its increasing value.

Stage 4: A substantial fuel wood harvest and market appear, with a considerable proportion of the land devoted to fuel wood production.

Stage 5: Farmers do not abandon their land and continue living in their native village.

Why, in other words, did the rising market price of fuel wood lead to wiping out the forest? Why did the farmers not act to make themselves better off by conserving and even increasing the production of an increasingly valuable resource?

One part of the answer is property rights. Most of the forested land was not owned by individuals or small groups, but was essentially an open-access resource. Anyone who wanted to harvest wood from these lands had the right to do so. In **Chapter 4** we examined a simple model of an open-access resource showing that individuals making decisions on the basis of benefits and costs to themselves will overlook **common-property externalities** they inflict on others. A resource of this type often will be overexploited. Viewed from another angle, when there is open access to a resource, the incentive that any individual might have to reduce the rate of use and conserve the resource is totally undermined. If someone reduces his or her harvest, others will simply take what has been left. Open-access resources promote a "use-it-or-lose-it" situation.

Thus, in the example, one of the root causes of the deforestation, which began the whole unraveling process, was an institutional one, a property rights system that created incentives for wiping out the resource even though rising scarcity was making it socially desirable to conserve it. This problem has occurred with historical regularity in developing countries, especially with land and forest resources. The most straightforward response would seem to be to change the property rights system so that the normal incentives for conservation can operate. This means instituting a system of individual or small-group property rights.

We have to keep in mind that like any single policy recommendation, this one is no panacea for all of the environmental problems of developing countries. It will work in some situations and not in others. Overuse of resources, such as the deforestation mentioned previously, can occur on "private" lands if the owners cannot effectively defend their boundaries and keep out would-be encroachers. This means, among other things, that there have to be effective and equitable legal institutions to settle land-use conflicts. Establishing private property rights in developing countries also means facing the demographic realities. In places with great population pressure, private property rights would hardly be feasible if they cut off a substantial proportion of the population from resources needed in order to subsist. Even in places without noticeable population pressure, essentially the same problem could occur if the property rights are distributed inequitably in the first place.

There are many other dimensions to the property rights issue. It is a topic of great controversy, and the debate is often carried out in overly simplistic terms. It is clear, however, that widely ranging resource and environmental problems in developing countries have been made much worse by ill-defined property rights and the open-access externalities to which these give rise. In those situations, innovations in property rights institutions can be effective.

Population Policy as Environmental Policy

Many people feel that the only effective way to control environmental destruction in developing countries is to control the number of people in those countries. In the simplest possible terms, the total impact of a group of people on its environmental resources can be expressed in the following way:

$$\text{Total environmental impact} = \text{Environmental impact per person} \times \text{Number of people}$$

It is clear that total environmental impact can increase as a result of increases in either or both of these factors. The contrary is also true: Decreases in total impact can result from decreases in either or both of the factors. More complicated scenarios are possible: Changes in technology, economic structure, consumption patterns, and so on, that lower the per capita environmental impacts in a country can be more than offset by population increases. Yet both factors are involved. Population declines or declines in the rate of population increase may be very helpful, but they are not sufficient in themselves to ensure a reduction in aggregate environmental degradation.

The world population is generally expected to increase from the current 8.0 to 9.7 billion in 2050. It's expected that about two-thirds of this increase will occur in countries of the developing world. Whether the increase is at the high end of this range or substantially lower depends in large part on the long-run behavior of **fertility rates.**[12] Although fertility rates in developing countries are sometimes very high, many have started to decline in recent years. To some extent this is a reflection of rising incomes, because increasing incomes are almost always associated with lowered fertility rates. Other important causal factors are a reduction in infant mortality, increased availability of family planning services,

---

12. The fertility rate is the average number of children born per woman over her lifetime; a rate of 2.0 implies zero population growth. Some developed countries have fertility rates of less than 2.0. In the developing world although fertility rates are falling, they range from 1.4 in Mauritius to 6.8 in Niger.

and increases in educational opportunities for women. Continued emphasis on these factors is in the best interest of people in the developing world, for environmental reasons, to reduce poverty directly, and to make it easier to institute developmental changes.

Although reductions in population growth rates can certainly help to reduce the overall impacts any group of people has on its environmental resources, it is no substitute for undertaking environmental policies in their own right. For one thing, diminished population growth rates do not necessarily automatically imply diminished environmental damages. Even with comparatively lower populations, it is anticipated that developing countries will continue to experience marked increases in **urbanization.** Unless confronted directly, this will lead to more severe air and water pollution in these burgeoning urban areas. As another example, decreases in agricultural populations may not be accompanied by reduced resource damages if, simultaneously, a shift to chemical agriculture occurs without proper safeguards against water pollution and increased pest resistance. In other words, although population policies may facilitate reduced environmental damages, they are no substitute for direct environmental policy itself.

Policy Choice in Developing Countries

We come, therefore, to the important question of the types of environmental policies that are most appropriate for developing economies. We have stated several times, in the context of developed economies, that no single policy approach will be the best for all environmental problems: certain problems call for one approach; others call for something else. And many situations call for combinations of policies. The same is true of developing countries. Beyond this, it needs to be asked if anything characterizing the developing world might cause policymakers to rely more heavily on one type of policy than another. The main argument in developed economies is the choice between **command-and-control** and **incentive-based** policies.

One especially relevant factor is that developing countries can ill afford, given the resource requirements of economic development, to devote more resources to environmental quality improvement than is necessary. This is an argument for making sure that the pollution-control policies adopted are **cost-effective,** and this in turn is an argument in favor of incentive policies. We have seen repeatedly throughout this book that incentive-type policies, in situations where monitoring emissions is possible and where materials-balance problems are addressed, can be expected to be substantially more cost-effective than command-and-control strategies. They make it possible to take advantage of different abatement costs across sources and also provide long-run incentives for firms to search for cheaper ways of reducing emissions.

To date many other countries have been following in the early footsteps of the developed economies; that is, they have relied primarily on command-and-control policies. There are some exceptions. Emission charge plans have been instituted in Colombia, China, Malaysia, and the Philippines. A tradable permit system has been initiated by authorities in Chile to address air pollution in Santiago.[13] Singapore led the world in 1975 with congesting pricing by instituting a program to charge drivers for using urban roads during heavily congested peak-use times of the day. Today, the program has moved from a flat fee to one based on time-of-day and the amount of congestion.[14]

---

13. Jacqueline Cottrell et al., *Environmental Tax Reform in Developing, Emerging and Transition Economies*, German Development Institute, 2016.
14. One-Motoring, Singapore Land Transport Authority, Electronic Road Pricing (ERP), from 13 Feb 2023, https://onemotoring.lta.gov.sg/content/onemotoring/home/driving/ERP.html.

Nevertheless, command and control is still the dominant trend in environmental policy in most developing countries. This may be the result of relatively weak policy institutions. It is a common observation that the capacities and performance of public regulatory agencies are relatively weak in many developing countries. This problem, of course, is not unique to them; administrative deficiencies in developed countries account for part of the large gap between the laws and their enforcement. But most observers agree that this is a particularly thorny problem for developing countries. It is not solely a matter of professionalism and lack of political clout. It is also generally true in the developed world that public concern and activist political participation by private environmental interest groups are often weak. Corruption, civil war, and lack of consistent institutional oversight in some nations can inhibit policy implementation and monitoring.

Perhaps a partial resolution of this question rests on recognizing that the category "developing countries" actually includes a wide range of experience. At one end of the spectrum are countries that are still almost totally agricultural, substantially uniform technologically, and with only the beginnings of a modern economic sector. At the other end of the spectrum are countries that have developed relatively large industrial, financial, and transportation sectors; important economic links to the rest of the world; and, most important, comparatively sophisticated political institutions. In the former countries, simple command-and-control approaches are likely to be best—a prohibition on a certain pesticide, for example, or limits on a certain irrigation practice. These may be enforced without sophisticated monitoring, and technical uniformity among producers means that these steps will be reasonably cost-effective.

In more advanced developing countries, incentive-based policies have much more to recommend them. Here the necessary political institutions may have been put in place, technological complexity makes it much more difficult to achieve acceptable levels of cost-effectiveness with command-and-control approaches, and strong long-run incentives for continued technical innovation in pollution control are of paramount importance. **Exhibit 21.1** discusses a policy initiative to develop incentive-based approaches, in the form of payments (subsidies) for providing environmental services, which have become popular in many developing economies.

EXHIBIT 21.1 Conditional Cash Transfers and Payments for Environmental Services

Payments for Environmental Services (PES) are incentive-based programs that give individual decision-makers monetary incentives for adopting certain behaviors, in this case, to preserve ecosystems and biodiversity. With a PES, monetary payments are given to people who engage in environmental conservation activities such as maintaining an area in forest cover or refraining from cultivating steeply sloped lands.

PES programs identify farmers or other landowners who might be expected to convert ecological land, then offering them payments, cash or otherwise, to refrain from that action. Of course it is based theoretically on the notion that land conversion

(Continued)

EXHIBIT 21.1 *(Continued)*

often produces external costs, in the form of, for example, downstream siltation or flooding, habitat loss, or atmospheric carbon release. Payments are justified by these avoided external costs.

PES programs are likely to be:

- Institutionally simpler;
- More cost-effective in delivering benefits to buyers;
- More effective in generating economic growth among suppliers by improving cash flow, diversifying income sources, and reducing income variance; and
- Sources of finance for conservation.

Some PES examples handled by the African Development Bank (AfDB) are the Watershed Services in the East Usambara Mountains of Tanzania and Trees for Global Benefit project in Uganda. The AfDB stresses the need for local community involvement for success. PES programs for forest ecosystem conservation in Costa Rica have benefited more than 18,000 families from 1997 to 2019; the benefiting community uses the money for repairs or construction of schools, streets, and health centers.

One issue has been the question of "additionality," simply the question of whether in many cases landowners are being compensated for actions they might have undertaken anyway, even without the program.

Nevertheless, PES programs are a good example of an incentive-based approach to environmental conservation. Although usually land-based, PES has been applied to fisheries management in Bangladesh and Mozambique.

Source: African Development Bank, *A Promising Tool for Natural Resources Management in Africa*, AfDB, 2015; United Nations, *Payments for Environmental Services Program Costa Rica*, United Nations Framework Convention on Climate Change, 2020.

The Paris Agreement and Developing Countries

Prior to the Paris Agreement on climate change, most of the action on climate matters was among countries of the developed world. Developing countries often emphasized that their needs in terms of economic development overshadowed efforts to mitigate global climate change. In fact, climate change has severe effects on countries of the developing world.

Many of these countries realize, just as they have in the developed world, that community resilience in the face of climate change is a critical concept. Community **resilience** is the ability to re-build and adapt relatively quickly after a calamity hits a community. Often the calamity results from a natural disaster, such as a hurricane or tsunami, floods and landslides, or forest fires. The intensity and frequency of these events have been magnified with climate change. Besides affecting weather patterns, climate change is impacting sea levels which affect people living in low-lying areas in many developing countries. Natural disasters displaced 21.5 million people since 2008. Climate refugees are mostly in the Asia-Pacific region which is prone to deadly flooding. In many countries, poverty can be acerbated by these effects and will probably intensify in the future. Specifically, we may expect:

- Increases in refugees due to population displacement from natural disasters
- Increases in the number of people moving inland and away from coasts and rising sea levels, perhaps adding to population pressures in urban areas

- Displacement of livelihoods, particularly in agriculture and fishing, as people need to seek other means of employment

The Paris Agreement on climate change resulted in consensus among developed, developing, and the least-developed countries and provides a platform for sharing solutions to climate change problems within the context of widespread poverty in developing countries. The agreement includes:

- Implementing National Adaptation Plans (NAPs) with international cooperation and sharing of earth-friendly technology; however, specific and adequate funding for developing countries is not identified
- Adopting Nationally Determined Contributions (NDCs), which are the accountability mechanisms through which countries report their progress every five years on achieving long-term goals for reducing GHG emissions and adapting to impacts of climate change
- Mobilizing private and public climate financing; however, there are no binding commitments or specific monies identified for specific developing countries
- Amending trade rules to include carbon-labeling and carbon taxes; however, this could alter the trade balance of developing countries and increase the transactions costs of trade. The World Trade Organization (WTO) will play a part in alignment and disputes among countries.

COP27 (the 2022 UN Climate Change Conference) established an international fund to enable the transfer of resources from richer countries to developing countries for GHG mitigation and adaptation. The Loss and Damage Fund inherently acknowledges global climate justice for climate-vulnerable developing countries.

21-4 The Role of the Developed Countries

Developing countries are struggling with a wide array of economic, political, and social problems that stand in the way of lasting economic modernization. To graft environmental concerns onto the process puts an added burden on everyone in these countries, whatever their position. The developed countries have an important role to play in helping to make this transition, not just for humanitarian reasons but also because many environmental problems are becoming increasingly global in scope. As these countries develop, their technical choices and emission-control efforts will have a direct bearing on important global problems, such as carbon emissions and climate change, toxic chemical releases, nuclear radiation emissions, and so on.

Technology Transfer

By **technology transfer** we refer to the transfer, from developed to developing countries, of technologies and skills that can provide the impetus for economic development with lower environmental impacts than could be attained without the transfer. The focus is on the transfer of knowledge that citizens of developing countries themselves can adapt to their own needs and styles of operation. Technology transfer means making technology available to countries so that their pace of economic development can be increased; this will have a positive impact on the demand for improved environmental quality, as discussed earlier. Transfer of environmental technology has the objective of reducing the environmental impacts of economic development, below what would occur otherwise, and perhaps below what has occurred historically in the developed world. It has become evident that if the rest of the world goes through the same high-pollution course of development as the developed countries have done, the drain on world resources will be enormous and the impact on the global environment potentially disastrous.

Green technology transfer, with accompanied financing from developed to developing countries, will be necessary to continue addressing poverty in conjunction with climate change effects. Building internal country resilience could improve government responses to natural disasters and the implications of internal migration.

In the long run, efficient use of world resources can increase when developing countries are able to adopt a cutting-edge technology from the developed world without expending resources on technological intermediary steps. For example, cell phone use was widely and readily adopted in developing countries without the extensive and costly build-out of landline technology which was experienced in developed countries. This technology leapfrog also applied to wireless internet access rather than first implementing wired services.

Concrete provisions for the transfer of technology have been written into some international environmental treaties in several ways[15]:

- Provide technical assistance
- Make new, environmental technology available affordably
- Access to public investment funds for environmental projects
- Raise private venture capital for environmental projects

The objectives include investing in such activities as clean technology, sustainable forestry and agriculture, waste-management systems, energy efficiency technologies, and increased use of renewable energy.

Technology transfer has two important parts:

- The first is the initial development of new technologies and procedures.
- The second is the actual transfer and adoption of the technology.

Research and development are a product of innovation in industries searching for ways of reducing emissions and in the pollution-control industry itself. Thus, one element in technology transfer is the provision of incentives for a brisk level of innovation in the originating countries. This implies pollution-control policies that provide these incentives, about which we have said a lot in earlier chapters. In particular, we have discussed the positive incentives for innovation provided by economic-incentive types of policies and the negative effects provided by technology-based standards.

The second element of environmental technology transfer is getting the ideas, technical means, and necessary training effectively into the receiving countries. The word *effectively* is important because history is full of cases in which transferred techniques have failed to

---

15. Chapter 19 contains a discussion of international environmental treaties in general, including the specific provisions of the Montreal Protocol and the Basel Convention. Other groups include the Nordic Environment Finance Corp., Global Environmental Fund Management Group (GEF) and the Overseas Private Investment Corporation (OPIC).

work as anticipated. It is much more than just moving a machine from one location to another; a tremendous array of problems must be worked out to bridge the informational, cultural, commercial, and political gaps that separate people in different countries. At the end of the process, which normally will involve many different business, trade, political, and environmental groups, the objective is to transfer technology that is compatible with local skills and labor availabilities.

Most environmental technologies in the developed world have been developed by firms in the private sector. In the United States, the **envirotech sector** consists of thousands of large and small firms in all phases of environmental activity. Getting technology and practices transferred and adopted in the developing world, therefore, involves creating effective connections between these firms and the responsible public and private agencies of the developing world.

Technology transfer must be looked at in the light of concerns about globalization. This concept has come to mean a lot of different things, one of which is the quality of the commercial contacts between multinational firms (and firms of the developed world) and people in the developing world. At issue is whether envirotech firms with potential technology treat this as an opportunity simply for short-run profit maximization, or whether they address environmental justice and make sure that technology is adapted to the long-run needs and capabilities of people in developing nations.

Environmental Values in International Development Banks

Some of the most egregious cases of environmental damage in developing countries actually have stemmed from projects initiated and funded by international aid organizations, whose objectives are primarily to help these countries develop economically. A classic example is the project funded partly by the World Bank to build roads and encourage colonization in the northwestern part of Brazil. The building of the roads attracted many more migrants into the area than was anticipated, "making already underfunded public agencies even less capable of controlling large-scale deforestation."[16] Many international donors have leaned toward the big project: dams, power stations, infrastructure, etc. These have often been pursued in ways that were not sensitive to environmental impacts because the donors, together with governments in recipient countries, have been so focused on spurring economic growth.

What this problem calls for is a more complete adoption of the general benefit–cost approach, interpreted broadly to mean the accounting for, and comparison of, all benefits and costs, whether or not they can be monetized in a formal framework. They should also include the environmental impacts. Now many international lending organizations take the environmental issues of developing countries more seriously. The World Bank, along with other regional multilateral development banks, requires complete environmental assessments for all projects and takes these into account in making lending decisions.

Summary

Environmental problems in developing countries have become increasingly important in the last few decades. While the appearance of global issues has helped people to see that all countries are inextricably linked in the global environment, more attention has also

---

16. World Bank, *Development and Environment,* World Development Report 1992, Oxford University Press, New York, 1992, 80.

been directed at traditional air- and water-pollution problems of developing countries. The issue of long-run sustainability of the natural resource and environmental assets of these countries has become a policy focus point.

Analysis of past trends shows that development tends to make some environmental problems worse and others better. Some phenomena, such as SO_2 pollution, seem to get worse as countries initially begin to develop rapidly and then improve as development leads to higher per capita incomes.

Policy institutions in developing countries historically have been relatively weak, but this is changing. Most environmental policy in these countries has followed the lead of the developed world, in terms of being based on command-and-control principles. Some have suggested that developing countries should emphasize incentive-based policies so as to achieve higher levels of cost-effectiveness.

Finally, the developed world can play a substantial role in helping countries develop without large-scale environmental destruction. The primary mechanism for this is through technology transfer, understood broadly to include the transfer of skills and technological capabilities that are culturally sound and not solely the transfer of capital goods.

Questions for Further Discussion

1. What is the relationship between economic growth, population growth, and environmental quality in developing countries?
2. Environmental pollution is, for the most part, reversible, in the sense that it can be decreased if the appropriate steps are taken. What are the pros and cons, therefore, of using sustainability as a criterion for evaluating environmental policies?
3. When a multinational business from the developed world opens operations in a developing nation, should it be held to the environmental standards of its country of origin or to those of the country in which it is operating? Discuss.
4. Suppose we introduce a new criterion, "administrative feasibility," for evaluating environmental policies in developing countries. How might this affect choices among different types of policies?
5. Refer to **Figure 21.1.** How would a technology transfer from country A to country B alter the PPC?
6. How could a PES program give incentive for people to migrate away from flood-prone areas in developing countries?

For additional resources pertaining to the material in this chapter, see the list in **Appendix B.**

Appendix A

Abbreviations and Acronyms Used in the Book

AfCFTA	African Continental Free Trade Agreement
AFFF	Aqueous film forming foam
APCA	Air Pollution Control Act
APTA	Asia-Pacific Trade Agreement
AQA	Air Quality Act
BACT	Best available control technology
BAT	Best available technology
BCT	Best conventional technology
BMP	Best management practice
BOD	Biochemical oxygen demand
BPT	Best practicable technology
Btu	British thermal unit
CAA	Clean Air Act
CAC	Command and control
CAFE	Corporate average fuel economy
CAP	Cap and trade
CCR	Coal combustion residues
CDM	Clean development mechanism
CERCLA	Comprehensive Environmental Response, Compensation, and Liability Act
CFC	Chlorofluorocarbon
CH$_4$	Methane
CITES	Convention on International Trade in Endangered Species of Wild Fauna and Flora
CO	Carbon monoxide
CO$_2$	Carbon dioxide
CO$_2$e	Carbon dioxide equivalent
COD	Chemical oxygen demand
COI	Cost of illness
COP	Conference of Parties
CPSC	Consumer Products Safety Commission
CV	Contingent valuation
CWA	Clean Water Act
DfE	Design for the environment

DO	Dissolved oxygen
DOD	Department of Defense
DOE	Department of Energy
DOI	Department of the Interior
DOT	Department of Transportation
DRT	Drift reduction technology
ECHA	European Chemical Agency
EFSA	European Food Safety Authority
EIA	Environmental impact analysis
EIS	Environmental impact statements
EPA	Environmental Protection Agency
EPC	Emergency Planning and Community Right-to-Know Act
ERP	Electronic road pricing
ESA	Endangered Species Act
EU	European Union
EU ETS	European Union Emissions Trading Scheme
EV	Electric vehicle
EVFTA	European Union Vietnam Free Trade Agreement
EVM	Electric vehicle miles driven
FC	Fecal coliform
FDA	Food and Drug Administration
FDCA	Food, Drug, and Cosmetic Act
FIFRA	Federal Insecticide, Fungicide, and Rodenticide Act
FTC	Federal Trade Commission
GATT	General Agreement on Tariffs and Trade
GDP	Gross domestic product
GEF	Global Environmental Fund
GHG	Greenhouse gas
GMP	Global Methane Pledge
GPS	Global positioning system
GWP	Greenhouse Warming Potential
HCFC	Hydrochlorofluorocarbon
HEW	Health, Education, and Welfare Administration
HFC	Hydrofluorocarbons
HLW	High-level waste
I&M	Inspection and maintenance
IB	Incentive based
ICE	Internal combustion engine
ICEM	Internal combustion engine miles driven
ICJ	International Court of Justice
IMF	International Monetary Fund
INDC	Intended Nationally Determined Contribution
IPCC	Intergovernmental Panel on Climate Change
IPM	Integrated pest management
kwh	kilowatt hour
LAER	Lowest achievable emission rate
LCR	Lead and Copper Rule

LEED	Leadership in Energy and Environmental Design
LEV	Low-emission vehicle
LLW	Low-level waste
MAC	Marginal abatement cost
MACT	Maximum available (or achievable) control technology
MATS	Mercury and Air Toxic Standards
MC	Marginal cost
MCL	Maximum containment level
MCLG	Maximum containment level goal
MD	Marginal damages
MEC	Marginal external costs
MOS	Margin of safety
MPC	Marginal private costs
mpg	miles per gallon
MSHA	Mine Safety and Health Administration
MSW	Municipal Solid Waste
MWTP	Marginal willingness to pay
NAAQS	National ambient air quality standards
NAP	National adaptation plan
NCP	National contingency plan
NDC	Nationally Determined Contribution
NEPA	National Environmental Policy Act
NH_3	Ammonia
NMOG	Non-methane organic gas
NOx	Nitrogen oxides
NPDES	National Pollutant Discharge Elimination System
NPDWR	National Primary Drinking Water Regulation
NPL	National priorities list
NPS	Nonpoint source
NSPS	New-source performance standards
NSR	New source review
NWR	National Wildlife Refuge
O_3	Ozone
ODP	Ozone Depleting Potential
ODS	Ozone depleting substance
OECD	Organization for Economic Cooperation and Development
OEM	Office of Environmental Management
OPIC	Overseas private investment corporation
OSHA	Occupational Safety and Health Administration
OSV	Oversnow vehicle
PAYT	Pay-as-you-throw
PES	Payment for environmental services
PFOA/PFOS	Per- and polyfluoroalkye
PM 2.5	Particulate matter smaller than 2.5 micrometers in diameter
PM 10	Particulate matter smaller than 10 micrometers in diameter
POP	Persistent organic pollutant

APPENDIX A: Abbreviations and Acronyms Used in the Book

POTW	Publicly owned treatment works
PPC	Production possibility curve
ppm	parts per million
PPP	Polluter pays principle
PRP	Potentially responsible party
PS	Point source
PSD	Prevention of significant deterioration
RACT	Reasonably available control technology
RCRA	Resource Conservation and Recovery Act
R&D	Research and development
REACH	Registration, Evaluation, Authorisation and Restriction of Chemicals
RECLAIM	Regional Clean Air Incentive Market (of Southern California)
REGGI	Regional Greenhouse Gas Initiative of Northeastern States
RFF	Resources for the Future
RIA	Regulatory impact analysis
RM	Recycled materials
SCC	Social cost of carbon
SDWA	Safe Drinking Water Act
SIP	State implementation plan
SMSA	Standard metropolitan statistical area
SO$_2$	Sulfur dioxide
SRF	State Revolving Fund
TBES	Technology-based effluent standard
TDP	Transferable discharge permit
TM	Total materials
TMDL	Total maximum daily load
TOC	Total organic carbon
TRI	Toxics release inventory
TSCA	Toxic Substances Control Act
TSS	Total suspended solids
ULEZ	Ultra low emissions zones
UNEP	United Nations Environment Program
UNFCCC	United Nations Framework Convention on Climate Change
USDA	United States Department of Agriculture
USMCA	United States–Mexico–Canada Agreement
UV	Ultraviolet
VM	Virgin materials
VOC	Volatile organic compound
VPP	Victim Pays Principle
VPRP	Voluntary pollution reduction program
VSL	Value of a statistical life
WEEE	Waste from Electrical and Electronic Equipment
WIFIA	Water Infrastructure Finance and Innovation Act
WMO	World Meteorological Organization
WPCA	Water Pollution Control Act
WQA	Water Quality Act

WtE	Waste to Energy
WTO	World Trade Organization
WTP	Willingness to pay
WWTP	Wastewater treatment plant
ZEV	Zero-emission vehicle
ZPG	Zero population growth

Appendix B
Additional Websites

Section 1
There are no additional websites for this section.

Section 2
Chapters 3, 4, and 5

- For seeing environmental economics in action, a useful source is Resources for the Future:
  - www.rff.org
- The U.S. Environmental Protection Agency (EPA) is a good source for material on the subject; search "environment economics":
  - www.epa.gov/environmental-economics
- The Organization for Economic Cooperation and Development (OECD) has much useful global information; search "environment tools and evaluation":
  - www.OECD.org/evn/tools-evaluation/
- More global material is at the World Bank; search "pollution management" and "environmental health program":
  - https://www.worldbank.org/en/programs/pollution-management-and-environmental-health-program
- An important source for international environmental data is the World Resources Institute:
  - www.wri.org
- Basic economic concepts in video are included in the Economics Classroom by Jason Welker.

Section 3
Chapters 6, 7, and 8

- Resources for the Future has numerous reports available in which benefit-cost techniques are applied to environmental problems:
  - www.rff.org/topics/environmental-economics/benefit-cost-analysis/

- The Inter-American Development Bank (IADB) historically has developed benefit-cost techniques to apply to development projects:
  - https://www.iadb.org/en/topics-effectiveness-improving-lives/cost-benefit-analysis
- The Federal Emergency Management Agency (FEMA) has a toolkit for benefit-cost analysis:
  - https://www.fema.gov/fact-sheet/fema-bca-toolkit-60-installation-instructions
- The Organization for Economic Cooperation and Development (OECD) has information on benefit-cost analysis for environmental projects and policy use:
  - https://www.oecd.org/governance/cost-benefit-analysis-and-the-environment-9789264085169-en.htm
- For environmental damage assessment, see the National Environmental Policy Act:
  - https://ceq.doe.gov/get-involved/international_impact_assessment.html
- See the Society for Benefit-Cost Analysis for discussions about theory and practice:
  - https://www.benefitcostanalysis.org/
- Costs are affected by pollution-control technologies available, and there are sites featuring information on this. For example, Green Pages—The Global Directory for Environmental Technology:
  - www.eco-web.com

Section 4

Chapters 9, 10, 11, 12, and 13

- For some of the science that underlies environmental regulation explore Science Direct (please note you have to register to use):
  - https://www.sciencedirect.com/topics/
- For summaries of Environmental Laws and Executive Orders, go to the Environmental Protection Agency (EPA):
  - https://www.epa.gov/laws-regulations/laws-and-executive-orders#majorlaws
- The Congressional Research Service publishes informational reports on various aspects of U.S. environmental policy:
  - https://www.loc.gov/crsinfo/about/
- The Organization for Economic Cooperation and Development (OECD) is very good on different types of environmental policies in the various OECD countries:
  - http://www.oecd.org/env/tools-evaluation/
- The Environmental Law Institute has reports on the legal status of many environmental regulations:
  - www.eli.org/programs

- See the Natural Resources Defense Council for legal aspects of environmental regulation:
    - https://www.nrdc.org/
- Organizations such as the Property and Environmental Research Center (PERC) and the Foundation for Research on Economics and the Environment (FREE) specialize in environmental policy based on liability laws and property rights:
    - www.perc.org
    - www.free-eco.org
- A good compendium of material on the enforcement of environmental regulations and business environmental law is available at the Schnapf Environmental Law Center:
    - www.environmental-law.net
- There are sites for information on cap-and-trade programs and carbon taxes, some examples are:
    - Environmental Defense Fund: www.edf.org/climate/how-cap-and-trade-works
    - Union of Concerned Scientists: https://www.ucsusa.org/
    - Carbon Tax Center: www.carbontax.org
    - Environmental Tax Policy Institute at the Vermont Environmental Law Center: https://www.vermontlaw.edu/academics/centers-and-programs/environmental-law-center
- There are private firms and organizations in the emission-trading space:
    - Environmental Markets Association: www.emahq.org
    - Element Markets: www.elementmarkets.com

Section 5
Chapters 14, 15, 16, and 17

Webpages dealing with current environmental policy for water:

- Environmental Protection Agency, search water and other specific environmental issues:
    - https://www.epa.gov/regulatory-information-topic
- The U.S. Army Corps of Engineers is important in water policy:
    - https://www.usace.army.mil/
- European Environmental Law Forum:
    - https://www.eelf.info/home-7.html
- The Organization for Economic Cooperation and Development (OECD):
    - https://www.oecd.org/water/
- The Brookings Institute has useful material:
    - https://www.brookings.edu/topic/environment/

- Many states have developed policies and programs focused on water-quality trading; for instance, search for Minnesota's:
  - **www.pca.state.mn.us/water/water-quality-trading**
- Search water at the World Resources Institute:
  - **https://www.wri.org/**
- Many universities have water resources centers and institutes:
  - At the University of Massachusetts Amherst: **https://wrrc.umass.edu/**
  - At the University of California Division of Agriculture and Natural Resources: **https://ciwr.ucanr.edu/**
  - At Missouri State University: **https://oewri.missouristate.edu/**

Webpages dealing with current environmental policy for Air:

- Details about air pollution CAP programs and clean air markets are available at the EPA's Clean Air Power Sector Programs:
  - **https://www.epa.gov/power-sector**
- For a discussion of eco-markets, see the Ecosystem Marketplace:
  - **www.ecosystemmarketplace.com**
- Technical issues related to the control of mobile-source emissions are covered by the National Center for Vehicle Emissions Control and Safety:
  - **https://www.epa.gov/vehicle-and-fuel-emissions-testing**
- Search the U.S. Energy Information Administration (EIA) for data on energy use:
  - **https://www.eia.gov/**
- The California Air Resources Board has information on all aspects of air pollution control:
  - **www.arb.ca.gov/homepage.htm**

For policy issues on toxic and hazardous substances:

- EPA's National Service Center for Environmental Publications: **http://www.epa.gov/nscep/**
- For information on pesticides and chemical regulation, see the Pesticide Action Network, and the National Pesticide Information Center:
  - **www.panna.org**
  - **www.npic.org**
- For international information, search the United Nations Food and Agriculture Organization:
  - **www.fao.org**

- Resources for the Future has many writings on the economic issues associated with toxic and hazardous materials:
  - www.rff.org
- National Oceanic and Atmospheric Administration (NOAA) has a site about toxic chemicals in coastal environments:
  - www.response.restoration.noaa.gov
- Search the "EPA Toxics Release Inventory" to track the Toxics Release Inventory (TRI) data:
  - https://www.epa.gov/toxics-release-inventory-tri-program

State-level environmental policy and recycling:

- The Environmental Law Institute has many reports on state-level environmental programs:
  - www.eli.org
- The Environmental Council of the States (ECOS) monitors state-level environmental issues:
  - www.ecos.org
- For websites about recycling, see the Global Recycling Network:
  - www.grn.com
- For municipal programs, see the West Coast Environmental Law site:
  - www.wcel.org
- Science Direct has a site on municipal solid waste (please note you have to register to use):
  - www.sciencedirect.com

Land use:

- For land use issues, see the Urban Institute:
  - www.urban.org
- See the Lincoln Institute of Land Policy:
  - www.lincolninst.edu

Section 6

Chapters 18, 19, 20, and 21

Global Warming:

- Intergovernmental Panel on Climate Change (IPCC):
  - www.ipcc.ch

- Center for Climate and Energy Solutions (C2ES):
  - www.c2es.org
- The EPA has a major webpage on the issue; search "EPA Climate Research":
  - https://www.epa.gov/climate-research
- The United Nations Framework Convention on Climate Change (UNFCCC) has information about the Paris Agreement:
  - www.unfccc.int

International Environmental Treaties:

- Many of the international treaties mentioned in the text have their own webpages:
  - The Basel Convention on Transboundary Movement of Hazardous Wastes:
    - www.basel.int
  - The Convention on International Trade in Endangered Species of Wild Fauna and Flora:
    - www.cites.org
  - Resource indicators are available from the Center for International Earth Science Information Network:
    - www.ciesin.columbia.edu

For a review of the state of the environment in many countries around the world:

- The Global Council for Science and the Environment:
  - https://www.gcseglobal.org/
- The European Environment Agency is a source of material on the European Union:
  - www.eea.europa.eu
- The United Nations Environment Program (UNEP) has information for initiatives around the world:
  - www.unenvironment.org
- A source of environmental information in developing countries is the Organization for Economic Cooperation and Development:
  - http://www.oecd.org/environment/
- The World Bank has data on the environment for individual countries and information on economic development and environmental protection:
  - http://data.worldbank.org/topic/environment
- Another site is the World Resources Institute:
  - www.wri.org

Name Index

A
Acey, Charisma, 383n
Adamowicz, W., 131n
Aliya, A.A., 132n

B
Bansal, Arun, 383n
Banzhaf, H. Spencer, 130, 135, 135n, 302n
Barma, Naazneen H., 365e
Becker, Randy, 154n
Bell, Beverly, 162n
Bergin, Michelle S., 13e
Bergstrom, John C., 135n
Blaufelder, Christopher, 237n
Blomquist, Glenn C., 128n
Boylan, James W., 13e
Boyle, Kevin J., 133n
Braden, John B., 31, 128n
Brookshire, David S., 133n
Brown, Gardner M., Jr., 125n
Brown, Thomas C., 133n
Burtraw, Dallas, 135n, 164n

C
Caffera, Marcelo, 15e
Carson, Rachel, 284
Carson, Richard T., 133n
Champ, Patricia A., 133n
Chaudhry, Pradeep, 383n
Coase, Ronald H., 176n
Codur, Anne-Marie, 10e
Cosbey, Aaron, 370e
Cottrell, Jacqueline, 387n
Covich, Alan, 135n
Cropper, Maureen L., 128n
Cummings, Ronald G., 133n
Cushing, Lara, 234n
Cushman, Colin, 383n
Czajkowski, Mikolaj, 135, 135n

D
Davis, Robert K., 135, 135n
Dechezleprêtre, Antoine, 136n
Delucchi, Mark, 125n
Dorfman, Robert, 379n

E
Evans, David, 135n

F
Farhani, Sahbi, 383n
Fausch, Kurt, 135n

Field, Barry C., 20n, 383n
Field, Sidney M., 332e
Field, Tory, 162n
Flitter, Emily, 183e
Fraas, Arthur G., 9e
Frankel, Jeffrey A., 369n
Freeman, A. Myrick, III, 121n, 128n
Fullerton, Don, 216n

G
Garbe, Paul, 123
Goodkind, Andrew L., 4, 66n
Graham, John D., 9e
Gillingham, Kenneth, 281n
Guesmi, Khaled, 383n

H
Hammitt, J.K., 131n
Hand, M., 146
Haninger, K., 131n
Hanley, Nancy, p. 135n
Hardin, Garrett, 68n
Harr, Jonathan, 173e
Harrington, Winston, 104n
Harris, Jonathan M., 10e
Heinzerling, Lisa, 104n
Hesselman, Marlies, 239e
Holland, Stephen P., 66n
Holmes, Thomas P., 135, 135n
Holmstead, Jeff, 9e
Holzinger, Katharina, 369n

J
Jebli, Mehdi Ben, 383n

K
Kaiser, K., 365e
Kask, Susan B., 135n
Keiser, David A., 254n
Kejun, Jiang, 370e
Kent, Paula, 135n
Kim, H.J., 125n
Kniesner, T.J., 130
Kochi, 135n
Kolbert, Elizabeth, 339n
Kolstad, Charles D., 128n
Kopelias, Pantelis, 67
Krupnick, Alan J., 13e, 135n
Krutilla, John V., 351n
Kuwahara, Robin, 123

405

L

Lai, Himanshe, 239e
Lanz, Bruno, 128n
Lass, Dan, 383n
Lave, Lester B., 122n
Learner, Howard A., 321n
Leigh, J.P., 130
Levy, Cindy, 237n
Lobell, David, 125n
Loomis, John, 135, 135n
Lott, J.R., 130

M

Magraw, Daniel Barstow, 350n
Manning, R.L., 130
Mannion, Peter, 237n
Mansur, Erin T., 66n
Maples, B., 146
Maxwell, Keely, 304n
McConnell, Virginia, 281n
McCubbin, Donald, 125n
Meredith, Sam, 183e
Metcalf, Gilbert E., 216n, 332n
Minh, T., 365e
Mitchell, Robert Cameron, 133n
Mitropoulos, Lambros K., 67
Moné, C., 146
Moore, M.J., 130
Morgenstern, Richard D., 104n
Muller, Nicholas Z., 66n
Murphy, Deborah, 370e
Murphy, James, 125n

N

Newcombe, Kenneth J., 384n
Nitze, William A., 350n
Nurmagambetov, Tursynbek, 123
Nyborg, Karina, p. 135n

O

Odman, M. Talat, 13e
Olivier, J.G.J., 325e
Orgill-Meyer, Jennifer, 134n
Orr, Fritz, III, 135n

P

Palmer, Karen, 281n
Pasurka, Carl, Jr., 154n
Peters, J.A.H.W., 325e
Pigou, A.C., 205n
Pinner Dickon, 237n
Plummer, Mark L., 125n
Polasky, S., 66n
Prevedouros, Panos D., 67
Provins, Allen, 128n

Q

Qiao, Dan, 135, 135n

R

Rai, Rajesh K., 383n
Rennert, Kevin, 338n
Repetto, Robert, 379n
Ritz, Beate, 122n
Roach, Brian, 10e
Rodziewicz, D.C., 132n
Rose, Andrew K., 369n
Rose, J., 130
Russell, Armistead G., 13e

S

Scarborough, Helen, 383n
Schlosberg, David, 302n
Schramm, Gunter, 384n
Schulze, William D., 133n
Schure, K.M., 325e
Segerson, Kathleen, 31
Seskin, Eugene P., 122n
Shadbegian, Ronald J., 154n
Shapiro, Joseph S., 254n, 273n
Sharma, M.P., 383n
Sheldon, Ian, 369n
Shih, Jhih-Shyang, 13e
Sigman, Hilary, 351n
Singh, G., 383n
Sjöberg, Eric, 310n
Smith, A., 146
Sommerer, Thomas, 369n
Sorkin, Andrew Ross, 183e
Stevens, T.H., 383n
Strange, Liz, 135n

T

Tiemann, Mary, 255n

V

Viscusi, W. Kip, 129n, 130
Viñela, L., 365e

W

Walker, Reed, 273n
Walls, Margaret A., 300n
Wang, Jess, 238n
Warford, Jeremy J., 384n
Wilkinson, James G., 13e
Wook, C., 130

Y

Yates, Andrew J., 66n

Z

Zhang, Y., 122n
Ziliak, J.P., 130

Subject Index

Pages number followed by e, f, n, t, indicate exhibits, figures, footnotes, tables, respectively.

A

Abatement costs.
  See also Marginal
    abatement cost functions
  aggregate, 88f
  balanced with damages, 158, 308
  calculating total, 195n5
  changes in, 87, 92–93
  defined, 77, 82
  difference in costs of, 83
  of emissions, 206–208, 207f, 210, 211f
  functions of, 83–85
  in international agreements, 355
  pseudo-efficient outcomes, 150
  subsidies, 220–223, 221t
  technical change, 52, 94, 142, 152, 198
  total, 86
  upper limit of, 86
Abatement subsidies, 220–223
Abatement technology, 249–250
Ability to pay, 40, 333
Absence of markets, 179
Acid-mine drainage, 246
Acid rain, 32, 33, 268, 273, 348, 349, 350n3, 351
Adaptation
  economics of, 336–338
  of humans, 328
Adirondack Council, 231
Administrative process of standards, 191
Afforestation, 330
Aggregate, marginal abatement cost function, 88–89, 88f
Aggregate demand curve, 43–44, 44f44n2
Aggregate economy, 26, 43–44
Aggregate level of output, 376
Aggregate willingness to pay, 43–44
Agricultural crop losses, 357

Agricultural economics, 20
Agricultural pesticides, 219
Agricultural pollution, 259
Agricultural subsidies, 143, 384
Agriculture
  biodiversity in, 339
  commercial, 341
  dependence on, 115, 379
  effects of global warming on, 327
  ozone elimination effects on, 125
  pesticide resistance weeds, 294e
  pollution from, 219, 246, 260–262
  reduction of pollution in, 329
  urbanization's effect on, 387
  willingness to pay for, 71, 73
Air pollution
  causes of, 13, 264–265
  damages of, 77
  effects of, 122, 124–125
  history of federal air policy, 266–269
  human health impacted by, 264–265
  interstate, 136t, 274
  potential air pollutants, 264
  reduction of in California, 310
  states' role in controlling, 309
Air pollution control. *See also*
  Clean Air Act (CAA)
  differentiated control, 271–273
  fairness of, 160
  international agreements, 346t–347t
  multilateral treaties of, 348
  national policy for, 264–282
  standards for, 13e, 269–270
  technology-based effluent standards, 271
Air Pollution Control Act (1995), 266t

Air Quality Act (AQA) (1967), 266, 267t
Ambient air quality standards, 192, 269–270
Ambient-based orientation of water pollution control, 259
Ambient damage functions, 78
Ambient pollutant levels, 96
Ambient quality
  of air, 132f
  defined, 22
  emission charges based on, 210
  environmental damages of, 31f, 78
  levels of, 31
  primary and secondary air standards for, 269, 270t
  standards for, 187, 188, 192, 249, 269–270, 309
Analysis
  of abatement costs, 87
  averting-cost, 128
  benefit-cost, 11–13, 12e–13e, 104–115, 121–140, 141–156, 382–383
  contingent valuation methods, 305
  cost-effectiveness, 102
  damage, 102–103
  dose-response, 116, 126
  economic, 3–4, 250
  of enforcement costs, 93–94
  impact, 100–101
  regulatory impact, 101, 338
  risk, 115–118
  for setting standards, 256
  of social costs, 90
  tools of, 2
Analytical models, 3
Antibiotic resistance, 294n4
Aquifers, 298
Asbestos, 293
Assimilative capacity, 21
Asthma, 122, 123t, 264

407

Asymmetric information, 160
Atmospheric gases, 264
Australia, 16t
Automobiles
  electric vehicles, 278–279
  cost-effectiveness of fuel efficient, 330
  emissions from, 125, 265
  emission standards for, 275–282
  external costs of driving, 67e
  GHG restrictions on, 329–330, 343
  internal combustion engine (ICE), 188, 189, 265, 276, 279, 283
  pollution-control equipment on, 278
Averting behavior, 126
Averting costs, 127, 128

B
Bacillus thuringiensis, 294e
Balancing mode, 39
Bald Eagle Protection Act (1940), 340
Bargaining issues, 353–354
Barriers to trade, 365
Barter economy, 39
Basel Convention on Transboundary Movements of Hazardous Wastes, 372
Baseline analysis, 142
Basic sedimentation process, 253
Before/after principle, 142
Behavioral economics, 4, 281
Benefit-cost analysis
  basic steps of, 118–119
  benefit-cost ratio, 106, 108
  of coal-fired power plants, 107e
  compare benefits and costs, 106
  cost estimate of, 156
  defined, 11–12, 104
  in developing countries, 382–383
  discounting, 109–110, 112e
  distribution issues in, 113–115
  framework of, 104–106
  horizontal equity, 113
  net benefits, 106

perspective of, 105
and pollution-control program, 106
scope of program, 106–109
sensitivity analyses of, 108
vertical equity, 113
with/without principle of, 142
Benefits
  benefit-cost analysis, 11–13, 104–115
  defined, 45–46
  demand curves of, 45f
  discounting, 109
  estimating of, 121, 137–139, 351
  external, 70–73
  of international agreements, 350, 351n6
  net benefits, 106, 110
  perceived, 349
  from reduced production costs, 124f
Bequest values, 139
Best available technology (BAT), 249
Best conventional technology (BCT), 250
Best-management practices (BMP), 191, 248, 259
Best practicable technology (BPT), 249
Best system of emission reduction (BSER), 271
Bilateral agreement, 348, 349–351
Bilateral transboundary pollution, 349f
Biochemical oxygen-demand (BOD)
  in developing countries, 14e–15e
  effects of, 245–246, 245n2, 246f
  removal of, 253
  in sugar-beet processing, 249–250
Biodiversity, 21, 339, 341, 340n7
Biofuel, 329
Biological uniformity, 339
Biotechnology, 339
Boston Harbor, 68, 83, 84f, 88
Bottom-up approach, 154

Brazil, 16t
Bronchitis, 122, 264
Brownfields, 304–305
Brundtland Report, 380n3
Burden of proof, 290

C
California Air Resources Board (CARB), 122, 232e
California carbon market, 232e
California Trading Program, 230t
Canada, 7e, 16t, 232e, 295e, 333, 343, 348, 351n5, 371
Cap-and-trade plan (CAP)
  for air pollution-control, 273–274
  for carbon emissions, 330–332, 332e
  competition in, 234
  defined, 226
  enforcement of, 234
  example of, 226–229
  gains from trade, 228–229
  for greenhouse gas emissions, 334
  incentive for research and development, 235
  initial rights allocation, 229–231
  issues with, 164
  for mercury, 273
  for nitrogen oxide emission reduction, 273
  in nonuniform emissions areas, 232–234
  permit price, 228
  permits reduced in, 231
  quantity-based system, 236
  safety valve of, 236
  transferable discharge permit, 240
  uncertainty's effect on, 236
  for volatile organic material, 274
  zoned emission system, 233
Capital, 154
Capital construction costs, 254
Carbon dioxide (CO_2), 326t.
  See also Greenhouse gases (GHG)
  cap-and-trade plan, 330–332
  centralized policy for, 309

Subject Index

costs of reducing emissions of, 10e
defined, 6
emissions of, 329
global warming caused by, 15, 325
per capita with emissions of, 16t
produced per unit of energy used, 328
taxes on, 219–220, 220f
Carbon footprint, 220, 220f, 370, 370e
Carbon market, 232e, 238e
Carbon taxes, 219–220
 in European Union, 331, 331e
 international program of, 7e, 332
 proposed in the United States, 331–332
 reduction of carbon footprint, 220
 setting of, 338
Carbon tetrachloride, 357–358
Carcinogens, 255
Cars. See Automobiles
Cause-and-effect relationship, 33
Centralized policy, 158, 226, 309
Charges (taxes), 204
Chemical exposure levels, 288
Chemical oxygen demand (COD), 245
Chemicals
 cost-benefit of regulating exposure, 288f
 globalization's effect on, 293
 governing use of, 286–295, 286t–287t
 London Guidelines on Chemicals, 372
 technological change in, 291
 testing of, 290
Chesapeake Bay Agreement, 230t
Children's health, 130–131
Chile, 14e, 387
China
 China-Australia Migratory Bird Agreement, 348
 emission charges in, 387
 emissions in, 16t

GHG emissions of, 237, 274, 325e
global trade in, 363
growing chemical use in, 291
Montreal Protocol, 357
trading programs in, 230t
China-Australia Migratory Bird Agreement, 348
China Trading Program, 230t
Chlorine, 356
Chlorofluorocarbon (CFC), 293, 356, 358–360
Circular economy, 26, 311
Clean Air Act (CAA) of (1963), 266t
 amendments of (1970), 266, 267t, 269, 271, 277
 amendments of (1977), 267t, 268, 267t
 amendments of (1990), 230t, 265, 267t, 267t, 268, 282, 309, 360
 command-and-control policies, 164
 enforcement of, 201
 Extension of (1966), 266t
 offset trading, 226
 sulfur dioxide trading scheme, 226
 trading program of, 230t
Clean development mechanism, 226, 334
Clean energy, 179–180
Clean Water Act (CWA)
 of (1972), 259
 of (1977), 247t, 249, 251
Climate change
 climate-economy simulation models, 338
 global, 67, 324–329, 341
 and globalization, 369–370
 mobile-source standards, 279–280
 Paris Agreement on, 389–390
 research into, 328n1
Coal, 220f
Coal combustion residues, 107e
Coastal zone flood insurance, 143
COI. See Cost of illness (COI)
Cold war, 305
Collective action, 337
Columbia, 14e–15e

Columbia River Treaty, 348, 351n5
Command-and-control (CAC) policies
 of air pollution control, 269
 of CAA, 164
 defined, 6, 186
 in developing countries, 387–388
 equimarginal principle in, 195–196
 for hazardous waste disposal, 306
 incentives in, 196–199
 in international agreements, 353
 standards approach for, 187–196
 strategies of, 186
 use of, 14, 201
Common law, 171–174, 172n2, 173e
Common-property exploitation, 374
Common-property externalities, 70, 385
Community pressure, 182–183
Community resilience, 389
Community wastewater treatment, 254
Comparative-risk analysis, 118
Compensation, 169
Competition, 63, 234
Competitive pressures, 208
Complementary, 379
Compliance, 186, 200, 208, 252
Comprehensive Environmental Response, Compensation and Liability Act (CERCLA), 102, 174, 299t, 303, 305, 306, 310
Conditional cash transfers (CCT), 388e–389e
Conservation reserve program, 330
Constitutional issues of environmental federalism, 308
Consumer products, 286–295, 286t–287t
Consumer Product Safety Act (1972), 286t
Consumers, 23–24, 23f, 318–319
Consumer subsidies, 274, 275f
Consumption, 19

410 Subject Index

Consumption residuals, 22
Contingent valuation (CV), 127, 135
 methods, 133–137, 305
Continued compliance, 201, 252
Continuous emissions, 245
Continuous measurement, 200
Continuous pollutants, 34
Control costs, 250
Convention, 348
Conventional pollutants, 245, 252
Convention on International Trade in Endangered Species of Wild Fauna and Flora, 372–374
Corporate Average Fuel Economy (CAFE) law, 280, 280t, 308, 329
Cost analysis, 141, 145–147, 148–155
Costa Rica, 14e–15e
Cost curves, 48–49, 48f
Cost data, 149
Cost-effective data, 102
Cost-effective emission reductions, 159
Cost-effectiveness
 analysis, 102
 of emission charges, 210–212
 of environmental policies, 159–160
 of greenhouse gases emission reduction, 329
 of methane reduction, 102
 pollution-control policies, 387–388
 of reducing CO_2 emissions, 330t
Cost-effective policy, 159–160, 160f
Cost-effective pollution control, 14e–15e, 86
Cost-ineffective policy, 159–160, 160f
Cost of illness (COI), 123
Cost perspective, 141
Costs. *See also* Abatement costs; Enforcement costs; Environmental costs; External costs; Marginal abatement costs; Marginal costs; Opportunity costs; Social costs; Total costs

actual vs. minimum, 149–150
averting costs, 127, 128
benefit-cost analysis, 11–13, 104–115
concepts of, 143–145
curves, 48–49, 48f
defined, 46
distribution of, 143, 353–356
effect of output adjustments on, 150–152
future, 155
of illness, 123
of industry regulating, 148–149
of international agreements, 349, 351
of local regulations, 147–148
low labor costs' effect on globalization, 368
misrepresentation of, 149
for mitigation, 145
out-of-pocket, 47
pollution's effects on production costs, 124–125, 124f
private, 48, 64
of single facilities, 145–147
surveys of, 149
technology's effect on, 52
time factor of, 49
transactions costs, 172
travel, 132–133
of wind turbine power plant, 146, 146t
Cost surveys, 149
Covid-19, 122, 276, 325e, 326, 363
Credit trading, 273
Criteria pollutants, 266
Cross-border pollution, 371
Cross-media transfer problems, 166
Cultural homogenization, 363
Cumulative pollutants, 32–33
Current multilateral agreements, 344, 344–347t
Current policies, altering, 383

D

Damage assessment, 102–103
Damage costs, 123–126
Damage functions
 changes in, 80–81
 marginal damage function, 78, 78f

material damage measured with, 126
physical aspects of, 121–122
problems estimating, 82
of rural area, 92n8
time's effect on, 82
types of, 78
uncertainty of, 81–82
Damages
 abatement costs balanced with, 158, 308
 control costs balanced with, 250
 defined, 22
 direct damage approach, 126
 from emissions, 31f
 from hazardous waste disposal, 298
 material damage, 125–126
 to natural resource, 305
 standards incorporation in, 191
 thresholds of, 79
 trade-off of environmental degradation, 77
Danger levels of toxic pollutants, 285
Dangerous Cargo Act (1871), 299t
DDT, 284, 310
Decentralized bargaining, 176
Decentralized market, 226
Decentralized policies, 158, 169–184, 308–309
Declaration of the 1972 United Nations Conference on the Human Environment, 350
Deep Water Horizon oil rig, 171–172, 257f
Deforestation, 324, 376, 384–385, 392
Degradable pollutants, 245–246, 245n1
Degradable wastes, 245n1
Degradation process, 246
Degree of risk, 337
Demand, 41–43
Demand curves
 aggregate, 44, 44f
 to determine benefits, 45–46
 factors of, 42–43
 intersection with supply curves, 73

issues with, 46
  for lowering lake pollution, 72
  market model, 63, 63f
  of social costs, 65, 66f
  typical curves, 42f
Denmark, 7e, 205e, 367
Department of Interior
    (DOI), 102
Deposit-refund systems,
    222–223, 297, 300
Design of environmental policy,
    7–9
Design standards, 189, 258
Detergents, 245
Developed countries, 14, 377,
    389–392
Developing countries, 14, 14e–
    15e, 377–378
  Paris Agreement and, 389
Differentiated control, 271–273,
    289–290
Diffusion models, 121
Dimensions of globalization,
    362–363
Diminishing willingness to
    pay, 40
Dinosaurs, 339
Diplomacy, 350
Direct costs, 123
Direct damage approach, 126
Direct-survey approach, 127
Dirty dozen chemicals, 293
Discharge permit, 227, 227f,
    248, 252
Discounting, 109–110, 112–113,
    112e, 137–138, 382, 382n4
Dispersion of toxic
    chemicals, 297
Dissolved oxygen, 245–246, 246f
Distortions in local
    economy, 384
Distributed of costs, 143
Distribution, 19, 113–115
Distributional impact,
    113–115, 216
Distributional issues, 113, 301
Distribution of income, 382
Domestic wastes, 253
DO profile, 246
Dose-response analysis, 116, 126

E
Earth summits, 343n1, 350
Eastern Europe, 4, 333

Ecological, 27
Economic analysis, 2–4
Economic burden, 9
Economic development,
    376–393
Economic equality, 59
Economic functions, 19
Economic growth
  defined, 376–377
  environmental regulations
    impact on, 101
  impact on environment, 11,
    11e, 378–381
  priority of, 376
Economic impact analysis, 101
Economic-incentive policies,
    5, 251
Economic institutions, 363
Economics
  behavioral, 280
  of bilateral transboundary
    pollution agreements, 349f
  of chlorofluorocarbon
    controls, 358–360
  defined, 2
  of enforcement, 199–202,
    199f
  growth vs. development of,
    376–377
  of handling hazardous waste,
    300–306
  homogenization, 363
  inequalities in, 363
  interconnection through
    trade, 362
  of international environmen-
    tal agreements, 349–352
  issues of mobile-source pollu-
    tion control, 282–282
  migration, 362
  normative, 3, 76n1, 92
  of pest resistance, 293–294
  political-economic aspects of
    standards, 198–199
  positive, 3, 76n1, 92
  recessions' effect on
    emissions, 333
  of recycling, 315–319
  of standards, 191–196
  system of, 19
  of what is, 92
  of what ought to be, 92
Economic structure, 9
Economists, 100, 104, 111

Economy
  aggregate, 26
  climate-economy simulation
    models, 338
  defined, 19
  distortion in, 384
  economic growth with open
    economy, 365e
  environment as asset of,
    26–27
  fundamental balance with
    environment, 23–26, 23f
  growth compared to environ-
    mental health, 29–30
  producers and consumers,
    23–24
  relationship with
    nature, 19
Ecosystem, 31f, 284–285,
    327–329, 339
Ecotourism, 341
Efficiency
  of agreements, 349–352, 349f,
    355–356, 355f
  economic, 17, 59, 60–61, 192,
    308–310
  of environmental policies,
    158–159
  vs. equity, 61
  fuel efficiency, 197
  regional variation of, 193f
  social, 161–162
  standards issue of, 192
  of technology-based effluent
    standards, 250
Efficient level of emissions,
    89–93, 92f, 95–96, 349
Effluent, 22, 166,
    182, 249
Effluent charges. See Emission
    charges
Egg Products Inspection Act
    (1970), 287t
Electric power plants, 208
Electric vehicles, 87, 145, 188,
    240, 267t, 276, 278–279,
    310
Electromagnetic radiation, 356
Emergency Planning and
    Community Right to
    Know Act (1986), 183, 297
Eminent domain, 320
Emission abatement
    technology, 249t

Emission charges
advantages and disadvantages of, 223–224
on carbon dioxide, 220f
for consumers, 319
cost-effectiveness, 210–212, 214–215
defined, 7, 205
deposit-refund systems, 222–223
in developing countries, 387–388
for disposal of toxic chemicals, 297
distributional impact of, 216
economics of, 206–208, 207f
enforcement costs of, 218–219
function of, 205–206
impact of, 216
indirect, 224
innovation incentives, 217–218
level of, 208–209
nonuniform emission and, 212–214
price-based system, 236
research and development incentives, 217f
standards approach vs., 208, 212
tax revenues of, 215–217
in world of uncertainty, 214–215, 215f
zoned, 213–214, 214f

Emission-control model, 107
Emission damage functions, 78
Emission permits
in decentralized market, 226
EPA role in, 274
RECLAIM trading credits, 273
Emission rate trading, 226, 239–240
Emission reduction credits, 360
Emission rights, 229–231
Emissions. *See also* Carbon dioxide (CO_2); Greenhouse gases (GHG)
abatement costs for reducing, 85n6
aggregate anthropogenic carbon dioxide, 333
ambient quality, 30–32, 31f, 187–188
automobiles standards, 198n6

benefit-cost analysis for controlling, 136t
cap-and-trade plan, 227–228, 229
carbon dioxide per capita, 16t
changes caused by, 30
changes in efficient levels of, 92–93
control model for, 107
control of quantities of, 215
cost-ineffective policy's effect on, 160
costs of reducing, 10e, 33
defined, 22
domestic greenhouse gases reduction, 329–330
efficient level of, 89–93, 92f, 95–96
enforcing standards, 199–200
equimarginal principle for reduction of, 94–96, 95t, 198t
federal policy on toxics in water and air, 295–297
from fossil fuels, 324
future repercussions of, 82
international reduction of, 343
lowest possible levels, 86
marginal damage function of, 78–79, 78f
measuring of, 121
mercury reduction, 273
mobile sources, 265, 275–282
national estimates of, 265
nitrogen oxide reduction, 12e–13e
nonpoint-source, 219
nonuniform, 212–214, 232–234
per unit of output, 197
from power plants, 267
residuals reduction, 85–86
socially efficient levels, 89–93, 90f
standards for, 195f, 188–189, 196–199
stationary sources, 265
in sugar-beet processing, 249–250, 249n4, 249t
of sulfur dioxide, 265, 267
taxes activities leading to, 259
transfer coefficient, 213n3
types of, 245–246

uncertainty of damages caused by, 81–82
waterborne, 253
Emissions damage function, 121
Emission standards
for air pollution-control, 270
for automobiles, 199–200, 266, 269, 276–278, 277t
defined, 187f
enforcing of, 199–200
incentives in, 196–198
pretreatment standards of wastewater, 254
for protecting human health, 367
types of, 187–189
weakness of, 235, 251
Emission taxes. *See* Emission charges
Emission trading
for air pollution-control, 273–274
growth of, 231, 334
in China, 230t
in developing countries, 230t
in Europe, 230t, 332
in water pollution control, 260–262
Emphysema, 122, 264
Employment taxes, 215
Endangered species, 391f, 377–378
Endangered Species Act (ESA) (1973), 340
Endangered species trade, 373
End-of-pipe pollution control, 251, 252f
Energy crisis, 64
Energy economics, 20
Energy efficiency factors, 328
Energy-efficiency gap, 281
Energy intensity, 328
Enforceability of environmental policies, 162–164
Enforcement
agency of, 201–202
of cap-and-trade plan, 234
economics of, 199–202, 199f
importance of, 163e
of international environmental agreements, 343–344
of international greenhouse gas agreements, 336
monitoring, 163

Subject Index

sanctioning, 163
of technology-based effluent standards, 201, 251–252
trade-offs in, 200
Enforcement costs analysis of, 201–202
defined, 39
of emission charges, 94f, 218–219
of environmental regulations, 145
in model of pollution control, 93
Enforcing agency, 201–202
Engineering judgment, 150
Environment
economic development relationship with, 376–393
economic growth and, 9–11, 12e, 378–381
economy balanced with, 23–26, 23f
globalization's effect on, 16–17
political policy environment, 17
valuing of, 13
Environmental amenity, 134–135
Environmental assets, 380
Environmental benefit, 11–12
Environmental costs, 144–143, 146t, 352
Environmental damages, 35, 79, 170, 170n1. *See also* Damages
Environmental databases, 307
Environmental degradation, 3, 65–66, 377–378
Environmental disincentives, 383–384
Environmental economics, 2, 3, 19, 46, 139
Environmental economists, 17
Environmental federalism, 308–310
Environmental growth, 9–11
Environmental impact analysis (EIA), 100–101
Environmental implications, 4
Environmental improvement programs, 125, 381–382
Environmental industry, 152e–153e

Environmental issues, 14–16
Environmental justice, 46, 115, 119, 162, 234, 238, 301–302, 311, 335–336, 392
Environmental laws, 191
Environmental management, 24
Environmental media, 30
Environmental models, 39
Environmental policies. *See also* Command-and-control (CAC) policies; policies
for air pollution control, 264–282
centralized, 158, 226, 309
concepts for effective, 88
cost-effectiveness of, 159–160, 160f, 387–388
cost-ineffective, 159–160, 160f
decentralized, 169–184, 170f, 308–309
design of, 7–9
economic-incentive, 5, 251
efficiency of, 158–159
effluent charges, 210–212
enforcement of, 163
equity in, 160–161
evaluation criteria of, 158
fairness of, 160–161
flexibility of, 164
government failure of, 167
for hazardous waste disposal, 298, 299
materials balance issues in, 166
moral consideration of, 166–167
morality, 160
perverse incentives in, 8
politics' effects on, 17
pollution-control, 143, 199–202, 228–236, 272–273
pollution control for, 76–77
pollution prevention, 25
scientific basis for, 76
socially efficient, 159–160
standards approach, 186–202
states role in, 161–162, 307–308
on toxic water and air emissions, 295–297
in United States, 247–248, 264–282

Environmental Protection Agency (EPA)
administration of treatment plant subsidies, 254
burden of proof, 290
formation of, 248
importance of environmental policy, 7
industry regulating costs of, 148–149
National Primary Drinking Water Regulation (NPDWR), 256e
permits establishment by, 231
role of, 249, 274, 288
setting maximum contaminated level goal, 256
standards establishment by, 249–250, 267
technology designation by, 271
Toxic Release Inventory, 297, 297n5
use of risk-benefit analysis, 118
water-polluting industries designation, 250
willingness to pay studies, 136t
Environmental quality
benefits of reduced damages, 122
defined, 22
in developing countries, 376, 379–380
economic approach to, 3
estimating benefits in, 121
expressed in house prices, 131–132
global issues of, 6
impact of economic growth on, 11
improvements, 5, 73
income's relationship with, 381
long-run growth rates' effect on, 381
macroeconomics behavior's relationship to, 9
models of, 3
nonuse values of, 138–139
policy for, 76
public goods of, 73, 178–179

414 Subject Index

Environmental quality (*Continued*)
  for minorities and low-income people, 161
  standards approach for, 186–187
  travel costs value expressed by, 132–133
  unmarketed types of outputs, 104
  willingness to pay, 127
Environmental regulations community level, 319–320
  constitutional issues of, 308
  costs of, 147–148, 153–155
  decentralization to individual states, 308
  economic efficiency in, 308–310
  economic growth effect of, 9–10
  effects on domestic production and imports, 366f
  impact, 101, 368
  issues with industry wide regulations, 150
  race to the bottom, 310, 368
  regulatory impact analysis of, 101
Environmental resources, 2
Environmental scientists, 77, 82, 100
Environmental services, 177–178, 178e
Environmental subsidies, 222e
Environmental sustainability, 28–30
Environmental taxes, 204–205, 205e
Environmental trade restrictions, 365–367, 371–374
Environmental values, 64, 392
Envirotech industries, 10, 152, 166, 392
Epidemiologists, 82, 115, 122
Episodic emissions, 34, 35e, 174, 245
Equimarginal cutbacks, 195
Equimarginal principle
  application in emission reductions, 95t
  compliance costs of, 212t
  defined, 53–54, 53f
  emission charges' application of, 211f

emission reductions' application of, 94–96
  in mobile-source air pollution control, 276
  policy of effluent charges, 210–212
  in standards, 193–196, 202
Equimarginal reduction, 195t
Equiproportionate
  in command-and-control policies, 94–96, 195
  climate change and, 333
  compliance costs of, 212, 212t
  examples of, 195n4
  perverse incentives of, 198n7
Equity
  defined, 59, 61
  in environmental policy, 160–161
  horizontal, 113
  intergenerational, 382–383
  of international agreements, 351
  vertical, 113
  vs. efficiency, 61
Ethiopia, 384
Europe, 204, 205e, 293, 319, 331e–332e
European Trading Scheme (ETS), 230t, 331e–332e
European Union, 226, 289e, 293, 331, 331e–332e, 333, 371
EV intensity, 279
Evaluation criteria of environmental policies, 158
E-waste, 319
Excess profits, 359
Existence value, 139
Expected value, 116
Exposure analysis, 116
Exposure standards, 287
External benefits, 70–73, 74
External costs, 64–70, 66f, 67e, 73–74, 144
Extinction of species, 339, 377
Exxon *Valdez*, 257, 305

F

Facility-type projects, 145
Fairness in environmental policy, 160–161
Federal government

air policy, 266–269
animal protection statutes, 340
mobile-source pollution-control program, 275–282
preempt state policies, 308
public wastewater treatment plants grants, 250
subsidies, 253
toxics in water and air emissions policy, 295–297
water pollution-control policy, 244, 246–248, 247t, 309
Federal Hazardous Substances Act (1960), 286t
Federal Insecticide, Fungicide, and Rodenticide Act (1972), 286t, 288, 288n2, 306
Federal Meat Inspection Act (1907), 287t
Federal Mine Safety and Health Act (1977), 287t
Federal Railroad Safety Act (1970), 299t
Federal Strip Mining Control and Reclamation Act (1977), 310
Federal Trade Commission (FTC), 238e
Feedstock taxes, 297
Fee systems, 309
Fertility rates, 386, 386n12
Fertilizers, 245
Financial assurance rules, 301
Financial capital, 16
Financial fund, 303
Finland, 7e
Fire retardants and the replacement cycle, 291–292e
Flat tax, 209
Fleet turnover ratio, 277
Flexibility mechanisms, 334
Flexibility of environmental policies, 164
Flora and fauna international agreements, 345t–346t
Fluorine, 356
Food, Drug, and Cosmetic Act (1938), 286t, 288, 306
Food Quality Protection Act (1996), 287t
Ford Motor Company's Core Recovery program, 319

Forest economics, 20
Forestry, 327
Former USSR. *See* USSR
Fossil fuels, 179, 180f, 219–220, 324
Frac Focus, 183
Fracking, 257
France, 7e, 16t, 205e
Free-riding behavior, 72–73, 179, 179
Free trade, 365–367
Fuel, 197, 278, 329
Fundamental balance, 23–26
Future costs, 155

G

Gains from trade, 228
Galapagos Islands, 341
GEF Management Group, 391n15
General Agreement on Tariffs and Trade (GATT), 365n1
Genetic capital, 340–341
Germany, 223, 353, 370e
Global climate change, 6, 279, 279–280, 324–329, 325e
Global environment, 15, 324, 333
Global Environment Fund Management Group (GEF Management Group), 391n15
Global greenhouse effect, 324–326, 377
Globalization
  benefit-cost analysis with worldwide perspective, 105
  carbon footprint of, 370, 370e
  climate change and, 369–370
  defined, 16
  effect on chemical uses, 293
  environmental implications of, 368–369
  impact of, 362–364
  pollution-haven issue, 368
  race to the bottom, 368
  technology transfer impact on, 392
Global meteorological system, 351n6
Global Methane Pledge (GMP), 335
Global pollutants, 33–34

Global positioning systems (GPS), 70
Global public goods, 351
Global warming
  causes of, 265, 324–326
  defined, 6, 15
  deforestation's effect on, 377–378
  human choices in, 327–329
  international efforts for addressing, 333–336
  prevention of, 10e
  regressive impact of, 115
Goods and services, 25, 39–40
Government failure, 167
Green GDP, 29–30
Green power, 180
Green gross domestic product (GDP), 29–30
Green technology transfer, 391
Greenhouse effect, 6, 15, 226, 264, 324–326, 329
Greenhouse gas emissions, 205, 231, 232e
Greenhouse gases (GHG)
  effects of, 324–326, 341
  reducing emissions of, 329–332, 330t
  social costs of, 338
  sources of, 326t
Greenhouse phenomenon, 327
Greenwashing, 239e
Gross domestic product (GDP), 10, 29–30, 328
Groundwater aquifer systems, 244
Groundwater contamination, 256e, 303

H

Habitats, 20, 340, 341
Halocarbons, 356
Hazardous Materials Transportation Act (1975), 299t
Hazardous waste. *See also* Toxic pollutants; Basel Convention on Transboundary Movements of Hazardous Wastes
  cleanup criteria, 304
  defined, 300
  disposal laws of, 296, 299t, 306

disposal sites for, 284, 298, 303
economic issues of handling, 303–306
financing for site cleanup, 303–304
management of, 298–299, 298t, 306
nuclear buildup cleanup, 305
of radioactive wastes, 302
reduction of, 296–297
states regulation of, 310
subsidies for proper disposal of, 300
uneven generation of, 298
Health. *See* Human health
Hedonic analysis, 131n16
High-level wastes (HLW), 302
Homeowners' association, 73
Honeybees, 289e
Horizontal equity, 113
Hotspot problem, 232
Household environments, 286
House prices, 131–132, 132f
Human capital, 154
Human exposure, 121
Human health
  chlorofluorocarbon impact on, 357
  in developing countries, 377–378
  factors effecting, 122
  measurement of damages, 121
  measuring costs of, 123
  outcomes, 135–136
  primary and secondary ambient air quality standards for, 269, 270t
  restrictions on products impacting, 366
  toxic pollutants impact on, 284–285
  value of expressed as averting costs, 128
Human life
  cultivation of animals and plants for, 339
  global climate change impact on, 324, 327–329
  value of, 128–130
Human resources, 2
Hydrofluorocarbons (HFCs), 326t
Hydrological phenomena, 188

I

Iceland, 7e
Illegal dumping, 145
Illness, 123
Impact, definition of, 100
Impact environmental impact analysis (EIA), 100
Impact of emission charges, 216–217
Impact reduction through technology, 165–166
Import controls, 373, 374
Inanimate capital, accumulation of, 154
Incentive-based policies (IB)
  in developing countries, 14, 14e–15e, 387–388
  emission charges and subsidies, 204–224
  emission charges or taxes, 7
  market-based systems, 204
  market-based trading programs, 7
Incentives
  for air pollution-control, 269
  based policies in international agreements, 353
  in cap-and-trade plan, 227–236
  and climate change, 6
  economic, 5
  for greenhouse gas emissions reduction, 330–332
  for habitat preservation, 341
  for hazardous waste disposal, 300–301
  household example of, 5–6
  importance of, 4–5
  incentive-based policies, 6–7
  to innovate, 217–218
  nonmaterial, 5
  perverse, 8, 230n1
  profit motive, 4
  standards use of, 196–199
  take-back programs, 319
  for technological innovations, 165–166
Increased land values, 125
India, 16t
Indirect costs, 123
Indirect dischargers, 254
Indirect emission charges, 224
Individual action, 337
Individual values, 40

Indonesia, 16t
Industrial activities, 66
Industrial countries, 377n1
Industrial facilities, 249
Industrial Revolution, 286, 324
Industrial wage rate studies, 129
Industry regulating costs, 148–153
Inflation Reduction Act (IRA) of 2022, 267t
Informal economic pressure, 183e
Informal pressure, 182–183
Information, 183
Information of toxic materials, 297, 372
Information sectors, 26
Infrastructure, demand for, 337
Initial compliance, 201, 252
Initial rights allocation, 229–231
Innovation, 165–166, 217–218, 310
Innovative property rights plan, 179
Inputs, 143n1
Insecticides, 289e
Inspection and maintenance (I&M), 279, 278, 281
Institutional policy, 384–386
Institutions, 4n1, 340
Instrument choices, 158n1
Insurance market, 297
Integrated pest management (IPM), 147
Intergenerational equity, 382–383
Internalize externalities, 177–180
International Court of Justice (ICJ), 336
International development banks, 392
International emission trading, 334
International environmental agreements, 343–361, 355f, 358t
International environmental issues biological diversity in, 339–341
  defined, 15–16
  enforcement for reduction of, 343–348

  incentive-based approaches to, 330–332
  physical problems of, 324–326
  scope of, 343n1
International environmental treaties, 391, 391n15
International market, 368, 373, 373f
International Monetary Fund (IMF), 363
International response to ozone-depletion, 357–358
International river agreements, 344t–345t
International trade, 16, 343
Interregional equity, 161
Interstate air pollution, 274
Interstate compact agreements, 302
Intertemporal dimensions, 21
Intertemporal trade-offs, 21
Ireland, 7e, 205e
Ivory, 374

J

Japan, 7e
Joint and several liability, 171
Joint implementation, 334
Judgments, 3
Justice, 46, 115, 119, 162–164, 234, 238, 283, 301–302, 311, 35–336, 340, 392

K

Kyoto conference, 15
Kyoto Protocol
  bases of drafting new global agreement, 334
  Clean Development Mechanism in, 226, 230t
  expiration of, 15
  international reduction of greenhouse gases, 333–334, 341

L

Labor market, 130t, 290–291
Land disposal of hazardous waste, 298t
Land economics, 20
Landfills, 312–314
Land-use controls, 320
Latin America, 14e–15e
Latvia, 205e

Law of conservation of matter, 24
Laws of nature, 19
Lawsuits, 172
Lead-Based Paint Poison Prevention Act (1991), 286t
Lead-free gasoline, 239–240
Least possible costs, 94
Leftover waste products. *See* Residuals
Legal arrangements, 19
Legal institutions, 386
Legal standing, 172
Liability
  defined, 169
  development of through common law, 171–174
  of hazardous waste disposal sites, 304
  incentives for proper hazardous waste disposal, 301
  incentives for waste reduction, 297
  issues with, 172
  laws of, 169–175, 170f
  natural resources damage provision of, 303
  penalty function terms of, 199n8
Liquid hazardous waste, 298
Local environmental regulations, 319–320
Local nuisance laws, 266
Local pollutants, 33–34
Local regulations, 147–148
London Guidelines on Chemicals, 372
Long Island Sound Nitrogen Trading Program, 230t
Long-run decisions, 28, 381
Long-run economic change, 154, 380
Long-run technical change, 152–153
Lost productivity, 382
Lost value of resource, 102
Love Canal, 284, 303
Low-carbon fuels, 329
Lowest achievable emission rate, 271, 271n2
Lowest possible marginal abatement costs, 86
Low-income populations near disposal sites, 301

Low-Level Radioactive Waste Policy Act of 1980 (amended 1985), 299t, 302
Low-level wastes (LLW), 302
Lung cancer, 264

M
Macroeconomics, 2, 9–11, 10e, 141
Macroeconomics data, 141
Macroeconomics modeling, 154
Maintenance of habitats, 340
Managed trade, 363
Manifest system, 299
Manure, 245
Maquiladora program, 371
Marginal abatement cost functions. *See also* Abatement costs
  actual marginal costs in, 86
  aggregate, 88f
  anatomy of curve of, 85f
  of changing emissions, 235n4
  concept of, 83–85
  of cost-effective policy, 159–160
  of cost-ineffective policy, 159–160, 160f
  efficient level of emissions, 89–91, 91f
  of emission-control model, 107–109, 108f
  mistakes in, 93n9
  representative figures of, 84f, 83n5
  of socially efficient levels of emissions, 89–91
Marginal abatement costs, 83, 85f, 88–89, 96
  compliance costs of, 212t
  of emissions standard, 187f
  equal marginal damage costs, 90–91
  equimarginal principle for, 211f
  for equiproportional cutbacks, 195–196
  functions of, 83–87
  in international agreements, 355
  lowering through innovation, 218
  lowest possible, 86

reduction promotes industry growth, 152
  research and development effect on, 235
  in standards, 202
  for two sources, 193
  uncertainty of curve of, 214–215
Marginal costs actual, 86
  concept of, 48f
  defined, 48
  economic efficiency, 60–61
  equimarginal principle, 53–54
  of producing organic apples, 50e–51e
  supply effected by, 54–55, 55f
  technology's effect on, 51–53
  typical curves, 50f
Marginal damage costs, 90–91
Marginal damage function
  causes of change in, 82
  damages curve of, 80n3
  defined, 78, 96
  of emission-control model, 107–108, 108f
  of emissions standard, 187f
  equations of, 80–81
  of populous urban area, 92n8
  reductions in emissions, 80f
  representative figures of, 78f
  of socially efficient levels of emissions, 90
  for standards, 191–192
  time specific, 80
Marginal emission damage function, 78, 78f
Marginal external costs, 65, 65n3, 66f
Marginal penalty function, 199–200, 199n8
Marginal production cost curve, 61
Marginal recycling costs, 318
Marginal savings, 61n1
Marginal social costs. *See* Social costs
Marginal willingness to pay, 41–44, 60–61, 60f
Margin of safety (MOS), 269, 282
Marine economics, 20
Marine Mammal Protection Act (1972), 340

Marine pollution international agreements, 344t
Maritime oil spills, 174
Maritime Protection, Research, and Sanctuaries Act (1972), 299t
Market, 4n2, 62, 229f
Market adjustments, 150–152
Market analysis, 104
Market-based systems
  for air pollution-control, 269
  carbon offset markets, 238–239e
  incentive-based policies, 204
  socially efficiency of, 61–64
  willingness to pay, 40
  workings of, 59
Market-based trading programs, 7
Marketed output, 378, 379f
Market failure, 64, 70, 73
Market for green power, 179–180
Market model, 63f, 73
Market outcomes, 66
  and external costs, 66f
Markets, 290. *See also* Permit market
Maryland, 103e
Materials balance, 166, 313
Materials damage, 125–126
Materials/energy balance, 24–25
Materials intensity, 313
Maximum achievable control technology (MACT), 268, 273, 282, 296
Maximum contaminant level goal (MCLG), 255
Maximum contaminant levels (MCLs), 255
Media, environmental, 30
Mercury, 273
Meteorological patterns, 326
Meteorological phenomena, 188
Methane, 6, 32, 102, 102t, 213f, 232e, 237, 256e, 325, 326t, 336, 341
  global pledge, 335
Methyl chloroform, 357, 358t
Mexico, 7e, 16t, 339, 371
Microbes, 255
Microeconomics, 2, 39
Midnight dumping, 145
Migration economics, 362

Mineral economics, 20
Minimum abatement costs, 85
Minority populations near disposal sites, 301
Miscellaneous international agreements, 347t
Mitigation costs, 145
Mitigation of greenhouse gases emissions, 329
Mobile-source air pollution, 188, 265, 275–282, 310, 329
Models, 3
Modern production technology, 83
Monitoring emissions
  in cap-and-trade plan, 235
  for emission charges, 218, 224
  with emission-control technology, 251
  for emission standards, 163, 199–200
  for international greenhouse gas agreements, 336
Monitoring requirements, 219
Monopoly profits, 359f
Montreal Protocol
  environmental trade restrictions in, 371–374
  issue of surface ozone, 356
  multilateral fund, 358
  phaseout schedule of, 358t
  on Substance that Deplete the Ozone Layer, 357, 360
  technology transfer, 353
  trade restriction in, 343, 359
Moral approach, 3
Moral consideration, 166–167
Morality in environmental policy, 160
Moral suasion, 180–182, 343
Morbidity, 122n2
Motor Vehicle Air Pollution Control Act (1965), 266t
Motor Vehicle Exhaust Study Act of (1960), 266t
Motor vehicles and fuel, 268
Multicountry environmental solutions, 343–344
Multilateral agreements, 344, 344t–347t, 348, 351–352
Multilateral fund, 358
Multinational agreements. *See* International environmental agreements

Multinational firms, 16
Multiple sources, 94
Municipal solid waste (MSW), 6, 300n6, 309, 311–314, 312t, 314t
Municipal Wastewater Treatment Construction Grant Amendments 1981, 248t
Municipal wastewater treatment plan
  subsidy program, 253–254

N
Nanotechnology, 291
National ambient air quality standards (NAAQS), 269–270, 274
National Contingency Plan (NCP), 303
National Defense Authorization Acts, 299t
National economy, 153
National Environmental Policy Act of 1970 (NEPA), 100
National Highway Traffic Safety Administration, 280
National Primary Drinking Water Regulation (NPDWR), 256e
National Priorities List (NPL), 303, 310
National Renewable Energy Laboratory, 146, 146t
National system of pollution control, 308
Natural assets, 19
Natural capital, 29–30
Natural environments, 81
Natural gas, 220f
Natural resource damages, 305
Natural resource economics, 19–22
Natural resource injury, 103e
Natural resources, 103e, 143n1
Natural scientists. *See* Environmental scientists
Nature, relationship with economy, 19
Nature conservancy, 179
Nature Conservancy group, 179n4
Nauru, 365e
Negligence liability, 171
Neonicotinoids, 289e

Subject Index 419

Nepal, 383
Net benefits, 107, 110, 338
Netherlands, 205e
New-car certification program, 279, 277, 277t
New-car emission standards, 276–278
Newly-industrialized countries, 377n1
New-source bias, 271, 289
New Zealand Trading Program, 230t
Nitrogen, 245
Nitrogen oxide emissions, 12e, 326t
Nitrogen oxide trading plan, 226
Nitrogen trifluoride, 326t
Noise pollutants, 32
Nominal interest rates, 111
Nonattainment areas, 268
Nonconventional pollutants, 245
Noncumulative pollutants, 32–33
Nondiscriminatory standards, 366–367
Nonhazardous-waste landfills, 300n6
Nonhuman ecosystem, 77
Nonhuman resources, 2
Nonjoint liability, 171
Nonmarket, 13
Nonmaterial incentives, 5
Nonpoint-source emissions, 34, 218, 248, 321
Nonrenewable resources, 21, 380
Nontariff barriers, 366
Nonuniform emissions, 212–214, 233
Nonuse values, 138–139
Nordic Environment Finance Corporation, 391n15
Normative economics, 3, 76n1, 92
North American Free Trade Agreement (NAFTA), 371
Norway, 7e, 16t, 205e, 223
Nuclear international agreements, 346t
Nuclear Waste Policy Act of 1982 (amended 1987), 299t, 302
Nuclear weapons, 305
Nutrient pollution trading, 261e

O

Occupational Safety and Health Act (1970), 287t, 306
Offset trading, 226, 236–240
Off-shore oil drilling platform, 257–258
Ohio Wetlands Mitigation Program, 230t
Oil Pollution Act (1990), 174, 257, 305
Oil spills, 257–258, 257f
Open-access pasture, 68n6
Open-access resources, 68–70, 68n6, 385
Open economy, 365e
Opportunity costs
 of abatement subsidies, 220–223
 concept of, 156
 defined, 47
 of local regulations, 147–148
 of single facilities, 147
 types of, 143–144
Option value, 139
Output
 adjustments' effect on costs, 150–152, 151f
 aggregate level of, 376
 emissions per unit of, 197
 per capita, 376
 standards based on, 198
 unmarketed types of, 104
Overexploitation of species, 339
Ozone-depleting pollutants, 33, 357–358
Ozone-depleting potential (ODP), 360n9

P

P–234, 233f
Paris Agreement, 334–336
 developing countries and, 389
Pay-as-you-throw (PAYT), 5, 6e, 316
Payment for environment services (PES), 177e–178e, 179, 388e–389e
Penalty function terms, 199–200, 199n8
Per capita output, 376
Perfluorocarbons, 326t
Performance standards, 189, 329
Permit market
 competition in, 234
 defined, 228
 for discharge permits, 229f
 EPA's role in, 274
 prices in, 236
 reducing amount of, 231
Permits
 cap-and-trade plan use of, 227–236
 carbon dioxide emission, 232
 for discharge, 229f
 fees system for, 309
 initial rights allocation, 229–231
 limiting number of permits, 229
 reducing amount of, 231
Permitting system, 309
Persistent organic pollutants, 293
Persistent water pollutants, 245, 246
Perverse incentives, 8, 198, 230n1
Pesticides, 294e
Pest resistance, 293–294, 294e
Petroleum, 220f
PFAS/PFOA/PFOS, 392e
Phosphate, 365e
Phosphorous, 245
Physical impacts, 122
Physical projects, 105
Pigouvian taxes, 205n2
Pipeline spills, 34
Plastics, cumulative pollutants, 32
Poachers, 374
Point-source emissions, 245
Point-source pollutants, 34
Poison Prevention Packaging Act (1970), 286t
Police power, 320
Policies. *See also* Command-and-control (CAC) policies; Environmental policies
 centralized, 158, 226, 309
 cost-effective, 159–160, 160f
 in developing countries, 381–389
 incentive-based, 6–7, 14, 14e–15e, 204–224, 387–388
 initiative for, 204
 international environmental agreements, 343–361

Subject Index

Policies (*Continued*)
  politics' effects on, 17
  public, 7–8, 11, 73, 76, 157
  source reduction, 25
  of states, 307–311
  trade-off, 192
  trade policy, 373f
Policy choices, 387–388
Policy initiative, 204
Policy options, 170f
Policy trade-off, 192
Political policy environment, 17
Political power
  realignments, 363
Political process, 191
Politics, 17, 198–199, 254, 275, 384–386
Pollutants.
  criteria, 266
  defined, 22
  multiple sources of, 94
  national estimates of, 265t
  types of, 32–35, 245–246
Polluter pays principle (PPP), 333, 350
Pollution, 122. *See also* Air pollution; Water pollution
  of air, 122
  calculating cancer deaths from, 117t
  causes of, 3
  control model, 76–77
  damages of, 77–82
  defined, 22
  effects on production costs, 124–126, 124f
  environmental, 61n1
  external costs of production, 65, 67, 67e
  managing episodic sources of, 35e
  oil spills, 257–258, 257f
  pollution-control technologies, 6
  prevention, 25, 252f
  reduction of health-related costs, 123
  of smoke, 264
  standard enforcement procedures, 6
  uncertainty of damages caused by, 81–82
Pollution-abatement
  technology, 272

Pollution control
  approach for, 152
  cost effective, 14e–15e, 250
  efficiency in, 159, 250
  emission standards for, 187f, 186, 188–189, 196–197, 200, 235
  enforcement costs of, 93
  equipment installation, 252
  federal policy for water, 244–262
  private information of costs of, 196
  technology-based effluent standards, 249–252
Pollution-control costs
  actual *vs.* minimum, 149–150
  economic burden of, 9–10
  long-run technical change of, 152–153
  as private information, 160
Pollution control
  equipment, 278
Pollution control model, 76–77
Pollution control policies.
  See also Environmental policies
  for air pollution-control, 271–273
  cap-and-trade plan, 227–236
  criteria for, 272–273
  enforcement of, 199–202
  output adjustments to, 151f
  penalty terms in, 200
  social costs of, 143
Pollution-control technologies
  adoption of, 165–166
  alternative, 249
  costs of, 160
  emission standards tied to specific, 249
  incentives for, 6–7
  marginal abatement costs differ based on, 228–229
Pollution damages, 77–82
Pollution havens, 17, 368
Pollution prevention, 25
Pollution Prevention
  Act (1990), 183
Pollution reduction
  programs, 181t
Population, 81, 328, 364, 386–387
Population pressure, 341

Ports and Waterways Safety Act (1972), 299t
Portugal, 7e
Positive economics, 3, 76n1, 92
Potentially responsible parties (PRP), 303
Poultry Products Inspection Act (1957), 287t
Precautionary principle, 293
Predictable consequence of environmental
  impact, 383n5
Preemption, 308
Preferences, 39–40, 382
Prescription drugs, 339
Present value, 109–110
Pretreatment standards, 250, 254
Prevention of significant deterioration (PSD), 268, 268n1, 271, 272t
Price elasticity of
  demand, 180n5
Prices, 49, 143, 236
Primary standards of air pollution control, 269, 270t
Primary treatment, 253
Private costs, 48, 64, 144
Private enterprise economies, 4
Private information, 160, 196
Private market system, 66, 72, 73
Private sector, 11, 111
Privatization, 16
Probabilistic basis, 171
Probability distribution, 116–117, 117t
Probability of accidental emission release, 34
Producers, 23, 23f
Production, 19, 64, 286–295, 286t–287t
Production costs, 124–125, 124f
Production limits, 359f
Production possibility curve (PPC), 26–27, 27f, 27n4
Production residuals, 22
Profit-loss statements, 47, 64
Profit motive, 4
Profits, 64
Progressive impact, 114
Property rights
  decentralized policy approach, 170f

defined, 68
in developing countries, 384–386
for genetic resources, 341
principle of, 175–176
problems with, 177–180
rules and conditions for, 177
Proportional impact, 114
Protected status, 340
Protocol, 343
Pseudo-efficient outcomes, 150
Public agencies, 165n5
Public analysis, 105
Public boards of health, 246n3
Public decisions, 104
Public environmental agencies, 201
Public environmental programs, 105, 139
Public goods
defined, 71–73, 73n7
environmental quality improvements are, 178–179
as external benefit, 73
of international agreements, 351
Public health, 269, 282
Publicly held resources, 171
Publicly-owned treatment works (POTWs), 249, 254, 254t
Public policies
importance of, 7–9
problems with, 157
on public goods, 73
Public program, 108f
Public resources, 305
Public sector, 11, 104, 113
Public trust doctrine, 171
Public wastewater treatment plants, 145, 250, 254
Public welfare, 269

Q
Qatar, 16t
Quantitative targets for greenhouse gases reduction, 334
Quantity -based system, 236
Quantity of emissions reduced, 85n6

R
Race to the bottom, 310, 368–369

Radiation exchange, 264
Radiation Exposure Compensation Act of 1990, 174
Radioactive waste, 32, 246, 302, 306
Rate of reuse, 313
Real interest rates, 111
Reasonably available control technology (RACT), 271, 272t
Recovery operations for hazardous waste, 298t
Recreational uses of water, 245
Recyclable materials, 251
Recycled-content standards, 318
Recycled materials, 311–313, 316–318, 317f
Recycling
alternative to waste disposal, 313
consumer's decisions for, 318–319
defined, 22
economics of, 315–319
increasing, 26
marginal costs of, 318
process of, 315f
ratio of, 317
of residuals, 296
single stream recycling, 316
states and communities action of, 314t
take-back programs, 319
technology, 251
voluntary programs for, 314
Reduction of goods, 25
Reduction of residuals, 25
Reformulated fuels, 278
Refuse Act 1899, 247, 247t
Regional Clean Air Incentive Market (RECLAIM), 273
Regional differences in costs, 143
Regional Greenhouse Gas Initiative (REGGI), 230t, 231, 331
Regional pollutants, 33
Regional trade agreements, 348, 371–374
Regional variation of efficiency levels, 193f
Registration, Evaluation, Authorization, and Restriction of Chemicals (REACH), 293

Regressive impact, 114
Regulatory control, 227
Regulatory criteria, 287–289
Regulatory impact analysis, 101, 338
Regulatory programs, 105
Remote monitoring technology, 200
Renewable Energy Certificates, 230t
Renewable resources, 20, 180, 180f, 278, 328, 380
Replacement cycle, 292e
Representative firm approach, 149
Research and development (R&D)
cap-and-trade plan incentive for, 235
importance of, 52
incentives for, 197, 202, 217–218, 217f, 273
reducing long-run technical costs, 152–153
technological innovations of, 165–166
technology standards' effect on, 197
Residuals
abatement costs of, 82–83
benefits and costs of coal combustion residues regulations, 107e
damage functions, 78
defined, 19, 22
equations of, 23f
intensity of production of, 25
production of, 24
recycling of, 296
reduction of, 25–26, 296
Residual treatment phase, 251
Resilience planning, 337
Resistant bugs, 294e–295e
Resource Conservation and Recovery Act (1976), 107e, 299t, 300, 300n6
Resources, 77n2, 102, 143n1, 385
Resources for the Future, 111, 111n9
Resource-use rate, 21
Restoration costs, 103
Restoration plan, 103e

Revealed preference methods, 127–128
Reversible damage, 82
Risk, 35e
 analysis, 115–116
 assessment, 116
 averse, 118
 benefit analysis, 118
 characterization, 116
 management, 116, 118
 neutral behavior, 117–118
 valuation, 116–118
River pollution, 77
Rivers and streams, 188
Rules and conditions of property rights, 177
Rural economy, 384
Russia, 16t

S

Safe Drinking Water Act (SDWA) (1974), 247t, 255–257
Safety valve, 236
Salmon and Steelhead Conservation and Enhancement Act (1980), 340
Salt caverns, 298
Saltwater resources, 244
Sanctioning polluters, 163, 199, 200
Sanitary awakening, 246
Scientific analysis, 38
Scientific basis, 76
Scientific estimates of pollution, 81
Scope of program, 106–109, 108f
Scrubber, 189n1
Sea level rise, 326, 338
Secondary standards, 269
 of air pollution control, 270t
Secondary treatments, 253
Sectoral shift, 25
Self-monitoring, 200
Sensitivity analyses, 108
Sewage, 245
Ship-breaking industry, 368
Short-run decisions, 28
Short-run environmental damage, 170n1
Side payments, 350–351, 353
Silent Spring (Carson), 284
Single stream recycling, 316

Skin cancer, 357
Sludges, 298
Smoke pollution, 264
Smokey Bear, 181
Snowmobile standards, 190e
Social arrangements, 19
Social asset, 26–27
Social choice, 27
Social concern, 3
Social cost of carbon (SCC), 338
Social costs
 defined, 48, 142
 of environmental regulations, 143
 of integrated pest management, 147
 private costs plus external costs, 65, 143
 of solid waste disposal, 318–319
Social efficiency
 changes in levels of emissions, 92–93
 defined, 161
 environmental policies, 159–160
 external costs, 65
 levels of emission, 89–93, 338
 of market economy, 62–64
 outcomes, 73
 in output, 60–61, 60f
Social marginal costs, 68–69
Social opportunity costs, 144
Social value, 13
Social willingness to pay, 70
Solid hazardous waste, 298
Solid waste disposal, 6e, 311–314
South Africa, 16t
South Coast Air Quality Management District, 310
Southern California Reclaim, 230t
Spain, 7e
Spillover effect, 65n2
Standard enforcement procedures, 6
Standard metropolitan statistical areas (SMSAs), 122
Standards
 acceptable chemical uses, 287
 automobile emission standards, 198n6
 drawbacks, 199–201, 204

economics of, 191–196
emission charges vs., 208, 212
equimarginal principle of, 193–196
hazardous waste disposal, 300
importance of, 186–187
incentives and, 196–199
lowest achievable emission rate, 271
national ambient air quality standards, 269
output-based, 198
political-economic, 198–199
popularity of, 202
setting, 198–199
setting the levels of, 191–192
for snowmobiles, 190e
thresholds for, 191
toxic pollution control, 290–291
types of, 187–191
uniformity of, 192–193
used in combination, 191
zero-risk level, 191
Stated preference method, 127, 133–134
State hazardous-waste regulations, 310
State implementation plans (SIP), 269, 309
State inspection and maintenance (I & M), 268
State revolving funds (SRF), 254
States, 307–308, 310, 320–321
Stationary-source control, 270–275
Stationary sources of emissions, 265, 266, 329
Statistical life, 128–129, 130t
Statutory law, 174–175
Statutory pollution-control laws, 174
Stewardship value, 139
Stockholm Convention on Persistent Organic Pollutants (POP), 293, 347t
Strategic possibilities, 353
Stratosphere, 264
Stratospheric ozone, 15, 265, 268, 268, 356
Strict liability, 171, 304
Subsidies
 consumer, 274, 275f

Subject Index 423

deposit-refund systems, 222–223
   for emission abatement, 220–223
   federal, 253
   firm responses, 204
   municipal wastewater treatment plan, 253–254
   for non-point source pollution, 258–259
   producer technologies, 275
   for proper hazardous waste disposal, 300
   types of, 222e
Subsistence-based economies, 363
Substitute chemicals, 358
Substitutes, 379
Sugar-beet processing plants, 249–250, 249n4, 249t
Sulfur dioxide trading scheme, 226
Sulfur hexafluoride, 326t
Sunshine laws, 183
Superfund, 303–304, 310
Superfund sites, 103e, 304
Supply, marginal costs determine, 54–55
Supply curve, 54–55, 55f, 63, 63f, 73
Surface air, 264
Surface ozone, 356
Surface-water system, 244
Sustainability, 21, 380
Sweden, 7e, 205e, 223
Switzerland, 7e
System of property rights, 341

T
Take-back programs, 319
Taxes, 7e, 219–220, 300. *See also* Charges taxes
Tax revenues, 215–217, 215f
Technical capacities, 27
Technical change in enforcement, 94
Technological arrangements, 19
Technological change, 51–53
Technological specifications, 279
Technology
   abatement costs changed by, 83, 87, 93
   best available technology, 249, 271

best conventional technology, 250
best practicable technology, 249
changes in, 155, 235f
choices of, 381
costs savings of, 197f
effects on marginal costs, 51–53
effluent-control, 251
equimarginal principle, 53–54
forcing, 165, 199, 277
fuel efficient equipment, 329
for hazardous waste reduction, 296
improvements of, 52f
incentives for innovations in, 165–166
mandated, 329
maximum achievable control technology, 268
monitoring polluters, 163
pollution-abatement, 272
pollution control for automobiles, 278
pollution-control technologies, 6, 96, 160
for production of green power, 179–180
reasonably available control technology, 271
for recycling, 251
remote monitoring, 200
specification for automobile pollution, 269
standards approach for, 189, 196
transfers, 353, 390–392
Technology-based effluent limitation guidelines, 249
Technology-based effluent standards (TBES)
   for air pollution-control, 271, 272t, 282
   for control of toxic pollutants, 296
   cost-effectiveness of, 250–251, 272
   defined, 249
   efficiency of, 250
   enforcement of, 252, 268
   establishment of, 249–250

   incentives in, 251–252
   results of, 251
   weakness of, 251–252
Technology-based system, 249
Technology forcing, 198, 277
Technology-forcing regulations, 165
Technology standards, 189, 196, 197, 201
Technology transfer, 353, 390–392
Temperature inversion, 81, 265
Tertiary treatments, 253
Testing of chemicals, 290, 291
Thermal treatment of hazardous waste, 298t
Third-party costs, 65n2
Thresholds, 79, 191, 270
Top down approach, 154
Total costs
   of abatement, 86, 208
   defined, 48
   socially efficient levels, 60–61
Total damage, 78
Total maximum daily load (TMDL) program, 191, 259–262
Total organic carbon (TOC), 245
Total production costs, 49, 53
Total suspended solids (TSS), 14e–15e, 245
Total tax payments, 208
Toxic air pollutants, 268
Toxic emissions, 295–297
Toxic pollutants, 245, 246
   effect on honeybees, 289e
   in Bhopal, India, 284
   DDT, 284
   development of, 284
   differentiated control of, 289–290
   dirty dozen, 293
   federal policy on toxics in water and air emissions, 295–297
   at Husky Energy Refinery explosion in Wisconsin, 284
   primary regulatory approach to controlling, 296
   state standards for waterborne, 309

Toxic Substances Control Act (1976), 288
  uniform standards for control of, 290–291
  unique characteristics of monitoring and control, 285
Toxic Release Inventory (TRI), 297, 297n5, 310
Toxic Substances Control Act (1976), 287t, 288, 289–290, 306, 321
Trade
  environmental restrictions vs. free trade, 365–367
  growth of, 16
  interactions with environment, 364–367
  policy, 373f
  regional agreements, 371–374
  restriction of, 359
  world, 365e
Trade constraints, 373
Trade-off
  across technologies and environmental media, 166
  defined, 26
  in enforcement, 200
  of environmental quality in developing countries, 379
  in pollution control, 256, 282
  in standards, 192
Trading plans
  in nonuniform emissions areas, 232–234
  for nutrient pollution, 261e
Trading programs, 230t
Trading rules, 231
Trading systems
  carbon dioxide multicountry trading plan, 226
  nitrogen oxide trading plan, 226
  reduction of lead-based gasoline, 239–240
  sulfur dioxide trading scheme, 226
  types of, 226
"Tragedy of the Commons" (Hardin), 68n6
Trail Smelter case (1935), 350
Transactions costs, 172, 178
Transferable discharge permit, 240, 268, 267t
Transferable quota program, 359

Transfer coefficient, 213n3, 232
Transfer payments, 144, 208, 209f
Travel costs, 132–133
Travel times related to number of cars, 69t
Treatment plants, 253–254
Treaty, 344
Troposphere, 264
Trust funds, 309
Two-part emission charge, 209

U
Ubiquitous nature of toxic pollutants, 285
Ultraviolet radiation, 264
Uncertainty of world, 214–215, 215f, 236
Underground depository, 302
Undervalued genetic capital, 340
Uniformity of standards, 192–193, 202
Uniform standard of toxic pollution control, 290–291
United Kingdom, 7e, 8e, 16t, 205e
United Nations, 333, 336, 364, 378
United Nations Environment Program (UNEP), 293, 343n1, 347t
United States
  ambient air quality standards, 192
  carbon dioxide emissions of, 16t, 21, 238
  carbon taxes proposed in, 332
  chlorofluorocarbon bans in, 373
  Columbia River Treaty, 348, 351n5
  deposit-refund systems used in, 222–223
  emission charges, 205
  environmental industry in, 152e–153e
  episodic emissions in, 35e
  estimated costs of asthma in, 123t
  generation of hazardous wastes in, 298
  GHG standards for automobiles, 280t

  growing chemical use in, 293
  habitat preservation in, 340
  history of federal water pollution-control policy, 246–248
  leading role in World Bank, 392
  Montreal Protocol in, 358–359
  national air pollution policy in, 264–282
  National Environmental Policy Act of 1970, 100
  nitrogen oxide trading plan, 226
  North American Free Trade Agreement, 371
  states role in environmental policy, 161–162, 307–308
  sulfur dioxide trading scheme, 226
  urbanization, 378
  use of benefit-cost analysis in, 104
United States Flood Control Act of 1936, 104
United States–Mexico–Canada Agreement (USMCA), 371
Unit pricing, 5
Unmarketed types of outputs, 104
Upper limit of abatement, 86
Upstream taxing, 220, 220f
Urban air quality, 268
Urbanization, 378, 387
U.S. Army Corps of Engineers, 247, 247t
U.S. CAFE and GHG Standards for Automobiles, 280t
USSR, 4
U.S. Oil Pollution Act of 1990, 174
U.S. Toxic Release Inventory, 183

V
Valuation, 117, 383
Value of physical impacts, 122
Value of restoring resources, 102
Value of statistical life (VSL), 128–130, 130t, 135
Vehicles. See Automobiles
Vertical equity, 113, 114t
Victim pays principle (VPP), 350

Virgin materials, 312–313
Visual pollutants, 33
Voluntary action, 180, 181t
Voluntary recycling programs, 314

W

Wage differential, 129
Wage rates, 128–130
Waste-disposal facilities, 298
Waste-end taxes and charges, 300
Waste from Electrical and Electronic Equipment (WEEE), 319
Waste heat, 245n1
Waste product disposal, 4
Waste reduction, 296
Waste-treatment facilities, 248, 377
Waterborne emissions, 245, 253, 309
Water contamination, 256e
Water economics, 20
  demand for, 43e, 254n6
Water pollution
  coastal, 244, 257, 320
  defined, 244
  effect of, 122, 124
  types of, 245–246
  in urban areas, 387
Water pollution-control
  ambient-based orientation of, 259
  conventional pollutants, 246
  in developing countries, 377–378
  emission trading, 260–262
  history of, 246–248
  major legislation on, 247–248t

nonpoint-source, 258–259
technology-based effluent standards, 249–252, 262
toxic pollutants, 246
Water Pollution Control Act (WPCA) (1948), 247t, 248
Water Pollution Control Act Amendments (1956), 247t
Water Pollution Control Act Amendments (1972), 247t, 248, 249, 254
Water Quality Act (1965), 247t, 248
Water Quality Act (1987), 248, 248t, 259
Water quality trading and offset programs, 260
Water resource system, 244
Wealth, 40, 380
Wildlife refuge services, 179
Willingness to accept, 138–139
Willingness to pay (WTP)
  approach to environmental damages valuing, 381–382
  balanced with marginal costs, 60–61
  for children's health, 130–131
  concept of, 39–43, 41f
  contingent valuation methods, 133–137
  demand curves of, 45f
  equal to benefits, 121
  estimating methods, 127
  expressed in house prices, 131–132, 131n16, 132f
  for external costs damages, 67–68
  limits of, 40n1
  nonuse values, 138–139
  preference methods, 127–137

total, 41, 60–61
underestimated in damage function, 126
valuing with, 128, 129, 131–133, 134–137
vs. willingness to accept, 138–139
Wind patterns, 349n2
Wind turbine power plant costs, 146, 146t
With/without principle, 142
Woodsy Owl, 181
Work environments, 286
Workers' compensation laws, 174
Workplace safety, 286
World Bank, 363, 365e, 378, 384n11, 392n16
World market for genetic information, 341
World trade, 365e
World Trade Organization (WTO), 363, 365–367, 365n1, 371–374, 390

Y

Yellowstone National Park, 190e, 191

Z

Zero-emission vehicles (ZEV), 278
Zero population growth, 25
Zero-risk level, 191
Zoned emission charge, 213–214, 214f
Zoned emission system, 233–234